April 25–26, 2016
Edinburgh, Scotland, UK

Association for Computing Machinery

Advancing Computing as a Science & Profession

L@S 2016

Proceedings of the Third (2016) ACM Conference on
Learning @ Scale

Sponsored by:

ACM

Supported by:

Google, Oracle Academy, edX, Canvas, and Microsoft Research

Association for
Computing Machinery

Advancing Computing as a Science & Profession

The Association for Computing Machinery
2 Penn Plaza, Suite 701
New York, New York 10121-0701

Notice to Past Authors of ACM-Published Articles
ACM intends to create a complete electronic archive of all articles and/or other material previously published by ACM. If you have written a work that has been previously published by ACM in any journal or conference proceedings prior to 1978, or any SIG Newsletter at any time, and you do NOT want this work to appear in the ACM Digital Library, please inform permissions@acm.org, stating the title of the work, the author(s), and where and when published.

ISBN: 978-1-4503-3726-7 (Digital)

ISBN: 978-1-4503-4477-7 (Print)

Additional copies may be ordered prepaid from:

ACM Order Department
PO Box 30777
New York, NY 10087-0777, USA

Phone: 1-800-342-6626 (USA and Canada)
+1-212-626-0500 (Global)
Fax: +1-212-944-1318
E-mail: acmhelp@acm.org
Hours of Operation: 8:30 am – 4:30 pm ET

Printed in the USA

Learning at Scale 2016 Preface

It is our great pleasure to present the Proceedings of the Third Annual ACM Conference on Learning at Scale, L@S 2016, held on April 25-26 at the University of Edinburgh, UK, the first time for the conference to be held outside of North America.

This conference series is a venue for discussion of the highest quality research on how learning and teaching can be transformed when done at scale. This conference was created by the Association for Computing Machinery (ACM), inspired by the emergence of Massive Open Online Courses (MOOCs) and the accompanying shift in thinking about education. This area of research is interdisciplinary, sitting at the intersection of the learning sciences, education, computer science, educational data mining, and learning analytics.

"Learning at Scale" refers to new approaches to teaching and learning that involve large numbers of students, thousands or even tens of thousands. It covers face-to-face settings as well as settings in which learners work remotely, whether synchronous or asynchronous. It is concerned with the challenges and affordances of scale: What are innovative forms of learning and instruction that can be orchestrated with very large numbers of learners? Specific topics include, but are not limited to: Pedagogies that enhance learning as scale; personalization and adaptation of learning at scale; self- and co-regulation of learning at scale; platforms, tools, and architectures for learning at scale; usability studies; tools for automated feedback and grading; learning analytics; analysis of log data; studies of application of learning theory; and finally, investigation of student behavior and correlation with learning outcomes, depth and retention of learning, and motivational and affective outcomes.

The call for papers attracted submissions from all over the world, covering a broad range of topics from the theoretical to the pragmatic. All papers were reviewed according to stringent criteria. Full Papers were reviewed by at least three program committee members, Work-In-Progress Papers and Demo Descriptions by two. Final decisions for acceptance of Full Papers were made by the program committee as a whole, often after extensive discussion of the merits of the paper. Whereas Full Papers present work that is innovative and mature, WiPs and Demos offer a forum for the newest and emerging work at earlier stages, offering pointers to future directions. As such, they fulfill a key role in this fast moving area. An industry session reflects the importance of L@S for the commercial world and for real world deployment.

As may be clear from the following analytics, the conference is highly selective in the work it accepts.

	Full Papers	**Work in Progress**	**Demos**
Submitted	79	66	8
Accepted	18	39	7
Accepted as Poster	24		
Acceptance Rate	23%	59%	88%

The overall submission numbers did not differ substantially from those of the previous year. Thus, the conference is successfully migrating from the continent of its birth, indicating its international relevance. How could it be different, as Learning at Scale is a truly international phenomenon?

We are fortunate to have three outstanding keynote speakers. Sugata Mitra, Professor of Educational Technology and Newcastle University, UK and winner of the 2013 TED Prize presents on "The

Future of Learning." Mike Sharples, Chair in Educational Technology, Institute of Educational Technology at The Open University, UK will share insights on "Effective Pedagogy at Scale, Social Learning and Citizen Inquiry." Ken Koedinger, Professor of Human Computer Interaction and Psychology, Director, Pittsburgh Science of Learning Center at Carnegie Mellon University, USA presents the final keynote, shared with the co-located Learning Analytics & Knowledge Conference on the topic, "Practical Learning Research at Scale."

Learning@Scale 2016 and edX.org introduce a new interactive format for conference sessions, namely, flipped sessions. Research shows that a flipped format of instruction is effective – in this format, classroom sessions are used for active learning and less interactive forms of learning are done at home. However, most conferences still preserve the decades-old format of mini lectures... Not anymore! Learning@Scale 2016 features flipped conference sessions. Authors of accepted papers, posters, and demos were invited to create online resources, "mini courses," for their contributions, to be hosted by edX. Conference participants familiarize themselves with these resources ahead of the conference. During the session, they discuss the papers and develop relevant themes and ideas based on these papers. After the conference, the platform will remain available for on-going discussions and sharing. The community supported the idea with an overwhelming response.

Learning at Scale 2016 was truly a community effort. We first thank the authors for their creativity and rigor. We are grateful to the program committee and all the reviewers for their thoughtful and constructive evaluation of the submitted papers, and their careful shepherding. ACM was our rock. Finally, the conference received invaluable sponsorship fromOracle Academy and Google at the gold level, as well as from edX, Instructure, Inc., and Microsoft Research at the bronze level.

We hope that the conference will be a forum for wonderfully interesting exchanges between researchers and practitioners from institutions around the world. While the proceedings may not capture the live excitement, they present a permanent record. May they be a valuable resource for many researchers interested in Learning at Scale in the years to come!

Vincent Aleven
Carnegie Mellon University, USA
L@S 2016 Program Co-Chair

Judy Kay
University of Sydney, Australia
L@S 2016 Program Co-Chair

Jeff Haywood
University of Edinburgh, Scotland
L@S 2016 Conference Chair

Ido Roll
University of British Columbia, Canada
L@S 2016 Program Co-Chair

Table of Contents

Demonstrations

Keynote Address

Session: Automated Assessment

Flipped Session - Crowdsourcing the Feedback

Flipped Session - Outside the MOOC

Keynote Address

Learning at Scale 2016 Organization

General Chair: Jeff Haywood *(The University of Edinburgh, UK)*

Program Co-Chairs: Vincent Aleven *(Carnegie Mellon University, USA)*
Judy Kay *(University of Sydney, Australia)*
Ido Roll *(University of British Columbia, Canada)*

Local Organization Chair: Dragan Gašević *(The University of Edinburgh, UK)*

Web & Communications Chair: Vitomir Kovanović *(The University of Edinburgh, UK)*

Flipped Sessions Coordinator: Piotr Mitros *(edX)*

Steering Committee: Ryan Baker *(Teachers College, Columbia University, USA)*
Armando Fox *(University of California at Berkeley, USA)*
Marti Hearst *(University of California at Berkeley, USA)*
Gregor Kiczales *(University of British Columbia, Canada)*
Scott Klemmer *(University of California at San Diego (USA)*
Ken Koedinger *(Carnegie Mellon University, USA)*
John Mitchell *(Stanford University, USA)*
Carolyn Penstein Rosé *(Carnegie Mellon University, USA)*
Jeremy Roschelle *(SRI International, USA)*
Daniel Russell *(Google, USA)*
Mehran Sahami *(Stanford/ex officio ACM Ed Board, USA)*
Karen Swan *(Univ of Illinois, Springfield, USA)*
Yan Timanovsky *(ACM Staff Liaison, USA)*
Beverly P. Woolf *(University of Massachusetts Amherst, USA)*

Program Committee: Tiffany Barnes *(North Carolina State University, USA)*
Yoav Bergner *(Educational Testing Service, USA)*
Marie Bienkowski *(SRI International, USA)*
Christopher Brooks *(University of Michigan, USA)*
Emma Brunskill *(Carnegie Mellon University, USA)*
Ulrike Cress *(Knowledge Media Research Center, Germany)*
Pierre Dillenbourg *(École Polytechnique Fédérale de Lausanne, Switzerland)*
Douglas Fisher *(Vanderbilt University, USA)*
Armando Fox *(University of California at Berkeley, USA)*
Kobi Gal *(Ben Gurion University, Israel)*
Dragan Gasevic *(University of Edinburgh, UK)*
Art Graesser *(University of Memphis, USA)*
Philip Guo *(University of Rochester, USA)*
Marti Hearst *(University of California at Berkeley, USA)*
Neil Heffernan *(Worcester Polytechnic Institute, USA)*
Daniel Hickey *(Indiana University, USA)*
Ulrich Hoppe *(University of Duisburg-Essen, Germany)*
Juho Kim *(Massachusetts Institute of Technology, USA)*

Program Committee (continued):

Kenneth Koedinger *(Carnegie Mellon University, USA)*
Chinmay Kulkarni *(Carnegie Mellon University, USA)*
Marcia Linn *(University of California at Berkeley, USA)*
Marsha Lovett *(Carnegie Mellon University, USA)*
Rose Luckin *(The London Knowledge Lab, UK)*
Manolis Mavrikis *(The London Knowledge Lab, UK)*
Robert Miller *(Massachusetts Institute of Technology, USA)*
John Mitchell *(Stanford University, USA)*
Piotr Mitros *(edX, USA)*
Antonija Mitrović *(University of Canterbury, New Zealand)*
Zachary Pardos *(University of California at Berkeley, USA)*
Beverly Park Woolf *(University of Massachusetts, USA)*
Jeremy Roschelle *(SRI International, USA)*
Carolyn Rose *(Carnegie Mellon University, USA)*
Daniel Russell *(Google, USA)*
Mehran Sahami *(Stanford University, USA)*
Eileen Scanlon *(Open University, UK)*
Daniel Seaton *(Massachusetts Institute of Technology, USA)*
Karen Swan *(University of Illinois, Springfield, USA)*
Candace Thille *(Stanford University, USA)*
Astrid Wichmann *(Ruhr-University Bochum, Germany)*

Additional reviewers:

Seth Adjei
Katerina Avramides
Christa Cody
Mutlu Cukurova
Vania Dimitrova
Yihuan Dong
Rachit Dubey
Mingyu Feng
Susan Goldman
Beate Grawemeyer
Tobias Hecking
Drew Hicks
Wayne Holmes
Iris Howley
Srecko Joksimovic
Łukasz Kidziński
Molly Kleinman
Scott Klemmer
Vitomir Kovanovic
Nancy Law
Ran Liu
Zhongxiu Liu
Christopher Maclellan
Sven Manske
Gregor Miller
Behrooz Mostafavi
Benjamin Nye Korinn Ostrow
Mykola Pechenizkiy
Joshua Peterson
Chris Piech
Thomas Price
Beat Schwendimann
Avi Segal
Douglas Selent
John Stamper
Dan Suthers
Steven Tang
Craig Thompson
Eric Van Inwegen
Kurt VanLehn
Katrien Verbert
Hao Wan
Marcelo Worsley
Xiaolu Xiong
Nesra Yannier
Hezheng Yin

Learning at Scale 2016 Sponsor & Supporters

Sponsor:

Gold Supporters:

Bronze Supporters:

The Civic Mission of MOOCs: Measuring Engagement across Political Differences in Forums

Justin Reich
MIT
Cambridge, MA
jreich@mit.edu

Brandon Stewart
Princeton
Princeton, NJ
bms4@princeton.edu

Kimia Mavon
Harvard
Cambridge, MA
kmavon@seas.harvard.edu

Dustin Tingley
Harvard
Cambridge, MA
dtingley@gov.harvard.edu

ABSTRACT
In this study, we develop methods for computationally measuring the degree to which students engage in MOOC forums with other students holding different political beliefs. We examine a case study of a single MOOC about education policy, *Saving Schools*, where we obtain measures of student education policy preferences that correlate with political ideology. Contrary to assertions that online spaces often become echo chambers or ideological silos, we find that students in this case hold diverse political beliefs, participate equitably in forum discussions, directly engage (through replies and upvotes) with students holding opposing beliefs, and converge on a shared language rather than talking past one another. Research that focuses on the civic mission of MOOCs helps ensure that open online learning engages the same breadth of purposes that higher education aspires to serve.

Author Keywords
MOOCs; civic education; discourse; text analysis; political ideology; structural topic model

ACM Classification Keywords
K.3.1. Computer Uses in Education.

INTRODUCTION
Political theorists have long argued that exposure to diverse perspectives is vital to a robust civil society and to the development of citizens [7]. Democratic discourse requires engaging with people who hold different perspectives, and differing perspectives are often a function of different life circumstances. One serious threat to contemporary civic education, therefore, is the growing homogeneity of school populations. In the United States, residential segregation has lead to growing de facto K-12 school segregation [8], while admissions processes and self-selection has resulted in class segregation in higher education.

ACM 978-1-4503-3726-7/16/04…$15.00 .
DOI: http://dx.doi.org/10.1145/2876034.2876045

Open online education offers one pathway for students to join communities of diverse learners beyond the bounds of geography [13]. Demographic research into massive open online courses (MOOCs) has shown that these courses are among the most diverse "classrooms" in the world, with students of different ages, levels of education, and life circumstances [5]. A globally diverse online learning community, however, does not guarantee that students encounter and consider different perspectives. Internet researchers have posed two competing theories for how people confront differences on the Web [6]. One theory holds that the Internet is a series of "silos" where individuals seek out media and communities that conform to their established beliefs [9]. Another theory holds that the Internet contains many interest-driven spaces that serve as ideological "bridges" [15], where people attracted to these interest-driven spaces can be diverse across many dimensions. At present, we know little about which of these theories best characterizes open online courses.

In this study, we investigate whether students in online course forums are building silos or bridges. We examine a case study of the HarvardX course HKS1368x, Saving Schools, a course on U.S. education policy. Using survey data, we locate student political beliefs along an education policy ideology spectrum—from left-leaning supporters of unions and school boards to right-leaning supporters of vouchers and charters—and then we analyze how political beliefs predict engagement in the course.

We present two approaches to evaluating whether students in MOOC forums engage across their political differences. First, by examining the connections between posts, replies, and upvotes in forum threads, we evaluate the degree to which students in forums respond directly to students with differing opinions. Second, we use text analysis to evaluate whether the use of language in online forums converges or diverges among students with different political beliefs. Even if students with different beliefs form integrated networks, it may still be possible for students to use siloed language to talk past one another. For instance, in a conversation about guns in American society, conservatives might address Second Amendment rights whereas liberals might discuss issues of public health. We hypothesize that in high-quality discussions in which students directly address each others' ideas, computational text analysis will reveal modest differences in the language used by people with opposing political beliefs.

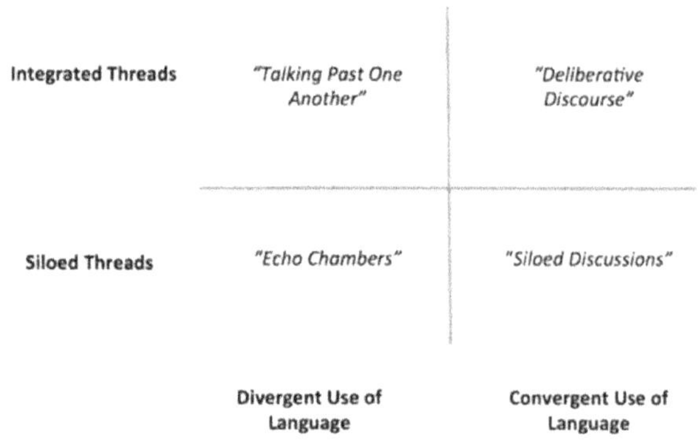

Figure 1*:* **Two-by-two schematic of dimensions of engagement in online discussion forums.**

Based on these two analyses, we propose a two-by-two matrix to summarize dimensions of engagement across political differences in online discussion forums, shown in Figure 1. The bottom left quadrant describes forums where people with different political beliefs separate into silos and use different language; these are the echo chambers of Internet discourse. The top left quadrant describes integrated threads in which partisans use different language; these are spaces where students with different beliefs talk past one another. In the bottom right quadrant, students discuss topics using a shared language, but they divide themselves into conversational silos with like-minded others. In the top right quadrant is the ideal condition of deliberative discourse, where people with diverse beliefs converse with a common vocabulary. This initial study, part of a larger project on measuring engagement across political differences in open online courses [18], presents early efforts at measuring these two dimensions.

We address four specific research questions in this study. First, do students with diverse political beliefs register for Saving Schools? Second, political belief correlate with course participation patterns? Specifically, do people with left- or right-learning beliefs on education reform participate more in the course forums? Third, do students in online discussion forums engage directly, through replies and upvotes, with students with different political beliefs? Fourth, do students with different political beliefs use different words and language to discuss topics, or do students converge on a shared language?

In addressing these questions, we respond to Siemens's [17] call to focus MOOC research not just on individual cognitive development but on improving society. As occurs in all sectors of education, there is constant tension between the many possible purposes of MOOCs: as online job and workforce skill training, as a stimulating leisure activity for lifelong learners, or as a modern Agora where citizens from a global commonweal can learn and share together. The pivot of MOOCs towards workforce development is not a foregone conclusion [3]. Research that examines the quality of engagement across political differences in MOOCs can lead the field towards more investigations of the potential of open online learning to benefit civic education and civil society.

This paper proceeds in four parts. We introduce the Saving School course, its students, and their political beliefs. We then present descriptive statistics on how political beliefs correlate with course participation. Next, we present social network analyses of the forum interactions of participants. Finally, we use Structural Topic Models, a method of text analysis, to evaluate the degree to which students with diverse political beliefs converge on a shared language [16].

SAVING SCHOOLS: THE COURSE AND PROFESSOR

Saving Schools is a course about U.S. education policy and reform offered by HarvardX on the edX platform that ran from September 2014 to March 2015. The course is taught by Paul Peterson, Director of the Program on Education Policy and Governance at Harvard University and Editor-In-Chief of *Education Next*, a journal of opinion and research. The course was designed around Peterson's (2010) book *Saving Schools* and consisted of four mini-courses based chapters of the book: "History and Politics of U.S. Education," "Teaching Policies," "Accountability and National Standards," and "School Choice."

Each mini-course was 5-6 weeks long, with content released in weekly bundles according to topic. Each week included a package of materials, such as video lectures, assigned reading, multiple choice questions, and discussion forums. For example, in the second Saving Schools module, "Teaching Policies," the weekly modules included discussions of "Teacher Compensation" and "Class Size Reduction." The "Teacher Compensation" module included three video lectures with the homework questions "are teachers paid too little?"; "are teachers paid too much?"; and "are teachers paid the wrong way?" Students were then instructed to read two opposing *Education Next* pieces on teacher pay and to respond in the forums to a discussion prompt on that topic. Some weeks, students were split into discussion cohorts by letter of last name or date of birth. Learners earning a certificate were required to post at least once in the discussion forum each week.

The politics of U.S. education reform do not perfectly align with conservative/liberal distinctions, but Paul Peterson's education policy preferences are generally associated with conservative positions. His journal, *Education Next*, is considered one of the leading publications for conservative viewpoints on education policy issues, and executive editor Martin West was an educational advisor to Mitt Romney's presidential campaign. Peterson is a proponent of free market reforms, school and teacher accountability [11], charter schools [10] and standardized testing [11]; and he has been critical of policies advocated by labor unions and schools boards. Our informal assessment of Saving Schools is that Petersen provides multiple perspectives on issues and gives each side a fair hearing, though he also makes clear his own, generally conservative, policy preferences.

	Participants	Survey Respondents	U.S. Forum Posters
Total (n)	5,408	1,982	592
Median age	32 years	36 years	40 years
US learners	76%	69%	100%
Percent female	55%	58%	64%
Bachelor's degree or above	79%	78%	88%
Average median grade	41%	67%	93%
Ever taught		55%	63%
Now teaching		26%	45%
Intent to complete course		57%	75%
Intent to audit course		31%	18%

Table 1: Demographics of Saving Schools participants.

The Students of Saving Schools

Demographics

There were 10,478 students who registered in at least one of the four modules for Saving Schools. As is typical for HarvardX MOOCs, about half of registrants did not ever actually enter the courseware, leaving 5,408 participants. Demographic data for these participants is shown in Table 1: 55% were female, 79% had a Bachelor's degree or advanced degree, 76% were participating from an IP address registered in the United States, and the median age was 32. The median grade, calculated by averaging the median grade of all four modules among students who got at least one graded problem correct, was 41%.

Of the 5,408 participants, 1,982 students completed the pre-course survey. Survey respondents are demographically similar to participants as a whole. Among these respondents, 55% report that they have worked as a teacher or instructor, and 26% report currently teaching. Respondents from the United States were asked questions, derived from a national survey conducted by *Education Next* [12], about their education policy preferences.

In this study, we focus our attention on the 592 students from the United States who both participated in the forum and completed the pre-course survey. Of the 1,008 students who posted in forums at least once, 613 were in the United States, and 592 American forum posters took the course survey, for a response rate among this group of 96%. These students differ in key dimensions from other course participants: on average they are older, more likely to be female, more likely to have a Bachelor's degree, more likely to have taught, more interested in earning a certificate, and more likely to actually do so. This group is our sample of interest for the remainder of the study.

Do you think that [government funding/taxes] for public schools in your district should increase, decrease, or stay about the same?				
Greatly increase	**Increase**	**Stay about the same**	**Decrease**	**Greatly decrease**
19%	42%	33%	4%	2%
Do you favor or oppose giving low-income families attending failing public schools the choice to attend private schools instead, with government assistance to pay the tuition?				
Strongly favor	**Somewhat favor**	**Neither favor nor oppose**	**Somewhat oppose**	**Strongly oppose**
18%	30%	5%	23%	24%
Do you favor or oppose tenure for teachers?				
11%	20%	7%	33%	27%
Do you think teacher unions have a generally positive or negative effect on schools?				
Strongly positive effect	**Somewhat positive effect**	**Neither positive nor negative effect**	**Somewhat negative effect**	**Strongly negative effect**
7%	29%	16%	34%	15%

Table 2: Responses by Saving Schools U.S. forum posters to politically salient questions derived from *Education Next* poll (*n*= 592)

Political Beliefs

In the pre-course survey, students from the United States were given a set of questions taken from the *Education Next* poll, a commissioned annual public opinion poll. (The authors had no involvement in creating the survey; these were secondary data) Of the various questions asked, we identified four questions that are most strongly correlated with measures of political partisanship [12]: questions about school taxes, school vouchers, unions, and teacher tenure. In Table 2, we show the distribution of responses to these four questions among the 592 U.S. survey respondents who were also forum posters. While the respondents generally favored increasing taxes and funding for public schools, with 61 percent in favor and only 6 percent opposed (perhaps unsurprisingly given the number of enrolled educators), beliefs varied more widely for the other three questions. Among respondents, 48 percent favored vouchers while 47 percent were opposed; 31 percent favored tenure while 60 percent were opposed; and 36 percent favored unions while 49 percent were opposed. In the 2015 *Education Next* poll, 50 percent of the public supported increased school funding, 42 percent supported vouchers, 29 percent favored tenure, and 30 percent favored unions [4].

Our assessment of these survey results is twofold. First, Saving Schools attracted students with diverse political beliefs about education policy. This alone is an important finding: MOOCs have the capacity to enroll students with diverse beliefs even when the faculty is recognized for having partisan beliefs. Second, U.S. forum posters' policy preferences are similar to those of the general U.S. public.

To generate a composite representation of a student's political ideology, we use principal components analysis (PCA) to reduce these four responses into a single representation of political ideology, drawing on all 1,295 U.S. students (out of 1,982 total pre-course survey respondents) who completed the *Education Next* poll questions (Table 3).

Factors	Political Ideology	Comp. 2	Comp. 3	Comp. 4
Eigenvalue	1.79	.92	.83	.45
Weights				
Taxes	0.3601	-0.8084	0.4286	0.1823
Vouchers	-0.4059	0.273	0.8714	-0.0366
Tenure	0.5688	0.4768	0.143	0.6547
Unions	0.6181	0.2113	0.1909	-0.7327

Table 3: Four factors derived from a Principal Components Analysis of 1,295 U.S. Saving Schools student responses to four *Education Next* questions.

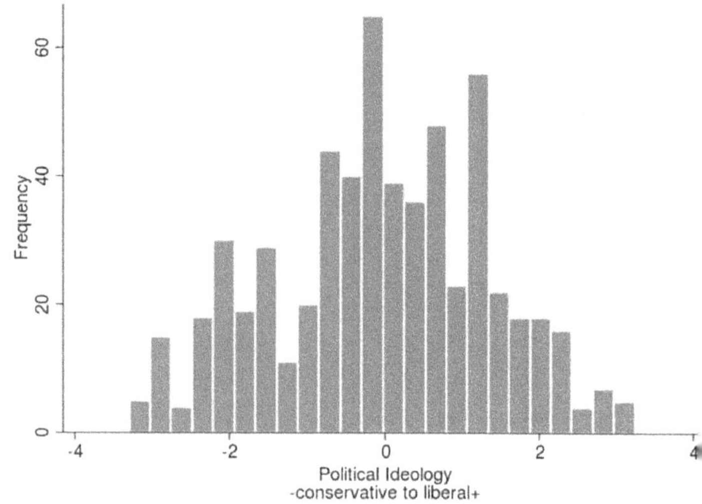

Figure 2: Distribution of political ideology scores of all U.S. Saving Schools survey respondents who posted in the forums (*n*=592).

The first principal component eigenvalue is substantially larger than the others and is the only component above one. As expected, this principal component has positive loadings for the questions related to taxes, tenure, and unions, and negative loading on the question related to vouchers. Given these favorable qualities for a summary measure, we call this new variable Political Ideology, where positive values are associated with typical liberal positions and negative values are associated with typical conservative positions. In Figure 2, we show the distribution of political ideology across all U.S. Savings Schools forum posters.

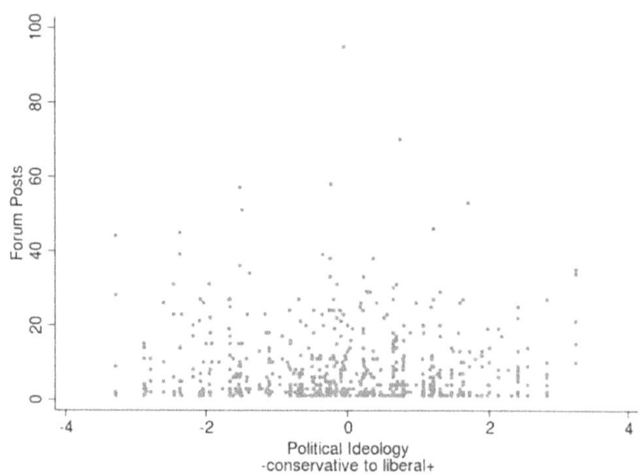

Figure 3: Scatter plot of U.S. Saving Schools forum posters by political ideology and number of forum posts (*n*=592).

FORUM ACTIVITY IN SAVINGS SCHOOLS: DOES POLITICAL BELIEF PREDICT STUDENT FORUM PARTICIPATION?

The corpus of discussions across all four modules includes 8,649 posts from 1,008 participants. The number of posts written per learner throughout the course varied from 1 to 95 among those who completed the *Education Next* poll. In Figure 3, which shows a scatterplot of the number of forum posts and political ideology, we see little relationship between political ideology and posting behavior, with posting behavior evenly distributed across conservative, neutral, and liberal political ideology scores. Moreover, choosing to post at least once is uncorrelated with political ideology. We conducted a logistic regression model where the outcome is posting at least once for the 1,166 U.S. students who completed the political survey and demographic questions. Controlling for gender, education, and age, we find no relationship between political ideology and posting at least once (β=.03, SE=.04, p=.50).

Students with different political beliefs participated in the Saving Schools forums at equitable rates. We turn to forum activity analysis and text analysis to examine whether these diverse students talk with one another.

Network Structure by Political Affiliation

For students to build "bridges" in their online course forums, it is first necessary that forum threads include a range of political perspectives. In this section we assess whether individual forum threads contain contributions from posters with a diversity of political beliefs. We then consider whether partisanship is a determinant of patterns in whom individuals post in response to and who they upvote.

Categorizing threads

Threads provide a natural mechanism for partitioning separate conversations in the forum. Different forum threads serve different purposes in MOOCs [19, 20]. Some serve an administrative function, such as having students introduce themselves, making announcements about the timing of homework, or providing feedback from the teaching staff. Others contain content of a more political nature such as discussions of collective bargaining, the common core, or vouchers. While engagement on all sides of the political spectrum may be of interest in administrative threads, we are particularly interested in whether people with different political beliefs engage in politically-salient threads.

To identify the threads of interest for this analysis, one researcher manually coded the initial topic of all 476 threads of the course into three categories: administrative, low political salience, and high political salience. Administrative threads included questions or comments about how to use the EdX platform to turn in homework assignments and a thread at the start of each mini-course inviting each student to share something about his/herself. Topics related to education policy but not demarked as controversial topics within the Saving Schools course were coded for low political salience. An example includes threads looking at the relationship between economic growth and education that began: "I certainly agree that economic growth and education are closely related. All the countries that scored low in the [international assessment] do not have an outstanding economic growth. Schools are the main source for human capital." Topics coded as high political salience included posts addressing themes in U.S. educational policy demarked as controversial or worthy of further discussion in the Saving Schools course, such as high stakes testing, the No Child Left Behind Act (NCLB), the Common Core, teachers' unions, and charter schools.

Threads vary substantially in both size and content. In order to ensure that our analysis was not dominated by low participation threads, we limit our analysis to threads that contain more than 10 posts, which leaves 76 threads containing 7677 posts. Of these 76, 15 were administrative, 11 were high political salience, and 50 were low political salience. There are 136 and 114 posts on average for high and low political salience threads compared to 64 for administrative threads.

Threads Have Ideologically Diverse Posters

We first address the question of whether posters segregate themselves across threads. In Figure 4, we show the average ideology level (as measured in the factor analysis above) for each thread, organized by our salience coding. Each point represents a thread and the intervals around them are 95% confidence intervals around the estimates of the average ideology of the posters in that thread. Almost all of the confidence intervals cover zero, which indicates

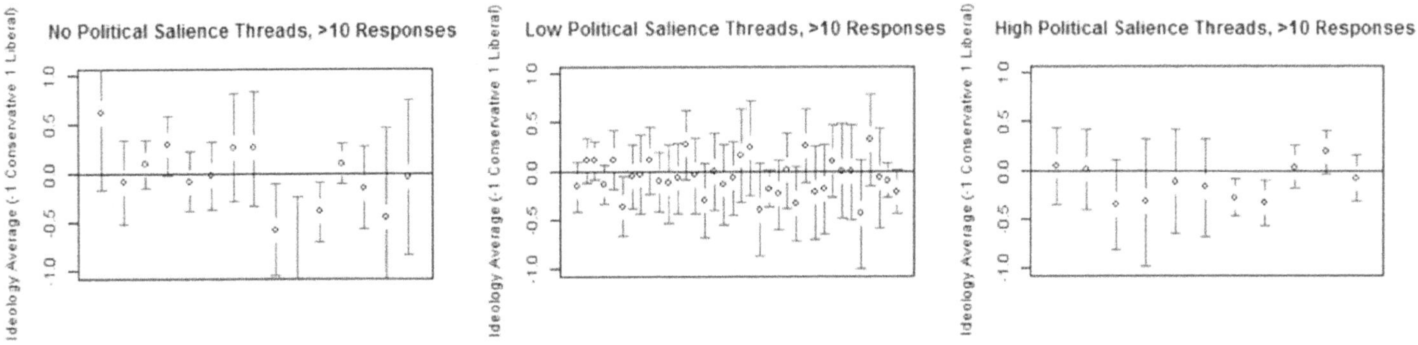

Figure 4: Ideological average in Saving Schools forum threads with more than 10 posts.

that individual threads are not being dominated by a single perspective. Even among high political salience threads the ideological average never strays far from the global mean.

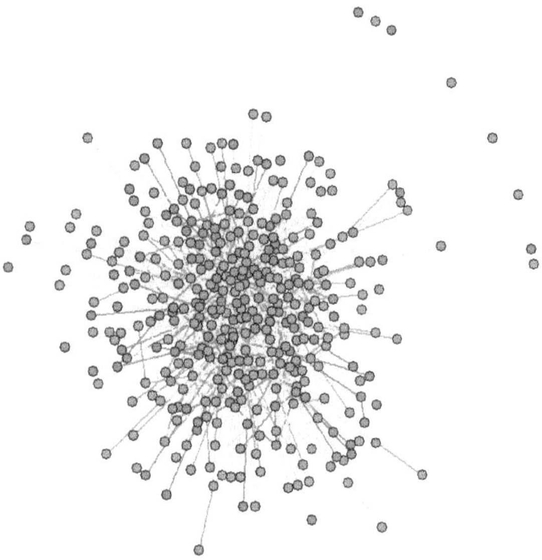

Figure 5: Exploratory social network graph of Saving Schools threads with >10 responses

We plot the network in Figure 5. We label nodes of liberal forum posters as blue, moderates as magenta, conservatives as red, and exclude non-respondents. Edges represent direct responses in threads with at least 10 posts. Edges are same color for matched nodes, and green otherwise. Nodes are laid out using the Fruchterman-Reingold layout. We attempted numerous community detection techniques including stochastic blockmodels, mixed-membership stochastic blocks and latent space models. None yielded a clustering consistent with political ideology, and the assortativity coefficient is small (0.037 using the continuous ideology measure).

One metric of engagement across partisan difference is the expected number of replies for a given poster. If a post generates only responses from authors of the same ideological type, it suggests little opportunity for bridging dialog. Figure 6 shows the patterns of posts and replies by post-type category. Along the x-axis we have the poster ideology, represented in a common U.S. tripartite division of liberal, moderate, and conservative, and the y-axis gives the expected number of replies by the replying author's ideology. Particularly in the high salience setting, an individual posting is likely to get at least one response from another forum participation with different beliefs. This is a necessary if not sufficient condition for bridging dialog.

Posting in a thread with politically diverse perspectives indicates engagement with thread participants but it does not necessarily imply acknowledgement of alternative arguments or perspectives. For this we turn to upvote behavior, which is how forum participants signal their positive response to specific posts. While there are multiple possible meanings to an upvote, we view it as an explicit action to promote the visibility of a post and thus the poster's argument. If an individual upvotes a post written

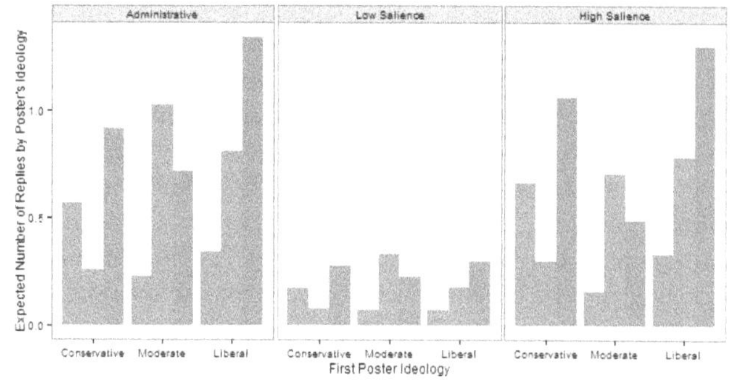

Figure 6: For each category of post, the expected number of comments per response post by response poster's ideology and commenter's ideology.

by someone of a different ideology in a politically salient thread, we take this as an indicator of a bridging action and an acknowledgment of alternative views.

Upvoting is a less frequent activity than posting within this particular class. There are 822 upvotes in the 76 threads we consider. Each thread contains 10.8 upvotes on average (coming from 5.7 unique voters) in comparison to 101 posts per thread on average. We have the voter's and the original poster's political ideology score for 285 upvotes.

To investigate whether people upvote across political differences, we look at upvotes where the voter and the post author have political ideology scores that are more than a standard deviation apart. For each thread for which we have both the original poster's and the upvoter's political scores, we calculate the percentage of upvotes that are made by a voter whose political ideology differs from that of the poster. The average thread-level percentages indicate a high rate of difference upvotes: 55% (administrative threads), 48% (low salience threads), and 49% (high salience threads). These rates are all consistent with rates we would expect if upvotes were assigned randomly across upvoted posts. This suggests that participants upvote posts that reflect an opposing ideology at the same rate as they

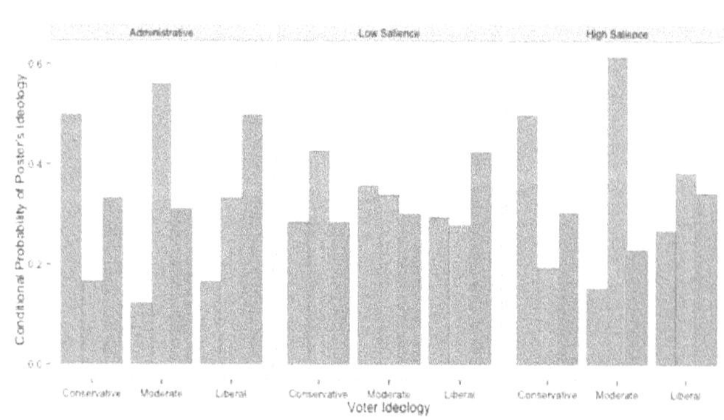

Figure 7: Conditional probability of poster ideology by upvoter ideology among upvotes in Saving Schools

upvote posts reflecting their own ideology. These results hold for metrics of assortativity on the bipartite graph of voters and posters. The assortativity coefficient on the continuous ideology score is 0.049.

We can also conceptualize upvote patterns in terms of categories of ideological affiliation. We split the voters and posters into terciles for conservative, moderate, and liberal. For each type of thread, we compute the conditional probability of the poster's ideological label given the voter's ideological label, displayed in Figure 7. We notice that the probabilities are roughly equal in the low salience group, and a chi-square test fails to reject the null distribution of independence. This suggests engagement across partisan differences. For the high salience threads, moderates show a clear preference for upvoting the posts of moderate posters. Conservatives show a preference for upvoting the posts of conservatives but also are willing to bridge, while liberals show a preference for moderates and other liberals. Interestingly, the administrative threads show a tendency for each group to vote for their own type.

The overall picture of forum activity in *Saving Schools* is one of enagement across diverse beliefs. Threads with more than 10 posts almost universally include an ideologically balanced mix of contributors. When looking at upvoting behavior, we find evidence that students indicate approval of posts by other students with substantially different political beliefs. We see some ideological preferences in upvoting behavior, but also upvoting of posts by peers with differing beliefs. Overall, the structure of forum activity suggests that in this one politically-salient MOOC, ideologically diverse students engage directly with one another over politically contentious issues.

Language Use by Political Affiliation

In this section, we investigate whether people with different beliefs use different language to discuss similar topics, or whether they converge on a shared language. We hypothesize that measurable differences in language use by partisan groups may represent situations where partisans "talk past one another," discussing the same issue in different terms that limit meaningful exchange. To examine these patterns, we a form of unsupervised text analysis from the topic modeling tradition [2] called the Structural Topic Model [14, 16]. Topic models are designed to identify sets of words, "topics," that tend to occur together.

We focused our analysis on two different forum threads that dealt with politically contentious issues: the Common Core State Standards and vouchers for private schools. For both threads we estimated a separate STM to evaluate whether particular topics are more likely to be discussed by students from one side of the political ideology scale. Differences in the distribution of topic usage by one partisan group may be evidence of fracturing discussions.

Common Core

Students were asked to respond to a prompt about the Common Core: "Based on this week's videos and readings, what is your opinion of the Common Core debate? Do you support states adopting the Common Core standards or do you oppose them doing this." From this data we have 195

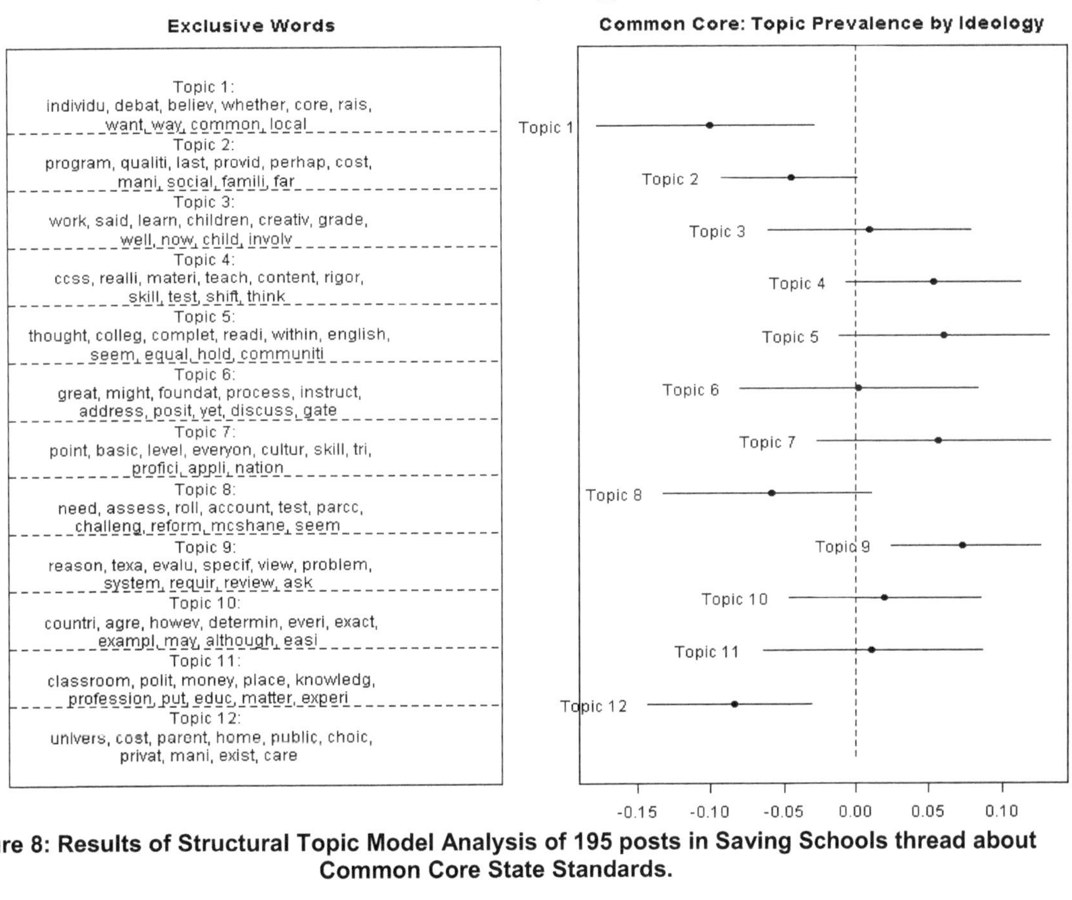

Figure 8: Results of Structural Topic Model Analysis of 195 posts in Saving Schools thread about Common Core State Standards.

posts for which we have political ideology information on the poster. Figure 8 plots two sets of results from a 10-topic model for the Common Core thread. On the left side are sets of words, known in the literature as FREX words [1, 16], that are associated with a specific topic while being less likely to appear in other topics. We use these FREX words as well as examples of posts highly representative of particular topics (as identified by the STM model) to semantically interpret these topics. For example, topic 3 deals in part with individual student needs and the need to encourage creativity. Topic 8 focuses on the role of tests and assessments in reforms based on the Common Core.

An advantage of the Structural Topic Model over other topic modeling algorithms is that we can incorporate information about the person who makes a forum post. In particular, we analyze whether liberals and conservatives write about different topics more or less frequently. The STM estimates several important quantities. First, like other topic models, it estimates a set of topics, which are defined as a set of words that tend to occur together. More specifically, it estimates a probability distribution where for each topic, each word has an associated probability of belonging to that topic. Second, and unique to the STM, it estimates the relationship between metadata that we know about a post, here whether it was written by a liberal, moderate, or conservative, and the proportion of the post belonging to a particular topic. Due to our focus on these political categories, we created a tripartite coding of the ideology data. We classified conservatives as those between 0 and the 33rd tercile, moderates between the 33rd and 66th tercile, and liberals from the 66th to 100th tercile.

We investigated representative posts from the three topics that did see a difference in frequency among liberals versus conservatives. Topic 9 focused on problems with the Common Core, and it was more likely brought up by liberals. As one student wrote in a representative post, "Actually, some [of] the greatest criticisms of the CC come from K and early elementary teachers -- saying that the standards are too high for student development (and they might be totally right, as no K-3 teachers were involved in

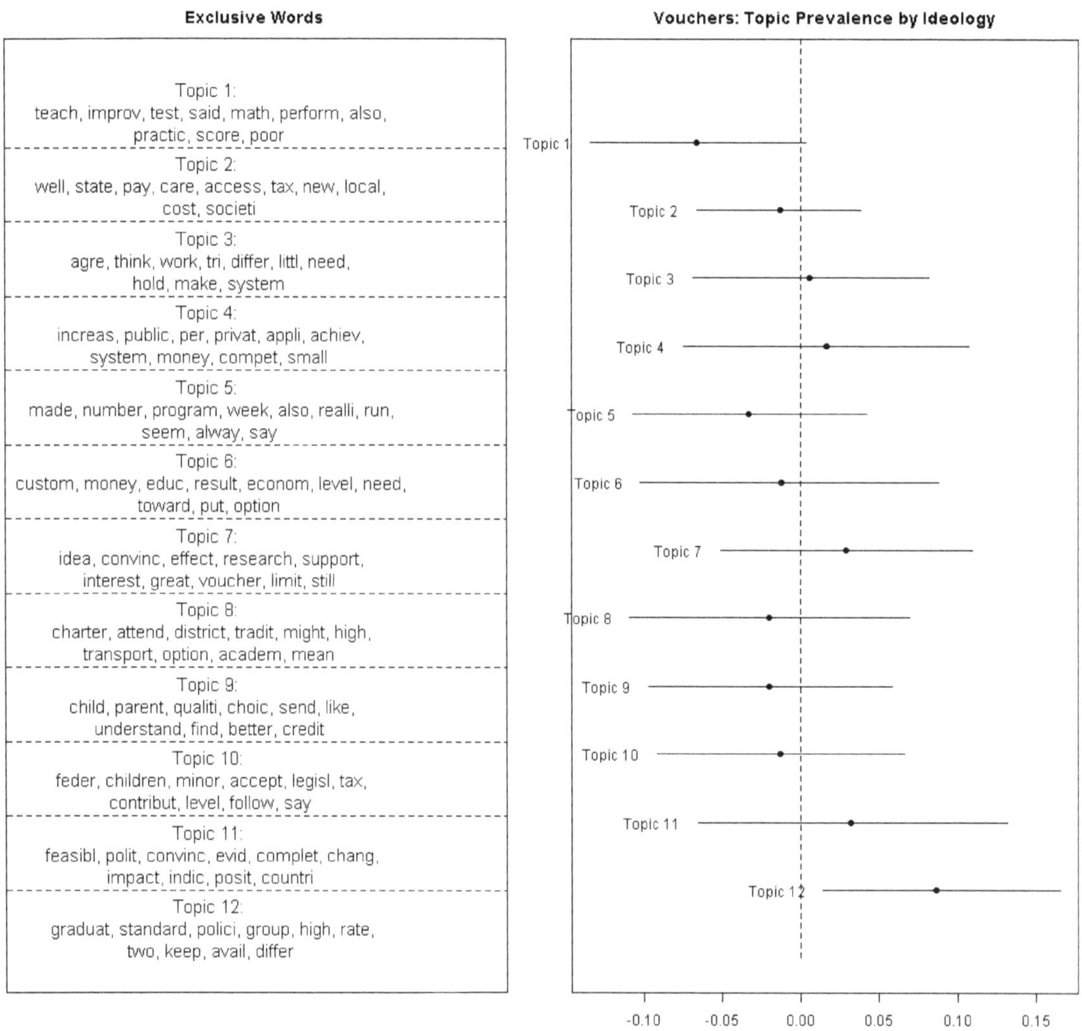

Figure 9: Results of Structural Topic Model analysis of 155 posts about vouchers.

the development of the standards)." Close inspection of these posts reveals that not every post is actually critical, however, and some address criticisms positioned by others. For example, one student responded to another, "As a public high school teacher, I totally agree with you that diversity and letting parents take the lead is absolutely important (and, clearly, that is something that you have set as a priority for your own children). However, the Common Core standards are about public schools -- cases in which parents have not chosen to take the lead." These examples show that even in topics where we see some quantitative evidence of partisan difference in topic distribution, meaningful exchange can be occurring.

Topics 1 and 12 were more associated with conservative posters. Topic 12 dealt with issues of costs, federal and state funding, and school choice. For example, one post read "NCLB is still on the books, so this will not permit some states to benefit from federal funds unfairly and without solvency while others balance budgets and invest in youth. Meanwhile, those states that CHOOSE to act by doing nothing will be identified as such. Liberty and freedom means CHOICE. But choice can be good and bad." Topic 1 dealt with how the debate about the common core had become politicized at the national level. For instance, a poster wrote, "Diversity and letting parents take the lead will always win out here against national curriculum that gets dumbed down to the lowest common denominator and politicized so as not to offend any group or to cater only to the largest sections of the population."

While these differences reveal some differences in how Liberals and Conservatives emphasized different language in the Common Core debate, overall, there were few significant differences in the topic distributions among students with different political beliefs in this thread.

Vouchers

Our second analysis focuses on a discussion thread about vouchers. Our results identified patterns of ideological engagement similar to those in the Common Core thread. For this thread, the discussion prompt was "Are you convinced by the evidence presented in the videos and readings in support of vouchers? If not, where do you think the evidence is lacking? If you are convinced, do you think vouchers are politically feasible?"

We analyzed the 155 posts for which we had a political ideology score using a Structural Topic Model with 12 topics. The left hand side of Figure 9 presents the words most exclusive to each topic. The right hand side presents estimates of whether the prevalence of a topic in a forum post varied between conservatives and liberals. Across all 12 topics we see only two significant differences. Topic 1, which dealt with opportunities for improvement in teaching practices, was more likely to be brought up by conservatives. Topic 12, on the other hand, was more likely to be brought up by liberals. This topic dealt with the need to keep graduation standards high. As with our analysis of the discussion about the Common Core, our text analyses reveal minimal differences in patterns of language used by liberals and conservatives. Tentatively, we present this as evidence that students with different political beliefs are engaging directly with one another in the forums, using a common set of themes and discussion topics.

In these threads about the Common Core and vouchers, and every other individual thread that we examined, we found little evidence of different distributions of topics among posts from liberals and conservatives. One possible interpretation of these findings is that our text analysis instruments are not sensitive enough to pick up on important differences in language use. Another interpretation is that in the forums, a meaningful exchange of ideas on controversial topics using a shared language is taking place. In the context of our other findings—the even distribution of political beliefs among students, the even forums participation of students with different beliefs, and the lack of evidence of assortative mixing in forums—we believe the latter interpretation is plausible.

DISCUSSION

Saving Schools represents a potentially surprising example of a politically-charged MOOC, taught by a professor with transparently partisan positions, that engages a politically diverse community of online students. Contrary to the concerns of observers that the internet has become a place of echo chambers and silos, we find evidence that Saving Schools is a space in the contentious debates over U.S. education reform where people with different opinions can learn and engage together. We found that the student body, at least among U.S. students, contained participants with diverse education policy preferences. Only a subset of participants chose to engage in online forum discussions, but the subset that did so was politically representative of the full set. Within forums, we found that most threads contained a balanced proportion of liberal and conservative posters, that liberals and conservatives directly responded to each others' posts, and that liberals and conservatives upvoted posts across partisan lines. Text analysis of student forum posts suggests that students with different political beliefs tend to discuss similar topics in roughly equal proportion. We find little evidence of students segregating themselves within rhetorical frames that inhibit meaningful discussion. Returning to our two-by-two schematic of online discourse from Figure 1, we argue that Saving Schools presents a case study where at least the pre-conditions of deliberative discourse appear to be met.

The most obvious limitation of this current work is that we lack any kind of "ground truth" with which to calibrate our instruments designed to measure engagement across political difference. In future studies, we hope to triangulate our forum analysis and text analysis with more robust and systematic qualitative evaluations of forum threads, conducted by coders with expertise either in online learning or in the substantive subject of the discussion. We also hope to include self-reported data from students about their experiences and their perceptions of engagement across political differences in the course. Finally, we hope that in future case studies, we might find evidence of assortative mixing, and then use experimental interventions to increase engagement across political differences and evaluate how our measures respond to those interventions.

Ultimately, our hope is that greater research and attention to non-cognitive and civic outcomes in MOOCs can broaden the conversation about the purposes of open online learning. Historically, public education has not only served the purpose of developing young people for professions but also for their roles as citizens in civil society. MOOC research should engage with questions as broad as our hopes for higher education.

ACKNOWLEDGMENTS

We gratefully acknowledge grant support from the Spencer Foundations New Civics initiative. We also thank the Saving Schools course team, the Harvard VPAL-Research Group for research support, and Lisa McKay for edits.

REFERENCES

1. Jonathan M. Bischof and Edoardo M. Airoldi. 2012. Summarizing topical content with word frequency and exclusivity. In *International Conference on Machine Learning* (ICML), 201–208. http://www.icml.cc/2012/papers/113.pdf
2. David M. Blei, Andrew Y. Ng, and Michael I. Jordan. 2003. Latent dirichlet allocation. *The Journal of Machine Learning Research* 3: 993-1022.
3. Max Chafkin. 2014. Udacity's Sebastian Thrun, Godfather Of Free Online Education, Changes Course. Retrieved October 27, 2015 from http://www.fastcompany.com/3021473/udacity-sebastian-thrun-uphill-climb
4. *Education Next.* 2015. Results from the 2015 *Education Next* Poll. Retrieved October 27, 2015 from http://educationnext.org/2015-ednext-poll-interactive
5. Andrew Dean Ho, Isaac Chuang, Justin Reich, Cody Austun Coleman, Jacon Whitehill, Curtis G Northcutt, Joseph Jay Williams, John D Hansen, Glenn Lopez, and Rebecca Petersen. 2015. HarvardX and MITx: Two Years of Open Online Courses Fall 2012-Summer 2014. HarvardX & MITx Working Paper No. 2.
6. Howard Gardner, Katie Davis. 2013. *The app generation: How today's youth navigate identity, intimacy, and imagination in a digital world.* Yale University Press
7. Joseph Kahne, Ellen Middaugh, Nam-Jin Lee, and Jessica T. Feezell. 2012. Youth online activity and exposure to diverse perspectives. *New Media & Society* 14,3: 492-512. doi:10.1177/1461444811420271
8. Gary Orfield, John Kucsera, Genevieve Siegel-Hawley 2012. E pluribus… separation: Deepening double segregation for more students. Working Paper.
9. Eli Pariser. 2012. *The filter bubble: How the new personalized Web is changing what we read and how we think.* Penguin Books.
10. Paul E. Peterson. 2010 Let the Charters Bloom. Retrieved August 7, 2015 from http://www.hoover.org/research/let-charters-bloom
11. Paul E. Peterson. 2015. No Child Left Behind and testing help hold schools accountable. Retrieved August 7, 2015 from http://www.latimes.com/opinion/op-ed/la-oe-peterson-nclb-defense-of-testing--20150224-story.html
12. Paul E. Peterson, Michael Henderson, and Martin R. West. 2014. *What Americans Think about Schools and How to Fix Them*. Brookings Institution Press.
13. Justin Reich, Anna L. Romer, and Dennis Barr. 2014. Dialogue across difference: A case study of Facing History and Ourselves' Digital Media Innovation Network. In *#youthaction: Becoming Political in a Digital Age*, Ben Kirshner and Ellen Middaugh. (Eds.). Information Age Publishing.
14. Justin Reich, Dustin Tingley, Jetson Leder-Luis, Margaret E. Roberts, and Brandon M. Stewart. 2015. Computer-Assisted Reading and Discovery for Student Generated Text in Massive Open Online Courses. *Journal of Learning Analytics*. 2, 1:156-184.
15. Howard Rheingold. 2000. *The virtual community: Homesteading on the electronic frontier*. MIT Press.
16. Margaret E. Roberts, Brandon M. Stewart, Dustin Tingley, Christopher Lucas, Jetson Leder-Luis, Shana Kushner Gadarian, Bethany Albertson and David G. Rand. 2014. Structural Topic Models for Open-Ended Survey Responses. *American Journal of Political Science*. 58, 4: 1064-1082.
17. George Siemens. 2015. Keynote Address at Learning with MOOCs Conference, Teachers College, Columbia University.
18. Spencer Foundation. 2015. Computational Measures of Engagement Across Difference in Online Courses. Video. (2 October 2015). Retrieved October 27, 2015 from https://www.youtube.com/watch?v=9v_vJJfdqIY
19. Glenda S. Stump, Jennifer DeBoer, Jonathan Whittinghill, Lori Breslow. 2013. Development of a framework to classify MOOC discussion forum posts: Methodology and challenges. In *NIPS Workshop on Data Driven Education*.
20. Miaomiao Wen, Diyi Yang and Carolyn Penstein Rośe. 2014. Linguistic reflections of student engagement in massive open online courses. In *Proceedings of the International Conference on Weblogs and Social Media*, 525-534

Mobile Devices for Early Literacy Intervention and Research with Global Reach

Cynthia Breazeal
MIT
Cambridge, MA
cynthiab@media.mit.edu

Robin Morris
Georgia State University
Atlanta, GA
robinmorris@gsu.edu

Stephanie Gottwald
Tufts University
Medford, MA
steph.gottwald@tufts.edu

Tinsley Galyean
Curious Learning
Cambridge, MA
tgalyean@curiouslearning.org

Maryanne Wolf
Tufts University
Medford, MA
maryanne.wolf@tufts.edu

ABSTRACT
Extensive work focuses on the uses of technology at scale for post-literate populations (e.g., MOOC, learning games, Learning Management Systems). Little attention is afforded to non-literate populations, particularly in the developing world. This paper presents an approach using mobile devices with the ultimate goal to reach 770 million people. We developed a novel platform with a cloud backend to deliver educational content to over a thousand marginalized children in different countries: specifically, in remote villages without schools, urban slums with overcrowded schools, and at-risk, rural schools. Here we describe the theoretical basis of our system and results from case studies in three educational contexts. This model will help researchers and designers understand how mobile devices can help children acquire basic skills and aid each other's learning when the benefit of teachers is limited or non-existent. !

Author Keywords
Open platform for education; early literacy; reading brain; virtual preschool; pre-k learning and technology; global literacy project

ACM Classification Keywords
K.3.1. Computers and Education: Computer Use in Education.

INTRODUCTION
Never has full literacy been more important to a child's future, or more possible, due to unprecedented access to knowledge and the ubiquity of low cost mobile devices. Access, however, requires literacy. The reality is that over 57 million children have no school and will never become literate. Another 100 million attend such inadequate schools that they will remain functionally non-literate. Environmental degradation and increased refugees will swell that figure. Further, universal attendance in brick-and-mortar schools will not be reached until 2050, and global teacher shortages are expected to worsen [12]. Alternative approaches must be explored.

Mobile devices offer the potential for providing educational content to children in multiple settings [9], but little comprehensive data exists on their efficacy [2]. This paper describes the design, deployment and early impact of an open platform for conducting global education research at scale and to collect data about engagement and learning. First, we describe a novel open platform that addresses the deployment and learning challenges faced by under-resourced communities, particularly their limited access to literacy instruction. This platform is presently deployed in Ethiopia, Uganda, India, South Africa and rural United States and serves 1000 children (see Figure 1). The second innovative aspect involves 1) *content curation* grounded in principles from cognitive neuroscience about the reading brain; and 2) an *educational strategy* informed by principles of social constructivist learning. Finally, we present results from three pioneering studies, each of

Figure 1: Children at our deployment sites using the tablets together. From left to right, in a remote Ethiopian village, in a school in South Africa and in a preschool in Alabama.

L@S 2016, April 25-26, 2016, Edinburgh, Scotland Uk
© 2016 ACM. ISBN 978-1-4503-3726-7/16/04...$15.00
DOI: http://dx.doi.org/10.1145/2876034.2876046

which represents an under resourced community: 1) children with no access to schools in Ethiopia; 2) children in schools with 50 to 100:1 student- teacher ratio in South Africa; and 3) an at-risk, underserved community in the United States. Each study follows controlled designs that address the challenges of conducting rigorous study in these communities. Our cumulative work indicates the potential of this approach to continue to scale successfully to serve under-resourced communities around the world.

Scenario	Deployment	Description
Disconnected-Remote Tablet Groups	e.g., Ethiopia	No or very infrequent Internet connectivity on site. Data stored on tablets (e.g, SD card). Manual intervention for data collection is required, aggregating the data at a central, better-connected workstation, and then uploading the data to the server.
Directly-Connected Remote Tablet Group	e.g., USA schools	WiFi or cellular connectivity to regularly contacted central server to upload data and receive updates. Frequency of uploads can be throttled.
Indirectly-Connected Remote Tablet Group	e.g., South Africa, school-home use, etc.	Strong, but intermittent Wi-Fi or cellular connectivity. Tablets make high-speed connection to local server cache, which trickles data to center server through more stable connection. Meant for deployment protocols in which tablets to return to central location for charging and data uplink.

Table 1: The platform currently supports three kinds of deployment scenarios

PLATFORM

Our technology design goals are 1) to monitor devices remotely; 2) to adjust educational content for learners and populations over time and with varied needs (see Table 1); and, 3) to deploy in conditions where Internet connection is difficult. Thus, our system is designed to:

- **Work without an Internet connection** by buffering data and providing alternate transmission paths.
- **Support remote administration** including the ability to monitor device health and remotely update content.
- **Simplify maintenance and administration** to support technical and non-technical local support personnel.
- **Provide a path to scalability** of a large number of sites and tablets.
- **Limit usage to educational content**, thus making it more accessible to a pre-literate population as well as reducing risk of theft.

The overall architecture is agnostic of any particular mobile device. This implementation uses android tablets because of: 1) the accessibility of the open source operating system; 2) affordability; and 3) availability to our populations. The current price (under $70) provides economic incentives, compared to traditional costs of education. Note that in developing countries an average of $100 USD/year is spent on education, compared to $10,000 USD/year in the USA [8; 11]. This intervention can be delivered for far less, with continuous efficacy data. Further, the number of smartphones in developing countries is projected to be 1.4 billion by 2018 [5], that points to how quickly scalability could occur.

Data Collection

There are three types of usage data collected: 1) device health (e.g., battery level, accelerometer data, etc.); 2) educational apps (e.g., app launches, time used); and, 3) specific response data within apps (e.g., words touched, performance, repetitions of activities). This system is based on the Funf Open Sensing Framework [1] that runs on Android devices without user intervention. It consists of software on both the mobile device side, that collects and stores the data, transporting it when an Internet connection allows; and the server side, that processes and analyzes the data [3].

Administrative Tools

An administrative web interface helps to monitor device health and organize tablet information online. It also allows for web-based remote commands to be sent to tablets (e.g., updated content) while they are in the field. This essential component allows us to iterate rapidly to improve the intervention and the learners' experience.

STUDY OBJECTIVES

The four major challenges faced by children with no or marginal schools were the basis for intervention objectives:

- **Technological familiarity**. To benefit from this intervention, children need sufficient familiarity with the tablets and to acquire a basic level of computer literacy, based largely on innate curiosity with no direct instruction.
- **Basic conceptual knowledge and vocabulary.** To benefit from the apps available, children need to understand basic concepts and vocabulary.
- **Early literacy skills.** To acquire basic literacy, children need exposure to precursor skills at the pre-k and first grade level (e.g., letter recognition, sight word reading, writing letters).
- **Engagement and behavior.** To sustain engagement, usage and literacy assessment data was used to update content.

LITERACY INTERVENTION

Our approach for tablet content design marries well-established theoretical cognitive neuroscience principles for how the young brain learns to read [13; 14] with social constructionist principles of how children learn with others [4, 15], even in minimally invasive education environments [10].

Tablet Content

Reading is not natural to humans. It involves creating a new circuit in the brain by connecting linguistic, visual, cognitive and affective regions. These regions are responsible for the phonological, orthographic, semantic, and comprehension processes necessary for fluent reading to develop. Theoretically curated and designed apps were chosen or designed to develop children's three critical precursor skills: alphabetic knowledge [13; 14], vocabulary knowledge, and letter-sound correspondence rules. Additional apps were then chosen to introduce the next, early reading skills of blending and decoding using basic vocabulary words. Complimentary e-books and videos reinforce print knowledge, vocabulary, and new concepts. The resulting collection of over 70 apps in English includes multi-level interactive games, e-books, videos and creativity apps (e.g., drawing, music) that foster the developing reading circuit, the discovery of new types of learning, maintaining engagement, and better understanding of others.

Tablet Exposure

Social constructivist models of learning emphasize curiosity-driven exploration, collaboration among learners, and the ability of each child to construct meaning from well-designed content and interaction with peers. Studies in minimally invasive education environments show the key role that social learning context plays in promoting learning [16, 17]. Children self-organize into learning cells, often of 4-6 children, who explore, play, and discover. Leader and connector roles emerge, where certain children take on the task of sharing discoveries with others. Within this social learning framework, we worked with the communities to ensure children have a place to congregate to play with the tablets together, guided by their own curiosity and each other's.

Method	Site
Receptive Vocabulary 1. **Peabody Picture Vocabulary Test** (PPVT-4) [6]; Children hear a word; see four pictures; and are asked which picture matches the word. 2. **PPVT-4 adapted measure**; Specific to conceptual vocabulary content on tablet. Consists of a random sample of 17-20 words.	USA Ethiopia and South Africa
Phonological Awareness and Literacy Screening (PALS-PreK) [7]. 1. **Letter Identification:** Children name random letters pointed to by the tester. 2. **Alphabet Recital:** Children are asked to recite the alphabet. 3. **Letter Naming**: Children are asked to name the sound that the letter represents. 4. **Letter Sounds:** Children are asked to give the sound(s) a letter makes. 5. **Letter Writing:** Children were asked to write the alphabet from memory. 6. **Rhyming Tasks:** Children are asked to complete rhyming tasks.	USA and adapted versions for Ethiopia and South Africa
Basic Sight Words Only children who performed with 80% accuracy on vocabulary and alphabetic tasks were asked to read a short list of basic sight words that represented known concepts in apps (e.g., baby, mother, father, etc.), and a selection of easily decodable words (e.g., bat, tap).	Ethiopia and South Africa

Table 2: Literacy measures per corresponding study site.

MEASURES

Table 2 summarizes literacy measures used for each case study. Their specific purpose was to determine if children were able to acquire pre-literacy skills (e.g., knowledge of sounds {phonemes} in words, names of uppercase and lowercase letters) and to expand English vocabulary based on the intervention.

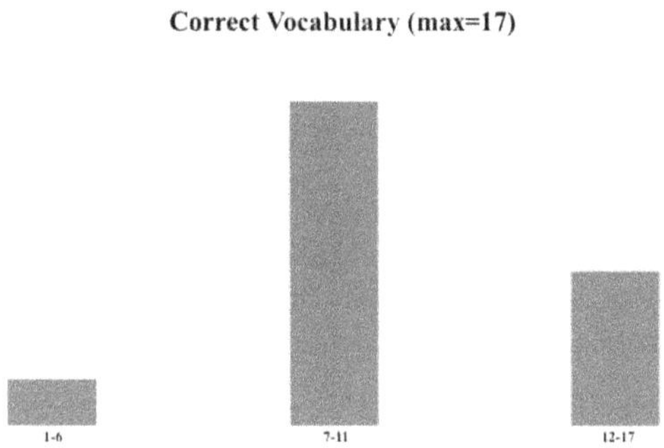

Figure 2: Results from Ethiopia. Number of subjects able to correctly identify vocabulary items.

Engagement Data

Usage data collected on the tablets were used to assess children's engagement with the intervention as summarized in the description of the platform above. We focus on battery level, app launches, and amount of time spent per app.

OVERVIEW OF PARTICIPANTS AND SITES

In the following, we present the design, measures and results from three first-of-their-kind studies. Each design mitigates the specific challenges of conducting a rigorous study in these communities. Participants and sites were chosen to explore distinct use cases, representative of under resourced communities:

- **Case Study 1:** Children in Ethiopia with no access to schools.
- **Case Study 2:** Children in a South African school with at 50+:1 student- teacher ratio.
- **Case Study 3:** Children at an at-risk, underserved community in the United States.

CASE STUDY 1: ETHIOPIA

Two villages were chosen as representative of Ethiopia's pastoral populations with no access to schools. The villagers speak a dialect of Oromo and have very rarely heard English or seen written language. There were no appropriate apps or digital activities available in the children's native Oromo language. However, learning to speak and read in English is highly aspirational with improved employment opportunities in the future. Local government and relevant leaders requested an English deployment for these reasons. There was no electricity and no electronic devices in the village. The deployment team provided solar charging equipment and training to village adults. All children in the villages between the approximate ages of 4-11 were given a tablet.

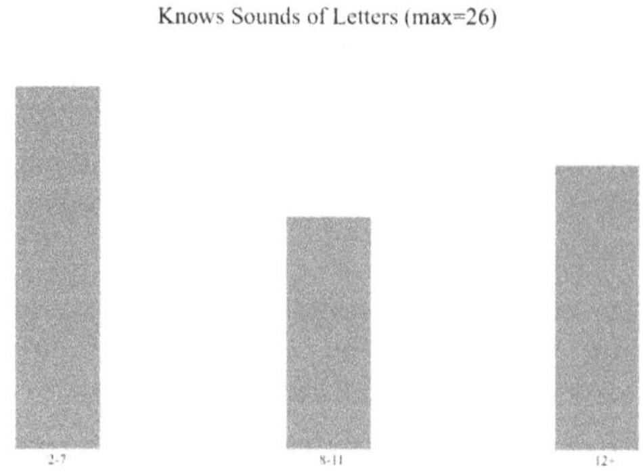

Figure 3: Results from Ethiopia. Number of subjects identifying sounds of letters.

Study Design

The study design and protocol involved only one condition: every child between the ages of 4-11 years began the study fully illiterate, with no prior exposure to such technology, to school or literate adults. Each child received a tablet (n=40, about 20 tablets in each village). Children freely shared and exchanged tablets over one year, followed by post-testing.

Measures

In Ethiopia, a member from our US team, our two Ethiopia deployment partners, and a translator administered formal assessments (see Table 2) in both Ethiopian villages at 12 months. Usage data, a measure of engagement, was collected by the tablets.

Literacy Data Results

Taken as a whole, the literacy assessment and behavioral data document the emergence of literacy in a group of children who have never seen symbolic text, but are motivated to learn.

Vocabulary and Concepts

See Figure 2. All children knew at least 4 tested English vocabulary words; over half knew more than 50% of tested words. This result is promising, particularly because tested words were randomly chosen out of many possible words on tablets, and because the children had no environment in which to practice.

Literacy Precursors

See Figure 3. All children tested knew at least 2 letter-names, all but 4 recognized and could name 10 or more English letters in an array, and most importantly, 14 could read a least one of the tested sight words. This group rivaled U.S. Kindergarten-level proficiency.

Usage Data Results

Technology Use

All children became "computer-literate" with the tablets. In the first village, all children learned to turn on their tablets within the first day without instruction. In the second village, by the second day all apps were engaged. By the end of the first month every app had been activated with the children totally "at home" with tablets.

Engagement

Observational data from our deployment team, including videos and photographs, indicate that a dynamic, curiosity-driven learning environment emerged in both groups of children. A collaborative atmosphere appeared in which kids of greater ability helped other children by taking a leadership role. Battery and usage data indicate that children used the tablets about 6 hours a day. Usage data from the first village over the year are illustrative. See Figure 3. First, over 325 apps were opened and explored, an example of children's innate curiosity. Second, based on the 20 tablets most used by children, over 85,000 app opening events occurred. Third, peak app use occurred during weeks 3 and 4 with over 9883 apps opened; lowest use occurred during the summer (averaging 405 apps opened during August), potentially related to the local environment. Fourth, children developed favorite apps, with 20 apps accounting for 25 percent of all activities (over 20,000 app opening events), a majority of which were literacy-focused. Thus, as the year progressed, children opened fewer apps, but spent much more time using specific apps, indicating more in-depth engagement with preferred apps over time.

CASE STUDY 2: SOUTH AFRICA

This study took place in a primary school just outside the town of KwaDukuza on the north coast of KwaZulu-Natal. The area surrounding the school consists of very poor, informal settlements with low levels of education and high unemployment rates. Electricity and Wi-Fi connectivity was available at the school. Participants included children in Reception/ Kindergarten year through Grade 3 (Ages 5-8).

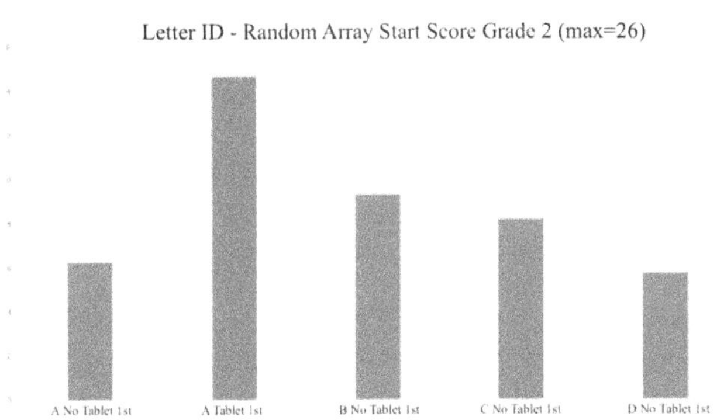

Figure 4: South Africa: Letter Identification at the start of grade 2. Comparing students who had tablets (A Tablet) during previous school year in the 1st grade for approximately 6-months compared to students who did not have tablets in 1st grade previously.

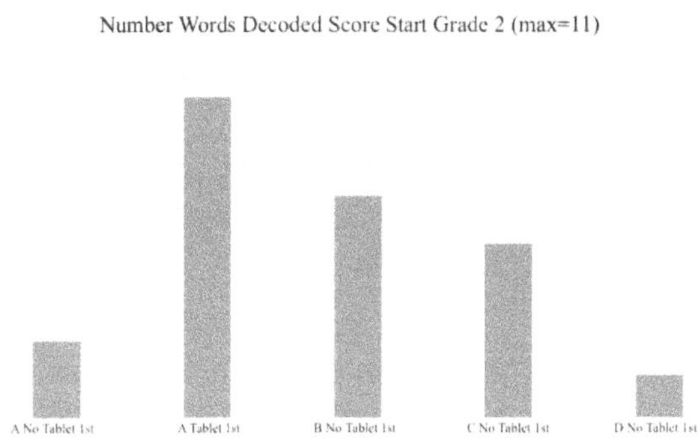

Figure 5: South Africa: Number of Words Decoded at start of grade 2.

Study Design

The initial study design and protocol included one condition: 25-30 tablets were provided to each classroom of children on rotating schedules during a typical school day throughout the week. Class sizes range from 50-99 children per class level. Four Kindergarten level and three 1st grade classes received 3 hours a week of tablet time, while three 2nd grade and three 3rd grade classes received 4 hours a week of tablet time. A total of n=551 children participated.

The deployment team was comprised of local educational and technology staff working in conjunction with project staff in the U.S. This initial study took place at one school to evaluate the short-term impact of this model on learning over approximately a 5-month period (August to early December, 2014). Children freely exchanged and shared the tablets with peers throughout class periods, making child-specific data not possible. Rather, class level assessment data was collected on children when the tablets were distributed, and at the start of the next school year.

Measures

In South Africa, all student testing was completed by local evaluators using literacy measures shown in Table 2. Usage data, as a measure of engagement, was collected by the tablets.

Literacy Data Results

Children who received the tablets in Grade 1 (Aug 2014) in School A were tested at the start of Grade 2 (Feb 2015) and were compared to Grade 2 children who did not receive tablets from the same school (A) and from other regional schools (B-D). Figures 4 and 5 indicate that children with

Condition	Scenario	Population	Tablet Exposure
Whole Day Pre-K Class (WD) n = 18	Traditional all-day Pre-K class staffed by a teacher and aide. State classroom curriculum. Pre-testing.	5 children baseline knowledge over 20 upper case letters. 61% received free/reduced cost lunches. 66% female.	20 minutes during class M-F. One night at home.
Half- Day Pre-K Class (HD) n = 16	Half-day Pre-K class staffed by teacher. State classroom curriculum. Pre-testing.	3 children baseline knowledge over 20 upper case letters. 100% received free/reduced cost lunches. 50% female.	Daily per teacher's class plan M-F. Home use M-Th.
Off-campus Virtual Pre-K (OC) n=20	No Pre-K class (lottery outcome). Parents brought children to school once a week for educational and support sessions. Pre-testing.	12 children baseline knowledge over 20 upper case letters. 45% received free/reduced cost lunches. 55% female.	24/7, full-week access to tablet at home.
Head Start/ No Tablet (HS) n= 12	Local Head Start class, staffed by teacher and aide. State preschool curriculum. No pre-testing.	100% received free/reduced cost lunches. 42% female	None.
No Pre-K/No Tablet Group (NO) n= 68	Children who did not take part in school district's Pre-K class or Head Start. No pre-testing.	100% received free/reduced cost lunches. 42% female,	None.

Table 3: Rural US study conditions and descriptions

tablets (A Tablet) had higher scores on letter identification (random array) and words decoded. Not all areas of assessment showed as clear differentiation.

Usage Data Results

Technology Use

South African children quickly learned to turn on and utilize the tablets, and opened and explored all apps. On average, over 3957 app openings occurred during school days when tablets were available.

Engagement

During weeks 1-3, the average time spent on an app was .49, .43 & .51 minutes. At the end of the pilot (14-15 weeks later) the average times spent on an app was .82 and .72 minutes. Peak number of apps used occurred during weeks 11-12, with average times .63 and .61 minutes. These results again suggest that children decrease the number of apps opened over time and then become more engaged with a few favorite apps.

CASE STUDY 3: RURAL UNITED STATES

The US study took place in a rural school district in Alabama (39 people per square mile) with a total elementary student population of 491. Eighty percent of students qualify for free/reduced cost lunch; 40% are African-American, 58% Caucasian. The district had limited preschool options and community had small Head Start program. Participants in the study were four years of age before September 2013.

Study Design

A quasi-experimental, controlled evaluation was performed. There was an inability to completely randomize participants within conditions due to a Pre-K lottery process. The study covers a pilot 4-month deployment. Four conditions were investigated in this case study (Table 3) that represent different levels of traditional Pre-K classroom instruction supplemented with tablet use. Participants were individually assigned a specific tablet (only the school district had access to names for confidentiality purposes). Children in the Off Campus condition (OC) were not enrolled in Pre-K classes, but parents wanted some Pre-k services. This group, therefore, used tablets at home (a virtual Pre-K), and they brought the children to school once a week for parent education and to work with a teacher.

Measures

Pre-K tablet-condition enrolled children (WD, HD, OC) were assessed on literacy measures in Table 2 in early January 2014 and again at end of school year in April. Further assessment of the 3 experimental (WD, HD, and OC) and the 2 non-tablet comparison groups (HS and NO) were conducted at Kindergarten entry in August 2014.

Literacy Data Results

This study demonstrates the set of challenges in quasi-experimental designs in schools. Demographic information and literacy measures document the non-random biases in group assignments and small samples (n=16-20). There were significant group differences in percentage of children receiving free and reduced lunches (OC=45%, WD=61%, HD=100%), an index of socioeconomic status, as well as differences in beginning early literacy knowledge (already

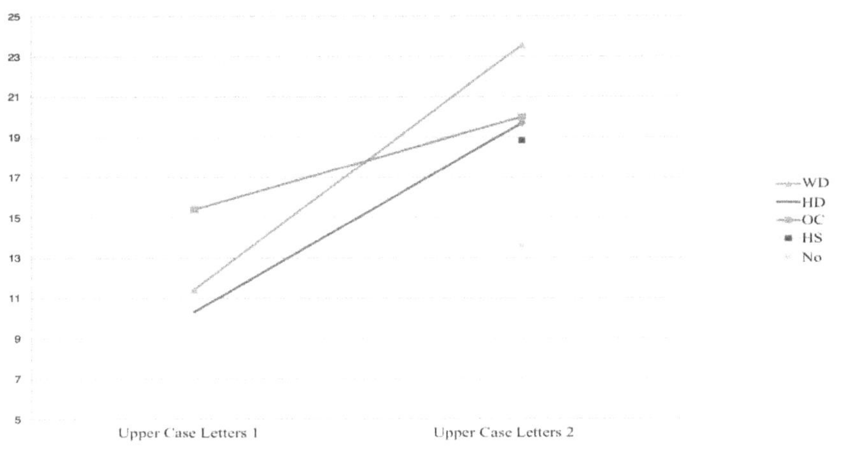

Figure 6: US Deployment. Number of uppercase letters named on PALS-Pre-K (max=26).

knew 16+ uppercase letters at baseline, OC=65%, WD=28%, HD=31%). These results suggest that the OC group had significantly higher language and early literacy knowledge at baseline. Such differences, along with the brevity of the study (4-months), make the interpretation of the promising potential of the tablets preliminary.

Within that context, the results of the PALS-Pre-K upper case letter naming evaluation (one of the better predictors of later reading) are of particular interest. Seen in Figure 6, all three tablet-using groups made significant changes in letter naming abilities during this study --- not surprising given that two groups (WD, HD) were placed in preschool classrooms with experienced teachers. Although the WD groups makes the largest gains, the HD group also made significant gains despite much less classroom time. Both groups had large percentages of children now meeting benchmarks of at least 16 letters (HD=75%, WD=94%) compared to baseline. Similar significant changes were found in their ability to provide letter sounds (Figure 7). Interestingly, the HD group made greater gains than the

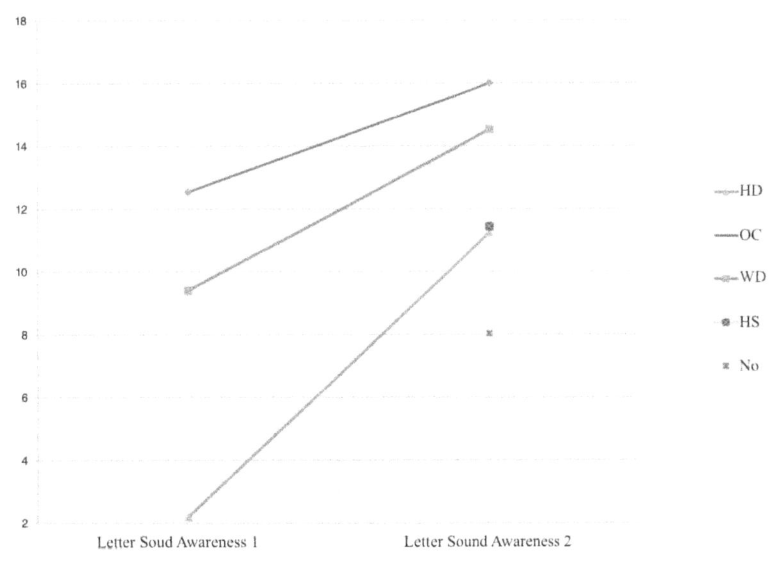

WD class. The amount of change on a receptive vocabulary measure was not significant, although the WD group's change was borderline. This result was expected given the short duration of the study.

None of the children in the HS or NO conditions were given tablets as part of this study. They were comparable to the HD group on socioeconomic status. Neither of these groups had baseline testing, but were tested at entry to Kindergarten like the other children in the tablet study. Their results, shown in each of the figures, indicate the HS group had similar early literacy outcomes as the tablet-use groups, except for significantly lower receptive vocabulary. The NO group showed significantly lower outcomes across all areas evaluated. Such results confirm the well-documented benefits of quality preschool programs, such as HS, for at-risk children. Without baseline data in the HS and NO groups, it is not possible to make further evaluation of the change that occurred in their abilities.

Usage Data Results

Technology Use

As in their African counterparts, US children quickly learned to turn on and utilize the tablets, and opened and explored all apps. Over 4000 app openings occurred during those days when school was in session. Peak tablet use occurred around 12-13 weeks post-initiation in the classrooms.

Engagement

We examined the first four weeks of engagement data across the three tablet-use groups to see how engagement level with tablets might change. In particular, we used "dwell time", the number of seconds a child keeps an app open as a proxy measure of engagement. As mean dwell time increases, children are switching less between apps and more focused on a single app. Repeated-measures ANOVA over the first four weeks for the two preschool (WD, HD) conditions showed dwell time was statistically significantly different across the first four weeks, $F(3,45) = 2.95$, $p = 0.04$, partial η 2 = 0.16. Duration in WD significantly increased from 146.6 ± 37.5 seconds in week 1, to 177.6 ± 58.1 seconds in week 2, to 184.7 ± 41.2 seconds in week 3 to 204.4 ± 73.3 seconds, but not HD. We speculate that as children have less time in the HD preschool to use tablets, the teachers prioritized other activities than tablet use. We also examined the difference between use of tablets in the classroom compared to use at home. Since the data has timestamps, we determined when children used the tablets at school or at home. Dwell time was statistically significantly higher when tablets were used at home (Mdn = 153.8 seconds) than in the classroom (Mdn = 138.6 seconds), $U=14,332.0$, $z=-2.48$, $p = 0.01$.

An important question is whether this tablet use impacts changes in the early literacy knowledge and outcomes indicated by the post-test scores. The simple index we used is how many apps children opened. Because of the difference in the samples, only the WD and HD groups with their more similar starting abilities and demographics were compared. Also, children who named 16 or more uppercase letters (25% of the subjects) were excluded from the analysis because of a concern for ceiling effects on the results.

In Figure 8 there is a systematic relationship ($r=0.43$) between number of apps opened and the number of uppercase letters learned over the study period for these

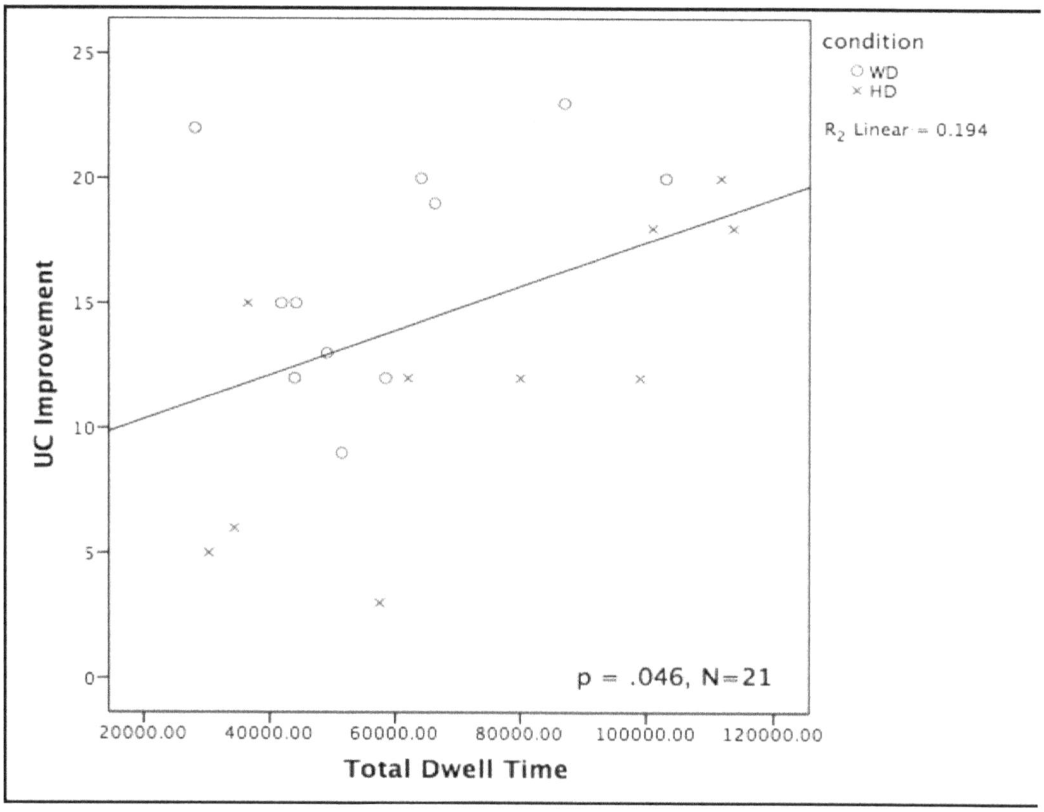

Figure 8: US Deployment. Total dwell time by change in letter naming performance

groups of children. Such results suggest a potential relationship between tablet use and change in early literacy abilities. Although these results are encouraging, given the limitations of these samples, over-interpretation of their impacts should be avoided.

SUMMARY

Each of these studies represents a first-of-its kind effort. They provide beginning evidence for the potential of this platform to benefit students across diverse under-resourced educational settings. We are most encouraged that despite challenges faced by each study population (i.e., no access to schools; or schools with 50-100:1 student-teacher ratio in developing countries; or low SES at-risk communities in developed countries), our three independent literacy and vocabulary pilot assessments suggest better performance overall when compared to similar grade students who did not have access to the tablets. We are also realistic about the range of challenges in this work; we believe the lessons learned below pave the way for future developments and advances.

LESSONS LEARNED

A number of key lessons will have great impact on the success and scalability of future deployments, and these may vary depending on the resources available, the context and location, and the number of children. However some common aspects can be found which greatly influence the outcome of projects. For example, having well-organized and established, on-the-ground deployment partners increases the credibility with community adults and facilitates a productive relationship with the community leaders. Related to this is the importance of building in processes that facilitate informing and eliciting consent from the community members. While initially cumbersome due to the lack of literacy in community members, the need to train facilitators and the necessity of recording responses, we found that formal procedures of consent created buy-in and enthusiasm for what was being offered. We also learned that common assumptions regarding data collection in education technology may be unnecessary. In this project we do not track the identity of individual children on a particular tablet. Not only is a sign-in process almost impossible for pre-literate children, anecdotally we find that unstructured tablet time involves a great deal of tablet exchange which we are hesitant to limit. While still observational, our conclusion so far is that such an environment facilitates a steeper learning curve.

There are a number of different logistical lessons learned that we have begun to capture in a set of deployment "recipes", that can be found along with many other deployment details at wiki.curiouslearning.org.

FUTURE LEARNING AT SCALE

In the context of this work we have come to believe there are many opportunities for how the technical capabilities, research agenda, and deployments can expand in the future to support learning at scale. Three areas are key: content expansion, peer learning, and technological innovation.

Content Expansion

There are clear and exciting opportunities for data-driven improvement, and the refinement and expansion of content. Additional apps need to be developed to support literacy beyond the early reading skills focused upon here. Based on our cognitive neuroscience framework, significant content lacunae exist in phonological, semantic, early decoding and blending processes that, when addressed, may propel children's reading acquisition, and ultimately their deepening comprehension abilities. Furthermore, education developers can introduce new content areas to the platform, both to other academic subjects (e.g., STEAM), as well as to provide resources concerning daily life (nutrition, health and hygiene, ethical development).

New apps and new forms of data analysis can help us understand how best to create engaging experiences that can live within both physical and networked virtual social environments to foster learning across deployment sites on a global scale. Our current work has emphasized peer-peer learning among children for a given deployment site. However, there is a compelling opportunity to connect children across sites through the tablets -- where children's curiosity about each other, and their desire to communicate with others across the world can motivate self-expression and sharing through reading and writing.

Understanding Peer Learning

From a research perspective, a wider range of deployments across even more diverse sites, and the resulting rich and standardized data provided by the platform from each, will make important cross-site and population analyses possible. The platform has already produced a unique cross-cultural data set to establish a data-driven science to understand children's curiosity-driven and peer learning and the efficacy of different content emphases on this. The resulting insights will help communities to better evaluate the critical dimensions that attract these early learners' attention, and engage them over time in tasks that lead to successful learning outcomes. There are also opportunities to develop new literacy and cognitive assessments that can be seamlessly integrated into the tablet experience, either as apps or woven into apps, to supplement traditional pre- and post- testing by trained personnel. Such assessments would generate more longitudinal and finer grained evidence-based assessment of engagement and learning gains. This would not only support evaluating the efficacy of the platform, but would support data-driven improvement of the tablet content and activities.

Technology Innovation

There are computational science opportunities for machine learning and AI methods to continuously adapt the experience to the needs of any learner anywhere. Capturing longitudinal data on learner's usage and behavioral outcomes can be leveraged to build adaptive learning models that scaffold the individual's learning with apps based on their interests and needs, while preserving the learners' ability for choice. Such a model fosters exploration and curiosity for learning, while providing content based on developmental principles.

Growing Community

The vision of this ongoing project is to support a connected community of contributors for the creation and deployment of educational content to 100s of millions of learners across many different cultures. To achieve this goal, we will continue to improve the platform to simplify the process of commissioning and distributing tablets. We also seek to empower communities to create and distribute mother-tongue apps and interactive storybooks so that children can learn to read in their home language. By making the device side software (both content management and data collection) open source, we can engage a community of developers to help the system reach as many devices as possible.

ACKNOWLEDGMENTS

We thank all of our deployment and content partners. We are especially grateful for the support provided by the Italian Development Council, Markos Lemma, Michael Girma, the MRP Foundation, Creesen Naicker, Roanoke County Schools and Dr. David Crouse. We appreciate the generosity of our content partners who donated copies of their software for us to test with our subjects. The children enjoyed them greatly. We would also like to thank Curious Learning (curiouslearning.org), the new nonprofit that is formed to facilitate this approach and to support the platform at scale, as well as provide the platform as a research platform for partners. If you have an interest in becoming a research partner, please contact them. Finally, we are deeply indebted to the children, parents, teachers and communities who participated in these studies.

REFERENCES

1. Aharony, N., Pan, W., Ip, C., Khayal, I., & Pentland, (2011). Social fMRI: Investigating and shaping social mechanisms in the real world. *Pervasive and Mobile Computing*, *7*(6), 643–659. http://dx.doi.org/10.1016/j.pmcj.2011.09.004
2. Baron, N. (2014) Words Onscreen: The Fate of Reading in a Digital World. Oxford , New York : Oxford University Press.
3. Bowman, M., Debray, S. K., and Peterson, L. L. 1993. Reasoning about naming systems. *ACM Trans. Program. Lang. Syst.* 15, 5 (Nov. 1993), 795-825. http://doi.acm.org/10.1145/161468.161471.
4. Chang, A., Breazeal, C., Faridi, F., Roberts, T., Davenport, G., Lieberman, H., Monfort, N. (2012) Textual tinkerability: encouraging storytelling behaviors to foster emergent literacy, *Proceedings CHI '12 Extended Abstracts on Human Factors in Computing Systems*, ACM, New York, NY, pp 505-520. http://dx.doi.org/10.1145/2212776.2212826
5. Dediu, H. (2014) When will smartphones saturate? Retrieved October 22, 2015 from http://www.asymco.com/2014/01/07/when-will-smartphones-saturate/
6. Dunn, M., & Dunn, L. M. (2007). *Peabody Picture Vocabulary Test—4*. Circle Pines, MN: AGS.
7. Invernizzi, M., Sullivan, A., Meier, J. & Swank, L. (2004). *PALS-PreK technical reference*. Richmond, VA: University Printing Services.
8. Kena, G., Musu-Gillette, L., Robinson, J., Wang, X., Rathbun, A., Zhang, J., Wilkinson-Flicker, S., Barmer, A., and Dunlop Velez, E. (2015). *The Condition of Education 2015* (NCES 2015-144). U.S. Department of Education, National Center for Education Statistics. Washington, DC. Retrieved October 22, 2015 from http://nces.ed.gov/pubs2015/2015144.pdf.
9. McManis, L. D. (2012). Achieving School Readiness & Success Using Tablets and Content. Hatch Innovations. https://www.hatchearlylearning.com/?wpfb_dl=8
10. Mitra, S. and Rana, V. (2001) Children and the Internet: Experiments with minimally invasive education in India. *The British Journal of Educational Technology*, volume 32, issue 2, pp 221-232. http://dx.doi.org/10.1111/1467-8535.00192
11. UNESCO Institute for Statistics. (2014) Government expenditure per student, primary. Retrieved September 1, 2015 from http://data.worldbank.org/indicator/SE.XPD.PRIM.PC.ZS/countries.
12. UNESCO Institute for Statistics. (2013) A Teacher for Every Child: Projecting Global Teacher Needs from 2015-2030. Retrieved September 1, 2015 from http://www.uis.unesco.org/Education/Documents/fs27-2013-teachers-projections.pdf.
13. Wolf, M. (2007) Proust and the Squid: The Story and Science of the Reading Brain. New York: Harper Collins
14. Wolf, M., & Gottwald, S. (2015). Android App Survey (Unpublished).
15. Vygotsky, L. (1978). Mind in Society. London: Harvard University Press.

Online Urbanism: Interest-based Subcultures as Drivers of Informal Learning in an Online Community

Ben U. Gelman, Chris Beckley, Aditya Johri, Carlotta Domeniconi, and Seungwon Yang*
George Mason University, 4400 University Drive, Fairfax, VA 22030, U.S.A.
*Louisiana State University, 267 Coates Hall, Baton Rouge, LA 70803, U.S.A.
{bgelman, cbeckley, johri, cdomenic}@gmu.edu; *seungwonyang@lsu.edu

ABSTRACT
Online communities continue to be an important resource for informal learning. Although many facets of online learning communities have been studied, we have limited understanding of how such communities grow over time to productively engage a large number of learners. In this paper we present a study of a large online community called Scratch which was created to help users learn software programming. We analyzed 5 years of data consisting of 1 million users and their 1.9 million projects. Examination of interactional patterns among highly active members of the community uncovered a markedly temporal dimension to participation. As membership of the Scratch online community grew over time, interest-based subcultures started to emerge. This pattern was uncovered even when clustering was based solely on social network of members. This process, which closely resembles *urbanism* or the growth of physically populated areas, allowed new members to combine their interests with programming.

Author Keywords
Informal Learning; Online Communities; Interest-based Subcultures; Scratch; Programming.

INTRODUCTION
Recent studies suggest that many youth have adopted information and communication technologies as learning tools outside of school. Levin & Arafeh [35], in a national survey of US teens, reported a 'digital disconnect' between students and their schools. Students reported limited use of the Internet in school when compared to how they used the Internet outside of school – finding virtual textbooks, backpacks, study groups, and guidance counselors. In another study of 4000 middle school students in the USA, students recounted their technology-using practices outside of school and suggested that more 'creative,' 'interactive,' and 'media oriented' uses of technology in school would lead to their increased engagement [34]. The debate on the role of technology in schooling is ongoing but there is enough evidence to suggest that learners are increasingly engaging in opportunities outside of school to advance their learning. In many cases learners' motivation might be more collaborative and enjoyment driven, but the use of online communities is increasing. As Ito et al. [31] found from their extensive study of youth and use of technology, "A smaller number of youth also use the online world to explore interests and find information that goes beyond what they have access to at school or in their local community." They argue that participation in online groups enables youth to connect to peers "who share specialized and niche interests of various kinds, whether that is online gaming, creative writing, video editing, or other artistic endeavors." Youth find these activities fulfilling as they are "fuelled by their interest but also a lack of support for interest-based activities in formal education." Ito et al. argue that in these "interest-driven" networks "youth may find new peers outside the boundaries of their local community. They can also find opportunities to publicize and distribute their work to online audiences and to gain new forms of visibility and reputation (pg. 1)."

In this paper we present a study of an interest-based online community, Scratch ™, designed specifically to provide an informal learning environment for developing programming skills [22]. The research question that motivated our study was: What structural and interactive patterns define a growing online community? As scholars looking at homophily in social networks have suggested [42], there is a need to understand the "ways in which networks evolve over time through cumulative processes of tie creation and dissolution (pg. 438)." We use clustering to examine how the community grew over time to better understand the role of the community aspects – interactions and connections – on informal learning. We found that as the community expanded it supported the development of interest-based subcultures thereby providing users the ability to develop and align with their identities while creating projects that are meaningful to them. We term this phenomenon "online urbanism". Similar to the rise of urbanism in cities, we found that new participants coalesced around new ideas or created artifacts that reflected new ideas [1].

L@S 2016, April 25-26, 2016, Edinburgh, Scotland Uk
© 2016 ACM. ISBN 978-1-4503-3726-7/16/04...$15.00
DOI: http://dx.doi.org/10.1145/2876034.2876052

LITERATURE REVIEW

Informal Learning

The term "informal learning" is often used as a contrast against didactic teaching in formal environments [36] and constitutes a multitude of activities that are "predominately unstructured, experiential, and non-institutional" [39, p.4] and are likely to take place outside the classroom [38]. Other characteristics associated with informal learning include unplanned and incidental cognition which occurs in daily routines [38] or intentional cognition with a particular emphasis on collaborative knowledge building [37]. Bell et al [28] argue that informal environments are shaped by individuals' cultural-historical backgrounds and prior knowledge, identity, and interests are especially important in informal environments, "where opportunities to learn can be fleeting, episodic, and strongly learner-driven" [28, p. 297]. And, "informal environments may particularly foster capacities that are unlikely to register traceable effects on conventional academic measures, notably around interest and motivation and identity" [28, p. 304]. Informal learning requires higher levels of self-regulation and a stronger sense of belonging and identity and often learners have to rely on the community.

Online Learning Communities

Online communities have become a core foundation of how the Internet and the Web are used for a range of issues from health and wellbeing to disaster management. They have also emerged as a popular mechanism for supporting informal learning [22, 40], either through communities designed directly to support learning (e.g. CSILE) [37] or indirectly through efforts such as Citizen Science [28], discussion forums or Q&A sites [44]. Given the overall popularity of online communities, their formation, growth, and decline of online communities have been areas of great interest and there is robust literature around motivation to participate, design of online interactions to increase participation and contributions, the problems faced by communities as they grow, and the need for a critical mass of participants for sustenance [43]. In spite of numerous research studies on this topic, we have limited understanding of structural changes over time, particularly when a community is going through a growth period. This is an interesting issue to examine if we want to better understand what drives the growth of online learning communities – what makes participants both stick around as well as what activities can attract new participants – so that we can design and sustain more productive online learning communities [40].

RESEARCH CONTEXT: SCRATCH ONLINE COMMUNITY

Online communities take many different forms such as discussion forums, question and answer (Q&A) communities, those where knowledge sharing and helping behaviors are critical, or communities such as Wikipedia, where user contributions are essential for the growth of the community. The research context for this study, Scratch, has been characterized by Sylvan as an Online Community of Creators (OCOC) [13]. OCOCs, according to her, are social network sites where the core activity of members is sharing personal and original creations [13]. This characterization of Scratch as an OCOC is of particular relevance within the context of this study. A community of creators offers its participants some unique ways to contribute that differ from other popular online communities such as discussion forums or Q&A sites and sites that only allow sharing of content, for instance photo sharing sites like Flickr. In addition to question and response and commenting on content, an OCOC allows participants to remix and appropriate content based primarily on the interest of the contributors. This process is organic and changes as participants with new interests join

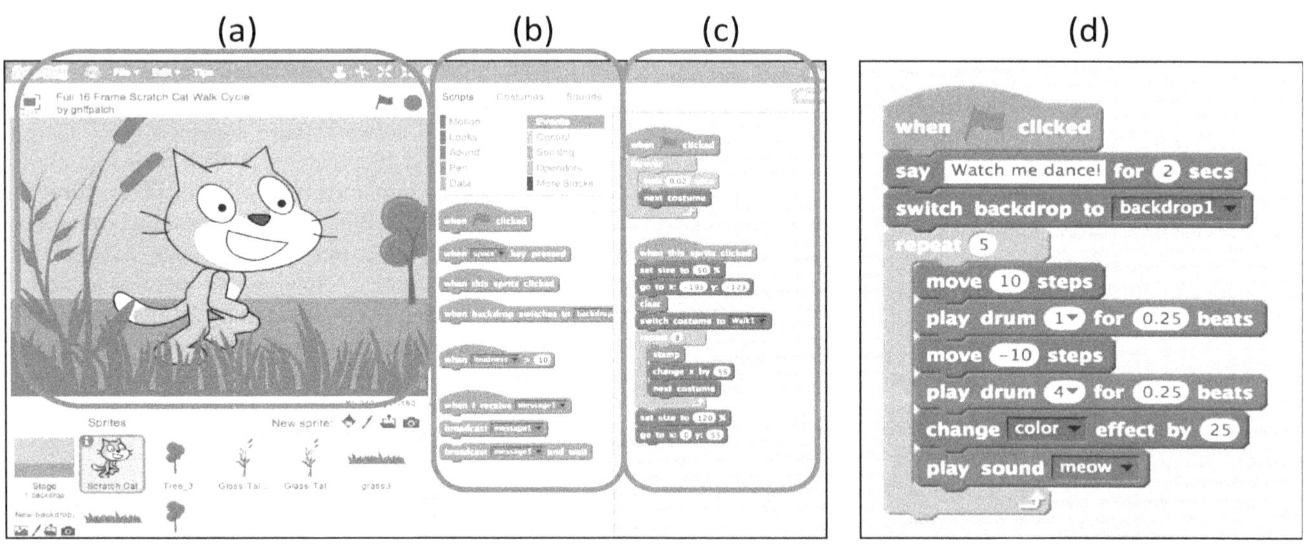

Figure 1. Scratch interface: (a) a project window, (b) blocks, (c) scripts, and (d) a script constructed with blocks.

the community. Also, unlike sites such as Wikipedia where all edits are monitored, Scratch is not a moderated platform.

Scratch is a programming language designed to teach programming basics through a visual, user-friendly interface. The primary target audience is people between the ages of 8 and 16 but the language is open to all [10, 23]. A core goal of Scratch is to make the creation and sharing of interactive content easy for users. As shown in Figure 1, the Scratch programming environment enables users to create programs with blocks, which map to programming constructs and allow users to manipulate data, including media content (e.g., sounds, videos, and images). Users can then share these interactive creations on the Scratch website [24]. The website is an online community where users may run and build on others' ideas and projects. Members can import the source code of any project into their own workspace and remix it. The Scratch website permits a user to view the code of any shared projects. Users may also extend an existing project and make it their own by "remixing". Each user creates a profile on the Scratch website where he shares his creations. Other users can show their interest by tagging projects using tags such as "love" or "favorite" or comment on these projects. Users may also choose to follow others, which allows them to see tags and project uploads of users they follow. Finally, users can chat, discuss project ideas, and work collaboratively in "studios."

In addition to its goal of creating and sharing programs, a fundamental element behind its creation has been to provide an alternate model for how the Web can be used for learning. The Scratch team envisioned learning outcomes related to programming and math skills as well as skills in design, creativity, communication, and so on. Learning is inherently a collaborative process that occurs across communities of practice. The Scratch community was created with the goal to foster learning among users through interaction and sharing of ideas and projects. Resnick et al. wrote about the Scratch in 'Programming for all' and their goal has always been to develop an approach to programming that would appeal to people who had not considered themselves programmers [19]. In May 2007, a website was launched to allow for more sharing of projects on the Web. Maloney et al. studied the use of Scratch at a Computer Clubhouse where urban youth between the age of 8-18 used Scratch [14]. The findings from this research indicated that users learned key programming concepts even in the absence of instructional interventions or experienced mentors. The ease of use for the Scratch platform and its interactivity made it attractive for users.

Data Description and Selection

The Lifelong Kindergarten Group at the MIT Media Lab created the Scratch dataset from the Scratch Online Community [24, 25]. The data set contains 1,056,950 registered users and 1,928,699 projects created between March 5, 2007 and April 1, 2012. Demographics of users are not published due to privacy concerns considering that the majority of Scratch users are kids and teens. This dataset was made publicly available by the Scratch team [26]. The number of users in the community shows a steep linear increase starting from around 100,000 users in March 2008 to slightly over one million users in March 2012 (Figure 2). The attributes associated with users include follower/followed connections, join dates, and number of projects. Project attributes include creation dates, types of code blocks used to create the project, and whether the project was remixed from others. The number of followers and the number of projects are highly skewed, with the majority of the population making 0 or 1 follower connection and/or project (see Figures 3 and 4 respectively). Of the total number of users, 143,234 users (13.55% of total users) have at least one follower, and 304,357 users (28.80% of total users) have created and shared at least one project. Overall, 66.68% of all users (704,820) has never shared a project or followed other users. This long-tail phenomenon is similar to user activity in other online communities [4].

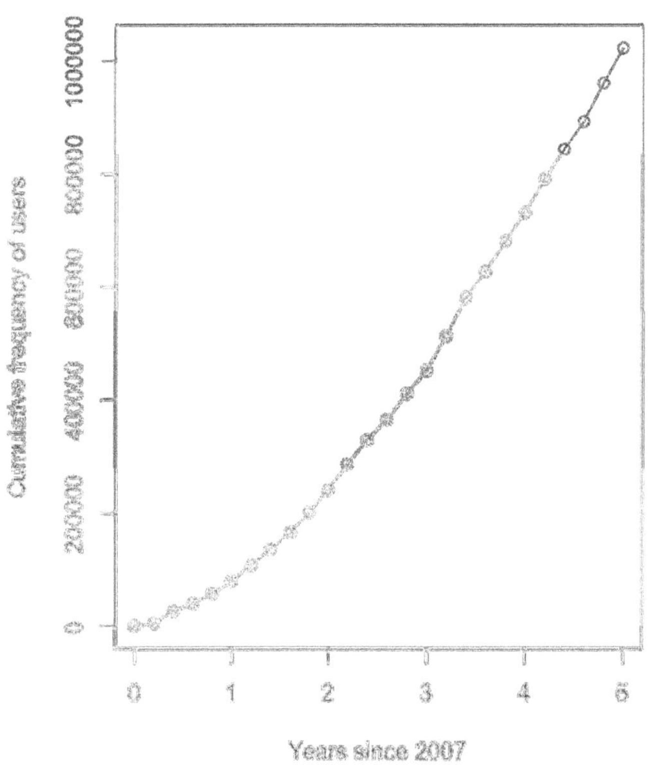

Figure 2: The growth of Scratch users ('0' in the x-axis represents March 5, 2007, and '5' represents March 5, 2012).

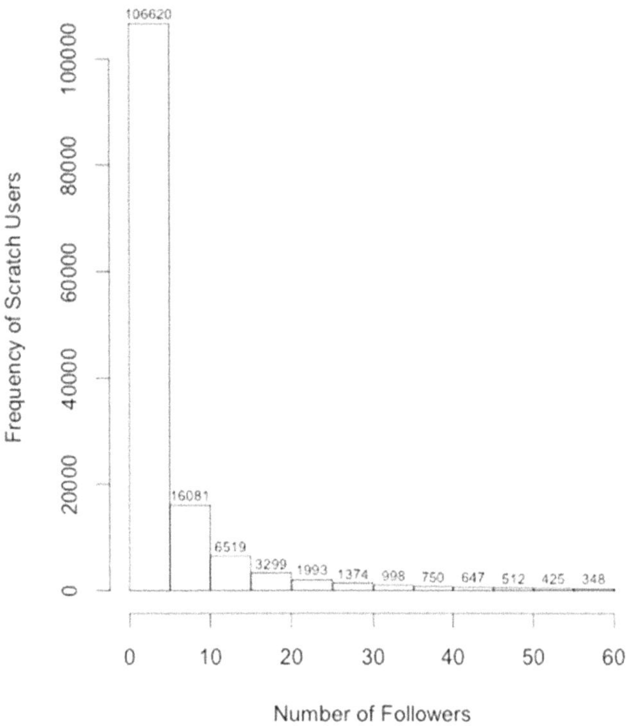

Figure 3: Frequency of Scratch users by the number of followers.

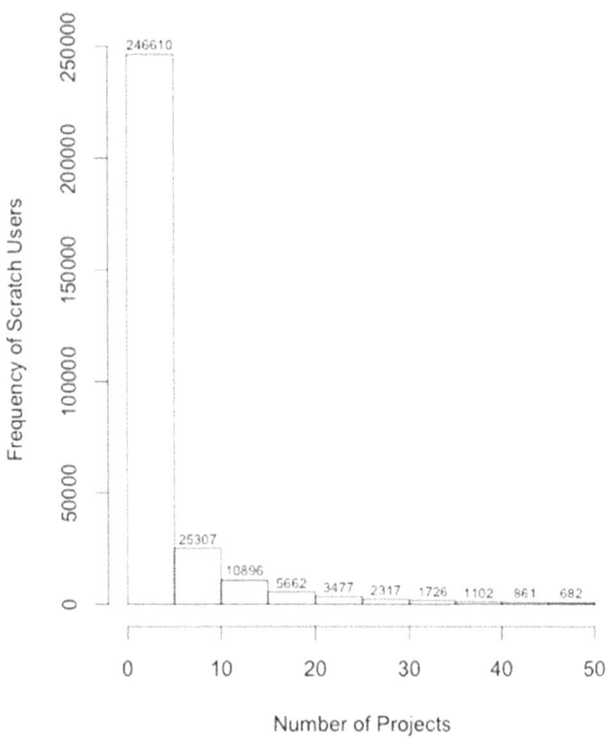

Figure 4: Frequency of Scratch users by the number of projects.

Follower-Followed Relationship as a Measure of Social Ties in Scratch

As recommended by [21], the investigation of social ties, beyond kinship, is critical for understanding subculture formation. Therefore, to select core active members in the community we leveraged the "follower/followed" relationships between pairs of users, rather than the number of projects a user has produced. In fact, the number of followers was a better indication of a user's activity: a user may attract followers if s/he not only is highly active, but also creates projects of interest to others. To generate a list of core active contributors, we adapted the concept of k-core of a graph introduced in [6]. Given the directed graph representing the follower relationship between users, we selected the users with at least k followers (i.e. the nodes with in-degree larger than k). The selection was performed once and not recursively as in [6]. As a result, our notion of k-core is less restrictive: for example, if a node n has in-degree k, and some of the followers have in-degree less than k, n is still considered as a k-core user.

Number of followers	Number of users
1+	95,780
10+	18,835
25+	8,154
50+	4,228
75+	2,738
100+	1,971

Table 1: Cumulative user counts with varying followers.

As shown in Table 1, we investigated different cutoff values for k and eventually settled on k = 25. We observed that at higher thresholds there was a slight bias towards long-term users as they had more time to accumulate followers. For instance, a cutoff value of k = 100 resulted in interactions and project themes of 1,971 users. In contrast, a cutoff value of 25 resulted in 8,154 active users including those who joined the community recently. Considering that the users with 25+ followers gave us a more representative sample, we performed in-depth analysis for these 8,154 users and their 468,057 follower/followed relationships.

Analysis: Identification of Subgroups

In recent years, several studies have examined different models of community growth over time to understand how members' behavior and dynamics impact community participation [4]. In this study, we used clustering techniques to examine growth in community participation. We used highly active core members as proxies for community activity as their participation significantly shapes communities' persistence and growth particularly during periods of high growth [2]. To achieve a better understanding of the collaborative nature of online communities scholars have focused primarily on structural features such as the underlying social networks within the communities. Within this tradition, multiple quantitative methods have been proposed for identifying the structure of a community. For instance, [15] has used hierarchical clustering whereas [16] used a behavioral method to classify members. Researchers have also used a 'sense of community' instrument [17] and [18] used a k-plex analysis to identify sub-communities as cohesive subgroups within a community.

OpenOrd Clustering

The OpenOrd layout in Gephi [5] was used to map the structure. OpenOrd is a multi-level, force-directed layout and uses average-link clustering based on both edge weights (if present) and distance, where distance is determined using a force-directed algorithm [8]. Clusters of nodes are replaced by single nodes, and the clustering is repeated until a certain distance threshold between the nodes is reached. After the clustering is complete, the graph is expanded by replacing the individual nodes with the original graphs in each cluster [8].

Clustering of Users with 25+ Followers

We clustered 8,154 users who have at least 25 followers, and identified five large clusters as shown in Figure 5. Cluster A was the oldest of the three – in terms of the average join dates of its members – and heavily featured early Scratch developers from MIT. Other users in the cluster developed complex projects that stretched the limits of Scratch as a programming language. Cluster B was younger on average than cluster A, and users began to focus more heavily on making games. Cluster C was the youngest of these three clusters, and contained users who had a large variety of projects. Cluster D was the largest and the main project theme of this cluster was games. Various types of game projects were identified – from simple ones involving small number of characters and limited use of media, to complex ones having multiple levels of difficulty and advanced multimedia support. Cluster E was the second smallest one and its users were mainly focused on art projects. Especially, the canine and feline images and characters were often appearing in the projects. We present the details of the temporal analysis for A-E in the next section.

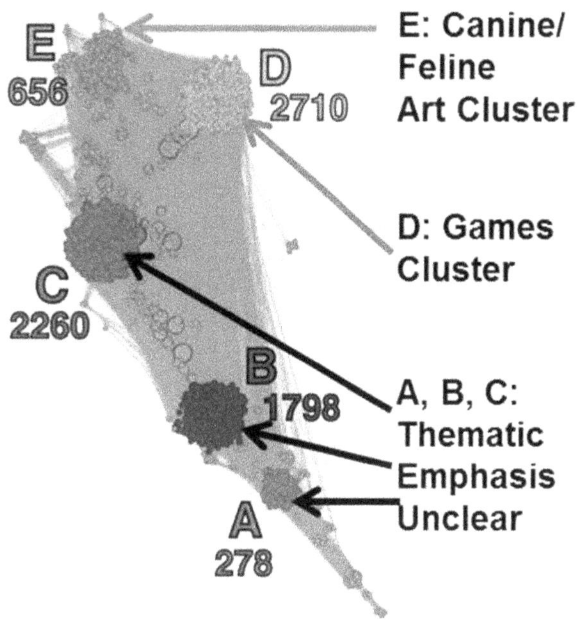

Figure 5: Users with 25+ followers. The number under each cluster label represents the size of the cluster.

To further investigate clusters A-E and uncover similarities within the cluster, we used a text mining approach (Table 2). By concatenating project titles, descriptions, and tags for all projects within each cluster, we represented each cluster as a document with a bag-of-words approach. For each term we calculated the term frequency * inverse document frequency (TFIDF) value [11]. The TFIDF allows uncovering discriminant terms by favoring frequent terms within a cluster, at the same time, penalizing common terms across clusters [11]. Prior to the analysis, all terms were stemmed using the Porter stemmer. The top frequent terms in Cluster A did not indicate any trend. For clusters B and C, certain commonality emerged among the top words. Terms such as "mario," "game," "pokemon," and "sonic" (as in Sonic the Hedgehog™) were present suggesting a slight emphasis on gaming. Cluster D showed a significant increase in the uniformity of the top terms. "Super Mario," "sonic," and "press" (as in "press these keys to play the game") constituted a larger percentage of the total terms as

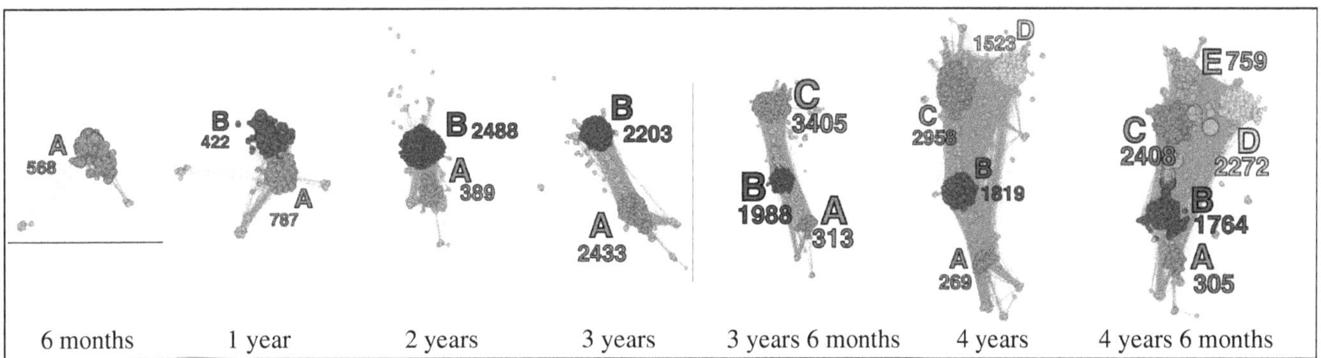

Figure 6: Cluster evolution: Cumulative time of the slicing is marked for each network graph.

compared to clusters B and C, suggesting specialization on gaming within cluster D. Cluster E exhibited top terms that were considerably different from other clusters but the terms had a high degree of uniformity.

In order to examine this cluster further, we selected a sample of the projects from the cluster and inspected them manually. We found that the projects heavily featured canine and feline art. The terms "art" and "contest" (as in a drawing contest) support these findings. Thus, the top terms for cluster E demonstrate a thematic uniformity of feline/canine art. Another reason D and E are interest-driven is the fact that the interest-specific terms also make up a higher percentage of the total terms in those clusters. Although the thematic emphasis of clusters was evident, we informally observed that there was a temporal characteristic to these clusters as well. To further investigate this aspect empirically, we developed the concepts of "Scratchage" and "Scratchend" (see [14] who use a similar methodology).

Temporal Emergence of Subgroups

Scratchage

Scratchage refers to the age of a user's account, measured in years. A user's Scratchage is relative to the end of our dataset. Thus, users who created their account on the last day of our dataset (April 1, 2012) have the youngest Scratchage of zero, and the users who created their account on the first day of our dataset (March 5, 2007) have the oldest Scratchage of 5.08 years. We found a trend among the clusters where as we progressed from cluster A to cluster E the Scratchage of the users decreased even though we did not use any temporal data for clustering (first column in Table 3). We believe that this occurred because of users tend to follow their contemporaries, rather than inactive users.

Scratchend

To measure and explore inactivity in the Scratch community, we created an attribute called "Scratchend," which is the amount of time in years between the final activity of a user and the end of the dataset (April 1, 2012). Our definition of "final activity" is either the final time a user follows someone else, or the final time he/she shares a project (whichever occurs last). For example, cluster D has a Scratchend of 0.37, meaning that, on average, it has been 0.37 years from the last user activity to the end of the dataset. Users who have reached their Scratchend are not likely to obtain any new followers. If a user is not developing friend connections with newer users, who have been joining at an increasing rate, then OpenOrd layout's repulsion forces will push these older, less connected users away. We see this trend in Figure 6, where the oldest clusters A and B are well separated from the younger clusters C, D, and E. We hypothesize that the users in the older clusters A and B joined Scratch, befriended their contemporaries, and then became inactive over time. Along with the increasing rate of new users, this explains why we see a temporal separation of clusters as well as newer clusters C and D with significantly more users.

Cluster	SA: Avg.	SA: SD	SE: Avg.	SE: SD
A	4.85	0.25	3.80	1.28
B	4.11	0.46	2.43	1.25
C	2.79	0.68	1.19	0.86
D	1.69	0.89	0.37	0.46
E	1.25	0.72	0.23	0.30

Table 3: Summary of Scratchage and Scratchend

Community Evolution

In order to dynamically visualize the evolution of the Scratch community, we used a modified version of Falkowski's overlapping sliding window approach [3]. The method involves slicing our dataset at various points in time, clustering each data slice via OpenOrd, and then comparing clusters across time slices. We began by slicing the dataset at one-year intervals. After clustering and sampling each frame, we added certain half-year intervals to observe incremental changes between large transformations in the graph. The initial text analysis of the clusters that we presented in Table 2 is paramount in tandem with the evolution of the Scratch community. The top terms displayed virtually no thematic uniformity in Cluster A, minor uniformity in clusters B and C, and significant uniformity in clusters D and E. This increase in thematic uniformity of the clusters directly corresponds to the age and growth of the clusters. The clusters in Figure 7 are labeled and colored to show the evolution and migration

Cluster	Top Words (TFIDF Values as percentage of Total Terms)
A	comput (5.3); time (4.7); make (4.4); space (4.4); random (4.0); new (3.8); stupid (3.6); first (3.2)
B	waffle (19.3); mario (17.6); game (12.3); super (9.5); tag (9.3); fun (8.5); pokemon (8.0)
C	funni (16.2); waz (15.0); wuz (15.0); tag (11.8); pokemon (10.4); good (8.6); add (8.6); sonic (8.5)
D	mario (22); epic (20.7); tag (16.3); press (12.2); sonic (9.8); super (8.4); add (6.2); scratch (4.2)
E	warrior (11.5); wolf (9.6); yay (8.8); cat (7.9); contest (7.7); pleas (7.0); art (5.7); pie (5.7)

Table 2: Summary of stemmed top frequent words in each cluster.

of users in the clusters over the five years of the dataset. Initially, all users were clustered into one large community (surrounded by small niche communities). This primordial community contained the majority of users at the time. By the first year, some users began to go inactive, and so the initial cluster, A, started to split in two, as new users arrived and friended the active existing members. This active/inactive separation continued until, directly after the beginning of the third year, cluster B burst and formed a third major cluster, C. Between the years 4 and 4.5, clusters D and E emerged from the enormous C cluster.

DISCUSSION

We draw on the "Subcultural Theory of Urbanism" proposed by Fischer [19]-[20] as framework for interpreting our findings. Within the realm of urbanism, subcultural theory proposes that city life is relatively unconventional (defined broadly) and cities stimulate unconventionality because population concentration generates a variety of subcultures. These subcultures can be seen as a "set of interconnected social networks" with common norms and habits. Unlike other theories of urbanism that argue that city life or urbanism results in breakdowns and thus leads to subgroups, the subculture theory argues that population growth provides the opportunity to find others with whom one can take part in a common way of life through mutual sharing of traits, interests and/or values. *Therefore, in the case of Scratch what we identify through our analysis as subgroups can be better understood as subcultures.* Furthermore, according to Fischer [20], the larger the place the more specialized are the subcultures since the population is higher and therefore there is more cultural heterogeneity. Although heterogeneity might exist in small places as well, the critical mass needed for a subculture is reached only in larger places.

Another characteristic of this theory identified by Fischer is that "subcultural theory is, at core, an ecological theory, not a theory about persons." Therefore, although aggregated individual level data is often used to identify and study urban subcultures, a more ecological approach using techniques such as clustering are appropriate. Subcultures are emergent and rather than *a priori* determination of the unit of analysis, it is more appropriate to let the data determine the unit and "its ultimate tests require place-level analyses and, ideally, emergent, place-level measures [20, pg. 548]." We argue that this theory is applicable in the context of online learning communities since, as Fischer himself contends [20, pg. 549], "subcultural theory is largely about the ability of subculture members to communicate", a prerequisite also for learning. He further argues that "specialized and unconventional aspatial subcultures should emerge for those populations with access to modern means of communication and transportation [20, pg. 550]", which is reflected in the online nature of learning and participation by users from across the world. Overall, according to Fischer, the diversity of urban life actually enhances the number of social ties, in particular those that are voluntaristic in nature. In urban conditions individuals have greater freedom in choosing whom they associate with, other than their kin, ties which are often forced. More than physical proximity, self-selection is the important criteria for subcultures to emerge. From an empirical perspective, to better understand the emergence of subcultures it is important to be able to look at social ties [21] and the concentration of these ties based on cultural affiliation (and not just physical proximity).

Online communities provide an interesting context to test the theory since physical proximity is not usually the cohesive factor in online communities (there are some exceptions), a large community in terms of member size provides an ideal context to test this theory. This theoretical perspective provides a unique lens to examine online communities as participation is largely voluntary and based on some form of affiliation beyond kinship. Our interest in using this framework emerged concurrently with our analysis of the community as we saw similar features – such as interest-based subcultures – emerge in our analysis.

One explanation for the emergence of interest-based

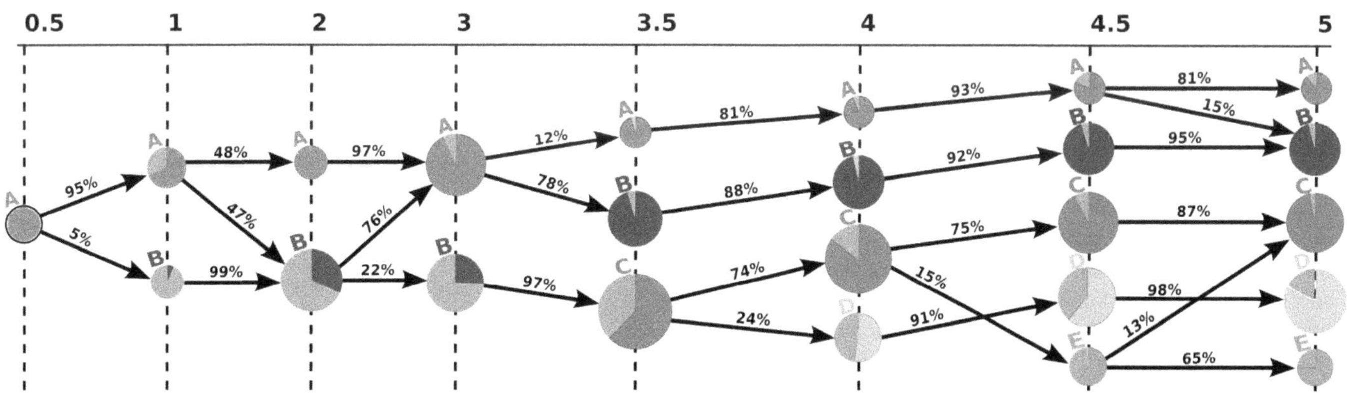

Figure 7: Scratch Community Evolution: Pie-charts' diameters are scaled to represent size of cluster; Light gray indicates new users in each cluster; Colors indicate migrated users in a cluster; Arrows indicate migration (percentage over time).

subculture might be Azevedo's [29] concept of "lines of practice" which suggests that "interests are realized in the specific fabric of activities that a person fashions himself or herself and that by definition extends into many realms of the person's life [29, pg. 505]." So, if learners are engaged with games in their lives, working on designing or programming of games is a natural extension of the "lines of practice." Azevedo [29] further argues that "an interest does not have a core whose essence is topic/domain centered—as when one says, for instance, that a student has an interest in biology, or science, or algebra, or technology, or programming, or physics, and so on, or when one speaks of students developing specific mathematical or scientific identities. Rather, being interested in a practice requires weaving it with many other concerns, domains, values, goals, and practices in one's life space, which makes the practice of interest meaningful in the short and long hauls [29, p. 505]." From this perspective as well we can see how learners create subcultures that allow them to develop an identity not only as a programmer, or someone learning how to program, but also align it with games or animations or with cats. Newcomers to these subcultures are able to see and remix projects from other participants, that is, they can participate peripherally, before contributing complex projects of their own – a core process in learning [45].

In this paper, we show how the Scratch community grew into interest-based subcultures, which act as important building blocks of the community structure that provide benefits to the community members with varying interests. As Azevedo, [29, pg. 464] defines, "interest-based engagement in a practice refers to self-motivated, often self-guided, short- and long-term participation in the fabric of activities that make up the practice." Interest-driven learning is usually differentiated into situational and personal interest [30, 32]. Situational interest refers to a temporary or fleeting engagement often triggered by the task environment. In contrast, an individual or personal interest refers to a person's long-term disposition to engage in a topic or domain. Personal interest and is usually associated with high knowledge and high value of such a topic/domain. The role of online communities in fostering interest-driven learning is consistent with the literature. For instance, Azevedo [41] demonstrated that the level to which students engage with an activity is often highly dependent on infrastructure, physical and digital, that allows students the opportunity to tailor the activities to their interests. This, when combined with the ability to pursue both self-initiated detours and multiple activities, enhances participation and learning [29, pg. 466]. Hidi [33], in her review paper, further emphasizes the importance of interest in learning and development. She argues that interest facilitates learning, improves understanding and stimulates effort as well as personal involvement. This focus on interest was diminished during behaviorism and the subsequent cognitive revolution but has garnered attention as neuroscientists have rediscovered the importance of emotions and feelings and psychologists have started to look at affective variables. Recent findings show positive influences of interest on attention, quantity and quality of learning, and improvement in learners' organization of tasks and their goals and choices. For example, within Scratch, a user can access a large number of projects created by others in the same subculture. Accessing such projects may promote learning of new Scratch blocks through remixing, and eventually enhance sustainability of the community by motivating the user to create similar or more sophisticated projects. The ability to join or create new subcultures provided users with an opportunity to express themselves, to find others with whom they shared interests and ideas, and have their own 'space'. In real world communities whereas subcultures evolve around shared societal goals, similar educational and socio-economic background, shared lifestyle choices, and so on, in Scratch the subcultures evolved around shared thematic interest, in addition to the shared interest in programming.

By examining the subcultures in Scratch, as well as the evolution of the entire community over time, we found a pronounced evolutionary trend. In the beginning, the community existed as a single entity where most active users followed each other and created projects with diverse themes. As the community grew massively and suburbanized over time, many of the initial users became inactive, while others migrated to new subcommunities that attracted new users. Eventually, the newer communities began to diverge from each other and formed distinct entities based upon certain, targeted interests such as games, animations, and arts. Since studies of online communities first appeared, scholars have argued that in many respects the social interactions on them mirror what we find in offline communities [27].

Our study supports as well as extends this view by demonstrating that not only in terms of social interactions at the dyadic or small group level but even looking at larger assemblages and longer term interactions we find that online communities can mirror offline communities. In keeping with the view of the subcultural theory of urbanism [9], we provide an ecological understanding of an online community and show how certain interest areas first thrive and then lose participants as other areas emerge and attract users. This process continues and in time the overall fertility increases providing newcomers with more and more options of subcultures. This work contributes to research on newcomer participation in online communities [43] by demonstrating the strong influence of affinity based participation. With the opportunity to attach themselves to interest-based subgroups, newcomers are able to self-select into subculture that appeal to them [43]. Although we are unable to comment directly on demographic homophily due to the lack of relevant data [42], our findings demonstrate the emergence of interest-based homogeneity at the level of social networks within a larger community.

Implications

There are several implications of this study. When designing online communities, users can be better supported by providing them the opportunity to create interest-based subgroups. Clustering can be used to choose projects that are highlighted in the community. Projects can be introduced strategically to increase visibility of active users from different subcultures. Our analysis highlights both the promises and pitfalls of community dynamics. It suggests that providing users a place to find people like them and to be able to explore their interests is critical in creative communities. On the other hand, this can also lead to divisions but we found a few users acted as brokers and were connected with multiple subcultures.

Limitations

Our study has several limitations:

- Lack of demographic data: This data was not released considering that the majority of Scratch users are minors. Richer analysis of subcultures in Scratch might have been available with this data.
- Selection of k = 25: In our analysis, we included users only with 25 or more followers. With k < 25, a more detailed analysis for the evolution of the community as well as diverse subcultures may have been possible. With k > 25 coupled with user account time stamps, may have allowed us to better understand the subcultures of highly active/long-term participants.
- Cumulative data of follower/followed relationships: Our analysis for the community evolution considers user relationships in a cumulative way. Thus, relationships that are inactive for a while may also have been included in the analysis. However, this cumulative relationship data enabled us to trace the evolution of the community throughout its lifecycle.

Future Work

The primary suggestion for future work is to examine in more detail individual learner's interest development, not just on the Scratch community platform but across their learning ecology. A comprehensive study of this sort will be able to shed light on the overall four-phase model of interest development and provide further guidance on how to better design online communities for learning. It will also allow us to evaluate how to integrate such communities in formal learning environments and understand what Azevedo [29] articulates as "lines of practice".

CONCLUSION

This study sheds new light on the participation of core active members over the lifecycle of an online community. As the population of Scratch grew at a higher rate after it became popular, users split into interest-based groups. Newer users conformed to these groups, thus perpetuating the interest-based communities. Although Scratch has a very specific goal – teaching computer programming – it resembles other OCOCs and online communities in general and these findings are broadly relevant.

ACKNOWLEDGEMENTS

We appreciate the Lifelong Kindergarten group at MIT for publicly sharing the Scratch datasets. This work is partly based upon research supported by U.S. National Science Foundation (NSF) Award#DUE-1444277 & EEC-1408674.

REFERENCES

1. Alba, R., Logan, J., Stults, B., Marzan, G., & Zhang, W. (1999). Immigrant groups in the suburbs: A reexamination of suburbanization and spatial assimilation. *American Sociological Review,* 446-460.
2. Butler, B., et al. (2002). Community effort in online groups: Who does the work and why? *Leadership at a Distance* (2002): 171-194.
3. Falkowski, T. et al. (2006). Mining and Visualizing the Evolution of Subgroups in Social Networks. *IEEE/VIC/ACM Int. Conf. Web Intelligence.*
4. Grabowski, A., Kruszewska, N., & Kosiński, R. A. (2008). Properties of on-line social systems. *European Physical Journal B*, 66(1), 107-113.
5. Jacomy, M., Venturini, T., Heymann, S., Bastian, M. (2014) ForceAtlas2, a Continuous Graph Layout Algorithm for Handy Network Visualization Designed for the Gephi Software. *PLoS ONE* 9(6): e98679.
6. Kumar, R., Novak, J. & Tomkins, A. (2010). Structure and evolution of online social networks. *Link mining: models, algorithms, and applications*. Springer New York, 337-357.
7. Manning, C., Raghavan, P. & Schütze. H. (2008). *Introduction to information retrieval.* Cambridge University Press.
8. Martin, S. et al. (2011). OpenOrd: An open-source toolbox for large graph layout. *IS&T/SPIE Electronic Imaging.*
9. Massey, D. & Denton, N. (1988). Suburbanization and segregation in US metropolitan areas. *American Journal of Sociology*, 592-626.
10. Resnick, M., et al. (2009). Scratch: programming for all. *Communications of the ACM*, 52(11), 60-67.
11. Robertson, S. (2004). Understanding inverse document frequency: On theoretical argument for IDF. *Journal of Documentation*, 60(5), 503-520.
12. Scratch. http://scratch.mit.edu/about/
13. Sylvan, E. (2010). Predicting Influence in an Online Community of Creators. *CHI 2010*, pp. 1913-1916.
14. Raban, D. R., Moldovan, M., & Jones, Q. (2010). An empirical study of critical mass and online community survival. *Proceedings of CSCW* (pp. 71-80).
15. Hopcroft, J., Khan, O., Kulis, B., & Selman, B. (2004). Tracking evolving communities in large linked networks. *PNAS*, 101, 5249-5253.

16. Chin, A., & Chignell, M. (2006). A social hypertext model for finding community in blogs. *Proceedings of Hypertext and Hypermedia* (pp. 11-22).
17. McMillan, D. W., & Chavis, D. M. (1986). Sense of community: A definition and theory. *Journal of community psychology*, 14(1), 6-23.
18. Chin, A., & Chignell, M. (2007). Identifying active subgroups in online communities. *Proceedings of Center for advanced studies on Collaborative research* (pp. 280-283).
19. Fischer, C. S. (1975). Toward a subcultural theory of urbanism. *American journal of Sociology*, 1319-1341.
20. Fischer, C. S. (1995). The subcultural theory of urbanism: A twentieth-year assessment. *American Journal of Sociology*, 543-577.
21. White, K. J. C., & Guest, A. M. (2003). Community lost or transformed? Urbanization and social ties. *City & Community*, 2(3), 239-259.
22. Yang, S., Domeniconi, C., Revelle, M., Sweeney, M., Gelman, B. U., Beckley, C., & Johri, A. (2015). Uncovering Trajectories of Informal Learning in Large Online Communities of Creators. *Proceedings of Learning @ Scale* (pp. 131-140). ACM.
23. Maloney, J., Peppler, K., Kafai, Y.B., Resnick, M., Rusk, N. (2008). Programming by Choice: Urban Youth Learning Programming with Scratch. *Proc. Of SIGCSE*, 367-371. New York, NY: ACM Press.
24. Scratch™ Online. Retrieved: http://scratch.mit.edu.
25. Scratch™ Online Statistics. Retrieved from http://scratch.mit.edu/statistics/.
26. Scratch Research Data Sharing Agreement. Retrieved from http://llk.media.mit.edu/scratch-data/.
27. Wellman, B., & Gulia, M. (1999). Net surfers don't ride alone: Virtual communities as communities. *Networks in the global village*, 331-366.
28. Bell, P., Lewenstein, B., Shouse, A. W., & Feder, M. A. (2009). *Learning science in informal environments: People, places, and pursuits*. National Academies Press.
29. Azevedo, F. S. (2013). The tailored practice of hobbies and its implication for the design of interest-driven learning environments. *Journal of the Learning Sciences*, 22(3), 462-510.
30. Renninger, A., Hidi, S., & Krapp, A. (2014). *The role of interest in learning and development.* Psychology Press.
31. Ito, M., Horst, H., Bittanti, M., Boyd, D., Herr-Stephenson, B., Lange, P. G., ... & Robinson, L. (2008). *Living and Learning with New Media: Summary of Findings from the Digital Youth Project.* John D. and Catherine T. MacArthur Foundation.
32. Hidi, S., & Renninger, K. A. (2006). The four-phase model of interest development. *Educational psychologist*, 41(2), 111-127.
33. Hidi, S. (2006). Interest: A unique motivational variable. *Educational Research Review*, 1(2), 69-82.
34. Spires, H. A., Lee, J. K., Turner, K. A., & Johnson, J. (2008). Having our say: Middle grade student perspectives on school, technologies, and academic engagement. *Journal of Research on Technology in Education*, 40(4), 497-515.
35. Levin, D., & Arafeh, S. (2002). The digital disconnect: The widening gap between Internet-savvy students and their schools. *Pew Internet & American Life Project.* http://www.pewinternet.org/reports/toc.asp?Report=67/
36. Eraut, M. (2000). Non-formal learning and tacit knowledge in professional work. *British Journal of Educational Psychology*, 70(1), 113-136.
37. Bereiter, C., and Scardamalia, M. (1989). Intentional learning as a goal of instruction (Bereiter & Scardamalia, 1989). In L. B. Resnick (Ed.), *Knowing, learning, and instruction: Essays in honor of Robert Glaser* (pp. 361-392). Hillsdale, NM: Lawrence Erlbaum.
38. Hodkinson, P., Colley, H., & Malcolm, J. (2003). The interrelationships between informal and formal learning. *Journal of Workplace Learning*, 15, 113-318.
39. Marsick, V. J., & Volpe, M. (1999). The nature of and need for informal learning. In V. J. Marsick & M. Volpe (Eds.), *Advances in developing human resources: Informal learning on the job* (pp. 1–9). Baton Rouge, LA: AHRD.
40. Barab, S., Kling, R., & Gray, J. H. (2004). *Designing for virtual communities in the service of learning*. Cambridge University Press.
41. Azevedo, R. (2007). Understanding the complex nature of self-regulatory processes in learning with computer-based learning environments: An introduction. *Metacognition and Learning*, 2(2-3), 57-65.
42. McPherson, M., Smith-Lovin, L., & Cook, J. M. (2001). Birds of a feather: Homophily in social networks. *Annual review of sociology*, 415-444.
43. Kraut, R. E. & Resnick, P. (2012). *Building successful online communities: Evidence-based social design.* Cambridge, MA: MIT Press.
44. Teo, H. J. & Johri, A. (2014). Fast, functional, and fitting: expert response dynamics and response quality in an online newcomer help forum. *Proceedings of CSCW 2014*, pp.332-341.
45. Lave, J. & Wenger, E. (1991). *Situated Learning: Legitimate Peripheral Participation*. Cambridge University Press.

Effects of In-Video Quizzes on MOOC Lecture Viewing

Geza Kovacs
Department of Computer Science, Stanford University
geza@cs.stanford.edu

ABSTRACT

Online courses on sites such as Coursera use quizzes embedded inside lecture videos (*in-video quizzes*) to help learners test their understanding of the video. This paper analyzes how users interact with in-video quizzes, and how in-video quizzes influence users' lecture viewing behavior. We analyze the viewing logs of users who took the Machine Learning course on Coursera. Users engage heavily with in-video quizzes – 74% of viewers who start watching a video will attempt its corresponding in-video quiz. We observe spikes in seek activity surrounding in-video quizzes, particularly seeks from the in-video quiz to the preceding section. We show that this is likely due to users reviewing the preceding section to help them answer the quiz, as the majority of users who seek backwards from in-video quizzes have not yet submitted a correct answer, but will later attempt the quiz. Some users appear to use quiz-oriented navigation strategies, such as seeking directly from the start of the video to in-video quizzes, or skipping from one quiz to the next. We discuss implications of our findings on the design of lecture-viewing platforms.

Author Keywords

in-video quizzes; lecture viewing; lecture navigation; seeking behaviors; MOOCs

ACM Classification Keywords

H.5.m. Information Interfaces and Presentation (e.g. HCI): Miscellaneous

INTRODUCTION

In-video quizzes are short, automatically-graded questions shown to users upon reaching a certain point in a lecture video, as shown in Figure 1. They are commonly found in MOOCs on Coursera.

In-video quizzes are beneficial because they provide learners with a way to test themselves on the material, which helps long-term retention (a finding known as the *testing effect*) [10]. They are particularly valuable in the context of MOOCs, because many learners interact primarily with videos and do not engage with assignments or exams [8] [2].

L@S 2016, April 25–26, 2016, Edinburgh, UK.

ACM 978-1-4503-3726-7/16/04 ...$15.00.
DOI: http://dx.doi.org/10.1145/2876034.2876041

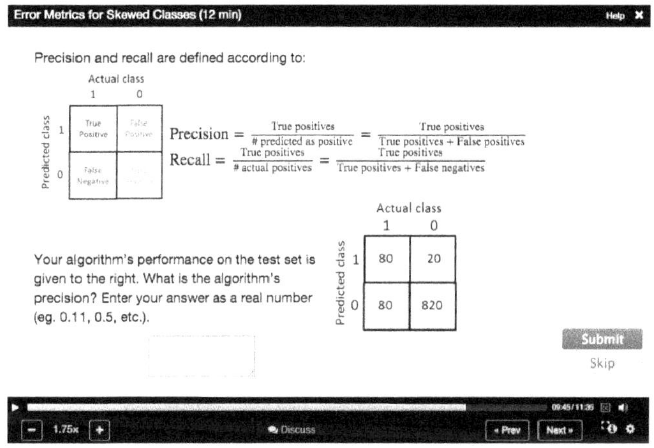

Figure 1. An in-video quiz on Coursera. In-video quizzes are short questions that are shown upon reaching certain points in the video.

In-video quizzes differ from other assessments in that they are displayed directly in the video viewer, so users can easily seek elsewhere upon encountering the quiz – seeking backward to review material related to the quiz, seeking forward to skip the quiz, etc. The presence of in-video quizzes inside videos can thus influence users' video viewing behaviors, potentially causing nonlinear navigation patterns such as seeking.

In this paper, we aim to learn more about how learners engage with in-video quizzes, and how video interaction patterns differ in the portions surrounding in-video quizzes. We do this by analyzing the video-viewing logs of the Machine Learning course on Coursera (ML4). We discovered the following interaction patterns associated with in-video quizzes:

- Users engage heavily with in-video quizzes – in lectures with quizzes, 74% of viewers will attempt to answer one.
- Users commonly seek forward to in-video quizzes, and seek backwards from in-video quizzes.
- Most backwards seeks from in-video quizzes occur after the user has seen the question, but before they answer it. This suggests that users are reviewing the preceding section to help them answer the quiz.
- Users do not tend to skip over in-video quizzes, either in the forward or backward direction.
- Users sometimes jump directly from the start of the video to in-video quizzes, or jump from one quiz to the next.
- Most users answer in-video quizzes correctly, with 76% answering correctly on their first try.
- In-video dropout is lower in lectures that have in-video quizzes, compared to lectures that lack in-video quizzes.

RELATED WORK

Kim et al performed an analysis of reasons for peaks in viewing and seeking while viewing lectures [7]. They found that users steadily leave videos over time, a phenomenon known as *in-video dropout*, and that visual transitions (such as slide transitions) tend to result in *interaction peaks*, with peaks in events such as users seeking back to the previous slide. They also presented a video viewer that encourages video navigation to interaction peaks [6]. However, the courses that they perform their video log analysis on do not have in-video quizzes, hence they are unable to report on interaction peaks that result from in-video quizzes. We similarly found in our own analysis that while there are many peaks in seeking behavior that can be accounted for by slide transitions, in-video quizzes tend to also be a major factor for determining where interaction peaks occur.

Guo and Kim analyzed the effects of video properties such as video length on viewer engagement [3]. They found that users become less engaged as videos grow longer, which is related to the problem of in-video dropout. However, they did not analyze the effects of in-video quizzes on viewer engagement, because the courses they analyzed do not have in-video quizzes. Our findings suggest that in-video quizzes may encourage viewer engagement, as indicated by the increase in rewatching and seeking behavior in the regions of the video surrounding the in-video quiz.

Guo and Reinicke investigated factors that contribute to nonlinear navigation through MOOCs [4]. They discuss examples of nonlinear navigation such as jumping back to previous lectures, rewatching videos, and going back from assessments to refer to lectures. Our present work focuses on navigation within videos as opposed to within MOOCs. However, we find that in-video quizzes, which are effectively assessments that are embedded into lecture videos, trigger similar backjumps and reviews within a video that Guo and Reinicke discuss at the course-level in their paper.

Anderson et al found that learners differ in the ways they engage with online courses: some only watch videos ("viewers"), some only complete assignments ("solvers"), and some engage in both ("all-rounders") [2]. Kizilcec et al discover similar engagement patterns [8], and discuss how these engagement patterns may be a result of learners' motivations for taking the course [9]. These differences between learners' engagement patterns are relevant to our work analyzing in-video quizzes, as they help explain why we find that some users' viewing behaviors seem to be aimed towards solving in-video quizzes. Additionally, the large population of users who engage primarily with videos underscores the importance of in-video quizzes as a means to test users' knowledge, which helps them retain the material [10].

In-video quizzes are not new; there are many past systems that embed quizzes into multimedia [1]. In-video quizzes are believed to have positive effects on learning [5], as testing helps in long-term retention of material [10]. However, to our knowledge, our paper is the first analysis of the effects of in-video quizzes on learners' rewatching and seeking behavior in the context of MOOCs.

Type of event or data within the ML4 course on Coursera	Value
Users who registered for the course	96,195
Users who started viewing at least 1 lecture	61,453
Users who reached the end of at least 1 lecture	41,643
Users who answered at least 1 in-video quiz	42,437
Users who downloaded at least 1 lecture video	28,369
Users who had a nonzero grade (submitted an assignment/review exercise)	26,035
Users who earned at least 80% of total points (threshold for certificate)	8,615
Number of lecture videos	113
Average length of a lecture video (in seconds)	621
Number of in-video quizzes	109
Number of slide transitions	339
Number of external multiple-choice assessments ("review exercises")	18
Number of distinct lectures which the user started viewing, across all users	1,495,954
Number of distinct lectures watched until end, across all users	976,933
Number of distinct in-video quizzes answered, across all users	1,031,061
Number of distinct review exercises answered, across all users	229,556
Total number of seek events	6,442,590
Total number of seek chains *(see Methodology section)*	2,103,336
Average length of video skipped over by a seek event (in seconds)	31
Average length of video skipped over by a seek chain (in seconds)	96

Table 1. Summary statistics for the ML4 course.

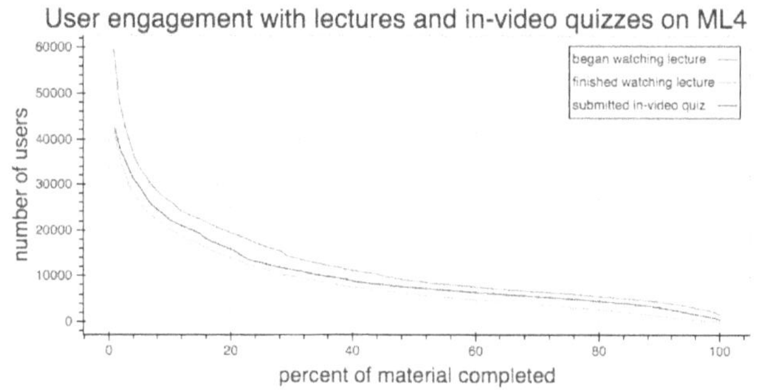

Figure 2. Response rates to the 109 in-video quizzes were similar to the viewing rates of the 113 lecture videos.

DATASET AND ENGAGEMENT LEVELS

The course we are analyzing in this work is the fourth iteration of the Machine Learning course on Coursera (ML4), which operated from October 2013 to January 2014. Our dataset contains data from 96,195 users, of whom 61,453 viewed at least one video. There are 113 lecture videos in the course, totaling 19.5 hours of video content, with an average length of 10 minutes per video. With 109 in-video quizzes over 19.5 hours of video, this averages out to one in-video quiz for every 11 minutes of video.

Of the 113 videos, 92 videos (81%) have 1 in-video quiz, 14 videos (12%) have no in-video quizzes, 6 videos (5%) have 2 in-video quizzes, and 1 video (1%) has 3 in-video quizzes. Videos with no in-video quizzes tend to be optional lectures covering interesting applications of machine learning, or are introductory videos that explain what will be covered next in the course.

Engagement with in-video quizzes is high: as shown in Figure 2, the answering rate of in-video quizzes closely mirrors the viewing rates for videos. In fact, the number of users who answer the in-video quiz is higher than the number who finish watching the video – if we look at the 92 videos that have one in-video quiz, 74% of users who begin watching a video submit an answer to its in-video quiz, whereas only 66% watch it to completion. This is likely because users often leave the

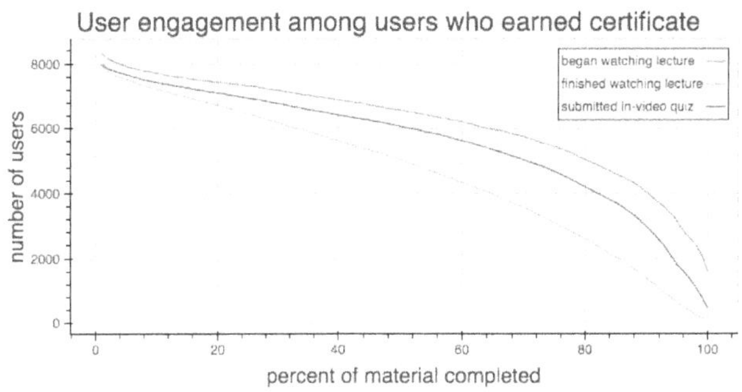

Figure 3. Users who earned certificates answered most of the in-video quizzes, even though in-video quizzes and lecture viewing do not count towards their scores.

video after completing the quiz, instead of watching it to the end (50% of in-video quizzes occur in the last 1/10 of the video, so the part following the quiz is often just a recap or preview). These high engagement rates with in-video quizzes contrast with the lower engagement rates typically observed for traditional assessments placed outside of the video [8] [2].

Certificate-earners (users who earned a grade of at least 80% – note that in-video quizzes and lecture viewing do not count towards grades) also engage heavily with in-video quizzes, as shown in Figure 3. If we look at the 92 videos that have one in-video quiz, 79% of certificate-earning learners who begin watching a video submit an answer to its in-video quiz, whereas only 72% watch it to completion. That said, even certificate earners skip a few videos and in-video quizzes; the ones they tend to skip are optional lectures, early material reviewing prerequisite math such as matrices, and tutorial videos about Octave (a software package used by the course).

Other summary statistics are shown in Table 1. Coursera provides users the ability to download videos and view them offline – meaning they will not see in-video quizzes, and their viewing activity will not appear in the logs. However, as we see in Table 1, the number of users who download videos is less than half of those that view videos online.

METHODOLOGY

Determining Portions of Video Seen

The Coursera logs we used for our analysis are labelled with an action (such as play, pause, or seek) associated with a point in the video, and a timestamp. We use these logs to reconstruct the portions of the video that the user has seen, with a technique similar to the one described in [7]. If we observe a play event associated with video position p, followed by another event at video position p+i, we can assume that the user watched that segment of the video.

Reconstructing Seek Source Positions

The seek events in Coursera's logs only specify the destination of the seek and the timestamp at which it occurred, but not the origin (the logs tell us where in the video the user seeked to, but not where the user seeked from). However, we were able to reconstruct the seek source positions based on the previous event – for example, if the user started playing from video position p at timestamp t, and we observe a seek

Event type	Seek chains going forward		Seek chains going backward	
	% of all seek chains	# seek chains, normalized by the length of the seek target (seconds). Ratio to baseline in parentheses	% of all seek chains	# seek chains, normalized by the length of the seek target (seconds). Ratio to baseline in parentheses
All seek chains	56%	16.40 (baseline)	44%	12.86 (baseline)
Seek chains going to in-video quizzes (and their surroundings)				
Seeks to quiz (+/- 0.5 sec)	0.35%	**67.43 (4.1x)**	0.20%	38.21 (3.0x)
Seeks to 10 seconds preceding quiz	3.35%	**62.17 (3.8x)**	1.82%	34.58 (2.7x)
Seeks to 10 seconds following quiz	1.15%	21.89 (1.3x)	0.70%	13.33 (1.0x)
Seek chains going to slide transitions (and their surroundings)				
Seeks to slide transition (+/- 0.5 sec)	0.22%	13.60 (0.8x)	0.35%	20.89 (1.6x)
Seeks to 10 seconds preceding slide transition	2.49%	15.04 (0.9x)	3.41%	20.63 (1.6x)
Seeks to 10 seconds following slide transition	3.54%	21.42 (1.3x)	2.33%	14.11 (1.1x)
Seek chains coming from in-video quizzes (and their surroundings)				
Seeks from quiz (+/- 0.5 sec)	0.36%	**67.17 (4.1x)**	3.79%	**713.4 (55x)**
Seeks from 10 seconds preceding quiz	0.65%	12.30 (0.8x)	0.96%	17.99 (1.4x)
Seeks from 10 seconds following quiz	1.89%	35.95 (2.2x)	1.63%	30.76 (2.4x)
Seek chains coming from slide transitions (and their surroundings)				
Seeks from slide transition (+/- 0.5 sec)	0.30%	18.22 (1.1x)	0.27%	16.22 (1.3x)
Seeks from 10 seconds preceding slide transition	6.72%	40.68 (2.5x)	2.27%	13.73 (1.1x)
Seeks from 10 seconds following slide transition	2.78%	16.81 (1.0x)	3.98%	24.10 (1.9x)

Table 2. Sources and destinations of seek chains. Users tend to seek backward from in-video quizzes (55x higher than baseline back-seek rate), and forward to in-video quizzes and the 10 seconds immediately preceding them (4x higher than baseline forward-seek rate)

event at timestamp t+i, then we assume the seek originated from video position p+i (or p+2i if the user is playing back the video at 2x speed, etc).

Grouping Seek Events into Seek Chains

Additionally, we observed that many seek events tend to occur in rapid succession as the user narrows down on the actual target. For example, when users seek via the keyboard, if they are at the beginning of the video and their seek target is 3 minutes into the video, they will press the right-arrow repeatedly until they reach the destination, resulting in a large number of small, noisy seek events, rather than a single seek from 0 to 3 minutes that we are interested in analyzing. Because we are primarily interested in where the user ends up seeking to, rather than the individual seek operations that got them to that point, if there are seek events that occur within 5 seconds of each other, we group them together into a single unit which we will call a *seek chain*. Using this approach, we reduced the 6,442,590 total seek events in our dataset into 2,103,336 seek chains. When we analyze seeking in this paper, as well as seek sources and destinations, we will be analyzing seek chains rather than raw seek events, to reduce noise from repeated seeks. That said, our main findings about peaks in seeking around in-video quizzes also hold if we analyze raw seek events instead of seek chains.

Limitations of Coursera's Dataset

Since Coursera's logs do not record when a user closes their browser window or the network disconnects, the full duration of what users finished watching may be underestimated. For example, if a user starts playing a video at time t, and this play event is the last logged event, we know that the user must have closed their browser prior to the next in-video quiz or the end of the video (otherwise a pause event would have been logged), however we do not know exactly when the browser was closed. We address this ambiguity by treating it as though the user had immediately stopped watching after that last play

Event type	value
Forward seek chains	
Total # of forward seek chains	1169873 (55.6% of seeks)
Average length of a forward seek chain, in seconds	129 seconds
Average # of times each second of video was seeked forward over	2153 (baseline forward seek rate)
# forward seek chains crossing slide transitions (339 slide transitions total)	909675 (43.2% of seeks)
# forward seek chains crossing each slide transition	2683 (1.25x baseline)
# forward seek chains crossing quizzes (109 quizzes total)	98613 (4.69% of seeks)
# forward seek chains crossing each quiz	905 **(0.42x baseline)**
Backward seek chains	
Total # of backward seek chains	933463 (44.4% of seeks)
Average length of a backward seek chain, in seconds	54 seconds
Average # of times each second of video was seeked backward over	719 (baseline backward seek rate)
# backward seek chains crossing slide transitions (339 slide transitions total)	301129 (14.3% of seeks)
# backward seek chains crossing each slide transition	888 (1.24x baseline)
# backward seek chains crossing quizzes (109 quizzes total)	47184 (2.24% of seeks)
# backward seek chains crossing each quiz	432 **(0.60x baseline)**

Table 3. Lengths of seek chains, and portions of the video that they skip over. Users typically do not seek forward or backward across in-video quizzes.

event, so we do not include the last (unknown) segment that was watched after their final interaction with the video.

AGGREGATE SEEK CHAIN STATISTICS

Sources and Destinations of Seek Chains

The sources and destinations of seek chains are shown in Table 2. We see that in-video quizzes are a popular destination of seeks, particularly in the forward direction – users seek forward to an in-video quiz at 4x the baseline rate of all seek chain destinations. In other words, users are 4 times more likely to seek to the second of video where an in-video quiz is located, than to an arbitrary second of video. Given the high answering rate for in-video quizzes we showed in Figure 2, this suggests that these seeks originate from users who want to answer the in-video quiz at that point. Note that Coursera's interface does not have any UI features for seeking to in-video quizzes apart from the progress bar, so the only way to reach the in-video quiz is to seek to a segment of video right before it. Hence, we consider seek chains which terminate at most 10 seconds before the in-video quiz to represent users intending to jump to the in-video quiz. We normalized this value by the length of the seek target – 10 seconds – so the unit of all measurements is seeks per second of video.

Users also seek backward from in-video quizzes at 55x the baseline rate. As we will show, these represent users reviewing the preceding section, likely trying to find material that will help them answer the in-video quiz.

Lengths and Directions of Seek Chains

As shown in Table 3, on average forward seek chains tend to be over longer distances, while backward seek chains tend to be of shorter duration. A potential explanation is that forward seeks aim to go to some salient part of the video – for example, an in-video quiz – whereas backward seeks aim to review a part of the video that was just missed. We also observe that users seek forwards more than backwards overall, including across slide boundaries; however, they tend not to seek forward over in-video quizzes. As we will see, this is because

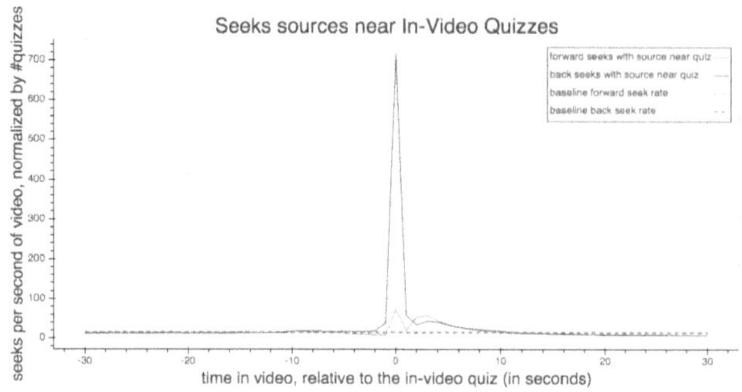

Figure 4. Seek chains with sources near in-video quizzes, averaged across all 109 in-video quizzes in the ML class. There are many backward seeks originating at the in-video quiz, reflecting users wanting to review the preceding material.

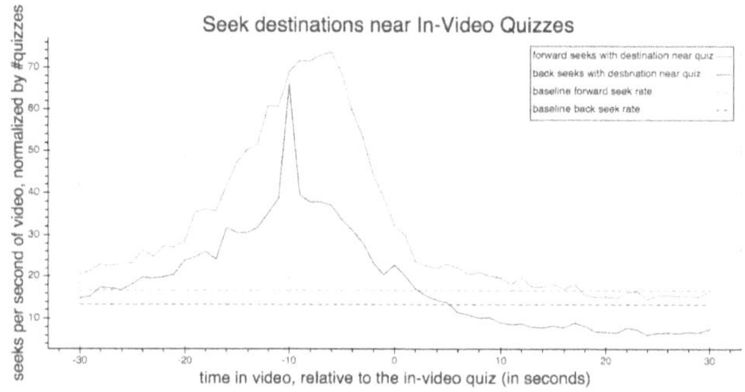

Figure 5. Seek chains with destinations near in-video quizzes, averaged across all 109 in-video quizzes in the ML class. The portion immediately preceding the in-video quiz is a common destination of both forward and backward seeks. The peak in forward seeks reflects users seeking forward to the in-video quiz, while peak in back seeks at 10 seconds before the video is likely due to users seeking back with their keyboard.

they are seeking to right before the in-video quizzes, either to view the quizzes, or to search for answers to quizzes.

Seek Sources and Destinations near In-Video Quizzes

As we saw in Table 2, there are many seeks originating from and terminating near in-video quizzes. In this section we will analyze seek chains near in-video quizzes in more depth.

Seek Sources near In-Video Quizzes

Figure 4 illustrates the sources of seek chains near in-video quizzes, averaged across all 109 quizzes. As we can see, there are a large number of backward seeks originating from in-video quizzes. These reflect users who, having seen the in-video quiz, are reviewing the preceding section to find information to help them answer the question. However, there are also many forward seeks originating from the in-video quiz as well as the portion that immediately follows it. These likely reflect users who, having looked at or completed the in-video quiz, are seeking forward to preview the next section.

Seek Destinations near In-Video Quizzes

Figure 5 illustrates where users seek to near in-video quizzes, averaged across all 109 quizzes. As we can see, the 10 seconds immediately preceding the in-video quiz are a popular destination of seeks, both in the forward and backward directions. Seek chains in the forward direction arriving just before the in-video quizzes may reflect users who intend to go to the in-video quiz – Coursera's interface does not provide a means of going directly to an in-video quiz, other than seeking to the immediately preceding portion and playing the video. Seek chains in the back direction arriving just before the in-video quizzes may reflect users who are reviewing the video to help them answer the in-video quiz. We observe a spike in back-seek destinations at exactly 10 seconds before the in-video quiz. This is likely users who are seeking backwards from the in-video quiz using the back arrow key on their keyboards, which causes a backward seek of exactly 10 seconds.

VIEWING BEHAVIOR IN AN INDIVIDUAL LECTURE

Visualization of Seeks and Watching

In order to explain why users are seeking to and from in-video quizzes, let us first visualize a representative video before moving on to all videos in aggregate. This is Lecture 13 from ML4, titled "Matrices and Vectors". We chose it because it has 2 in-video quizzes, and neither is located at the very end of the video, so results should not be overly influenced by the position of the in-video quizzes.

Figure 6 presents the seek chain sources and destinations in this video as a scatter plot. It illustrates users seeking forward to in-video quizzes and going back to the preceding section to look for answers. It also show how seek chains do not tend to cross forward or backward across in-video quizzes. Thus, the in-video quizzes subdivide the video into smaller sections that users do not tend to skip between.

As shown in Figure 7, in-video quizzes are a popular destination of seeks. Many of these seeks originate from the preceding section, confirming the statistics we saw in Table 2. This suggests that users may have found the answer to the quiz, and are seeking forward to answer the in-video quiz. However, there are also many seeks to the in-video quiz from the start of the video and from the previous in-video quiz. This suggests some users might be following a quiz-centric navigation strategy of seeking directly to the quiz to preview it before they watch the video.

Increased Rewatching near In-Video Quizzes

We hypothesized that if users search for relevant material in the preceding segment upon encountering an in-video quiz, this should be reflected in the viewing logs. Namely, we would expect to see increased re-watching of the portion prior to the in-video quiz. We would also expect to see seeks that originate from the in-video quiz and go backwards to the preceding section, which contains material related to the quiz. We show examples of these phenomenon in this section.

We see in Figure 7 E that the portion of the video surrounding the in-video quiz tends to receive more views. We also observe a trend of fewer views for portions of the video that occur later, which can be explained by in-video dropout [7].

We believe the increase in the number of views surrounding the in-video quiz is due to users rewatching the portion preceding the in-video quiz, perhaps searching for material that will help them answer the quiz. Indeed, if we exclude each user's first-time watch, and look only at what users are rewatching in aggregate, we still observe this peak in number of rewatches around the first in-video quiz, as shown in Figure 7 F.

Because Coursera does not require users to take in-video quizzes, we wondered whether users explicitly skip across in-video quizzes to avoid taking them. As illustrated in Figure 7 B, we found that this does not seem to be the case. On the contrary, there is actually a dip in the number of forward seeks that cross over the in-video quiz, so users are explicitly trying not to skip the in-video quizzes. This low number of forward seeks crossing over the last in-video quiz in this example might be attributed to the fact that it is located towards the end of the video, so the user may be aware that there is no new content to find towards the end. However, if we look at the first in-video quiz in the example, we also observe a dip in the number of forward-seeks over the in-video quiz, even though there is important content in the video after it.

Thus, we observed that users rewatch the regions surrounding in-video quizzes, tend to backseek to review the materials preceding the quiz, and do not forward-seek over quizzes.

VIEWING BEHAVIOR IN ALL LECTURE VIDEOS

In this section, we analyze seek chains in all videos to learn how in-video quizzes influence users' viewing behavior.

Forward Seeking to In-Video Quizzes

Figure 8 shows the destinations of forward seeks for each of the 113 videos in the course. Each horizontal line represents a video, where darker shades indicate more seek chains going to a particular segment of the video. We label the locations of in-video quizzes (red) and slide transitions (green).

In-video quizzes are a popular destination of seeks, as indicated by the black streaks immediately preceding the in-video circles (recall that Coursera does not let users seek directly to in-video quizzes, but requires them to seek to the segment right before the quiz if they want to take it). As we showed in Table 2, forward seek rates to the in-video quizzes are 4 times higher than the baseline rate.

If we look at lectures 25-30 in Figure 8, they do not visually match the pattern we see in the other lectures. This is because they're optional videos discussing applications of Machine Learning, which don't have in-video quizzes.

Video Parts Skipped Back Over

As we can see in Figure 9 and Table 2, in-video quizzes are a major source of backward seek chains. As we can see in Figure 9, if we look at all portions of the video that are skipped backwards over by seek chains, it is primarily the segments preceding the in-video quizzes. This can be explained by users searching in the preceding segment for the answer to the in-video quiz.

Interestingly, we observe that when the last in-video quiz occurs at the midpoint of a video, as is the case with Lecture 19 in Figure 9, there is little back-seeking which occurs after the quiz. This suggests that the back-seeking phenomenon which occurs directly before a quiz is indeed a result of the in-video

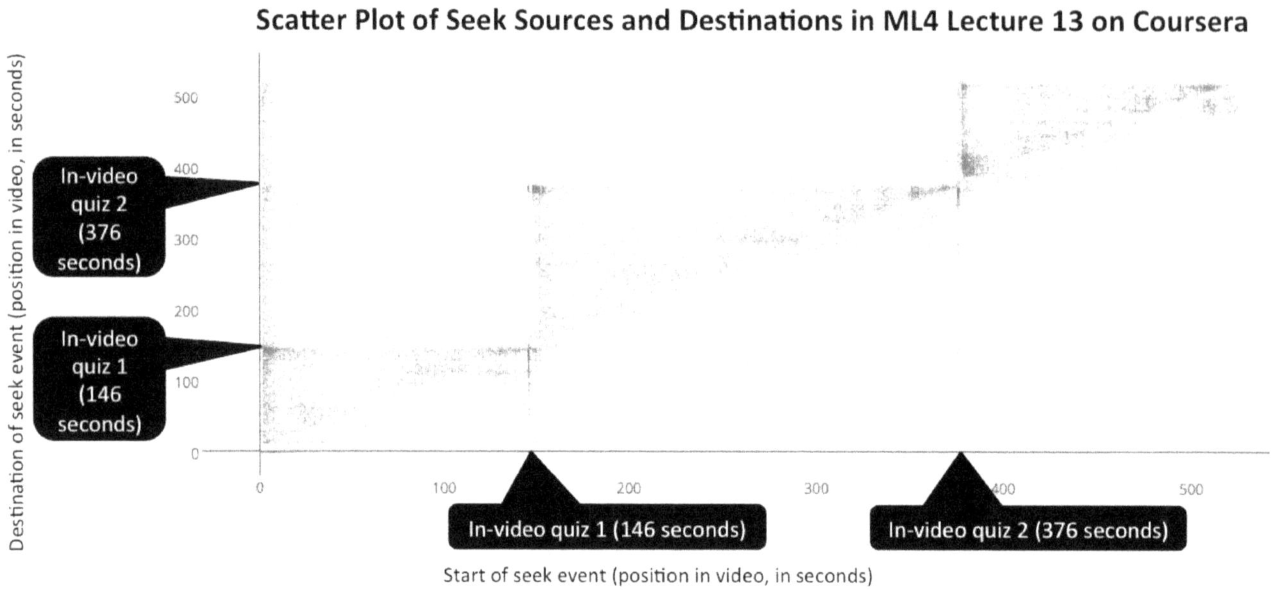

Figure 6. Seek sources and destinations in a lecture with 2 in-video quizzes. Each point at (x,y) represents a seek from time x to y. There are many seeks to in-video quizzes from the start of the video, the previous section, and between quizzes.

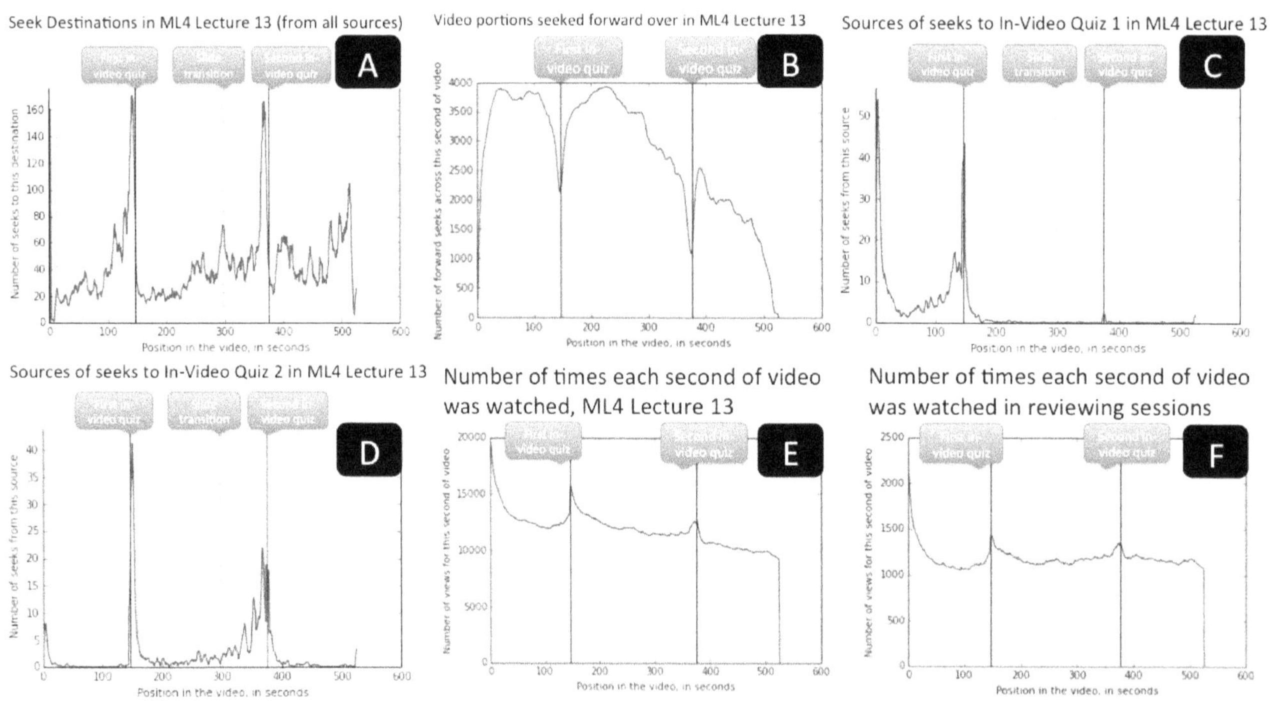

Figure 7. A) in-video quizzes are a popular destination of seeks. B) users do not tend to skip forward over in-video quizzes. C) seeks to in-video quizzes tend to be from the preceding section. D) some users are seeking directly from one in-video quiz to the next. E+F) local peaks in viewing occur around in-video quizzes.

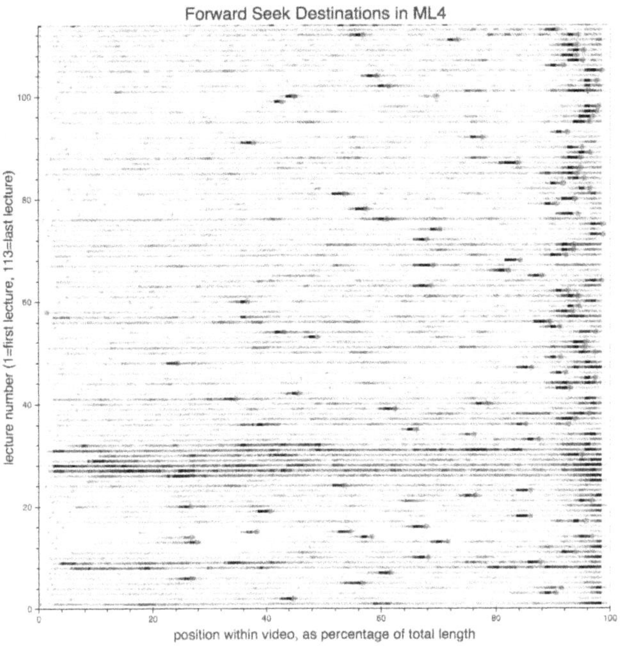

Figure 8. Destinations of forward seek chains in all videos. Each horizontal line represents a video; darkness of a segment indicates the number of seek chains going to that part of the video. Red dots indicate in-video quizzes, and green diamonds indicate slide transitions. Users tend to seek forward to in-video quizzes.

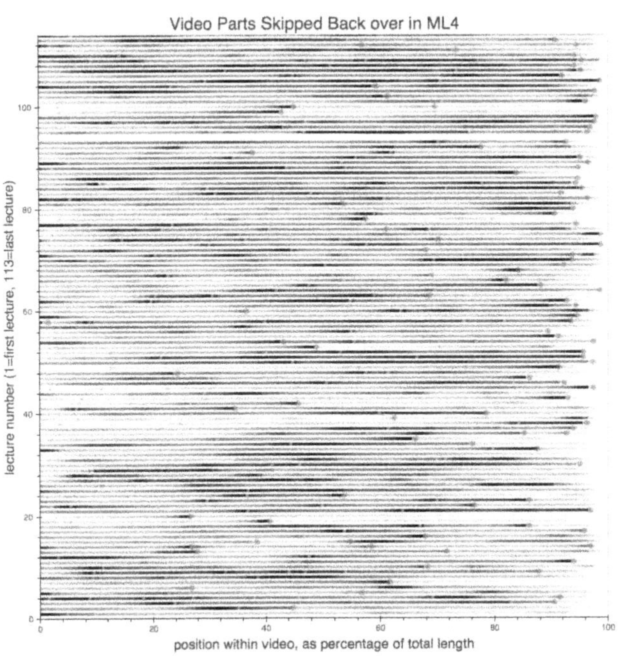

Figure 9. Parts of the video skipped over by backwards seek chains. They tend to be the portions preceding the in-video quizzes, reflecting that users are reviewing the video in response to seeing the in-video quiz

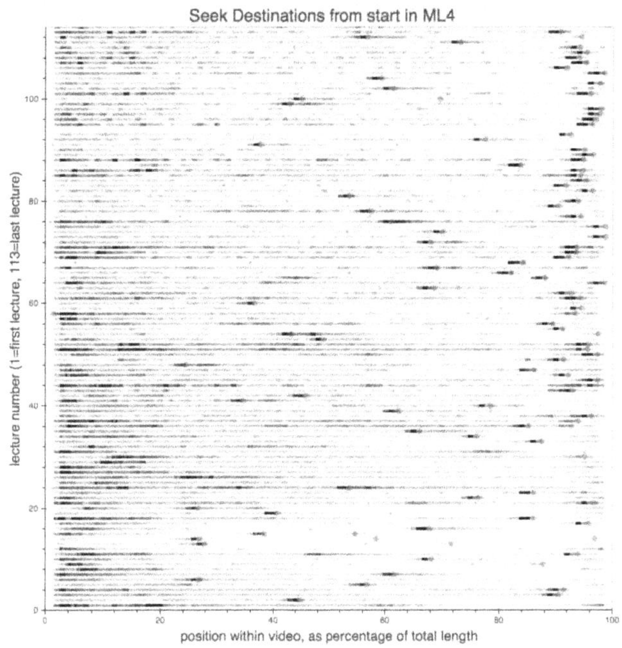

Figure 10. Seek destinations from the start of the video. Many users seek directly from the start of the video to the in-video quizzes.

quiz causing users to seek backwards more, as opposed to being a side-effect of in-video quizzes tending to occur near the end of the video.

Seek Destinations from the Start of the video

As we can see in Figure 11, many users jump directly from the start of the video to in-video quizzes. This suggests that these users might be previewing the quizzes before they watch the video, or they are using the quizzes as a navigational tool to help them decide which parts of the video they need to see and review.

DO LECTURES WITH IN-VIDEO QUIZZES HAVE HIGHER ENGAGEMENT AND LOWER IN-VIDEO DROPOFF?

We saw previously that there are bursts in seeking, viewing, and reviewing near in-video quizzes. This leads us to ask whether lectures with in-video quizzes have higher engagement (viewing and seeking), and lower in-video dropoff.

In Table 4, we compare engagement metrics in videos with in-video quizzes to videos without in-video quizzes. On average, videos with in-video quizzes have more seek chains per viewing session. However, the increased seeking may also be attributable to video length – lectures with in-video quizzes tend to be slightly longer. Users who start watching a video with in-video quizzes will also view a larger percentage of that video before leaving the video. This increased viewing is in spite of video length – previous studies have found that users tend to stop viewing longer videos, especially videos longer than 6 minutes (this is known as *in-video dropout*) [7].

That said, although this data suggests that in-video dropout is lower in lectures with in-video quizzes, it does not prove a

Type of data	Lectures with no in-video quizzes	Lectures with 1 in-video quiz	Lectures with 2 in-video quizzes
Number of lecture videos	13	92	7
Average lecture video length (in seconds)	534.8	628.7	704.9
Average number of seconds of video watched per viewing session	333.8	492.4	528.7
Average percent of video watched per viewing session	59.3%	79.1%	75.6%
Percentage of viewers who start watching the video that reach the end	61.9%	67.5%	62.8%
Average number of seek chains per viewing session	1.16	1.43	1.78
Percentage of viewers who seeked at least once while viewing the video	36.2%	42.7%	47.5%

Table 4. Users watch a larger portion of lecture videos that contain in-video quizzes during viewing sessions, and have more seeking activity.

causal relationship. It may simply be the case that the videos with quizzes happen to have more engaging content.

HOW MUCH EFFORT DO USERS INVEST IN ANSWERING IN-VIDEO QUIZZES?

In this section, we will look at how many attempts users make to answer in-video quizzes, and how much time they spend between attempts. As shown in Table 5, 76.0% of users will answer the in-video quiz correctly on their first try.

Among the users who answered an in-video quiz incorrectly on their first try, 76.5% will submit a correct answer within the next 30 minutes. Users who submit an incorrect answer first but later submit a correct answer submit an average of 1.28 incorrect times before they finally submit a correct answer (72.5% submit one incorrect answer before getting a correct answer, and 27.5% submit two incorrect answers before submitting a correct answer). Users who submit an incorrect answer first but later submit a correct answer spend a median of 13 seconds (mean=32, σ=85) from when they submit their first incorrect answer until when they submit a correct answer.

Users who submit an incorrect answer and never submit a correct answer submit an average of 2.68 incorrect answers (13.8% submit one incorrect answer and give up, 4.4% submit two incorrect answers and give up, and 81.8% submit 3 times, at which point Coursera will show them the correct answer). They spend a median of 13 seconds (mean=29, σ=71) from when they submit their first incorrect answer until when they submit their final (incorrect) answer.

Let us now return to the users who first submit an incorrect answer but later (within the next 30 minutes) submit a correct answer. Between the period when a user submits the incorrect answer and when they submit the correct answer, 9.1% of these users will make a seek. Among those, 97% seek backward, while 3% seek forward. Users who perform a seek will spend a median of 115 seconds (mean=218, σ=278) before they submit a correct answer. As indicated by the backwards seek chain, the user is presumably using this time to review the preceding section. In contrast, the users who do not perform a seek spend a median of 11 seconds (mean=23, σ=53) before submitting a correct answer.

Type of interaction with in-video quiz				Percentage of users	Median time spent between initial and final answer (seconds)	Mean number of incorrect attempts
Answers in-video quiz correctly on first try				76.0%		
Answers in-video quiz incorrectly on first try				24.0%	13 (mean=31, σ=83)	1.54
	Will not submit a correct answer within the next 30 minutes			23.5% (4.3% of total)	13 (mean=29, σ=71)	2.68
	Will submit a correct answer within the next 30 minutes			76.5% (18.4% of total)	13 (mean=32, σ=85)	1.28
		Does not seek before submitting answer		90.9% (16.7% of total)	11 (mean=23, σ=53)	1.28
		Makes a seek before submitting answer		9.1% (1.7% of total)	115 (mean=218, σ=278)	1.51
			Backward seek	97.0% (1.6% of total)	116 (mean=217, σ=275)	1.51
			Forward seek	3.0% (0.1% of total)	56 (mean=229, σ=367)	1.48

Table 5. Most users answer in-video quizzes correctly on the first try. Among users who seek back to review the preceding section after answering a question incorrectly, they spend almost 2 minutes before they submit the correct answer.

Thus, most users who attempt an in-video quiz (94.4%) will submit a correct answer within 30 minutes, with the majority answering correctly on their first try. However, most users who answer incorrectly simply answer again within the next 13 seconds, without referring to the rest of the video.

WHEN AND WHY DO USERS SEEK BACKWARDS FROM IN-VIDEO QUIZZES?

There are several possibilities for when backwards seek chains could occur in the context of in-video quizzes. Users might see the in-video quiz, realize they don't know the answer, and then seek back to review the preceding section. Or, users might try answering the in-video quiz, get the answer wrong, and then seek back to the review the preceding section. We sought to see which of these reviewing strategies was the most popular, as shown in Table 6.

It turns out that the former strategy – of seeing the in-video quiz, and seeking back to review before attempting to answer the quiz – is the most widely used. Of all backwards-seeking that occurs starting from an in-video quiz, a total of 60.5% actually occurs before the user attempts to answer the in-video quiz (but after they have seen the question). Of these, after the user returns to the in-video quiz, they will answer it correctly 62.4% of the time. It is rather peculiar that this is lower than the overall rate at which users correctly answer quizzes on their first attempt (76.0%); one possible explanation is that the learners who needed to review the preceding section did not understand the material as well as those who felt they could answer the quiz as soon as they saw it.

14.4% of backwards seeking from the in-video quiz occurs after the user submitted an incorrect response. Of these, 81.8% will eventually submit a correct response after reviewing, 9.4% will submit at least one more incorrect response but will never submit the correct response, and 8.8% will never attempt the problem again.

3.0% of backwards seeking from the in-video quiz occurs after the user submitted a correct response. These users are presumably just reviewing the video for purposes other than

Context in which backwards seek chain from in-video quiz occurred		Percentage of backwards seek chains from quiz
Seeked back to review preceding section before first attempt to answer the quiz		60.5%
	User's first attempt to answer the quiz will be correct	62.4% (37.8% of total)
	User's first attempt to answer the quiz will be incorrect	37.6% (22.8% of total)
User never attempts to answer the in-video quiz		19.4%
Seeked back to review preceding section after submitting an incorrect response		14.4%
	Will eventually submit a correct response after reviewing	81.8% (11.8% of total)
	Will submit at least one more incorrect response (but will never submit a correct response)	9.4% (1.3% of total)
	Will never attempt to answer the quiz again (will submit neither incorrect nor correct responses)	8.8% (1.3% of total)
Seeked back to review preceding section after submitting a correct response		3.0%

Table 6. Most backwards seek chains from in-video quizzes occur after the user has seen the question, but before they have submitted an answer to it.

to answer the in-video quiz. In the remaining 19.4% of backwards seek chains starting from in-video quizzes, the user saw the question, but will never submit any answer to it.

Thus, most (75%) backwards seek chains from in-video quizzes occur before the user answers the quiz correctly and are followed by an answer attempt within the next 30 minutes, while only 3% occur after the user submits a correct answer. This suggests that the reason why users seek backward from in-video quizzes is to review the preceding section to help them answer the in-video quiz.

DISCUSSION AND CONCLUSION

In this paper we sought to characterize the ways in which users engage with in-video quizzes, and how they affect users' video viewing behavior. We did so by analyzing the video viewing logs in Coursera's Machine Learning course.

We found that users engage heavily with in-video quizzes, with a similar fraction of learners answering in-video quizzes as those who finish watching videos, as shown in Figure 2. We also found certain video viewing patterns emerge in regions surrounding in-video quizzes, specifically:

- Users engage heavily with in-video quizzes – in lectures containing a quiz, 74% of viewers will answer the quiz.
- There are peaks in seeking and rewatching activity in the regions surrounding the in-video quiz.
- In-video quizzes are a common source of seek chains within videos. Users most frequently seek backward from the in-video quiz to the preceding section. Most backwards seek chains from in-video quizzes occur after the user has seen the question, but before they answer it. This suggests that users are reviewing the preceding section to help them answer the quiz.
- In-video quizzes are a common destination of seek chains. Users most commonly seek from the preceding video segment, which contains material relevant to the quiz.
- Users do not tend to skip forwards or backwards over in-video quizzes. They thus segment the video into isolated subsections that users rarely seek between.
- Some users follow quiz-oriented navigation strategies, jumping straight to the quiz from the beginning of the video, or jumping from one in-video quiz to the next.
- In-video dropout is lower in lectures that have in-video quizzes, compared to lectures that lack in-video quizzes.
- Most users answer in-video quizzes correctly on the first try. Among those who answer incorrectly, the median time until they answer correctly is just 13 seconds.

Our results suggest future work investigating the effects of in-video quizzes on in-video engagement rates. Previous work (on videos lacking in-video quizzes) has shown that there is a steady drop-off in users watching lectures, particularly in longer lecture videos [7]. We saw in Table 4 that in-video dropout is lower in lecture videos that have in-video quizzes, compared to videos that don't have in-video quizzes. However, this may be caused by differences in the lecture content, rather than the presence of in-video quizzes. Additionally, as we also saw in Figure 7 E, the drop-off in number of views appears to temporarily decline in the area surrounding the in-video quizzes. Thus, because we found that users tend to answer in-video quizzes and not skip over them, and we found peaks in seeking activity around in-video quizzes, this leads us to wonder whether in-video quizzes could help counteract the disengagement patterns that occur in longer lecture videos. However, A/B tests would be required to actually verify the effects of in-video quizzes on engagement rates.

The peaks in seeking towards in-video quizzes suggest a number of possible interface modifications that could be explored. Coursera currently does not allow users to easily skip directly to in-video quizzes, instead requiring them to go to the preceding few seconds of videos. Since in-video quizzes were one of the most common destinations for seek chains, particularly in the forward direction, one might investigate the effects of modifying the interface to make it easier to seek to in-video quizzes. We also observed that users often seek back from in-video quizzes to the preceding section, upon seeing the in-video quiz. Hence, another interface modification that may be worth exploring is to let users preview the in-video quizzes, and see whether this allows them to navigate the lecture more effectively.

In-video quizzes have many appeals, such as the potential for improving engagement by making lectures more interactive and enabling users to test their understanding of the material. We have examined users' interaction patterns with lecture videos in the context of Coursera's in-video quizzes, and hope that our findings can inform future improvements to the design of interactive lecture-viewing systems.

REFERENCES

1. Robert Allen. 1998. The Web: interactive and multimedia education. *Computer Networks and ISDN Systems* 30, 16 (1998), 1717–1727.

2. Ashton Anderson, Daniel Huttenlocher, Jon Kleinberg, and Jure Leskovec. 2014. Engaging with massive online courses. In *Proceedings of the 23rd international conference on World wide web*. International World Wide Web Conferences Steering Committee, 687–698.

3. Philip J Guo, Juho Kim, and Rob Rubin. 2014. How video production affects student engagement: An empirical study of mooc videos. In *Proceedings of the first ACM conference on Learning@ scale conference*. ACM, 41–50.
4. Philip J Guo and Katharina Reinecke. 2014. Demographic differences in how students navigate through MOOCs. In *Proceedings of the first ACM conference on Learning@ scale conference*. ACM, 21–30.
5. Mina C Johnson-Glenberg. 2010. Embedded formative e-assessment: who benefits, who falters. *Educational Media International* 47, 2 (2010), 153–171.
6. Juho Kim, Philip J Guo, Carrie J Cai, Shang-Wen Daniel Li, Krzysztof Z Gajos, and Robert C Miller. 2014a. Data-driven interaction techniques for improving navigation of educational videos. In *Proceedings of the 27th annual ACM symposium on User interface software and technology*. ACM, 563–572.
7. Juho Kim, Philip J Guo, Daniel T Seaton, Piotr Mitros, Krzysztof Z Gajos, and Robert C Miller. 2014b. Understanding in-video dropouts and interaction peaks in online lecture videos. In *Proceedings of the first ACM conference on Learning@at Scale conference*. ACM, 31–40.
8. René F Kizilcec, Chris Piech, and Emily Schneider. 2013. Deconstructing disengagement: analyzing learner subpopulations in massive open online courses. In *Proceedings of the third international conference on learning analytics and knowledge*. ACM, 170–179.
9. Rene F Kizilcec and Emily Schneider. 2015. Motivation as a Lens to Understand Online Learners: Towards Data-Driven Design with the OLEI Scale. *ACM Transactions on Computer-Human Interaction (TOCHI)* 22, 2 (2015), 5.
10. Henry L Roediger III and Andrew C Butler. 2011. The critical role of retrieval practice in long-term retention. *Trends in cognitive sciences* 15, 1 (2011), 20–27.

Brain Points: A Deeper Look at a Growth Mindset Incentive Structure for an Educational Game

Eleanor O'Rourke[1], Erin Peach[1], Carol S. Dweck[2], and Zoran Popović[1]
[1]Center for Game Science, Department of Computer Science & Engineering, University of Washington
[2]Department of Psychology, Stanford University
{eorourke, epeach, zoran}@cs.washington.edu, dweck@stanford.edu

ABSTRACT
Student retention is a central challenge in systems for learning at scale. It has been argued that educational video games could improve student retention by providing engaging experiences and informing the design of other online learning environments. However, educational games are not uniformly effective. Our recent research shows that player retention can be increased by using a brain points incentive structure that rewards behaviors associated with growth mindset, or the belief that intelligence can grow. In this paper, we expand on our prior work by providing new insights into how growth mindset behaviors can be effectively promoted in the educational game *Refraction*. We present results from an online study of 25,000 children who were exposed to five different versions of the brain points intervention. We find that growth mindset animations cause a large number of players to quit, while brain points encourage persistence. Most importantly, we find that awarding brain points randomly is ineffective; the incentive structure is successful specifically because it rewards desirable growth mindset behaviors. These findings have important implications that can support the future generalization of the brain points intervention to new educational contexts.

Author Keywords
Educational games; growth mindset; incentive structures.

INTRODUCTION
One of the biggest challenges facing systems for learning at scale is student retention. Only a small percentage of students in Massive Open Online Courses (MOOCs) complete the courses they begin [10], and little is known about how to engage students in online learning environments. In contrast, video games are famous for their ability to motivate players to perform complex tasks over long periods of time. This has inspired a growing interest in leveraging games to engage students in educational settings [5, 22, 20]. Game incentive structures, the systems or rewards given to successful players, have attracted particular attention for their ability to motivate students [12]. As a result, there is great potential for educational games to provide engaging learning experiences at scale, and to inform the design of formal online learning experiences.

While educational games can motivate students, not all designs are equally effective. Our recent work shows that player persistence can be increased by modifying game incentives to reward behaviors associated with the growth mindset [24]. The growth mindset is the belief that intelligence can be increased over time through hard work and good strategies [21]. Psychology research shows that the growth mindset can be taught, and that growth mindset interventions can have a positive impact on students' motivation, reaction to failure, and academic achievement [2, 3, 6]. In our prior work, we encouraged growth mindset behaviors in the game *Refraction* using a novel "brain points" incentive structure that directly rewards students for their effort, use of strategy, and incremental progress [24]. While this research provides new insights into how persistence can be encouraged in online settings, the original study leaves a number of important questions unanswered.

In this paper, we expand on our previous work to gain a deeper understanding of the growth mindset intervention. The original intervention was composed of three central components: a growth mindset narrative, the brain points incentive structure, and a progress visualization. We study how each of these components contributes to the intervention's effects on student persistence, use of strategy, and reaction to challenge in the educational game *Refraction*. We developed four new versions of the intervention: one without a mindset narrative, one without brain points, one with brain points that are awarded randomly, and one without a progress visualization. Each version was created to explore a specific question about the intervention design. We present results from an online experiment with 25,000 students that compares each modified intervention to the original intervention design.

Our findings have a number of implications for the design of educational systems that aim to increase student retention by teaching the growth mindset. We found that fewer children persist when the growth mindset narrative is included because they quit during the game's introductory animation. This suggests that animations that interrupt gameplay are not effective at encouraging persistence. However, we found that the brain points incentive structure did increase persistence. More interestingly, we confirmed that rewarding players for their effort

L@S 2016, April 25-26, 2016, Edinburgh, Scotland Uk
© 2016 ACM. ISBN 978-1-4503-3726-7/16/04$15.00
DOI: http://dx.doi.org/10.1145/2876034.2876040

at random times is not effective; brain points are successful specifically because they reward productive struggle. This highlights the importance of developing intelligent behavioral metrics that can detect growth mindset behaviors when applying this approach to new learning environments. Finally, we found that visualizing player progress increases retention, suggesting that student data can be used as an effective motivator. We believe these findings make an important contribution that will help researchers generalize the brain points intervention to other online learning contexts in the future.

BACKGROUND

High rates of student attrition are common in online learning environments. In a meta-analysis of MOOC courses, Jordan found that completion rates range between 1% and 40%, with an average of 15% [10]. Researchers have cautioned against interpreting this high attrition rate as a failure of MOOCs because students begin courses with a diverse set of motivations, intentions, and circumstances that impact completion [14, 15, 27]. However, students who report that they are taking a course to earn a certificate still have low completion rates [15, 27], suggesting that there is room to improve.

While researchers have begun to explore methods of improving retention [7, 13, 16], we still have a limited understanding of how to motivate student to persist in online learning environments. However, we believe there is great potential for learning theory and educational games to inform the design of platforms for online learning. Psychologists have studied the relationship between motivation and academic achievement for decades, providing valuable insights that can inform the design of educational technologies. Game incentive structures have also been cited as a potentially valuable method of motivating students in a variety of learning environments [12].

In this section, we describe the theory behind the growth mindset and review related work on educational games. Then we provide an overview of our original work on incentivizing the growth mindset in games, and discuss the research questions left unanswered by our first study.

Theories of Intelligence

Extensive research in psychology shows that students' beliefs about intelligence can have a strong effect on their motivation, reaction to challenge or failure, and academic achievement [3, 6, 9]. Individuals who have a *fixed mindset* believe that they are born with a certain amount of intelligence, and that this is an unchangeable attribute. However, individuals who have a *growth mindset* believe that intelligence is malleable, and that it can be increased through hard work and good strategies [21]. These beliefs can impact both behavior and academic achievement; Blackwell et al. conducted a study that showed that holding a growth mindset predicted improving grades over the two years of middle school, while holding a fixed mindset predicted static or decreasing grades [3].

Fortunately, studies show that the growth mindset can be taught [21, 3, 2, 6, 11]. For example, growth mindset behaviors can be encouraged by changing the praise given to successful students. Multiple studies have shown that students who are praised for their ability after success ("you must be smart at these problems") react poorly to a subsequent failure, while students who are praised for their effort ("you must have worked hard at these problems") react favorably [11, 21]. The growth mindset can also be taught directly. Blackwell et al. taught middle-school students about the growth mindset through readings and discussions about the neural connections that form in the brain when it works hard. Before the intervention, students' math grades had been steadily decreasing, but after the workshop their grades improved significantly [3]. Aronson et al. report similar results in a study of an intervention for college students [2].

Growth mindset interventions have great potential to increase student motivation and performance at scale. As a result, recent efforts have explored methods of teaching the growth mindset online. Brainology, a for-purchase online program based on the Blackwell intervention, teaches students the scientific basis of the growth mindset through readings and interactive exercises [1]. Paunesku et al. studied the effectiveness of an online growth mindset intervention, delivered through two 45-minute sessions involving reading and writing exercises, and found student grades in core academic courses increased in comparison to a control [25]. However, little is know about how to teach the growth mindset through educational games.

Educational Games

Video games are increasingly recognized as a compelling platform that could be used to improve student motivation in educational settings [5, 22, 20]. Although empirical studies suggest that educational games can have mixed effects on learning outcomes [8, 18, 20], a number of clear successes highlight their potential as instructional tools. Mayo reviewed a variety of STEM game studies, and found that games can produce up to a 40% positive increase in learning outcomes [20]. Games have also been shown to increase student motivation [26] and time-on-task [18, 17]. Researchers note that successful educational games are typically designed around effective pedagogical practices [20, 22], highlighting the importance of grounding educational games in validated theory.

Researchers have explored methods of integrating learning theory into games to maximize student motivation, persistence, and learning [18, 4]. For example, Chase studied task framing in a genetics game, and found that students who are told their performance depends on both chance and skill persist longer after failure than those who are told their performance depends on skill alone [4]. Researchers have also studied methods of increasing persistence by adding game-like elements to formal learning environments [12]. Krause et al. found that student performance and retention improved when social gamification elements were added to a MOOC course [16]. This research suggests that games can be optimized for student motivation and persistence, and that incentive structures can be used to engage students outside of game environments. However, the relative impacts of varying game elements on student motivation are still not well understood.

[1]Brainology: http://www.mindsetworks.com/webnav/program.aspx

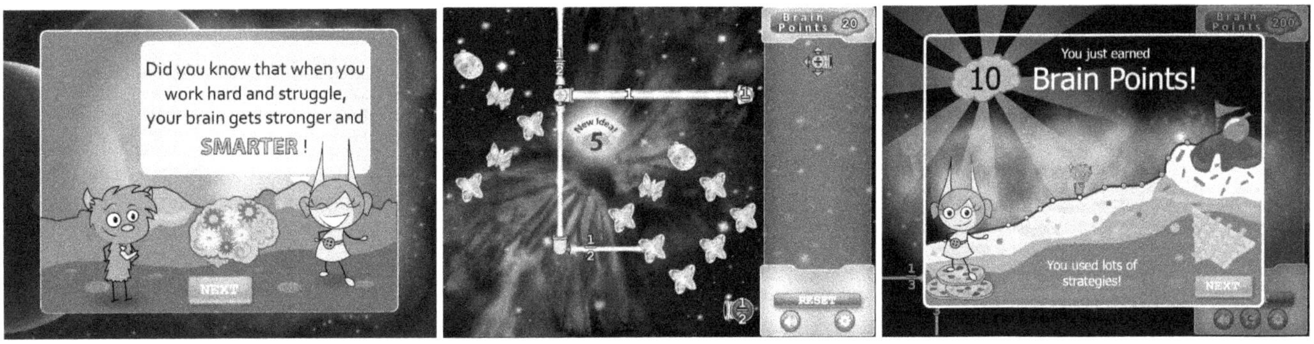

(a) (b) (c)

Figure 1. Screenshots of three central components of the brain points intervention for the educational game *Refraction*. Figure (a) shows a single panel from an introductory animation that teaches the growth mindset directly. Figure (b) shows brain points being earned during a game level. Figure (c) shows the brain points summary screen that displays a mountain that visualizes player progress.

The Brain Points Intervention

In recent work, we presented a new approach for promoting growth mindset behaviors in an educational game called *Refraction* [24]. This intervention is focused around a novel "brain points" incentive structure that directly rewards students for their effort, use of strategy, and incremental progress as they play. However, the intervention also includes a growth mindset narrative presented through an animated dialog, and a visualization of student progress that is displayed after each completed level. Screenshots of these three components of the intervention are shown in Figure 1.

In our first paper, we evaluated the intervention through an online study of 15,000 students [24]. This experiment compared the growth mindset version of *Refraction* to a control version with a standard incentive structure that awarded points for each completed level. We found that children in the mindset condition played longer and completed more levels than those in the control, suggesting that the intervention encouraged persistence. These children also used more strategy, suggesting that they learned the behaviors rewarded by the brain points incentive structure. Finally, more struggling players persisted in the growth mindset condition, suggesting that the intervention improved children's reaction to challenge. These findings indicate that the brain points intervention encouraged students to adopt growth mindset behaviors during play. However, this study left a number of important questions unanswered.

It is not currently clear whether the mindset narrative, brain points incentive structure, or progress visualization had the strongest effect on player behavior. Since previous work shows that the growth mindset can be taught directly [3], it is possible that the narrative contributed the majority of the effect. Furthermore, the original study compared brain points awarded during gameplay to a control where points were awarded after each completed level. It is possible that children simply enjoy earning points while playing, and that rewarding growth mindset behaviors is unimportant. Finally, it is unclear whether the progress visualization contributes to the observed effects.

In this work, we explore these unanswered questions through a large-scale experiment that compares five alternate versions of the growth mindset intervention. Our goal is to expand on our prior work; the design of the original brain points intervention is not a contribution of this paper. Instead, we provide new insights about the design of the brain points intervention that improve our understanding of how to promote growth mindset behaviors through educational games. We believe our findings will prove instrumental for future efforts to generalize this approach to other learning contexts.

EXPERIMENT DESIGN

To tease apart the impact of the different components of the brain points intervention, we designed an experiment that compares five different versions of the educational game *Refraction*. The first version is a control that uses a lightly modified version of our original intervention [24]. The remaining four versions either remove or modify components of the intervention to address specific research questions. In our analysis, we compare each modified version to to the control version, which allows us to measure the added impact of each component of the design. We leave pairwise comparisons of the modified versions for future work. In this section, we provide an overview of *Refraction* and describe the control version of the game. Then we present our four research questions and the versions of *Refraction* that we use to address each question.

Refraction

Refraction is a Flash puzzle game that was created by game researchers and learning science experts at the Center for Game Science to teach faction concepts to elementary school students. The game was designed to support a conceptual understanding of fractions rooted in the concept of splitting [19]. To play, a child interacts with a grid that contains laser sources, target spaceships, and asteroids, as shown in Figure 2. The goal of the game is to satisfy target spaceships by avoiding asteroids and splitting the laser into the correct fractional amounts. The player uses pieces that change the laser direction or split the laser into two or three equal parts to achieve this goal. To win, the player must correctly satisfy all the target spaceships at the same time.

Refraction uses an adaptive level progression that allows players to advance through concepts at their own pace. The progression covers eleven fraction concepts, ranging from split-

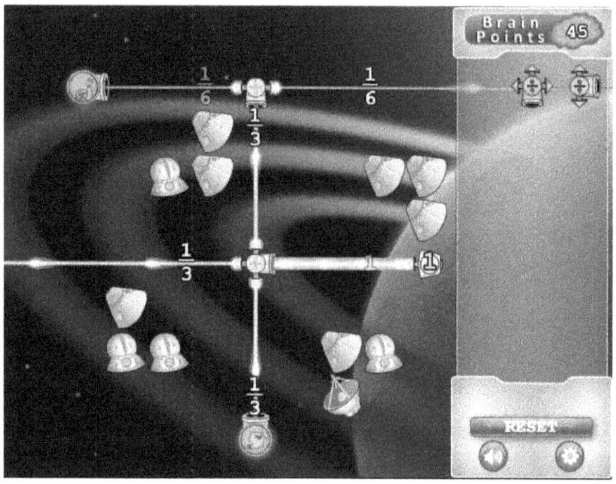

Figure 2. A level of Refraction. The pieces on the right are used to split lasers into fractional amounts and redirect them to satisfy the green target spaceships. All ships must be satisfied at the same time to win.

ting a laser into halves to splitting a laser to create both sixths and ninths. The game provides ten levels for each concept: one tutorial level with only required pieces, and nine puzzle levels that involve choosing between splitter pieces to produce the correct fractions. Each player begins with the tutorial level, and then continues to solve puzzle levels either two are solved under a mastery threshold or all nine puzzles are completed. To achieve mastery, the player must complete the level in 1.5 times the minimum required moves without making mathematical errors. The levels are always presented in the same order, so all children play the same first three levels, and some continue with additional puzzles until mastery is reached.

Control

To provide context for the four new versions of *Refraction* created for this study, we give a brief overview of the control version. For more detail on the intervention design see [24].

Narrative

The intervention includes a growth mindset narrative that is communicated through animations. A 25 second animation at the beginning of the game introduces the brain points incentive structure and teaches the growth mindset using language based on the Brainology curriculum and the Blackwell intervention [3]. This is followed by three additional animations, shown after the player completes the first three *Refraction* planets, which provide additional detail about the growth mindset. The animations are designed to directly teach the growth mindset and reinforce the value of strategy use and productive struggle.

Incentive Structure

The "brain points" incentive structure was designed to reward players for their effort, use of strategy, and incremental progress. Players earn brain points as they work to solve levels. We designed four metrics that capture desirable growth mindset behaviors in the game. The *new hypothesis* metric triggers when a player makes two new moves in a row. The *empty board* metric triggers when at least two pieces are on the board and the player returns all pieces to the starting bin. The *math* metric triggers when the player makes a target fraction for the first time. Finally, the *moves* metric triggers when the player makes ten distinct moves. These metrics capture desirable learning strategies and productive persistence in *Refraction*.

To make the system more difficult to game, a player must trigger two of these metrics to earn points. For example, a player will earn points if she first clears the board and then tries a new hypothesis. This allows the system to reward desirable behaviors without being overly transparent. Brain points are awarded to players in increments of five. When points are earned, a small animated brain icon with a short message is displayed, as shown in Figure 1(b). The message reflects the last metric the child triggered. The messages associated with the four metrics are "New Idea" for the *new hypothesis* metric, "Fresh Start" for the *board cleared* metric, "Math Effort" for the *math* metric, and "Working Hard" for the *moves* metric.

Progress Visualization

The *Refraction* world has seven different planets, and players advance to a new planet every time they collect 50 points. After each level, a summary screen showing the player's progress through the current planet is displayed, as shown in Figure 1(c). This visualization shows a mountain with ten dots. The player climbs one dot for every five points earned, symbolizing the player's hard work. At the top of the summary screen, a message highlights the number of points earned during the previous level. At the bottom, a message praises the player's work, reinforcing the growth mindset narrative and highlighting the connection between using growth mindset learning strategies and solving levels.

RQ1: Does the growth mindset narrative matter?

The first question we wanted to explore was whether the growth mindset narrative presented through the sequence of four animations have a strong impact on player behavior. We hypothesized that the narrative would make an important contribution, increasing persistence and improving players' reaction to challenge. To answer this question, we created a version of *Refraction* that did not include the four animations. After loading this version of the game, players are immediately dropped into the first level, without any introduction to the growth mindset or the brain points incentive structure. Players receive points just as they would in the control version, and they see the progress visualization after each level.

RQ2: Do brain points matter?

Next we wanted to explore whether brain points impact the effectiveness of the intervention. We hypothesized that points would contribute to encouraging growth mindset behaviors. However, since many effective mindset interventions focus exclusively on textual narratives [3], it is possible that brain points have no impact on student persistence, strategy use, and reaction to challenge. To explore this question, we created a new version of the intervention that included the growth mindset animations but no points.

In this version, players begin by watching a modified version of the introductory animation that teaches the growth mindset but does not mention the brain points incentive structure. After the animation, children play the game exactly as they would in the control condition, except that that no points are earned

Figure 3. A screenshot of the neutral dialog box displayed after each level in the version of *Refraction* that does not include brain points.

during gameplay. Since the progress visualization displayed after each level is centered around earning points, we removed the summary screen in this version. Instead, we display a neutral dialog box, shown in Figure 3. While players do not earn points in this version, we silently calculate the number of brain points each player would have earned. We use this point count to determine when to advance players to the next *Refraction* planet, so that players advance at the same rate that they would have in the control condition.

RQ3: Do brain points need to reward specific behaviors?

We were also interested in studying whether brain points are more effective when they reward specific behaviors. We hypothesized that rewarding growth mindset behaviors would contribute to the effect. However, it is possible that players simply enjoy earning points during gameplay, and that rewarding growth mindset behaviors is unimportant. To explore this question, we developed a version of the game that awarded points randomly, rather than in response to strategic behavior.

In this version, players view the same growth mindset narrative and progress visualization as in the control condition. Players still earn points during gameplay, but we do not use the combined strategy metric to determine when to award points. Instead, we set a timer to award points after a certain number of seconds. When the random points timer finishes, we wait until the player makes a move, and then award brain points. We chose this approach to make the points seem less random, since earning points when you have not made any move feels unnatural. When players earn random points, the "Working Hard" message is displayed to insinuate that the points are rewarding effort. The "Working Hard" message is always displayed on the summary screen in this version.

To ensure that random points are awarded at the same rate as brain points, we randomly select each wait time from the distribution of times between brain points in the data set collected for the original experiment [24]. However, as we discuss in detail in the analysis section, random points are awarded significantly more often than brain points. This is because we award random points using this time distribution during all levels the game. In the control condition, it is more difficult to earn brain points during the four tutorial levels at the beginning of the game because these levels do not include fractions.

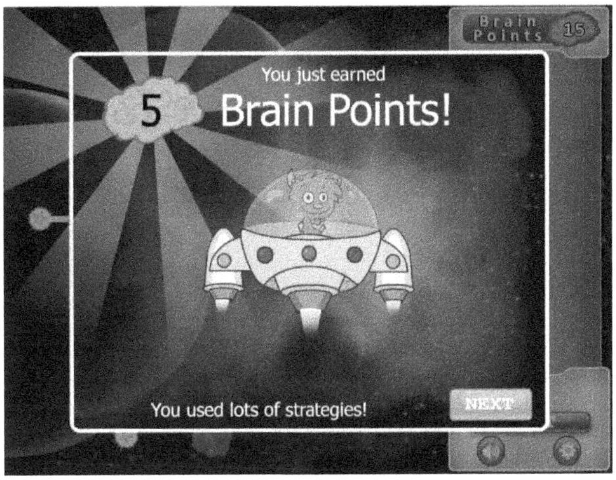

Figure 4. A screenshot of the summary screen without the mountain visualization that displays player progress through the current *Refraction* planet. We display a neutral animation of a spaceship in this summary screen instead.

RQ4: Does the progress visualization matter?

Finally, we wanted to study whether the progress visualizations displayed on the summary screens contribute to the effects measured in the original study. We hypothesized that the visualization would contribute to engagement, since it provides a clear indication of player progress through the game. However, it is possible that the visualization and mountain metaphor are too abstract to have a strong impact on children. To study this question, we created a version of the intervention that showed a summary screen without the mountain visualization. The summary still displays the points earned during the previous level and the growth mindset message. However, the mountain is replaced by an animated image of a spaceship, as shown in Figure 4.

METHOD

To address our research questions, we studied how children played the five versions of *Refraction* on the educational website BrainPOP [2]. BrainPOP is a popular resource in the United States, where it is used in around 20% of elementary schools (Traci Kampel, personal communication). The website provides extensive curriculum materials for teachers, and also includes an educational game portal designed for use in the classroom. This is the same website that was used to conduct the original brain points study reported in [24].

BrainPOP is a valuable resource for studying the impact of educational game interventions because it provides researchers with access to a large, diverse population of students. However, as is common with online platforms, we know very little about the students who visit BrainPOP. While the website is primarily used in schools, we have no information about the contexts in which students play. We use random assignment

[2]BrainPOP: http://www.brainpop.com/

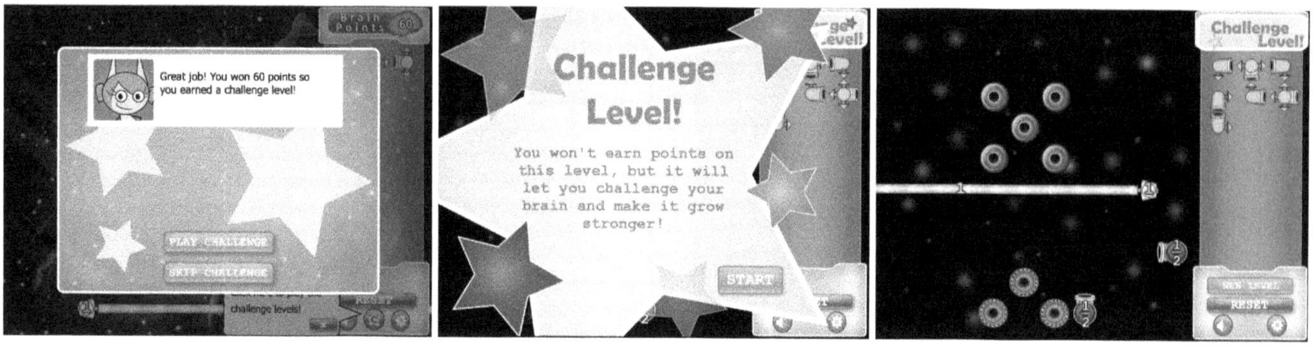

(a) (b) (c)

Figure 5. We designed a "challenge level" to observe how children react in the face of a particularly difficult puzzle. Figure (a) shows the message displayed when the player earns the challenge level. Figure (b) shows the introductory message displayed when the player starts the challenge level. Figure (c) shows the challenge level interface. The player can skip the challenge at any point by clicking the "New Level" button. For the no points condition, all textual references to points are removed from these dialog boxes.

and large sample sizes to mitigate the effects of any uncontrolled variables. We are also unable to administer pre- and post-tests to formally measure learning. Instead, we measure how our interventions impact observable in-game behaviors.

Behavioral Metrics

We use a variety of metrics to capture behaviors associated with the growth mindset, which we describe in detail below. As children play *Refraction*, we log all interactions with the game or its interface to capture behavior so that we can calculate these metrics for our analysis.

Persistence

To capture student persistence, we use two outcome measures: the amount of time children spend playing the game, and the number of levels they play. We calculate the amount of active time played by counting the number of seconds children spend interacting with the game, excluding menu navigation and idle periods with more than thirty sections between actions. We calculate the number of levels played by counting levels with at least one game action. Since *Refraction* uses an adaptive level progression, each child plays a different set of levels based on their incoming skill. However, we expect incoming skill to be evenly distributed across conditions because we assign players randomly.

Growth Mindset Behavior

We also wanted to measure whether students exhibit the growth mindset behaviors rewarded by brain points. To capture these behaviors, we use an outcome measure that combines the four metrics used to award brain points in the control version of *Refraction*. As mentioned in the Experiment Design section, we use the *new hypothesis*, *empty board*, *math*, and *moves* metrics to determine when to award points. In all five versions of *Refraction*, we log an event every time one of these metrics is triggered. We sum the number of times each of the four metrics is triggered during play to calculate overall strategy use. Then to control for amount of time played, we divide this combined metric by the number of minutes of active time. This produces a final outcome measure that captures the average number of metrics triggered per minute during play.

Reaction to Challenge

In addition to observing behavior during standard game levels, we wanted to measure how children are impacted by a particularly challenging level. Previous studies show that children react differently to failure on a challenging problem when they receive fixed and growth mindset praise [21]. We use a similar test in *Refraction* by giving players access to a "challenge level" when they earn sixty points. This level presents a unintuitive spatial problem that is tricky for adults to solve. The challenge is framed as a special reward given to players for their progress in the game. Screenshots of the challenge level and associated messages are shown in Figure 5.

Players are given the option of either playing the challenge level immediately or skipping the level. Players can return to the challenge at any point during gameplay by clicking the "C" button on the game's sidebar. This allows persistent children to attempt the challenge multiple times. We wanted to measure whether effects produced by the growth mindset intervention would transfer to levels where effort is not explicitly rewarded, so no points were given during the challenge level. Players could exit the challenge at any point by clicking the "New Level" button on the game sidebar. The challenge-related text is identical in all versions of the game except the "no points" version, in which references to points are removed.

We capture player behavior in relation to the challenge level using four different metrics. For all of these analyses, we only include children who play the game long enough to earn the challenge level. First, we calculate the number of times each player attempts the challenge level. Next, we calculate whether each player wins the challenge level. Since the level is very difficult, and players can skip the level at any time, we expect only a small percentage of children to win. We capture persistence by calculating the amount of active time each player spent on the challenge level. Finally, we calculate the average number of growth mindset behaviors per minute using the combined measure described above. These measures provide us with a robust picture of how children in each condition react to a particularly challenging level.

Condition	Active Time Played			# Levels Played			Growth Mindset Behavior Per Minute		
Control	2.54 min	$N = 10,000$	$p < 0.0001$	4 levels	$N = 10,000$	$p < 0.0001$	2.40	$N = 10,000$	$p < 0.0001$
No Narrative	3.01 min	$Z = -5.05$	$r = 0.05$	4 levels	$Z = 4.74$	$r = 0.05$	2.61	$Z = 7.08$	$r = 0.07$
Control	2.54 min	$N = 10,000$	$p < 0.0001$	4 levels	$N = 10,000$	*n.s.*	2.40	$N = 10,000$	$p < 0.0001$
No Points	2.21 min	$Z = -4.89$	$r = 0.05$	4 levels	$Z = -1.49$		2.71	$Z = 8.47$	$r = 0.09$
Control	2.54 min	$N = 10,000$	$p < 0.01$	4 levels	$N = 10,000$	$p < 0.0001$	2.40	$N = 10,000$	$p < 0.0001$
Random Points	2.19 min	$Z = -2.66$	$r = 0.03$	3 levels	$Z = -5.62$	$r = 0.06$	2.02	$Z = -7.22$	$r = 0.07$
Control	2.54 min	$N = 10,000$	$p < 0.0001$	4 levels	$N = 10,000$	$p < 0.005$	2.40	$N = 10,000$	*n.s.*
No Progress Viz	2.26 min	$Z = -3.80$	$r = 0.04$	3 levels	$Z = -2.89$	$r = 0.03$	2.46	$Z = 0.63$	

Table 1. Results from the statistical tests analyzing children's behavior while playing *Refraction*. We report the amount of active time children spend playing the game, the number of levels attempted, and the average number of growth mindset behaviors they exhibit per minute during the game. In each column, the median values are reported to the left of each cell.

Condition	# Challenge Attempts			Challenge Win Rate			Active Time Played			Growth Mindset Behavior Per Minute		
Control	1 attempt	$N = 1,580$	*n.s.*	7.69%	$N = 1,580$	*n.s.*	2.08 min	$N = 1,580$	*n.s.*	0.99	$N = 1,580$	*n.s.*
No Narrative	1 attempt	$Z = 0.05$		5.75%	$\chi^2 = 2.38$		2.06 min	$Z = 1.12$		0.87	$Z = 1.52$	
Control	1 attempt	$N = 1,309$	$p < 0.05$	7.69%	$N = 1,309$	$p < 0.05$	2.08 min	$N = 1,309$	$p < 0.05$	0.99	$N = 1,309$	$p < 0.05$
No Points	1 attempt	$Z = 2.07$	$r = 0.06$	11.19%	$\chi^2 = 4.67$	$v = 0.06$	2.48 min	$Z = 1.99$	$r = 0.06$	1.10	$Z = 2.47$	$r = 0.07$
Control	1 attempt	$N = 1,326$	$p < 0.01$	7.69%	$N = 1,326$	*n.s.*	2.08 min	$N = 1,326$	$p < 0.05$	0.99	$N = 1,326$	$p < 0.005$
Random Points	1 attempt	$Z = -2.78$	$r = 0.08$	7.69%	$\chi^2 = 0.00$		1.86 min	$Z = -2.50$	$r = 0.07$	0.73	$Z = -2.87$	$r = 0.08$
Control	1 attempt	$N = 1,325$	*n.s.*	7.69%	$N = 1,325$	*n.s.*	2.08 min	$N = 1,325$	*n.s.*	0.99	$N = 1,325$	*n.s.*
No Progress Viz	1 attempt	$Z = 1.51$		9.55%	$\chi^2 = 1.14$		2.33 min	$Z = 1.06$		1.06	$Z = 1.37$	

Table 2. Results from the statistical tests analyzing children's behavior while interacting with *Refraction*'s challenge level. Players earn a challenge level after collecting 60 points, giving us an opportunity to observe how they react to a difficult puzzle. We report the number of times children attempt the challenge level, their win rate, the amount of active time they spend working on the challenge, and the average number of growth mindset behaviors they exhibit per minute during the level. In each column, the median values are reported to the left of each cell.

Data Collection

To collect our data, we modified *Refraction* to randomly assign BrainPOP players to one of the five versions of the game. We only include new players in our analysis, and only use data from a player's first game session to control for issues with shared computers in school. We track players by storing information in the Flash cache, which allows us to exclude returning players. One disadvantage of this approach is that a player who clears the cache or switches computers will be treated as a new player in our experiment. However, this effect is distributed evenly across conditions due to randomization.

We collected data on BrainPOP between September 3 and October 28, 2015. *Refraction* was featured on the front page of the BrainPOP game portal once per week during this period, allowing us to attract large numbers of students. Our data set contained a total of 26,662 players. We randomly selected 5,000 players from each condition to include in our analysis.

DATA ANALYSIS AND RESULTS

We study the effects of our modified versions of the growth mindset intervention by comparing each to the control version of the intervention. We chose not to compare the four experimental versions to each other because this would result in a large number of pairwise comparisons. As a result, we are not able to formally reason about the relative impacts of the four versions. However, this analysis allows us to effectively explore our four research questions, which focus on understanding the added impact of each aspect of the intervention design. We leave comparative analyses of the four modified intervention designs for future work.

Before performing our analysis, we evaluated the Kolmogorov-Smirnov test to assess the normality of our data, and found that it was statistically significant for all of our outcome measures. As a result, we chose to use non-parametric statistical methods. We use a Wilcoxon rank sums test and an r measure of effect size for continuous variables, and a Chi-square statistic and a Cramer's V measure of effect size for nominal variables. We report effect sizes in addition to p-values to show the magnitude of the differences between our populations, since we are likely to find many significant differences due to our large sample sizes. For both tests, effect sizes with values less than 0.1 are considered *very small*, 0.1 are *small*, 0.3 are *moderate*, and 0.5 or greater are *large*. The results of our statistical analyses are reported in Tables 1 and 2. We describe these results and their implications in the following sections.

Growth Mindset Animations Provide No Added Benefit

We expected the growth mindset narrative presented through animations to encourage persistence and strategic behavior. However, our analysis showed the opposite effect. Children in the no narrative condition played significantly longer, a median of 3.01 minutes compared to 2.54 minutes for the control. They also completed significantly more levels; the median was 4 levels for both conditions, but children in the no narrative condition completed a mean of 8.08 levels compared to a mean of 7.65 levels for the control. Finally, players who did not see the animations were more strategic, exhibiting a median of 2.61 growth mindset behaviors per minute compared to 2.40 per minute for those in the control.

These results surprised us. Previous research shows that interventions that teach the growth mindset directly can be effective [2, 3]. On the other hand, this is the first intervention to attempt to teach the growth mindset through in-game animations, and games research has shown that players dislike tutorials that interrupt gameplay [1]. This made us wonder if a large percentage of players quit during the introductory animation itself, leading to lower overall persistence. To explore this question, we performed a follow-up analysis that only included players in both conditions who completed the first level of the game.

This analysis tells a different story. A larger number of children complete the first level in the no narrative condition, 3,536 players compared to 3,278 players in the control. However, we found no significant difference in the amount of time played ($Z = 1.32$, $N = 6,814$, *n.s.*), with medians of 6.09 minutes for the no narrative condition and 6.38 minutes for the control. There was also no significant difference in the number of levels completed ($Z = -0.14$, $N = 6,814$, *n.s.*), with medians of 8 levels for both conditions. Finally, we found no significant difference in the number of growth mindset behaviors observed per minute ($Z = 0.57$, $N = 6,814$, *n.s.*), with medians of 2.95 for the no narrative condition and 2.93 for the control.

This analysis suggests that the growth mindset animation dissuades some children from playing the game, reducing overall engagement. However, the animations do not have a negative impact on children's persistence or growth mindset behavior. This interpretation is further reinforced by our analysis of children's behavior during the challenge level. As reported in Table 2, there were no significant differences between these two conditions for any of our challenge level measures.

There are a number of possible explanations for this result. It may be that children do not like watching animations during gameplay, and that those who persist through the animation do not pay attention to its content. We display growth mindset messages throughout the game, on the summary screens at the end of each level and on the brain points themselves. It is therefore possible that reinforcing the growth mindset narrative through animations is not necessary. We will need to confirm this hypothesis through further studies, however our findings indicate that growth mindset animations are not necessary to effectively promote desirable behaviors in *Refraction*.

Brain Points Increase Player Retention

We expected the control version of *Refraction* with the brain points incentive structure to be more effective at encouraging growth mindset behaviors than the version without points. Our analysis confirms that children in the no points condition play for less time, a median of 2.21 minutes compared to 2.54 minutes for the control. However, there is no significant difference in the number of levels completed. More surprisingly, players in the no points condition exhibit significantly more growth mindset behaviors during gameplay, a median of 2.71 per minute compared to 2.40 per minute for the control.

A smaller number of children persist until the challenge level in the no points condition, 581 compared to 728 in the control. However, our analysis of challenge level behavior shows that players in the no points condition are more persistent and strategic. They attempted the challenge level significantly more times; the median number of attempts was 1 for both conditions, but players in the no points condition tried the challenge slightly more often, a mean of 1.06 times compared to 1 time for players in the control. Players in the no points condition spent more time on the challenge, used more growth mindset strategies, and won the challenge more often.

There are a number of possible interpretations of these results. It may be that the no points version of *Refraction* is more effective at encouraging use of strategy and persistence in the face of challenge. However, our analysis also shows that children in the no points condition completed the same number of levels as those in the control condition in less time. It is therefore more likely that the players who choose to persist in the no points version are more skilled at *Refraction*. In a recent study of player demographics on the homeschooling website K12.com, we found that older players exhibit more growth mindset behavior per minute than younger players [23]. Since older players are typically more skilled at the game, this suggests that the combined growth mindset behavior metric may be correlated with incoming ability.

Further research is needed to understand the full implications of these results. It is clear from this analysis that brain points encourage a larger number of players to persist for long periods of time in *Refraction*. While it is likely that players who persist in the no points condition exhibit more strategic behaviors because they have a high level of incoming ability, it is not possible to confirm this hypothesis through our current study.

Rewarding Players Randomly is Not Effective

We expected that rewarding players with brain points randomly, instead of in response to growth mindset behaviors, would be less effective. Our analysis confirms this hypothesis. Players who received points randomly played for significantly less time, a median of 2.19 minutes compared to 2.54 for the control. They also played significantly fewer levels, a median of 3 compared to 4 for the control. Finally, they exhibited significantly less growth mindset behavior, a median of 2.02 per minute compared to 2.40 per minute for the control.

Fewer players persist until the challenge level in the random points condition, a total of 598 compared to 728 in the control. Those that did make it to the challenge level played fewer times; while the mean was 1 attempt for both conditions, those in the no points condition made a mean of 0.92 attempts, compared to 1 attempt for those in the control. Children in the random points condition spent less time working on the challenge level, used less strategy, and were less likely to win.

To confirm that brain points are not awarded more frequently than random points, we compared the number of points earned per minute in each condition. Recall that points are awarded in increments of five in both versions. We found that players in the random points condition received points significantly more often ($Z = 31.72$, $N = 10,000$, $p < 0.0001$, $r = 0.3$), a median of 5.31 points per minute compared to 2.39 per minute for the control. However, this difference is driven by a difference in earned points on the tutorial levels. Brain points are challenging to earn during the tutorial levels, but random points are awarded at the same rate on all levels.

These results suggest that randomly praising students for their effort is not effective. While it is possible that random points are less engaging because they are given out more frequently, this would not explain the differences in observed growth mindset behaviors and students' reaction to challenge during gameplay. As a result, it appears that the brain points incentive structure is successful specifically because it rewards students for their productive struggle and use of strategy. This finding has important implications. In order to effectively integrate this intervention into a new context, it will be necessary to develop new behavioral metrics that accurately capture growth mindset behaviors to determine when to award points.

The Progress Visualization Increases Player Retention

We hypothesized that the summary screen progress visualization would contribute to player engagement. Our analysis confirmed this hypothesis. We found that players with no visualization played for significantly less time, a median of 2.26 minutes compared to 2.54 minutes for the control. They also completed significantly fewer levels, a median of 3 levels compared to 4 levels for the control. However, the progress visualization had no impact on growth mindset behaviors. There was no significant difference in the growth mindset behavior per minute, nor in any of the challenge level measures.

This finding suggests that showing players their progress, where progress measures growth mindset behavior rather than number of levels completed, increases player retention. This suggests that children may be motivated by seeing their progress and anticipating the reward of moving on to the next *Refraction* planet. The progress visualization is therefore a worthwhile addition to the growth mindset intervention.

CONCLUSION

In this work, we provide new insights into the design of a brain points incentive structure to promote the growth mindset in an educational game. We follow up on our previous research on brain points [24], exploring questions left unanswered by the original study. In particular, we explore the impact of the growth mindset narrative, brain points incentive structure, and summary screen progress visualizations on player persistence, use of strategy, and reaction to challenge. We find that narrative animations provide no added benefit to the intervention, and cause many players to quit before trying the first game level. However, we find that the progress visualizations and the brain points incentive structure both increase player persistence. Most importantly, we find that brain points are effective specifically because they reward desirable growth mindset behaviors. A similar incentive structure that rewards players at random intervals fails to encourage strategy use and persistence in the face of challenge.

While these results provide a deeper understanding of the design brain points intervention, a number of questions remain unanswered. We found that growth mindset animations had no positive impact on player behavior, however we cannot confirm why these animations were disengaging. It is possible that players never enjoy watching animations in casual games, however it's also possible that the cartoony style of the animations was unappealing to older students. We also found that players who did not receive brain points were more strategic and persistent in the face of challenge than players who did. This may be because more skillful players choose to persist in the no points version of the game, but we cannot confirm this hypothesis with the current data. Further research is needed to explore these open questions.

Despite these limitations, our findings make an important contribution to our understanding of growth mindset interventions for educational games. We believe the brain points incentive structure could be generalized to other educational games, and could even be used to gamify more formal learning environments. Online interventions that teach the growth mindset have been shown to be effective [25], and it is possible that growth mindset theory could be adopted into systems for learning at scale to improve student retention. We hope to explore this important research area in the future.

ACKNOWLEDGMENTS

We thank creators of *Refraction* for making this work possible. In particular, we would like to recognize Barbara Krug and Marianne Lee who created the incredible art and animations for this study. We also thank Allisyn Levy of BrainPOP for promoting *Refraction*. This work was supported by the Office of Naval Research grant N00014-12-C-0158, the Bill and Melinda Gates Foundation grant OPP1031488, the Hewlett Foundation grant 2012-8161, Adobe, and Microsoft.

REFERENCES

1. Erik Andersen, Eleanor O'Rourke, Yun-En Liu, Rich Snider, Jeff Lowdermilk, David Truong, Seth Cooper, and Zoran Popović. 2012. The impact of tutorials on games of varying complexity. In *Proceedings of the 2012 ACM annual conference on Human Factors in Computing Systems (CHI '12)*. ACM, New York, NY, USA, 59–68. DOI: http://dx.doi.org/10.1145/2207676.2207687
2. Joshua Aronson, Carrie B. Fried, and Catherine Good. 2002. Reducing the Effects of Stereotype Threat on African American College Students by Shaping Theories of Intelligence. *Journal of Experimental Social Psychology* 38 (2002).
3. Lisa S. Blackwell, Kali H. Trzesniewski, and Carol Sorich Dweck. 2007. Implicit Theories of Intelligence Predict Achievement Across an Adolescent Transition: A Longitudinal Study and an Intervention. *Child Development* 78, 1 (2007), 246–263.
4. C. Chase. 2012. The interplay of chance and skill: Exploiting a common game mechanic to enhance learning and persistence. In *Proceedings of the 2012 International Conference of the Learning Sciences*.
5. James P. Gee. 2008. *What Video Games Have to Teach Us About Learning and Literacy*. St. Martin's Press.
6. Catherine Good, Joshua Aronson, and Michael Inzlicht. 2003. Improving adolescents' standardized test performance: An intervention to reduce the effects of stereotype threat. *Journal of Applied Developmental Psychology* 24 (2003), 645–662.
7. Philip J. Guo, Juho Kim, and Rob Rubin. 2014. How Video Production Affects Student Engagement: An Empirical Study of MOOC Videos. In *Proceedings of the First ACM Conference on Learning @ Scale Conference (L@S '14)*. ACM, New York, NY, USA, 41–50. DOI: http://dx.doi.org/10.1145/2556325.2566239
8. Erik Harpstead, Brad A. Myers, and Vincent Aleven. 2013. In search of learning: facilitating data analysis in educational games. In *Proceedings of the SIGCHI*

Conference on Human Factors in Computing Systems (CHI '13). ACM, New York, NY, USA, 79–88. DOI: http://dx.doi.org/10.1145/2470654.2470667

9. Gail D. Heyman and Carol S. Dweck. 1998. Children's Thinking about Traits: Implications for Judgments of the Self and Others. *Child Development* 64, 2 (1998), 391–403.
10. Katy Jordan. 2015. MOOC Completion Rates: The Data. (2015). http://www.katyjordan.com/MOOCproject.html
11. Melissa L. Kamins and Carol S. Dweck. 1999. Person Versus Process Praise and Criticism: Implications for Contingent Self-Worth and Coping. *Developmental Psychology* 35, 3 (1999), 835–847.
12. Karl M. Kapp. 2012. *The gamification of learning and instruction: game-based methods and strategies for training and education*. San Francisco, CA: Pfeiffer.
13. Hanan Khalil and Martin Ebner. 2014. MOOCs Completion Rates and Possible Methods to Improve Retention-A Literature Review. In *Proceedings of the World Conference on Educational Multimedia, Hypermedia and Telecommunications*. 1236–1244.
14. René F. Kizilcec and Sherif Halawa. 2015. Attrition and Achievement Gaps in Online Learning. In *Proceedings of the Second (2015) ACM Conference on Learning @ Scale (L@S '15)*. ACM, New York, NY, USA, 57–66. DOI: http://dx.doi.org/10.1145/2724660.2724680
15. René F. Kizilcec and Emily Schneider. 2015. Motivation As a Lens to Understand Online Learners: Toward Data-Driven Design with the OLEI Scale. *ACM Trans. Comput.-Hum. Interact.* 22, 2, Article 6 (March 2015), 24 pages. DOI: http://dx.doi.org/10.1145/2699735
16. Markus Krause, Marc Mogalle, Henning Pohl, and Joseph Jay Williams. 2015. A Playful Game Changer: Fostering Student Retention in Online Education with Social Gamification. In *Proceedings of the Second (2015) ACM Conference on Learning @ Scale (L@S '15)*. ACM, New York, NY, USA, 95–102. DOI: http://dx.doi.org/10.1145/2724660.2724665
17. Jeremy Lee, Kathleen Luchini, Benjamin Michael, Cathie Norris, and Elliot Soloway. 2004. More than just fun and games: assessing the value of educational video games in the classroom. In *CHI '04 Extended Abstracts on Human Factors in Computing Systems (CHI EA '04)*. ACM, New York, NY, USA, 1375–1378. DOI: http://dx.doi.org/10.1145/985921.986068
18. Conor Linehan, Ben Kirman, Shaun Lawson, and Gail Chan. 2011. Practical, appropriate, empirically-validated guidelines for designing educational games. In *Proceedings of the SIGCHI Conference on Human Factors in Computing Systems (CHI '11)*. ACM, New York, NY, USA, 1979–1988. DOI: http://dx.doi.org/10.1145/1978942.1979229
19. Taylor Martin, Carmen Petrick Smith, Erik Andersen, Yun-En Liu, and Zoran Popović. 2012. Refraction Time: Making Split Decisions in an Online Fraction Game. In *American Educational Research Association Annual Meeting (AERA)*.
20. Merrilea J. Mayo. 2009. Video Games: A Route to Large-Scale STEM Education? *Science* 323 (2009), 79–82.
21. Claudia M. Mueller and Carol S. Dweck. 1998. Praise for Intelligence Can Undermine Children's Motivation and Performance. *Journal of Personality and Social Psychology* 75, 1 (1998), 33–52.
22. Harold F. O'Neil, Richard Wainess, and Eva L. Baker. 2005. Classification of learning outcomes: evidence from the computer games literature. *The Curriculum Journal* 16, 4 (2005), 455–474.
23. Eleanor O'Rourke, Yvonne Chen, Kyla Haimovitz, Carol S. Dweck, and Zoran Popović. 2015. Demographic Differences in a Growth Mindset Incentive Structure for Educational Games. In *Proceedings of the Second (2015) ACM Conference on Learning @ Scale (L@S '15)*. ACM, New York, NY, USA, 331–334. DOI: http://dx.doi.org/10.1145/2724660.2728686
24. Eleanor O'Rourke, Kyla Haimovitz, Christy Ballweber, Carol Dweck, and Zoran Popović. 2014. Brain Points: A Growth Mindset Incentive Structure Boosts Persistence in an Educational Game. In *Proceedings of the SIGCHI Conference on Human Factors in Computing Systems (CHI '14)*. ACM, New York, NY, USA, 3339–3348. DOI: http://dx.doi.org/10.1145/2556288.2557157
25. David Paunesku, Gregory M. Walton, Carissa Romero, Eric N. Smith, David S. Yeager, , and Carol S. Dweck. 2015. Mind-Set Interventions Are a Scalable Treatment for Academic Underachievement. *Psychological Science* 26, 6 (2015), 784–793. DOI: http://dx.doi.org/10.1177/0956797615571017
26. Katrina E. Ricci, Eduardo Salas, and Janis A. Cannon-Bowers. 1996. Do Computer-Based Games Facilitate Knowledge Acquisition and Retention? *Military Psychology* 8, 4 (1996), 295–307. DOI: http://dx.doi.org/10.1207/s15327876mp0804_3
27. Julia Wilkowski, Amit Deutsch, and Daniel M. Russell. 2014. Student Skill and Goal Achievement in the Mapping with Google MOOC. In *Proceedings of the First ACM Conference on Learning @ Scale Conference (L@S '14)*. ACM, New York, NY, USA, 3–10. DOI: http://dx.doi.org/10.1145/2556325.2566240

Explaining Student Behavior at Scale: The Influence of Video Complexity on Student Dwelling Time

Frans van der Sluis
Online Learning Lab
Center for Innovation
Leiden University
The Hague, The Netherlands
f.van.der.sluis@fgga.leidenuniv.nl

Jasper Ginn
Online Learning Lab
Center for Innovation
Leiden University
The Hague, The Netherlands
j.h.ginn@fgga.leidenuniv.nl

Tim van der Zee
Leiden University Graduate
School of Teaching
Leiden University
Leiden, The Netherlands
t.van.der.zee@iclon.leidenuniv.nl

ABSTRACT

Understanding why and how students interact with educational videos is essential to further improve the quality of Massive Online Open Courses (MOOCs). In this paper, we look at the complexity of videos to explain two related aspects of student behavior: the dwelling time (how much time students spend watching a video) and the dwelling rate (how much of the video they actually see). Building on a strong tradition of psycholinguistics, we formalize a definition for information complexity in videos. Furthermore, building on recent advancements in time-on-task measures we formalize dwelling time and dwelling rate based on click-stream trace data. The resulting computational model of video complexity explains 22.44% of the variance in the dwelling rate for students that finish watching a paragraph of a video. Video complexity and student dwelling show a polynomial relationship, where both low and high complexity increases dwelling. These results indicate why students spend more time watching (and possibly contemplating about) a video. Furthermore, they show that even fairly straightforward proxies of student behavior such as dwelling can already have multiple interpretations; illustrating the challenge of sense-making from learning analytics.

Author Keywords

MOOCs; video; information complexity; dwelling time; learning analytics; student behavior.

INTRODUCTION

MOOCs have enjoyed increasing attention and popularity in recent years. The enthusiasm surrounding MOOCs is related to their ability provide large and previously hard-to-reach audiences with easy access to open content and for bringing students the autonomy to learn at their own pace [16]. Despite the recent successes of MOOCs, they have also been criticized due to unsatisfactory learning outcomes and poor implementation of instructional design principles [25]. Their scale, one-size-fits-all approach, and lack of face-to-face interaction limit MOOCs in their ability to sufficiently support the learning process of students [17].

Compared to traditional classroom education, online education distinguishes itself in two important ways. Firstly, it lacks the control over the learning process that is typical for the classroom situation. An in-class teacher has a vast array of interventions available to steer the behavior of his or her students. To the contrary, MOOCs offer no such flexibility. Secondly, online education offers an opportunity to evaluate and explain student behavior through the vast amounts of data that can be gathered online. Essentially, online education exchanges control over the learning process for an abundance of data with which to monitor learners at scale. The challenge is to leverage this data to explain and steer student behavior.

Videos make up most of the educational content in MOOCs. This makes it important to better understand how students interact and engage with educational videos. By sensing the clicks of students as they navigate through the content of a course, we can create models that have the potential to predict various aspects of the learning process. For example, [23] evaluate how click actions (pauses, seeking, skipping, replaying) reflect the perceived difficulty of a video, whereas [32] use click sequences to predict in-video dropouts, dwelling time, complete course dropouts, and subsequent clicks. However, the analysis of student behavior through clicks tends to be too granular for sense-making; that is, to be able to unambiguously assign meaning to clicks and subsequently explain student behavior [28].

One of the key aspects that explains student behavior while watching a video is, evidently, the video itself. Numerous studies have attempted to identify optimal MOOC video attributes, mostly by looking at measures related to a student's dwelling time: the amount of time students spend watching a video. Video production variables (short length, informal talking heads, etc.) have been found to affect student engagement, as measured by dwelling time and post-video quiz participation [10]. A different study identified video length, abrupt visual transitions, and interface characteristics as reasons for in-video dropouts [18]. We only have a limited understanding why certain characteristics of videos affect student behavior and, more importantly, how we can turn this understanding into appropriate online interventions in support a student's

L@S 2016, April 25–26, 2016, Edinburgh, UK.

DOI: http://dx.doi.org/10.1145/2876034.2876051

learning process. Nonetheless, several studies have proposed guidelines on creating "good" videos for MOOCs based on analyzing dwelling time, such as [19]. A particular popular guideline is the 'less than 6 minutes' recommendation, proposed by [10], which is also based on analyzing dwelling times.

Student background is an important factor in explaining the time that students spend on watching a video. When students re-visit a course, re-watch a particular video, or watch an educational video as part of an on-campus education, they tend to be more selective about which parts of the video they view [3, 18, 23]. Furthermore, perceived difficulty is a confirmed factor for lower dwelling time. That is, difficulty correlates negatively with dwelling time [23].

Most insights on dwelling time come from studies looking to explain how humans read and use text. For the most part, such studies focus on the relevance of - and interest for - a text. Regarding the relevance of search results, [6] show that the difference in readability between document and search result snippet negatively predicts dwelling time, explaining 69% of its variation in the first 120 seconds. Likewise, for the interest in text, [31] show that interested readers have a lower reading time than non-interested readers. In turn, this can also be explained by textual complexity, such that complexity increases interest up to the point that it becomes too difficult to understand and slows down reading [33, 14]. Similarly, a lack of complexity reduces interest, causing readers to be more easily distracted while reading [31]. We can conclude from research on reading that information complexity is a key factor of dwelling time. In this paper, we explore whether similar effects can be seen for educational videos as for text. We hypothesize that:

1. Dwelling time increases in videos with high information complexity, and that;
2. Dwelling time increases in videos with low information complexity.

In order to (dis)confirm these hypotheses, we aim to make two contributions. First, we formalize both information complexity and student dwelling time within the context of videos by proposing a mathematical definition for both. Then, we explore whether, and if so *how* dwelling time is explained by information complexity. To this end, we look at the dwelling time of 471,179 episodes of students watching a (part of a) video. These contributions have the potential to attach meaning to a student's dwelling rate by showing how it relates to one of its causes - the information complexity. In turn, they put the basis for using video complexity as a metric that can hypothetically be optimized for a student's learning process. This approach aims for sense-making by interpreting large-scale data on student behavior in a theoretically sound and meaningful way. Moreover, it aims to turn this understanding into actionable learning analytics by subsequently formalizing the causes of student behaviour.

This paper is organized as follows. First, the *Scalable Definitions* section introduces and defines, respectively, measures of information rate and dwelling rate for videos. In turn, the *Methodology* and *Results* describe a study on the relation between these variables for 104 educational videos. Finally, the *Discussion* interprets and discusses the theoretical as well as the practical implications of the findings on the influence of video complexity on student dwelling time.

SCALABLE DEFINITIONS

Dwelling rate

In its most basic definition, dwelling time is the time that users spend on a piece of content [6]. This is a variant of a time-on-task measure, where viewing content is only one of many possible tasks that a student undertakes during learning. In the case of educational videos, we can not only estimate the dwelling time but also the dwelling rate. Whereas dwelling time refers to how much time students spend watching a video, the dwelling rate refers to how much of the video they actually see. To compare across videos and with the information conveyed within a video, we will define both measures as relative to the duration of the video.

Measuring time-on-task is complicated because most Learning Management Systems (LMS) only record events spread out over time (e.g., login, submit assignment), but do not record actual activity (e.g., working on an assignment) [20]. Time-on-task can only be estimated given a sufficient level of density and detail in the recorded events. The click events recorded by modern LMSs contain such detail, showing precisely which actions students take while watching a video (e.g., seeking, pausing) and when the video starts and ends. However, such time-on-task measures are based on the assumption that the time spent between two actions is spent on a task. This section discusses how video dwelling can be estimated from such sparse events.

Time-on-task estimation

Current efforts already seek to leverage click-stream logs to estimate how students watch a lecture video. For example, [18] analyze particular re-watching activity by looking at local peaks in backward seek actions. Similarly, [23] analyze forward seeking frequency and skipped video length. However, timed-based task estimators have been shown to work better than frequency-based estimators, explaining up to 15% more variance in learning behavior and outcomes [20]. [28] reach similar conclusions. Whereas it is difficult to unambiguously assign meaning to clicks (see *Introduction*), time-based estimators give a more precise estimation of student activity. In order to arrive at a reasonable estimation of dwelling time and dwelling rate, we extend on current efforts to analyze click-stream data [18, 23] by using these recent insights on deriving student activity from events [20].

Table 1 gives an example of a typical in-video click-stream trace. It shows a hypothetical activity log within one user session. To define a session, we adopt the common cut-off point of 30 minutes . The in-video *actions* commonly recorded are play, pause, seek, stop, and rate-change actions. This last action changes the *speed* at which the video is played. Furthermore, *time* denotes a time stamp at which an action is performed and *pos* the position in the video when an action is recorded. Several pre-processing steps are required before

Table 1. Example click-stream trace log and analyses

Data				Analyses			
row (i)	pos	time	action	t_Δ	s	pp	p_Δ
1	0	0	play	0	0	0	0
2	10	20	seek	20	1	20	20
3	20	30	pause	10	1	20	10
4	10	40	seek	10	0	20	0
5	10	50	play	10	0	10	0
6	40	70	seek	20	1	30	10
7	60	90	pause	20	1	60	20

Note. Data: in-video position (pos), timestamp (time), and play rate (rate).

Note. Analyses: time increment (t_Δ), play state (s), initial position (pp), and4tu position increment (p_Δ).

defining dwelling rate and related features, the results of which are also included in Table 1. Each will be explained next.

The time spent in between two consecutive actions i and $i-1$ forms the basis for any time-on-task measure [20]. Given the time of action i, t_Δ can be defined as:

$$t_\Delta(i) = \text{time}(i) - \text{time}(i-1).$$

To determine whether a video is actually running, the play state is derived from the action trace. Since we are interested in the period and with that the play state up to the point that an action is performed, this variable is defined as the play state s up to and excluding the action i itself:

$$s(i) = \begin{cases} 1 & \text{if action}(i-1) = \text{'play'} \\ 0 & \text{if action}(i-1) = \text{'pause'} \\ \text{pos}(i-1) & \text{otherwise} \end{cases}$$

The value of $s(0)$ is to be set to either 0 or 1, depending on whether a video is already playing at the moment the video is opened by a student.

As Table 1 illustrates, the position pos can change due to viewing as well as through seek actions. This makes it difficult to determine how much of a video the student actually viewed. Moreover, it complicates the procedure by which we assign an in-video action to a section of the video. To mitigate this difficulty, we define the initial position pp of an action i based on the previous action $i-1$:

$$pp = \begin{cases} \text{pos}(i-1) & \text{if s(i)} = 0 \\ \text{pos}(i-1) + t_\Delta(i) & \text{otherwise} \end{cases}$$

To determine how much of a video a student watched, the change in video position p_Δ is derived from the action trace. Since it is not straightforward to derive a p_Δ measure solely from the changes in position pos(i) alone, we use the initial position pp to define p_Δ:

$$p_\Delta(i) = \begin{cases} 0 & \text{if s(i)} = 0 \\ pp - \text{pos}(i-1) & \text{otherwise} \end{cases}$$

Combined, the preceding set of features allows us to estimate the time-on-task.

Towards a measure of dwelling time and rate

Using the click-stream trace data and aforementioned analyses, we define two aspects of dwelling: time and rate. We define dwelling time as the total time that a student spends on watching a video relative to the nominal length of that video. As such, we regard pause time as integral to the time spent on watching a video:

$$\frac{\sum_i t_\Delta(i)}{\text{video duration}} \tag{1}$$

Making dwelling time a function of video duration allows us to compare the amount of information viewed per amount of time (see next section).

We define dwelling rate as how much more or less a student watches of a video relative to the nominal length of that video. Formally, the dwelling rate is expressed as:

$$\frac{\sum_i p_\Delta(i)}{\text{video duration}} \tag{2}$$

This measure of dwelling rate has the particular advantage of only looking at (re-)watching, where re-watching is a particular method that helps understanding complex videos by spreading the same amount of information over a longer period of time.

By definition, dwelling time includes time spent on activities other than watching the video. This follows an assumption common to time-on-task measures that the time spent in between the recorded actions is spent on the attributed task. This is a fairly flexible definition, which can not only include time to think but also time to find background information on external websites. Since this can make the dwelling time a multiple of the video length, it is likely that this has a substantial effect on the variance. On the contrary, the definition of dwelling rate excludes most of the variance that would otherwise occur in dwelling time.

Information rate

Whereas measures of complexity are fairly well-defined for text [2], similar metrics for the complexity of the information in videos are scarce. Video adds both a time and visual dimension to textual information, making such a metric more complicated than for text. Notwithstanding, the heavy reliance on spoken words in educational videos in MOOCs opens up the possibility to derive a complexity measure from video transcripts. Even though this focus on transcripts disregards both the visual and auditory channel, a substantial part of the educational content is embedded in what is being said. This possibility is further supported by evidence that language presented either verbally or visually is processed in the same working memory component, the so-called phonological loop [1, 27, 9].

The focus on transcripts allows us to apply and benefit from the successes on predicting textual complexity. Two specific modeling challenges need to be solved for a successful application of complexity models to educational videos. Firstly, one needs to identify plausible and robust features of textual information complexity. Secondly, one needs to extend textual information complexity to information rate by including the time dimension. Both challenges will be addressed in the subsequent sections.

Features of textual complexity

Since Lively and Pressey [24] introduced the first readability indicator roughly a century ago, many additional models of textual complexity have been created. Many of these models have since been criticized for their utilization of surface-level indicators as proxies for complex cognitive processes that occur when reading a text [2]. This argument is similar to that of [28], who argues that it is difficult to unambiguously assign meaning to surface-level indicators such as a certain number of words per sentence. Notable exceptions are in [34, 33], who apply deep syntactic-semantic analyses to better reflect the complex cognitive processes during reading.

To define a plausible and robust measure of complexity, we adopt a set of features introduced by [33]. Each of these features are based on well-known psycholinguistic findings on the causes of reading difficulty and are designed to be robust against overfitting. The applicability and robustness of this model has been shown elsewhere. The model used in [33] predicted human ratings of complexity with $r = .442$ on a new data set not used during model training. We will describe each of the features shortly. Domain-specific language aspects are deliberately not included, as the goal is to formalize a general model of information complexity which can be broadly applied.

Word length is a classic approach to inferring readability, having a central role in nearly all formulas concerning readability. The importance of word length is well supported. Longer words give higher fixation durations during reading [15], whereas shorter words are more likely to be skipped while reading [4]. Word length is generally defined in the following two ways:

$\text{len1} = |c \in w|$, word length in characters c per word w;

$\text{len2} = |s \in w|$, word length in syllables s per word w.

Sentence length is related to syntactic difficulty [7]. A sentence consisting of more words is likely to have more dependencies connecting them. The most common measure of sentence length is calculated by looking at the number of words.

$\text{wps} = \log|w \in S|$, words w per sentence S.

A logarithm is added to counter a long tail in the length of sentences.

Lexical familiarity indicates how familiar a reader is with a word. It influences a reader's fixations, such that more frequent words take less initial processing time [13] and high-frequency words are more likely to be skipped than less frequent words [29]. The most salient measure of lexical familiarity is printed word frequency. This can generally be approximated with two metrics. Based on the occurrence of a word on either the Dale list of 3000 common words [5] or on a large representative collection of writing:

$\text{fam1} = \frac{|\{w \in T | w \in D\}|}{|w \in T|}$, the frequency of words w on the Dale list D relative to all the words in a text T.

$\text{fam2} = \log_{10}\text{cnt}(w)$, the logarithm of the term count cnt per word w.

For this study, the Google Books N-Gram corpus will be used for the term count function cnt.

Character and word density. Numerous studies related to priming have shown that a target string is better identified when it shares letters with a prime. This holds for identity priming (repeating the prime), form priming (using a partly different string) [11], as well as over longer distances [21].

Repetition creates a form of redundancy which can be measured in terms of entropy. It defines the number of bits needed to encode a message [30]. Since the aim is not to measure text size but instead, to measure size-invariant information density, a sliding window is applied within which local entropy is calculated. Given the probability p of a sequence $x_1 \dots x_n$, the Sliding Window Entropy (SWE) $H_{w,n}$ over X can be defined as:

$$H_{w,n}(X) = \sum_{i=w}^{N} \frac{1}{N-w} H_n \circ \{x_j : j = i - w + 1, \dots, i\}$$

$$H_n(X) = -\sum_{x_1,\dots,x_n \in X} p(x_1,\dots,x_n)^2 \log p(x_1,\dots,x_n)$$

Here, w is the window size. Using $H_{w,n}$ two features are defined:

$\text{cha}_n = H_{w,n}(C)$, n-gram SWE over characters C.

$\text{wor}_n = H_{w,n}(W)$, n-gram SWE over words W.

Dependency Locality Theory (DLT) states that a reader, while reading a sentence, performs a moment-by-moment integration of new information sources [8]. The amount of cognitive resources (i.e., integration costs) that this requires has been shown to account for differences in reading time across a range of linguistic effects [22]. Integration costs are dependent on the distance between the to be integrated head and its referent, where distance is measured by the number of intervening discourse elements [8]. This effect is also present in learning from educational videos [27, 26], and is stronger for more complex videos [9]. This is approximated by defining a (new) discourse referent as a noun or verb (phrase).

Given a dependency d connecting words a and b. Let Y_d be a collection containing each part-of-speech tag y for the words and phrases between and including word a and b, then the dependency length of dependency d is given by:

$\text{int} = \sum_{d \in D} \log|\{y \in Y_d | y \in \{\text{noun}, \text{verb}\}\}|$, integration costs of dependencies D in a sentence.

A logarithm is added to counter a long tail in integration costs.

Towards a measure of information rate

The different features are combined in a model of textual complexity similar to [33]. The model is trained on a data set using

Table 2. Coursera click-stream data

course	videos	data.points	included	
configuringworld001	37	159,625	46,839	(29.34%)
globalorder001	21	283,807	112,744	(39.73%)
humanlanguage001	27	925,599	270,333	(29.21%)
internationaltaxation01	10	166,864	34,213	(20.50%)
metals001	6	20,361	6,356	(31.22%)

distinctive levels of complexity, namely on two 'languages' from Wikipedia: Simple English and regular English. The details of this model generation step are explained further on in the *Methodology* section.

Given the resulting metric of *complexity*, a measure of information rate can be defined as follows:

$$\textit{complexity} \times \textit{words per second} \qquad (3)$$

Since words are the common information-bearing tokens in communication [14], this measure includes the time dimension through *words per second.*

By formalizing information rate in Equation 3, a scalable definition is given based on the spoken words in a video. This definition relies on a robust set of features which is expected to be applicable to video transcripts, even though they are likely distinct from normal texts. Furthermore, it relies on a plausible set of features which is expected to result in a meaningful, interpretable, outcome.

METHODOLOGY

Data sets

Wikipedia articles

Two 'languages' from Wikipedia were used to train a model of textual complexity: Simple English and regular English. These two languages are intended to be distinctive in their level of complexity as authors are instructed to use easy words and shorter sentences, but not to include less information. Only articles that occurred in both languages were selected, allowing for a pair-wise comparison, and which were neither a stub (i.e., incomplete) nor a special, redirect, or disambiguation page. Based on the Simple English creation date the oldest 10,000 pairs, a total of 20,000 articles, were used for classification purposes. The underlying assumption being that more matured articles better reflect the intended writing style. As these articles address a wide range of topics they were deemed especially relevant for constructing a model of general information complexity which is not biased towards a certain domain.

The following pre-processing steps were performed on the Wikipedia data set. The data consisted of two dumps from August 3, 2011, containing all articles encoded as wiki-text for both languages. Using JWPL [35], both dumps were imported into a MySQL database and subsequently parsed to plain text. All templates and links to files and images were removed.

Coursera videos, transcripts and click streams

The data used in our study comes from five MOOCs (see Table 2). These courses were organized by Leiden University between 2014 and 2015. The MOOC videos differ substantially in the topics being discussed, such as environmental issues, political affairs, linguistics, and tax law. The most common production style used throughout the videos is the 'talking head' setup. In certain videos this was supplemented or mixed with additional graphics or text. As is typical for MOOCs, the videos can be considered the core educational content of the MOOCs.

Of the five MOOCs, the data of a total of 104 videos were analyzed. The original transcripts, originally uploaded by the administrators of the respective courses, were extracted for each video. The transcript of each video was analyzed to determine its complexity. Function words such as "[SILENCE]" were removed and the transcripts were split per paragraph before analysis. We define a paragraph within a video based on the locations of the in-video questions. The complexity analysis was performed on the paragraphs, in order to make any local difficulties more apparent in the analyses and reduce the influence of confounding effects that can occur over a longer time period.

Click-stream data from students interacting with the selected courses was examined as proxy of student behavior. To this end, users not registered as students (for example, course administrators) were excluded from the data. Click-stream actions were attributed to video paragraphs using *pp* from Table 1. The total amount of watching episodes before further filtering was 1,556,256.

We filtered for only those students who finished watching a video paragraph. Given the fact that we want to measure dwelling time, this approach allows us to examine user sessions for which we can accurately compute the time spent on a task. Whether a student reached the end of a section was determined based on an auto-generated pause action at the time of an in-video question. Because a student often skips the final seconds of the video, preventing a pause-action from being generated, we look at any action in the last ten seconds of a video to estimate whether a student finished the final paragraph. Furthermore, only those sessions were included in which students did not change the play rate of the video. We chose to do this such as to prevent any complicating factors to the analysis, given its influence on both information rate and dwelling rate and time. After filtering the resulting data set contained 471,179 unique user sessions with any of the videos.

Feature computation

For feature computation we used the following toolkits and, if applicable, settings. For all complexity features, the OpenNLP word and sentence tokenizers were used. For feature *len2* the number of syllables per word was measured using the Fathom toolkit. For feature *fam2* the Google Books N-Gram corpus was used as model representative for common English. The word counts were summed for each lower-cased word over the years starting from the year 2000. For feature *dlt* the Stanford Parser was used to parse sentence dependencies. For the SWE features (*cha* and *wor*) entropy was based on n-grams of length $n = 1 \ldots 3$ and windows of size $w = 15$ for words and $w = 50$ for characters. For feature *wor* in particular, the Snowball stemmer was used to reduce words to their root form. Stemming reduces simple syntactical variance and, in turn, gives more significance to the semantic meaning of a word.

We used the R statistical language to compute all features relating to clickstream behaviour. We further used the *rmongodb* and *RmySQL* packages to query data, and the *data.table*, *rjson*, *stringr* and *parallel* packages to clean and process the data.

Statistical methods

All statistical analyses were implemented using R [12].

Classifier. A Logistic Regression Model (LRM) was trained on the paragraphs from each of the pre-selected 10,000 articles per Wikipedia language. To decrease the importance of the particular data set used and increase the importance of the individual features, an LRM was chosen as a simple, linear classifier.

As a first pre-processing step, features containing more than 10% of missing values were removed, after which any observations containing missing values were removed. The data was balanced to assure it contained an equal number of simple and normal paragraphs. To select the best possible subset of features, both forward and backward stepwise search through the feature set was applied. As tuning parameter $k = log_{10}(n)$ was set, where n is the number of observations, specifying a penalty for the number of variables included in a model. To validate the classification performance the classifier was trained on 80% and tested on 20% of the data set.

Graphical fit. To illustrate the relation between an independent and a dependent variable, in Figure 2 a smoothing technique was used. This technique fits a polynomial surface determined by the independent variable based on local fitting. At a point x a fit is made using all other points weighted by their distance from x[1]. Standard parameters were used for the weights (i.e., $(1 - \frac{\text{distance}}{\text{maximumdistance}}^3)^3$). We set the span parameter to use all the data points when determining the fit. This is a strong smoother that was necessary to reduce noise, in particular with dwelling time. To indicate a goodness-of-fit, the 95% confidence intervals were included in the figures as well. The graphs were based on a random selection of 2,000 data points to keep its computation efficient, yet not overestimate the statistical confidence (intervals).

Polynomial model. We used a simple 2-level linear regression model to evaluate the evidence for our hypotheses. The model was fitted using a least-squares estimation. We report the R^2 as well as the standard error, the latter of which can be compared to the range of the dependent variable to give an evaluation of the model.

[1]See http://stat.ethz.ch/R-manual/R-patched/library/stats/html/loess.html

Table 3. Summary statistics

	r_{pb}	Wikipedia Simple	Wikipedia English	Coursera
wps	.272	1.20	1.31	1.14
len1	.231	4.73	5.01	4.74
len2	.268	1.38	1.47	1.43
fam1	.089	0.76	0.66	0.75
fam2	.098	7.46	7.40	7.83
wor_1	.063	3.72	3.73	3.72
wor_2	.023	3.79	3.79	3.79
wor_3	.004	3.70	3.70	3.70
cha_1	.057	3.88	3.89	3.82
cha_2	.097	5.29	5.31	5.27
cha_3	.077	5.49	5.51	5.49
int	.237	0.52	0.67	0.42

Note. r_{pb} denotes the point-biserial correlation coefficient for distinguishing between Simple and English Wikipedia.

RESULTS

Video Complexity

Table 3 gives the summary statistics for each feature on both the Wikipedia and Coursera data sets. The table shows that the features give similar results on both data sets, indicating the possibility of applying the Wikipedia data set features to analyze Coursera transcripts.

Using each of the features from Table 3 as input, a LRM was trained with stepwise feature selection. The model is able to predict whether a paragraph was either Simple English or English with 68.03% accuracy. The resulting regression equation is:

$$\begin{aligned} \text{complexity} = & -11.64 + 2.54 \times \text{wps} + 3.22 \times \text{len2} \\ & + 1.18 \times \text{cha}_1 - 0.23 \times \text{fam2} + 3.40 \times \text{cha}_3 \\ & - 4.16 \times \text{wor}_3 - 0.27 \times \text{fam1} + 0.26 \times \text{int} \\ & - 0.53 \times \text{wor}_0 \end{aligned} \quad (4)$$

All predictors are significant at a $p < .001$ probability. Whilst these features can distinguish well between articles (with 90.87% accuracy, see [33]), the problem of distinguishing between paragraphs seems substantially more challenging with an accuracy of 68.03%. Even though the performance on this data set is fairly low, the model is based on few, yet meaningful features to support the aim of using the resulting model for explaining student behavior.

The application of the resulting model of complexity in Equation 4 to analyze articles and transcripts is shown in Figure 1. The histograms show how the predicted levels of complexity are distributed for each data set, differentiating between Simple English and regular English for Wikipedia and showing a normal distribution for the Coursera data set. The normal distributions suggest that the model can be applied to Coursera

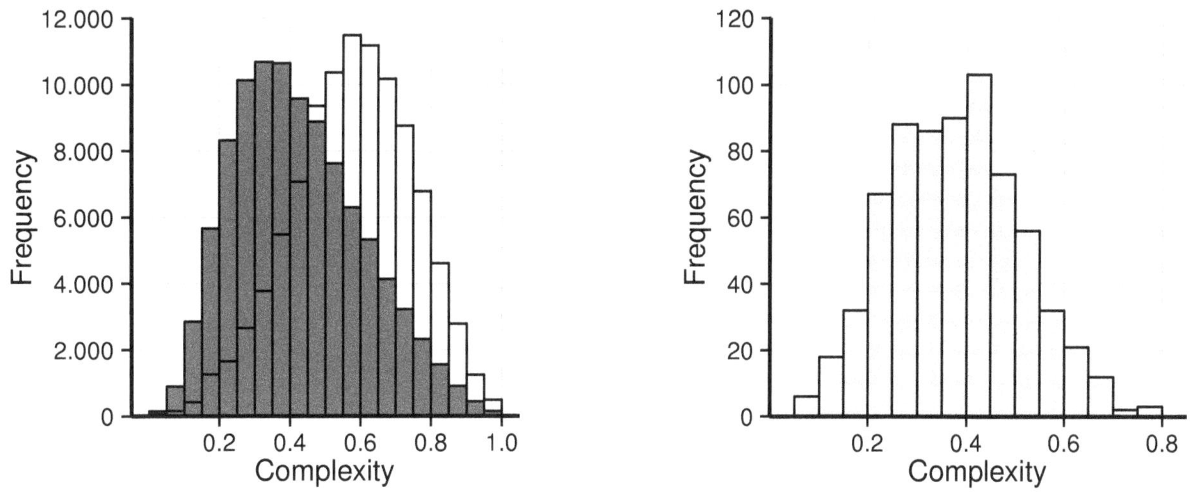

(a) Wikipedia (b) Coursera

Figure 1. Histograms of complexity analysis.

transcripts in the same way as it can be for the Wikipedia paragraphs. However, one notable difference is the overall lower level of complexity for the Coursera transcripts in comparison to English Wikipedia.

Dwelling Time

Figure 2 compares information rate with how long and how much students watch a video paragraph for those students who finished watching a paragraph. The graphs are based on a fit line, suppressing details yet highlighting an overall trend. A similar trend is apparent for both graphs, showing an increased student dwelling at the lower as well as at the higher ranges of information rate. This trend suggests a confirmation of our hypotheses.

Remarkable differences are, for dwelling time, a sharper increase at both a low and high information rate and in general substantially more variation. These differences can be expected from dwelling time in comparison to dwelling rate, as the dwelling time includes time that students did not spend on watching the video but instead on activities such as finding more information.

The trends described in Figure 2 are explained using two linear regression models. The resulting models confirm the trend for dwelling rate, explaining $R^2 = 22.44\%$ of variance ($SE = 1.32$, $F(2, 451679) = 65330$, $p < .001$). Yet, the models do not confirm the trend for dwelling time, explaining only $R^2 = 1.43\%$ of variance ($SE = 10.67$, $F(2, 451679) = 3268$, $p < .001$). This difference can be expected given the naturally higher variance in dwelling time. For the confirmed model of dwelling rate, the resulting model equation is:

$$\text{dwelling rate} = 3.20 - 5.37 \times \text{information rate} + 3.02 \times \text{information rate}^2 \quad (5)$$

All parameters are significant at $p < .001$.

DISCUSSION

Understanding how students interact with videos and what causes this behavior is of great importance to improve future MOOCs. Our work consists of two contributions towards this goal. Firstly, we demonstrated a formalization of information rate and dwelling in educational videos. Secondly, we showed how a student's dwelling rate is a function of information rate. The relationship between information rate and dwelling rate follows a polynomial pattern, such that high dwelling times are typical for videos having either low and high rates of information. A similar trend was found for the relation between information rate and dwelling time. These findings are remarkable, as it is typically assumed that high dwelling rates and times would only be associated with high rates of information.

The value of both contributions is confirmed by two regression models. For information rate, a LRM gave 68.03% accuracy on distinguishing Simple English from regular English in our ground truth, on an 80%/20% train/test split of 20,000 Wikipedia paragraphs. Although this accuracy is not as high as desired, it does indicate the model is successful. In particular, the accuracy confirms the model's value on a ground truth that is challenging due to the short length of the paragraphs. For dwelling rate, the polynomial regression model gave an explained variance of 22.44% by information rate. This is a particular high value, especially since it explains actual student behavior on a real-world data set and at scale.

Video Complexity

The computational model of information complexity for videos was successful in explaining meaningful student behavior. This shows the validity of applying the textual model to spoken words, in line with earlier findings showing that language is (partly) processed in similar ways irrespective of the presentation modality [27, 26, 9]. Furthermore, this suggests the importance of measuring theoretically well-supported aspects of text.

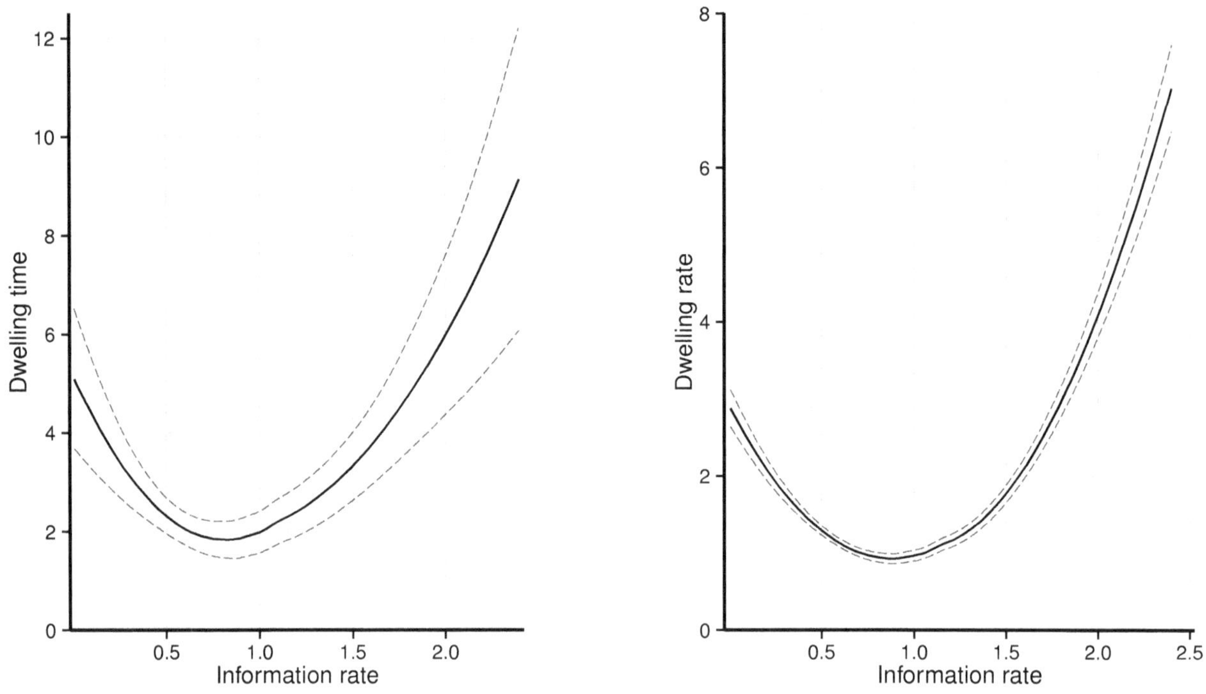

(a) Dwelling time (b) Dwelling rate

Figure 2. Fit-line with confidence intervals showing the relation between information rate and either relative dwelling time (a) or rate (b).

This study calls attention to several novel aspects of video transcripts which may commonly be ignored when considering information complexity. Other than straightforward characteristics such as sentence and word length, complexity is also based on lexical familiarity, character and word density, and distances between related words. The advantage of these metrics is that they are not based on assumptions or purely data-driven correlations but on a long tradition of experimental research in the field of psycholinguistics. Although our proposed definitions and formalizations need to be enhanced, they provide a strong foundation to conceptualize and operationalize video information complexity in a theoretical sound way.

As the current paper is focused on universal aspects of human information processing, the algorithms used were based on generic text corpora and language characteristics. As such, certain course- or domain-specific aspects might have been left out. Although videos from five different courses were analyzed, the observations may be limited to online courses with a specific type of content or a particular pedagogical approach.

Dwelling time and rate

The empirical and theoretical soundness of information complexity measures allow us to attach meaning to dwelling time and rate and, accordingly, confirm our hypotheses. Namely, that student dwelling increases, although not to a great extent, with a low information rate. This is as expected: a lower information rate can make it difficult for students to keep focus, which in turn necessitates them to re-watch parts of the video where they lost focus. Moreover, student dwelling increases with a high information rate. This is also as expected: a higher information rate can make it difficult for students to understand the content, making it necessary to re-watch parts of the video.

These findings are unique in showing a fairly complex relation on a large scale with data from actual student behavior. However, this also means that the data includes high variances and large extremes, an effect which is exacerbated by the use of a fit line which extends the discovered trends into the outer ranges. The variance is particularly high for dwelling time. In comparison to dwelling rate, dwelling time includes the time spend on activities other than watching the video. This will have a stronger effect of concentration difficulties and accordingly will show more variance. High variance is typical for complex material, as the effects of many instructional design aspects become more salient with rising complexity.

The results show that dwelling rate gives a good picture of student behavior, whereas dwelling time gives likely a more realistic one. Yet both measures stay a proxy of actual student's attention, motivation and actions. The current study can pinpoint a particular salient determinant of student behavior, namely the information rate. However, the student's interest or motivation for watching the videos was not taken into consideration. Likewise, no measures of learning results were taken into account. The relationship between video watching behavior, information rate and learning results is an important topic; the current study contributes to the advancement of this research direction. Knowing how the information rate influences a student's understanding, engagement, and learning requires further research.

Towards sense-making

To a large extent, dwelling rate is predicted by the information rate. In and of itself, dwelling rate is not directly interpretable and as such cannot function as a proxy measure of (perceived) difficulty nor of other related constructs. That is, a high dwelling rate is typical for videos both with a low or high information rate, thus troubling any inference which does not account for information rate. For example, [32] and [10] assume that dwelling rate equals user engagement, yet we have shown that the interpretation of dwelling rate is not straightforward. In a similar vein, earlier work has even demonstrated that interest is negatively correlated with reading time, such that engaged users will typically spend less time watching or reading and not more [31].

Our findings highlight the importance of using well-established definitions from experimental research in order to go beyond black-box predictions. This is a particular salient conclusion when compared to more ambiguous measures such as granular click-stream data [1, 2]. Any interpretation of a proxy of behavior becomes plausible once controlling for related variables - such as video complexity - that are theoretically expected to explain it. To allow for sense-making, it is critical to select well-supported metrics with known theoretical relations.

Towards optimal video complexity

Two of the practical implications of the gained insights and presented computational model will be highlighted.

Video guidelines

The insights gained on the importance of information rate cast doubts on straightforward guidelines for "good videos", such as a desired maximum length of a video. For example, the popular '6 minutes' rule proposed by [10] is based on correlational data of dwelling time. Our contributions suggest that correlations between length and desired behavior or learning outcomes might be influenced by another factor, as the role of video length can be overshadowed by information rate. In other words, it might not be the length of a video, but the complexity that causes people to quit watching a video.

Instead of presenting guidelines on "good videos", we provide MOOC video design teams with several key concepts to consider when designing educational videos. As we have shown, information rate is a substantial predictor of student watching behavior. By extension, this provides us the ability to influence behavior through manipulation of the video information rate. When designing MOOC videos, attention should be paid to carefully apply these insights to reach the desired level of information complexity.

Actionable learning analytics

The algorithms and resulting computational model discussed in this paper can be used as a diagnostic tool to evaluate the complexity of videos. Although there is not yet enough evidence to make specific recommendations for making better videos, it does provide MOOC teachers with feedback on their videos and directions for improvement. The discussed individual textual aspects of information complexity as well as the temporal aspect can be manipulated, or an ideal level can be decided on before a video is being produced. Note that more research is needed to further verify the effects of manipulating video information complexity and to establish specific guidelines.

The formalized definitions of dwelling time and information rate open possibilities for more adaptive learning environments. When combined with measures of prior knowledge and learning results, these insights will help us to present users with automatically adapted videos according to their needs. In terms of actionable learning analytics, the formalized aspects of video complexity lend themselves for video selection and retrieval considerations. Based on the learning goal for a video and the desired student watching behavior, we can aim for a specific level of information complexity.

CONCLUSIONS

The information rate of a MOOC video is a substantial predictor of dwelling time and rate. However, the relationship between these two variables is complex, as high dwelling is typical for videos with both high and low rates of information. This signifies the importance of information rate, and opens up the possibility of information rate to be taken into account when studying or trying to influence student video watching behavior. With our contributions we have provided a foundation to further expand research in this area, allowing for further sense-making and to solidify actionable learner analytics.

REFERENCES

1. Alan Baddeley. 2003. Working memory: looking back and looking forward. *Nature reviews neuroscience* 4, 10 (2003), 829–839.
2. Rebekah Benjamin. 2012. Reconstructing Readability: Recent Developments and Recommendations in the Analysis of Text Difficulty. *Educational Psychology Review* 24, 1 (2012), 63–88. Issue 1.
3. Derek O Bruff, Douglas H Fisher, Kathryn E McEwen, and Blaine E Smith. 2013. Wrapping a MOOC: Student perceptions of an experiment in blended learning. *MERLOT Journal of Online Learning and Teaching* 9, 2 (2013), 187–199.
4. Marc Brysbaert, Denis Drieghe, and FranÃğoise Vitu. 2005. *Word skipping: Implications for theories of eye movement control in reading.* Oxford University Press, Chapter 6, 1–29.
5. Jeanne S. Chall and Edgar Dale. 1995. *T1 - Readability Revisited: The New Dale-Chall Readability Formula.* PB - Brookline Books, Cambridge, Mass.
6. Kevyn Collins-Thompson, Paul N. Bennett, Ryen W. White, Sebastian de la Chica, and David Sontag. 2011. Personalizing web search results by reading level. In *Proceedings of the 20th ACM International Conference on Information and Knowledge Management (CIKM '11)*, Bettina Berendt, Arjen de Vries, Wenfei Fan, Craig Macdonald, Iadh Ounis, and Ian Ruthven (Eds.). ACM, New York, NY, USA, 403–412.
7. Edward Fry. 2002. Readability versus leveling. *Reading Teacher* 56, 3 (2002), 286.
8. E. Gibson. 2000. The dependency locality theory: A distance-based theory of linguistic complexity. In *Image, language, brain: Papers from the first mind articulation project symposium.* 95–126.

9. Paul Ginns. 2006. Integrating information: A meta-analysis of the spatial contiguity and temporal contiguity effects. *Learning and Instruction* 16, 6 (2006), 511–525.
10. Philip J. Guo, Juho Kim, and Rob Rubin. 2014. How Video Production Affects Student Engagement: An Empirical Study of MOOC Videos. In *Proceedings of the First ACM Conference on Learning @ Scale Conference (L@S '14)*. ACM, New York, NY, USA, 41–50.
11. Glyn Humphreys, Lindsay Evett, and David Taylor. 1982. Automatic phonological priming in visual word recognition. *Memory & Cognition* 10 (1982), 576–590. Issue 6.
12. Ross Ihaka and Robert Gentleman. 1996. R: A Language for Data Analysis and Graphics. *Journal of Computational and Graphical Statistics* 5, 3 (1996), 299–314.
13. Albrecht Inhoff and Keith Rayner. 1986. Parafoveal word processing during eye fixations in reading: Effects of word frequency. *Attention, Perception, & Psychophysics* 40, 6 (1986), 431–439. Issue 6.
14. T. Florian Jaeger and Harry Tily. 2011. On language utility: processing complexity and communicative efficiency. *Wiley Interdisciplinary Reviews: Cognitive Science* 2, 3 (2011), 323–335.
15. M.A. Just and P.A. Carpenter. 1980. A theory of reading: From eye fixations to comprehension. *Psychological Review* 87 (1980), 329–354.
16. Judy Kay, Peter Reimann, Elliot Diebold, and Bob Kummerfeld. 2013. MOOCs: So Many Learners, So Much Potential ... *IEEE Intelligent Systems* 28, 3 (2013), 70–77.
17. Hanan Khalil and Martin Ebner. 2014. MOOCs Completion Rates and Possible Methods to Improve Retention - A Literature Review. In *Proceedings of EdMedia: World Conference on Educational Media and Technology 2014*, Jarmo Viteli and Marianna Leikomaa (Eds.). Association for the Advancement of Computing in Education (AACE), Tampere, Finland, 1305–1313.
18. Juho Kim, Philip J. Guo, Daniel T. Seaton, Piotr Mitros, Krzysztof Z. Gajos, and Robert C. Miller. 2014. Understanding In-video Dropouts and Interaction Peaks Inonline Lecture Videos. In *Proceedings of the First ACM Conference on Learning @ Scale Conference (L@S '14)*. ACM, New York, NY, USA, 31–40.
19. René F Kizilcec, Kathryn Papadopoulos, and Lalida Sritanyaratana. 2014. Showing face in video instruction: effects on information retention, visual attention, and affect. In *Proceedings of the SIGCHI Conference on Human Factors in Computing Systems*. ACM, 2095–2102.
20. Vitomir Kovanović, Dragan Gašević, Shane Dawson, Srećko Joksimović, Ryan S. Baker, and Marek Hatala. 2015. Penetrating the Black Box of Time-on-task Estimation. In *Proceedings of the Fifth International Conference on Learning Analytics And Knowledge (LAK '15)*. ACM, New York, NY, USA, 184–193.
21. Kerry Ledoux, C. Christine Camblin, Tamara Y. Swaab, and Peter C. Gordon. 2006. Reading Words in Discourse: The Modulation of Lexical Priming Effects by Message-Level Context. *Behavioral and Cognitive Neuroscience Reviews* 5, 3 (2006), 107–127.
22. Richard L. Lewis, Shravan Vasishth, and Julie A. Van Dyke. 2006. Computational principles of working memory in sentence comprehension. *Trends in Cognitive Sciences* 10, 10 (2006), 447 – 454.
23. Nan Li, Łukasz Kidziński, Patrick Jermann, and Pierre Dillenbourg. 2015. MOOC Video Interaction Patterns: What Do They Tell Us? In *Design for Teaching and Learning in a Networked World*, Gránne Conole, Tomaž Klobučar, Christoph Rensing, Johannes Konert, and Élise Lavoué (Eds.). Lecture Notes in Computer Science, Vol. 9307. Springer International Publishing, 197–210.
24. Bertha A. Lively and Sidney L. Pressey. 1923. A Method for Measuring the "Vocabulary Burden" of Textbooks. *Educational Administration and Supervision* 9, 7 (1923), 389–398.
25. Anoush Margaryan, Manuela Bianco, and Allison Littlejohn. 2015. Instructional quality of Massive Open Online Courses (MOOCs). *Computers & Education* 80 (2015), 77 – 83.
26. Richard E Mayer and Roxana Moreno. 2003. Nine ways to reduce cognitive load in multimedia learning. *Educational psychologist* 38, 1 (2003), 43–52.
27. Roxana Moreno and Richard E Mayer. 1999. Cognitive principles of multimedia learning: The role of modality and contiguity. *Journal of educational psychology* 91, 2 (1999), 358.
28. Justin Reich. 2015. Rebooting MOOC Research. *Science* 347, 6217 (2015), 34–35.
29. Erik D. Reichle, Alexander Pollatsek, Donald L. Fisher, and Keith Rayner. 1998. Toward a model of eye movement control in reading. *Psychological Review* 105, 1 (1998), 125–157.
30. Claude E. Shannon. 1948. A Mathematical Theory of Communication. *Bell System Technical Journal* 27, 7, 10 (Jul, Oct 1948), 379–423, 625–656.
31. Larry L Shirey and Ralph E Reynolds. 1988. Effect of interest on attention and learning. *Journal of Educational Psychology* 80, 2 (1988), 159.
32. Tanmay Sinha, Patrick Jermann, Nan Li, and Pierre Dillenbourg. 2014. Your click decides your fate: Inferring Information Processing and Attrition Behavior from MOOC Video Clickstream Interactions. In *Empirical Methods in Natural Language Processing Workshop on Modeling Large Scale Social Interaction in Massively Open Online Courses*. Doha, Qatar.
33. Frans Van der Sluis, Egon L. Van den Broek, Richard J. Glassey, Elisabeth M. A. G. van Dijk, and Franciska M. G. de Jong. 2014. When Complexity becomes Interesting. *Journal of the American Society for Information Science and Technology* 65, 7 (2014), 1478–1500.
34. Tim Vor der Brück, Sven Hartrumpf, and Hermann Helbig. 2008. A Readability Checker with Supervised Learning Using Deep Indicators. *Informatica* 32, 4 (2008), 429–435.
35. Torsten Zesch, Christof Müller, and Iryna Gurevych. 2008. Extracting Lexical Semantic Knowledge from Wikipedia and Wiktionary. In *Proceedings of the 6th International Conference on Language Resources and Evaluation*. Marrakech, Morocco.

The Future of Learning

Sugata Mitra
Professor of Educational Technology
Winner of the 2013 TED Prize
Newcastle University, the UK
sugata.mitra@newcastle.ac.uk

ABSTRACT

In this talk, Sugata Mitra will take us through the origins of schooling as we know it, to the dematerialisation of institutions as we know them.

Thirteen years of experiments in children's education takes us through a series of startling results – children can self organise their own learning, they can achieve educational objectives on their own, can read by themselves. Finally, the most startling of them all: Groups of children with access to the Internet can learn anything by themselves.

From the slums of India, to the villages of India and Cambodia, to poor schools in Chile, Argentina, Uruguay, the USA and Italy, to the schools of Gateshead and the rich international schools of Washington and Hong Kong, Sugata's experimental results show a strange new future for learning.

Using the TED Prize, he has now built seven 'Schools in the Cloud', of which some glimpses will be provided in the talk.

BIOGRAPHY

Prof. Sugata Mitra is Professor of Educational Technology at the School of Education, Communication and Language Sciences at Newcastle University, UK.

He is the instigator of the Hole in the Wall (HIW) experiment, where in the year 1999 a computer was embedded within a wall in an Indian slum at Kalkaji, Delhi and children were allowed to freely use it. The experiment aimed at proving that kids could be taught computers very easily without any formal training. Sugata termed this as Minimally Invasive Education (MIE). The experiment has since been repeated at many places. He is the recipient of many awards from India, the UK, USA and many other countries in the world.

His interests include Children's Education, Remote Presence, Self-organising systems, Cognitive Systems, Physics and Consciousness.

L@S 2016, April 25–26, 2016, Edinburgh, UK.
ACM 978-1-4503-3726-7/16/04.
http://dx.doi.org/10.1145/2876034.2876053

The Hole in the Wall experiment has left a mark on popular culture. Indian diplomat Vikas Swarup read about Mitra's experiment and was inspired to write his debut novel that went on to become the Oscar winning movie of 2009 - Slumdog Millionaire.

He is a PHD in Physics credited with more that 25 inventions in the area of cognitive science and educational technology. He was conferred the prestigious Dewang Mehta Award for Innovation in Information Technology in the year 2005. Amongst many other awards, he was awarded the 1 million dollar TED Prize in 2013.

Starting with molecular orbital computation in the 1970s, Mitra discovered that the structure of organic molecules determine their function more than the constituent atoms.

After a Ph.D. in Solid State Physics from the IIT, Delhi, he went on to research energy storage systems, first at the Centre for Energy Studies in the IIT and then at the Technische Universität, Vienna, Austria. This resulted in a new design for Zinc-Chlorine batteries.

His interests in the flow of electricity through biological systems, a consequence of his Ph.D. research on exciton dissociation in organic semiconductors, led on to a seminally speculative paper on why the human sense organs are located where they are.

His interest in computer networking led him towards the emerging systems in printing in the 1980s. He set up India's first local area network based newspaper publishing system in 1984 and went on to predict the desktop publishing industry. This in turn led to the invention of LAN based database publishing and he created the "Yellow Pages" industry in India and Bangladesh.

His interest in the human mind once again led him into the areas of learning and memory and he was amongst the first in the world to show that simulated neural networks can help decipher the mechanisms of Alzheimer's disease.

He was amongst the first people in the world to invent Voluntary Perception Recording (a continuously variable voting machine) and a hyperlinked computing environment, several years ahead of the Internet.

Professor Mitra's work at NIIT created the first curricula and pedagogy for that organisation, followed by years of research on learning styles, learning devices, several of them now patented, multimedia and new methods of learning. Culminating and, perhaps, towering over his previous work, are his "hole in the wall" experiments with children's learning. Since 1999, he has convincingly demonstrated that groups of children, irrespective of who or where they are, can learn to use computers and the Internet on their own using public computers in open spaces such as roads and playgrounds. He brought these results to England in 2006 and invented Self Organised Learning Environments, now in use throughout the world. In 2009, he created the Granny Cloud, of teachers who interact with children over the Internet.

In 2013, he was awarded the first $1 million TED prize, to put his educational ideas together to create seven laboratories called 'Schools in the Cloud'. Here he intends to study learning as emergent phenomena in an educational self organising system.

Since the 1970s, Professor Mitra's publications and work has resulted in training and development of perhaps a million young Indians, amongst them some of the poorest children in the world. The resultant changes in the lives of people and the economy of the country can only be guessed at.

Using Multiple Accounts for Harvesting Solutions in MOOCs

Jose A. Ruiperez-Valiente[a,b,c,*], **Giora Alexandron**[a,*], **Zhongzhou Chen**[a], **David E. Pritchard**[a]
[a] Massachusetts Institute of Technology, Massachusetts Ave 77, 02139 Cambridge (MA) USA
[b] Universidad Carlos III de Madrid, Av. Universidad 30, 28911 Leganés (Madrid) Spain
[c] IMDEA Networks Institute, Av. del Mar Mediterráneo 22, 28918 Leganés (Madrid) Spain
{jruipere, giora, zchen22, dpritch}@mit.edu

ABSTRACT
The study presented in this paper deals with copying answers in MOOCs. Our findings show that a significant fraction of the certificate earners in the course that we studied have used what we call *harvesting* accounts to find correct answers that they later submitted in their main account, the account for which they earned a certificate. In total, ~2.5% of the users who earned a certificate in the course obtained the majority of their points by using this method, and ~10% of them used it to some extent. This paper has two main goals. The first is to define the phenomenon and demonstrate its severity. The second is characterizing key factors within the course that affect it, and suggesting possible remedies that are likely to decrease the amount of cheating. The immediate implication of this study is to MOOCs. However, we believe that the results generalize beyond MOOCs, since this strategy can be used in any learning environments that do not identify all registrants.

Author Keywords
Academic dishonesty; educational data mining; learning analytics; MOOCs

ACM Classification Keywords
H.2.8. **[Database Management]**: Database Applications - *Data mining*; J.1. **[Computer Applications]**: Administrative Data Processing - *Education*; K.3. **[Computing Milieux]**: Computers and Education - *Computer and Information Science Education: Information systems education*

INTRODUCTION
The issue of academic dishonesty in higher education has been studied for at least half a century. According to McCabe and Trevino [4], studies report that between "13 to 95 percent of college students engage in some form of academic dishonesty" (p. 523). The survey study by Davis [3] reported cheating rates of up to 88%. The specific numbers depend on how one defines and measures academic dishonesty, but the overall picture is that of a severe, widely spread phenomenon. Singhal [9] described cheating as one of the major problems in education today.

Massive Open Online Courses (MOOCs) offer free access to complete courses often containing both lectures and problems. Students who demonstrate a satisfactory level of achievement can earn a certificate of accomplishment. While these certificates currently do not have formal value, the fact that many people tend to include them in resumes and professional social networks indicates that they are perceived by some as an indication of knowledge and proficiency. There is also evidence that they have value in the job market[1]. Another use of MOOC certificates is in academic admissions, e.g. Wharton Business School announced that it will use its MOOCs as an additional tool for selecting MBA candidates [2]. This can explain, at least partially, the motivation of some students looking for easy ways to earn MOOC certificates.

In this study we detect the use of multiple accounts by the same student for copying answers. The method works as follows. The student uses one or more harvesting accounts (the *harvester/s*) to obtain the correct answer, and then submits it in the *master* account, the account for which the student intends to earn a certificate. Finding the answer in the harvester account can be done either by asking to see the correct answer after using all the attempts ('show answer' on the edX platform), or by exhaustive search (e.g. pure guessing for multiple choice questions) until the correct answer is found. This is a clear case of academic dishonesty since it explicitly violates the edX honor code (which all registrants agree to) that requires that users "Maintain only one user account", and "Not engage in any activity that would dishonestly improve my results"[2]. The findings that we present below show that this phenomenon is quite widespread. For example, about 5% of the certificate earners in our course harvested at least 10% of their correct answers; 2% used it for more than 70% of their correct answers.

The phenomenon of using harvesting accounts was also reported by Northcutt, Ho, and Chuang, who examined multi-

* The two first authors have contributed equally to this work

[1] http://www.pcworld.com/article/2071060/employers-receptive-to-hiring-it-job-candidates-with-mooc-educations.html

[2] https://www.edx.org/edx-terms-service

L@S 2016, April 25-26, 2016, Edinburgh, Scotland Uk
© 2016 ACM. ISBN 978-1-4503-3726-7/16/04 $15.00.
http://dx.doi.org/10.1145/2876034.2876037

ple courses offered by MITx and HarvardX [6]. They coined the term CAMEO (Copying Answers using Multiple Existence Online) for this phenomenon, and we adopt this term. In the context of cheating in digital learning environments, another closely related work is the one by Palazzo et al. [8]. They studied the amount of copying answers from another student using the same online homework tutor, and found that the fraction of copied answers ranged between 3 and 11%. CAMEO also resembles what Baker et al. [1] defined as *gaming the system* – "Attempting to succeed in an interactive learning environment by exploiting properties of the system rather than by learning the material" – both in terms of the motivation (improving grades), and in terms of the method (exploiting technical features of the system).

The rest of the paper is organized as follows. In the next section we define the phenomenon and the detection method. In the Results section we present the results of applying the method on a specific course. In the Discussion section we discuss the findings, followed by summary and main conclusions in the last section.

HARVESTING SOLUTIONS USING MULTIPLE ACCOUNTS

This section is organized as follows. First, we define the phenomenon. Second, we state the criteria that we use for identifying an answer as having been harvested. Third, we define behavioral patterns. Fourth, we give a high-level description of the algorithm that implements the patterns.

Defining the phenomenon

CAMEO refers to an event in which a user uses one or more accounts to find the correct answer to a question, and then submits this answer in his/her main account. We refer to the account(s) used for finding the solution as the harvesting accounts (or the *harvester/s*), and to the account in which the answer is submitted as the *master* account. A CAMEO event can thus be described as a triplet of the form <*master, harvester, question*>. The criteria for identifying CAMEO events are described below.

Criteria

Each triplet must also adhere to the following criteria:

1. ***Harvester and master belong to the same IP group.*** IP group is a group of accounts that shared the same IP at least once in the course, or are connected through an account with whom both shared an IP (this criterion is applied recursively). It is defined as follows. Let $G=(U, I, E)$ be a bipartite graph in which U represents the set of the users, I represents the set of the IPs, and E are the edges between U and I, when an edge (u,i) denotes that user u has used IP i at some point in the course. For each *connected component cc* within G (a connected component is a subgraph in which there is a path between each two nodes), then the nodes of cc that belong to U (the 'user' nodes) form an IP group. Identifying connected components in a graph is a basic problem in graph theory, and can be computed in linear time.

2. ***Harvester does not have extrinsic motivation.*** This is operationalized as harvester does not earn a certificate. The rationale is clear - earning a certificate indicates that the user seeks a reward from time invested in this account, reducing the likelihood that this is a 'service' account. We note that this requirement may ignore 'heavy' harvesting accounts, i.e., accounts that accumulate enough course credits to earn a certificate solely due to extensive harvesting.

3. ***Harvested questions are actually used in the master account.*** The rationale that underlies this criterion is that if a student establishes an account to harvest answers, then most of the questions done by this account will be used by a master account. Thus, we require that at least 85% of the solutions obtained by the harvester were actually used by a master. We picked 85%, and not 100%, to allow for some flexibility, for example in case that the user solves a question in the harvester account, but then decides to skip it in the master account because he/she realizes that it is a random question (thus the solution in the master account can be different; we elaborate on the effect of randomization below).

4. ***Master harvests at least 10 answers.*** The intention is to increase our certainty that the student used this pattern to harvest answers; therefore this filter adds a minimum count of harvested answers to consider the student as using the pattern. This threshold represents about 1% of the questions required for a certificate.

5. ***Master account is not used for harvesting solutions.*** The rationale is similar to the one in criterion 2, in the opposite direction.

Harvesting patterns

We define two CAMEO patterns: *Immediate*, and *delayed batch*. In both patterns, a harvesting event is composed of the harvester getting the correct answer in his/her account either using 'show answer' or by using exhaustive search, followed by the master submitting the correct answer in his/her account. The harvester and master should also adhere to the criteria listed above (the Criteria subsection). The patterns are described below. A graphical representation of them is given in Figure 1.

Immediate mode. This pattern refers to a situation in which the user harvests the solution in the harvesting account, and inserts it in the master account shortly after. The threshold that we use is of up to 15 minutes between the two events. The main hypothesized modus operandi behind this pattern is that of a user who is progressing in the two accounts simultaneously, using two browsers (in order to login with two accounts at the same time). In this case we require that both actions were done by the same IP address.

Delayed batch mode. This pattern refers to a situation in which the user harvests the solution for multiple answers, and then submits them in a rapid sequence in the master account. The main hypothesized modus operandi behind this pattern is of a user who harvests multiple solutions, stores them, and later submits them in a batch, possibly in a different physical location and/or using a different machine, but one in the same

IP group as explained in the first criterion. The threshold that we use for the length of the sequence is of (at least) 10 correct submissions, and the threshold that we use for 'rapid' is less than 20 seconds between two consecutive ones. To avoid overlap with the *immediate* mode, we also require that there will be at least 15 minutes gap between the last harvesting event and the first master event in this sequence. We note that cheating events that are part of a batch mode sequence, but with less than a 15 minutes delay, will be caught by the *immediate* mode. So in such cases the event would still be detected.

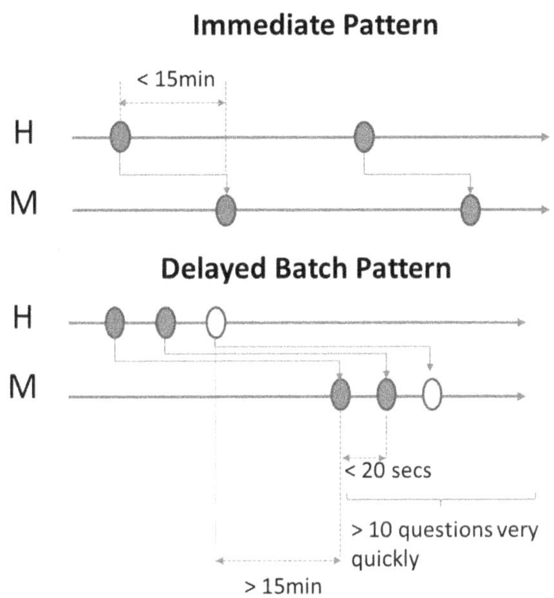

Figure 1. Schematic representation of the two harvesting patterns (H=Harvester, M=Master)

Completeness of the two patterns. We note that the two patterns do not fully cover the range of harvesting possibilities. For example, a sequence consisting of less than ten questions that are harvested and then submitted by the master more than fifteen minutes after they were harvested will not be detected. Also, we have used global thresholds that were not adjusted for specific questions. We deliberately picked very strict definitions so as to follow our general approach that in the study of academic dishonesty, it is better to decrease the false positive ratio at the expense of increasing the false negative one. The implication is that our algorithm is probably not detecting all the harvesting events. Still, the results are quite significant. Thus, we believe that at this stage it is more important to bring this issue to the attention of the community, rather than to polish the patterns in order to identify all of the harvesting events.

Algorithm

Below we give a high-level description of the algorithm. Its input is the tracking logs of the course, processed to create per-user, time-sorted log files. Each event in the tracking log represents a student action, and contains the IP from which the action that this event represents arrived. A submission to a question creates an event that contains, among other things, information about the question (i.e., question ID), the student, the answer, and whether it is correct or not (more information on edX tracking logs can be found on edx.org).

1. Process the user log files to build two dictionaries - one that maps each student to all the IPs used by this student, and one that maps an IP to all the students who used it at least once during the course.
2. For *immediate pattern*: Per user *U*, for each successful submission to a problem *P* at time *t*, search if any student *V* from that IP group has submitted a correct answer, or a request to see answer, to *P* in the 15 minutes before *t*, from *ip*. If so, add the triplet to the list of harvesting events.
3. For *delayed batch pattern*: Per user *U*, for each sequence of ten or more successful submissions to questions *Pi...Pk*, with no more than 20 seconds between each consecutive submissions, search if any students *V* in the IP group of *U*, got the answer to *Pi...Pk* in a similar pattern to the one described in 2. If so, add the triplets <*U, V, Pi*>...<*U, V, Pk*> to the list of harvesting events.
4. Test for the criteria described in the Criteria subsection. Remove entries that contain items that do not fulfill these criteria.

While we hope that this description can be a sufficient starting point for ones who wish to implement this algorithm, we intend to make the source code of the algorithm publicly available.

RESULTS

In this section we present the results of running our algorithm on the data from edX.org MOOC 8.MReVx given in summer 2014. First, we describe the setting. Second, we present the findings.

Context - Introductory Physics MOOC 8.MReV

Population: The MOOC 8.MReVx was run on edX.org in Summer 2014. It attracted about 13500 registrants, of which 502 earned a certificate. Gender distribution was 83% males, 17% females. Education distribution was 37.7% secondary or less, 34.5% College Degree, and 24.9% Advanced Degree. Geographic distribution includes US (27% of participants), India (18%), UK (3.6%), Brazil (2.8%), and others (total of 152 countries). (All numbers are based on self-reports.)

Course structure: The course covers the standard topics of a college introductory mechanics course with an emphasis on problem solving and concept interrelation. It lasted for 14 weeks, with content divided between 12 mandatory units and two optional ones on advanced topics. The course contains 273 e-text pages, 69 videos, and about 1000 problems. The problems include checkpoints problems embedded within the e-text and videos, and homework and quiz questions which are given at the end of the units.

Tracking logs: The interaction data of the students with the learning environment is saved on edX servers and was downloaded and delivered to us through MITx, according to the

	#Master accounts	#Harvester accounts	#Harvested answers
All students	99 (6.3%)	112	19602 (3.06%)
Certificate earners	52 (10.3%)	63	12396 (3.09%)
Non-certificate earners	47 (4.35%)	49	7206 (3%)

Table 1. Amount of CAMEO in our course

usage agreements between edX, MITx and us. The interaction logs were subdivided by user and sorted by time.

Findings

This subsection presents the results of applying the script that implements the criteria described above on the tracking logs of 8.MReV. For the purpose of this study, we consider only students who completed at least 5% of the questions in the course - a total of 1581 students. Among these, 502 earned a certificate. The output of the CAMEO detection script is a list of such triplets <*master, harvester, question*> labeled as 'immediate' or 'batch'. This list could be then analyzed and combined with other information on the course to obtain various statistics. The findings are divided into 4 subsections. In the first we present an overall view of the amount of cheating in the course. In the second we compare the performance of the master and the harvester accounts with the rest of the students. In the third we give some descriptive statistics about CAMEO events. In the fourth we show findings regarding question characteristics and amount of cheating.

Amount of CAMEO

Number of master and harvester accounts. In total, we identified 99 master accounts, and 112 harvester accounts, which constitute 6.3% of the 1581 who completed at least 5% of the questions in the course. Among the 99 master accounts, 52 were certificate earners (10.3% of the 502 certificate earners) and 47 were non-certificate earners (4.35% of the non certificate earners who completed at least 5% of the questions). We note that some masters operated more than one harvester account. The rationale is probably to enable exhaustive search on questions for which the number of allowed attempts is not enough to find the solution. See Table 1.

CAMEO among submissions. Approximately 3% of all the correct submissions in the course were harvested (19602 out of 639863 correct submissions). See Table 1.

CAMEO among certificate earners. Figure 2 shows the amount of cheating among certificate earners. A point on the graph represents the amount of the certificate earners who harvested at least y% of their correct submissions. For example, 5.37% of certificate earners harvested ≥10% of their correct answers. About 2.5% of the certificate earners harvested more than 50% of their correct answers. We judge that to the left of the shoulder at (2, 70%) are students 'harvesting for a certificate' without any attempt to master the required knowledge.

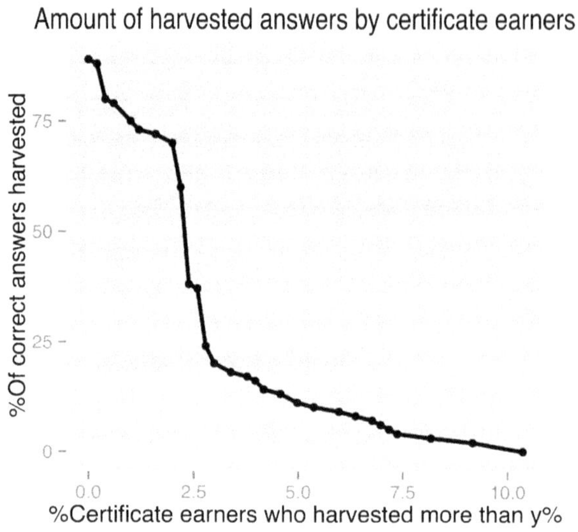

Figure 2. Percentage of cheating by certificate earners

Cheaters compared with other students

Success rate and response time among certificate earners. The findings show that within the certificate earners, masters tend to have a very high average success rate on individual problems, and very fast response time (elapsed time between opening a problem and answering it correctly), compared with the rest of the students. (Here we focus only on certificate earners in order to compare groups of students that answered similar numbers of questions). This is illustrated in Figure 3. The x-axis shows the percentage of correct submissions at the first attempt, and the y-axis shows the average time needed for a correct submission. Master accounts are marked in red, with the size of the circle proportional to the fraction of answers that they harvested. As can be seen, there is a cluster of red points on the bottom right part of the figure (fast and correct). In general the trend is that the bigger the red circle (more cheating), the higher the success rate and the faster the submission. Also, the top three performers of the course in terms of minimum time and performance at first attempt are cheaters. Additionally, we also found that it was statistically significant that cheaters have better performance in first attempt submissions and require less time for correct submissions.

Distribution of performance among masters, harvesters, and the rest of the students. The distribution of performance among masters, harvesters, and the rest of the students (ones who attempted more than 5% of the questions) is presented in Figure 4. In terms of mean values, masters have a success rate of 82.5%, harvesters have a success rate of 43.9%, and the rest of the students have a success rate of 61.6%. The results of an ANOVA test confirm that the success rate (masters) >success rate (rest of students) >success rate (harvesters). ($F=72.43$, $p=10^{-16}$).

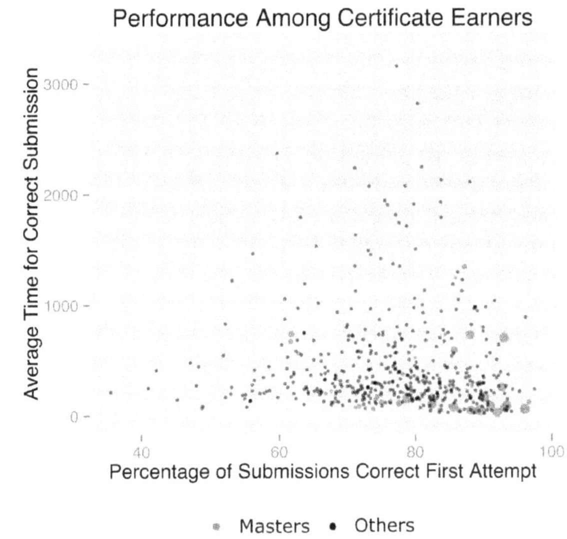

Figure 3. Response time vs. percentage correct for certificate earners; size of red dot indicates amount of cheating

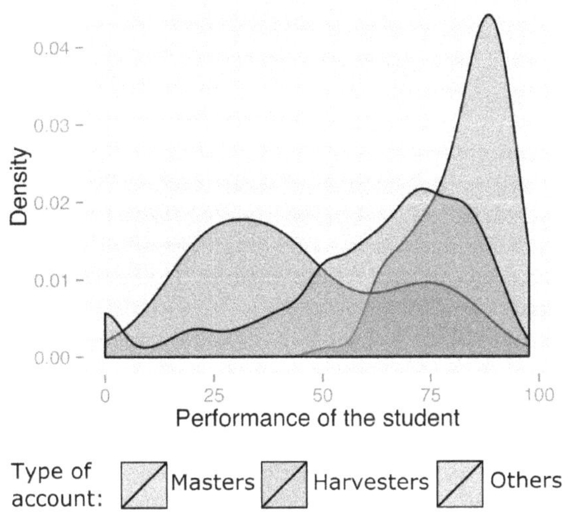

Figure 4. Distribution of performance

Characteristics of CAMEO events

Distribution of harvesting between patterns. Approximately 90% of the harvesting events followed the immediate pattern, and 10% followed the delayed batch pattern.

Harvesting technique. 53.5% of the cheating events were harvested by asking to see the answer ('show answer' button). 46.5% were harvested using exhaustive search.

Harvesting precedes first master answer. 91% of the harvested answers preceded the masters first attempt (which was therefore correct).

Delay of the cheating event. Figure 5 shows the distribution of the elapsed time between the harvesting event and the submission in the master account for events in which this delay was less than 5 minutes (90% of the CAMEO event detected). The median is 27 seconds with mode=5 seconds; 75% of the *immediate* mode submissions were done within 72 seconds after the harvesting event.

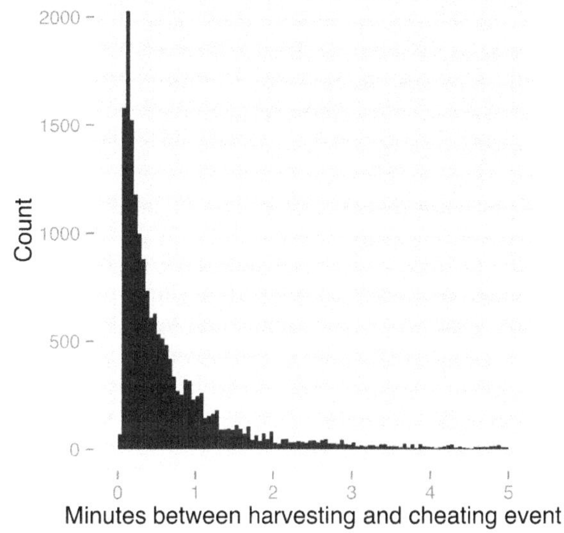

Figure 5. Delay between harvesting and submission: *Immediate* mode

Factors that correlate with cheating

This subsection presents results on the relation between characteristics of problems and the amount of cheating on these problems. The main objective is to focus on aspects that we believe can help instructors design their course in a way that is less vulnerable to CAMEO.

More harvesting on high-stake questions. Our course contains three types of problems - quizzes, homework and checkpoints. Additionally, we also have a midterm and a final exam, not included in the analysis for this subsection. In terms of contribution to the final grade, quiz questions have the highest weight, then homework questions, then checkpoints. The information about the weight of the questions is given in the syllabus of the course, so we can assume that students are aware of it.

We calculated the average percentage of harvested submissions per type of assignment. On average, the fraction of harvested submissions for quizzes, homework and checkpoints is 1.2%, 0.98% and 0.77%, respectively (of the total submissions; we note that the 3% in Table 1 refers to the percentage of *correct* submissions). An ANOVA test confirms that this difference is statistically significant ($F = 3.03$, $p = 0.046$).

Limiting feedback reduces harvesting. We have several places where questions that are similar in terms of weight are accompanied by different levels of feedback regarding the correct answer. The 'show answer' feature was not available before the deadline for quizzes except for one quiz (due to a mistake in settings). On this specific quiz, harvesting accounted for 3.77% of correct answers, vs. 1.25% on those without show answer.

Similar findings were obtained when looking at the midterm and final exams. On the midterm, with the 'show answer' disabled, the average amount of cheating was 1.2%, while on the final exam, on which 'show answer' was enabled, the average amount of cheating was 2.6%. It might have been higher except that students who harvest a majority of their answers tend to stop out when they reach the passing grade and make little of no effort on the final exam. These results clearly show that limiting the feedback reduces harvesting. That it does not reduce it further reflects that students can still harvest solutions using exhaustive search utilizing the correct/wrong feedback that is always given.

Randomization reduces harvesting. In most of the questions in our course requiring a numerical (vs. algebraic) answer, the question parameters are randomized (for example, the angle of an inclined plane), so different accounts see numerically different variations of the same problem.

We found that there is less cheating on randomized questions, both globally – the total amount of cheating events, and after normalizing by the total number of submissions to the problem.

For randomized questions, the percentage of cheating is 5.84%, while for non-randomized questions, it is 9.23%. In terms of absolute numbers, the average number of submissions that were harvested per problem with randomized variables was 10, whilst for the rest of the questions, it was 20. The normalized results are statistically significant, with p-value under 0.01 for both the normalized and the absolute comparisons. Although this was not a randomized trial, we believe that this indicates a causal relationship, namely, that randomization decreases cheating by making the harvesting more difficult. This is further discussed in the next section.

DISCUSSION

Significant use of CAMEO

The findings that we have presented above reveal that a significant fraction of the certificate earners in our course - almost 10%, used CAMEO to obtain at least $\sim$1% of their correct answers. Moreover, they reveal that $\sim$2.5% of the certificated users obtained most of their points by using this method, typically without even inspecting the questions to see if they might answer them legitimately. Our study is consistent with the hypothesis that the main motivation for this kind of cheating is to earn a certificate. Although the observation that a significant amount of cheating was by non-certificate earners seems to contradict this, we note that the non-certificate earners that used CAMEO tended to drop out from the course early, but till then, actually harvested a higher fraction of their answers than the certificated CAMEO users. Thus our conclusion is that they started the course with the intention of earning a certificate dishonestly, but decided to quit for various reasons (for example, our many questions, or the many randomized questions that thwart CAMEO), maybe even moving their CAMEO efforts to somewhere else. This is also consistent with the finding of Northcut et al. that CAMEO is more prevalent among users who have many certificates [6].

We were surprised by the relatively large number of students who used CAMEO in our course. One would expect that people would be interested in earning a certificate without actually learning something in courses that can be used for gaining external benefits, such as an advantage in the labor market. This is more naturally associated with programming and engineering courses, and less with introductory physics course as ours. So there is no specific reason to believe that the amount of cheating in our course is particularly high.

The high level of CAMEO may well result from the fact that MOOCs share features identified by previous work on academic dishonesty as associated with more cheating. For example, in [5] it was reported that cheating is more likely to happen in large and public institutions (vs. small private ones). According to the analysis of around 80 studies done in [7], Classroom Environment also has a considerable effect, with cheating more associated with bigger classrooms in which there is less individualized attention. Also, according to [4], cheating is restricted by what is perceived to be the social norm.

Altogether, due to the characteristics of MOOCs, of cheating being a phenomenon that tends to spread, and of MOOC certificates becoming more valuable, we can expect to see an increase in the amount of CAMEO in MOOCs, making it a more significant issue.

Implications

The most important finding of our work is that CAMEO is quite widespread. Furthermore, CAMEO is only one form of academic dishonesty: we are not detecting when answers obtained by one student are given to another student, which has been observed to occur in $\sim$ 11% of all answers [8] (vs the 3% CAMEO found here). Nor have we investigated the availability of plagiarizing answers from solutions found on the Internet. So cheating is undoubtedly highly prevalent in MOOCs.

The main threat is that CAMEO (and other forms of cheating) will decrease the confidence that the certificates provide a reliable evidence of knowledge and competency. Thus we believe that it is important to address CAMEO and other methods of academic dishonesty that are possible in online learning environments before they jeopardize the value of the MOOC certificates. We note that the current 'verified certificates' take steps to assure that the name on the certificate belongs to the individual who entered the answers in the master account, but is not a good defense against CAMEO and other forms of academic dishonesty.

Besides being a threat to the integrity of MOOC certificates, CAMEO also interferes with educational research. Our findings show that the users with the highest skill accounts in our course are masters, and that the lowest skill accounts are harvesters. This means that any research that tries to study the behavior of successful students vs. that of unsuccessful ones, might be heavily influenced by these two outlying groups. For example, if we try to identify the variables that most strongly correlate with student's skill, this subset of harvester and master accounts would have a significant effect on the results.

CAMEO almost certainly impacts learning. Users employing batch mode are foregoing the struggle of trying to answer questions on their own, and it seems obvious that this will have a negative effect on their learning. However, it is not clear that students who use a harvester account to find the answer to a few percent of the questions that they have struggled with is hurting their learning - indeed it might even be beneficial. Certainly this is a topic for future research.

Remedies

We now discuss steps that our research shows should reduce, or at least frustrate, CAMEO.

Our findings clearly show that using randomization of the numbers in questions reduces CAMEO. Randomization of question parameters is already supported by the edX platform, and we recommend that instructors use it where possible, certainly in preference to multiple choice (which can be harvested using exhaustive search). Randomizing does not completely defeat CAMEO. A more general form of randomization would be using question pools, i.e., group of questions that require very similar skills at similar level of difficulty, but have significantly different surface features (i.e. wordings or symbols chosen for various quantities).

A much simpler-to-implement prevention method is to avoid giving any feedback on important questions such as exams - including even the usual true/false feedback. Even allowing 'show answer' after the due date enables students to harvest the answers for use the next time the course is given. The obvious disadvantage of omitting feedback is that it compromises the learning experience, since immediate feedback is very important for learning. Individual instructors will have to trade off whether they want to help the great majority of students that wants to learn vs assuring the security of the edX.org certificate.

In the future, CAMEO can be addressed on the platform level, by adding cheating detection, and by supporting more general classes of randomization and question pooling along with algorithms for fairly grading students who do not do exactly the same questions.

SUMMARY, CONCLUSIONS AND FUTURE WORK

In this paper we have presented research on academic dishonesty in MOOCs. The specific method that we have studied, termed CAMEO [6], is based on using multiple accounts to harvest solutions. Our results show that a significant fraction of the certificate earners in our course - about 10%, have used this method to some extent, and that 2.5% of them obtained the majority of their correct answers by using it. We also showed that students who used CAMEO tended to have high success rate and fast response time compared with the other students. We then found that a question's characteristics correlate strongly with the amount of cheating on it. This led to our suggestions for instructional design practices that are less vulnerable to CAMEO.

Our main conclusions are as follows:

1. CAMEO is already significant among MOOC students, our study represents a lower bound on CAMEO, and does not include other forms of academic dishonesty like copying from other students. Our results suggest that cheating can jeopardize the validity of the MOOC certificate system.
2. The main motivation for CAMEO appears to be earning a certificate, consistent with our observation that questions that weigh heavily towards the overall grade are most likely to be cheated upon.
3. We show that delaying feedback and using randomization of problems can reduce CAMEO. Instructors can employ these with trade-off between pedagogy, prevention, and the amount of extra work required.

Though the research was conducted in MOOCs, the results and conclusions are also relevant to other learning environments that allow users to register additional accounts under a different user name. This research is only a first step into studying this phenomenon. Our plans for future research include:

Generalizing the results. In order to get a better estimation of the severity of CAMEO, our plan is to extend our research, and analyze a larger sample of courses. We also intend to make the source code publicly available.

Run-time detection. In addition to using methods for preventing CAMEO, it is important to detect it while it happens, so timely intervention can be made. Thus, we plan to develop a run-time version of the algorithm. Since the algorithm is quite scalable, and with small optimizations can be made linear in the amount of actions in the course, the cost in performance should be minimal. Also in the context of the algorithm, we are interested in developing a detector that does not rely on the IP, as sophisticated users can use various method to hide their IP address.

Understanding CAMEO. Pedagogy-wise, we are interested to understand the specific purposes for using CAMEO (for example, is it a *help seeking* strategy?). Among other things, this will extend our understanding of the motivation of learners in MOOCs, and eventually, can help to improve them.

ACKNOWLEDGMENTS

The first author wants to thank the projects 'eMadrid' (Regional Government of Madrid) under grant S2013/ICE-2715 and 'RESET' (Ministry of Economy and Competiveness) under grant RESET TIN2014-53199-C3-1-R for partially supporting this work. The authors would like to thank Christopher Chudzicki for his help in carrying out this study, and to Curtis Northcutt, Isaac Chuang, and Andrew Ho for useful discussions. We also thank the anonymous reviewers for their useful comments.

REFERENCES

1. Baker, R., Corbett, A., Koedinger, K., Evenson, S., Roll, I., Wagner, A., Naim, M., Raspat, J., Baker, D., and Beck, J. Adapting to when students game an intelligent tutoring system. In *Intelligent Tutoring Systems*, M. Ikeda, K. Ashley, and T.-W. Chan, Eds., vol. 4053 of *Lecture Notes in Computer Science*. Springer Berlin Heidelberg, 2006, 392–401.
2. Byrne, J. A. Wharton Using MOOCs To Recruit MBAs. http://poetsandquants.com/2015/02/11/wharton-using-moocs-to-recruit-mbas/, 2015. Accessed: 2015-10-30.
3. Davis, S. Academic dishonesty in the 1990s. *The Public Perspective* (1993).
4. Donald L. McCabe, L. K. T. Academic dishonesty: Honor codes and other contextual influences. *The Journal of Higher Education 64*, 5 (1993), 522–538.
5. McCabe, D. L., Trevino, L. K., and Butterfield, K. D. Cheating in Academic Institutions: A Decade of Research. *Ethics & Behavior 11*, 3 (July 2001), 219–232.
6. Northcutt, C., Ho, A. D., and Chuang, I. L. Detecting and preventing ”multiple-account” cheating in massive open online courses. *CoRR abs/1508.05699* (2015).
7. Palazzo, D. J. Detection, patterns, consequences, and remediation of electronic homework copying, 2006. Masters Thesis.
8. Palazzo, D. J., Lee, Y.-J., Warnakulasooriya, R., and Pritchard, D. E. Patterns, correlates, and reduction of homework copying. *Phys. Rev. ST Phys. Educ. Res. 6* (Mar 2010), 010104.
9. Singhal, A. C. Factors in students’ dishonesty. *Psychological Reports 51*, 3 (2015/10/29 1982), 775–780.

How Mastery Learning Works at Scale

Steve Ritter
Carnegie Learning, Inc.
437 Grant St.
Pittsburgh, PA 15219
sritter@
carnegielearning.com

Michael Yudelson
Carnegie Mellon
University
5000 Forbes Avenue
Pittsburgh, PA 15213
myudelson@
cs.cmu.edu

Stephen E. Fancsali
Carnegie Learning, Inc.
437 Grant St.
Pittsburgh, PA 15219
sfancsali@
carnegielearning.com

Susan R. Berman
Carnegie Learning, Inc.
437 Grant St.
Pittsburgh, PA 15219
sberman@
carnegielearning.com

ABSTRACT
Nearly every adaptive learning system aims to present students with materials personalized to their level of understanding (Enyedy, 2014). Typically, such adaptation follows some form of mastery learning (Bloom, 1968), in which students are asked to master one topic before proceeding to the next topic. Mastery learning programs have a long history of success (Guskey and Gates, 1986; Kulik, Kulik & Bangert-Drowns, 1990) and have been shown to be superior to alternative instructional approaches.

Although there is evidence for the effectiveness of mastery learning when it is well supported by teachers, mastery learning's effectiveness is crucially dependent on the ability and willingness of teachers to implement it properly. In particular, school environments impose time constraints and set goals for curriculum coverage that may encourage teachers to deviate from mastery-based instruction.

In this paper we examine mastery learning as implemented in Carnegie Learning's Cognitive Tutor. Like in all real-world systems, teachers and students have the ability to violate mastery learning guidance. We investigate patterns associated with violating and following mastery learning over the course of the full school year at the class and student level. We find that violations of mastery learning are associated with poorer student performance, especially among struggling students, and that this result is likely attributable to such violations of mastery learning.

Author Keywords
Adaptive educational systems; intelligent tutors; mastery learning; big data; longitudinal data; educational outcomes.

L@S 2016, April 25 - 26, 2016, Edinburgh, Scotland, UK.

ACM 978-1-4503-3726-7/16/04...$15.00.
DOI: http://dx.doi.org/10.1145/2876034.2876039

INTRODUCTION
Nearly every adaptive learning system aims to present students with instructional materials appropriate to their level of understanding (Enyedy, 2014). Typically, such adaptation follows some form of mastery learning (Bloom, 1968), in which students are asked to master one topic before proceeding to the next topic. Mastery learning programs have a long history of success (Guskey and Gates, 1986; Kulik, Kulik & Bangert-Drowns, 1990), predating computer-based instruction. The use of computers to implement mastery learning has popularized the approach and changed the process in several ways. Computer-based systems are able to determine mastery at a much more fine-grained "knowledge component" level (Koedinger et al., 2012), using techniques like Bayesian Knowledge Tracing (BKT; Corbett and Anderson, 1995). The use of computers to track mastery also enables mastery learning systems to more easily track mastery at the individual student level. In individualized mastery models, each student can move at his or her own pace, as opposed to class-level mastery models, where the teacher paces the class, based on class-level measures of student understanding (Block & Burns, 1976).

The ability to implement mastery learning at the individual level, using fine-grained knowledge components seems to be a clear pedagogical advantage over class-based mastery, but it requires a change from typical classroom practice, where teachers control the pace of instruction. In a typical school environment, in which learning time and course objectives are relatively fixed, teachers may feel pressure to "cover" each topic, regardless of mastery. In a teacher-led classroom, most student questions will pertain to the topic the teacher has chosen to address in the particular class period. In contrast, when teachers are assisting students using a mastery-based adaptive learning system, students will typically be learning different topics during the same class period. Thus, on any particular day, a teacher may be asked for assistance on any of a wide range of topics, which may be more challenging for them than the teacher-paced model.

For individualized mastery learning to scale, it needs to work in real classrooms within traditional school environments. While it may be tempting to dismiss

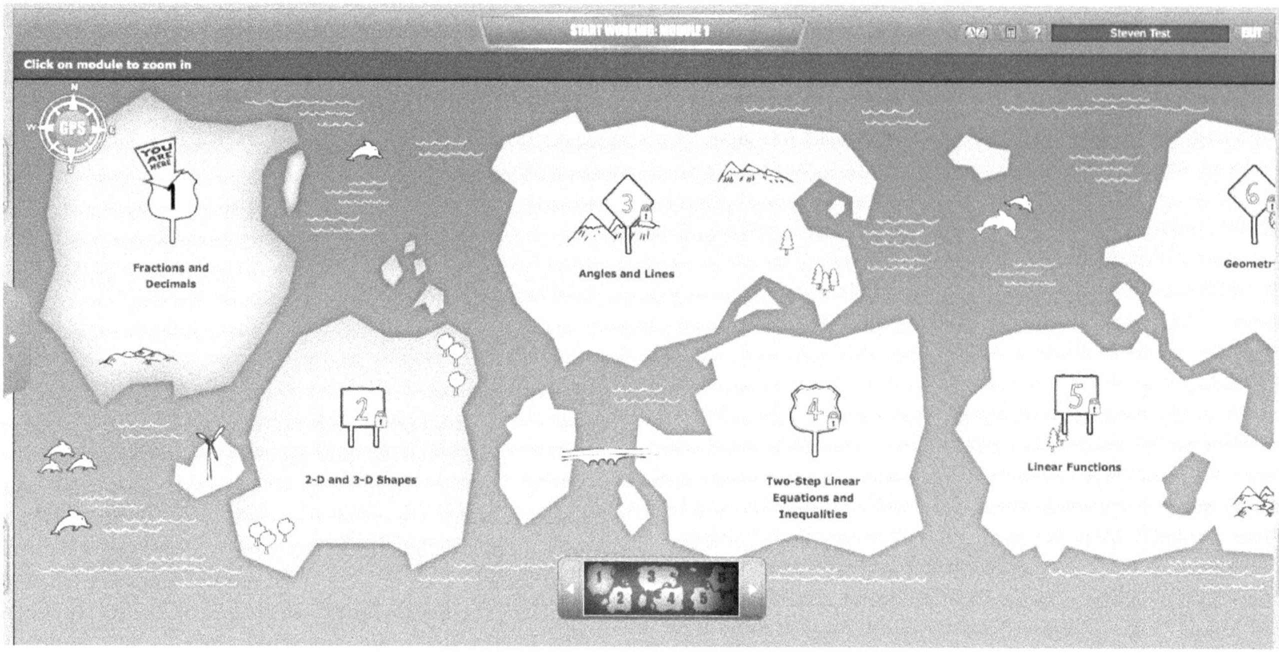

Figure 1. View of curriculum within Carnegie Learning's Cognitive Tutor used at the middle school level. Each island represents a module or major topic within the course. Within each island are roads representing units and sections. In this view, all modules but the first are locked. When the student completes the first module, the second automatically unlocks. If the student is following a mastery sequence, only one island will be unlocked at a time. If the teacher allows mastery to be violated, she may open multiple islands for the student. (© Carnegie Learning, Inc.)

teachers' concerns about strict implementation of mastery, it is not at all clear that strict adherence to the individual mastery model is necessary to produce superior outcomes. With fixed instructional time, there can be a tradeoff between mastering a small number of topics and covering a larger number of topics in less depth. It is possible that teachers are aware of this tradeoff and make decisions on pacing to optimize performance. Teachers may also be sensitive to particular student abilities (such as prior knowledge of a particular topic) that might justify skipping a student past that topic. In Carnegie Learning's Cognitive Tutor, the system explored in this paper, as in all real-world implementations of adaptive learning systems, teachers (and, in some cases, students) have some ability to override strict mastery learning prescriptions. The ability to violate mastery learning is intended to allow flexibility for unusual circumstances but also to account for the fact that teachers have information about student knowledge and abilities from sources unknown to the adaptive system, such as external exams or prior-year reports.

Our question in this study is whether these violations of mastery learning are likely to enhance or hinder student learning. The theory of mastery learning predicts that students who are allowed to master prerequisites before proceeding to the next topic will perform better on subsequent topics. If violations of mastery learning reflect accurate assessments of student knowledge unavailable to the adaptive learning system, then we would expect such practices to benefit students. If, on the other hand, such violations take place regardless of student knowledge, we might expect students to be harmed by this practice. Furthermore, we would expect this effect to become more pronounced over time. Later in the school year, students might find themselves missing more and more prerequisites and thus falling further and further behind in their understanding. We would expect this effect to be particularly pronounced among the worst prepared students, since they are the ones who we would expect to miss the greatest number of prerequisites.

COGNITIVE TUTOR

Carnegie Learning's Cognitive Tutor is used by over 450,000 students each year in middle schools and high schools across the United States (Ritter et al., 2007). It is most often delivered as a blended curriculum, where students spend 40% of their class time using the mastery-based and self-paced intelligent tutoring software and 60% of their class time using print-based materials. Numerous studies, including a recent large-scale study performed by RAND Corporation (Pane et al., 2014), have confirmed its effectiveness in real-world situations.

The Cognitive Tutor software divides a math course up into major topics called modules (see Fig. 1). Each module contains one or more units, which are divided into sections, representing subtopics. Each section contains a number of knowledge components on which mastery is evaluated. Students complete problems within the section until they are judged (by BKT) to have mastered each knowledge component, at which time they automatically move to the next section (or unit or module, if they have completed the last section in the previous). Although the software is delivered with modules, units and sections aligned with academic standards, teachers and school administrators can construct custom versions of the sequence to suit their needs. They may also add pre- and post-tests before and after any module.

The system provides teachers with two ways to violate mastery learning. They can unlock a module for a student, prior to the student having mastered the previous module. This allows students to work on any unlocked modules, possibly skipping prerequisites. Teachers can also change the student's placement within a module (from one unit or section to another).

DATA

We used a large dataset of over 11,000 students enrolled in grades 6-8 in 49 schools and 280 classes in a single countywide school district in the Southeastern United States. Data were collected by Carnegie Learning's MATHia software, based on Cognitive Tutor, for Middle School Math in the 2014-2015 school year. Classes implemented a blended learning curriculum, with a target of 40% of class time using the software and 60% of class time using Carnegie Learning's text-based activities.

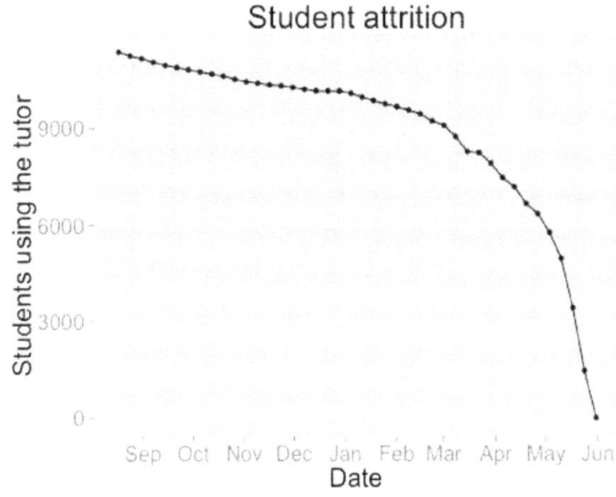

Figure 2. Number of students using the tutor over time.

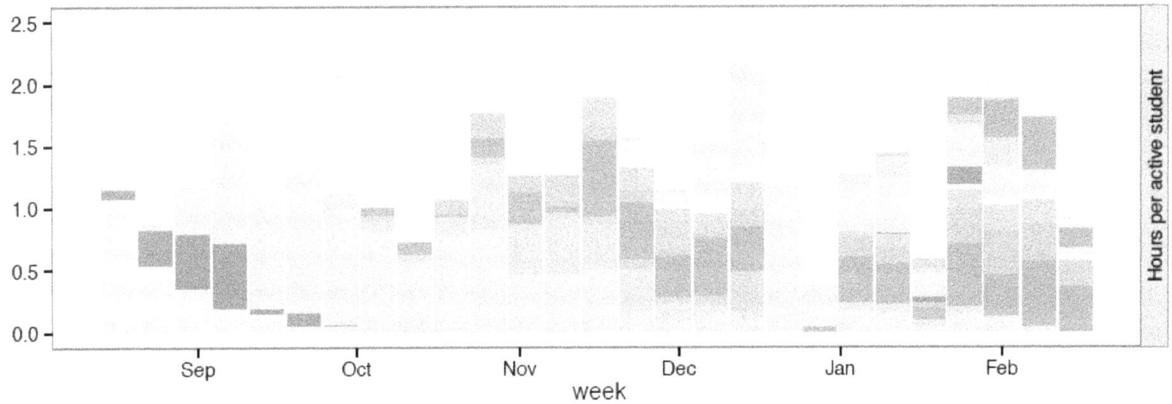

(a) class following mastery learning

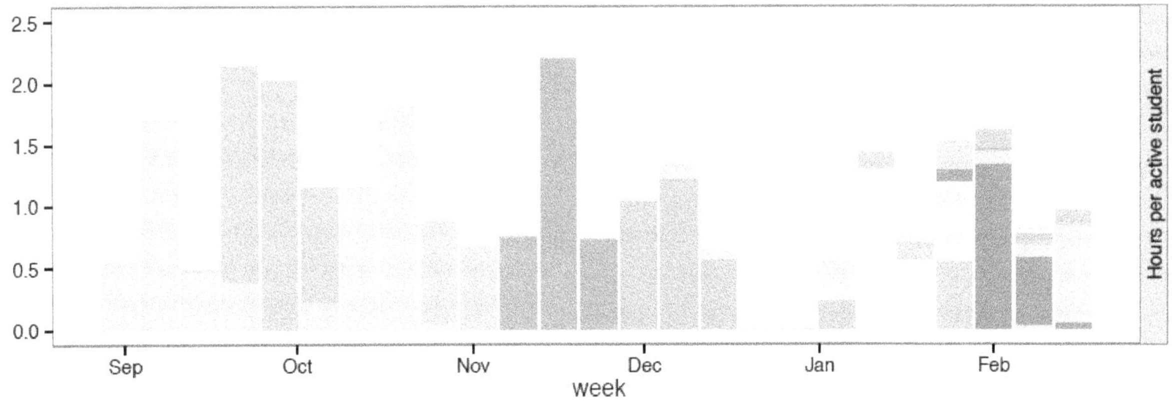

(b) class not following mastery learning

Figure 3. Progress through the curriculum in two classes used in this study. Each bar represents one week. The height of the bar represents the average time per student (in hours) spent using the tutor in that week. The colors of the bars represent time spent in specific content modules. Blank space in the second half of December in the lower graph means no student activity. (©Carnegie Learning, Inc.)

Figure 2 displays the number of students using the tutor over time. From the start of the school year in late August of 2014, the number of students slowly declined, with the decline accelerating in March. This date corresponds to the standardized end-of-course and state test dates, which likely accounts for the decline in usage. It is important to consider this attrition in examining the data presented in this study. Many trends change in mid-March and April due to such attrition.

School administrators in this district constructed custom curricula to be used by students in each course. These custom curricula defined very small modules (most containing only a single unit). For this reason, most violations of mastery learning take the form of the teacher opening a module and asking the student to start working on a new module, without completing the previous module.

Since the decision to either follow or violate mastery learning is made by teachers, we expect that some classes will be found to follow mastery learning, while others may not. Figure 3 illustrates the difference between a class following mastery learning and one moving students along at the teacher's pace. The class illustrated in Figure 3a (the top illustration) shows a pattern typical in a class using mastery learning. All students start off in the same module (indicated by a color in the graph). In the second and third week, some students have completed the first module and started the second or third modules. This leads to a wave pattern and, later in the school year, a wide range of content being addressed within the class in any given week. The class represented by Figure 3b (the bottom illustration) is one in which students make progress through the curriculum at the same pace. For the first three weeks, all students are working on the same module. In the fourth week, almost all time is spent on the second module. This pattern continues through most of the school year. In any given week, just about all work is within a single module.

ANALYSIS AND RESULTS

Class-Level Analysis

While the patterns shown in Figure 3 are illustrative of progress within classes either largely following or largely violating mastery learning, many classes fall somewhere in between. In a class where students are keeping up with the teacher's pace, there may be few observed violations of mastery learning, because teachers have no need to move students ahead.

In order to perform a more fine-grained analysis of the effects of mastery learning, we examined the data to determine, for each student, the average proportion of times a module was left incomplete or the teacher moved a student from one unit to another. This is our measure of mastery learning violations. We then aggregated per-student ratios of mastery violations by class and computed a

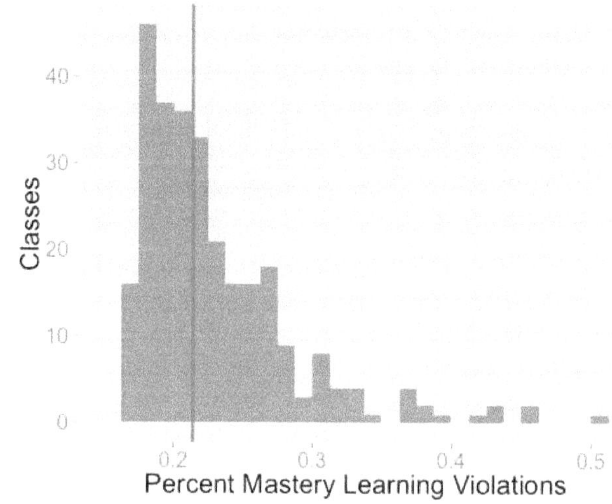

Figure 4. Distribution of the class median percent teacher moves (sections moved out of over sections encountered).

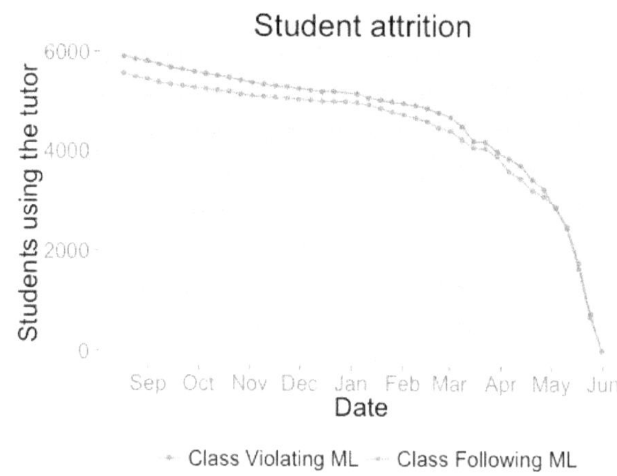

Figure 5. Number of students using the tutor over time for classes following and violating mastery.

per-class median mastery learning violations across all its students. The resulting distribution is shown in Figure 4. The median of the distribution is 0.21 (marked as a vertical red line). We find this number to be surprisingly high even in the absence of a prior expectation for this value. It means that in a typical class students are not finishing every fifth section.

For our further analyses we will split classes into two groups around the median. We label a class with median mastery violations of 0.21 or less "Mastery followed"; otherwise, the class would be labeled "Mastery violated." As we saw in Figure 3, attrition is a concern. Figure 5 shows attrition, split by mastery categorization. There is a small difference in student population sizes, but overall attrition patterns are similar.

Our primary concern is whether following or violating mastery learning is associated with differential student outcomes. To examine this question, we consider two metrics: errors per problem per hour and sections mastered per hour. Errors per problem per hour is a twice normalized measure of error commission. Number of sections mastered per hour is a metric we have previously found to be strongly correlated with achievements on standardized and state tests (Ritter et al., 2013). With respect to our discussion, the number of sections mastered per hour is a less sensitive measure, since sections can be completed (all problems attempted) without mastering all skills. Figure 6 shows both of these metrics for classes that either followed or violated mastery.

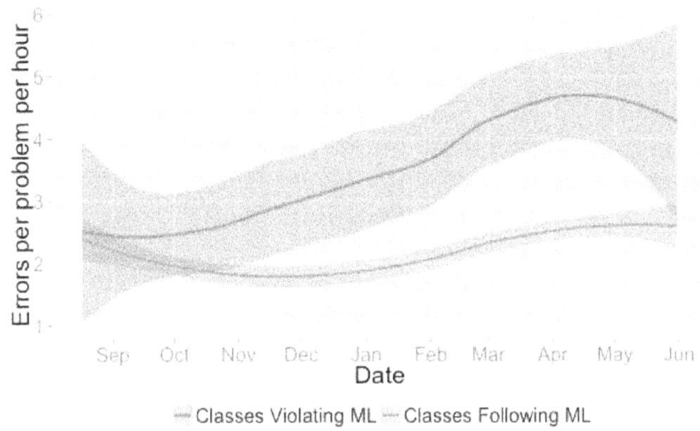

(a)

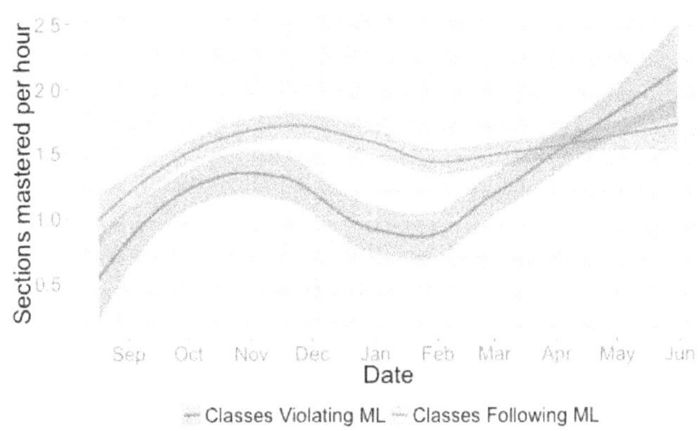

(b)

Figure 6. Number of errors per student per problem per hour (a) and number of sections mastered per hour (b) for classes either violating or following mastery learning. Student data is aggregated weekly, and graphs are smoothed using local regression (LOESS smoothing). Shaded areas show variability around smoothed curves.

In Figure 6a we can see that the normalized error rate for students in classes following mastery learning is relatively stable. This is exactly what we expect in a self-paced class. If the tasks get harder as students learn more, then they should be making about the same number of errors every week (Ritter, et al. 2007). For the classes in which mastery learning is frequently violated, on the other hand, error rates go up over time. The variability is notably larger as well. This pattern is consistent with the hypothesis that, over time, students who are frequently allowed to skip prerequisites find themselves with more gaps in their knowledge and are thus less able to complete more advanced tasks without making errors. The increased variability might result from the fact that, in these classes, some students are able to master prerequisites within the time the teacher allows (and thus don't increase their error rate). There may also be an affective component to this result, as students in classes violating mastery learning become more frustrated and less engaged with the class.

As shown in Figure 6b, students in classes following mastery learning master more sections each hour. In such classes, the number of sections mastered per hour is also relatively stable. In contrast, in classes where mastery learning is frequently violated, the number of sections mastered per hour is generally lower with the exception of the end of the school year, where heavy attrition introduces substantial noise.

Student-Level Analysis

The previous analyses proceed from an assumption that teachers are either predisposed to generally allow students to master material at their own pace or to take action to ensure that all (or most) students in a class move through the curriculum at the same pace. Our class-level analyses indicate that students in classes that are generally following mastery learning show fewer errors over all and that students in classes where mastery learning is frequently violated show increasing error rates. However, our hypothesized model of the effects of mastery learning violations makes some predictions at the student level. Specifically, we believe that, in any class, there may be students who are able to progress more quickly than the pace that the teacher sets, some who can match the teacher's pace and some who generally progress slower than the teacher's pace. For students matching the teacher's pace, the teacher's intentions with regard to following mastery learning matter little. Those students master the topics they encounter quickly enough that teachers don't skip them past many. Students mastering topics at a pace faster than that set by the teacher might either be allowed to race ahead or else be held back in various ways (including completing enrichment activities, being given time off or being asked to help slower students). While these students' experience in classes that generally violate mastery learning is affected by the mastery learning policy of the class, the effect of such policies on those students may vary. Our strongest student-level hypothesis is that violating mastery learning will have the greatest detrimental effect on students who are mastering material at a pace slower than that set by the teacher. These students are not allowed to master prerequisites.

In order to investigate hypothesized effects on students of varying ability, we classified students based on their performance on the first two pretests they encountered (preceding a student's first two modules). By using only the first two pretests, we hope to capture student ability prior to any substantial effects of the mastery learning policy in the class.

Approximately 4,900 students were the low pre-test group and roughly 5,800 in the high pre-test group (misbalance is due to the high cardinality of the subset of students with a pre-test result equal to the median).

Figure 7(a) shows the student distribution of pretest scores. Figure 7(b) shows the distributions for classes that either generally followed or generally violated mastery learning. We can see the students in classes that tend to violate mastery learning generally perform more poorly on the pretest. This should not be surprising; the teacher's decision to violate mastery learning is likely to be influenced by the fact that the class is not mastering material quickly enough to cover the entire curriculum before the end of the school year (or the date of a state exam). Table 1 summarizes student counts across two median splits: by performance on first two pretests and by mastery learning violations on the student level. Here we can see that students with lower pre-test performance tend to be subjected to mastery learning violations more frequently, while students with higher pre-test performance tend to be following mastery learning with fewer violations. This is to be expected, since lower levels of preparation are likely to lead to smaller portions of the curriculum covered, given relatively fixed time on the software. Further, teachers are less likely to manually advance better-prepared students.

Table 1. Student counts with respect to pre-test performance and mastery learning violations

Student mastery learning violations	Performance of first two pre-tests	
	Low	High
Violated	2674	2345
Followed	2218	3432

Figure 8 provides support for our hypothesis that weaker students are more hurt by violating mastery learning (ML). In Figure 8(a) and Figure 8(b), error rates for ML followers and ML violating students are compared within low- and high-pretest subgroups; this comparison reveals that that error curves for weaker students rise faster and remain at higher levels than those for students following mastery learning. Similarly, the number of sections mastered per hour – our closest proxy of overall student success in the course – is reliably higher for classes with stronger students that follow mastery learning (Figure 8(d)). Differences for weaker students (Figure 8(c)) are less pronounced, perhaps because such students struggle to master topics, even when in a class that is generally following mastery. If a student has done a large number of problems in a topic without reaching mastery, Cognitive Tutor automatically moves the student to the next topic and signals the teacher that the student has not mastered the prerequisite. Thus, even in a class that is following mastery, some weaker students may not master the material. Figure 8(d) is consistent with clear benefits to following mastery learning, since even high-performing students appear to be hurt when they violate mastery learning.

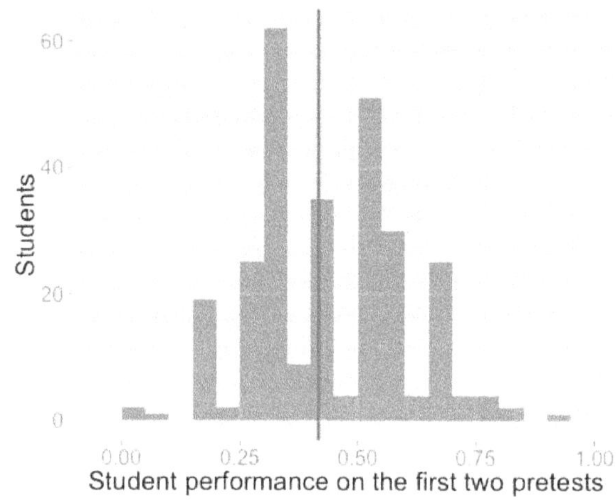

(a)

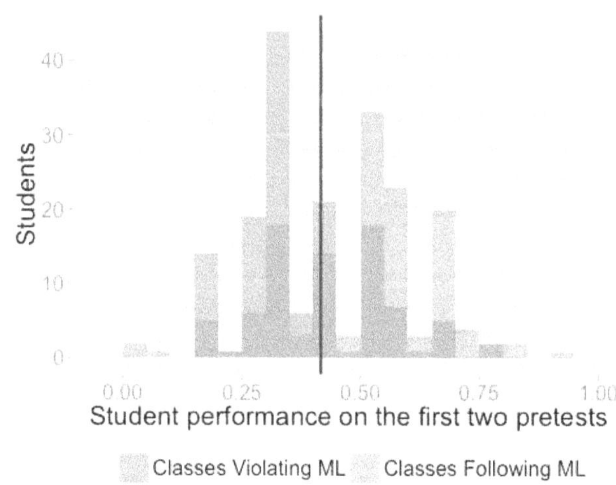

(b)

Figure 7. (a) Distribution of class median for the first two student pretest results. The median is marked by a vertical red line. (b) Distributions of class median for first two student pretest results for classes that are violating and following mastery learning (ML). The overall median is marked by a blue line.

Figure 8(e, f) is a regrouping of data from Figure 8(c, d). In these graphs, we can see that, when following mastery learning, better prepared students have a clear advantage over weaker students all through the year (cf. Figure 8(e)). When it comes to students who violate mastery learning, weaker students with low scores for the first two pretests master more sections per hour starting in November and until mid-April. However, as we can see by comparing purple curves from Figure 8(a, b), weaker students achieve this higher graduations per hour rate at the expense of visibly higher error rates.

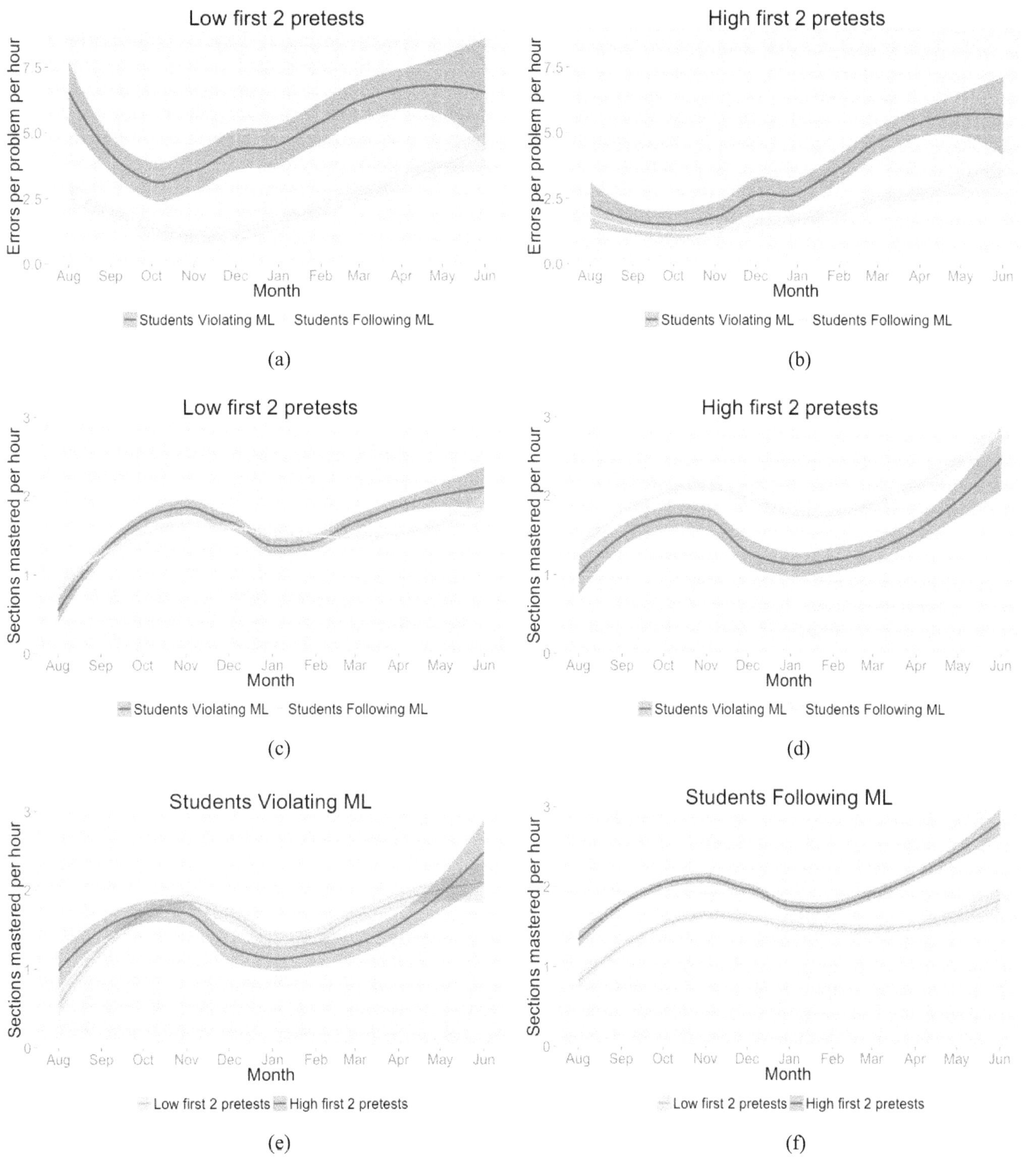

Figure 8. Monthly student median errors per problem per hour and monthly student median sections mastered per hour for the two student performance groups.

Note that, starting in February, students with a large number of mastery learning violations experience a period of intensive growth in number of mastered sections. While that should generally be viewed as a positive phenomenon, this intensification is not paralleled with the reduction of errors (Figure 8a,b) and that downplays the otherwise positive trend. To this point, we have shown data for students based on whether the student's class generally followed or violated mastery learning.

DISCUSSION

Adaptive educational systems are based on a strong assumption that varying instruction to fit individual student needs will result in improved outcomes. The most common form of adaptation and the one with the strongest base of research evidence is mastery learning. Mastery learning involves selecting content that is appropriate to the student's current level of knowledge. However, in order to scale in schools, adaptive learning systems need to adapt not just to the student but also to the needs of the instructional environment.

Schools, typically, have a fixed amount of instructional time (especially in-class time), in which students are expected to learn particular content. Teachers may be required to follow pacing guides that define the order in which content is taught and when particular content needs to be completed. They may believe that exposing students to all content expected to be on the exam is preferable to allowing students to master only a subset of that material and have no exposure to some. Teachers may believe that violating mastery learning in this way is a reasonable strategy for balancing coverage against robust understanding. Our analyses provide evidence that this belief is misguided. Students who are allowed to follow mastery learning make fewer mistakes in more advanced topics, and the decision to violate mastery learning hurts struggling students the most.

We intend to use these results as part of professional development materials demonstrating to school officials and, most importantly, teachers that mastery learning works to their advantage even if it is not directly evident to them. Teachers enable student use of the Cognitive Tutor and make decisions on whether to go against its recommendations and move students along in the curriculum. Complete elimination of violations of mastery learning may be impractical in many cases, for it would require a different paradigm of education to be deployed at scale. However, any reduction of mastery learning violations could be seen as potentially having a positive effect on student learning.

These results, to the best of our knowledge, are the first attempt to demonstrate the benefits of adhering to mastery learning on a large-scale dataset covering records of thousands of students across hundreds of classes. The result is also a testament to how hard it can be for teachers to "trust the machine" and let it handle the complexities of determining appropriate activities for students. While we do not intend to make strong causal claims from our correlational study, our results are not easily amenable to plausible alternative explanations. It is possible that changes in student errors and mastery rates result from student or teacher factors other than a propensity to follow mastery learning. However, any such explanation would need to explain not just the difference between students who followed mastery learning and those who didn't but the fact that these means and variances change over time. The hypothesis that these changes are due to the use of mastery learning predicts both group differences and changes over time.

Given the factors that drive teachers to violate mastery learning, one complication arises out of the fact that weaker students (i.e., those with lower pre-test scores) *necessarily* are those for whom violations of mastery learning are likely to occur. That is, mastery learning violations are targeted, by their very nature, at weaker students. While this may confound our ability, in this study, to exactly estimate the magnitude of the effect of mastery learning violations, our results are consistent with the hypothesis that such violations genuinely drive poorer learning and performance, especially as demonstrated by the increase in error rates (and variability in error rates) over time for students who have not been following mastery learning. As they move through the school year, such students tend to be increasingly confronted with topics that require pre-requisites that they have not yet mastered. These effects appear to be particularly harmful for weaker students. Having said that, and given the median split that we did, in nearly half of the cases, students (stronger and weaker alike) appear to be disadvantaged by being moved in the curriculum. Students being manually moved by teachers against mastery learning recommendations have consistently higher error rates. In terms of sections successfully mastered per hour, following mastery learning or being a stronger student could be seen as having an obvious advantage. That advantage can be effectively cancelled by violating intelligent tutor's mastery learning recommendations.

CONCLUSION

Mastery learning is an old and widely validated practice. While it is commonly used in adaptive learning systems, it is far from a frequent practice in typical classrooms. Our analysis suggests that mastery learning, despite its educational effectiveness, is not always a natural fit for traditional school environments, where many aspects of the instructional environment assume that students proceed at a common pace.

In order for mastery learning and, by implication, adaptive learning systems to succeed at scale, we need to demonstrate that the educational advantages of the approach override any mismatch between the approach and the school environment. Our analyses suggest that this is the case.

To our knowledge, all adaptive learning systems in regular use have provisions for teachers and/or students to override their suggestions. A major concern for the effectiveness of adaptive learning systems deployed at scale relates to whether such systems' recommendations are central to instructional effectiveness and, if so, how such systems can gain the trust of their users (both teachers and students) so that their recommendations are followed as frequently as possible.

We hope that the demonstrated shortcomings of violating mastery learning will encourage teachers and practitioners to, if not completely avoid violating mastery learning-based recommendations, at least significantly reduce the number of cases when they resort to it. We believe that data like this demonstrating the effectiveness of following our mastery learning recommendation will be influential on teachers implementing adaptive learning systems.

ACKNOWLEDGEMENTS

We would like to thank Ambarish Joshi for designing and developing some of the preliminary analyses and visualizations used in this work.

REFERENCES

1. Block, J. H., & Burns, R. B. (1976). Mastery learning. In L. Shulman (Ed.), Review of research in education (Vol. 4, pp. 3–49). Itasca, IL: Peacock.
2. Bloom, B. S. (1968, May). Mastery learning. In Evaluation comment (Vol. 1, No. 2). Los Angeles:University of California at Los Angeles, Center for the Study of Evaluation of Instructional Programs.
3. Corbett, A.T., Anderson, J.R. (1995). Knowledge Tracing: Modeling the Acquisition of Procedural Knowledge. User Modeling and User-Adapted Interaction, 1995, 4, 253-278.
4. Enyedy, N. (2014). Personalized Instruction: New Interest, Old Rhetoric, Limited Results, and the Need for a New Direction for Computer-Mediated Learning. Boulder, CO: National Education Policy Center. Retrieved 10/29/2015 from http://nepc.colorado.edu/publication/personalized-instruction.
5. Guskey, T. R., & Gates, S. L. (1986). Synthesis of research on the effects of mastery learning in elementary and secondary classrooms. Educational Leadership, 43 (8), 73-80.
6. Koedinger, K.R., Corbett, A.C., & Perfetti, C. (2012). The Knowledge-Learning-Instruction (KLI) framework: Bridging the science-practice chasm to enhance robust student learning. Cognitive Science, 36 (5), 757-798.
7. Kulik, C.-L., Kulik, J. A., & Bangert-Drowns, R. L. (1990). Effectiveness of mastery learning programs: A meta-analysis. Review of Educational Research, 60, 265-299.
8. Pane, J.F., Griffin, B.A., McCaffrey, D.F., & Karam, R. (2014). Effectiveness of Cognitive Tutor Algebra I at scale. Educational Evaluation and Policy Analysis, 36 (2), 127-144.
9. Ritter, S., Anderson, J.R., Koedinger, K.R., & Corbett, A. (2007) The Cognitive Tutor: Applied research in mathematics education. Psychonomics Bulletin & Review, 14(2), pp. 249-255.
10. Ritter, S., Joshi, A., Fancsali, S. E., Nixon, T. (2013). Predicting standardized test scores from Cognitive Tutor interactions. In Proceedings of the 6th International Conference on Educational Data Mining (Memphis, TN, 2013). 169 – 176.

$1 Conversational Turn Detector: Measuring How Video Conversations Affect Student Learning in Online Classes

Adam Stankiewicz
Carnegie Mellon University
Pittsburgh, PA, USA
stankiewicz@cs.cmu.edu

Chinmay Kulkarni
Carnegie Mellon University
Pittsburgh, PA, USA
chinmayk@cs.cmu.edu

ABSTRACT
Massive online classes can benefit from peer interactions such as discussion, critique, or tutoring. However, to scaffold productive peer interactions, systems must be able to detect student behavior in interactions at scale, which is challenging when interactions occur over rich media like video. This paper introduces an imprecise yet simple browser-based conversational turn detector for video conversations. Turns are detected without accessing video or audio data. We show how this turn detector can find dominance in video-based conversations. In a case study with 1,027 students using Talkabout, a video-based discussion system for online classes, we show how detected conversational turn behavior correlates with participants' subjective experience in discussions and their final course grade.

ACM Classification Keywords
H.5.3. Information Interfaces and Presentation (e.g. HCI): Group and Organization Interfaces; K.3.1 Computers and Education: Computer Uses in Education

Author Keywords
video discussions, turn taking, peer learning

INTRODUCTION
At their best, interactions between peers can improve students' sense of belonging [22], communication skills [21], and can form the basis for powerful learning mechanisms, such as peer tutoring. These peer learning techniques can be designed to scale with the size of the classroom and have the potential to improve massive-scale education.

However, one challenge for peer learning opportunities that depend on direct interactions among peers, such as peer tutoring, is that peers may not spontaneously engage in productive interactions. For example, when students tutor each other, they are likely to dominate the conversation and lecture to their partner, rarely elaborating on their explanations or allowing their partner to apply information on their own [10].

L@S 2016, April 25–26, 2016, Edinburgh, Scotland, UK.

ACM 978-1-4503-3726-7/16/04 ... $15.00.
DOI: http://dx.doi.org/10.1145/2876034.2876048

Scaffolding peer interactions helps students engage in more productive interactions. Research on text-based peer interactions already shows the benefits of scaffolding. Structuring the activities peers participate in [4] as well as scaffolding their turn-by-turn conversations is beneficial [17]. Indeed, dynamic conversation support for discussions yields learning gains similar to intelligent tutoring [17].

Could similar support be useful for video conversations? For example, if the system can detect when the peer tutor is dominating the conversation, it may be able to suggest ways in which the tutee could take a more active role. Synchronous channels (e.g., video discussions) improve participants' sense of belonging and willingness to collaborate [25]. Further, communication channels, like video, support multimodal communication and nonverbal cues that are better suited to ambiguous discussions [5] and complex sense-making [7].

Because it is more difficult to gather semantic information from video than from text due to the richness of video (e.g., [19]), existing systems do not scaffold video conversations dynamically. Furthermore, because of the greater trust [25] (and thus higher self-disclosure [29]) in video discussions, semantic extraction (such as transcripts) may not even be desirable. For example, consider a global classroom discussion on racial prejudice, as described by the designers of Talkabout, a video-based discussion system [16]. Students may not participate in conversations as candidly if they knew conversations were being recorded. Because video data is more identifiable than text chats, it may also actively put students at risk (consider a discussion on human rights with some participants who live in countries with oppressive regimes).

This paper introduces a browser-based conversational turn-detector that could be the basis of dynamic conversation support. This conversational turn-detector does not store (or use) any recording of conversations. We call this a $1 turn detector because it is cheap yet imprecise. This turn detector only detects yielded turns (where one speaker stops speaking as another starts), but it can run in real time with commodity video conferencing software such as Google Hangouts. We demonstrate how this turn detector can be used to detect dominance in a conversation.

We also present a case study of how turn-taking behavior measured by our $1 detector correlates with student performance and experience with Talkabout. Approximately 6,000 students have used Talkabout with more than two dozen classes.

This paper presents results from 1,027 participants that used Talkabout to participate in 392 discussion groups.

Through this case study, we present evidence that our $1 turn detector can detect dominance as experienced by participants. We also find correlations between detected turn-taking behavior and performance measures like course grades and self-reported survey responses. For example, we find that while participants' perception of how much they learned in a discussion depends on how much they spoke, their willingness to meet the other participants again in a future discussion depended only on how much others spoke and was not statistically correlated with their duration of speaking.

Through this work, we make two contributions. First, we introduce an imprecise yet privacy-sensitive turn-detector and demonstrate how it can detect dominance in conversations at large scale. To encourage other researchers and designers to use the detector to provide active conversation guidance, we are providing it as BSD-licensed open-source[1]. Second, through our case study, we offer suggestions to designers on how to design video-discussion structures that improve students' learning experiences.

RELATED WORK

Prior research has shown that peer learning activities are an effective approach to learning [12, 28]. Participating in structured activities, such as talking with peers in small groups to discuss conceptual questions and solve problems, enables learners to collaborate with other students who are at similar levels of understanding. When students have to explain material to a peer (e.g. via tutoring), they also recall it better and transfer their learning to new problems more successfully [11, 32].

Despite the benefits of peer interactions, there are several challenges in successfully adopting structured peer learning. At scale, without the ability for instructors to intervene, it is difficult to get students to coordinate and collaborate productively in synchronous communication channels [15, 23]. For example, more competent students dominate discussions [14, 6, 9], and rarely allow less competent partners in a tutoring session to apply information on their own [10].

Monitoring and facilitating discussions in real-time may help students engage in more productive small-group conversations [31, 13]. Providing real time, personalized feedback to participants in text-based group chats (e.g., *"Be sure to pay attention to what others are saying."*) improved group dynamics [31]. Monitoring a face-to-face conversation in real time to create representations of dominance allowed participants to censor their own behavior and reduce dominance [13].

Despite the benefits of the dynamic conversation support [31, 13], these approaches do not take users' privacy into account which might make users feel uncomfortable in self-disclosing personal information. For example, a real time language feedback typically relies on the words used in a group conversation (e.g., [31]). Additionally, an analysis of participants' chat transcripts are commonly used to measure performance (e.g., [17]).

[1] https://github.com/adamstankiewicz/talkabout-turntaking

Our conversational turn detector, however, only uses low-level behavior (i.e., when a new participants begins speaking) instead of accessing the transcripts or video feeds of the group discussion.

In a conversation, turn-taking is used to manage the exchange of speaking turns between participants using signals that dictate when a turn has ended or will continue further [8]. Occasionally, participants will speak over each other by using backchannel signals to acknowledge understanding or interest in the speaker [26]. Thus, one way that dominance can be detected is through monitoring conversational turn-taking behaviors.

Dominant behavior directly affects group dynamics. While a dominant participant may have a negative effect on a group's effectiveness by limiting the opportunity for others to speak [31], dominance is a characteristic of a leader or mediator [13]. Therefore, systems that foster small-group discussions may be able to capitalize on an emergent dominant speaker by scaffolding them into a successful mediator who can balance participation among group members by encouraging others to contribute to the conversation.

By analyzing turn-taking behaviors in conversations, it becomes possible to detect dominant behavior. Dominance is expressed through social signals such as being verbally intrusive and speaking more than others [18]. Therefore, an individual with longer turn durations might indicate an increased level of dominance.

Several studies have explored dominance as measured by conversational turn-taking behaviors. For example, groups that had dominant people had a lower group intelligence than groups with a more equal distribution of turns [33].

DETECTING TURNS IN COMMODITY VIDEO-CONFERENCING

We wanted to create a system that could collect data at large scale, and therefore, we did not consider solutions that required participants to install software on their computers. Our turn detector is implemented entirely in Javascript, and runs within a browser (for Google Hangouts).

Our turn detector is designed for commodity video conferencing software such as Skype or Google Hangouts, which offer third-party developers the ability to create extensions (or "apps") but do not provide them with direct access to the video or audio stream. For example, Google Hangouts provides the Hangouts Developer API [1] to enable a programming interface for developers to control various features (e.g., adjusting video camera settings) and share data between the video conferencing software and third-party extensions.

We discovered that while most extension APIs do not provide direct access to video streams, they do allow third-party apps to see when participants' primary video feed (i.e., who participants see they are talking to) changes. Combined with the observation that video conferencing systems focus on the participant who is speaking, this enables detecting conversational turns without directly accessing video from the conversation. We consider a conversational turn to be the time from when one participant begins speaking to when a different participant begins speaking (i.e., when the primary video feed changes).

This detection method has two limitations. First, if a conversation only involves two participants, participants' primary video feed does not change (each participant always sees the other). Therefore, our turn detector only records turns when more than two participants are present in a conversation. Second, the displayed participant changes after a short delay, so this method is unable to detect overlapping turns. Because we are unable to detect overlapping turns, we also cannot detect unyielded turns or backchannel, where a participant continues speaking even as other participants speak (e.g., to indicate agreement, saying "yes", or "um-hm").

There are two other challenges. If a participant started speaking themselves, their display remains focused on the previous speaker. Also, participants may enter and leave the conversation at any time. To address these challenges, we choose two participants who both report turns in a conversation. In a second step, we process the detected turns to remove duplicates.

To choose two participants to act as reporters, we give each participant a unique, but arbitrary identifier. When a new participant joins (or leaves) a conversation, the two participants with the lowest identifiers act as reporters. However, if the two reporters are engaged in a back-and-forth conversation, turns may go unreported. Therefore, when a reporter is speaking (i.e., in the primary video feed of the group conversation), a third reporter is temporarily chosen to report turns.

This reporting mechanism leads to each turn being reported multiple times. In a post data collection step, we group together subsequent reports that a participant has begun speaking into a single turn.

This turn detection scheme is admittedly simple, and does not detect all turns (especially unyielded turns). Still, we find that these approximate turns are useful to detect dominance, as well as yield some insights into participants' discussion experience.

In summary, our turn detector uses the Google Hangouts API to detect when a speaker's display changes to a new participant (i.e., when the audio channel switches to a different speaker). When this occurs, Talkabout logs the event onto its private servers including a timestamp and a unique identifier for the new speaker. To help other researchers use this \$1 conversational turn detector, we are making a Javascript implementation available under a BSD license. We are also releasing analysis scripts in Python and R that process raw turn data[2].

Calculating dominance

Speakers in a conversation might assert dominance in a variety of ways. For example, they may speak more loudly, use a different tone of voice, frequently interrupt other speakers, or not yield the floor when someone else is speaking at the same time.

[2]https://github.com/adamstankiewicz/talkabout-turntaking

Our detector cannot detect most of these channels, and instead our dominance metric considers only the duration for which participants hold the floor for each turn, and the frequency of their turn. In particular, we consider a conversation to be dominated when there is a larger inequality of either the number and duration of turns for individual participants.

This accounts for two kinds of dominant behavior: 1) a participant might speak for the majority of the discussion in very few turns; and 2) a participant might dominate the discussion by frequently interrupting other students with short turns. To account for these two types of behavior, we operationalize dominance for both the number of turns and duration of turns as two Gini coefficients, a non-binary classification of inequality, as shown in Equation 1:

$$G = \left| 1 - \sum_{k=1}^{n} \left[(X_k - X_{k-1})(Y_k + Y_{k-1}) \right] \right| \qquad (1)$$

where X_k is the cumulative proportion of the population variable, for $k = 0, \ldots, n$, with $X_0 = 0$, $X_n = 1$ and Y_k: cumulative proportion of the total number and duration of turns per participant, for $k = 0, \ldots, n$, with $Y_0 = 0$, $Y_n = 1$.

Gini coefficients are typically used to show income distributions (e.g., for the bottom x% of a population, what percentage of the total income they have). Here, we propose using Gini coefficients as a means to demonstrate the inequality of conversational turns among participants in video conversations, both in quantity (number of turns per participant) and in time (duration of turns per participant). For example, the Gini coefficient for the inequality in number of turns per participant is measured between 0 (all group members contributed an equal number of turns) and 1 (a single group member contributed the entirety of turns in the group).

To create a uniform measure of dominance regardless of the kind of dominant behavior, we compute our dominance measure $\mathcal{D}$ as the average of both the Gini coefficient for number of turns and the Gini coefficient for the duration of turns in each group:

$$\mathcal{D} = \frac{1}{2}\left[Gini_{duration of turns} + Gini_{number of turns} \right] \qquad (2)$$

While dominance in group conversations may be useful in certain situations (e.g., an explanation from a learner who has a firm understanding of a concept and can clearly articulate their understanding to other learners), the next section describes how we find that dominance typically detracts from learners' experience in video conversations by limiting the opportunity for others to actively contribute to the discussion.

CASE STUDY: TALKABOUT

To illustrate how the \$1 turn detector can yield useful design insights, we applied video discussions on the Talkabout platform [16], which enables learners in MOOCs to participate in small-group discussions with peers from around the world. The discussion groups are conducted using Google Hangouts.

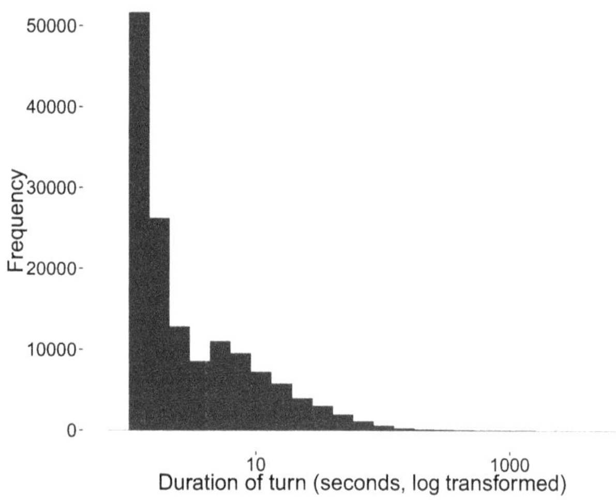

Figure 1. Most detected turns were short; the mean turn duration was 7.5 seconds, the median turn duration was 2 seconds.

As learners log in to Talkabout at a predetermined day and time, they are assigned into a group until it reaches its size limit (instructors choose group sizes) at which point a new group is formed.

In addition to the conversational turn-taking behavior, we also captured information about student demographics and performance. We looked at the behaviors of 392 Talkabout discussion groups, consisting of 1,027 unique participants from 104 countries.

The case study demonstrates how our turn detector can model dominance in video conversations and relate participants' turn behavior with their subjective experiences. The exploratory study design affords us the ability to make correlational (rather than causal) observations that may form the basis of future interventions using our conversational turn detector.

Talkabout discussions, student demographics, and course grades

We determined each participant's country by performing an IP lookup; participants also provided their gender when they signed up for Talkabout.

Discussion groups ranged in size from 2 to 7 participants (mean = 4.59; SD = 1.24) and 2 to 5 countries (mean = 2.96, SD = 0.93). On average, there were 1.63 participants per country (SD = 0.50), producing an average of 527.60 (SD = 365.90) conversational turns and 61.85 (SD = 25.65) minutes per discussion group. Each discussion group had an average of 8.03 (SD = 4.51) turns per minute (Figure 1).

After each Talkabout discussion, we prompted participants to fill out a survey about their experience (Table 1). Three of the questions were answered on an ordered rating scale whereas the final question elicited an open-ended response.

The *Share knowledge* question was intended to capture whether participants' felt they were able to contribute their personal experiences and opinions to the other members of their group. It had three possible responses: "Not at all", "Occasionally", and "Frequently." Out of 394 responses, the median response was "Frequently."

Label	Question
Share knowledge	I shared my personal experience and opinions with others in this group. *(Likert)*
Learned	I learned a great deal from my discussion with group. *(Likert)*
Meet again	I would like to be paired with this discussion group for future discussions in this class. *(Likert)*
Personal experiences	Among the personal experiences and ideas your classmates shared in your hangout, describe two specific experiences/ideas that you personally found most interesting. *(Open response)*

Table 1. Survey questions and labels.

The *Learned* question pertained to understanding whether participants felt they had learned as a result of participating in Talkabout discussion groups. It had 5 possible responses ranging from "Strongly disagree" to "Strongly agree." In 402 responses, the median response was "Agree."

The *Meet again* question was intended to act as an approximization for the overall quality of the discussion, gauging students' interest in joining another Talkabout discussion with the same group members in the future. It had 5 possible responses ranging from "Never" to "All of the time." Out of 398 responses, the median response was "Often."

Additionally, for one class using Talkabout, we obtained a small sample (n = 53) of students' final grade (50% quizzes, 50% final exam) that we matched with their discussion behavior and demographic information.

FINDINGS

We present our results in two parts. First, we examine if dominance in discussions as measured by our turn-detector corresponded to students' subjective experience of dominance. To do so, we look at how our measure of dominance correlates with group attributes such as group size which students associated with dominance. Next, we examine if other turn behaviors measured by our detector, such as the number and duration of both individual and others' turns, predict self-report measures from the survey and performance in the course.

Correlating measured dominance with subjective perceptions

Consistent with prior work (e.g., [9]), several learners' open-ended survey responses suggested they experienced dominance negatively:

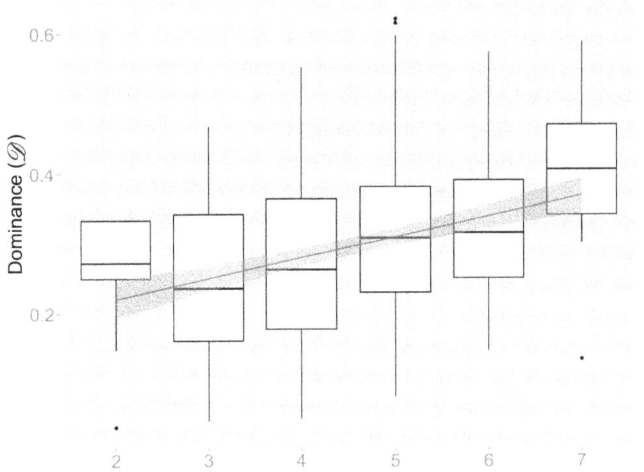

Figure 2. Dominance increases as the number of participants in a group (group size) increases.

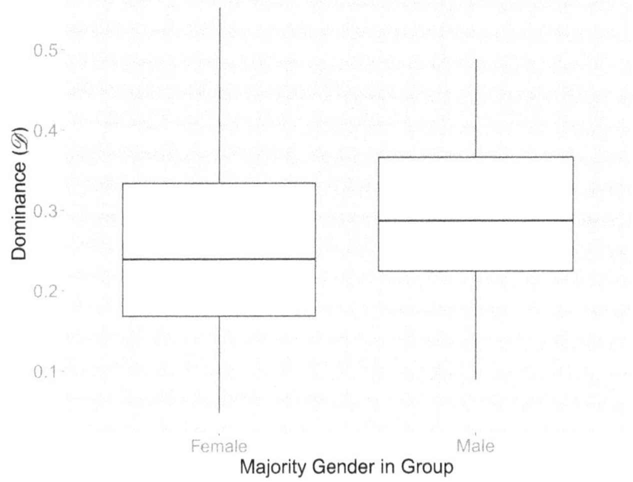

Figure 3. Majority male groups exhibit more dominant behavior than majority female groups.

It was the first Hangout with 6 people. I found it much more difficult than with four people. Specially, if you had one person talking very long time.

These responses also suggested that dominance increased with group size, for example:

Our group was small. However, it allowed us more time to have a meaningful discussion on our interests and the course itself.

This led us to ask if the dominance measured by our system similarly increased with group size.

Measured dominance increases with group size

Figure 2 shows how dominance increases as the number of participants in a group increases. A linear regression model found that dominance does significantly increase with group size (adjusted R^2 = .09, F(1,390) = 40.83, p < .001). This suggests dominance as operationalized (our $\mathscr{D}$ measure) corresponded to students' subjective experience.

Majority male groups are more dominant

In studies with in-person groups, dominance is perceived to increase with a larger fraction of male participants [33]. To examine whether the gender makeup of a group affected measured dominance, we split the groups into majority (> 50%) male and majority female groups. This was done only for groups where the gender was known for all participants, resulting in 39 majority male groups (41% of groups) and 57 majority female groups (59% of groups).

As shown in Figure 3, majority male groups (mean $\mathscr{D}$ = .30, SD = .11) demonstrated significantly more dominant behavior than majority female groups (mean $\mathscr{D}$ = 0.25, SD = .12), t(88.50) = 2.14, p < .05, which is consistent with prior work [33].

Having a direct measure of dominance enables us to investigate this behavior more deeply. For example, we found no significant difference in the duration or number of turns between genders in groups consisting of mostly males. This suggests that while majority male groups exhibited more dominance than majority female groups, both genders were equally likely to dominate majority male groups.

Dominance unaffected by geographic diversity

While there was a significant relationship between dominance and the number of countries present in the group (adjusted R^2 = .02, F(1, 390) = 10.52, p < .01), we found no significant improvement in model fit after controlling for group size (F(1, 389) = .03, n.s.). This suggests that increased geographic diversity does not increase dominance.

Correlating measured turn-taking and discussion outcomes

In this section, we look at how measuring turns directly (albeit approximately) allows us to estimate participants' course grades and responses to the survey questions (see Table 1).

In addition to dominance, we captured students' turns in conversations, and how long they spoke. In our data collection, we found that the number of turns and duration of total turns were significantly correlated (r = 0.67, $t(1379)$ = 33.25, p < .001). Therefore, we only use duration of total turns as a predictor in our analysis.

Learners who speak longer had a higher grade

A linear regression model shows a significant relationship between the total duration of a student's turns and his or her grade (adjusted R^2 = .08, F(1,51) = 5.26, p < .05). We also consider the number and duration of other participants' turns as potential factors that contribute to students' final course grade. However, neither the number of other group members' turns (adjusted R^2 = .02, F(1,51) = 1.85, n.s.) nor the duration of other students' turns (adjusted R^2 = .00, F(1,51) = .86, n.s.) are significantly related to students' grade.

Therefore, students who take an active role in the Talkabout conversations have a larger benefit on their course grade than those who listen to other group members' contributions.

Learned

A linear regression model shows a significant relationship between whether participants felt they learned from the discussion and how long they spoke during the conversation (adjusted $R^2 = .01$, $F(1,400) = 4.99$, $p < .05$).

We also consider the duration of other students' turns in the group (i.e., the total group duration minus the duration of the participant's own turn duration) as a potential factor.

In contrast to the effect on students' grades, a linear regression model shows a significant, potentially larger, relationship between students' self-reported learning and the duration of others' turns (adjusted $R^2 = .02$, $F(1,400) = 10.32$, $p < .01$). Controlling for the number and duration of participants' own turns, we see a significant improvement in model fit ($F(1,398) = 9.83$, $p < .01$) suggesting that students believe they learned more as the duration of other members' turns increases. Therefore, students perceived they learned not only through speaking (and sharing their knowledge), but through participants speaking as well.

Taken together, one interpretation of these data is that higher-scoring students are more likely to speak than to listen, and that learning is perceived both through processes such as perspective-taking [2] (i.e., developing deeper mental models by taking others' perspectives that conflict with their own), and elaboration [30], where students develop more elaborate mental models by speaking about class topics.

Additionally, we find that students' self-perceived learning does not significantly correlate with dominance in discussion groups ($r_s = -0.05$, n.s.). This suggests that dominance does not play a role in whether students felt they learned from the discussion.

Shared knowledge

As expected, we found that a linear regression model shows that students felt they shared knowledge with the group more often when they spoke for longer (adjusted $R^2 = .03$, $F(1,392) = 12.53$, $p < .001$).

Responses to the open-ended survey question voice participants' concern about not being able to share what they knew:

> *Problem is many participants means you do more listening (sometimes to points repeated over and over again) than discussing.*

However, the relatively low model-fit (adjusted $R^2 = .03$) for talk duration predicting knowledge shared suggests that detecting when knowledge is shared requires more semantic knowledge about what was spoken. Survey responses demonstrate the patterns of sharing that we are unable to detect:

> *The opportunity given to talk to people all over the world is great. Hear the stories people shared and reflect on my own. It is truly wonderful experience!*

We also see a significant relationship between participants' *share knowledge* self-report measure and the dominance portrayed in their respective groups. Learners in more dominant groups felt they had less opportunity to express their own opinions and experiences ($r_s = -.12$, $p < .05$).

Meet again

We find that whether students wanted to meet their group again was significantly correlated with the duration of other students' talk (adjusted $R^2 = .01$, $F(1,396) = 5.32$, $p < .05$), but not the duration of their own talk (adjusted $R^2 = 0.0$, $F(1,396) = 1.50$, $p = 0.13$). This suggests that while students might feel they shared knowledge when they have a chance to speak, they recognize that discussions are more valuable based on what others say.

Our analysis also suggests that students' desire to meet the same group again was influenced by a large number of factors. For example, students are explicitly told Talkabout is a way to meet peers around the world, so we would expect that students who discussed with a diverse group might want to do so again. As expected, we find a significant relationship between geographic diversity and the desire to meet again (adjusted $R^2 = .02$, $F(1,396) = 8.49$, $p < .01$). While the number of participants in a group is correlated with geographic diversity ($r = .52$, $p < .001$), we found no increase in students' desire to meet a large group again after controlling for diversity. However, the R^2 value is similarly small, suggesting that diversity is just one of many factors that influences students desire to meet their discussion group again.

Moreover, we find no significant relationship between whether learners want to meet again with their group and dominance ($r_s = .03$, n.s.). Taken together, our analysis provides initial evidence that equal participation in conversations may encourage students to meet their peers again just as higher geographic diversity does.

DISCUSSION

This paper presents a low-cost approach to detecting turn taking in video conversations using commodity software like Google Hangouts. While this detection scheme is inherently imprecise, we demonstrate how results from this scheme are consistent with more elaborately gathered data from prior work. For example, we found that majority male groups were more dominant than groups that consisted mostly of females, replicating prior research [33]. This suggests that a low-cost method such as our $1 conversational turn detector can gather low-level turn data as effectively as more sophisticated approaches at scale.

Our experience suggests that low-level features such as turns, even when imprecisely detected, still yield useful insights. In particular, we see three applications for such techniques: a privacy-sensitive estimator for discussion quality, large-scale data that informs design, and active scaffolding that improves student discussions.

Even though participants in discussions may be dominant in many ways that our $1 turn detector cannot capture (e.g., by speaking more loudly, using a different tone of voice, not yielding the floor when two participants speak at the same time), we find that a combined Gini coefficient that comprises turn duration and frequency captures some dominant behavior as experienced by participants. In scenarios where a more intrusive collection of data is difficult, methods like ours may be suitable.

As a method to collect large-scale data to inform design, we can already see the value of the $1 turn detector. For example, we find that while balance is useful for outcomes like how much students felt they learned through discussions, other outcomes like students' willingness to discuss with a group again depends on how much other participants speak, but not how much participants themselves speak. This may enable us to extend previous interactive systems that deal with dominance in conversations, which seek to always balance participants' speaking (e.g. [13, 3]). Our findings suggest a more nuanced approach may be beneficial: for example, systems might encourage students who repeatedly report not wanting to be paired with their discussion partners to listen more.

Low-cost turn detection can also enable more dynamic conversation support. For example, if we are able to detect when a discussion is becoming dominated by one (or more) learners, the system might be designed to remind the dominant speaker(s) to encourage other group members to contribute. A designated facilitator to attend to group dynamics in distributed teams improves team outcomes [20, 27], yet the designers of Talkabout found that static moderation assistance with a volunteer moderator led to discussions that were less motivating and where students were less willing to meet with the same group again [16].

Still, this low-cost method has its limitations. Prior research has shown that low-level features, such as patterns of conversational turns cannot predict learning gains for students as well as semantic indicators (e.g., such as the transcript of what was spoken) [24]. This is consistent with our analysis, which shows that our data cannot capture higher-level subjective information (e.g., students' perceptions of how much knowledge was shared in their discussion).

CONCLUSIONS AND FUTURE WORK

This paper presents an imprecise but practically useful turn-detector for video-conferencing based conversations. Through a case study of a discussion system used in many MOOCs, we examine the benefits and limitations of this approach.

Through our work, we find that even simple turn detection may be useful for certain applications, such as detecting dominance. However, semantic information is necessary to accurately predict other outcomes, such as grades and participants' subjective approval of their discussion partners.

We see three opportunities for future work. First, we are investigating how approximate turn information can be composed into metrics beyond dominance. For instance, without access to the conversation itself, could we detect that some participants are performing facilitation behaviors such as choosing discussion topics or asking other participants to contribute? Ideally, such predictions would be available to system designers in real time. Second, we are investigating how the $1 conversational turn detector can be used to provide active conversation support. Even knowing the state of a discussion may help designers better structure discussions. Finally, low-level signals like detected turns could be combined with high-level signals, such as participants' self-reported measures, not only to improve current discussions, but also to choose better discussion partners and teams.

ACKNOWLEDGMENTS

We thank Julia Cambre for her initial implementation of a turn-taking system in Talkabout. We sincerely thank the anonymous reviewers' for their generous feedback; Coursera and the OpenEdX teams for platform integration; and the instructors and students of the MOOCs who use Talkabout. This research was funded in part through NSF grants #1351131 and #1444865.

REFERENCES

1. *Google Hangouts Developer API.* https://developers.google.com/+/hangouts/. Accessed on October 31, 2015.
2. Edith Ackermann. 1996. Perspective-taking and object construction: two keys to learning. *Constructionism in practice: designing, thinking, and learning in a digital world, Lawrence Erlbaum, Mahwah, NJ* (1996), 25–35.
3. Tony Bergstrom and Karrie Karahalios. 2007. Seeing more: visualizing audio cues. In *Human-Computer Interaction–INTERACT 2007.* Springer, 29–42.
4. D Coetzee, Seongtaek Lim, Armando Fox, Bjorn Hartmann, and Marti A Hearst. 2015. Structuring interactions for large-scale synchronous peer learning. In *Proceedings of the 18th ACM Conference on Computer Supported Cooperative Work & Social Computing.* ACM, 1139–1152.
5. Richard L Daft and Robert H Lengel. 1986. Organizational information requirements, media richness and structural design. *Management science* 32, 5 (1986), 554–571.
6. Myron H Dembo and Timothy J McAuliffe. 1987. Effects of perceived ability and grade status on social interaction and influence in cooperative groups. *Journal of Educational Psychology* 79, 4 (1987), 415.
7. Gerardine DeSanctis, Anne-Laure Fayard, Michael Roach, and Lu Jiang. 2003. Learning in online forums. *European Management Journal* 21, 5 (2003), 565–577.
8. Starkey Duncan. 1972. Some signals and rules for taking speaking turns in conversations. *Journal of personality and social psychology* 23, 2 (1972), 283.
9. Nicolas Fay, Simon Garrod, and Jean Carletta. 2000. Group discussion as interactive dialogue or as serial monologue: The influence of group size. *Psychological Science* 11, 6 (2000), 481–486.
10. Lynn S Fuchs, Douglas Fuchs, Johnell Bentz, Norris B Phillips, and Carol L Hamlett. 1994. The nature of student interactions during peer tutoring with and without prior training and experience. *American Educational Research Journal* 31, 1 (1994), 75–103.
11. Marti A Hearst. 2015. Can Natural Language Processing Become Natural Language Coaching?. In *Proceedings of the 53rd Annual Meeting of the Association for Computation Linguistics.* ACL, 1245–1252.

12. David W Johnson, Roger T Johnson, and Karl A Smith. 1991. Active learning: Cooperation in the college classroom. (1991).

13. Taemie Kim, Agnes Chang, Lindsey Holland, and Alex Sandy Pentland. 2008. Meeting mediator: enhancing group collaborationusing sociometric feedback. In *Proceedings of the 2008 ACM conference on Computer supported cooperative work*. ACM, 457–466.

14. Alison King. 1997. ASK to THINK-TEL WHY: A model of transactive peer tutoring for scaffolding higher level complex learning. *Educational psychologist* 32, 4 (1997), 221–235.

15. Yasmine Kotturi, Chinmay Kulkarni, Michael S Bernstein, and Scott Klemmer. 2015. Structure and messaging techniques for online peer learning systems that increase stickiness. In *Proceedings of the Second (2015) ACM Conference on Learning@ Scale*. ACM, 31–38.

16. Chinmay Kulkarni, Julia Cambre, Yasmine Kotturi, Michael S Bernstein, and Scott R Klemmer. 2015. Talkabout: Making distance matter with small groups in massive classes. In *Proceedings of the 18th ACM Conference on Computer Supported Cooperative Work & Social Computing*. ACM, 1116–1128.

17. Rohit Kumar, Carolyn P Rosé, Yi-Chia Wang, Mahesh Joshi, and Allen Robinson. 2007. Tutorial Dialogue as Adaptive Collaborative Learning Support. *Artificial Intelligence in Education: Building Technology Rich Learning Contexts that Work* 158 (2007), 383.

18. John M Levine and Richard L Moreland. 1990. Progress in small group research. *Annual review of psychology* 41, 1 (1990), 585–634.

19. Michael S Lew, Nicu Sebe, Chabane Djeraba, and Ramesh Jain. 2006. Content-based multimedia information retrieval: State of the art and challenges. *ACM Transactions on Multimedia Computing, Communications, and Applications (TOMM)* 2, 1 (2006), 1–19.

20. Gloria Mark, Jonathan Grudin, and Steven E Poltrock. 1999. Meeting at the desktop: An empirical study of virtually collocated teams. In *ECSCW '99*. Springer, 159–178.

21. Penelope L Peterson and Susan R Swing. 1985. Students' cognitions as mediators of the effectiveness of small-group learning. *Journal of Educational Psychology* 77, 3 (1985), 299.

22. Paul R Pintrich and Akane Zusho. 2007. Student motivation and self-regulated learning in the college classroom. In *The scholarship of teaching and learning in higher education: An evidence-based perspective*. Springer, 731–810.

23. Roy Rada. 1998. Efficiency and effectiveness in computer-supported peer-peer learning. *Computers and Education* 30, 3 (1998), 137–146.

24. Carolyn Rosé, Yi-Chia Wang, Yue Cui, Jaime Arguello, Karsten Stegmann, Armin Weinberger, and Frank Fischer. 2008. Analyzing collaborative learning processes automatically: Exploiting the advances of computational linguistics in computer-supported collaborative learning. *International journal of computer-supported collaborative learning* 3, 3 (2008), 237–271.

25. Andrew John Saltarelli. 2012. *Effects of Belongingness and Synchronicity on Face-to-face and Computer-mediated Online Cooperative Pedagogy*. Ph.D. Dissertation. East Lansing, MI, USA. Advisor(s) Roseth, Cary J. AAI3505186.

26. Emanuel A Schegloff. 2000. Overlapping talk and the organization of turn-taking for conversation. *Language in society* 29, 01 (2000), 1–63.

27. Pao Siangliulue, Kenneth C Arnold, Krzysztof Z Gajos, and Steven P Dow. 2015. Toward Collaborative Ideation at Scale: Leveraging Ideas from Others to Generate More Creative and Diverse Ideas. In *Proceedings of the 18th ACM Conference on Computer Supported Cooperative Work & Social Computing*. ACM, 937–945.

28. Michelle K Smith, William B Wood, Wendy K Adams, Carl Wieman, Jennifer K Knight, Nancy Guild, and Tin Tin Su. 2009. Why peer discussion improves student performance on in-class concept questions. *Science* 323, 5910 (2009), 122–124.

29. Jennifer L Steel. 1991. Interpersonal correlates of trust and self-disclosure. *Psychological Reports* 68, 3c (1991), 1319–1320.

30. Cynthia S Symons and Blair T Johnson. 1997. The self-reference effect in memory: a meta-analysis. *Psychological bulletin* 121, 3 (1997), 371.

31. Yla R Tausczik and James W Pennebaker. 2013. Improving teamwork using real-time language feedback. In *Proceedings of the SIGCHI Conference on Human Factors in Computing Systems*. ACM, 459–468.

32. Keith J Topping. 1996. The effectiveness of peer tutoring in further and higher education: A typology and review of the literature. *Higher education* 32, 3 (1996), 321–345.

33. Anita Williams Woolley, Christopher F Chabris, Alex Pentland, Nada Hashmi, and Thomas W Malone. 2010. Evidence for a collective intelligence factor in the performance of human groups. *Science* 330, 6004 (2010), 686–688.

Course Builder Skill Maps

Boris Roussev
Google, Inc.
1600 Amphitheater Parkway
Mountain View, CA 94043 USA
borislavr@google.com

Pavel Simakov
Google, Inc.
1600 Amphitheater Parkway
Mountain View, CA 94043 USA
psimakov@google.com

John Orr
Google, Inc.
1600 Amphitheater Parkway
Mountain View, CA 94043 USA
jorr@google.com

Amit Deutsch
Google, Inc.
1600 Amphitheater Parkway
Mountain View, CA 94043 USA
amitdeutsch@google.com

John Cox
Google, Inc.
1600 Amphitheater Parkway
Mountain View, CA 94043 USA
johncox@google.com

Michael Lenaghan
Google, Inc.
1600 Amphitheater Parkway
Mountain View, CA 94043 USA
mlenaghan@google.com

Mike Gainer
Google, Inc.
1600 Amphitheater Parkway
Mountain View, CA 94043 USA
mgainer@google.com

L@S 2016, April 25-26, 2016, Edinburgh, Scotland UK
ACM 978-1-4503-3726-7/16/04.
http://dx.doi.org/10.1145/2876034.2893374

Abstract
In this paper, we present a new set of features introduced in Course Builder that allow instructors to add skill maps to their courses. We show how skill maps can be used to provide up-to-date and actionable information on students' learning behavior and performance.

Author Keywords
Skill Maps; Adaptive Learning; Learning Analytics; MOOCs

Introduction
On-line learners need up-to-date information on their progress, areas of strength and weakness, how to adapt their learning behavior, and personalized paths through the material they are learning [7]. Instead, they often get static information presented to them, with interactivity and personalization limited to scores on graded, summative assessments. Instructor visibility into student performance is often limited to averages and distributions of class scores. Worse, gathering this data usually happens after, rather than during, student engagement with a unit of content [5].

To address these shortcomings, online learning platforms employ learning analytics [5]. To implement these analytics for specific pieces of content, course designers need to define the knowledge domain of their course, and understand student learning states.

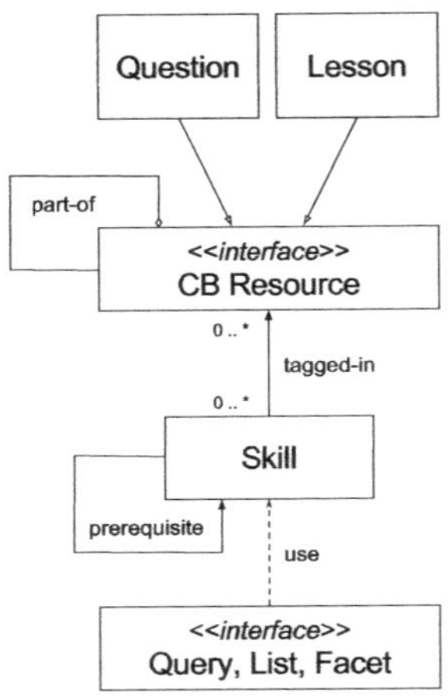

Figure 1. UML diagram of the Course Builder skill map and its relationship to learning resources.

Course Builder (CB) is an open-source platform developed by Google for delivering online courses at scale. Over the past four years, Google, nonprofit organizations and universities have used CB to create hundreds of online courses in multiple languages reaching over 2 million students worldwide. CB version 1.10 includes new features that allow instructors to add skill maps to their courses. This paper describes the approach taken in CB and compares related approaches.

Course Builder Skill Map Model

In the CB model, a skill is any unit of knowledge in the course which can be taught or assessed. In CB lessons contain course material such as text, videos, and activities. Lessons within a course are usually presented linearly. Now each lesson can also be tagged with the *skills* taught. A skill may depend on several previous skills taught elsewhere in the course, and it may have zero or more follow-on skills that depend on it. Navigating the course by skill, rather than lesson, allows students to traverse the course nonlinearly. For example, students interested in just one skill may view only the subset of lessons that teach that skill.

In addition to lessons, instructors are able to tag questions and other learning resources with skills as illustrated by the Unified Modeling Language diagram in Figure 1. The *Query*, *List*, *Facet* interface and the *use* association model a set of classes implementing functionality for querying, grouping, aggregating, and faceting the skill map. The recursive *part-of* association on Resource defines the course resource graph through aggregation and transclusion.

Course Builder Skill Map Features

We have extended the instructor's view of the course outline to show the skills taught in all lessons. We have also added a skill map dashboard with a tabular and graphical view. On the tabular view the instructor can see all the skills, their prerequisites, follow-ons, and what lessons they are taught in. In the graphical view the instructor can see the web of dependencies between skills. Here, the instructor can focus in on a particular skill or rearrange the layout of the graph to understand better the intricate relationships of the skills.

Figure 2. Student's perspective of the lesson view

The student's perspective of the lesson view is shown on Figure 2. It has a collapsible knowledge panel listing the skills taught in a particular lesson. The knowledge panel shows details about the skills in a lesson, including name, description, and level of mastery; it also shows the lesson's prerequisite skills and the skills that follow-on from it. Each skill on the panel links to the content unit where it is taught, so students who want to find their own pathways through the course

For the instructor, the skill map opens up interesting new analytics information. We have added two new views to the analytics dashboard. The first displays the student proficiency distributions for all skills in a unit, see Figure 3. The second draws a chart that compares student progress on selected skills over the lifetime of a course.

From a pedagogical point of view, skill maps enable a goal-oriented course design approach: course creators can start with the skills they want to teach and design the course content around them.

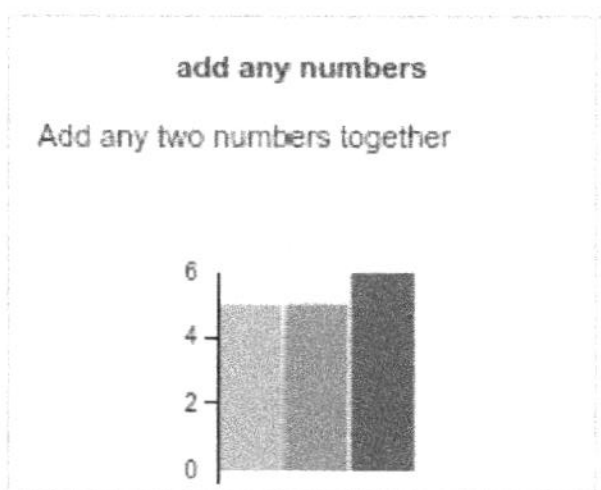

Figure 3. Analytics dashboard for skill competencies

and explore all the different links can use the panel to personalize their learning experience [6].

In addition to displaying information about the skills taught in a lesson, the knowledge panel provides a meta-cognitive signal, which may help students get deeper understanding of the content and explore the course in a way that meets better their personal needs.

Comparison with Two Related Systems

The Open Learning Initiative (OLI), which began at Carnegie Mellon University in 2002, creates web-based courses designed so students can learn effectively without an instructor. OLI uses a two-tiered model: high-level objectives which specify what students will be able to do at the end of each instructional module, backed by one or more skills representing a discrete concept or knowledge component [2]. Interactive activities and quizzes are used to assess students' learning of the various skills. OLI uses Bayesian Knowledge Tracing (BKT) to estimate the probability a student has learned each skill [1] and mastery of an objective is calculated by averaging the scores of the skills that make up the objective.

Unlike the OLI model, the CB skill map is single-tiered, with the addition of the prerequisite relation. The OLI model uses objectives in order to roll up aggregate data for reporting, since skill maps tend to be large and the fine-grained data of competency on a skill-by-skill basis is often not useful. However the OLI model encodes one particular set of roll-ups in the many-to-many mapping of skills to objectives. In our model, we recognize the need for rollups but leave open the possibility of aggregating along multiple different axes, e.g. by course section (that is, unit or lesson); by terminal skill (that is, skills which sit at the head of chains of dependencies); or by other categories. This flexibility is reflected in the Query/List/Facet interfaces in Figure 1 above.

The OLI model also does not include any prerequisite relation between skills. In CB, prerequisite relations make it possible to make inferences about the student learning state. If we conclude that a student knows a particular skill, we can reason probabilistically that the student also knows all its prerequisite skills. We can apply the same process of reasoning going from prerequisites to follow-on skills. This can be used in efficient adaptive testing.

Learning Space Theory (LST) is used as the theoretical basis for ALEKS. In LST, the basic unit of knowledge is a parameterized question [3] and the student knowledge state is the set of all questions in the domain that the student is capable of solving. Not all knowledge states are feasible; a student who cannot add single-digit numbers likely cannot add double-digit numbers either. The collection of all feasible states satisfying certain regularity conditions is called a *learning space*. At least initially, a learning space is designed using human experts. The time of these experts is expensive, so a major issue is state explosion. A learning space with *n* questions theoretically has 2^n states although in practice there are much fewer. Pruning the space is done with a series of entailment queries of the form "Do you believe a student who has failed questions $\{q_1 \ldots q_n\}$ would also fail question q_{n+1} ?" [3] and the number of queries required can easily grow to the thousands.

Unlike LST, CB explicitly defines the structure of the knowledge domain using the prerequisite relation. Our deterministic skill map model cannot express alternate sets of prerequisites, whereas in LST there may be more than one way to achieve mastery on a question. One could address this limitation by extending the base skill map model with a belief network derived from the skills graph with prior and conditional probabilities for the nodes.

Moreover, the trade-off for LST's generality is the complexity of validating the learning space. This commonly involves systematically questioning experts to capture their personal knowledge structure. The limitations include a lack of consistency between the experts' structures and the large number of questions the experts have to answer.

Because the CB prerequisite graph is designed by domain experts we can assume that it is *correct* but possibly *incomplete*. When course developers underestimate relationships between skills, they have failed to recognize their own *expert blind spots*: areas where the very understanding necessary to teach a domain leads experts to miss the learning needs of novices [4]. Thus we can use a validation algorithm which focuses only on adding the missing prerequisites.

References

[1] Ryan Baker, Albert Corbett, and Vincent Aleven. 2008. More Accurate Student Modeling through Contextual Estimation of Slip and Guess Probabilities in Bayesian Knowledge Tracing. Intelligent Tutoring Systems Lecture Notes in Computer Science, 406-415.

[2] Norman Bier, Sean Lip, Ross Strader, Candace Thille, and Dawn Zimmaro. 2014. An Approach to Knowledge Component/Skill Modeling in Online Courses. White paper. Retrieved October 5, 2015 from http://oli.stanford.edu/.

[3] Jean-Clause Falmagne and Jean-Paul Doignon. 2011. Learning Spaces. Interdisciplinary Applied Mathematics. Springer.

[4] Pamela Hinds. 1999. The curse of expertise: The effects of expertise and debiasing methods on prediction of novice performance. *Journal of Experimental Psychology: Applied*. 5, 2: 205-221.

[5] Marsha Lovett. 2012. Cognitively informed analytics to improve teaching and learning. Presentation at EDUCAUSE Sprint. Retrieved October 5, 2015 from http://www.educause.edu/ir/library/powerpoint/ESPNT122Lovett.ppt.

[6] Barbara Means, Yukie Toyama, Robert Murphy, Marianne Bakia, and Karla Jones. 2010. Evaluation of Evidence-Based Practices in Online Learning: A Meta-Analysis and Review of Online Learning Studies. US Department of Education. Washington, DC/

[7] Gilbert Paquette, Olga Mariño, Delia Rogozan, and Michel Léonard. 2015. Competency-based personalization for massive online learning. *Smart Learning Environments*. 2, 4.

Learning Student and Content Embeddings for Personalized Lesson Sequence Recommendation

Siddharth Reddy
Dept. of Computer Science,
Cornell University
Ithaca, NY 14850, USA
sgr45@cornell.edu

Igor Labutov
Dept. of Electrical and
Computer Engineering, Cornell
University
Ithaca, NY 14850, USA
iil4@cornell.edu

Thorsten Joachims
Dept. of Computer Science,
Cornell University
Ithaca, NY 14850, USA
tj@cs.cornell.edu

L@S 2016, April 25–26, 2016, Edinburgh, UK.
ACM 978-1-4503-3726-7/16/04.
http://dx.doi.org/10.1145/2876034.2893375

Abstract
Students in online courses generate large amounts of data that can be used to personalize the learning process and improve quality of education. In this paper, we present the Latent Skill Embedding (LSE), a probabilistic model of students and educational content that can be used to recommend personalized sequences of lessons with the goal of helping students prepare for specific assessments. Akin to collaborative filtering for recommender systems, the algorithm does not require students or content to be described by features, but it learns a representation using access traces. We formulate this problem as a regularized maximum-likelihood embedding of students, lessons, and assessments from historical student-content interactions. Empirical findings on large-scale data from Knewton, an adaptive learning technology company, show that this approach predicts assessment results competitively with benchmark models and is able to discriminate between lesson sequences that lead to mastery and failure.

Author Keywords
Probabilistic Embedding; Sequence Recommendation; Adaptive Learning

Introduction
The popularity of online education platforms has soared in recent years. Companies like Coursera and EdX offer

Massive Open Online Courses (MOOCs) that improve access to high quality educational content for anyone connected to the Internet. However, in these online environments learners often lack the personalized instruction and coaching that can potentially lead to significant improvements in educational outcomes. Furthermore, the educational content may be contributed by many authors without a formal underlying structure. Intelligent systems that learn about the educational properties of the content and guide learners through custom lesson plans could help learners take advantage of large and heterogeneous collections of educational content to achieve their goals.

Our aim is to build a domain-agnostic framework for modeling students and content that can be used for personalized lesson sequence recommendation. A common data source available in online learning products is *access traces* that log student interactions with modules of course content. These access traces have the form *Student A completed Lesson B* and *Student C passed assessment D*. *Lessons* are content modules that introduce or reinforce concepts, and *assessments* are content modules with pass-fail results that test student skills. We use access traces to embed students, lessons, and assessments together in a joint semantic space, yielding a representation that can be used to reason about the relationship between students and content (e.g., the likelihood of passing an assessment, or the skill gains achieved by completing a lesson). The model is evaluated on simple synthetic scenarios, as well as large-scale real data from Knewton, an education technology company that offers personalized recommendations and activity analytics for online courses.

Related Work Our work builds on the existing literature in psychometric user and content modeling, including the Rasch model [7], temporal and multi-dimensional item response theory [3, 8, 5], Bayesian knowledge tracing [2], sparse factor analysis [4], and deep knowledge tracing [6]. We extend this work in a multi-dimensional setting where student knowledge evolves over time in a continuous state space, and explicitly-modeled lesson prerequisites modulate knowledge gains from lesson modules.

Embedding Model

We now describe a probabilistic model that places students, lessons, and assessments together in a *latent skill space*. Students have trajectories through the latent skill space, while assessments and lessons are placed at fixed locations. Formally, a student is represented as a set of d latent skill levels $\vec{s} \in \mathbb{R}_+^d$; a lesson module is represented as a vector of skill gains $\vec{\ell} \in \mathbb{R}_+^d$ and a set of prerequisite skill requirements $\vec{q} \in \mathbb{R}_+^d$; an assessment module is represented as a set of skill requirements $\vec{a} \in \mathbb{R}_+^d$. A student can be tested on an assessment module with a pass-fail result $R \in \{0, 1\}$, where the likelihood of passing is high when a student has skill levels that exceed the assessment requirements and vice-versa. A student can also work on lesson modules to improve skill levels over time. To fully realize the skill gains associated with completing a lesson module, a student must satisfy prerequisites. Time is discretized such that at every timestep $t \in \mathbb{N}$, a student completes a lesson and may complete zero or many assessments. The evolution of student knowledge can be formalized as an *input-output hidden Markov model*.

Assessment results are modeled as follows: for student $\vec{s}$, assessment $\vec{a}$, and result R,

$$R \sim \text{Bernoulli}(\phi(\Delta(\vec{s},\ \vec{a}))) \tag{1}$$

where ϕ is the logistic function, and

$$\Delta(\vec{s},\ \vec{a}) = \frac{\vec{s} \cdot \vec{a}}{||\vec{a}||} - ||\vec{a}|| + \gamma_s + \gamma_a \tag{2}$$

where γ_s is a student-specific bias term and γ_a is an assessment-specific bias term. Student learning from lessons is modeled as follows: for student $\vec{s}$ who worked on a lesson with skill gains $\vec{\ell}$ and prerequisites $\vec{q}$ at time $t+1$, the updated student state is

$$\vec{s}_{t+1} \sim \mathcal{N}\left(\vec{s}_t + \vec{\ell} \cdot \phi(\Delta(\vec{s}_t,\ \vec{q})),\ \Sigma\right) \tag{3}$$

where the covariance matrix $\Sigma = I_d \sigma^2$ is isotropic. We estimate model parameters from log data using maximum-likelihood estimation with L_2 regularization, and select hyperparameters using cross-validation. Examples of embeddings trained on synthetic log data are given in Figures 1 and 2.

Experiments on Online Course Data

To evaluate the embedding model, we use data processed by Knewton, an adaptive learning technology company whose infrastructure uses access traces to generate personalized recommendations and activity analytics for online learning products. The data describes interactions between college students and two science textbooks, and collectively consists of 2.18 million access traces from over 7,000 students, recorded in 1,939 classrooms over a combined period of 5 months. The following summarizes the main findings – details and further results can be found in [1]. We first evaluate the embedding model on the task of predicting results of held-out assessment interactions, and find that the embedding performs comparably to benchmark models from item response theory. We then introduce a novel prediction task to more directly evaluate the embedding model on its ability to distinguish between lesson sequences that lead to mastery and failure on target assessments. Using *propensity score matching* [9] to de-bias the observational data from Knewton, we find that the model is generally able to recommend successful paths.

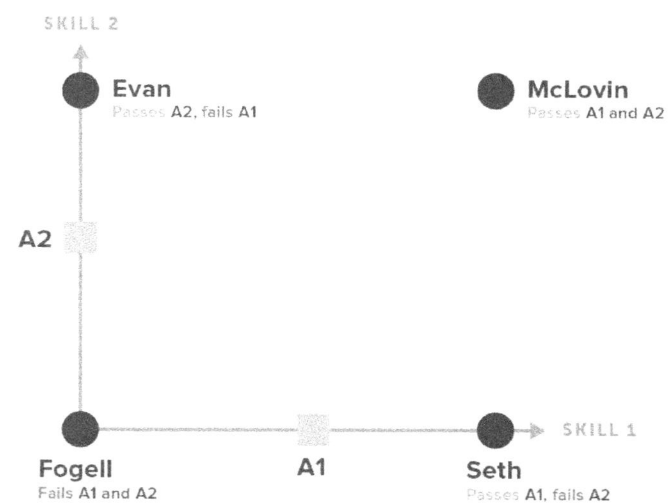

Figure 1: A two-dimensional embedding without lessons

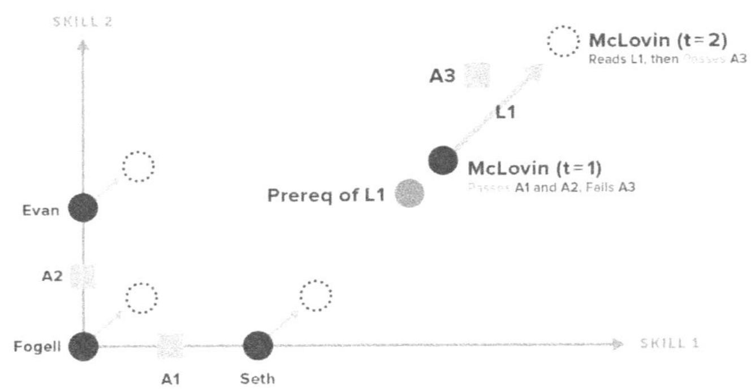

Figure 2: A two-dimensional embedding with lessons and prerequisites

Conclusions

We presented a general model that learns a representation of student knowledge and educational content that can be used for personalized instruction. The key idea lies in using a multi-dimensional embedding to capture the dynamics of learning and testing. Using a large-scale data set collected in real-world classrooms, we (1) demonstrate the ability of the model to successfully predict learning outcomes and (2) introduce an offline methodology as a proxy for assessing the ability of the model to recommend personalized learning paths. We show that our model is able to successfully discriminate between personalized learning paths that lead to mastery and failure.

An implementation of the Latent Skill Embedding and the IPython notebooks used to conduct experiments – as well as a full paper with a comprehensive description of our methods and results – are available online [1].

We thank Knewton for valuable feedback. This research was funded in part NSF Awards IIS-1247637, IIS-1217686, and IIS-1513692, a grant from the John Templeton Foundation provided through the Metaknowledge Network at the University of Chicago, and through the Cornell Presidential Research Scholars program.

References

[1] Latent skill embedding. http://siddharth.io/lentil.
[2] Corbett, A. T., and Anderson, J. R. Knowledge tracing: Modeling the acquisition of procedural knowledge. *User Modeling and User-Adapted Interaction 4*, 4 (1994), 253–278.
[3] Ekanadham, C., and Karklin, Y. T-skirt: Online estimation of student proficiency in an adaptive learning system. *Machine Learning for Education Workshop at ICML* (2015).
[4] Lan, A. S., Studer, C., and Baraniuk, R. G. Time-varying learning and content analytics via sparse factor analysis. In *Proceedings of the 20th ACM SIGKDD international conference on Knowledge discovery and data mining*, ACM (2014), 452–461.
[5] Linden, W., and Hambleton, R. K. Handbook of modern item response theory. *New York* (1997).
[6] Piech, C., Bassen, J., Huang, J., Ganguli, S., Sahami, M., Guibas, L. J., and Sohl-Dickstein, J. Deep knowledge tracing. In *Advances in Neural Information Processing Systems* (2015), 505–513.
[7] Rasch, G. *Probabilistic models for some intelligence and attainment tests*. ERIC, 1993.
[8] Reckase, M. D. *Multidimensional Item Response Theory*, first ed. Springer Publishing Company, Incorporated, 2009.
[9] Rosenbaum, P. R., and Rubin, D. B. The central role of the propensity score in observational studies for causal effects. *Biometrika 70*, 1 (1983), 41–55.

Supporting Scalable Data Sharing in Online Education

Stephen Cummins
Computer Laboratory
University of Cambridge
Cambridge, UK
Stephen.Cummins@cl.cam.ac.uk

Alastair R. Beresford
Computer Laboratory
University of Cambridge
Cambridge, UK
Alastair.Beresford@cl.cam.ac.uk

Ian Davies
Computer Laboratory
University of Cambridge
Cambridge, UK
Ian.Davies@cl.cam.ac.uk

Andrew Rice
Computer Laboratory
University of Cambridge
Cambridge, UK
Andrew.Rice@cl.cam.ac.uk

L@S 2016, April 25-26, 2016, Edinburgh, Scotland UK
ACM 978-1-4503-3726-7/16/04.
http://dx.doi.org/10.1145/2876034.2893376

Abstract
Online educational tools often generate learning data, and sharing such data between tutors and students can often improve learning outcomes. Unfortunately the process of sharing learning data today is not always transparent to students. Our aim is to improve the transparency and user control aspects of sharing data whilst maintaining the educational utility of data sharing between tutors and students. To do so, we start by surveying the possible methods of sharing data, and we use this to design a token-based scheme for facilitating data sharing. We implemented our scheme and observed it in use by 7,798 students over the course of one year. We find that our proposed scheme provides a good balance between transparency, user control, educational utility and scalability.

Author Keywords
Privacy; Authorisation; Review; Data Sharing

ACM Classification Keywords
K.3.1 [COMPUTERS AND EDUCATION]: Computer Uses in Education

Introduction
A key feature of supporting online learning at scale is to ensure safe and reliable data exchange between learners and any collaborators such as tutors or classmates. The is huge

value in the interaction between students and tutors, students and their peers, or indeed for tutors to make informed and targeted interventions during the learning process [1]. This human aspect is amongst the most important for providing motivational support, as well as much needed access to someone with an interest and expertise in the subject.

Learning data captures the personal journey of the student, and often includes metadata such as their name and contact details. Therefore a secure mechanism of sharing learner data is an important consideration when designing online platforms which support informal relationships between students and their tutors and peers.

Existing Models of Sharing Data

We have identified five different models which platforms could use to authorise and orchestrate the sharing of data between students and tutors. Not all these models are commonly used in the education sector today. We label the five models as *Public*, *Reciprocal*, *Anonymous*, *Enrolment*, and *Token*.

The *Public* model makes all data available to any user of the system. An example of this model in practice is the micro-blogging site, Twitter. Posts on Twitter are accessible to all users and non-users equally, with some profile information also publicly visible.

The *Reciprocal* model is used by platforms such as Facebook and LinkedIn. Users of these platforms search a public directory of user profiles to request access to more detailed information. If a request is granted, a bi-directional link is established such that each user may view detailed information of the other.

The *Anonymous* model aims to remove personally-identifiable information from any shared data. For example, previous studies have proposed the peer-wise sharing of marked work and any associated tutor feedback between students [2].

The *Enrolment* model involves users registering for a particular service, or joining an institution and thereby granting access to their data to other members of the service or organisation. Examples in the education sector include EdX, Coursera, or Moodle, where course registration is directly connected to a default data sharing policy.

The *Token* model relies participants sharing authorisation tokens between themselves to grant access to data items. Examples include shareable URLs to enable document collaboration using Google Docs. We have developed a token-based approach for our platform where a tutor can set students work by sending students a digital token generated by the platform. Independently, Khan Academy has recently adopted a token model to share learning data.

The enrolment model and the token model support different approaches to online learning. Under the enrolment model, a centralised approach to course delivery is required because course registration is directly couple with a structured approach to content delivery and an associated sharing policy for learning data. As a result, students trust the course provider to enrol suitable tutors, limiting transparency on what happens to their data. This approach also limits scalability – neither external tutors nor students cannot borrow or reuse course components delivered on these platforms in other contexts. Indeed, a common policy is that if a user wishes to withdraw their consent for data sharing they must deregister from the course and they can no longer access any content. An important benefit of the enrolment model is that students do not need to explicitly authorise access to their learning data – the platform does this automatically.

	Dimensions		
Platforms	*Model of Data Sharing*	*Who is granted access*	*Ability to withdraw*
Coursera	Enrolment	Organisation	Yes†
EdX	Enrolment	Organisation	Yes†
Isaac Physics	Token	Individual	Yes
Khan Academy	Token	Individual	Yes
Moodle	Enrolment	Organisation	No
SWATT	Anonymous	Group	No

Table 1: Classification of Learning Environments: †Indicates no further access to course materials if the user revokes access to their data.

The token model supports a decentralised approach to online learning. Students and tutors can bring together material in any order to build a course or programme of work. This approach is more scaleable because the delivery of content and provision of support is not contingent on any particular party. The disadvantage, when compared with the enrolment model, is the overhead associated with building the course, and configuring the data sharing policy – something which can no longer be automated since there is no centralised register of trustworthy tutors. In the token model, users are able to revoke access to their data at any time without penalty. Furthermore, course content is typically available for free without any connection to a tutor or course timetable or other structure.

Table 1 summarises six online learning platforms. With the important exception of Khan Academy, the popular platforms currently use the enrolment model.

The Isaac Platform & Data Sharing

Isaac Physics is a project funded by the Department for Education and Skills in England which Supports the transition between school and Higher Education. In particular, the project focuses on developing students' problem solving skills.

In order to support a decentralised model of online learning, we need a mechanism to support the sharing of learning data between tutors and students. We therefore implemented an out-of-band token-based model. First the tutor, teacher, or coach (T), asks the platform to generate a token for a specific activity or piece of work. Second, T shares the token with one or more students (S).

When a token is entered by S, the platform asks them if they would like to share their learning data with T. To provide some confidence to S of the provenance of T, the system exposes the name and email address of T. This allows S to be confident that they have entered the correct token.

The token itself is an eight-character alphanumeric code, for example HA12-PG8Y. A short token is important since it can be easily written by T on a whiteboard or copied into a notebook. The consequence of this is that rate limiting is required on the platform to prevent brute-force attacks in which a malicious S attempts to join an activity run by a tutor T who has not shared the token with S.

Once access has been granted by S, then T can view S's learning data, including any answers provided by S. S may revoke access to T, in which case T is informed that they no longer have access to view any of S's learning data.

Results and Discussion

The Isaac platform has been live since September 2014, and after one year, Isaac had 10,565 registered users (4,878 Male, 1,957 Female and 3,730 unspecified) and 105,124 anonymous users generating over 2,197,010 data points.

For the purpose of this paper, we excluded all users who we know are teachers in schools and all users who have not yet made at least one question attempt, either correctly or incorrectly. A total of 7,798 out of our 10,565 users are eligible under these criteria.

In total, 5,455 students (69.95%) engaged with the data sharing mechanism on the platform and 2,343 (30.05%) have not. A total of 27 (1.1%) students used the revocation option to prevent a previously authorised tutor from viewing their data.

We analysed the usage data of students who connect to a tutor (coached users) when compared to those who have not (uncoached users). Coached users attempt a Minimum (m), Median (M), and 90th percentile (P_{90}) of $m = 0$, $M = 55$, $P_{90} = 195$ questions, whereas uncoached attempt $m = 0$, $M = 16$, $P_{90} = 99$.

On average, coached users eventually answer more questions correctly ($m = 0$, $M = 22$, $P_{90} = 74$) compared to uncoached users ($m = 0$, $M = 5$, $P_{90} = 35$), but they also tend to answer more incorrectly ($m = 0$, $M = 9$, $P_{90} = 31$ vs. $m = 0$, $M = 3$, $P_{90} = 16$). This may be because coached users are aware that a tutor will see their end result, and not necessarily how many attempts they made at any particular question. This data does not necessarily suggest that the act of sharing learning data with a tutor directly leads to a difference in interaction; further work is needed to understand this relationship.

Conclusion & future work

We have reviewed a number of different strategies for sharing learning data in online learning platforms and we developed a token-based approach to support controlled sharing of learning data to support a decentralised learning model.

We found a difference in behaviour between users who have shared learning data with a tutor and those who have not. Students supported by a tutor attempt more questions than those who do not, which may be an indication of greater motivation. There are a number of possible explanations. A tutor who assigns work and monitor progress encourages engagement. Furthermore, access to external, tailored and targeted support maintains momentum and promotes student progression.

We intend to investigate the relationship between sharing learning data with tutors further. In addition we intend to enabling any users of Isaac to create data sharing links with each other, with the aim of fostering a peer-learning network.

REFERENCES

1. Michelene T. H. Chi. 2009. Active-Constructive-Interactive: A Conceptual Framework for Differentiating Learning Activities. *Topics in Cognitive Science* 1, 1 (Jan. 2009), 73–105.
2. Stephen Cummins, Liz Burd, and Andrew Hatch. 2011. Investigating shareable feedback tags for programming assignments. *Computer Science Education* 21, 1 (March 2011), 81–103.

Recommending Self-Regulated Learning Strategies Does Not Improve Performance in a MOOC

René F. Kizilcec
Stanford University
Stanford, CA, USA
kizilcec@stanford.edu

Mar Pérez-Sanagustín
Pontificia U. Católica de Chile
Santiago, Chile
mar.perez@ing.puc.cl

Jorge J. Maldonado
Pontificia U. Católica de Chile & Universidad de Cuenca, Ecuador
jjmaldonado@uc.cl

Author Keywords
Massive Open Online Course; Self-Regulated Learning.

ACM Classification Keywords: K.3.1. COMPUTERS AND EDUCATION: Computer uses in Education.

L@S 2016, April 25-26, 2016, Edinburgh, Scotland, UK
ACM 978-1-4503-3726-7/16/04.
http://dx.doi.org/10.1145/2876034.2893378

Abstract
Many committed learners struggle to achieve their goal of completing a Massive Open Online Course (MOOC). This work investigates self-regulated learning (SRL) in MOOCs and tests if encouraging the use of SRL strategies can improve course performance. We asked 17 highly successful learners about their strategies for how to succeed in a MOOC. Their responses were coded based on a SRL framework and synthesized into seven recommendations. In a randomized experiment, we evaluated the effect of providing the recommendations to learners in the same course ($N = 653$). Although most learners rated the study tips as *very helpful*, the intervention did not improve course persistence or achievement. Results suggest that a single SRL prompt at the beginning of the course provides insufficient support. Instead, embedding technological aids that adaptively support SRL throughout the course could better support learners in MOOCs.

Introduction
A primary goal of MOOCs is to provide people with an opportunity to learn. Although only a small number of those who start go on to complete the entire course, many online learners selectively engage with parts of the content [3,5,7]. This variation in behavior can be attributed in part to differences in motivation [8,15].

In fact, only around half of the survey respondents in a typical MOOC report an intention to complete the course to earn a certificate [8]. However, that leaves hundreds of thousands of committed learners who want to complete the course, but do not succeed. The main obstacle, according to recent surveys, is that learners do not have enough time to spend on the course [5,6]. While time is a finite resource, there are more and less effective strategies for time management, and more broadly, strategies for how to succeed in completing an online course. What are effective strategies to complete a MOOC and how can online learners be empowered to apply those strategies?

Self-regulated learning (SRL) strategies have been studied for decades in traditional classroom settings. SRL can be understood as the ability to control, manage, and plan learning actions and behavioral processes that increase goal attainment [12,17]. SRL skills improve as a person develops and keeps learning in pursuit of better academic outcomes. Students who apply SRL strategies are more successful in problem solving, and have higher academic achievement, intrinsic motivation, and task interests [12].

In addition, there is growing evidence for the role of SRL strategies in student achievement in online learning environments [4,10]. Multiple studies have shown that helping students apply metacognitive and resource management strategies is related to higher self-regulation and academic achievement in online environments [1,2,9,13]. Broadbent and Poon [4] found higher academic outcomes in online higher education settings among those who applied time management, metacognition, and effort regulation strategies. Moreover, research on MOOCs suggests that time management, planning, and self-monitoring skills are critical to succeed in these courses, but many learners struggle to engage in relevant self-regulation activities [8,15]. The absence of external pressure to make progress and clear social norms around completing these courses means that learners need to be highly self-directed to succeed. Littlejohn et al. [10] interviewed MOOC learners who were either high or low in self-regulation and identified behavioral differences between the two groups in terms of SRL sub-processes, including motivations and goal setting. In the current research, we asked successful learners about their own strategies to better understand SRL in MOOCs.

A relatively small amount of guidance could go a long way in supporting online learners. Self-regulation can be trained by helping learners apply SRL strategies, for instance, by providing additional scaffolding in the learning environment [17]. Several studies provide evidence that prompting SRL strategies can increase achievement [1,2,9,13]. For instance, prompting students either by suggesting metacognitive activities (e.g., thinking aloud about one's decisions) [2] or by asking them to explain their actions in pop-up windows [9] promoted self-regulation and raised performance. Thus, prior work in online environments suggests that prompting learners with SRL strategies can improve their performance.

Pilot: Strategies of the Most Successful

We conducted a pilot study of 17 highly successful MOOC learners who not only earned a Coursera certificate but additionally opted to take an in-person exam at Pontificia Universidad Católica de Chile to receive a certification recognized by the Chilean government. We surveyed these learners about the SRL strategies they found most useful for taking a MOOC. They wrote recommendations for other learners to help them succeed in the course. The 35 collected recommendations were coded independently by two researchers based on Pintrich's metacognitive and resource management categories [11]. We found seven strategies that these successful learners considered to be effective in MOOCs. Time management and effort regulation stood out as the most important strategies to succeed, consistent with prior work on SRL in online learning [4].

Study Tips Experiments

We leverage the SRL strategies that we had collected from successful learners in the form of study tips. Some learners were randomly assigned to receive study tips, while others completed a control activity. We assessed subsequent persistence and achievement outcomes to test the following hypothesis: *H1.* Prompting learners with SRL strategies improves persistence and achievement in a (self-paced) MOOC.

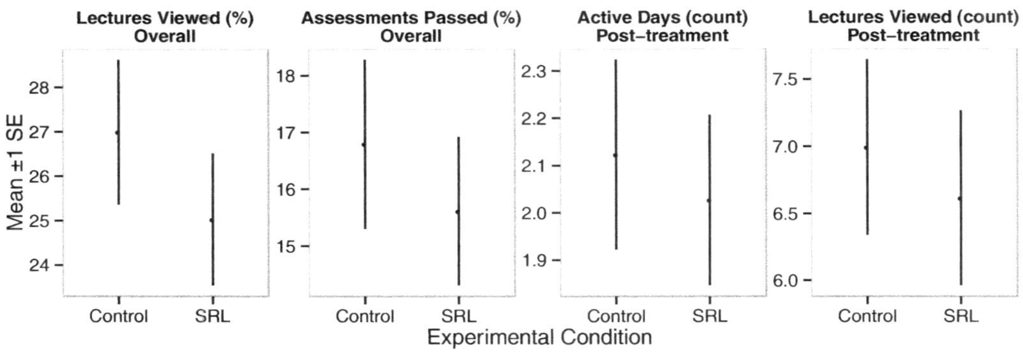

Figure 1. Course outcome measures examined as a function of experimental condition (N = 569).

Methods

The experiment was conducted several weeks later in the same MOOC as the pilot study. The experiment was embedded for 15 days in the course survey that was announced multiple times via email. Of the 820 survey responses, 741 reached the stage in the survey at which they were randomly assigned to conditions, and 653 unique participants who were not cross-exposed were retained in the final sample: 322 control and 331 SRL. The average age was 40 (SD = 10), 61% women, 89% with a bachelor's or higher degree. In the course survey, learners were randomly assigned to either a SRL condition or a control condition. In the SRL condition, participants were presented with seven recommended SRL strategies based on pilot findings.

They were told that "[w]e have interviewed people who have successfully completed the course to find out how they did it. The following strategies stood out as the most effective." Each strategy consisted of a brief label (review your goals constantly; take notes and summarize the course content to better understand it; apply what you learn; plan ahead; set yourself realistic goals; find fellow students; choose a good study environment) and a quotation collected in the pilot study. Participants rated how helpful they thought the strategies will be for them (from 1 to 5) and wrote a brief message addressed to new learners about the strategies to internalize them. In the control condition, participants were shown the official course description and course topics; rated how useful they thought the course will be for their career (from 1 to 5), and wrote a short message addressed to the course designers about the topics they found most/ least interesting. Behavioral data collected by the platform was available from months before the start of the experiment until 25 days after the start of the experiment. The main outcome measures were the percentage of lectures that learners' watched (i.e., persistence) and the percentage of assessments that learners' completed with a passing grade (i.e., achievement). Similar outcome measures were used in prior research with MOOCs [6,8]. Two additional behavioral outcomes were how many days learners were active in the course after taking the survey (post-treatment), and how many unique lectures they watched post-treatment. Corresponding pre-treatment measures served as covariates in the analysis. Participants also reported their gender, education level, course intentions, and prior experience with the topic.

Results and Discussion

Most learners who participated in the experiment had only recently started the course: 90% had been active for less than 2 weeks. However, 13% of survey respondents had already watched over 90% of lectures. They were excluded from further analysis, as the SRL strategies were intended to help learners at an earlier stage. Results were qualitatively equivalent when using an earlier cutoff. Moreover, random assignment was successful in providing two groups balanced in pre-treatment self-report measures ($ps > .35$) and behavioral measures ($ps > .48$). The control task provided a similar experience as in the SRL condition: Study tips were most commonly rated as *very helpful* (M = 3.87, SD = 0.88) in the SRL condition and course topics were rated as *very useful* (M = 4.20, SD = 0.78) in the control condition. In both conditions, around 72% of participants wrote a message (typed > 20 characters). A sample size of 569 yields 85% statistical power to detect effect sizes of only 0.25 SD. However, no significant benefit from providing SRL study tips over the control task was found for several course outcomes. The overall percentage of viewed lectures and passed assessments was similar in both conditions, and number of active days and viewed lectures following the intervention was almost identical (Fig. 1).

Covariate-adjusted OLS regression analyses with robust standard errors confirm this null result (*ps* > .56).

The findings suggest that merely telling MOOC learners about ways to engage in self-regulated learning does not lead to improvements in course persistence or achievement, despite our efforts to select especially relevant strategies and communicating them with authentic quotations. The prompt might have been too brief and insufficiently integrated with the rest of the course to scaffold the application of the strategies. Future work should focus on approaches to support SRL that are embedded in the course and adaptive to the learners' skills and motivations [10], such as activities to scaffold time management and metacognitive self-regulation strategies. Moreover, moving toward explanatory models for SRL interventions, a deeper understanding of learners' SRL profiles can support more targeted approaches to scaffolding the learning experience.

ACKNOWLEDGMENTS

This work was partially supported by the Project MOOC-Maker (14ENI2-26862) an the Fondecyt Project (11150231). Jorge Maldonado thanks the University of Cuen Ecuador for funding his doctoral studies a Pontificia Universidad Católica of Chile.

REFERENCES

1. R. Azevedo, D.C. Moos, J.A. Greene, F.I. Winters, & J.G. Cromley. 2008. Why is externally-facilitated regulated learning more effective than self-regulated learning with hypermedia? *Educational Technology Research & Development* 56, 1: 45–72.
2. M. Bannert & C. Mengelkamp. 2013. Scaffolding Hypermedia Learning Through Metacognitive Prompts. In *International Handbook of Metacognition & Learning Technologies Springer International Handbooks of Education*. 171–186.
3. L. Breslow, D. Pritchard, J. DeBoer, G. Stump, A. Ho, & D. Seaton. 2013. Studying learning in the worldwide classroom: Research into edX's first MOOC. *Research & Practice in Assessment* 8: 13–25.
4. J. Broadbent & W. Poon. 2015. Self-regulated learning strategies & academic achievement in online higher education learning environments: A systematic review. *The Internet & Higher Education* 27: 1–13.
5. A.D. Ho, I. Chuang, J. Reich, et al. 2015. HarvardX & MITx : Two Years of Open Online Courses Fall 2012-Summer 2014. *SSRN Electronic Journal*, 10: 1–37.
6. R.F. Kizilcec & S. Halawa. 2015. Attrition & Achievement Gaps in Online Learning. *Proceedings of the Second ACM Conference on Learning@Scale*, 57–66.
7. R.F. Kizilcec, C. Piech, & E. Schneider. 2013. Deconstructing Disengagement: Analyzing Learner Subpopulations in Massive Open Online Courses. *Proceeding s of the Third International Conference on Learning Analytics & Knowledge*, 170–179.
8. R.F. Kizilcec & E. Schneider. 2015. Motivation as a Lens to Understand Online Learners: Toward Data-Driven Design with the OLEI Scale. *Transactions on Computer-Human Interactions (TOCHI)* 22, 2: 24.
9. X. Lin & J.D. Lehman. 1999. Supporting Learning of Variable Control in a Computer-Based Biology Environment: Effects of Prompting College Students to Reflect on Their Own Thinking. *Journal of Research in Science Teaching* 36, 7: 837–858.
10. A. Littlejohn, N. Hood, C. Milligan, & P. Mustain. 2016. Learning in MOOCs: Motivations & self-regulated learning in MOOCs. *The Internet & Higher Education* 29: 40–48.
11. P.R. Pintrich. 1999. The role of motivation in promoting & sustaining self-regulated learning. *International journal of educational research* 31, 6: 459–470.
12. P.R. Pintrich. 2000. The Role of Goal Orientation in Self-Regulated Learning. In *Handbook of Self-Regulation*, Monique Boekaerts, P.R. Pintrich & M. Zeidner (eds.). Academic Press, 451–502.
13. M. Taub, R. Azevedo, F. Bouchet, & B. Khosravifar. 2014. Can the use of cognitive & metacognitive self-regulated learning strategies be predicted by learners' levels of prior knowledge in hypermedia-learning environments? *Computers in Human Behavior* 39: 356–367.
14. P. Virtanen, H. Niemi, A. Nevgi, O. Raehalme, & A. Launonen. 2003. Towards strategic learning skills through self-assessment & tutoring in web-based environment. *Paper presented at the European Conference on Educational Research, University of Hamburg*.
15. S. Zheng, M.B. Rosson, P.C. Shih, & J.M. Carroll. 2015. Understanding Student Motivation, Behaviors & Perceptions in MOOCs. *Proceedings of the 18th ACM Conference on Computer Supported Cooperative Work & Social Computing - CSCW '15*: 1882–1895.
16. C. Zhenghao, B. Alcorn, G. Christensen, N. Eriksson, D. Koller, & E. Emanuel. 2015. Who's Benefiting from MOOCs, & Why. *Harvard Business Review.*
17. B.J. Zimmerman. 2015. *Self-Regulated Learning: Theories, Measures, & Outcomes*. Elsevier.

Investigating the Use of Hints in Online Problem Solving

Stephen Cummins
Computer Laboratory
University of Cambridge,
Cambridge, UK
sac92@cam.ac.uk

Ian Davies
Computer Laboratory
University of Cambridge,
Cambridge, UK
ipd21@cam.ac.uk

Alistair Stead
Computer Laboratory
University of Cambridge,
Cambridge, UK
ags46@cam.ac.uk

Alastair R Beresford
Computer Laboratory
University of Cambridge,
Cambridge, UK
arb33@cam.ac.uk

Lisa Jardine-Wright
Cavendish Laboratory
University of Cambridge,
Cambridge, UK
ljw21@cam.ac.uk

Andrew Rice
Computer Laboratory
University of Cambridge,
Cambridge, UK
acr31@cam.ac.uk

L@S 2016, April 25-26, 2016, Edinburgh, Scotland Uk
ACM 978-1-4503-3726-7/16/04.
http://dx.doi.org/10.1145/2876034.2893379

Abstract
We investigate the use of hints as a form of scaffolding for 4,652 eligible users on a large-scale online learning environment called Isaac, which allows users to answer physics questions with up to five hints. We investigate user behaviour when using hints, users' engagement with *fading* (the process of gradually becoming less reliant on the hints provided), and hint strategies including *Decomposition*, *Correction*, *Verification*, or *Comparison*. Finally, we present recommendations for the design and development of online teaching tools that provide open access to hints, including a mechanism that may improve the speed at which users begin fading.

Author Keywords
Problem Solving; Scaffolding; Hints; Physics

ACM Classification Keywords
K.3.1 [Computer Uses in Education]: Distance learning

Overview
Supporting distance learners can be difficult. Lack of geographic and temporal co-location reduces opportunities for timely feedback and tailored interventions, making it difficult for students to sustain motivation. This reduces the efficacy of Massive Open Online Courses in particular.

Teaching effective problem solving strategies or heuristics is a common educational goal and is documented across various disciplines, particularly those considered more mathematical in nature [3, 2]. Teaching these skills is not trivial, and can be demanding in terms of cognitive load [1], making supporting the development of such skills in a distance learning context particularly difficult.

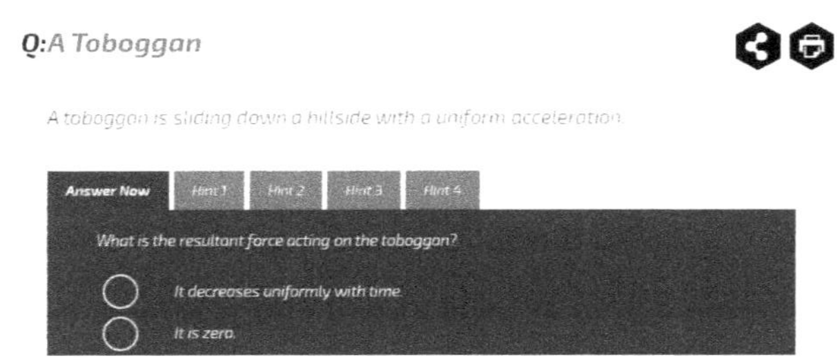

Figure 1: Typical hint layout to a question

Teachers often provide prompts or questions, referred to as scaffolding, to support inexperienced problem solvers. The Isaac platform provides a novel scaffolding mechanism that supports learners of physics at a large scale by providing a structured approach using hints that helps to decompose the problem. The steps in this mechanism consist of (1) Identify the questions goal and pertinent info, (2) Draw a Diagram (3) Identify useful concepts and tools, (4) Plan and implement your solution on paper, and (5) Check your working. Five hint types have been developed and used on Isaac to encourage these steps (see Figure 1). This paper presents early instrumentation data that shows students‘ use of hints during problem solving.

Method

We identified the following research questions: (1) How do people use hints to scaffold their learning? (2) What impact do using hints have on student success? (3) How do motivations for the use of hints differ between users? (4) To what extent do users voluntarily engage with fading? The data presented in this paper is based on usage log data and was collected between 20/09/2014 and 21/09/2015, and is derived from instrumentation logging. We exclude any data generated by known teachers and project staff. In our analysis, we make the assumption that users who view hints receive benefit from it, and therefore may behave differently from those who have not. We therefore track users' usage of hints across all sessions on the site. Approximately 74% of hints, or 679/908, of eligible questions follow the hint sequence strictly. Hint views are recorded when a user clicks on a hint tab, making it possible for multiple hint views per question or skipping hints entirely.

Results

Of the 4,652 users that answered a question, 456 always used all hints available on every question, 3,673 used at least some of the available hints on some of the questions, and 523 never used hints on any question. A total of 185,896 hint views were recorded over 816 questions of the 908 eligible questions where hints are available. Isaac contains 64 questions where every user attempting has viewed all the hints available, suggesting they are challenging. In total, there were 752 questions on which users used at least one hint. For each question where hints were used, a median of one user-hint was viewed.

Patterns in Hint Usage

Table 1 shows pairs of events within our users' *question interactions*. The shading highlights patterns of hint usage; for example 58% of people who view a Concepts hint then view the Info hint; 34% of people who view the Info hint view the Diagram hint and so on.

Event		Subsequent Event								
		End	Correct	Incorrect	Concepts	Info	Diagram	Equations	Video	Total
Event	Start	0.0	39.0	33.0	20.0	1.9	1.1	1.7	2.7	100
	Correct	90.0	5.6	0.62	1.8	0.32	0.35	0.48	1.0	100
	Incorrect	2.4	16.0	64.0	7.3	1.6	1.1	2.0	4.9	100
	Concepts	4.1	5.1	12.0	7.5	58.0	5.0	4.5	4.0	100
	Info	1.7	3.6	9.3	14.0	7.1	34.0	24.0	6.0	100
	Diagram	3.1	4.0	8.6	7.2	14.0	7.4	44.0	11.0	100
	Equations	3.1	4.3	10.0	9.0	15.0	15.0	7.4	36.0	100
	Video	8.5	11.0	25.0	12.0	5.6	5.2	19.0	13.0	100

Table 1: Percentage likelihood of users carrying out one event (column) after a given previous event (row). The table should be read row-wise only. (For example, for those users that enter an incorrect answer, 7% subsequently view a concept hint.

With user interactions of any length (i.e. not just those shown in Table 1) , if we denote correct answers with ✓ incorrect with ✗, and hints with **C**oncepts, **I**nformation, **D**iagrams, **E**quations and **V**ideos, the top 5 most frequent patterns were, in descending order, (1) C → ✓, (2) C (3) C → I → ✓, (4) C → I → D → E → V (5) V → ✓.

The most common strategy is to view the concept hint for problem decomposition and then submit a correct answer. The second is to use the concepts hint to determine if the question can be answered; a large proportion of users do this and never attempt to answer. The fifth top strategy – viewing the video without any other hints and answering correctly, may have been due to students learning which hints suit them best. While this may be evidence that some students do not follow our hint sequence, they have followed the steps independently, or simply opted to view the hint they perceive to be most valuable immediately. However, absolute data (on which Table 1 is based, but does not include) shows that viewing a video hint is the most likely hint to lead to a correct answer (0.9% compared with 0.47 0.35 0.26 0.38 for concepts, info, diagram and equations respectively), which indicates that users are not always using the hint that is most likely to lead to a correct answer. Even so, not all users viewed the video hints — this could be due to a number of factors (e.g. bandwidth, time required, school network restrictions).

Motivation for hint use

We have identified 4 different motivations for using hints: Decomposition, Correction, Verification and Comparison.

Decomposition

The user is unable to make a start and needs support decomposing it into solvable chunks. On Isaac, such students can be identified as those who do not answer before looking at the hints, or perhaps only use the hints that perform this initial decomposition activity for them. The data shows that this strategy is used by a high proportion of users: 3,086 of 4,652 (66.34%).

Correction
Further help is needed in response to an incorrect answer being received. The data shows that of the users who submitted incorrect answers, a high proportion viewed hints afterwards: 3,196 of 3,984 (80.22%). When a user is told they have provided an incorrect answer, Isaac attempts to provide them with tailored feedback if the answer is associated with a common error and therefore may provide sufficient support for the 788 users for whom no further hints are required.

Verification
The user has calculated an answer and wants to verify it before submitting. An early usability study of Isaac helped to identify this behaviour by finding that at least one student viewed hints after entering the correct answer but before pressing the 'check answer' button. Users who engage in this behaviour may be relying on scaffolding when it is not needed; this is a supporting case for enforced fading of the hints to take place. To develop effective problem solving skills we would prefer that users verify the correctness of their solutions themselves without relying on expert hints. Unfortunately, we are unable to accurately quantify the number of users who hold this motivation due to the many ways it could manifest. For example, users may calculate an answer on paper before using the hints.

Comparison
The user has already given a correct answer but wishes to compare the process used by an expert to their own by subsequently using hints. The data shows that this strategy is used by a moderate proportion of users who answered questions correctly: 1,179 of 4,075 (28.93%). This is an encouraging behaviour to observe as it is important to become familiar with different strategies of problem solving.

Future Work
We intend to investigate the popularity of different hint types by changing how we present hints to users so that we can observe which types are the most popular. As part of this future work we will more directly investigate how question difficulty affects how users use the scaffolding available.

Currently, Isaac supports the use of multiple choice and numeric questions. We are in the process of incorporating additional tools to support the entry, and automated assessment, of formulae as a new question type. This will allow students' to solve problems algebraically rather than numerically, which is an abstraction that is known to be challenging for physics students [2].

REFERENCES
1. Paul A. Kirschner, John Sweller, and Richard E. Clark. 2006. Why Minimal Guidance During Instruction Does Not Work: An Analysis of the Failure of Constructivist, Discovery, Problem-Based, Experiential, and Inquiry-Based Teaching. *Educational Psychologist* 41, 2 (June 2006), 75–86.
2. S.M. Ross and J.P.R. Bolton. 2002. Physica: A Computer Environment for Physics Problem-Solving. *Interactive Learning Environments* 10, 2 (Aug. 2002), 157–175.
3. A.H. Schoenfeld. 1992. *Learning to Think Mathematically: Problem Solving, Metacognition, and Sense Making in Mathematics Handbook of Research on Mathematics Teaching and Learning: A Project of the National Council of Teachers of Mathematics.* MacMillan Publishing, New York. 334–370 pages.

A Scalable Learning Analytics Platform for Automated Writing Feedback

Nicholas Lewkow
Jacqueline Feild
Neil Zimmerman
Mark Riedesel
Alfred Essa
McGraw-Hill Education
Boston, MA USA
firstname.lastname
@mheducation.com

David Boulanger
Jeremie Seanosky
Vive Kumar
Kinshuk
Athabasca University
Edmonton, AB Canada
vive@athabascau.ca

Sandhya Kode
IIIT Hyderabad
Hyderabad, India
sandhya.kode@gmail.com

Abstract
In this paper, we describe a scalable learning analytics platform which runs generalized analytics models on educational data in parallel. As a proof of concept, we use this platform as a base for an end-to-end automated writing feedback system. The system allows students to view feedback on their writing in near real-time, edit their writing based on the feedback provided, and observe the progression of their performance over time. Providing students with detailed feedback is an important part of improving writing skills and an essential component towards solving Bloom's "two sigma" problem in education. We evaluate the effectiveness of the feedback for students with an ongoing pilot study with 800 students who are using the learning analytics platform in a college English course.

Author Keywords
Analytic Tools for Learners, Automatic Essay Feedback, Scalable Analytics, Performance Feedback, Natural Language Processing

Introduction
Performance feedback is essential for self-regulated learning, which is an attribute of highly effective learners [3, 12]. Bloom has shown that providing formative feedback to students increases performance, compared to

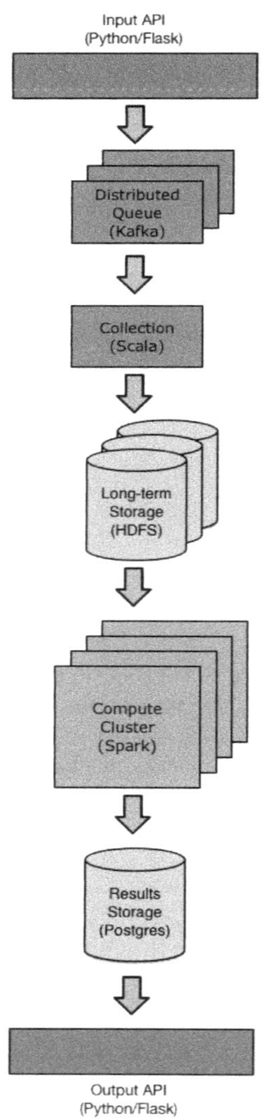

Figure 1: Architecture diagram of the learning analytics platform OpenACRE.

only providing final feedback [1]. This allows students to develop and implement actionable strategies for improving performance as they progress. Formative feedback is even more effective if it can be given in near real-time [5, 9].

In this paper we describe a scalable platform for learning analytics called OpenACRE (Analytics Collaborative Research Environment). OpenACRE allows for ingestion of heterogeneous educational data from multiple source systems, long-term storage of raw data, running arbitrary models on the raw data using a parallel analytics engine, and short-term storage of resulting analytics for use by students, teachers, and researchers. As a proof of concept, we implement an end-to-end writing feedback system utilizing OpenACRE. Writing feedback is especially hard to provide in real-time and at scale as it is computationally expensive, making it well suited for the capabilities provided by OpenACRE. There are several other existing writing feedback systems which provide various feedback to students, for example Revision Assistant, WriteToLearn, and Writing Pal [11, 10, 8]. While these systems provide useful information, they are either commercial black boxes which do not allow for modification, or are intelligent tutoring systems which provide writing instruction through customized modules. OpenACRE stands apart by providing the ability to develop and deploy new analytical models at scale, making it useful for researchers to test new feedback algorithms.

To evaluate our proof of concept system in a classroom setting, an efficacy study is currently underway to investigate the usefulness of the feedback to improve student performance. The study consists of 800 college students who are learning English at VNR VJIET in India.

OpenACRE

The OpenACRE platform consists of an input and output API, long- and short-term databases, and a parallel computation cluster. A low-level diagram is shown in Figure 1. This platform is designed to handle the challenges of scalability, resiliency to data loss, and fault tolerance. Additionally, OpenACRE is built to be extensible for future models, without the need for drastic modification to the system as a whole.

Learning event data is ingested into OpenACRE through the RESTful input API and persisted to the long-term data store. RESTful APIs are used because they are stateless, easily extended for future functionality, and agnostic to programming language. The input API accepts event data from external sources and temporarily stores the events in a queueing system. Next, a collection service takes events from the queue and stores them in a long-term data store. The event data is stored in its original "raw" form and is never altered. Storing unaltered event data allows for arbitrary computation and the implementation of future models without knowledge of those models beforehand.

Next, the computation engine runs analytical models by taking data from the long-term store and performing transformations/aggregations to create new output views. Apache Spark is used for our computation engine as it allows for user-friendly parallel computation and horizontal scalability on commodity hardware. The output views produced by the computation engine are persisted to the results store database. From there, they are provided to the RESTful output API which is accessible by other backend or user facing systems, such as dashboards.

The combination of all the OpenACRE components listed above results in a learning analytics platform which can

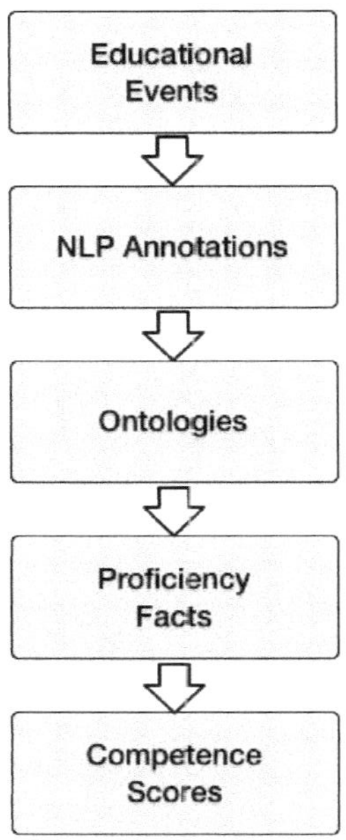

Figure 2: High-level diagram showing the flow of the OpenSCALE algorithm from educational events to competence scores.

ingest arbitrary learning event data, apply parallel analytic models to the data, and provide the results of the analytics to external systems and dashboards in a generic fashion.

End-to-end Writing Feedback System

As a proof of concept, we built an end-to-end writing feedback system with OpenACRE at the core. The end-to-end system includes the student facing system, which collects student writing data from their learning management system (LMS) and displays the automated feedback visualizations. It also includes the backend system, which stores and analyzes the student data.

The typical workflow for a student using this system includes editing a writing assignment and viewing automated feedback in a repeated fashion until the student is satisfied with their writing and submits their assignment. Since the LMS which students are using is instrumented to directly collect writing data, there is no need to use an additional system. This allows for an intuitive interaction between the student and their LMS, while collecting data for feedback at the same time.

The feedback given to students is developed from an existing collection of competencies which include traditional writing metrics such as spelling and grammatical accuracy as well as more advanced metrics that capture sentiment and writing flow [6]. Details of the writing feedback competencies are not included here for brevity.

We designed a custom dashboard to display feedback visualizations to students and instructors. These include both a snapshot of overall feedback and the progression of feedback over time.

The analytics model implemented in this automatic writing feedback system is called OpenSCALE [2]. This model parses text with Stanford CoreNLP library [7], creates ontologies and facts from the annotated text, and aggregates the facts into competence scores for students.

A high-level view of the transformations which go from text to competence scores is described in Figure 2. First, the text is annotated using the Stanford CoreNLP library. The annotations include tokenization of the text into words and sentences, part of speech tagging, syntactic parsing and sentiment analysis. These annotations are used to create an ontology of the relationships between words, sentences and paragraphs in the text, including both their structure and semantic meaning. For each piece of text, OpenSCALE creates one ontology which is put through an inferencing layer. This looks for patterns in the ontology that show evidence of students having a particular skill/competence and creates proficiency facts. Each fact includes information about the degree of competence (weight) exhibited by a unique student on a specific assignment at a given time. Finally, the proficiency facts are aggregated to generate final scores for each competence which are persisted in the results store.

Pilot Research Study

We are currently running a pilot research study to test the usefulness of the feedback system for increasing student writing performance. Eight hundred first year engineering students at VNR VJIET in India are using our system to complete up to twenty writing assignments. The students are using the Moodle LMS to answer essay assignment prompts and an external site for viewing their feedback visualizations.

The current pilot study is an observational study and will use the method of propensity score analysis to determine the effectiveness of the feedback visualizations [4]. Students will also fill out surveys about the feedback they received and its usefulness.

Conclusions

Providing real-time feedback to students is an important component to solving Bloom's two sigma problem. In this paper we described a scalable learning analytics platform which is able to ingest educational data from multiple external systems and provide analytics on that data in near real-time. We demonstrated the usefulness of this platform with the implementation of a writing feedback system and are currently running a pilot research study to evaluate its effectiveness with eight hundred first-year engineering students at a university in India. In the future, we plan to extend OpenACRE to incorporate additional data pipelines that consist of the ingestion of new types of data from different sources and new analytical models which act on that data.

Acknowledgements

This paper is based on work supported by the McGraw-Hill Education Digital Platform Group (MHE DPG). Despite provided support, any opinions, findings, conclusions or recommendations expressed in this paper are those of the authors and do not necessarily reflect positions or policies of the company.

References

[1] Bloom, B. S. The 2 sigma problem: The search for methods of group instruction as effective as one-to-one tutoring. *Educational researcher* (1984), 4–16.

[2] Boulanger, D., et al. Scale: A competence analytics framework. In *State-of-the-Art and Future Directions of Smart Learning*. Springer, 2016, 19–30.

[3] Butler, D. L., and Winne, P. H. Feedback and self-regulated learning: A theoretical synthesis. *Review of educational research 65*, 3 (1995), 245–281.

[4] Guo, S., and Fraser, M. W. Propensity score analysis. *Statistical methods and applications 12* (2015).

[5] Hattie, J., and Timperley, H. The power of feedback. *Review of educational research 77*, 1 (2007), 81–112.

[6] Kumar, V., et al. Mobile computing and mixed-initiative support for writing competence. *Intelligent and Adaptive Learning Systems: Technology Enhanced Support for Learners and Teachers: Technology Enhanced Support for Learners and Teachers* (2011), 327.

[7] Manning, C. D., et al. The stanford corenlp natural language processing toolkit. In *Proceedings of 52nd Annual Meeting of the Association for Computational Linguistics: System Demonstrations* (2014), 55–60.

[8] McNamara, D. S., et al. The writing-pal: Natural language algorithms to support intelligent tutoring on writing strategies. *Applied natural language processing and content analysis: Identification, investigation, and resolution* (2012), 298–311.

[9] Nicol, D. J., and Macfarlane-Dick, D. Formative assessment and self-regulated learning: A model and seven principles of good feedback practice. *Studies in higher education 31*, 2 (2006), 199–218.

[10] Pearson. The research behind writetolearn, 2007.

[11] turnitin. Turnitin revision assistant, 2015.

[12] Zimmerman, B. J. Self-regulated learning and academic achievement: An overview. *Educational psychologist 25*, 1 (1990), 3–17.

The Opportunity Count Model: A Flexible Approach to Modeling Student Performance

Yan Wang
Worcester Polytechnic Institute
Worcester, MA 01609, USA
ywang14@wpi.edu

Seth Adjei
Worcester Polytechnic Institute
Worcester, MA 01609, USA
saadjei@wpi.edu

Korinn Ostrow
Worcester Polytechnic Institute
Worcester, MA 01609, USA
ksostrow@wpi.edu

Neil Heffernan
Worcester Polytechnic Institute
Worcester, MA 01609, USA
nth@wpi.edu

L@S 2016, April 25-26, 2016, Edinburgh, Scotland UK
ACM 978-1-4503-3726-7/16/04.
http://dx.doi.org/10.1145/2876034.2893382

Abstract

Detailed performance data can be exploited to achieve stronger student models when predicting next problem correctness (NPC) within intelligent tutoring systems. However, the availability and importance of these details may differ significantly when considering opportunity count (OC), or the compounded sequence of problems a student experiences within a skill. Inspired by this intuition, the present study introduces the Opportunity Count Model (OCM), a unique approach to student modeling in which separate models are built for differing OCs rather than creating a blanket model that encompasses all OCs. We use Random Forest (RF), which can be used to indicate feature importance, to construct the OCM by considering detailed performance data within tutor log files. Results suggest that OC is significant when modeling student performance and that detailed performance data varies across OCs.

Author Keywords

Opportunity Count; Random Forest; Student Modeling; Next Problem Correctness; Intelligent Tutoring System

ACM Classification Keywords

I.6.5. Simulation and modeling: Model Development; K.3.0. Computers and education: General.

Helpful Definitions

Skill Builder: Skill Builders are a type of problem set within ASSISTments based on mastery learning. To master a skill, students must accurately answer three consecutive skill opportunities. High performing students are likely to have fewer OCs, while struggling students are likely to have higher OCs. As OC increases, data points grow scarcer as students master the skill or drop out of the assignment. Each Skill Builder is identified by a unique skill ID.

Random Forest: Random Forest is a proven method for making predictions when considering a variety of features [6]. The method trains regression trees based on decision splits made from a random subset of data features. The resulting output offers a prediction model based on an ensemble of regression trees. Random Forest can also be used to succinctly define the degree of importance a feature holds within a model.

Introduction

Despite the fact that detailed performance data has been shown to enhance student modeling within intelligent tutoring systems [1,2,5], little focus has been given to the critical significance of opportunity count (OC), or the compounded sequence of skill opportunities within a student's learning experience. It seems intuitive that the availability and importance of details within logged tutor data would vary based on OC: modeling certain performance details on a student's 3rd skill opportunity may reveal more about learning than modeling the same details on a student's 7th opportunity. Considering OC could also reduce the noise inherent to modeling few OCs through more flexible modeling of performance details.

The present work introduces the Opportunity Count Model (OCM) and investigates the significance of considering OC in student models. The OCM builds separate models for differing OCs by using Random Forest to determine fluctuations in the importance of student performance details across a dataset stratified by OC. We seek to validate the OCM, by answering the following research questions:

1. Can the accuracy of models predicting next problem correctness (NPC) be enhanced by aggregating separate models for differing OCs when considering additional details of a student's performance?
2. Is there variation in the importance of particular student performance details across OCs?

Dataset and Method

We examined the effectiveness of the OCM using a dataset comprised of student data logged between September 2012 and August 2013 within ASSISTments, a popular intelligent tutoring system for mathematics [3]. The dataset contained performance details for 85,862 problems logged by 3,210 unique students spanning 70 unique Skill Builders (see side panel).

The dataset included OC, student ID (St), skill ID (Sk), correctness (Ct), number of attempts (Att), first response time (FRT), percentage of hints requested (%H), first action (FA), and historical accuracy (% HA) (see final side panel for more detail). Table 1 depicts an example from the dataset. Student 34 has two skill opportunities for 'Skill 5', makes a single attempt on the first and two attempts on the second, and solves both in approximately 30 seconds. She immediately solved the first skill opportunity but required 60% of available hints on the second skill opportunity, requesting a hint before even attempting to solve the problem (FA = 1). Percentage values were discretized by units of 20% to simplify our modeling approach. For example, HA of 64% was discretized to 60%.

We used MATLAB's implementation of Random Forest (RF, see side panel) to build the OCM and make predictions about student performance [4]. We divided the dataset into training and testing segments, and developed 100 regression trees using the training set. Within this process, subsets of the training data were repeatedly sampled with replacement to construct the trees.

OC	St	Sk	Ct	Att	FRT(10s)	% H	FA	% HA
1	34	5	1	1	3	0	0	0
2	34	5	1	2	3	60	1	100
1	56	5	0	1	2	0	2	0

Table 1: A subset of data with OC and performance details.

Helpful Definitions

Out-of-bag Error [4]: A subset of training data is left out when building each tree, thereby leaving a portion of data "out of the bag." After building a tree, the out of bag subset is applied to the tree and arrives at a prediction. The root mean squared error (RMSE) of prediction for all out-of-bag cases becomes known as the out-of-bag error.

Feature Importance: When assessing the importance of a feature, *m*, values of *m* are randomly permuted in out-of-bag cases. A secondary measure of out-of-bag error is then calculated based on the permuted data. The difference between this secondary out-of-bag error and the original out-of-bag error is regarded as the importance of feature *m*. The larger the difference in error, the more important the feature is to the model. Negative values suggest a feature that is useless or even harmful in prediction.

As RF progresses through the process of building decision trees, subsets of features are chosen randomly to establish node splits. The number of features, *n*, in this subset can be limited to enhance predictive accuracy. For our current work, we explored a wide range of student performance details (or model features), ultimately retaining the *n* with minimum out-of-bag error (see side panel) when applying RF to the test set.

We ran and tested RF for each OC, using segments of the dataset. For comparison, we also constructed a Traditional Model (TM), or a single model encompassing all OCs. Within the TM, it is possible to consider or ignore OC as a feature, resulting in two types of TMs: TM without OC (TMNOC) and TM with OC (TMOC). The code used for this process is available at [7].

RF was used to examine the predictive accuracy of the TMNOC, the TMOC, and the OCM, and to quantify feature importance (see side panel) within each model. Five-fold cross validation was used to assess predictive accuracy. Predictive accuracy is represented here by the root mean squared error (RMSE) of test sets.

Results

Figure 1 shows the RMSE of model predictions for next problem correctness at various OCs. Data points at the 5th OC represent error in predicting correctness on the 6th OC. Feature importance was generated while running RF for each feature within each fold, and ultimately averaged across folds. Table 2 presents relative feature importance within the OCM.

Discussion

The OCM distinctly outperforms both TMs (except when OC = 11). This is not necessarily surprising. The OCM builds a separate model for each OC. In general, it has many more parameters (i.e., degrees of freedom) than TMs. While this observation is somewhat obvious, it suggests that OC is a critical feature to consider when modeling student performance (RQ1). We also observed a trend in the difference of prediction accuracy between models. The OCM is less accurate in later OCs. At the 11th OC, TMs begin to outperform the OCM within our dataset. We suspect that this is caused

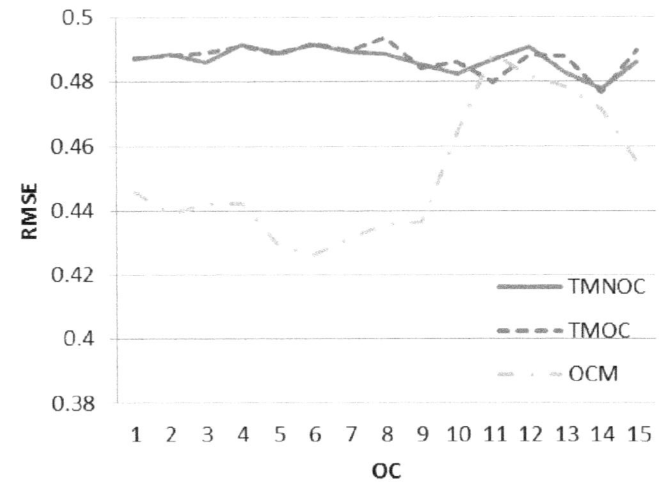

Figure 1: Prediction accuracy of three models. The point at the ith OC shows the prediction accuracy of $i^{th}+1$ correctness.

OC	Sk	Ct	Att	FRT (10s)	% H	FA	HA
1	6.31	0.85	0.80	1.16	0.73	0.69	0.00
3	7.12	1.10	0.23	1.36	0.71	0.64	1.86
5	6.06	0.69	0.48	0.91	0.39	0.66	0.42
7	2.87	0.57	-0.05	-0.17	0.33	0.19	0.46
9	3.25	0.42	0.17	0.17	0.18	0.11	0.23

Table 2: Feature importance within the OCM at different OCs.

Helpful Definitions

Correct (Ct): A binary measure of accuracy on first attempt.

Attempts (Att): The number of attempts made before arriving at a correct solution.

First Action (FA): The first thing a student does within a skill opportunity. Students may attempt to solve (0), request a hint (1), or request a scaffold (2).

First Response Time (FRT)(10s): The time between opening a skill opportunity and making a first action. This measure was groomed to remove outliers larger than 400ms (less than 1% data loss) and to simplify the time structure to 10-second increments.

Percent of Hints Used (%H): The percentage of available hints requested by a student within a skill opportunity.

Historical Accuracy (HA): Generated to compile a student's percentage of correctness across prior OCs within a skill.

by the reduction of data points as OC increases. As OC increases, data points grow scarcer as students either master the skill or drop out. Therefore, at later OCs, the OCM has fewer cases on which to train and test.

Findings also suggest that feature importance varies as OC changes, justifying use of the OCM when considering performance details in student modeling (RQ2). Results presented in Table 2 revealed that feature importance differed considerably with increases in OC. When considering an OC of 3, aside from the importance of the skill itself, the most relevant features within the model were first response time and historical accuracy. However, when considering an OC of 7, first response time was no longer important and may have actually hindered prediction accuracy. Examining feature variation in this way allows us to discriminate important factors across different phases of learning. For example, the skill itself is more important with fewer OCs, but with higher OCs, importance shifts to other features. This may suggest that at later modeling stages, researchers should focus less on the refinement of skill content and more on factors pertaining to individual students. While it is difficult to draw any specific conclusions here based on these results, it is worth future investigation.

Contribution

The present work revealed that OC is an important factor for the community to consider when modeling student performance. Further, our finding that the importance of features varies across OCs establishes a call for further examination of the significance of student performance details at different learning phases.

Acknowledgements

We acknowledge funding from the NSF (1316736, 1252297, 1109483, 1031398, 0742503), ONR's "STEM Grand Challenges," and the IES (R305A120125, R305C100024).

References

1. Duong, H.D., Zhu, L., Wang, Y. and Heffernan, N. 2013. A prediction model uses the sequence of attempts and hints to better predict knowledge: better to attempt the problem first, rather than ask for a hint. In *Proc of the 6th Int Conf on EDM*, 316-317.
2. González-Brenes, J.P., Huang, Y. and Brusilovsky, P. 2014. General features in knowledge tracing: Applications to multiple subskills, temporal item response theory, and expert knowledge. In *Proc of the 7th Int Conf on EDM*, 84-91.
3. Heffernan, N. and Heffernan, C. 2014. The ASSISTments ecosystem: building a platform that brings scientists and teachers together for minimally invasive research on human learning and teaching. *Int J of AIED*. 24, 4: 470-497.
4. MathWorks. 2015. TreeBagger. Retrieved 10/10/15 http://www.mathworks.com/help/stats/treebagger.html
5. Pardos, Z. A. and Heffernan, N. 2010. Using HMMs and bagged decision trees to leverage rich features of user and skill from an intelligent tutoring system dataset. *J of Machine Learning Research W & CP.*
6. Leo Breiman and Adele Cutler. Random Forests. Retrieved 10/10/15 https://www.stat.berkeley.edu/~breiman/RandomForests/cc_home.html.
7. Wang, Y. 2015. Data and code for "The Opportunity Count Model: A flexible approach to modeling student performance." http://tiny.cc/LAS2016-OCM

The Unexpected Pedagogical Benefits of Making Higher Education Accessible

David Joyner
Udacity, Inc.
2465 Latham Street NW
Mountain View, CA 94040
david.joyner@udacity.com

Georgia Institute of Technology
85 5th Street NW
Atlanta, GA 30332
david.joyner@gatech.edu

Ashok K. Goel
Georgia Institute of Technology
School of Interactive Computing
85 5th Street NW
Atlanta, GA 30332
ashok.goel@cc.gatech.edu

Charles Isbell
Georgia Institute of Technology
School of Computer Science
801 Atlantic Dr. NW
Atlanta, GA 30332
isbell@cc.gatech.edu

L@S 2016, April 25-26, 2016, Edinburgh, Scotland UK
ACM 978-1-4503-3726-7/16/04.
http://dx.doi.org/10.1145/2876034.2893383

Abstract
Many ongoing efforts in online education aim to increase accessibility through affordability and flexibility, but some critics have noted that pedagogy often suffers during these efforts. In contrast, in the low-cost for-credit Georgia Tech Online Masters of Science in Computer Science (OMSCS) program, we have observed that the features that make the program accessible also lead to pedagogical benefits. In this paper, we discuss the pedagogical benefits, and draw a causal link between those benefits and the factors that increase the program's accessibility.

Author Keywords
Online education; accessibility; higher education.

ACM Classification Keywords
K.3.2. Computer and Information Science Education.

Introduction
Recently, there have been several efforts to make higher education more accessible, with massive open online courses—MOOCs—leading this charge [1]; however, MOOCs have proved to be divisive in higher education, with some educators praising their potential to make educational content accessible [7], while other researchers have noted that MOOCs have not yet delivered on many of their original promises [3, 8].

Tools of the Program

- **Piazza:** The forum and de facto "classroom" for OMSCS classes, for class discussions, questions, announcements, and other virtual analogues of the in-class experience. Every OMSCS course heavily leverages Piazza.
- **Peer Feedback:** A tool developed at Georgia Tech for pairing students for peer reviews. Peer review is used as a learning activity, not to generate grades, although experiments have been performed on using peer review to support expert grading [4]. Roughly one third of the classes in the OMSCS use Peer Feedback.
- **T-Square:** The Sakai-based learning management system used for assignment submission and expert evaluation.
- **Udacity:** The host of the program's prepared lecture material, as well as interactive exercises and some class projects.

In the two years since the Georgia Tech online Masters of Science in Computer Science debuted, we have noted that in some ways, this program has delivered a superior pedagogical experience to the traditional residential program, specifically due to the factors that made the program accessible. Here, we describe and connect that accessibility, to the pedagogical benefits we have observed. We conclude that with the right planning, the relationship between accessibility and pedagogy can be mutualistic, not parasitic.

OMSCS Program

The Georgia Tech OMSCS program was developed through a partnership with AT&T and Udacity, and has since grown to over 3000 students in two years. The experience is similar to residential students: students apply for admission, pay tuition, earn grades, and complete the same assignments, projects, and exams. The chief difference is that class material is delivered via Udacity.com in lieu of classroom lectures.

Each OMSCS class is built around a MOOC developed by Udacity. However, the for-credit offering of the class includes individual instructor involvement, expert human grading, complex projects, and other factors that are uncommon in MOOCs. The courses themselves are similar to distance learning classes, with the MOOC as a textbook. The OMSCS, however, is built from the ground-up to take advantage of the internet; it is remarkably affordable compared to residential and distance learning degrees; it is capable of admitting a greater number of students; and it is an equivalent degree to the residential program. Thus, the OMSCS is large, flexible, affordable, and partially pre-produced like MOOCs, but is also rigorous, accredited, and subject to admissions and tuition like distance learning.

Increased Accessibility

The OMSCS program addresses four traditional barriers to access: scheduling, geography, cost, and exclusivity.

- **Schedule Flexibility.** OMSCS classes require no synchronous activities and present most class materials on the first day of the semester, allowing students to succeed without taking time off work.
- **Geographic Flexibility.** The OMSCS has no residency requirement. Students may succeed without uprooting their family or leaving their job for two years. One student wrote, "I wrote and submitted Assignment 1 from Liberia. Project 1 was coded in Israel, and submitted in Palestine. Assignment 4 was written and submitted from Mongolia. And Project 2, from home in Portland."
- **Economic Affordability.** The program costs approximately $8000 including books and fees. The low tuition and flexibility noted above dramatically reduce the true costs of the program. As a result, a plurality of students enroll in the program not for career benefits, but for personal enjoyment.
- **Enhanced Inclusivity.** The program has no physical barrier to create an artificial student capacity. As a result, while the on-campus program fills up with only 10% of applicants, the OMSCS accepts all qualified students. This creates a much more diverse student body, with backgrounds and experiences from outside computing.

Student Demographics

Table 1 compares the demographic information of the online and residential sections of CS7637 in Fall 2014 [2]. Notably, online students tend to be older, more educated, and more experienced. They are also more likely to be male, domestic, and employed, although

Student Profiles

	Online	Residential
Age		
<24	15%	82%
25-34	47%	17%
>35	39%	1%
Gender		
Female	10%	24%
Male	90%	76%
Location		
Domestic	87%	32%
International	13%	68%
Level of Prior Education		
Bachelor's	87%	94%
Master's	11%	6%
Ph.D.	2%	0%
Employment Status		
Full-Time	90%	5%
Part-Time	5%	15%
None	5%	80%
Prior Coding Experience		
<8 years	45%	90%
9-18 years	41%	10%
>18 years	14%	0%

Table 1: Comparison of online and residential students in the KBAI class in Fall 2014.

the different gender ratios are due to the drastically different international and domestic ratios between the programs. Within each location, the gender ratios are the same between the online and residential programs.

Pedagogical Benefits

The accessibility of the program has led to a student population that is more intrinsically motivated to learn, more experienced, and more professionally diverse. We argue this unique student body and the structure of the OMSCS combine to create unique pedagogical benefits.

Student-Initiated Discussions

In traditional residential classes, time is a finite resource that must be budgeted carefully. Online, there does not exist a finite amount of synchronous class time to budget, and thus student-initiated discussions do not compete with planned activities. In CS6460 in Fall 2015, for example, the class concluded with over 500 discussions initiated by students.

Parallel Discussions

In residential classes, students must take turns and the class (or groups within the class) may only discuss one topic at a time. This makes individualization difficult: a particular discussion may confuse the low-achieving students or bore the high-achieving students. Online, discussions may proceed in parallel, allowing students to self-select which discussions are appropriate for their ability. This also allows the volume of discussion to expand; in CS6460 in Fall 2015, ~100 students and instructors generated 11,000 posts in 17 weeks.

Extended and Self-Documenting Discussions

Because discussions in residential classrooms are time-boxed within the assigned class time and conducted verbally, the discussion must end with little left behind except students' notes and memories. Online, discussions have no need to come to an artificial end, and all discussions inherently self-document. In CS6460, for example, class projects are captured in single long-running threads that document the project team's progress across the entire semester.

Help-Seeking and Student-to-Student Interactions

In the OMSCS, students ask any questions on Piazza. While the question may be implicitly targeted to the instructor, students may enter and answer or follow-up. Thus, student-to-student interaction dominates the class experience. As a result, students receive rapid answers and feedback from that diverse and experienced student body instead of just instructors. The average time to receive an answer is 30 minutes.

De Facto Teaching Assistants

With most classes enrolling anywhere from 200 to 500 students, there are reliably certain students who are excessively helpful. To an outside observer, these students would appear to be teaching assistants with the extent to which they help their classmates. Anecdotally, it is not unusual for students to note that certain classmates dramatically improved their class experience. This has also allowed instructors to identify candidates for future teaching assistant positions.

Expert-Level Peer Feedback

As noted previously, many OMSCS use peer review [4] to allow students to review classmates' assignments. Although MOOCs often use peer feedback to generate assignment grades [6], the OMSCS program instead leverages the known pedagogical benefits of both giving and receiving peer review [5]. The unique student body present in the OMSCS means that experts are participating as peers in these exercises as well.

Organic Student-Instructor Interaction

As instructors, we have been struck with how the online forum structure creates a 24-hour classroom where we may come, view discussions in their entirety, and participate in every conversation, with everyone able to listen. This has led to the most common positive feedback we have received: students have commented that the student-instructor interaction in these classes exceeds any residential class they have taken.

Conclusion

In this paper, we have worked as participant-observers, noting pedagogical benefits to students in the OMSCS program not previously seen in residential classes. OMSCS students agree: in Summer 2015, 90% of online CS7637 students rated the course as better than residential courses. CS6460, a course that relies on the benefits outlined above, drew a similar assessment; 80% rated it as better than other courses. Students frequently praise the teaching teams' involvement, the chance to review classmates' work, and the active student communities, all of which come from efforts to increase accessibility. With the right circumstances and planning, the relationship between accessibility and pedagogy can be mutualistic, not parasitic.

Acknowledgements

The authors are instructors who have taught both OMSCS and residential classes. We thank Joe Gonzales, the creator of Peer Feedback and the staffs of the Georgia Tech College of Computing, Georgia Tech Professional Education, and Udacity for their support.

References

1. Daniel, J. (2012). Making sense of MOOCs: Musings in a maze of myth, paradox and possibility. *Journal of Interactive Media in Education*, *2012*(3), Art-18.
2. Goel, A., & Joyner, D. (2016). An Experiment in Teaching Artificial Intelligence Online. In D Haynes (Ed.) *International Journal for the Scholarship of Technology-Enhanced Learning(1)* 1.
3. Guzdial, M. (2014). Ubiquity symposium: MOOCs and technology to advance learning and learning research: limitations of MOOCs for computing education: addressing our needs. *Ubiquity*, *2014*(July), 1.
4. Joyner, D., Ashby, W., Irish, L., Lam, Y., Langston, J., Lupiani, I., ... Goel, A. (2016). Graders as Meta-Reviewers: Simultaneously Scaling and Improving Expert Evaluation for Large Online Classrooms. In *Proceedings from the Third ACM Conference on Learning @ Scale*.
5. Li, L., Liu, X., & Steckelberg, A. L. (2010). Assessor or assessee: How student learning improves by giving and receiving peer feedback. *British Journal of Educational Technology*, *41*(3), 525-536.
6. Lu, J., & Law, N. (2012). Online peer assessment: effects of cognitive and affective feedback. *Instructional Science*, *40*(2), 257-275.
7. Milheim, W. D. (2013). Massive open online courses (MOOCs): Current applications and future potential. *Educational Technology: The Magazine for Managers of Change in Education*, *53*(3), 38-42.
8. Popenici, S. (2015). Deceptive Promises: The Meaning of MOOCs. In McKay, E. (Ed.) *Macro-Level Learning Through Massive Open Online Courses (MOOCs): Strategies and Predictions for the Future*, 158-167.

Expert Evaluation of 300 Projects per Day

David Joyner
Udacity, Inc.
2465 Latham Street NW
Mountain View, CA 94040
david.joyner@udacity.com

Georgia Institute of Technology
85 5th Street NW
Atlanta, GA 30332
david.joyner@gatech.edu

L@S 2016, April 25-26, 2016, Edinburgh, Scotland UK
ACM 978-1-4503-3726-7/16/04.
http://dx.doi.org/10.1145/2876034.2893384

Abstract
In October 2014, one-time MOOC developer Udacity completed its transition from primarily producing massive, open online courses to producing job-focused, project-based microcredentials called "Nanodegree" programs. With this transition came a challenge: whereas MOOCs focus on automated assessment and peer-to-peer grading, project-based microcredentials would only be feasible with expert evaluation. With dreams of enrolling tens of thousands of students at a time, the major obstacle became project evaluation. To address this, Udacity developed a system for hiring external experts as project reviewers. A year later, this system has supported project evaluation on a massive scale: 61,000 projects have been evaluated in 12 months, with 50% evaluated within 2.5 hours (and 88% within 24 hours) of submission. More importantly, students rate the feedback they receive very highly at 4.8/5.0. In this paper, we discuss the structure of the project review system, including the nature of the projects, the structure of the feedback, and the data described above.

Author Keywords
Online education; evaluation; feedback.

ACM Classification Keywords
K.3.2. Computer and Information Science Education.

Evaluation Metrics

Quantity: On average, how many projects are reviewed each day? In the week preceding this analysis, 432 projects were reviewed per day, and 357 projects were reviewed per day for the previous four weeks.

Turnaround Time: On average, how long does a student have to wait to receive their feedback? The median turnaround time the previous seven days was 138 minutes, with 95% of projects returned to students within 24 hours.

Student Satisfaction: Students rate their satisfaction with the reviews they receive on a scale of 1 to 5. Are they satisfied with the feedback? The average rating received is 4.8/5.0, with roughly 29% of students rating their level of satisfaction.

Introduction

In October 2014, one-time MOOC developer Udacity launched its first collection of Nanodegree programs. Nanodegree programs were set apart from many other online offerings by their strong emphasis on projects. A Nanodegree program was primarily a collection of projects, with MOOC-based material to support the projects. Projects took on various forms, from web sites to Android applications to data reports [1].

Soon, a challenge emerged: assessment. The projects were too open-ended for automated evaluation, but they strived for a level of expertise that was believed to be impossible from peer review alone. Expert feedback was needed. But with programs quickly scaling up to hundreds of submissions a day, how would expert evaluation be possible?

To address this issue, Udacity set about recruiting freelance project reviewers. Project reviewers are paid per project, creating a gig economy surrounding project evaluation. After a year, the results have been striking: thousands of projects have been evaluated with rapid turn-around times and high student satisfaction.

In this paper, we present the structure of this system and evaluate its success across three metrics: number of projects handled, turn-around time, and student satisfaction. We close by noting a collection of pedagogical benefits present in this system.

Program Structure

Nanodegree programs are project-based vocational curricula aiming to prepare students for the job title given in the Nanodegree program's name. Each Nanodegree program is built around a series of projects. Each project is open-ended, allowing students significant leeway to decide how to approach the problem. Students are supplied a rubric for project evaluation, and are subsequently evaluated on their success according to the rubric. The ultimate goal of the projects is to give the student a strong portfolio of past work in the chosen field.

Each student is given a set of customized due dates based on their enrollment date. If a student misses a due date, their subsequent due dates are simply shifted backwards; there is no other penalty for missing a due date. Upon submission, projects are evaluated by an expert and returned to the student with written feedback. If the project meets expectations, the student receives credit for completing it; if not, the student may try again.

Each Nanodegree program is supported by Udacity's courseware, often available separately as independent MOOCs. Students are not required to watch these courses; if a student enters the program with sufficient knowledge to execute a project or would prefer to learn from another source, they may.

Project Review

The foundation for this system is the ability to rapidly review and return projects to students. There are over 10,000 students enrolled in Nanodegree programs, and thus, hundreds of projects are submitted each day. To address this, Udacity leverages a group of hundreds of individual project reviewers.

Project Reviewers

Initially, project reviewers were Udacity employees, but as the programs have scaled up, more and more Nanodegree graduates have been recruited to join Udacity's project review workforce. To become a project reviewer, the student must first complete the Nanodegree containing the project they want to review.

Then, they must complete the Udacity Code Reviewer course [6], as well as some additional project- or program-specific training. After demonstrating success in evaluating some sample projects, the reviewer may be selected as a full reviewer. Reviewers are paid between $5 and $50 per project reviewed, and they themselves regularly receive student feedback.

Project Submission And Assessment
As they progress through the Nanodegree program of their choice, students complete and submit projects. In addition to the code, papers, analyses, or other deliverables demanded by the project, students may also submit notes requesting certain types of feedback. Upon submission, the project is added to the list of projects awaiting evaluation, and any reviewer for that project may claim it and begin reviewing.

While reviewing, the reviewer has access to a number of resources to support their evaluation. They see the notes left by the student, as well as the history of project submission so they can check the feedback the student has received in the past and observe the progress the student has made. The reviewer then evaluates the project based on the rubric, supplying written feedback as well as a pass/fail ruling on each rubric category. Upon completion, this feedback is immediately returned to the student, at which point the student may optionally evaluate the feedback they received on a five-point scale and leave written feedback for the project reviewer.

Evaluation Metrics

This paper has thus far summarized the project review system used at Udacity for evaluating student work. There are a number of ways we can evaluate the success of this system. The left sidebar summarizes three: (a) its success at evaluating a large number of projects, (b) the average turnaround time between submission and evaluation, and (c) students' self-reported satisfaction with the evaluations they receive.

Table 1 summarizes the evaluation of the project review system for two time periods for which complete data is available. Due to these metrics, we consider the project review system implemented by Udacity to be successful at scaling up expert evaluation of student assignments to hundreds of assignments every day.

Pedagogical Benefits

These metrics evaluate whether or not the system employed here was successful at scaling up expert evaluation of projects. We speculate that there are pedagogical benefits in this project review system. In comparison to traditional academic settings, we observe three major benefits to the project evaluation model presented here: the rapidness of feedback, the emphasis on revision, and the flexibility of the deadlines. The combination of these three things results in evaluation being almost entirely framed as formative rather than summative assessment [3].

First, from the perspective of traditional higher education, it is often a struggle to return assignments quickly; a one-week turn-around time is anecdotally considered good. The model presented here, however, returns 95% of projects within 24 hours. Less than 1% of projects have to wait a week for feedback. Rapid feedback gives students more opportunity to iterate over their projects and learn from their reviews.

Second and relatedly, iteration and improvement are often absent in traditional higher education. This is the traditional grading model: each assignment is given a grade, and those grades together form the final score

	Last 7 days	Last 28 days
Projects Reviewed per Day	432	357
Median Turnaround Time (minutes)	138	168
% Returned within 24 Hours	95%	91%
Student Satisfaction	4.8/5.0	4.8/5.0

Table 1: Statistics for projects evaluated in the last 4 weeks and 7 days, respectively. In each case, the statistics are through October 27th, 2015.

in the class. In the Nanodegree model, however, if a project submission does not meet specifications, it is returned to the student for revision and resubmission. There is no Nanodegree equivalent of 'failing' a project: if a student 'fails' a project, that simply means they must try again. This puts puts formative assessment front and center in the evaluation process

One of the reasons why assignment submission is final in traditional higher education is the need for immovable due dates: the semester must end on a certain day, and the student must have a grade for the class by that day. For this reason, the third major pedagogical benefit of the model used in the Nanodegree programs is the flexible due dates. As with the emphasis on revision, a student in a Nanodegree program can never 'fail' an assignment. This retains the motivation provided by due dates [5] while removing their finality.

Conclusion

In scaling higher education, whether it be through MOOCs or simply through more accessible online programs, assessment remains one of the most significant considerations. In its Nanodegree programs, Udacity decided that expert evaluation was necessary for the type of outcomes it strived to achieve, and thus it set about finding ways to integrate expert evaluations into a large program.

The result: despite the submission of hundreds of projects every day, the project review system gets 50% of students feedback within 2.5 hours and 95% of students feedback within 24 hours, while maintaining a high student satisfaction rate with the feedback and creating other pedagogical benefits. Perhaps more significantly, there remains a significant wait list of students wanting to become project reviewers; it is feasible that this same model could easily be extended to tens of thousands of submissions a week.

ACKNOWLEDGMENTS

David Joyner is a course developer with Udacity and an instructor with the Georgia Tech Online MS in CS program. Although he works for Udacity, he was not involved in the development or administration of Udacity's project review system, and instead has evaluated it independently. We are grateful to Yael Goshen, Christine Hall, and Oliver Cameron for information supplied in support of this work.

References

1. Cameron, O. (2015, May 12). How a Udacity Graduate Earns $11k a Month Reviewing Code. *Medium.com.* Retrieved from http://bit.ly/1mbt87l
2. Georgia Tech. (2015). Online Master of Science in Computer Science [Web Site]. Retrieved from http://www.omscs.gatech.edu/
3. Harlen, W., & James, M. (1997). Assessment and learning: differences and relationships between formative and summative assessment. *Assessment in Education*, *4*(3), 365-379.
4. MIT. (2015). MITx MicroMasters Credential [Web Site]. Retrieved from http://micromasters.mit.edu/
5. Nesterko, S. O., Seaton, D., Reich, J., McIntyre, J., Han, Q., Chuang, I., & Ho, A. (2014). Due dates in MOOCs: does stricter mean better?. In *Proceedings of the First ACM conference on Learning @ Scale*. ACM.
6. Udacity. (2015). Becoming a Udacity Code Reviewer [Online Course] Retrieved from http://bit.ly/1OeUjIH
7. University of Illinois at Urbana-Champaign. (2015). iMBA [Web Site]. Retrieved from https://onlinemba.illinois.edu/

Metaphors for Learning & MOOC Pedagogies

Karen Swan
One University Plaza, MS BRK 377
Springfield, Illinois 62703
University of Illinois Springfield
kswan1@uis.edu

Scott Day
University of Illinois Springfield
One University Plaza, MS BRK 377
Springfield, Illinois 62703
217-206-7520
sday1@uis.edu

Leonard Bogle
University of Illinois Springfield
One University Plaza, MS BRK 377
Springfield, Illinois 62703
217-206-7824
lbogl1@uis.edu

L@S 2016, April 25–26, 2016, Edinburgh, UK.
ACM 978-1-4503-3726-7/16/04.
DOI: http://dx.doi.org/10.1145/2876034.2893385

Abstract
The research reported in this paper used a researcher developed tool to categorize the pedagogical approaches used in MOOCs. The Assessing MOOC Pedagogies (AMP) tool characterized MOOC pedagogical approaches on ten dimensions. Preliminary testing on 20 different MOOCs demonstrated >= 80% inter-reliability and the facility of the measure to distinguish differing pedagogical patterns. The patterns distinguished crossed content areas and seemed to be related to what Sfard (1998) identified as metaphors for learning; acquisition and participation approaches seemed to distinguish the pedagogies of differing MOOCs. A third, arguably important, pattern related to self-direction was also distinguished.

Author Keywords
MOOCs; Pedagogy; Metaphors for Learning

ACM Classification Keywords
H.5.m. Information interfaces and presentation (e.g., HCI): Miscellaneous;

Introduction
Since the development of the first Massive Open Online Courses, MOOCs have become one of the most talked about trends in higher education (1,

The AMP (Assessing MOOC Pedagogies) tool is based on a similar tool developed by Tom Reeves (25) for describing the pedagogical dimensions of computer-based instruction. In adapting Reeves' tool, the authors retained 10 of the 14 dimensions – (1) epistemology, (2) role of the teacher, (3) experiential validity (renamed "focus of activities"), (4) cooperative learning, (5) accommodation of individual differences, and (6) user role – albeit adapting these to the MOOC context, and added four other dimensions – (7) structure, (8) approach to content, (9) feedback, and (10) activities/assessment.

2). MOOCs have come to be viewed by some as the savior of higher education (53), and by others as the harbinger of its ultimate demise (3,4). As the promised transformation of higher education failed to arrive however, debate has focused on the flaws in the MOOC model – high drop-out rates, limited social interaction, heavy reliance on instructivist models, and, perhaps most importantly, a failure to impact the under-represented populations they were touted as serving (5). Indeed, research has found that people who enroll in MOOCs tend to be well-educated, already possess a college degree and are employed, and reside in developed countries – a far cry from the original intended audience for free online courses (6,7,8).

We believe that finding mechanisms to distinguish among MOOCs or evaluate their underlying components or characteristics should be a first step in the "research, evaluation, and assessment of learning" in MOOCs (9, p. 4). Moreover, while technologically sophisticated, most MOOCs have not been designed to take advantage of the affordances of sophisticated instructional designs or advances in learning technologies.

In this paper, the authors report on findings from their application of a tool they developed, not to rate the instructional quality of MOOCs, but rather to categorize the pedagogical approaches taken by them. They believe that identifying such approaches is an important first step in considering what pedagogical approaches best meet the often unique needs of MOOC participants. The AMP (Assessing MOOC Pedagogies) tool they developed characterizes the pedagogical approaches taken by individual MOOCs along ten dimensions. The authors used AMP to evaluate 20 MOOCs from five different providers and found that the pedagogical patterns that emerged suggested differing approaches related to metaphors for learning – acquisition, participation, (11) and self-directed learning.

THE AMP TOOL

The development of the AMP tool began with work conducted by the American Council on Education's (ACE) College Credit Recommendation Service to review MOOCs for college credit. While ACE reviewed MOOCs for content coverage, the authors developed a tool to categorize the pedagogical approaches taken by the same MOOCs (12) and was based on a similar tool developed by Tom Reeves.

Epitemology (1=objectivist/5=constructivist)*Role of the Teacher* (1=teacher centered/5=student centered)
Focus of Activities
(1=convergent/5=divergent)Structure (1=less structured/5=more structured)
Approach to Content (1=concrete/5=abstract)
Feedback (1=infrequent, unclear/5=frequent, constructive)Cooperative Learning (1=unsupported/5=integral)Accommodation of *Individual Differences*
(1=unsupported/5=multifaceted)
Activities/Assessments (1=artificial/5=authentic)
User Role (1=passive/5=generative)

METHODOLOGY

After initial revisions of the AMP instrument, four researchers independently reviewed the first thirteen MOOCs assessed by ACE. An initial inter-rater reliability across measures was greater than 80% on all MOOCs and increased to 100% through consensus. The courses approved by ACE were in the STEM areas, so four non-STEM courses offered by Coursera were added to explore other platforms.

The 20 courses were rated on each of the 10 dimensions in the AMP tool. Those ratings were plotted on matrix to give a visual representation of the pedagogical patterns in each MOOC.

RESULTS

Figure 1 shows the three distinct pedagogical patterns that emerged.

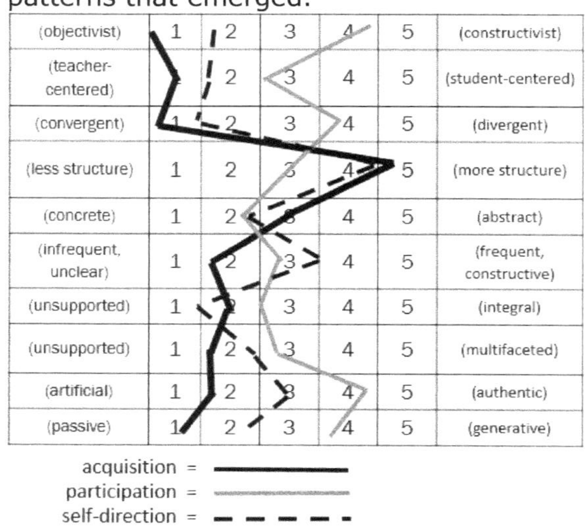

Two of those patterns can be linked to the two metaphors for learning identified by Anna Sfard (11) – the *acquisition* metaphor and the *participation* metaphor. The acquisition-type MOOCs have pedagogical approaches that seem to be based on an acquisition notion of learning, while the pedagogical approaches of participation-type MOOCs seem grounded in a participation metaphor. Eight acquisition-type and three participation-type MOOCs were identified. A third pattern falling mostly between the two was deemed to focus on learning as *self-directed.*

SIGNIFICANCE

The research reported in this paper identified three distinct pedagogical patterns in the MOOCs reviewed using the AMP tool. These patterns can be linked to particular metaphors for learning. These pedagogical patterns, in turn, seem suited to particular kinds of MOOC users. MOOCs that fall in the acquisition category, for example, seem particularly well suited to users new to a discipline, whether they be novice learners trying to prepare for higher education or retired folks just wanting to expand their knowledge. Participation-type MOOCs most likely are well suited to users who, no matter their expertise, are drawn to the social potential of MOOCs and enjoy working to create knowledge with others. Finally, the self-direction metaphor seems especially well suited to the way that many users pick and choose how they interact with MOOCs. Perhaps as MOOCs evolve they can experiment with designs that even more clearly embrace particular metaphors, or even better, offer different metaphors from which users can choose. The notion surely deserves further investigation.

REFERENCES

1. Markoff, J. (2011). Virtual and artificial, but 58,000 want course. *The New York Times*. Retrieved from: http://www.nytimes.com/2011/08/16/science/16stanford.html
2. Pappano, L. (2012, November). The year of the MOOC. *The New York Times*. Retrieved from: http://www.nytimes.com/2012/11/04/education/edlife/massive-open-online-courses-aremultiplying-at-a-rapid-pace.html
3. Friedman, T. L. (2013, January 26). Revolution hits the universities. *The New York Times.* Retrieved from http://www.nytimes.com/2013/01/27/opinion/sunday/friedman-revolution-hits-the-universities.html?_r=0
4. Vardi, M. Y. (2012). Will MOOCs destroy academia? *Communications of the ACM, 55*(11).
5. Carr, N. (2012, September). The crisis in higher education. *MIT Technology Review*. Retrieved from: http://www.technologyreview.com/featuredstory/429376/the-crisis-in-higher-education/
6. Siemens, G. (2015). The role of MOOCs in the future of education. In Bonk, C. J., Lee, M. M., Reeves, T. C., & Reynolds, T. H. (Eds) *MOOCs and Open Education Around the World*. New York: Routledge, xii-xvii.
7. Christensen, G., Steinmetz, A., Alcorn, B., Bennett, A., Woods, D., & Emanuel, E. J. (2013). The MOOC phenomenon: Who takes massive open online courses and why? Retrieved from http://papers.ssrn.com/sol3/papers.cfm?abstract_id=2350964
8. Guzdial, M., & Adams, J. C. (2014). MOOCs need more work; so do CS graduates. *Communications of the ACM, 57*(1), p. 18-19.
9. Sandeen, C. (2103). Integrating MOOCs into traditional higher education: The emerging "MOOC 3.0" era. *Change, 45*(5), 34-39.
10. Sfard, A. (1998). On two metaphors for learning and the dangers of choosing just one. *Educational Researcher, 27*(4), 4-13.
11. Swan, K., Day, S., Bogle, & van Prooyen, T. (2015). AMP: A tool for categorizing the pedagogical approaches of MOOCs. In Bonk, C. J., Lee, M. M., Reeves, T. C., & Reynolds, T. H. (Eds) *MOOCs and Open Education Around the World*. New York: Routledge, 105-118.
12. Reeves, T. (1996). *Evaluating what really matters in computer-based education.* Retrieved from http://eduworks.com/Documents/Workshops/EdMedia1998/docs/reeves.html

Observing URL Sharing Behaviour in Massive Online Open Courses

Silvia Elena Gallagher
Trinity College, The University of Dublin, Ireland
Sgallag1@tcd.ie

Timothy Savage
Trinity College, The University of Dublin, Ireland
tsavage@tcd.ie

L@S 2016, April 25–26, 2016, Edinburgh, UK.
ACM 978-1-4503-3726-7/16/04.
http://dx.doi.org/10.1145/2876034.2893387

Abstract
Information sharing is a key activity of Massive Online Open Courses (MOOCs) user behavior. Sharing Uniform Resource Locators (URLs) has been identified as a means for individuals in online spaces to generate social relationships, construct knowledge, and disseminate information; however this activity has not been investigated within the MOOC space. This paper presents an observational study of URL sharing within MOOCs, and explores how a MOOC learning community responded to this micro behaviour. The research explored 1,471 comments and 416 learners who displayed URL sharing behavior from two iterations of the 'Irish Lives' Futurelearn / Trinity College, University of Dublin MOOC. The analysis identified patterns of behavior within 'URL Sharers', and suggests that this activity could support greater learner interaction. Although causality is not implied, the results of this analysis contributes a tentative new understanding of URL sharing in MOOCs, and denotes a new MOOC micro behaviour. This can be useful for MOOC practitioners to facilitate design choices.

Author Keywords
Massive Online Open Courses; Uniform Resource Locators; Online learner behaviour.

Context
The data analyzed in this research originates from a six week Irish History MOOC developed by Trinity College, The University of Dublin and hosted on the Futurelearn platform.

A total of 29,346 users registered in two iterations of the Irish Lives MOOC, and of these, 7,257 learners posted at least one comment. 98,024 comments were posted in both iterations. Within these comments, 1,471 contained a URL which were posted by 416 (5.7%) learners. This cohort of 416 learners is denoted as 'URL Sharers'.

It is important to note that the MOOC structure did not ask learners to provide URLs in any of the learning steps.

ACM Classification Keywords
H.5.m. Information interfaces and presentation (e.g., HCI): Miscellaneous.

Introduction
Knowledge sharing between online learners is a key activity for knowledge acquisition and facilitating social interaction [1]. Massive Online Open Course (MOOC) learners share information asynchronously within discussion spaces in MOOC platforms, however there is a lack of understanding around the type, nature, and influence of information shared between learners. Uniform Resource Locators (URLs) have been investigated in the online space as being examples of connective information sharing tools [2], however little is known of their importance for MOOC learner interaction. This paper investigates the behavior of learners who share URLs in MOOCs, and hypothesizes on the impact of URL shared comments for user engagement. It contributes a original understanding of information sharing within the MOOC space, which could help MOOC practitioners consider design choices and encourage learner interaction.

URLs and Online Social Interaction
Uniform Resource Locators (URLs) are addresses of webpages (e.g. http://www.tcd.ie) commonly used to link information from different areas of the Internet. They are used both as a tool for technical development, and as a medium for individuals to share information online. Sharing URLs has been widely investigated in various online spaces such as micro blogs, social network sites, networked websites, and online communities; however, little research has investigated their presence in MOOCs.

URLs are described as connective tools that help online individuals direct each other, while also showing their own interests in a specific topic [2]. They are a simple way of providing context and promoting knowledge sharing in online environments and can help individuals expose themselves to information that they may not have found themselves. Link sharing could be considered an activity that supports the development of understanding relating to multiple representations of reality, and supporting the social negotiation of knowledge that underpins constructivist learning environments. Link sharing is also considered a critical attribute of connectivist learning whereby learners are bringing into, or connecting, information for the learning community [3].

URL sharing in MOOCs disseminates knowledge and ideas between online individuals; however it is questioned whether sharing URLs in MOOCs can also encourage social relationships and learner interaction.

This research examines the frequency of URLs within MOOC learner comments. It also investigates how a MOOC community responds to URL sharing, and questions whether URL Sharers can be conceptualized as a micro level MOOC learner role.

Methodology
In order to explore the behavior of URL sharing in MOOCs, a quantitative exploratory analysis was conducted on data from the Irish Lives Trinity College / Futurelearn MOOC. The data included 98,024 comments extracted from the Futurelearn platform, of which 1,471 contained a URL. Learners who shared a URL were extracted and termed as 'URL Sharers' (416 learners; 5.7%).

Results

The analysis found the average number of all comments posted by URL Sharers was 52.7 comments (48.8 with outlier removed), compared with 11.1 comments by non-URL sharers, suggesting that URL Sharers tend to comment more actively than non-URL Sharers.

Selected variables	Sept 2014	March 2015	Both
Number of registered learners	18,264	11,085	29,346
Number of comments posted	67,556	30,468	98,024
Number of learners who posted at least one comment	4,857 (26.5%)	2,400 (21.6%)	7,257 (24.7%)
(1) Number of comments containing a URL	937 (1.3%)	534 (1.7%)	1,471 (1.5%)
(2) Number of learners who shared a URL (URL Sharers)	280 (5.7%)	136 (5.6%)	416 (5.7%)
(3) Average number of all comments posted by a URL Sharer / non-URL Sharer	50.2 / 11.6	57.9 / 10	52.7 / 11.1
(4) Number of URL Sharers who provided multiple URLs	154 (55%)	67 (49.2%)	221 (53.1%)

Table 1: Variables examined in URL Sharers cohort

A large proportion of URL Sharers provided multiple sources of information, in the form of URLs, to the MOOC community. 221 URL Sharers (53.1%) provided URLs within multiple comments, with 83 URL Sharers (20%) providing 5 or more comments with URLs. This suggests that this cohort of users could be contextualized as either experts in the field, those with a particular interest in the topic under instruction, or particularly motivated to share other resources they had identified.

An analysis of the top 30 most active posters, denoted by frequency of comments, found that 56% (n=17) were URL Sharers. This could be seen as unsurprising, given that they are posting multiple times. However, it could also be a useful way of identifying power users early, and more research is needed to ascertain whether there is any correlation between these two variables.

Another key area of interest was to examine how the MOOC community responded to the provision of URLs. First, an examination of the average number of likes provided for URL comments and non-URL comments was conducted. It was found that a URL comment had a higher average number of likes than non-URL comments, with URL comments averaging 1.58 likes compared with 0.99 for non-URL comments. This suggests that providing a URL in a comment could elicit more learner engagement, in the form of likes, than not providing a URL.

Secondly, the comments containing URLs were extracted, and an analysis of whether these comments were within multi-comment threads was conducted. Multi-comment threads suggest greater community

Future Research

This preliminary analysis has provided an observational basis for future research in URL Sharing in MOOCs including:

- Comparative analysis across multiple MOOCs
- Modelling of time series data to understand if URL sharing promotes interaction
- Examining what factors promote interaction and whether these correlate with URL sharing
- Investigating and classifying micro level behaviors in MOOCs
- Investigating whether successful course takers spend more time in discussions that have URLs
- Using URL sharing as an activity within MOOCs to determine whether this encourages interaction
- URL sharing and completion rates
- Power users and URL sharing

engagement as learners are interacting with one another, in contrast with single comments where no additional interaction was generated. Of the 1471 comments containing URLs, 49% (n=734) were within multi-comment threads. In comparison with non-URL comments, only 27% (n=26,599) were contained within multi-comment threads. This could suggest that the act of sharing a URL is either encouraging discussion or is being provided in response to a comment.

In addition, the average number of comments within a multi-comment thread that contained or did not contain URLs was also examined. Multi-comment threads that contained a URL were more likely to have longer discussions, with on average 6 comments, compared with an average of 2 comments in a non-URL multi-comment thread. This cautiously suggests that URL comments tend to generate engagement between learners to a greater extent than non-URL comments.

Discussion

This observational study suggests that there is scope for additional analysis of URL sharers in MOOCs. It hypothesizes that URL sharing behavior could have an influence on learner behavior in MOOCs. There appears to be an intriguing correlation between URL sharing and learner activity in MOOCs but more research is needed to investigate the reasons behind this. It is important to stress that causality is not implied in this research.

The analysis contextualizes a cohort of leaners as 'URL Sharers', and described how URL sharing is a method of information dissemination and knowledge generation by learners. It suggests that URL Sharers could be added to the body of knowledge on MOOC user roles. Within this preliminary case study analysis, it is tentatively suggested that these users tend to post more frequently, add knowledge to the MOOC, and facilitate greater engagement between learners.

URL sharing showed increased engagement between users both in the form of 'likes' and multi-comment threads. The analysis of liking behavior brings up additional questions. If URL comments tend to get a larger number of 'likes' than non-URL comments, does this community reassurance encourage URL Sharers to continue sharing URLs or stay longer within the MOOC?

Future research should examine information sharing within MOOCs, and it is suggested that an improved classification of information sharing typologies should be conceptualized. In addition, micro level behavior within MOOCs, such as URL sharing, should also be investigated.

Acknowledgements

We would like to thank the staff at Futurelearn for providing baseline data for this research.

References

1. Ma, W.W.K. and Yuen, A.H.K., 2011. Understanding online knowledge sharing: An interpersonal relationship perspective. Computers & Education 56, 1 (1//), 210-219.
2. Holton, A.E., Baek, K., Coddington, M., and Yaschur, C., 2014. Seeking and Sharing: Motivations for Linking on Twitter. Communication Research Reports 31, 1, 33-40.
3. Siemens, G., 2005. Connectivism: A Learning Theory for the Digital Age. International Journal of Instructional Technology & Distance Learning 2, 1.

Illusion of Progress is Moar Addictive than Cat Pictures

Leo Leppänen
University of Helsinki
Helsinki, Finland
ljleppan@cs.helsinki.fi

Lassi Vapaakallio
University of Helsinki
Helsinki, Finland
lassi.vapaakallio@alumni.helsinki.fi

Arto Vihavainen
University of Helsinki
Helsinki, Finland
avihavai@cs.helsinki.fi

L@S 2016, April 25-26, 2016, Edinburgh, Scotland UK
ACM 978-1-4503-3726-7/16/04.
http://dx.doi.org/10.1145/2876034.2893388

Abstract
We conducted two studies on the effect of visual reward mechanisms for increasing engagement with an online learning material. In the first study, we studied the effect of showing cat pictures as a reward to correct and incorrect answers to multiple choice questions, and in the second study, we created an illusion of progress using a progress bar that showed step-wise increments as students answered to the questions. Our results show the use of cat pictures as a visual reward mechanism does not significantly increase students' engagement with learning materials. At the same time, students who were shown progress bars had a statistically significant increase in the quantity of answers – on average 88% more answers per day. However, our results also indicate that this effect declines over time, meaning that students catch up to the illusion.

Author Keywords
multiple choice questions, visual rewards, visual feedback, motivation, student engagement, gamification, pictures of cats, progress bar

Participant demographics

In the first study, 664 students answered more than three questions. Out of them, 314 were in the treatment group and 350 in the control group. In the second study, 411 students answered more than three questions, with 197 in the treatment group and 214 in the control group.

Introduction

Being active during a course leads to a significantly smaller risk of failing [5]. One way of increasing participation is to motivate students [2]. In any large enough course, not every student is intrinsically motivated to study [9]. Therefore, additional incentives can be helpful. A classical way is to offer partial course credit for assignments [7]. Another, more recent, way has been to employ *gamification* [3, 4], with the purpose of engaging and motivating the students.

In this study, we look at two possible ways of increasing student motivation via visual feedback for answering multiple choice questions (MCQs).

Research Design

Research Questions

The research questions for this study are as follows:

- **RQ1**: How does the use of cat pictures as a feedback mechanism for MCQs change students' behavior?
- **RQ2**: How does the use of progress bars as a feedback mechanism for MCQs change students' behavior?
- **RQ3**: If the students' activity increases or decreases due to the changed feedback mechanism, to what extent does the effect persist?

Context and Data

The study was conducted in an online programming course organized by the University of Helsinki during Spring 2015. The participants included students both affiliated and not affiliated with the university. See sidebar for demographics.

The students were expected to study a blended online material with programming assignments and embedded programming-related MCQs. The students did not receive course points for answering the questions, but they were told that the questions could be useful in rehearsal and as a way to test their understanding so far. Thus, studying the effect of visual rewards on the students' engagement with the questions was meaningful. The MCQs were designed so that the students could request new ones that would have some parts of the question altered. The system was inspired by the QuizPACK [10].

Methodology

Two subsequent 18-day randomized controlled trials were conducted. The students were randomly assigned into two groups that received different types of visual rewards after answering a question. In all studies, all groups received textual feedback in the form of a single word telling them whether the answer was correct, and in addition, the control group was always shown an icon indicating the correctness of their answer. Only users who answered at least 3 different questions were included in the studies.

In the first trial, the treatment group was shown a picture of a sad kitten for an incorrect answer, and a randomly chosen image of a cat with a positive or neutral expression for a correct answer. The cat pool used for the study contained over 1000 images. In the second trial, the treatment group was shown a progress bar that filled one third for every consequent correct answer, and emptied on a wrong answer. When the progress bar was filled completely after three consecutive correct answers, it changed color from blue to green.

Results

A statistical analysis performed on the differences between the groups of the first study ($p = 0.54$ and $df = 33.87$ for Student's T-Test) indicates that there is no statistically significant difference between the groups. The mean answers per day per student were 4.30 for the group that was shown pictures of cats and 4.10 for the control group.

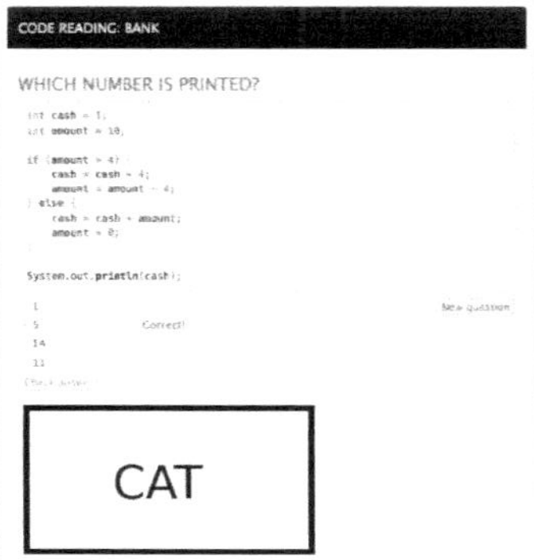

Figure 1: An embedded parameterized question in the course material.

For a correct answer, the shown cat was selected randomly from a database of over 1000 pictures, while an incorrect answer always led to the same picture of a sad cat.

The answer profiles of the student groups in the second study are different, confirmed by Student's T-Test ($p < 0.01$, $df = 26.57$). For the treatment group that was shown a progress bar, the mean answers per day per student was 9.32, while for the control group, the mean answers per day per student was 4.97. This means that the treatment group submitted around 88% more answers per day than those in the control group.

We also searched for statistical trends in all four groups. A Cox-Stuart test for trend showed that the treatment group from the second study — in which students were shown a progress bar — had a statistically significant ($p < 0.02$) decreasing trend. This indicates that the effectiveness of the progress bar diminishes over time. While the other groups also "lost" students over time, no statistically significant trends were found.

Discussion & conclusion

The lack of a statistical difference in student engagement between the groups in the first study suggests that a reward scheme based purely on pictures of cats does not significantly increase student engagement. It is possible that the pictures of cats ended up feeling cheesy or unnecessary in a fashion similar to the way some students perceived badges that were added to online exercises in the study conducted by Haaranen et al. [6]. While we did not study how the students perceived the images, negative perceptions that could be possible in our context have previously been observed by Berkling and Thomas [1]. Our data shows that a small amount of students did answer the questions with cat pictures extensively when they were first introduced, but this small population does not change the overall result. No observable trend was found that could tie the answering behavior to age, gender or previous programming experience.

Based on the above, the answer to our first research question is: "*pictures of cats as a feedback mechanism for MCQs does not increase student engagement with the material.*"

In the study with progress bars, we observed that the amount of students' answers in the treatment group was significantly higher than in the control group, with students answering up to 88% more questions. Therefore the answer to our second research question is: "*a progress bar as a feedback mechanism for MCQs significantly improves student engagement with the material.*"

This behavior with progress bars is interlinked with the *challenge*, an important part of gamification [8]. We postulate that the cat pictures did not present an interesting enough challenge for the student – in the case of the cat pictures, the challenge can be seen as "*can you find the right option for this question?*", whilst in the case of the progress bar the challenge can be seen as "*can you answer a question correctly three times in a row?*"

This result is consistent with the findings of Stott and Neustaedter [11]: overall, students answer more questions when the system has all four of *freedom to fail*, *rapid feedback*, *storytelling* and *progression*. In our case, only the study with the progress bars had a *progression* element.

However, our results also showed that there was a statistically significant decreasing trend in the number of answers in the treatment group with progress bars. Since only the progress bar group showed a statistically significant decreasing trend in the amount of answers, it seems that the other groups form a "baseline", towards which the progress bar group's activity declines. Based on this, our answer to the third research question is: "*the positive changes on student engagement decrease over time.*"

REFERENCES

1. Kay Berkling and Christoph Thomas. 2013. Gamification of a Software Engineering course and a detailed analysis of the factors that lead to it's failure. In *Interactive Collaborative Learning (ICL), 2013 International Conference on.* IEEE, 525–530.
2. Janet Carter, Dennis Bouvier, Rachel Cardell-Oliver, Margaret Hamilton, Stanislav Kurkovsky, Stefanie Markham, O. William McClung, Roger McDermott, Charles Riedesel, Jian Shi, and Su White. 2011. Motivating All Our Students?. In *Proceedings of the 16th Annual Conference Reports on Innovation and Technology in Computer Science Education - Working Group Reports (ITiCSE-WGR '11)*. 1–18.
3. Sebastian Deterding, Dan Dixon, Rilla Khaled, and Lennart Nacke. 2011a. From game design elements to gamefulness: defining gamification. In *Proceedings of the 15th International Academic MindTrek Conference: Envisioning Future Media Environments.* ACM, 9–15.
4. Sebastian Deterding, Miguel Sicart, Lennart Nacke, Kenton O'Hara, and Dan Dixon. 2011b. Gamification. using game-design elements in non-gaming contexts. In *CHI'11 Extended Abstracts on Human Factors in Computing Systems.* ACM, 2425–2428.
5. Scott Freeman, Sarah L Eddy, Miles McDonough, Michelle K Smith, Nnadozie Okoroafor, Hannah Jordt, and Mary Pat Wenderoth. 2014. Active learning increases student performance in science, engineering, and mathematics. *Proceedings of the National Academy of Sciences* 111, 23 (2014), 8410–8415.
6. Lassi Haaranen, Petri Ihantola, Lasse Hakulinen, and Ari Korhonen. 2014. How (not) to introduce badges to online exercises. In *Proceedings of the 45th ACM technical symposium on Computer science education.* ACM, 33–38.
7. Sean Kelly. 2008. What Types of Students' Effort Are Rewarded with High Marks? *Sociology of Education* 81, 1 (2008), 32–52.
8. Scott Nicholson. 2012. A user-centered theoretical framework for meaningful gamification. *Games+ Learning+ Society* 8, 1 (2012).
9. Richard M Ryan and Edward L Deci. 2000. Intrinsic and extrinsic motivations: Classic definitions and new directions. *Contemporary educational psychology* 25, 1 (2000), 54–67.
10. Sergey Sosnovsky, Olena Shcherbinina, and Peter Brusilovsky. 2003. Web-based parameterized questions as a tool for learning. In *World Conference on E-Learning in Corporate, Government, Healthcare, and Higher Education*, Vol. 2003. 309–316.
11. Andrew Stott and Carman Neustaedter. 2013. Analysis of gamification in education. *Surrey, BC, Canada* (2013).

Enabling Schema Agnostic Learning Analytics in a Service-Oriented MOOC Platform

Jan Renz
Hasso Plattner Institute
University Potsdam
jan.renz@hpi.de

Gerado Navarro-Suarez
Hasso Plattner Institute
University Potsdam

Rowshan Sathi
Hasso Plattner Institute
University Potsdam
rowshan.sathi@hpi.de

Thomas Staubitz
Hasso Plattner Institute
University Potsdam
thomas.staubitz@hpi.de

Christoph Meinel
Hasso Plattner Institute
University Potsdam
christoph.meinel@hpi.de

L@S 2016, April 25-26, 2016, Edinburgh, Scotland UK
ACM 978-1-4503-3726-7/16/04.
http://dx.doi.org/10.1145/2876034.2893389

Abstract
This paper at hand describes the design and implementation of an analytics service to retrieve live usage data from students enrolled in a service-oriented MOOC platform for the purpose of learning analytics (LA) research. A real-time and extensible architecture for consolidating and processing data in versatile analytics stores is introduced.

Author Keywords
Service oriented architecture, MOOC, Learning Analytics

ACM Classification Keywords
H.4 Information Systems Applications; H.5 Information interfaces and presentation; K.3.1 Computer Uses in Education;

Introduction
To be able to cope with the "massiveness" of MOOCs, the underlying Learning Management Systems (LMS) must be able to serve thousands of users at the same time. Service Orientated Software Architecture (SOA) using Microservices [1] is a popular pattern to achieve the required performance and scalability.

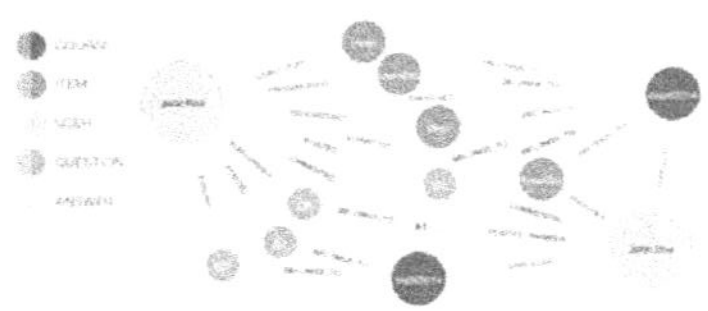

Figure 2: Experience Graph Schema showing the interconnection among different entities such as users, courses and learning items

Figure 3: Use Case Example: Showing the geo position of users To implement this feature and additional *transform* step has been added that converts the Users IP-Address to an approximate Geo Information and adds this information to the the tracked event. This information is then queried using *ElasticSearch*.

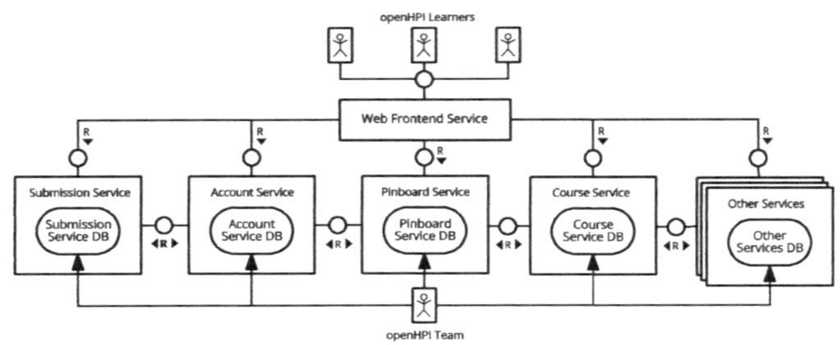

Figure 1: FMC diagram of an service orientated LMS architecture. While this architecture uses stand alone components that communicate with each other, it is notable that this is an internal architecture only.

Given a data analysts view, one of the major drawbacks of such a distributed architecture is the loss of a centralized place, where all the data (including all the learning analytics data) is stored. This complicates the retrieval of data, especially if the required data is spread across multiple services. Given an architecture as proposed in [2] and shown in Figure 1, a learner taking a course will produce data in the data storages of several services.

This paper will discuss two main research questions:

1. Facing a service-oriented MOOC platform, what is the best approach to collect and extract the relevant data?
2. What are appropriate schemas and technologies for storing, analyzing, and querying the data?

Service specific and cross service data

All data, that is contained within a single service can be retrieved by just querying this specific service. Given the course enrollments are managed by a specific service, retrieving data like enrollments per course or enrollments over time can be retrieved by querying this service or the underlying database. This does not require a dedicated analytics service.

But as soon as the required data is spread across multiple services (for example the overall course activity) or the data does not belong to any specific service (such as, e.g. UI interaction tracking data) a new service must be introduced to take responsibility of these tasks. We will call this service the Learning Analytics Service (Lanalytics). Its responsibility is the data collection, transformation, storage, and retrieval of all required learning analytics data. The service concept in brief is, an analytics service which collects or gathers the latest data from different services, perform additional processing steps, transforms the gathered data into different data schema and finally loads the transformed data into several data stores, called Analytics Stores (AS). Researchers and other services can access these AS to retrieve data or perform analyses.

Data collection

Traditional approaches, such as ETL (Extract, Transform and Load process), do not work in the current architecture as it does not support real time data processing and short term load peaks, which violates SOA principles, as it collects data directly from databases. Pulling data from the service interface also does not meet the data collection requirements of service oriented architecture. Data virtualization is an emerging approach which provides an abstraction layer on top of the database. This abstraction layer provides a unified access to retrieve data from the underlying infrastructure. The drawback of this approach is its complexity and the lack

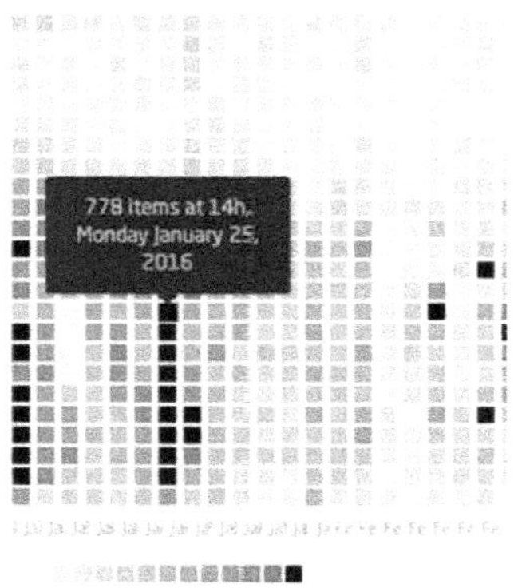

Figure 5: Use Case Example: Showing the overall course activity by hour.

of complete transparency for data and information management [3].

Therefore, an event driven push model for services is an appropriate option for data collection in this context. A combination of SOA and event-driven architecture is proposed as a solution for data collection, which is known as 'Event-Driven SOA' and used for this service.

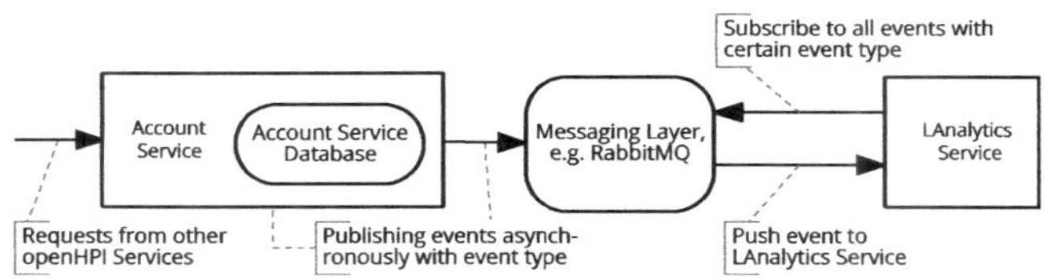

Figure 4: Overview of the event-driven concept for data collection

The events that are sent by the services follow a format inspired by the Experience API [5] in the form of: <Actor> <Verb> <Object>, with <Result> in <Context>. As shown in Figure 2 the *Lanalytics* service then subscribes to this events.

Data transformation and storage

After the service has received the subscribed events this data has than to be processed and stored. The service currently supports three different data schema, which will be described in the following paragraphs.

The **Experience Event schema** stores the processed events in *ElasticSearch* and *Postgres* as flat event data. The **Experience Graph Schema** uses the same data, but represents it in a graph model**.** Apart from directly mapped entities, there are some entities which describe the relationship among different nodes and thus, they are explicitly mapped to the edges. In the graph this relationship is seen as a statement where *Actor* is the origin of the edge, *Verb* is the type of the edge and *Object* is the destination of the edge. Additional parts of the statement such as *Result* and *Context* are added as properties of the edge. Therefore, by following the mentioned rules it is possible to create a graph that contains a) most entities of the platform, b) the relationships between these entities, c) the user activities represented similar to the Experience API statements, and d) the student profile data as the students are represented as nodes with all available data attributes. Figure 2 not only shows the interlinked data model but also shows the possibilities of finding similarities among learners and to compare the learning experience and outcome between two learners. This data is stored in a Graph database. Furthermore, it supports **the MOOCdb schema[8]**.

Data transformation is based on a processing pipeline, inspired by the *chain responsibility* and *command* pattern [6]. Each pipeline consists of *ExtractSteps*, *TransformSteps* and *LoadSteps* classes. *ExtractSteps* processes the raw input data into a container class *ProcessingUnit*. Then the pipeline passes the *PipelineUnit* to *TransformSteps,* which transforms the data by implementing a *transform()* method. The mapping is done in the *TransformStep*. As a part of this mapping, *TransformSteps* creates *LoadSteps*. A layer *LoadCommands* is introduced between *TransformSteps* and *LoadSteps* to ensure the modularity and extensibity of the LAnalytics Service. Finally, The *LoadSteps* excecutes the *LoadCommands* to update the respective analytics stores. The stored data can be retrieved via a REST interface. An example how this could be done can be found in [7].

Performance and scalability evaluation

As this communication is asynchronous, data processing will not not slow down the overall performance of the system on load peaks. If more events are sent than the Lanalytics service is able to process in real time, it will result in an increasing cue size and receiving slightly outdated data when retrieving data from this service. Given the service based architecture and the decoupling from other system components it can easily be scaled by deploying multiple instance or scaling the underlying data storages.

Conclusion

Introducing a dedicated service enables learning analytics for data that is spread across multiple service or not maintained by any service at all (, such as UI interactions). By using multiple analytic stores with different underlying technologies the advantages of these stores can be utilized to do complex analytic queries at a low implementation cost. While some storages and schemas are good for event based data, other represent graphs of interconnected entities. Since the rollout of the first version, most analytics tasks have been implemented using the the *Experience Event* schema running on ElasticSearch.

The major drawback is that every storage system has to be maintained. Furthermore, computing power and storage has to be provided for every single storage system.

References

1. Sam Newman. 2015. *Building Microservices*. " O'Reilly Media, Inc.".
2. Christoph Meinel, Michael Totschnig, and Christian Willems. 2013. openHPI: Evolution of a MOOC platform from LMS to SOA. In *Proceedings of the 5th International Conference on Computer Supported Education (CSEDU), INSTICC, Aachen, Germany*, Vol. 5.
3. Arcot Rajasekar, Mike Wan, Reagan Moore, and Wayne Schroeder. 2006. A prototype rule-based distributed data management system. In HPDC workshop on Next Generation Distributed Data Management, Vol. 102. Citeseer.
4. Learning Measurement for Analytics Whitepaper, https://www.imsglobal.org/sites/default/files/caliper/IMSLearningAnalyticsWP.pdf
5. Advanced Distributed Learning. 2013. The Experience API - Version 1.0.1. (2013). http://www.adlnet.gov/wp- content/uploads/2013/10/xAPI_v1.0.1- 2013- 10-01.pdf
6. Rebecca Ferguson and Simon Buckingham Shum. 2012. Social learning analytics: five approaches. In *Proceedings of the 2nd international conference on learning analytics and knowledge*. ACM, 23–33.
7. Jan Renz, Daniel Hoffmann, Thomas Staubitz, and Christoph Meinel, 2016, Using A/B Testing in MOOC Environments in *Proceedings of the 6th International Conference on Learning Analytics and Knowledge, ACM, http://dx.doi.org/10.1145/2883851.2883876*
8. Kalyan Veeramachaneni, Sherif Halawa, Franck Dernoncourt, Una-May O'Reilly, Colin Taylor, Chuong Do. MOOCdb: Developing Standards and Systems to Support MOOC Data Science. arXiv# 1406.2015

Designing Videos with Pedagogical Strategies: Online Students' Perceptions of Their Effectiveness

Chaohua Ou
Georgia Institute of Technology
Atlanta, GA 30332, USA
cou@gatech.edu

Ashok K. Goel
Georgia Institute of Technology
Atlanta, GA 30332, USA
goel@cc.gatech.edu

David A. Joyner
Georgia Institute of Technology
Atlanta, GA 30332, USA
joyner@cc.gatech.edu

Daniel F. Haynes
Georgia Institute of Technology
Atlanta, GA 30332, USA

L@S 2016, April 25-26, 2016, Edinburgh, Scotland Uk
ACM 978-1-4503-3726-7/16/04.
http://dx.doi.org/10.1145/2876034.2893391

Abstract
Despite the ubiquitous use of videos in online learning and enormous literature on designing online learning, there has been relatively little research on what pedagogical strategies should be used to make the most of video lessons and what constitutes an effective video for student learning. We experimented with a model of incorporating four pedagogical strategies, four instructional phases, and four production guidelines-in designing and developing video lessons for an online graduate course. In this paper, we share our experience as well as students' perceptions of their effectiveness. We also discuss what needs to be done for future research.

Author Keywords
artificial intelligence, educational videos, learning at scale, MOOCs, online learning

Introduction
Online instruction is provided predominantly through short content-based videos [5]. Despite the enormous literature on designing online learning, there has been relatively little research on what pedagogic strategies should be employed to make the most of the video lessons and what constitutes an effective video for teaching and learning [5,6, 7]. On the other hand,

Figure 1: Four-phase instructional structure

many computer scientists have examined students' different video interaction patterns and the potential of leveraging the patterns to provide insights for improving the MOOC learning experiences [4, 8, 9, 10, 11]. These analyses provide insights into how students interact with videos and how videos with different production styles and navigations make difference in student engagement. Although these studies examined and analyzed massive amount of data on students' video watching, students' perceptions of the effectiveness of the videos are generally lacking.

Goel & Joyner [2], experimented with a model of incorporating four pedagogical strategies, four instructional phases, and four production guidelines-in designing and developing 26 video lessons for an online graduate course. They also surveyed students on their perceptions of the video lessons' effectiveness. In this paper, we analyze the survey findings as well as our experience of designing and developing the videos. We also discuss about what needs to be done for further research on exploring the effectiveness of educational videos in online learning.

Design and Development of Video Lessons for Online KBAI

Knowledge-Based Artificial Intelligence (KBAI) is a core course in artificial intelligence. It has been offered online since Fall 2014 as part of the Georgia Tech Online Masters of Science in Computer Science program. In designing videos for this course, we tried to leverage the key strength of video as a medium by integrating the design with four pedagogical strategies [2]: (1) *learning by example*: Each video lesson presents an example of a real-world task for which we want to build an AI agent. This example is then used throughout the explanation of the method in that lesson to tie the method back to a particular practical problem; (2) *learning by doing*: Each video lesson includes several interactive exercises, one for each main concept in the class; (3) *adaptive learning*: We equipped the exercises with a tutor to give students targeted, personalized, just-in-time feedback on their responses to the exercises; and (4) *learning through reflection*: At the conclusion of each video lesson, the instructor recaps of the main points of the lesson and connects it to other parts of the course. Students are then asked to summarize and submit what they have learned. We created a coherent and dynamic instructional structure in every video lesson by adopting and applying the principle of four-phase instruction [12, 13] (see Figure 1). We adopted four video production guidelines from research literature that have been found to be effective in engaging students [4, 5, 14]: (1) *Keep it short and to the point*: The length of the video clips ranges from 1 to 5 minutes; (2) *Demonstrate by tablet capture*: A digital whiteboard is used to illustrate examples with instructor voiceover. Graphics, charts, animations, and instructor's handwriting are used for the demonstration; (3) *Pair teaching*: We experimented with pair teaching in some of our videos. We were hoping that the interactive conversation/discussion format of teaching would help build a connection between the presenters and the students, stimulating their interest and engaging them as well; and (4) *Provide learner control*: The 26 video lessons are organized based on the structure of the course topics and students are provided with a schedule on when they should finish studying each of the lessons. However, all the videos are available to the students and they are free to study at their own pace.

	Statement
Item 1	The lectures are informative and easy to understand.
Item 2	The exercises provided during the lectures kept me engaged.
Item 3	The feedback I received from the exercises enhanced my understanding of the lesson.
Item 4	Overall, the video lessons were valuable in helping me learn.

Table 1: The 4-item scale in end-of-course survey

Students' Perception of the Video Lessons' Effectiveness

We administered the end-of-semester survey in Fall 2014 and Spring 2015. A 4-item scale was used to get an insight into students' perceptions of the video lessons' effectiveness (see Table 1). Each item was rated on a 7-point scale (1 = strongly disagree, 7 = strongly agree). The results of multivariate analysis of variance (MANOVA) indicated that there was no significant difference on the ratings among students from two semesters on each of the four statements. The lectures were particularly highly rated in terms of being informative and easy to understand ($M = 6.43$). Students were very positive about the exercises. They agreed the exercises kept them engaged ($M = 6.01$) and the feedback from the exercises helped enhance their understanding of the lessons ($M = 5.70$). Overall, students strongly believed that the video lessons were valuable in helping them learn ($M=6.51$).

We asked student what, if any, course elements they would like to see in other online courses. There were 86 responses for Fall 2014 and 105 for Spring 2015. Among the total of 191 students who responded to the question, 46 (24.1%) of them recommended the video lessons among various course elements. Thematic analysis [1, 3] was used to analyze the 46 responses and these are the elements that the students liked about the video lessons: (1) Interesting, insightful, useful, and easy-to-understand lectures. (2) Pair teaching; (3) The interactive exercises. (4) Personalized feedback from the tutor; and (5) Instructional structure of the video lessons. We also asked students what changes they would recommend be made to the course or to the video lessons. In the Fall 2014 survey, a total of 97 students responded to the question regarding what changes they would recommend be made to the course and 10 of the students recommended changes be made to the video lessons. In the Spring 2015 survey, we specifically asked a question on what changes they would recommend to be made to the video lessons and 88 students responded to the question. However, 36 out of the 88 students responded by saying the video lessons were excellent and no changes were needed. Therefore, thematic analysis [1, 3] was conducted on 62 responses, 10 from the Fall survey and 52 from the Spring survey. Here are the two major changes they proposed: (1) Provide more exercises and more challenging exercises; and (2) Provide more examples, resources, and guidance on how concepts can be incorporated into course projects.

Discussion and Future Work

The preliminary findings of this study indicate that the model for designing and developing online KBAI video lessons was successful in creating an interactive learning environment to effectively engage students and improve their online learning experience. We hope this model will help instructors, instructional designers, and video production professionals make informed decisions on designing and developing educational videos.

In order to further accommodate students' needs, more exercises could be designed as optional exercises so that those who need more exercises could choose to practice more. To meet the needs of the students who want more challenging exercises while not making the exercises too difficult for other students, branching exercises could be used to achieve a balance. As for the learner support that students wanted for the course projects, case studies, project examples, and other resources could be provided as study guide instead. On the other hand, the current study only explored students' perceptions of the video lessons' effectiveness. Future studies are needed to explore how students' use of the video lessons affects their learning performance.

References

1. Braun, V., & Clarke, V. (2006). Using thematic analysis in psychology. *Qualitative Research in Psychology, 3*(2), 77-101.
2. Goel, A., & Joyner, D. (2016) An Experiment in Teaching Cognitive Systems Online. *International Journal of Scholarship of Technology-Enhanced Learning, 1(1):3-23.*
3. Guest, G., MacQueen, K.M. & Namey, E. E. (2011). *Applied thematic analysis*. London: Sage.
4. Guo, P. J., Kim, J., & Rubin, R. (2014). How Video Production Affects Student Engagement: An Empirical Study of MOOC Videos. In *Proceedings of the Second ACM Conference on Learning @ Scale.* ACM.
5. Hansch, A., Hillers, L., McConachie, K., Newman, C., Schildhauer, T., & Schmidt, P. (2015) Video and Online Learning: Critical Reflections and Findings from the Field. *HIIG Discussion Paper Series No. 2015-02*. Retrieved from http://ssrn.com/abstract=2577882
6. Hibbert, M. (2014). What Makes an Online Instructional Video Compelling? *EDUCAUSE Review*. Retrieved August 1, 2015, from http://www.educause.edu/ero/article/what-makes-online-instructional-video-compelling
7. Kay, R. H. (2012). Exploring the use of video podcasts in education: A comprehensive review of the literature. *Computers in Human Behavior, 28*(3), 820-831.
8. Kim, J., Guo, P. J., Cai, C. J., Li, S., Gajos, K.Z., & Miller, R. C. (2014a). Data-Driven Interaction Techniques for Improving Navigation of Educational Videos. *UIST 2014.*
9. Kim, J., Li, S., Cai, C. J., Gajos, K.Z., & Miller, R. C. (2014b). Leveraging Video Interaction Data and Content Analysis to Improve Video Learning. *CHI 2014 Workshop on Learning Innovation at Scale.*
10. Kim, J., Guo, P. J., Seaton, D.T., Mitros, P., Gajos, K.Z., & Miller, R. C. (2014c). Understanding In-Video Dropouts and Interaction Peaks in Online Lecture Videos. *Proceedings of the Second ACM Conference on Learning @ Scale.* ACM.
11. Li, N., Kidzinski, L., Jermann, P., & Dillenbourg, P. (2015). MOOC Video Interaction Patterns: What do they tell us? In *Design for Teaching and Learning in a Networked World* (pp. 197-210). Springer International Publishing.
12. Merrill, M. D. (2002). First principles of instruction. *Educational Technology Research and Development, 50*(3), 43-59.
13. Merrill, M. D. (2007). First principles of instruction: A synthesis. In R. A. Reiser & J. V. Dempsey (Eds.), *Trends and issues in instructional design and technology* (2nd ed., pp. 62-71). Upper Saddle River, NJ: Merrill/Prentice-Hall
14. Thomson, A., Bridgstock, R., & Willems, C. (2014). "Teachers flipping out" beyond the online lecture: Maximising the educational video potential of video. *Journal of Learning Design, 7*(3), 67-78.

Optimizing the Amount of Practice in an On-Line Learning Platform

Kim M. Kelly
Worcester Polytechnic Institute
Worcester, MA USA
kkelly@wpi.edu

Neil T. Heffernan
Worcester Polytechnic Institute
Worcester, MA USA
nth@wpi.edu

L@S 2016, April 25–26, 2016, Edinburgh, UK.
ACM 978-1-4503-3726-7/16/04.
DOI: http://dx.doi.org/10.1145/2876034.2893393

Abstract
Intelligent tutoring systems are known for providing customized learning opportunities for thousands of users. One feature of many systems is differentiating the amount of practice users receive. To do this, some systems rely on a threshold of consecutive correct responses. For instance, Khan Academy used to use ten correct in a row and now uses five correct in a row as the mastery threshold. The present research uses a series of randomized control trials, conducted in an online learning platform (eg., ASSISTments.org), to explore the effects of different thresholds of consecutive correct responses on learning. Results indicate that despite spending significantly more time practicing there is no significant difference on learning between two, three, four, or five consecutive correct responses. This suggests that systems, and MOOCS, can employ the simple rule of two or three consecutive correct responses when determining the amount of practice provided to users.

Introduction
Online platforms (Khan Academy, MOOCs, Webwork.org, etc.) are widely used in education to help improve student learning. One feature of such systems is their ability to personalize the learning experience for students by customizing the amount of practice provided to students. However, determining the optimal amount of practice, while essential, is not a trivial task. Clearly, determining the correct amount of practice is

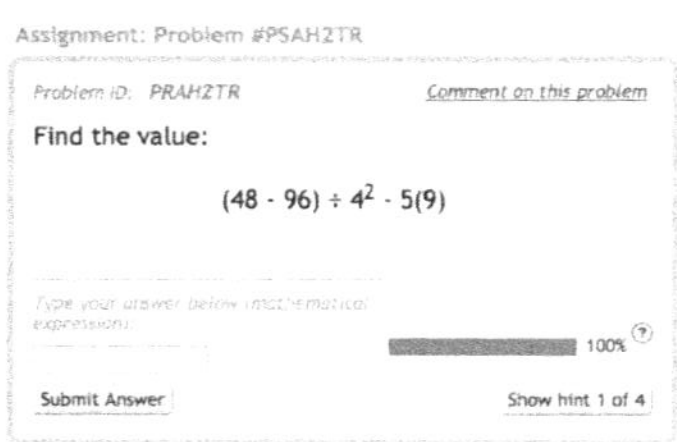

Figure 1. A sample order of operations problem students completed as part of Study 1.

Condition (Students who met the threshold)	Mean Post-Test Score	Mean # of questions	Mean minutes
2-CCR (n=69)	33% (48)	5.7 (3.9)	14.30 (10.90)
3-CCR (n=79)	34% (48)	7.5 (3.9)	17.36 (11.75)
4-CCR (n=66)	39% (49)	9.1 (5.1)	16.55 (12.48)
5-CCR (n=44)	36% (49)	13.1 (7.8)	23.45 (15.72)

Table 1. Study 1 mean post-test scores, number of questions completed by students, and number of minutes it took for students to complete the assignment by condition. Standard deviations are included in parenthesis.

critical because under-practice might not provide enough opportunities for a student to learn a skill, while over-practice might cause students and teachers to disengage with the system. To determine the correct amount of practice, systems attempt to identify the point in time when students have "learned" the skill, otherwise referred to as reaching mastery. Defining mastery may vary between systems.

Systems use a variety of methods to predict this latent variable, mastery. For example, some systems, such as Cognitive Tutor [4,6] rely on knowledge tracing. Knowledge tracing uses student performance to compute the probability that the student will answer the next problem correctly, as well as the probability that the student is in the known state [1]. More complicated methods, such as deep knowledge tracing [5] are currently being developed as well. However, a simpler method also exits. Systems, such as Khan Academy [2] and ASSISTments [3] use a predetermined number of consecutive correct responses (N-CCR) to predict mastery. This method is based on the assumption that if a student can answer a set threshold of consecutive questions correctly than the student has mastered the skill and additional practice is not needed.

N-CCR has the potential benefit of being simple to understand and interpret. Teachers, parents and students can easily understand what is required to complete an assignment. Additionally, a consecutive correct threshold is easy to implement in that it doesn't require complicated programming like knowledge tracing. This makes it particularly useful for simple systems and even MOOCs that are looking to customize learning experiences for thousands of users across the world.

So what is the optimal threshold? The present study uses the random assignment feature in ASSISTments to investigate whether additional attempts, due to a higher mastery threshold, will lead to improved learning as measured by performance on a transfer task.

Study 1- Method

Students from four different middle school classes were randomly assigned to one of four conditions: 2-CCR (n=103), 3-CCR (n=109), 4-CCR (104), or 5-CCR (n=96). The number indicates the threshold of consecutive correct responses that were required to complete the assignment. For example, a student in the 3-CCR condition would be required to answer three consecutive questions correctly without hints or support before reaching mastery. The topic for this assignment was order of operations (see Figure 1). Questions were all morphologically similar to each other. Once students reached the threshold for consecutive correct responses, they were immediately given a post-test that consisted of one transfer item. The transfer item required students to apply the current topic in a novel situation.

Results

In analyzing the data, it was noted that completion rates seemed to vary by condition. A chi-square test of independence was performed to examine the relation between students who finished and those who did not by the extreme conditions (2-CCR and 5-CCR). As expected, the relation was significant X^2 (2, N=199) = 9.06, p<0.01. This means that there was a disproportional amount of students who completed the assignment by condition. Reaching the 5-CCR threshold required students to complete more problems than the 2-CCR condition. Therefore more students in the 5-CCR condition quit the assignment before finishing than in the 2-CCR condition. This introduces a selection effect.

Presumably, students who persevered and completed the assignment with a higher threshold were higher knowledge students. This means that differences in post-test scores might be caused by student differences rather than the experimental manipulation.

Despite the probable selection effect, when examining post-test scores (see Table 1), an ANOVA revealed that there was no significant difference in performance on the post-test by condition ($F(3,258) = 0.21$, $p = 0.89$). Yet students in the 5-CCR condition completed on average twice as many questions and spent significantly more time than students in in the 3-CCR condition. To account for the differential completion rate by condition all students who did not complete the assignment were automatically assigned a post-test score of zero. As expected, post-test scores dropped. An ANOVA again revealed, no significant difference in post-test performance by condition ($F(3, 412) = 0.86$, $p = 0.46$).

A review of the 95% confidence interval shows that mean post-test performance for 2-CCR, 3-CCR, and 4-CCR conditions overlap. Remember, to account for the differential completion rate, students who failed to reach the threshold were assigned a post-test score of zero. As a result, the mean post-test score for the 5-CCR condition is greatly impacted by the increased number of students who did not complete the assignment.

Study 2- Method

In an attempt to generalize the findings of Study 1, an additional study was conducted simultaneously with a different mathematical topic. Again, students were randomly assigned to one of four conditions: 2-CCR (n=64), 3-CCR (51), 4-CCR (59), or 5-CCR (42). The topic for this assignment was the distributive property. Once students met the N-CCR threshold, they were immediately given a post-test that consisted of two transfer questions. The transfer questions required students to apply the skill in a more challenging problem.

Results

As expected, there was a differential completion rate by condition. However unlike Study 1, the difference between the two extreme conditions (2-CCR and 5-CCR) was not significant (X^2 (2, N=106) = 0.30, $p = 0.59$).

When considering only the students who met the threshold requirement for their condition, an ANOVA revealed that there is no significant difference in performance on the post-test by condition ($F(3, 162) = 1.35$, $p = 0.26$). See Table 2 for mean post-test scores.

Despite the lack of improved learning, students in the 5-CCR condition completed significantly more questions than those in the 2-CCR condition ($F(3, 163) = 25.24$, $p<0.0001$). An analysis of the 95% confidence intervals for number of questions completed reveals that 3-CCR does not appear different than 4-CCR in the amount of practice students receive.

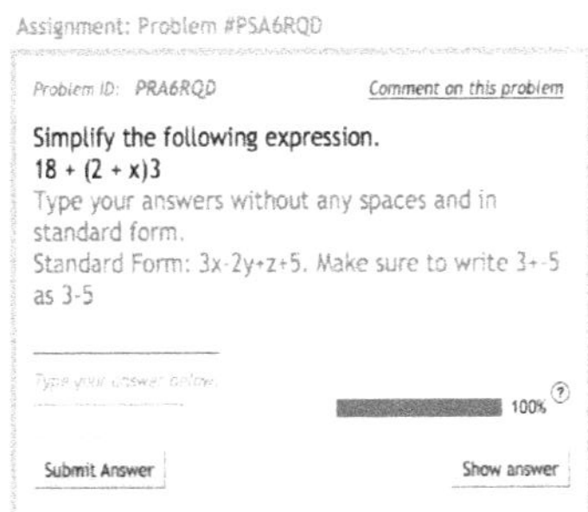

Figure 2. A sample distributive property problem students completed as part of Study 2.

Condition	Mean Post-Test Score	Mean Number of Questions
2-CCR (n=53)	46% (38)	2.9 (1.2)
3-CCR (n=38)	55% (39)	5.7 (3.8)
4-CCR (n=42)	38% (37)	6.6 (3.4)
5-CCR (n=33)	49% (39)	8.8 (4.1)

Table 2: For students in Study 2 who reached the N-CCR threshold and completed the assignment, the mean post-test scores by condition and mean number of questions completed by students are shown. Standard deviations are provided in parenthesis.

Conclusion

Determining the correct amount of practice students require to learn a skill is essential for the success of on-line learning environments. The present studies investigate different thresholds (including two, three, four, and five) of consecutive correct responses and find that there is no significant impact on learning as measured by performance on transfer tasks. However, as expected, higher thresholds force students to complete significantly more practice. This becomes a problem when it affects homework completion rates. Specifically, higher thresholds deter students from completing assignments, which may impact their future engagement with system and potentially their self-esteem.

This is a significant contribution to the field because as systems attempt to educate learners en masse, they must be able to easily, yet accurately customize practice opportunities. Future research should attempt to look at retention rates as an alternative measure of learning. Specifically, is there a difference in performance by condition on a post-test that is administered a week after students reach the N-CCR threshold? This might indicate that there is in fact a benefit to higher thresholds of N-CCR.

Acknowledgements

We thank multiple current NSF grants (ACI-1440753, DRL-1252297, DRL-1109483, DRL-1316736, DGE-1535428 & DRL-1031398) , the US Dept. of Ed (IES R305A120125 & R305C100024 and GAANN), and the ONR.

References

1. Corbett, A., Anderson, J. (1995). Knowledge Tracing: Modeling Acquisition of Procedural Knowledge. *User Modeling and User-Adapted Interaction,* 4, 253-278.
2. Faus, M. (2014). Improving Khan Academy's student knowledge model for better predictions. *MattFaus.com* [web log]. Retrieved October, 2014, from http://mattfaus.com/2014/05/improving-khan-academys-student-knowledge-model-for-better-predictions/
3. Feng, M., Heffernan, N. T., Koedinger, K. R.: Addressing the assessment challenge in an Intelligent Tutoring System that tutors as it assesses. *User Modeling and User-Adapted Interaction*, 19, 243-266 (2009)
4. Koedinger, K.R., Corbett, A.T. (2006). Cognitive tutors: Technology bringing learning sciences to the classroom. In Sawyer, R.K. (ed.). The Cambridge handbook of the learning sciences. Cambridge University Press, New York.
5. Piech, C., Bassen, J., Huang, J., Ganguli, S., Sahami, M., Guibas, L. & Sohl-Dickstein, J. Deep Knowledge Tracing. Retrieved from http://web.stanford.edu/~cpiech/bio/papers/deepKnowledgeTracing.pdf.
6. Timeline of Cognitive Tutor History. (2003-2013). Cognitive Tutoring Authoring Tools. Retrieved from http://ctat.pact.cs.cmu.edu/index.php?id=timeline

Optimally Discriminative Choice Sets in Discrete Choice Models: Application to Data-Driven Test Design

Igor Labutov
Cornell University
Ithaca, NY
iil4@cornell.edu

Kelvin Luu
University of Washington
Seattle, WA
kellu@cs.washington.edu

Hod Lipson
Columbia University
New York, NY
hod.lipson@columbia.edu

Christoph Studer
Cornell University
Ithaca, NY
studer@cornell.edu

L@S 2016, April 25–26, 2016, Edinburgh, UK.
ACM 978-1-4503-3726-7/16/04.
http://dx.doi.org/10.1145/2876034.2893394

Abstract

Difficult test questions can be made easy by providing a set of possible answer options of which most are obviously wrong. In the education literature, a plethora of instructional guides exist for crafting a suitable set of wrong choices (distractors) in order to probe the students' understanding of the tested concept. The art of multiple-choice question design thus hinges on the question-maker's experience and knowledge of the potential misconceptions. In contrast, we advocate a data-driven approach, where correct and incorrect options are assembled directly from the students' own past submissions. Large-scale online classroom settings, such as massively open online courses (MOOCs), provide an opportunity to design optimal and adaptive multiple-choice questions that are maximally informative about the students' level of understanding of the material. We deploy a multinomial-logit discrete choice model for the setting of multiple choice testing, derive an optimization objective for selecting optimally discriminative option sets, and demonstrate the effectiveness of our approach via a user study.

Introduction

A finite set of alternatives for the student to pick from—the key feature of multiple choice questions (MCQs) that makes them attractive in grading, is the very thing that makes *good* MCQs notoriously difficult to design [4]. Incorrect options, also known as distractors, should ideally be picked from a representative set of misconceptions that students commonly share. But even if this set is representative, the question might still fail to distinguish between students who were "close" to the correct answer and those who were clueless. In the adaptive testing literature [3], the questions are selected to be at a level appropriate for a given student, such that their responses result in the most accurate estimate of their knowledge. In this work, we pursue adaptive testing at a finer-grained level of *question design*.

The contributions of our work are summarized as follows:

- We derive an objective set function for selecting an optimal set of choices in a nominal choice model, given the estimated user ability.
- We collect and release a dataset used in our experiments: a "U.S. States Quiz" dataset, where users were given an MCQ quiz testing their knowledge of U.S. states.

Model

We require our model to have the following three features:

- The model specifies the probability of a student choosing a particular option as a function of that student's *ability* and that option's *correctness*, such that students with higher ability are more likely to pick the most correct option (we will discuss this aspect in detail below).
- An "ideal" student (with the greatest attainable *ability*) chooses the correct option with probability 1.
- A student with the least attainable *ability* makes their choice uniformly at random.

For simplicity, we require that there is one correct option, leaving the remaining options as distractors that lie on a continuum of *apparent correctness*, i.e., a measure that varies in how difficult it is to discern the distractor from the correct answer.

A multinomial logit model with a partial order constraint on the choices and a non-negativity constraint on the student's *ability*, exhibits all of the desired properties above. Specifically, we use the following model:

$$P(s_i \text{ picks option } j \mid \theta_i, \{\beta_j\}_{j\in Q}) = \frac{\exp(\theta_i\beta_j)}{\sum_{\beta_{j'}\in Q}\exp(\theta_i\beta_{j'})}$$

such that $\beta_{j*} > \beta_j,\ \forall\beta_j \in Q \setminus \beta_{j*}$, and $\theta_i \geq 0, \forall i.$

Here, s_i is student i with ability θ_i, $\{\beta_j\}_{j\in Q}$ is the set of option parameters of question Q that encodes the *apparent correctness* of each option, and β_{j*} is the correct option. Without the explicit partial order constraint on choices and the non-negativity constraint on subjects, the model would capture the relative preference of subjects towards choices. In psychometrics this would be known as the nominal response model [2], and is related to the more general multidimensional unfolding models often used to investigate the relationship between subjects and preferences. In our setting, the non-negativity constraints on the ability θ_i, combined with the partial order constraints on the option parameters are critical to obtain the desired interpretation of the θ_i parameters, namely as capturing the *ability* of the students. More importantly, performing optimal option subset selection under this model will result in subsets that are most informative about the students' *abilities*.

Optimal Choice Sets

We pose the problem of optimal choice set design in the traditional experiment-design setting: maximize Fisher information on the student ability parameter θ as a function of a selected observation (choice set). We can show that under the model formulated in the previous section, the optimal choice set of a maximum size K is a solution to the following discrete optimization problem:

$$\begin{aligned} \underset{\{x_i x_j\}}{\text{maximize}} \quad & \frac{\sum_{i,j} x_i x_j (\beta_i - \beta_j)^2 \exp(\theta[\beta_i + \beta_j])}{\sum_{i,j} x_i x_j \exp(\theta[\beta_i + \beta_j])} \\ \text{subject to} \quad & x_i \in \{0,1\}, \forall x_i \\ & \sum x_i \leq K \end{aligned}$$

User Study: "US States Quiz"

We performed a real-world study to evaluate the importance of data-driven choice set selection in the context of a quiz that asks users to name states of the United States. In this setting, we considered a *question* to be a specific state which the subject is required to identify by picking a correct choice out of a set of options. Each subject had to complete a task consisting of two stages, in the following order:

Stage I (fullMCQ): Subjects are presented with a map of the U.S. with a randomly highlighted state and 50 options, one for each state. This selection is made for every one of the 50 states, presented in a random order. Subjects are not revealed the correct answer.

Stage II (subsetMCQ): The same subject then repeats the test, but now with only 4 options for each of the 50 states. Options are chosen according to two strategies: **Random** and **Optimal** described in more detail below.

Each subject was randomly assigned to one of two experimental conditions: (**Exp1**, **Exp2**):

(Exp1) Random: ($N = 110$) During the second stage of the task (**subsetMCQ**), the choices are selected uniformly at random from the 50 options.

(Exp2) Optimal: ($N = 67$) During the second stage of the task (**subsetMCQ**), the choices are selected according to the optimization objective derived in the previous section. Data collected during the **Random** condition is used to fit the model parameters to be used for optimizing the subsets (described in detail next).

We propose two strategies for empirically assessing the quality of an MCQ test via two correlation metrics:

Within-subject correlation The performance of the subject at the first stage of the task (**FullMCQ**) serves as a ground-truth score of that subject's knowledge of the domain. The correlation of the performance score of the same subject on the same set of questions, but with only a subset of choices, provides a measure of quality of the presented choice sets. We observe in Figure 2 that the within-subject correlation between the scores improves significantly in the **Optimal** condition: Pearson's correlation in the **Optimal** condition is 0.89, vs. 0.78 in **Random**.

Between-subject correlation A good test should also discriminate between subjects of different levels of ability. If, for example, student A ranks higher that student B by their raw score on the **fullMCQ**, we should expect this ordering to be preserved if we were to instead rank the students based on their performance on the **subsetMCQ** test. We use Kendall Tau—a measure of rank correlation—on subsets of students ordered according to their performance in the **fullMCQ** and **subsetMCQ** tests. We observe (Figure 2) that rank correlation in the subjects exposed to the **Optimal** condition significantly outperforms

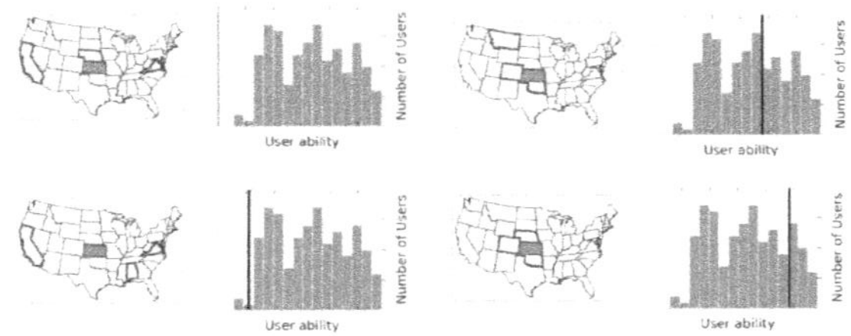

Figure 1: Visualization of optimal choice sets for the question "Kansas", as the student ability parameter increases (black vertical bar, displayed over the empirical distribution of inferred student abilities). Observe that as ability increases, choices become clustered closer to the true answer, making the correct answer progressively more difficult to discern. Note the first panel in the sequence, corresponding to the $\theta \approx 0$ case, i.e., user with low ability, where we observe an interesting behavior: two choices are selected to be at the endpoints of the interval.

rank correlation of the subjects in the **Random** condition, confirming our hypothesis: the test that optimizes information about the student's ability implicitly optimizes the accuracy of the ranking of the students.

Conclusion

We have proposed a method for optimal choice selection in the task of optimal test design. Our response model is closely related to a discrete choice model, where the variance parameter encodes the ability of the user. This formulation, unlike related models such as [2, 1], allows us to explicitly optimize for optimal choice sets, where optimality is specified in terms of estimator efficiency on the user ability parameter. We demonstrate (Figure 1) that the resulting choice sets are selected on the basis of how easily the choices are mistaken for one another, highlighting one of the principles of good multiple choice question design that good distractors must capture common misconceptions.

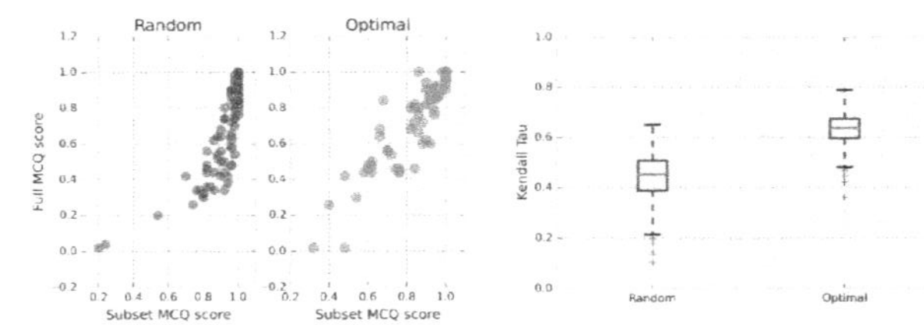

Figure 2: *Left:* Within-subject correlation between raw score attained on the **subsetMCQ** and **fullMCQ** tests separated by choice set design strategy. *Right:* Rank correlation between subjects according to the choice-set design strategy.

REFERENCES

1. Yoram Bachrach, Thore Graepel, Tom Minka, and John Guiver. 2012. How To Grade a Test Without Knowing the Answers—A Bayesian Graphical Model for Adaptive Crowdsourcing and Aptitude Testing. *arXiv preprint arXiv:1206.6386* (2012).
2. Gerhard H Fischer and Ivo W Molenaar. 2012. *Rasch models: Foundations, recent developments, and applications.* Springer Science & Business Media.
3. Frederic M Lord. 1980. *Applications of item response theory to practical testing problems.* Routledge.
4. Michael C Rodriguez. 2005. Three options are optimal for multiple-choice items: A meta-analysis of 80 years of research. *Educational Measurement: Issues and Practice* 24, 2 (2005), 3–13.

Identifying Student Misunderstandings using Constructed Responses

Kristin Stephens-Martinez
University of California
Berkeley, USA
ksteph@cs.berkeley.edu

John DeNero
University of California
Berkeley, USA
denero@berkeley.edu

An Ju
Tsinghua University
Beijing, China
ja12@mails.tsinghua.edu.cn

Armando Fox
University of California
Berkeley, USA
fox@cs.berkeley.edu

Colin Schoen
University of California
Berkeley, USA
cschoen@berkeley.edu

L@S 2016, April 25-26, 2016, Edinburgh, Scotland UK
ACM 978-1-4503-3726-7/16/04.
http://dx.doi.org/10.1145/2876034.2893395

Abstract
In contrast to multiple-choice or selected response questions, constructed response questions can result in a wide variety of incorrect responses. However, constructed responses are richer in information. We propose a technique for using each student's constructed responses in order to identify a subset of their stable conceptual misunderstandings. Our approach is designed for courses with so many students that it is infeasible to interpret every distinct wrong answer manually. Instead, we label only the most frequent wrong answers with the misunderstandings that they indicate, then predict the misunderstandings associated with other wrong answers using statistical co-occurrence patterns. This tiered approach leverages a small amount of human labeling effort to seed an automated procedure that identifies misunderstandings in students. Our approach involves much less effort than inspecting all answers, substantially outperforms a baseline that does not take advantage of co-occurrence statistics, proves robust to different course sizes, and generalizes effectively across student cohorts.

Author Keywords
constructed response questions, semi-automatic misunderstanding detection, introductory computer science, education, massive courses

Introduction
In contrast to selected response questions, such as multiple-choice, constructed response questions are much richer in assessing student knowledge and diagnosing student misunderstandings. However in large-enrollment courses, whether online or brick-and-mortar, it is infeasible to expect instructors to read and interpret the constructed responses for all students.

Our goal in this paper is to use these constructed responses at scale to identify misunderstandings in students. We will do this by magnifying a small amount of human labeling effort using trends among the answers from a large cohort of students.

Related Work
Intelligent Tutoring Systems (ITS) use a student model to inform how to help a student. A widely-used approach to create these models is combining an overlay model, in which the student's domain knowledge is represented as a subset of an expert's, with perturbation models, which capture (possibly incorrect) student knowledge not shared by experts [2]. The subset of knowledge representing misconceptions is sometimes called a *bug library*, and originally these were constructed manually by experts.

However, even with automation in creating these bug libraries, it takes much time and effort to create a student model [2]. We propose that by relaxing the desire to create a model that fully and accurately captures student misunderstandings, it is possible to create a practical model that diagnosis common misunderstandings in students without such large effort. Our main goal is the creation of this practical usable artifact for instructors.

Categories for Wrong Answers:

Correct: The answer is actually correct, but marked wrong due to a typo (Ex: `TRue` instead of `True`)

Not an answer (NA): The answer is actually an attempt to do something else, such as quit the interface (Ex: `eixt()`)

Wrong Answer: The answer is actually wrong.

Identifying Misunderstandings in Students
Definition of a Misunderstanding in a Student
A student demonstrates he has a misunderstanding if he responds with two distinct wrong answers that are evidence of that misunderstanding. This definition focuses our analysis on patterns of repeated mistakes.

Labeling Wrong Answers
We have instructors label the top K most common wrong answers (Top-K). To find these, we first remove each student's duplicate (question, wrong-answer) pairs – here on called a *wrong answer*. As a result, we have a series of distinct (student, wrong answer) pairs – here on called *responses*. Then we count the number of responses per wrong answer, sort by this count, and take the top K most common wrong answers across all questions within an assignment. For our evaluation we chose $K = 100$.

We use a two-step process when labeling wrong answers. First, the raters categorize a wrong answer using the categories listed in the margin. Second, for those categorized as wrong are given zero or more *misunderstanding labels*. If a wrong answer has no label, the rater could not determine what misunderstanding could have caused the wrong answer. In addition, an answer may be caused by multiple misunderstandings, hence the allowance for multiple labels.

Using the Label Map
Identifying a misunderstanding in a student involves two steps. Given a student's responses, we first find all labels that are shared by two or more wrong answers. These are identified as misunderstandings in the student.

Second, we propagate labels. A student has additional misunderstanding(s) if three conditions are met: (1) there are two wrong answers where one is not in the Top-K set,

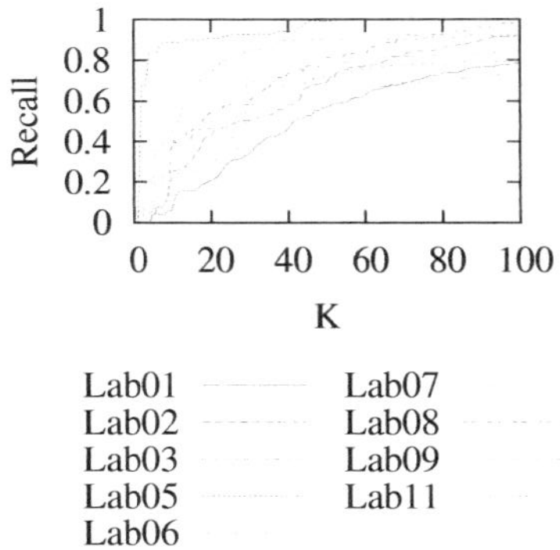

Figure 1: Recall of identified misunderstandings for the fully labeled student sample as K increases.

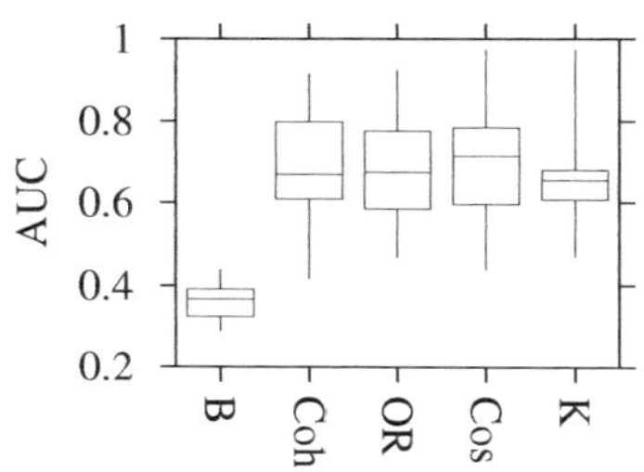

Figure 2: Boxplot of AUC across all labs for baseline and each co-occurrence metric. Note the y-axis does not start at zero.

(2) the wrong answer in Top-K has a misunderstanding label the student does not have, and (3) the two wrong answers have a high co-occurrence.

Case Study: Introductory Computer Science

Empirical Context

We collected wrong answers from UC Berkeley's introductory computer science class's code reading comprehension question sets in nine labs administered by OK [1]. Seven labs had disjoint topics and two were review (Lab03 and 08). Only Lab11 had $< 1,000$ students. The number of wrong answers per student ranged from 0 to 239, with a mean per-lab-median at 14.

Two raters categorized and labeled the Top-K, with $\mathsf{K} = 100$. For evaluation, the raters also inspected all wrong answers from a random 50 student sample from each lab – here on called *fully labeled samples*. The category raw inter-rater agreement is 0.92. The fraction of labels given by both raters over all labels given was 0.61. The number of misunderstandings per student in the fully labeled samples ranged from 0 to 15 with a mean per-lab-median of 3.

Given this context, there are ample wrong answers to use and potentially multiple misunderstandings to identify in the students in the fully labeled samples.

Top-100 Exploration

When inspecting what percentage of wrong answers need labeling with $\mathsf{K} = 100$, five labs required less than 5%, two required less than 10%, and the last two less than 20%. In other words, for a majority of labs the raters spent 95% less time than if all answers required inspection.

Figure 1 shows recall for identifying misunderstandings in the students in the fully labeled samples as K increases.

All labs have recall greater than 0.6 when $\mathsf{K} = 100$. This figure shows $\mathsf{K} = 100$ is potentially more than enough because marginal returns for each additional wrong answer quickly decrease and is small by the time $\mathsf{K} = 100$.

Co-occurrence Metrics Exploration

We considered four co-occurrence metrics: odds ratio, coherence, cosine, and kulcynski, mainly inspired by pattern mining literature [4]. We compared these metrics to an uninformed baseline where if a student has a wrong answer with an unshared label that student receives the label with a probability of p.

To compare the metrics and the baseline we chose to use the area under the curve (AUC). However, the high recall when $\mathsf{K} = 100$ and 1.0 precision by our definition of identifying misunderstandings in students needs to be handled. For easier comparison we anchored each graph at the baseline's extreme points, which are the same for all, and scaled the curve such that it fits inside a 1x1 square.

Figure 2 shows the AUC values across all labs for the baseline and metrics using a boxplot with quartiles. All metrics perform better than the baseline, except when Lab11's baseline AUC is higher than its coherence. These results show that the co-occurrence metric is providing useful information in propagating labels. However, which metric performs best is unclear.

Scaling and Stability of Top-K

To understand the scale of how many students are actually needed to achieve good recall for each lab and the stability of the Top-K wrong answers, we investigated the recall on the fully labeled sample and the overlap with the overall Top-100 for increasing values of N sampled students. We ran each N student sample 50 times and plotted the mean recall and percent overlap in Figure 3.

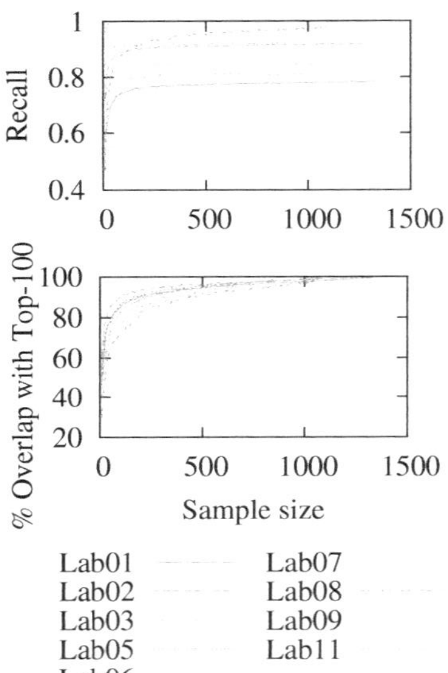

Figure 3: Comparison of recall with fully labeled samples and % of overlap with overall Top-100 for increasing samples of the students. Note neither y-axis starts at 0.

This figure shows that the number of students needed for reasonable scale and stability is only a few hundred.

Future Work

Co-Occurrence Metric Investigation for Propagation
While all metrics performed better than baseline, there was no clear best metric to use. We plan to investigate further in both which metrics to use and how to use these metrics to determine if a label should be propagated.

System Deployment for Guidance Messaging
To better understand the misunderstanding diagnostic model's performance, we plan to deploy it in OK. We will use it to decide what guidance message to give a student to help him learn the misunderstood concept.

In addition, we will investigate what kind of guidance best helps computer science learning and what factors need consideration. Education research has found many kinds of effective guidance messages and other factors which influencing message effectiveness [3]. We plan to compare concept reteaching and knowledge integration guidance, as well as investigate how message timing and student prior coding experience and achievement level influence the guidance's effectiveness.

Conclusion

Prior work expends much effort on creating student models to then identify misunderstandings. We propose a more practical way by relaxing the need to identify all misunderstandings to at least the common ones. Our empirical technique expends less effort than creating a student model, while successfully diagnosing misunderstandings in students.

Our model is based on instructors inspecting the top common wrong answers by categorizing and labeling them with associated misunderstandings. Then, using this mapping from wrong answers to labels, we identify misunderstandings in students by both using only the map and propagating labels using co-occurrence metrics. In our introductory computer science class case study, we inspected the top 100 most popular wrong answers. We achieved at least 0.6 recall and perfect precision across all nine lab assignments and when including propagation all metrics under consideration, in all cases but one, performed better than a random baseline.

Acknowledgements

This material is based upon work supported by the National Science Foundation Graduate Research Fellowship Program under Grant No. DGE 1106400.

References

[1] Basu, S., Wu, A., Hou, B., and DeNero, J. Problems before solutions: Automated problem clarification at scale. In *Proceedings of the Second ACM Conference on Learning@ Scale* (2015), 205–213.

[2] Holt, P., Dubs, S., Jones, M., and Greer, J. The state of student modelling. In *Student modelling: The key to individualized knowledge-based instruction.* Springer, 1994, 3–35.

[3] Shute, V. J. Focus on formative feedback. *Review of Educational Research* (2008), 153–189.

[4] Wu, T., Chen, Y., and Han, J. Re-examination of interestingness measures in pattern mining: a unified framework. *Data Mining and Knowledge Discovery* (2010), 371–397.

The Distributed Esteemed Endorser Review: A Novel Approach to Participant Assessment in MOOCs

Jennifer S. Kay
Tyler J. Nolan
Thomas M. Grello
Computer Science Department
Rowan University
Glassboro, NJ, USA
kay@rowan.edu
nolant3@students.rowan.edu
grellot6@students.rowan.edu

Abstract
One of the most challenging aspects of developing a Massive Open Online Course (MOOC) is designing an accurate method to effectively assess participant knowledge and skills. The Distributed Esteemed Endorser Review (DEER) approach has been developed as an alternative for those MOOCs where traditional approaches to assessment are not appropriate. In DEER, course projects are certified *in-person* by an "Esteemed Endorser", an individual who is typically senior in rank to the student, but is not necessarily an expert in the course content. Not only does DEER provide a means to certify that course goals have been met, it also provides MOOC participants with the opportunity to share information about what they have learned with others at the local level.

Author Keywords
Assessment; MOOC; DEER; Esteemed Endorser; Robot Programming; Educational Robotics.

Robot Programming for Absolute Beginners

What: Two MOOCs that introduce the basics of LEGO Mindstorms Robot Programming (NXT & EV3).

Asynchronous: Participants can join at any time, and have unlimited time to complete the course.

Target Demographic: School teachers with no prior experience in robotics or programming.

Participation to Date:
NXT MOOC: ~7K participants
EV3 MOOC: ~2K participants

Figure 1. The EV3 MOOC

L@S 2016, April 25-26, 2016, Edinburgh, Scotland UK
ACM 978-1-4503-3726-7/16/04.
http://dx.doi.org/10.1145/2876034.2893396

Figure 2. LEGO NXT & EV3 robots

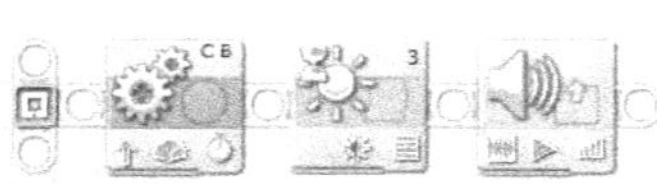
Figure 3. A simple NXT program

Figure 4. The Corresponding EV3 program

Introduction

One of the most challenging aspects of developing a Massive Open Online Course (MOOC) is designing an accurate method to effectively assess student knowledge and skills. As she was developing the two *Robot Programming for Absolute Beginners MOOCs* (RoboMOOCs)[5], Kay realized that traditional MOOC assessment techniques were inappropriate for these MOOCs, and so she developed an alternative approach, the Distributed Esteemed Endorser Review (DEER). In DEER, MOOC students are required to have course projects certified *in-person* by an individual (the "Esteemed Endorser") who meets certain qualifications specified in the MOOC. Typically, an Esteemed Endorser would be both senior in rank to the MOOC student and also a respected member of the student's community, but is not necessarily an expert in the course content.

Not only does DEER enable MOOC participants to receive course certification, but DEER also provides MOOC participants with the opportunity to share information about what they have learned with others at the local level.

Traditional Approaches to Assessing Student Learning in MOOCS

Automated Assessment Systems

One of the biggest benefits of automated assessment is the speed of its response. However, as the complexity of the assessment increases, the implementation of automated grading systems becomes correspondingly complex and has the potential to be controversial. For example, consider automated scoring of essays and free-response questions. Proponents of automated grading cite its value in high stakes writing tests, which by their very nature follow a very specifically designed format, [4] and claim that results are at least as consistent as human raters [1]. Nevertheless, despite automation's potential for vast cost savings, organizations such as the College Board continue to use human experts to grade free-response sections of the SAT college entrance exams [2] and there is strong opposition to automated essay grading by the National Council of Teachers of English [6].

Peer (and/or Self) Assessment

The accuracy of peer (and self) assessment is still an open question. In his 1998 review of (pre-MOOC) literature, Topping [8] found 18 studies that concluded that it was reliable, and 7 others that concluded that it was unreliable. More recently Wilkowski, et. al. [10] found that most self assessments in their two MOOCs were accurately graded. However, in their first MOOC, where students may have perceived the rewards of success to be significant, almost 20% of the students awarded themselves full credit for work that was blank, nonsense, or a duplicate of the work of others.

Peer assessment brings with it the potential to benefit both the assessor and the assessed. Sadler and Good concluded that the self-assessment process improves learning, but peer-assessment does not! [7] However, Topping [8] suggests that there is improved test and skill performance as the result of peer assessment.

Assessment by Subject-Matter Experts

There has been some experimentation with the use of online experts to grade in the MOOC and not-quite-so-massive course domain. Vogelsang and Ruppertz [9] experimented with hiring "Cloud Teaching Assistants" and Brooks et. al. [3] suggest that grading burdens can be eased by automatic clustering of similar responses.

The Need for an Alternative Approach

Our RoboMOOCs could not use traditional assessment approaches:

Automated Grading could have given participants instant feedback on their programs, but ...

- Locating and uploading source code would require our technological novices to leave the safe confines of the LEGO software environment.
- Identical programs can produce different behaviors on different robots e.g. due to physical design of robot and/or sensor accuracy.
- Creating an interpreter for these languages would have been a significant endeavor.

Peer Review would have allowed participants to share their work with others, but ...

- It might have been too challenging for our technological novices.
- The RoboMOOCs are asynchronous; participants may join at any time.

The Distributed Esteemed Endorser Review

We developed the DEER review as the result of recognizing that in the RoboMOOCs:

1. Our target demographic (K-12 teachers) had a supervisor that was easily identifiable (their school principal) and who would see their MOOC participation as beneficial.
2. We could create projects that would demonstrate understanding of MOOC content, but could be evaluated by individuals without an understanding of that content.

Assessment in the RoboMOOCs

In brief, the DEER assessment process that we implemented for the RoboMOOCs works as follows:

Simple Automated Assessments to Support Learning
Most lessons consist of a short video followed by some automatically graded multiple choice questions, intended to help participants assess their understanding of the material presented. Questions can be attempted multiple times without penalty, helpful feedback is provided for incorrect responses, and they have no effect on the participants' "final grade" in the course.

DEER Programming Projects for Participant Certification
At the beginning of the course, participants are introduced to the DEER process and provided with a letter of explanation to give to their school principal. The principal is asked to either assess the work him or herself, or to assign a trusted delegate to do so.

Over the course of the final 3 weeks of our 5-week course, participants are assigned a total of 5 robot programming projects, each of which includes:

- A clear specification of the work to be accomplished, designed to be understood by course participants.
- A second specification of how to assess a demonstration of the project, written for someone who is *not* familiar with the course material.

For example, in their second project, MOOC participants must program their robot to move back and for th to specific positions on a lin e while the robot displays specific images and plays specific sou nds. While the participant can only achieve success by correctly programming the robot to do these tasks, an evaluator does not ne ed any domain knowle dge to confir m that the robot's performance meets the specification.

Following each project, participants are asked to answer the following question:

- Did you suc cessfully complete Robot Project <number> and demonstrate it to a colleague?

With one of the following three responses:

- Yes
- Not yet, but I intend to do so later
- No, I have no plans to do so. I do no t want a certificate.

Once participants have affirmed successful completion and demonstration of all five projects (and optionally completed some survey information) they are eligible to download a certificate of completion which has a space for the principal's signature and clearly states "Not Valid Without Principal's Signature."

The principal's letter and project specifications for our MOOCs can be found at:

http://www.rowan.edu/cs4hs

DEER Guidelines

Specify the Esteemed Endorser (EE). Ideally the EE is senior in rank to the MOOC participant, a respected member of the participant's community, and has reason to value participation in the MOOC. The EE does not need to be an expert in course content.

Inform the EE about the Process through an open letter to EEs that is available outside of the MOOC.

Define the Assessment Criteria by providing clear specifications for the EE (or the EE's chosen delegate) of how to evaluate participant's work, which are available outside of the MOOC.

Provide a Certificate that participants can download when they *self-report* completion of course requirements. The certificate must have a space for the EE's signature and state that it is not valid without the EE's signature!

Conclusions

The DEER review is appropriate for populations of MOOC participants where:

- The typical MOOC participant is expected to be a part of a group that has super visors or mentors
- The supervisors or m entors recognize a value in MOOC participation
- MOOC assignments can be design ed in a manner that they can be ass essed by non-experts.

Beyond K-12 teachers, we can envision DEER reviews of students by their teachers, club members by their leaders, workers by their supervisors, etc.

In addition to facilitating assessment, the DEER review process expands the reach of a MOOC by introducing a senior member of the local community to what an individual participant learned in a MOOC that was developed thousands of miles away. Learning to program a robot on your own can be fun and educational, but sharing your success with your colleagues and supervisors has the potential to benefit both you (as others recognize your accomplishments) as well as the larger community - it is our hope that principals will get excited about the potential for introducing robots and programming into their schools!

Acknowledgements

This work was supported by a generous grant from Google CS4HS.

References

1. Stephen P. Balfour. 2013. Assessing writing in MOOCs: Automated essay scoring and calibrated peer review. Research & Practice in Assessment 8(1), 40-48.
2. College Board. 2015. Become an SAT Essay Reader. Accessed October 2015 from http://professionals.collegeboard.com/prof-dev/opportunities/become-sat-reader
3. Michael Brooks, Sumit Basu, Charles Jacobs, and Lucy Vanderwende. 2014. Divide and correct: using clusters to grade short answers at scale. In Proceedings of the first ACM conference on Learning @ scale conference (L@S '14). ACM, New York, NY, USA, 89-98.
4. Deborah Crusan. 2015. And then a Miracle Occurs: The Use of Computers to Assess Student Writing. International Journal of TESOL and Learning, 4(1), 20-32.
5. Jennifer S. Kay, 2015. Educational Robotics for Absolute Beginners. Accessed October 2015 from http://www.rowan.edu/cs4hs.
6. National Council of Teachers of English. 2013. NCTE Position Statement on Machine Scoring. Retrieved October 2015 from http://www.ncte.org/positions/statements/machine_scoring
7. Philip M. Sadler and Eddie Good. 2006. The Impact of Self- and Peer-Grading on Student Learning. Educational Assessment 11(1), 1-31.
8. Keith Topping. 1998. Peer Assessment between Students in Colleges and Universities. Review of Educational Research 68(3), 249-76.
9. Tim Vogelsang and Lara Ruppertz. 2015. On the validity of peer grading and a cloud teaching assistant system. In Proceedings of the Fifth International Conference on Learning Analytics And Knowledge (LAK '15). ACM, New York, NY, USA, 41-50.
10. Julia Wilkowski, Amit Deutsch, and Daniel M. Russell. 2014. Student skill and goal achievement in the mapping with google MOOC. In Proceedings of the first ACM conference on Learning @ scale, 3-10.

Evaluating the 'Student' Experience in MOOCs

Lorenzo Vigentini
School of Education & Learning & Teaching Unit - UNSW Australia
Sydney, Australia
l.vigentini@unsw.edu.au

Catherine Zhao
Learning & Teaching Unit UNSW Australia
Sydney, Australia
Catherine.zhao@unsw.edu.au

Abstract
Whilst most research on MOOCs makes inferences about the experience of learners from their interaction with the platform, few considered the rich feedback provided by learners. This paper presents the application of a conceptual model of student experience borrowed from higher education. Its relevance in the context of MOOCs was tested by using a range of questions and presentation methods in four MOOCs selected for their specific features. With varying response rates, results from over 8900 participants show how universities might view and evaluate the experience in MOOCs compared with that in traditional courses.

L@S 2016, April 25-26, 2016, Edinburgh, Scotland UK
ACM 978-1-4503-3726-7/16/04.
http://dx.doi.org/10.1145/2876034.2893469

Author Keywords
Student experience; MOOCs; surveys; evaluation.

ACM Classification Keywords
H.5.m. Information interfaces and presentation; J.1 Education

Introduction
Massive Open Online Courses (MOOCs) have offered an unprecedented opportunity for individuals from a diverse and often non-traditional backgrounds to access university level education [2,8], sparking a renewed interest in understanding how to create a learning experience that goes beyond the traditional brick-and-mortar courses. While there has been a rapid growth in research on learning, teaching and effectiveness of MOOCs, there appears to be a lack of work exploring the learning experience from the participants' perspective [9].

In a seminal work on student experience in higher education, Pascarella & Terenzini explored the variety of aspects that affect student experience [4]. Some of these are directly related to learning and teaching; others have to do with the life beyond class. These aspects affect the way students *experience* learning and influence their level of satisfaction. This work was extended in an institutional study in Australia [6] in which the authors proposed the articulation of a holistic conceptualization for student experience (Figure 1).

A1. Conceptual building blocks characterising the student experience

Course Enablers are the key features of the educational platform, the course designs and mode of teaching to support learning.

Precursors are students' prior academic and professional experience, motivations, aspirations and expectations of learning.

Engagement is the totality of learners' interactions with the platform, peers, and the course.

The ***Worth of Experience*** is what learners take away and project to their future, evaluating the learning experience, their satisfaction with the course, the perceived utility and effectiveness of the course for their learning, and/or for the development of knowledge and skills.

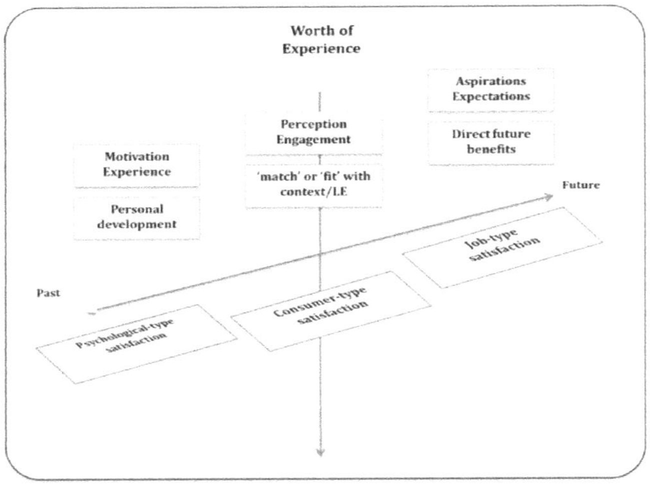

Figure 1: Holistic conceptualization of student experience [11].

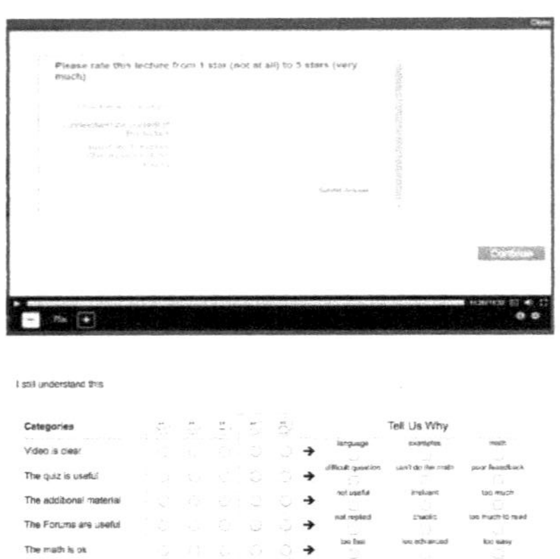

Figure 2. A snapshot of an In-Video-Survey 'in-video' (Top) and the Quick Evaluation Survey 'in-context' (Bottom).

This takes into account the individuals and their interactions with the learning context. It recognizes the value of the antecedents of learning: students' prior experiences with education, their motivations, previous performance and perceived effectiveness in learning. It also exposes the key role of engagement in learning with the learning environment, underpinned by a timeline projecting to direct future benefits realised in their expectations, aspirations and goals. In order to evaluate the learners' experiences in MOOCs, this paper focuses on four conceptual building blocks proposed in the model, testing whether these are relevant for MOOCs: **course enablers**, **learners' precursors**, **engagement** and **worth of experience** (aside A1).

UNSW Australia entered the MOOC space to experiment with pedagogical models at scale by combining different design features and modes of delivery. In the four MOOCs selected here, different models of *course design* (the way the course modules were released) and *course delivery* (how the teaching was structured throughout the MOOC) were tested blending course content, activities, assessment tasks, and support, to achieve the intended instructional design. Table 1 provides an overview of the MOOCs including the funnel of participation [1]. The high attrition widely reported [1,2] raises questions about the relevance of *completion* in relation to the idea of *student experience*. We specifically looked at active participants reporting the ongoing work evaluating the effectiveness of surveys in capturing responses that gauge motivation, engagement, and satisfaction of the learners' experiences with MOOCs and ultimately characterize their learning experience compared to students in traditional university courses.

	INTSE	LTTO	P2P	PMED
Duration (weeks)	9	6	9	8
Target Group	Engineers	Teachers	High school students & teachers	General public
Course Design	All-at-once	All-at-once	Sequential	Semi-sequential
Course Delivery	All-at-once	Staggered	Staggered	Staggered

	INTSE	LTTO	P2P	PMED
Registrants	32928	28864	22761	13185
Active learners	59.96%	62.59%	46.67%	35.44%
Completing	4.21%	4.45%	0.69%	3.92%

MOOC	#Active learners	Pre-course survey #	Post-course survey #	Pre-course survey %	Post-course survey %
INTSE	19708	2684	638	13.62%	3.24%
LTTO	18024	4409	313	24.46%	1.74%
P2P	10576	264	126	2.50%	1.19%
PMED	4673	401	72	8.58%	1.54%
TOT	52981	7758	1149		

Table 1. Overview of the MOOCs. **INTSE**= Introduction to system engineering; **LTTO**= Learning to teach online; **P2P**= Particles to planets; **PMED** = Personalized Medicine

2. METHODS

Two questions directed the analysis: 1) whether there are differences in the approaches to gathering feedback (the timeline, the mode of presentation and placement) and 2) whether the conceptual framework for 'student experience' has significance in MOOCs. Three methods were collated to generate the source data: the Coursera's standard demographic survey; the 'in-house' surveys experimenting with different questions and modes of delivery; and quick in-video evaluations (Figure 2).

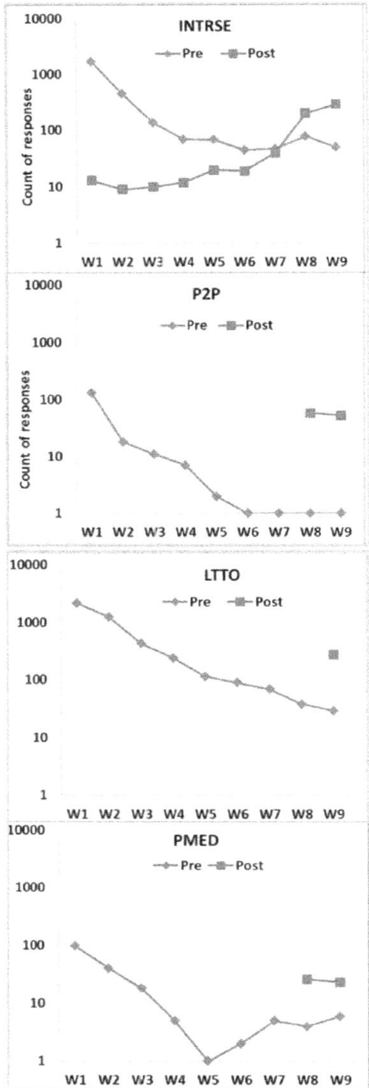

Figure 3. Counts of responses in the four MOOCs' course surveys (log scale) over 9 weeks. Note that in INTSE participants could complete post-surveys at any time

Variations in the questions asked reflected the needs of stakeholders. This also provided opportunities for benchmarking with internal course evaluations and with external tools as the pre-course survey validated at Stanford [5].

3. RESULTS

Response rates generally satisfied a 2% margin of error threshold. Unsurprisingly, the timeline of responses for pre- and post- surveys in Figure 3 shows that the total responses for the post-survey are smaller than the pre-survey. However, giving credit for participation (INTSE) made a difference not only in the cumulative responses over time, but keeping post-surveys open from the start allowed participants to 'complete' the MOOC at any time supporting the idea that MOOC is not a 'course' for everyone. LTTO recorded the highest number of responses in the pre-survey because this was fully embedded as first course activity. For what concerns the effectiveness of the two approaches to gather quick feedback – the IVS and Quick Evaluation (Figure 2), there is a larger difference in the interaction with the MOOC tools when the IVS are moved 'outside' the video as done in P2P (Figure 4). Furthermore there is a large difference between the responses in the two tools clearly showing the benefits of having in-video questions. All differences are statistically significant. Further analysis will be carried out to establish the relationship between formative feedback and overall satisfaction. To test the validity of the student experience framework, the 'experience', 'motivations' and 'satisfaction' subscales were tested. Cronbach alphas > .9 showed high internal reliability. Then, an exploratory factor analysis was carried out to test the conceptual underpinning of the aspects of experience. The factor structure across the MOOCs is almost identical, despite slight differences in the use of questions in the different surveys. The results also confirm a similar pattern to that observed in the university's end-of-semester survey with almost all items fitting under an 'overall satisfaction' construct. This is an important finding, suggesting that the conceptual framework to define the experience of learning does not change in MOOCs presenting similar characteristics to traditional courses.

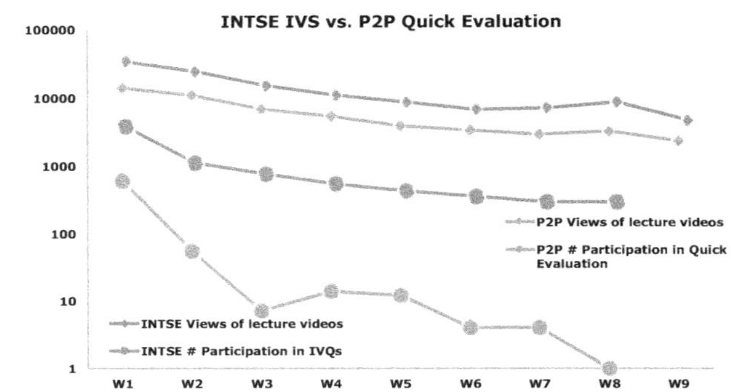

Figure 4. Interaction with the MOOCs: Lecture views vs N of respondents to 'quick evaluations' in INTSE and P2P.

4. CONCLUSION

Understanding the experiences of learners in MOOCs lays the foundation of making informed decisions on course design and teaching, as well as providing valuable information about how participants prefer to engage with learning at scale. Like for traditional courses, the robustness (quality) and the effectiveness (the appropriateness of implementation) of evaluation instrument should assure the quality of the data captured, yet MOOCs present a number of additional challenges [3,7]. We began to compare the enabling features of the MOOC design and how these affect participants' engagement. An A/B type testing with quick evaluations of the videos 'in-line' is described.

A2. Student Experience Questions

- Overall, I am satisfied with the quality of this course.
- The material of the course was presented in an engaging manner.
- Overall, this course met my expectations.
- Examples, illustrations or real-world cases were used effectively to explain things.
- The course encouraged my interest in this field of study.
- The goals and requirements of the course were made clear to me.
- Overall I have improved the knowledge/skills I will need.
- Quizzes helped me to evaluate my progress effectively.
- Interacting in the forums helped me to clarify things I did not understand.

This clearly points to the benefit of a seamless experience, embedding both content and evaluation questions in the user interface, gauging an immediate feedback about learners' perceptions about effectiveness. More is required to explore the relations between course characteristics (enablers) and the levels of engagement and satisfaction. The analysis of the ratings of videos seems to show that more committed learners (i.e. paying participants) report higher levels of satisfaction with the effectiveness of the lectures for their learning. Further analysis will be performed on the patterns of engagement related to the survey data with questions about the effectiveness of the features/designs, which scaffold learning. Finally, we set to evaluate the *worth* of learners' experience in participating in MOOCs. The analysis showed that the satisfaction with the MOOCs is generally positive, however this is the result of a complex combination of factors, which reflect the intricacy of the relations between enablers (course features), precursors (student characteristics) and actual engagement. An interesting future avenue will be to explore further the value of certification and accreditation [3,8] in relation to course design. More research will be required to further explore these relations and inform the future development of the courses.

References

1. Doug Clow. 2013. MOOCs and the Funnel of Participation. *Proceedings of the Third International Conference on Learning Analytics and Knowledge*, ACM, 185–189. http://doi.org/10.1145/2460296.2460332
2. Katy Jordan. 2014. Initial trends in enrolment and completion of massive open online courses. *The International Review of Research in Open and Distributed Learning* 15, 1. Retrieved May 7, 2015 from http://www.irrodl.org/index.php/irrodl/article/view/1651
3. Hamish Macleod, Jeff Haywood, Amy Woodgate, and Mubarak Alkhatnai. 2014. Emerging patterns in MOOCs: Learners, course designs and directions. *TechTrends* 59, 1: 56–63. http://doi.org/10.1007/s11528-014-0821-y
4. Ernest T. Pascarella. 2005. *How college affects students*. Jossey-Bass, San Francisco, Calif.
5. Emily Schneider and René F. Kizilcec. 2014. "Why Did You Enroll in This Course?": Developing a Standardized Survey Question for Reasons to Enroll. *Proceedings of the First ACM Conference on Learning @ Scale Conference*, ACM, 147–148. http://doi.org/10.1145/2556325.2567852
6. Lorenzo Vigentini, Catherine Zhao, and W Ashraf. 2013. A holistic view of Student Experience: the process, the problems, the methods and the rewards. *Proceeding of the AHEEF*.
7. Li Yuan, Stephen Powell, and JISC CETIS. 2013. *MOOCs and open education: Implications for higher education*. Retrieved October 21, 2015 from http://publications.cetis.org.uk/wp-content/uploads/2013/03/MOOCs-and-Open-Education.pdf
8. Chen Zhenghao, Brandon Alcorn, Gayle Christensen, Nicholas Eriksson, Daphne Koller, and Ezekiel J. Emanuel. 2015. Who's Benefiting from MOOCs, and Why. *Harvard Business Review*. Retrieved October 29, 2015 from https://hbr.org/2015/09/whos-benefiting-from-moocs-and-why
9. Samar Zutshi, Sheena O'Hare, and Angelos Rodafinos. 2013. Experiences in MOOCs: The Perspective of Students. *American Journal of Distance Education* 27, 4: 218–227. http://doi.org/10.1080/08923647.2013.838067

Personalized Adaptive Learning using Neural Networks

Devendra Singh Chaplot
School of Computer Science
Carnegie Mellon University
Pittsburgh, PA 15213, USA
chaplot@cmu.edu

Eunhee Rhim
Samsung Electronics Co., Ltd.
Suwon, South Korea
eunhee.rhim@samsung.com

Jihie Kim
Samsung Electronics Co., Ltd.
Suwon, South Korea
jihie.kim@samsung.com

L@S 2016, April 25-26, 2016, Edinburgh, Scotland UK
ACM 978-1-4503-3726-7/16/04.
http://dx.doi.org/10.1145/2876034.2893397

Abstract
Adaptive learning is the core technology behind intelligent tutoring systems, which are responsible for estimating student knowledge and providing personalized instruction to students based on their skill level. In this paper, we present a new adaptive learning system architecture, which uses Artificial Neural Network to construct the Learner Model, which automatically models relationship between different concepts in the curriculum and beats Knowledge Tracing in predicting student performance. We also propose a novel method for selecting items of optimal difficulty, personalized to student's skill level and learning rate, which decreases their learning time by 26.5% as compared to standard pre-defined curriculum sequence item selection policy.

Author Keywords
Adaptive Learning; Neural Networks; Learner Model; Instructional Model; Student Model; Personalized Item Selection.

Introduction
Adaptive learning refers broadly to a learning process where the content taught or the way such content is presented changes, or "adapts," based on the responses of the individual student [5]. It is the core technology for intelligent tutoring systems having 3

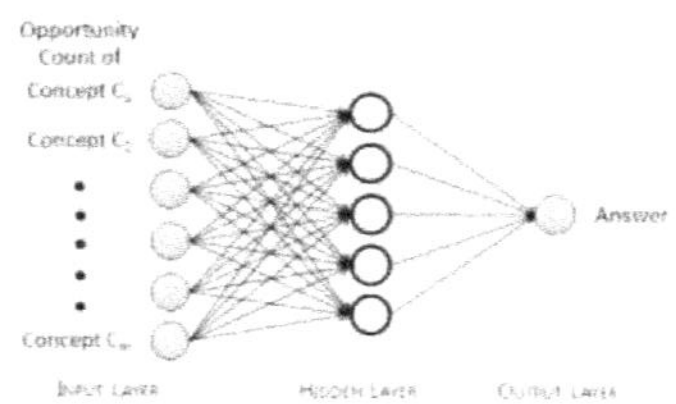

Figure 2: Artificial Neural Network used for Learner Model

Refined NN	Equation
NN-I	$f_{NN}(\boldsymbol{C}) + b_j$
NN-S	$\alpha_k f_{NN}(\boldsymbol{C})$
NN-SI	$\alpha_k f_{NN}(\boldsymbol{C}) + b_j$

Table 1: Equations for refined Neural Networks

major components: model of content to be learned (Content Model), model to estimate student proficiency (Learner Model) and a model to present content to the student in a personalized fashion based on his proficiency (Instructional Model).

The proposed adaptive learning system overcomes two important shortcomings of existing adaptive learning systems: (1) inability of Learner Model to handle multi-concept problems and (2) inability of Instructional Model to systematically select problems of appropriate difficulty for the student to maximize learning gain. We propose a new adaptive learning system architecture as shown in Figure 1, based on Artificial Neural Networks, which overcomes these shortcomings.

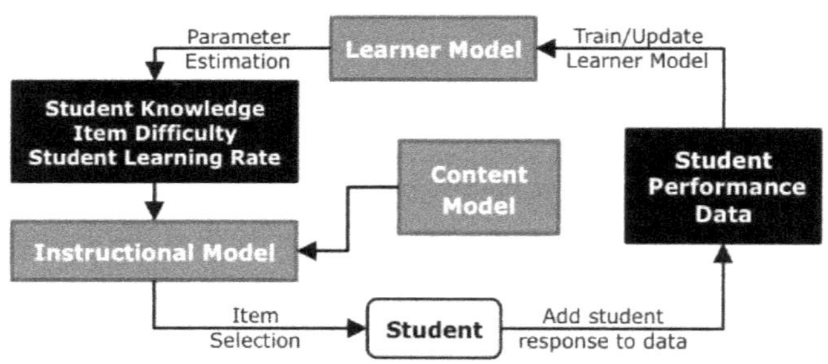

Figure 1: Adaptive Learning System Architecture

Content Model

The Content Model consists of a set of concepts, which are represented in a pre-requisite graph [1]. The pre-requisite graph is a directed acyclic graph with edges denoting the order in which concepts need to be mastered. The content model also consists of items. An 'item' refers to any entity like problem, question, step, quiz, etc. which is not broken down into smaller entities and involves certain concept(s).

Learner Model

Classical learner models in both Logistic Regression and Bayesian Knowledge Tracing (BKT) [2] families are unable to handle multi-concept items. Conjunctive BKT, Additive Factor Model and Conjunctive Factor Model were proposed to handle this problem, but they are limited by mathematical assumptions in the underlying cognitive model [3]. In order to handle multi-concept problems, we propose a new learner model using an artificial neural network, which does not assume any relationship between the inputs (concepts in Content Model) contrary to previous methods and can leverage huge amount of student performance data available for educational data mining to identify complex non-linear relationships between the concepts. Student performance data contains student-item transactions, each containing Student ID $T = T_k$, Item ID $M = M_j$, set of concepts involved in item M_j (denoted by S_j), Current Opportunity Count(s) (OC) [2] of concept(s) in set S_j and student response X_t (1 for correct, 0 for incorrect). The OC(s) of concept(s) involved in the item and corresponding student response are used as input and output, respectively, for training the Neural Network as shown in Figure 2.

Estimating Item Difficulty

Let's denote the output of the neural network for an item M_j, by $f_{NN}(OC_i: C_i \subseteq S_j)$. The output of the neural network is the mean of predicted performance over all items involving input concepts. We estimate difficulty b_j of item M_j, by calculating the average difference between predicted and real values of student performance on that item.

$$b_j = \frac{1}{n_j} \sum_{M=M_j} \left(f_{NN}(OC_i: C_i \subseteq S_j) - X_t\right)$$

Here, n_j is the number of transaction for item M_j.

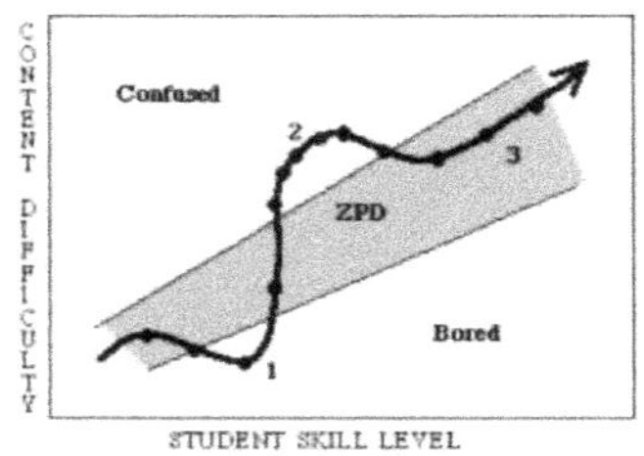

Figure 3: Zone of Proximal Development (ZPD) illustration [4]

ESTIMATING STUDENT LEARNING RATE

We create an individualized neural network for each student T_k, which is trained only on transactions by that student. Then we take the ratio of sum of outputs from individualized NN to the sum of outputs from general NN to estimate student learning rate α_k:

$$\alpha_k = \frac{\sum_{T=T_k} f_{NN_k}(OC_i : C_i \subseteq S_j)}{\sum_{T=T_k} f_{NN}(OC_i : C_i \subseteq S_j)}$$

Here, the individualized neural network for student k is denoted by f_{NN_k}. The original Neural Network can be refined using these estimates of item difficulty (NN-I), student learning rate (NN-S) or both (NN-SI) as described in Table 1.

Instructional Model

Instructional Model is responsible for selecting practice items of optimal difficulty, which maximize `Learning Gain' or the increase in student skill level. Theories of zone of proximal development (ZPD) [4] (See Figure 3) and item information function [1] indicate that an item of appropriate difficulty matches the current student skill level. Probability of solving an item correctly is analogous to the current student skill level on the concepts involved in the item (when difficulty is constant). As the item difficulty increases, the probability of correctly solving the item decreases, and vice versa. Consequently, we formulate `Learning Gain' of an item M_j as the geometric mean of both the quantities so that it is maximized when chances of correctness and difficulty are balanced:

$$LG\ (M_j) = \rho \sqrt{sigmoid(b_j) * P(X=1)}$$

where ρ is a constant
b_j is the difficulty of item M_j, $b_j \in (-\infty, \infty)$
$P(X=1)$ is the prob. of solving item correctly

Intuitively, a student with higher learning rate should be given more challenging items and should have higher learning gain than another student having the same skill level but a lower learning rate. Thus, we define 'Personalized Learning Gain' of an item M_j for student T_k, having learning rate $\alpha_k \in (0, \infty)$, as

$$PLG\ (M_j, T_k) = \rho \sqrt{sigmoid(b_j) * P(X=1)^{\frac{1}{\alpha_k}}}$$

The learning gain for each item can be calculated using estimates of b_j, α_k and $P(X=1)$ from the Learner Model.

We propose two item selection policies:

1. Max Learning Gain (NN): Selecting the item with highest LG.
2. Max Personalized Learning Gain (NN): Selecting the item with highest PLG.

In both the policies, if all concepts involved in an item are already mastered, then that item is discarded. Student response to the selected item is used to update the learner model, which is used to select the next item. This process is repeated until all concepts are mastered i.e. when probability of knowing the concept is greater than a particular threshold, typically 0.95.

Experiments & Results

PREDICTING STUDENT PERFORMANCE

Results on Algebra 2008-2009 Course Data from KDD Cup 2010 show that Neural Networks outperform standard and individualized BKT [6] on the task of predicting student performance, as shown in Table 2.

Method	Accuracy	RMSE	AUC
Standard BKT	82.7	0.363	-
Individualized BKT	82.8	0.361	-
Neural Network	88.3	0.320	0.687
NN-S	88.4	0.318	0.693
NN-I	88.8	0.308	0.708
NN-SI	**88.9**	**0.307**	**0.713**

Table 2: Comparison of Learner Models

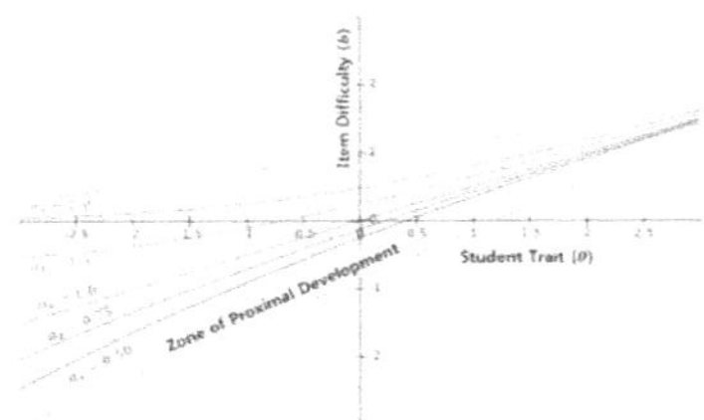

Figure 4: Optimal Item difficulty as a function of student trait for students with different pace of learning

COMPARING ITEM SELECTION POLICIES

We generated synthetic data simulating 3000 students and 183 items over 11 concepts in Grade 6 Expressions and Equations for validating item selection policies due to unavailability of real data. The most generic 4-parameter logistic model of IRT was modified to generate the data. We defined θ_i as the latent trait over each concept C_i rather than having a single latent trait and modeled learning gain over time as defined earlier. The prerequisite graph in the content model was incorporated by constraining θ_is of post-requisites to be always less than that of prerequisites.

We evaluate item selection policy by calculating the average number of items required by students to master all concepts. Pre-defined curriculum sequence is the most common item selection policy, which selects concepts in the order pre-defined in the curriculum. To evaluate the formulation of LG and PLG, we use Maximizing Learning Gain and Maximizing Personalized Learning Gain in idealized setting using real values of parameters (item difficulty and student learning rate), which were used to generate data. As the real values will not be available in practice, we also maximize LG and PLG using parameter estimates from Neural Networks. Results in Table 3 show that maximizing PLG (ideal) reduces items required to achieve mastery by 26.5% over pre-defined curriculum sequence policy. Max PLG (NN) is able to achieve learning efficiency comparable to the ideal scenario. The plot of optimal item difficulty (b), which maximizes personalized learning gain, as a function of Student Skill level (θ) for different values of α_k is shown in Figure 4. It shows that optimal item difficulty is not only proportional to the current student skill level but also consistent with the student pace of learning.

Item Selection Policy	Avg. #items to reach mastery
Pre-defined curriculum sequence	85.29
Max Learning Gain (ideal)	70.88
Max Personalized Learning Gain (ideal)	62.66
Max Learning Gain (NN)	69.96
Max Personalized Learning Gain (NN)	64.51

Table 3: Comparison of Item Selection Policies

Conclusion

We have proposed an adaptive learning system architecture based on Artificial Neural Networks which handles multi-concept items for effective prediction of student performance and selects practice items of optimal difficulty personalized to student's skill level.

References

1. Barla, M., Bieliková, M., Ezzeddinne, A. B., Kramár, T., Šimko, M., and Vozár, O. 2010. On the impact of adaptive test question selection for learning efficiency.*Computers & Education*, *55*(2), 846-857.
2. Corbett, A. T., and Anderson, J. R. 1994. Knowledge tracing: Modeling the acquisition of procedural knowledge. *User modeling and user-adapted interaction*, *4*(4), 253-278.
3. Koedinger, K. R., D'Mello, S., McLaughlin, E. A., Pardos, Z. A. and Rosé, C. P. 2015. Data mining and education. WIREs Cogn Sci, 6: 333–353
4. Murray, T., and Arroyo, I. 2002. Toward measuring and maintaining the zone of proximal development in adaptive instructional systems. In *Intelligent Tutoring Systems* (pp. 749-758)
5. Oxman, S., and Wong, W. 2014. White Paper: Adaptive Learning Systems. Snapwiz. *Integrated Education Solutions*, 1.
6. Yudelson, M. V., Koedinger, K. R., and Gordon, G. J. 2013. Individualized bayesian knowledge tracing models. In *Artificial Intelligence in Education* (pp. 171-180).

Understanding ESL Students' Motivations to Increase MOOC Accessibility

Judith Uchidiuno
HCI Institute
Carnegie Mellon University
Pittsburgh, PA 15213 USA
jio@cs.cmu.edu

Jessica Hammer
HCI Institute
Carnegie Mellon University
Pittsburgh, PA 15213 USA
hammerj@cs.cmu.edu

Amy Ogan
HCI Institute
Carnegie Mellon University
Pittsburgh, PA 15213 USA
aeo@andrew.cmu.edu

Evelyn Yarzebinski
HCI Institute
Carnegie Mellon University
Pittsburgh, PA 15213 USA
eey2@cs.cmu.edu

L@S 2016, April 25-26, 2016, Edinburgh, Scotland UK
ACM 978-1-4503-3726-7/16/04
http://dx.doi.org/10.1145/2876034.2893398.

Abstract
Massive Open Online Courses (MOOCs) have the potential to bridge education and literacy gaps by offering high quality, free courses to anyone with an Internet connection. MOOCs in their present state, however, may be relatively inaccessible to non-native English speakers, as a majority of MOOC content is in the English language. While a potential solution is to translate all MOOC content into all languages, it is not known whether this solution will satisfy the learning goals of all English as a Second Language (ESL) speakers. Through a series of interviews, we investigate ESL speakers' motivations for taking MOOCs and other online courses. Our findings show that ESL speakers have a variety of motivations for taking online courses that are not captured in current surveys, which implies that current one-size-fits-all approaches to increasing MOOC accessibility for learners with a first language other than English may not be effective. Rather, offering learners individualized tools based on their motivation and needs may be more effective.

Author Keywords
MOOCs; English as a Second Language; MOOC Accessibility; Learning Motivations.

Name & Age	Native Language	Current Country
Alina: 50s	Russian	USA
Filip: 30s	Polish	UK
Maria: 30s	Spanish	USA
Amit: 20s	Hindi	India
Carmen: 40s	Spanish	USA
Andrej: 20s	Serbian	Serbia
Jose: 30s	Spanish	USA
Ali: 20s	Urdu	Pakistan
Pooja: 20s	Hindi	India
Diego: 20s	Spanish	Peru
Minjun: 20s	Korean	USA
Aditi: 40s	Hindi	USA

Table 1. Participant pseudonym, age, native language, and current country of residence.

Introduction

Massive Open Online Courses (MOOCs) are online-only educational courses meant to provide open access to all learners, regardless of their educational background or geographic location [1]. However, issues such as a lack of infrastructure, digital literacy, and English language proficiency have been found to hinder MOOC adoption in developing areas [2]. Additionally, most MOOCs are aimed at English-speaking audiences. A review of all publicly available MOOC courses as of October 2015 reveals that about 75% of MOOC courses are offered in English [5], while native English speakers are only 6% of the world's population [4].

This disparity between worldwide native language populations and the language of MOOC content is well known, and there are ongoing efforts to make MOOCs more accessible to audiences for whom English is not a native language [6]. At the same time, a large percentage of current English-language MOOC users are non-native English speakers, also called English as a Second Language (ESL). By understanding the motivations of ESL learners who are already engaged with English-language MOOC content, we can better evaluate existing interventions for ESL MOOC accessibility, and design future interventions that address what ESL learners actually need.

To our knowledge, there are currently no research studies that propose generalizable design or implementation changes to MOOCs based on empirical knowledge of the actual needs and motivations of ESL learners. Additionally, these motivations may be difficult to obtain from analyzing ESL student behavior within MOOCs, as such motivations may not be observable in their MOOC activity. To address some of these gaps, we interviewed 12 online learners for whom English was not a first language, regarding their needs and motivations for taking MOOCs and other online courses. We look at the complexities of these learners' motivations and experiences to give us insights into designing the kinds of interventions that may be effective at supporting non-native English speakers in MOOCs.

Methodology

We conducted semi-structured interviews with 12 learners who were non-native English speakers, who had previously participated in MOOCs or online courses. Subjects were recruited through local community groups, Craigslist, and Facebook. Table 1 shows participant pseudonyms, ages, native languages, and current country of residence. The semi-structured interviews lasted roughly 35 – 60 minutes, were conducted in English, and took place in person or over Skype. We questioned participants about their motivations for participating in MOOCs and other online courses, their experience while taking these courses, and their learning needs. All interviews were audio-recorded and transcribed by the research team for analysis. The data was repeatedly reviewed and iteratively coded for themes around different motivations for participating in MOOCs. The codes and themes were continuously reviewed, until agreed upon by the entire research team.

Results and Discussion

The most salient themes of our analysis were the motivations that our ESL learners expressed, which we present here identified by the learners who discussed them. We additionally discuss implications for MOOC design and study, which these motivations suggest.

Motivation 1: Career Advancement by Mastering Course Material (Pooja, Diego, Andrej, Ali, Aditi, Amit)
One motivation for people to take online courses is to improve their knowledge of the subject area, which we observed in half of our participants (and which is shared by many non-ESL learners). For ESL learners with this motivation, however, it is important to design MOOC interventions that present the MOOC content with very little additional cognitive strain due to language. Presenting MOOCs in local languages, localizing examples, content and context dictionaries, or designating language-specific discussion forums may be particularly effective for supporting these participants' motivation to learn.

Motivation 2: Career Advancement by Obtaining MOOC Certificates in English (Jose, Carmen, Filip)
In contrast to those whose main goal was primarily to master the course material (irrespective of language), these participants enrolled in MOOCs to acquire English vocabulary in a specialized domain and obtain the course certificate for that specific content in English. This certificate would allow learners to demonstrate their mastery - which they may already have in their native language - in English. For such learners, administering placement tests when beginning the course to determine existing knowledge, providing non-linear navigation options to skip known content, or perhaps providing an additional certification verifying that all course content was completed in English may be more effective to better match their goals.

Motivation 3: Career Advancement for Future Opportunities and Geographic Mobility (Jose, Pooja)
Some of our participants sought out MOOCs or other online courses as a way of improving their geographic mobility. The MOOC served as an opportunity to engage with course content, but not for a specific test or milestone; rather, learners engaged with course content because they thought it would support them in an eventual move to an English-speaking country. MOOCs could intelligently match these learners with people who live or work in the countries they hope to move to, either on discussion boards or in live chat, so that they can learn about local culture and possibly even build useful contacts.

Motivation 4: Learning the English Language for Career Advancement (Jose, Maria, Diego)
These participants took MOOCs to improve their *general* English language abilities, as they needed mastery of the language to communicate and obtain the jobs they desired. Some fulfilled this need by taking English language courses, while others chose to simultaneously improve their subject area knowledge and their English language skills by enrolling in courses on topics of interest to them, which were offered in English. For such learners, studying in an English-language MOOCs is an additional chance to practice their language skills. This experience could be enhanced with tools such as language captions, content and context dictionaries, and spell-check enabled textboxes.

Motivation 5: Managing Daily Life (Jose, Alina)
Two learners enrolled in MOOCs not to master course content or to improve their academic English skills, but instead to improve their ability to manage the regular, unpredictable experiences of daily life such as going to get haircuts, shopping, or even talking to neighbors. This need encompassed both English language and culture, and was particularly relevant for ESL speakers already living in an English-speaking country. These

learners are very likely to benefit from support groups within MOOCs that allow people in a certain geographic location to meet and share their experiences adapting to a new culture, or to practice language together face to face. For these learners, it may be beneficial to introduce content in simple English and provide examples in the courses that will demonstrate how to navigate real life situations, rather than abstractions or examples only applicable to the workplace.

Motivation 6: Building Relationships (Pooja, Alina, Minjun)

Although MOOCs can emphasize content over fostering online relationships, for some learners, MOOCs served as a way of transcending cultural barriers and accessing a more valued community – one where they could achieve the class status or professional connections they sought. Course content was secondary to forming relationships with the "right" kind of person, or to transforming existing relationships by becoming the "right" kind of person oneself. Incorporating lessons from Connectivist MOOCs (cMOOCs)- where courses do not run on a single website or with a centralized core of content, and participants are encouraged to meet in locations of their choosing and organize themselves [3]- may be more appropriate to address this motivation.

Conclusion

Non-native English speakers are motivated to take MOOC courses for a diverse set of reasons – all factors that can potentially impact the ways to best scaffold their learning needs. Their needs are as diverse as the learners themselves, and our findings show that it is not sufficient to broaden MOOC accessibility by using one-size-fits-all approaches such as translating all MOOC content to learners' local languages. Instead, researchers must understand and support students' needs, presenting them with necessary and appropriate interventions to accomplish their goals.

Acknowledgements

We thank all the study participants that shared their time, learning experiences, and other feedback. We also thank Google for their support in this and related research through a Google Focus Award.

References

1. Tharindu Rekha Liyanagunawardena, Andrew Alexandar Adams, and Shirley Ann Williams. 2013. MOOCs: A systematic study of the published literature 2008-2012. *The International Review of Research in Open and Distributed Learning* 14, 3: 202–227.
2. J. Nyoni. 2013. The viral nature of massive open online courses (MOOCs) in open and distance learning: discourses of quality, mediation and control. *Mediterranean Journal of Social Sciences* 4, 3: 665.
3. Carol Yeager, Betty Hurley-Dasgupta, and Catherine A. Bliss. 2013. cMOOCs and Global Learning: An Authentic Alternative. *Journal of Asynchronous Learning Networks* 17, 2: 133–147.
4. 2015. English-speaking world. *Wikipedia, the free encyclopedia*.
5. Find MOOCs By Languages. *MOOC List*. https://www.mooc-list.com/languages?static=true
6. A new partnership to bring Coursera to the hundreds of millions of Chinese learners across the world. http://blog.coursera.org/post/63406806112/a-new-partnership-to-bring-coursera-to-the

LINK-REPORT: Outcome Analysis of Informal Learning at Scale

Xiang Fu
Dept. of Computer Science
Hofstra University
Hempstead, NY 11549
Xiang.Fu@hofstra.edu

Tyler Befferman
Dept. of Computer Science
Hofstra University
Hempstead, NY 11549
tbeff1@pride.hofsra.edu

M.D. Burghardt
Dept. of Engineering
Hofstra University
Hempstead, NY 11549
M.D.Burghardt@hofstra.edu

L@S 2016, April 25–26, 2016, Edinburgh, UK.
ACM 978-1-4503-3726-7/16/04.
http://dx.doi.org/10.1145/2876034.2893407

Abstract
We present LINK-REPORT, a distributed learning outcome analysis module that is integrated with the WISEngineering platform for supporting informal learning in engineering. LINK-REPORT provides a coherent workflow of outcome analysis: starting from development of learning outcome goals, to learner behavior collection, to automated grading of open ended short answer questions, and to report generation and aggregation. It generates learning data for research opportunities in modeling of learner traits.

Author Keywords
outcome assessment; automated grading

Introduction
As children spend over 80% of their time out-of-school [2], informal learning has been a crucial tool for engaging pre-college students and broadening their participation in science, engineering, and mathematics (STEM). The outcome assessment, however, is challenging because typical evaluation approaches in classroom teaching are not applicable. Therefore, collecting *more* and *better* data on learning outcomes is essential [1].

The evolving online education platforms such as Blackboard and edX have shed a light on this problem.

Figure 1: WISEngineering Tablet Portal. It delivers step by step instructions of an engineering project (e.g., creating a prosthetic leg for disabled people). Tools such as a design journal and design wall allow reflection and discussion. Distributed clusters at backend serve large volume of video and picture uploads from students.

For example, Yang et al. studied the learning data of Scratch [6], an informal learning platform for computer programming. In this study, learning processes are modeled as the cumulative trajectory of the programming blocks mastered by learners [10].

It is interesting to see how the data mining in [10] can be generalized to the analysis of a variety of learning outcome goals which will need to draw upon many different types of data. For example, in [1] a collection of six strands of learning goals are proposed for informal learning: O1: interests, O2: knowledge, O3: scientific reasoning, O4: reflection, O5: practice, and O6: identifying with scientific enterprise. It is a great challenge to collect and analyze the evidence data.

Extending the Web-based Inquiry Science Environment (WISE) from UC Berkeley [8], the WISEngineering system [4, 5] provides a tablet portal (shown in Figure 1) that offers hands-on engineering project activities and content for informal science settings. In our project, learners use a 7 inch tablet to collect data, plot and analyze information, reflect upon their designs, and share products with peers.

LINK-REPORT draws upon the existing WISEngineering system. It provides a coherent workflow to collect, tag, analyze, synthesize, and aggregate reports, leveraging auto-grading and machine learning algorithms. In this paper, We first present the learning dataset that is available in the WISEngineering system. Then we briefly introduce the workflow of LINK-REPORT and its software architecture. Finally, we present how learning indicators are modeled and assessed for the set of six learning goals in [1].

Raw Dataset

WISEngineering inherits the user management, curriculum design, and visual rendering module from Berkeley WISE [8]. All learner related data are stored in several MySQL databases. The data include the learner profile, session information (such as login/out time-stamp, duration of stay on each page), student responses (to multiple choice, match sequence questions, and open-response short answer questions).

LINK-REPORT also produces raw data. It injects an additional client-end script into the curriculum pages of WISE, and collects learner behavioral data such as keyboard and mouse events, which could be potentially used for user traits analysis in future.

Data Synthesis

Raw data is further processed for data mining and report aggregation in the next stage. LINK-REPORT provides a learning goal editor for defining learning outcome goals. Then a collection of indicators (called "grading criteria") can be defined for each learning goal. A learning indicator can be defined as the student performance over a specific question. The system has the capability to evaluate open-ended questions using multiple criteria (e.g., whether a learner is familiar with terminology used in the project, and the writing proficiency of the learner). As an example, Figure 2 shows that a learning goal "understanding engineering specification" is evaluated using three indicators in a project called "Balance Challenge".

One benefit of LINK-REPORT is that it leverages the use of machine learning for processing open-ended short answer questions and datasets that usually need labor intensive human evaluation. As shown in [3], a stacked generalization algorithm [9] is used for combining multiple

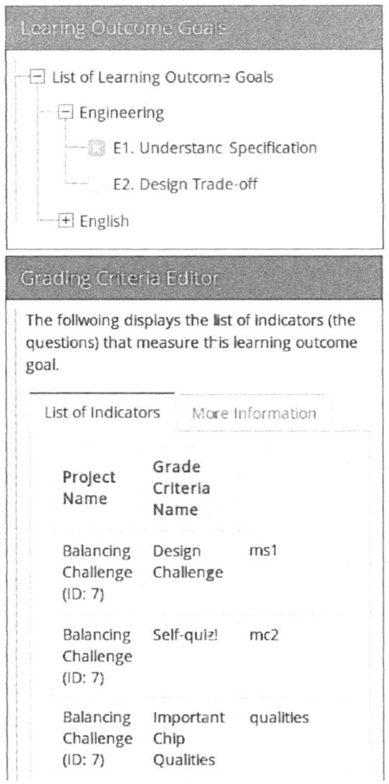

Figure 2: Indicator of Learning Goals. Three grading criteria (using multiple choice, match sequence, and auto-grading on short answer, respectively) are defined for a learning goal "understanding engineering specification".

machine learning/auto-grading algorithms (including the edX EASE engine [7]), for generating an optimized classifier as the auto-grader. We deployed these auto-grading classifiers in a distributed environment and can provide instant grading services for short answer questions [3]. Figure 3 shows an example of the summary page of a project and the statistics of its auto-graders.

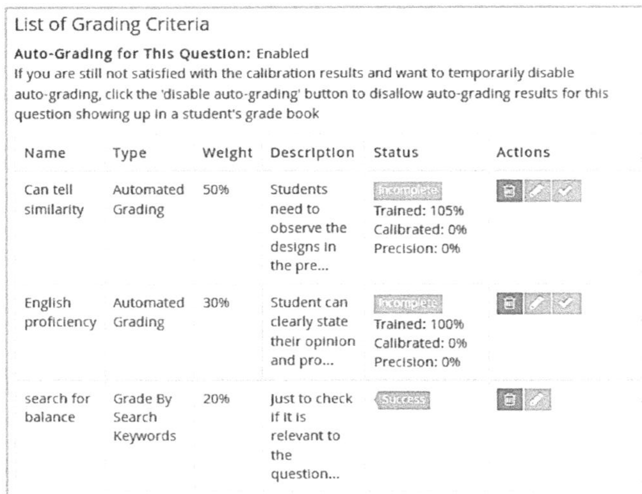

Figure 3: Auto-grading Training Statistics

Report Aggregation

WISEngineering [3] was designed to support nationally distributed informal science projects by learning communities. For example, the Wise Guys and Gals (WGG) project [4] leverages the national Boys and Girls Clubs for broadening the participation of middle school ages in engineering. These projects have multiple sites of implementation across the nation. One question that LINK-REPORT can address is how implementation and learning outcomes are similar and different across the various sites. Analysis can be broken down by site and compared.

To allow scalability WISEngineering adopts a loose confederation of servers. When a report is ordered, a template is sent to satellite servers, then these reports are aggregated.

On each satellite server, each learning outcome goal is assessed by aggregating the performance data on all the performance indicators associated with it (as shown in Figure 2). For example, the goal "understanding engineering specification" can be evaluated by a multiple choice question in one project, and another essay question which is graded by auto-grader.

```
$dtPost35 = array("type"=>"dataItem",
  "cols"=>array("Learning Outcome", "Club"),
  "presentation"=>array("approach"=>"histogram"),
  "function"=>"getOverallPerformance",
  "person_selector"=>array("type"=>"PERSONSEL_NONE"),
  "aggregate_op"=>array("type"=>"AGGREGATEOP_AVG"),
  "groupby_op"=>array("type"=>"GROUPBYOP_CLUBID"),
  "daterange_op"=> array("type"=>"GENBY_REPORT"),
  "histogram_op"=> array("frequency"=>"WEEKLY", "count"=>"10")
);
```

Figure 4: Code Snippet of Weekly Report Template

Data can be grouped by individual students, clubs and geographical districts. Figure 4 shows a snippet of a weekly report template. The report generation tool allows an educator to search data in a flexible way using different aggregation and grouping options.

Figure 5 shows a sample report generated by aggregating the reports from satellite servers. Using a simple weighted sum approach, the performance of all clubs on each learning outcome goal can be visually displayed and compared.

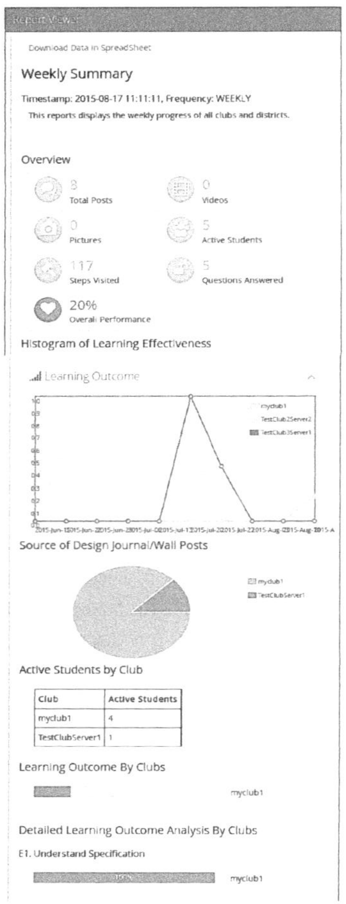

Figure 5: Sample Weekly Report. The clubs shown in the report are actually located on two separate physical servers. The bottom of the report shows the progress of each learning outcome goal at each club.

Work In Progress: Learning Model

LINK-REPORT is expandable. New learning indicators can be added into the system and be correlated with existing learning outcomes. We now briefly describe our plan to establish a collection of indicators for the six learning goals outlined in [1].

Most of the attitude outcomes (such as O1: interests in science and O6: identifying with scientific enterprise) can be assessed by online surveys built into the system. O2 (knowledge), O3 (scientific reasoning) and O4 (reflection) can be evaluated by standardized questions and short answer questions (graded by machine learning algorithms automatically). O5 (engagement in scientific practice) are related to the learner behavior data collected, such as the student tablet usage and activity records on design journals. We suspect that other usage data such as keystroke frequency and mouse events can also be used as indicators.

A learning indicator based on technology vocabulary can be established, similar to [10]. The "relevance" of terms can be automatically synthesized from semantic dictionary such as Wordnet, Wikipedia, and sample essays provided by human graders. Thus, by analyzing the bag of words, and their distance to the engineering discipline, auto-grader can assess the depth and effectiveness of a learner's use of scientific reasoning. Another direction is to assess the relevance and correlation between all indicators, so that the assessment model can be automatically adjusted.

Acknowledgments This material is based on the work supported by the National Science Foundation under grant DRL 1422436.

References

[1] Bell, P., Lewenstein, B., Shouse, A. W., and Feder, M. A. *Learning Science in Informal Environments: People, Places, and Pursuits*. National Academic Press, 2009.

[2] Cardella, M., Wolsky, M., Paulsen, C., and Jones, T. Informal pathways to engineering. In *ASEE Annual Conference* (2013).

[3] Fu, X., Befferman, T., Chiu, J., and Burghardt, M. Wisengineering: Achieving scalability and extensibility in massive online learning. In *Proc. Web Information System Engineering (WISE)* (2015), 323–337.

[4] Hofstra STEM Research Center. Research and Development: Advances in Wise Guys & Gals – Boys and Girls as WISEngineering STEM Learners. http://www.hofstra.edu/Academics/Colleges/SEAS/CTL/wise/research-development.html.

[5] Hofstra STEM Research Center. WISEngineering Web Portal. http://wgg1.hofstra.edu.

[6] MIT Media Lab. Scratch Online. http://scratch.mit.edu/.

[7] Paruchuri, V., Huang, D., Jarvis, J., Tauber, J., Aune, N., and Kern, J. EASE Auto-Grading Module. https://github.com/edx/ease.

[8] UC Berkeley. Berkeley WISE System. https://wise.berkeley.edu/.

[9] Wolpert, D. H. Stacked generalization. *Neural Networks 5* (1992), 241–259.

[10] Yang, S., Domeniconi, C., Revelle, M., Sweeny, M., Gelman, B. U., Beckley, C., and Johri, A. Uncovering trajectories of informal learning in large online communities of creators. In *Proceedings of 2nd ACM Conference on Learn at Scale* (2015), 131–140.

Beetle-Grow: An Effective Intelligent Tutoring System for Data Collection

Elaine Farrow
University of Edinburgh
School of Informatics
10 Crichton Street
Edinburgh, EH8 9AB, UK
elaine.farrow@ed.ac.uk

Myroslava O. Dzikovska[1]
University of Edinburgh
School of Informatics
10 Crichton Street
Edinburgh, EH8 9AB, UK
m.dzikovska@ed.ac.uk

Johanna D. Moore
University of Edinburgh
School of Informatics
10 Crichton Street
Edinburgh, EH8 9AB, UK
j.moore@ed.ac.uk

L@S 2016, April 25–26, 2016, Edinburgh, Scotland, UK.
ACM 978-1-4503-3726-7/16/04.
http://dx.doi.org/10.1145/2876034.2893408

Abstract
We present the BEETLE-GROW intelligent tutoring system, which combines active experimentation, self-explanation, and formative feedback using natural language interaction. It runs in a standard web browser and has a fresh, engaging design. The underlying back-end system has previously been shown to be highly effective in teaching basic electricity and electronics concepts.

BEETLE-GROW has been designed to capture student interaction and indicators of learning in a form suitable for data mining, and to support future work on building tools for interactive tutoring that improve after experiencing interaction with students, as human tutors do.

Author Keywords
intelligent tutoring; natural language; interaction data; conceptual learning; physics; electronics

Introduction
Many effective teaching techniques combine active experimentation, self-explanation, and formative feedback [1, 2, 7, 8, 9, 10]. In classroom situations, these rely heavily on dialogue with a teacher. Our work focuses on implementing similar techniques in an Intelligent Tutoring System (ITS) using natural language interaction.

[1] Myroslava Dzikovska is now at Google, London

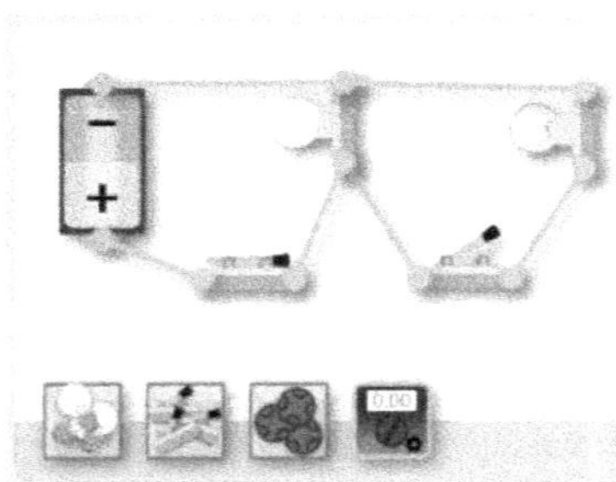

Figure 1: The graphics used in the interactive circuit workbench combine selective stylization with an element of realism to facilitate a constructivist learning approach [3], encouraging learners to experiment freely and learn from hands-on experience.

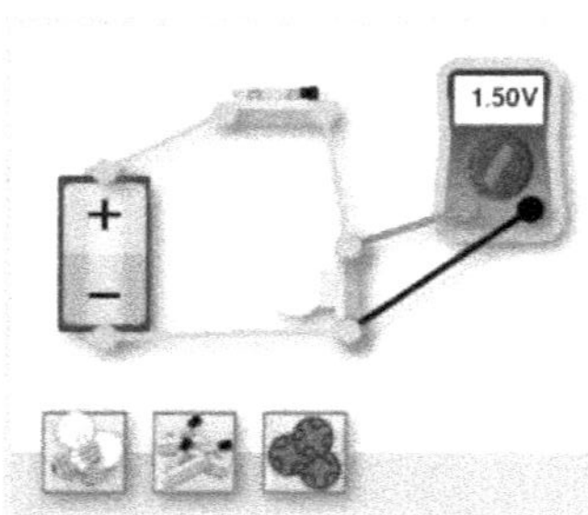

Figure 2: The circuit workbench communicates with a back-end circuit simulator to show the correct voltmeter readings and display each bulb at the appropriate level of brightness.

In learning environments with a very high student-teacher ratio such as MOOCs, it is clearly not practical for every learner to engage in extended dialogue with an expert human tutor. A dialogue-based ITS can promote learning by guiding experimentation, eliciting predictions and explanations, and generating tailored formative feedback automatically for a large population of learners.

Automated methods for analyzing student input often use statistical models trained on large corpora of student language [6]. We would like to go beyond identifying correct and incorrect student answers in text and start to use interaction data to learn effective feedback tactics. This would allow a future ITS to improve from interaction with students, just as human tutors do [11]. A necessary first step is to collect the required training data.

The BEETLE-GROW system we describe in this paper is designed for large-scale data collection, while also delivering a valuable learning experience in its own right. An interactive demonstration of the system can be accessed at `http://beetle-grow.inf.ed.ac.uk`.

Background

BEETLE-GROW builds on the success of BEETLE II, a natural-language ITS which has been shown to be highly effective in teaching basic electricity and electronics, demonstrating effect sizes of d=1.72 [5]. BEETLE II combines natural language dialogue, guided experimentation, and adaptive feedback to implement the conceptual change [4] tutoring approach.

In BEETLE-GROW, we have added a new browser-based user interface, allowing multiple remote users to access the system concurrently. Since the only technical requirement is an HTML5 compliant browser (such as Google Chrome or Mozilla Firefox), the system can easily be made available to a wide variety of students. Student interaction data is logged in a format suitable for data mining and as training data for machine learning.

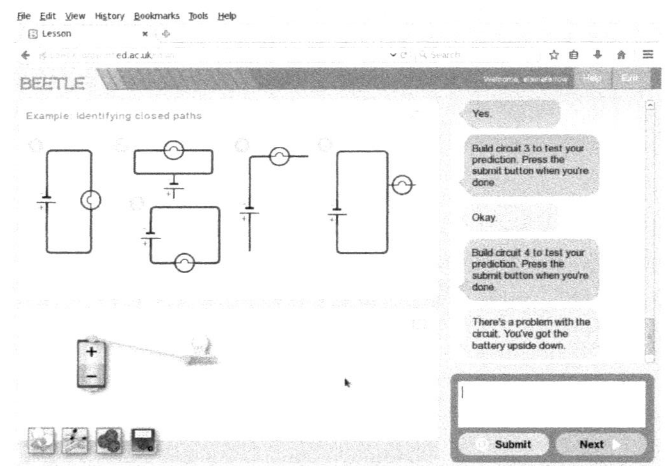

Figure 3: The browser-based user interface uses industry standard technologies: HTML5, CSS3, JavaScript, and the Play Framework, an open source web programming framework.

User Interface

The user interface (Figure 3) uses a responsive design optimized for modern browsers, including touch screen devices such as Android and iPad tablets. It is divided into panels corresponding to different aspects of the tutoring process: reading learning materials (Figure 4), interacting with the tutor (Figure 5), and experimenting with electrical circuits using a circuit simulator (Figures 1 and 2). The layout is similar to the BEETLE II interface, but redesigned with a friendly and contemporary look and feel, intended to be attractive to our target user group (students aged around 13-25).

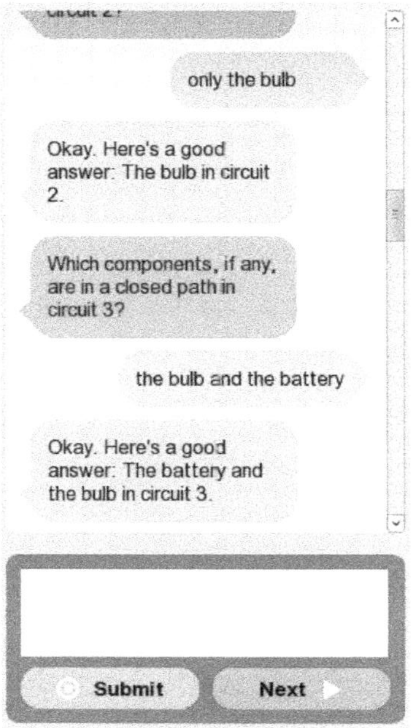

Figure 5: Student input is visually separated from tutor feedback and questions in the chat interface, making the dialogue easier to follow.

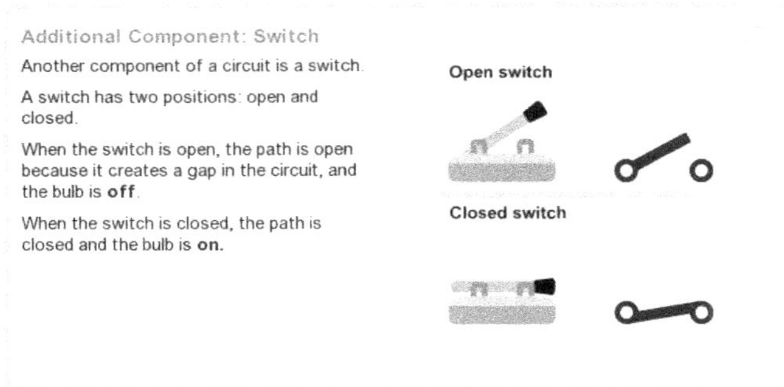

Figure 4: The learning materials are presented using HTML5, with scalable text and high quality graphics optimized for presentation in modern web browsers.

System Architecture

BEETLE-GROW is implemented as a distributed system, in which a web server accepts requests from the GUI and routes users to the correct page. Lesson progress is tracked in a database, allowing the student to exit the lesson at any time and resume later from the start of the last exercise attempted.

The curriculum covers ten main topics and includes over 150 questions. Some require the student to select and connect electrical components in the interactive circuit workbench to match a circuit diagram shown on screen. Others expect a written answer of one or two sentences. There are numerical and yes/ no questions, and questions asking the student to identify particular circuit components.

Student input consists of circuits built in the workbench, text entered in the chat window, and button presses to request help or to move through the learning materials. The dialogue manager is responsible for processing the input and deciding on the next action to take, such as presenting further learning materials, asking a question, or giving feedback on a student answer. It communicates with the back-end components retained from BEETLE II, which handle curriculum management, natural language processing, answer diagnosis, and tutorial planning.

The tutorial planner does not allow a student to move on from a question without supplying an answer in the expected form: either a circuit or some text. Submitted circuits are compared against the desired circuit answer, a diagnosis is made, and formative feedback is given; for example, "There's a problem with the circuit. The switch should not be open." After a third successive failure, the correct circuit is loaded into the workbench, allowing the student to proceed.

In contrast, no formative feedback is currently given for textual answers. Instead, the system simply states the expected answer and leaves the student to decide if their own answer was a close enough match. This behavior corresponds to the TELL condition reported in [5], which demonstrated that asking students for an explanation and then immediately giving away the correct answer was highly effective, despite the obvious potential to 'game the system' by typing minimal or nonsense answers. This approach also avoids the negative effect on student satisfaction and engagement seen in BEETLE II evaluations due to the limitations of the natural language understanding and feedback selection modules used there.

Conclusion and Future Work

BEETLE-GROW harnesses the proven educational potential of the BEETLE II system and makes it available to a new audience. The browser-based user interface makes deployment at scale straightforward. We have confidence that BEETLE-GROW will help students to learn, while simultaneously allowing us to collect a large corpus of interaction data for future analysis.

As our next step, we are interested in partnering with teachers and other education researchers to carry out large-scale user trials with BEETLE-GROW in the classroom and remotely. Data from such trials will generate new insights into the effect of active experimentation on learning in the domain of basic electricity and electronics.

Student answers and interaction data collected from these trials can also be used to train statistical algorithms, such as those described in [6], in order to provide better student feedback in a future version of BEETLE-GROW.

Acknowledgments
We thank the US Office of Naval Research for their financial support under Award number N000141410733, and our colleagues Mary Hutchison and Edmund Farrow for their contributions to the design and implementation of the new user interface.

References
[1] Chi, M., Jordan, P., VanLehn, K., and Litman, D. To elicit or to tell: Does it matter? In *Proceedings 14th International Conference on Artificial Intelligence in Education (AIED)* (Brighton, UK, 2009).

[2] Chi, M. T. H., de Leeuw, N., Chiu, M.-H., and LaVancher, C. Eliciting self-explanations improves understanding. *Cognitive Science 18*, 3 (1994), 439–477.

[3] Duffy, T. M., and Jonassen, D. H. *Constructivism and the technology of instruction: A conversation.* Hillsdale, NJ: Lawrence Erlbaum Associates, 1992.

[4] Duit, R., and Treagust, D. F. Conceptual change: A powerful framework for improving science teaching and learning. *International Journal of Science Education 25*, 6 (2003), 671–688.

[5] Dzikovska, M., Steinhauser, N., Farrow, E., Moore, J., and Campbell, G. Beetle II: Deep natural language understanding and automatic feedback generation for intelligent tutoring in basic electricity and electronics. *International Journal of Artificial Intelligence in Education 24*, 3 (9 2014), 284–332.

[6] Dzikovska, M. O., Nielsen, R., Brew, C., Leacock, C., Giampiccolo, D., Bentivogli, L., Clark, P., Dagan, I., and Dang, H. T. SemEval-2013 Task 7: The Joint Student Response Analysis and 8th Recognizing Textual Entailment Challenge. In *Proceedings of the 6th International Workshop on Semantic Evaluation (SEMEVAL-2013)*, Association for Computational Linguistics (Atlanta, Georgia, USA, 2013).

[7] Litman, D., Moore, J., Dzikovska, M., and Farrow, E. Using natural language processing to analyze tutorial dialogue corpora across domains and modalities. In *Proceedings of 14th International Conference on Artificial Intelligence in Education (AIED)* (Brighton, UK, 2009).

[8] Narciss, S. The impact of informative tutoring feedback and self-efficacy on motivation and achievement in concept learning. *Experimental Psychology 51*, 3 (2004), 214–228.

[9] Purandare, A., and Litman, D. Content-learning correlations in spoken tutoring dialogs at word, turn and discourse levels. In *Proceedings of the 21st International FLAIRS Conference* (2008).

[10] Shute, V. J. Focus on formative feedback. *Review of educational research 78*, 1 (2008), 153–189.

[11] VanLehn, K. The relative effectiveness of human tutoring, intelligent tutoring systems, and other tutoring systems. *Educational Psychologist 46*, 4 (10 2011), 197–221.

ASSISTments Dataset from Multiple Randomized Controlled Experiments

Douglas Selent
Worcester Polytechnic Institute
100 Institute Road
Worcester, MA 01609 USA
dselent@wpi.edu

Thanaporn Patikorn
Worcester Polytechnic Institute
100 Institute Road
Worcester, MA 01609 USA
tpatikorn@wpi.edu

Neil Heffernan
Worcester Polytechnic Institute
100 Institute Road
Worcester, MA 01609 USA
nth@wpi.edu

L@S 2016, April 25-26, 2016, Edinburgh, Scotland UK
ACM 978-1-4503-3726-7/16/04.
http://dx.doi.org/10.1145/2876034.2893409

Abstract
In this paper, we present a dataset consisting of data generated from 22 previously and currently running randomized controlled experiments inside the ASSIStments online learning platform. This dataset provides data mining opportunities for researchers to analyze ASSISTments data in a convenient format across multiple experiments at the same time. The data preprocessing steps are explained in detail to inform researchers about how this dataset was generated. A list of column descriptions is provided to define the columns in the dataset and a set of summary statistics are presented to briefly describe the dataset.

Author Keywords
ASSISTments; Randomized Controlled Experiments; Dataset.

ACM Classification Keywords
E.0. Data: General

Introduction
ASSISTments

ASSISTments is a freely available online learning platform mostly used in mathematic classes between grades 4-12 in the United States. ASSISTments currently has 140,032 users who have done 32,625,908 problems from years 2013-2015. Most of the users are middle school (grades 6-8) mathematic students, who are located in or near Massachusetts. Students use ASSISTments on classwork and homework, which may be done with or without the use of a paper copy. Instant feedback is typically provided to the students upon answering problems, so that students will immediately know if they have answered the problem correctly. Students are not allowed to skip any problems and must answer correctly in order to continue on to the next problem. If a student does not answer the problem correctly on their first attempt, the problem is marked as incorrect. Almost all problems in ASSISTments give the student the option to click on a hint button, which either offers additional help to the student or just gives the student the answer to the problem, so that he or she may continue.

Experiment Infrastructure

All of the experiments were created by either internal or external researchers working with ASSISTments. Dr. Heffernan was funded by NSF to create the ASSISTmentsTestBed.org to support external researchers to conduct studies. The ASSISTmentsTestBed.org is a reporting service that helps researchers retrieves data on experiments that have been run inside the ASSISTments system [1, 2]. This reporting service is also knows as the Assessment of Learning Infrastructure (ALI), which combines automated analysis with the data reporting [6]. Several of these experiments have been previously published, with topics ranging from student confidence, student choice, and buggy messages [3-5, 8].

Data Selection

In the ASSISTments online learning platform, there are several ways to build assignment structures which experiments can be embedded inside of. One type of structure is called a Skill Builder. A Skill Builder is an assignment type that consists of a large number of similar problems, where students must answer a specified number of problems (usually three) correctly in a row on the same day in order to finish the assignment. These problems are generated by variabilized templates, where several problem instances are generated from the same template with different numbers replacing the variables of the template [7]. We chose only to include experiments that leveraged the Skill Builder infrastructure because that was the most common assignment structure. We also chose to only use experiments with a control group and a single experimental group since that was the study design for most of the experiments. Using only Skill Builder assignments with a single experimental condition allows for a common set of independent and dependent variables to be used for all 22 experiments.

To ensure that there was a large enough sample of students for each experiment, only experiments that had over fifty students complete the assignment in all the conditions of the experiment were chosen. Also, only experiments that had less than 10% corrupted data were used.

Data Pre-Processing

The following steps were done to clean the data and transform all the experiment data into a canonical form for analysis. First, the original data was retrieved for all the assignments that were known to be experiments by using the ASSISTmentsTestBed.org. Once this data

Experiment Number	Students	Problems
1	1,204	7,657
2	695	9,466
3	381	5,105
4	627	9,771
5	1,864	12,549
6	457	1,861
7	515	2,068
8	540	2,212
9	402	2,213
10	545	8,030
11	412	2,612
12	335	1,817
13	497	3,930
14	704	3,197
15	523	2,967
16	136	1,526
17	428	2,930
18	745	3,776
19	1330	4,694
20	1,917	9,268
21	429	2,538
22	426	2,065

Table 1. Number of students and problems done for each experiment.

was retrieved, problems which were not common to all the experiments were removed. These problems included any pretest and posttest problems that an experiment may have contained as well as scaffold problems. Nearly all the prior experiments did not have pretest or posttest problems, since the ability to create such experiments did not exist in the ASSISTments system at the time those experiments were created. Scaffold problems are sub-problems for a given original problem, which break the original problem down into a few smaller sub-problems. Scaffold problems were removed because only eleven experiments contained scaffold problems and scaffold problems are considered a type of tutoring which does not count toward the correctness of the Skill Builder assignment.

A recent improvement to the ASSISTments system was the addition of logging the condition students were randomly assigned into. Unfortunately this data did not exist at the time most of the experiments were run, therefore the condition that students were assigned into was derived from the problems they had been assigned. The condition students were randomly assigned into was derived based on distinguishing problem numbers that the student had worked on.

Several experiments involved interventions containing video feedback, where students were required to have video in order to be considered part of the experiment. These experiments had an initial question to check on whether or not the student could see the video. The answers to these questions were analyzed to determine if the student was able to see video. An additional column was added to the dataset to indicate if the student could see video where applicable.

The two variables used for measuring student performance were whether or not the student completed the assignment and the mastery speed for those students who were able to complete the assignment. The number of problems it takes a student to complete a skill builder is also called mastery speed as defined in [10]. We believe these two variables are important measures, where mastery speed measures student learning and completion rate measures student persistence. There were a few cases where a small number of students did a large number of problems, which added skew to the distribution of mastery speed. A log transform was used so that these few students did not have large impact on the means for mastery speed.

Data Description

A description of the column names in the dataset are provided at the ASSISTments Data Dump Glossary webpage[1]. The dataset has 32 columns including a number of student covariates. The dataset is in the form of one row per student per assignment. Table 1 shows some basic summary statistics of the dataset, including the number of problems done for each experiment and the number of unique students in each experiment. A total of 102,252 problems were attempted by 8,297 unique students across 22 different experiments. Note that a single student could have participated in more than one experiment and not all students experienced the conditions of the experiment. This dataset can be downloaded at https://sites.google.com/site/las2016data/data/ThisOne.xlsx.

[1] http://www.assistmentstestbed.org/the-data/interpreting-your-data-v-1-0

CONTRIBUTIONS, FUTURE WORK, AND CONCLUSIONS

The contribution that this paper makes is the generation of a dataset consisting of 22 randomized controlled experiments run inside the ASSISTments online learning platform. What makes this dataset unique is that it is a combination of data from several different experiments all with a common design and common set of independent and dependent variables. We believe this dataset can be used for further analysis with a focus on finding general trends among independent variables across multiple experiments. It is currently being used in research to improve the detection of treatment effects in randomized controlled experiments [9].

Acknowledgements

We thank Yang Lu for creating large portion of the infrastructure to support the ASSISTments TestBed which we used to obtain our data. We also thank Anthony Botelho for his work on adding several of the features we used to the data reporting system.

We thank multiple NSF grants (ACI-1440753, DRL-1252297, DRL-1109483, DRL-1316736, DGE-1535428 & DRL-1031398), the US Dept. of Ed (IES R305A120125 & R305C100024 and GAANN), and the ONR.

References

[1] ASSISTmentsTestBed (2015) The ASSISTmentsTestBed. A website that supports researchers funded via the Heffernan (2014) grant. Retrieved from www.assistmentstestbed.org

[2] Heffernan (2014) "SI2-SSE: Adding Research Accounts to the ASSISTments' Platform: Helping Researchers Do Randomized Controlled Studies with Thousands of Students." An NSF proposal abstract

[3] Lang, C., Heffernan, N., Ostrow, K., & Wang, Y. (2015). The Impact of Incorporating Student Confidence Items into an Intelligent Tutor: A Randomized Controlled Trial. In Santos, et al. (eds.) Proceedings of the 8th Int Conf on EDM. pp. 144-149.

[4] Ostrow, K. S. (2015). A Multifaceted Consideration of Motivation and Learning within ASSISTments (Master's Thesis, Worcester Polytechnic Institute).

[5] Ostrow, K. S., & Heffernan, N. T. (2015, June). The Role of Student Choice Within Adaptive Tutoring. In Artificial Intelligence in Education (pp. 752-755). Springer International Publishing.

[6] Ostrow, K. S., Selent, D., Wang, Y., Van Inwegen, E. G., & Heffernan, N. T. (2015) Assessment of Learning Infrastructure (ALI): The Theory, Practice, and Scalability of Automated Assessment. Learning Analytics 2016.

[7] Razzaq, L., Patvarczki, J., Almeida, S. F., Vartak, M., Feng, M., Heffernan, N. T., & Koedinger, K. R. (2009). The Assistment Builder: Supporting the life cycle of tutoring system content creation. Learning Technologies, IEEE Transactions on, 2(2), 157-166.

[8] Selent, D., & Heffernan, N. (2015, June). When More Intelligent Tutoring in the Form of Buggy Messages Does not Help. In Artificial Intelligence in Education (pp. 768-771). Springer International Publishing.

[9] Thanaporn, P., Selent, D., & Heffernan, N., Beck, J., Zou, J. Using a Single Model across Multiple Interventions to Improve the Detection of Treatment Effects. The 9th International Conference on Educational Data Mining on Educational Data Mining (*in submission*)

[10] Xiong, X., Li, S., & Beck, J. E. (2013, May). Will You Get It Right Next Week: Predict Delayed Performance in Enhanced ITS Mastery Cycle. In FLAIRS Conference

Predicting Student Learning using Log Data from Interactive Simulations on Climate Change

Elizabeth McBride
UC Berkeley
4515 Tolman Hall
Berkeley, CA 94709
bethmcbride@berkeley.edu

Mario Martinez
UC Berkeley
Tolman Hall
Berkeley, CA 94709
mario.m.martinez@vanderbilt.edu

Jonathon M. Vitale
UC Berkeley
Tolman Hall
Berkeley, CA 94709
jonvitale@berkeley.edu

Zachary Pardos
UC Berkeley
4641 Tolman Hall
Berkeley, CA 94709
pardos@berkeley.edu

Hannah Gogel
UC Berkeley
Tolman Hall
Berkeley, CA 94709
hgogel@berkeley.edu

Marcia C. Linn
UC Berkeley
4611 Tolman Hall
Berkeley, CA 94709
mclinn@berkeley.edu

http://dx.doi.org/10.1145/2876034.2893410

Abstract
Interactive simulations are commonly used tools in technology enhanced education. Simulations can be a powerful tool for allowing students to engage in inquiry, especially in science disciplines. They can help students develop an understanding of complex science phenomena in which multiple variables are at play. Developing models for complex domains, like climate science, is important for learning. Equally important, though, is understanding how students use these simulations. Finding use patterns that lead to learning will allow us to develop better guidance for students who struggle to extract the useful information from the simulation. In this study, we generate features from action log data collected while students interacted with simulations on climate change. We seek to understand what types of features are important for student learning by using regression models to map features onto learning outcomes.

ACM Classification Keywords
K.3.1 [Computers and Education]: Computer Uses in Education.

Introduction
Interactive simulations are commonly used tools in technology enhanced education. Simulations have the unique affordance of being able to connect small-scale and

large-scale phenomena for students [5]. Connecting the smaller-scale science mechanism to the larger-scale outcome is often confusing for students. Simulations can be used as inquiry activities, especially in science disciplines. In inquiry activities, students are able to develop their own knowledge by asking scientific questions, answering those questions using evidence, developing explanations, and connecting explanations to scientific knowledge [4].

In this study we use a series of four simulations that were part of a week-long curriculum on global climate change. This curriculum was run using the Web-based Inquiry Science Environment (WISE). This particular unit on global climate change had two foci: establishing a causal mechanism between increased concentrations of carbon dioxide and temperature and confronting the commonplace but incorrectly held link between ozone depletion and atmospheric temperature.

We employ feature engineering to understand how students are using the simulations and which activities are most productive for learning, as evidenced by gains in pre- or posttest scores or embedded items. Previous studies have investigated clustering of similar features for use in predictor models [1, 2]. However, since our simulations were embedded within a longer unit, we are also interested in investigating student activity at different visits (first, second, etc.).

NetLogo Models

The four simulations in the unit progress in complexity between the first and the fourth. During the first simulation, students view solar radiation coming from the sun. The solar radiation is either absorbed or reflected by the surface of the earth. The temperature of the atmosphere is shown in a dynamically generated graph next to the simulation of temperature vs. time. In this simulation, students are able to use a slider to change the speed of the simulation or to highlight a single ray and watch it transform into heat, then into infrared radiation. In the second simulation (Figure 1), students are also able to add and remove greenhouse gases. A second graph is added, plotting concentration of carbon dioxide vs. time. In the third and fourth simulations students investigate the role of ozone in global warming, and can add and decrease ozone. We do not analyze the ozone simulation on its own here because there were not clear student gains from this portion of the curriculum. In each of the four simulations, students must press "Go" to start or restart the simulation. Students were able to visit simulations as many times as they wanted.

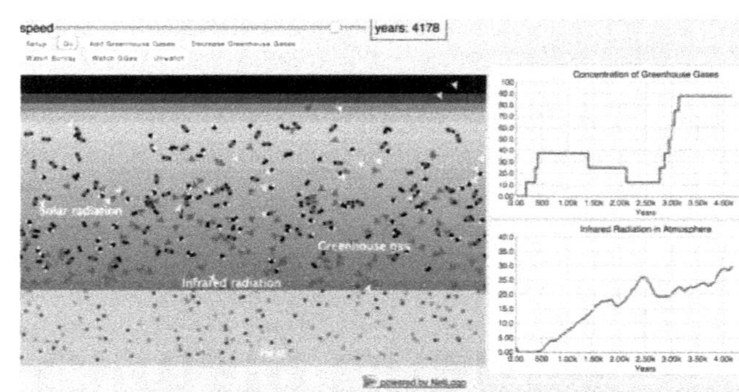

Figure 1: An Example of the NetLogo Simulations students interact with during the unit

Data

Our data on student interactions with simulations includes timestamped actions. Students also completed pre- and posttest items that measured student ability to differentiate between the effects of ozone depletion and

Variable	Mean	St.Dev.	Min	Max
Slider	33.35	126.6	0	1321
Go	21.44	16.92	0	135
Watch Ray	7.10	11.38	0	93
Graph Press	16.77	39.27	0	410
Time Spent (s)	1621.27	801.9	0	4478
Visits	6.49	5.21	1	56
Actions	328.17	288.15	2	1793

Figure 2: Descriptive statistics of generated features

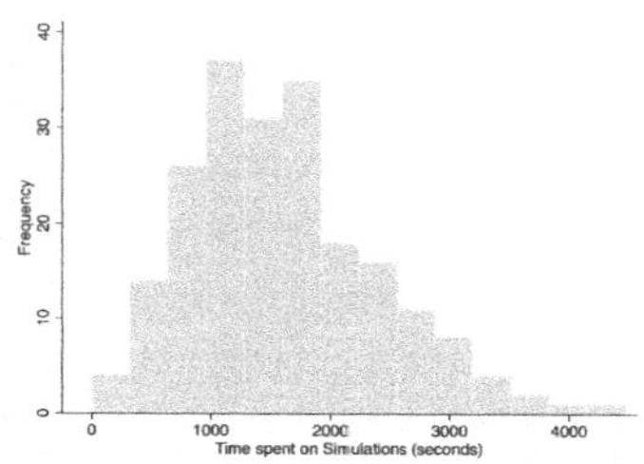

Figure 3: Amount of time (in seconds) spent on all four simulations

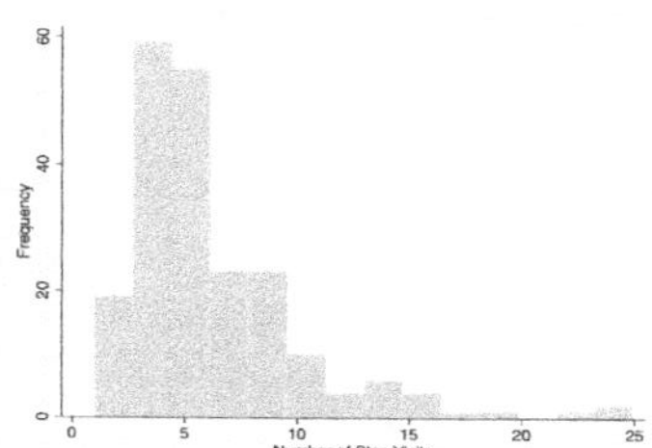

Figure 4: Number of visits students made to all four simulations

Variable	Mean	St.Dev.	Min	Max
Slider	10.06	55.18	0	752
Go	6.02	6.10	0	44
Watch Ray	2.80	5.99	0	46
Graph Press	4.67	13.60	0	131
Time Spent (s)	489.49	311.99	0	1690
Visits	3.40	2.42	1	13
Add GHGas	22.34	52.78	0	400
Decrease GHGas	28.74	47.50	0	367
Actions	117.3	154.06	1	1177

Figure 5: Descriptive statistics of generated features for only Simulation 2

greenhouse gases as well as ability to integrate ideas about energy transformation. Essay items were scored using a knowledge integration rubric [3]. Within the unit students engaged in concept mapping activities, also scored using knowledge integration rubrics [3].

The data comes from 422 students in three classrooms from two different schools. During simulations and the unit, students worked in pairs, but students were assessed individually at the pre- and posttests. We average pre/posttest scores across student pairs during this analysis.

Methodology

We engineered features from the action log data. Using these engineered features and student scores on both embedded and pre/post items, we run regression models. We also examine differences in features based on visit number. We analyze the entire dataset, which includes all four simulations, for productive patterns. Since some feature types differ between simulations, we also analyze a single simulation (simulation 2) to examine features that may be unique by simulation. We chose simulation 2 because it has a wider range of control options than simulation 1. Prior knowledge can be approximated using scores from the first concept mapping activity (after simulation 1).

Feature Generation

We generated features that relate the actions done by students and the time spent on simulations. Using all simulations, these features are: 1) Time spent on simulations, 2) Number of visits to simulations, 3) Number of actions done, 4) Number of times student used the speed slider, 5) Number of times the student pressed ''Go'' to restart simulation, 6) Number of times the student resized graphs, and 7) Number of times the student clicked ''Watch Ray''. Figures 2 - 4 show descriptions of these features.

Using only data from simulation 2, we use the same features as above and add two new features: 8) Number of times a student clicked ''Add Greenhouse Gas'', and 9) Number of times a student clicked ''Decrease Greenhouse Gas''. We also examine student interaction with the model based on the visit number.

Effects of Features on all Simulations

Using a regression model to predict posttest scores that includes the pretest score as well as all features listed above (features 1-7) as covariates, we find that the pretest score [$\beta = 0.81$, $p < 0.001$], features of time spent on simulations [$\beta = 0.0006$, $p < 0.001$], and number of times clicked on a graph [$\beta = -0.006$, $p < 0.05$] are significant. This model also only predicts posttest scores moderately well, with an R-squared value of 0.40. While the time spent on a simulation is an expected predictor, the number of clicks on a graph may be more interesting. Clicking on the graphs may be distracting for students, as shown by a negative regression coefficient, but this needs further investigation to differentiate between how different types of students utilize the graphs in different ways.

Effects of Features on One Simulation

Using data from Simulation 2 across all visits, we ran a regression model to find features that were important to learning. This regression attempts to predict the score of the second concept map activity that follows simulation 2 using the first concept map (done after the first simulation) as a covariate. We use all other features described above (features 1-9).

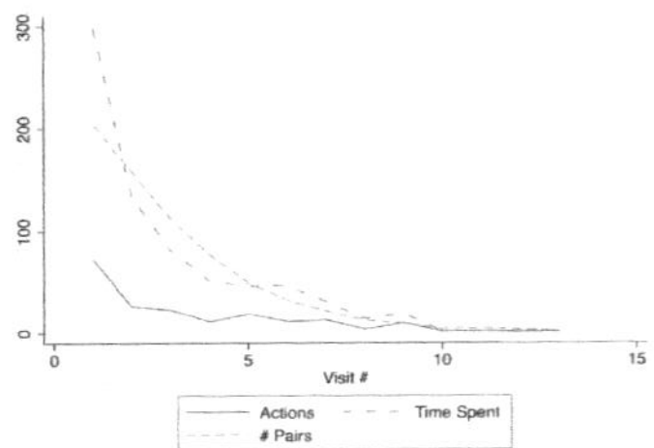

Figure 6: Averages of features by visit numbers

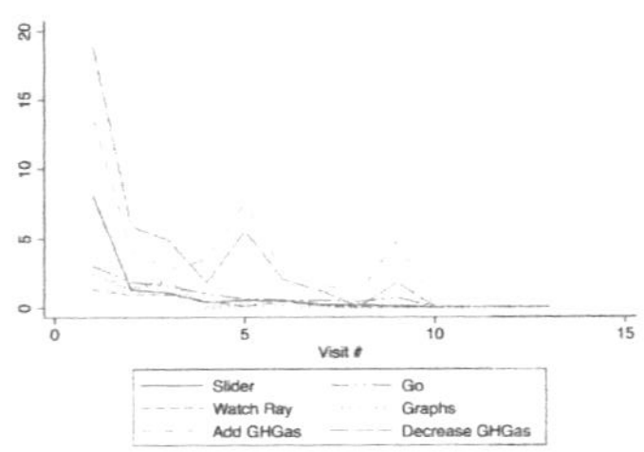

Figure 7: Averages of features by visit numbers

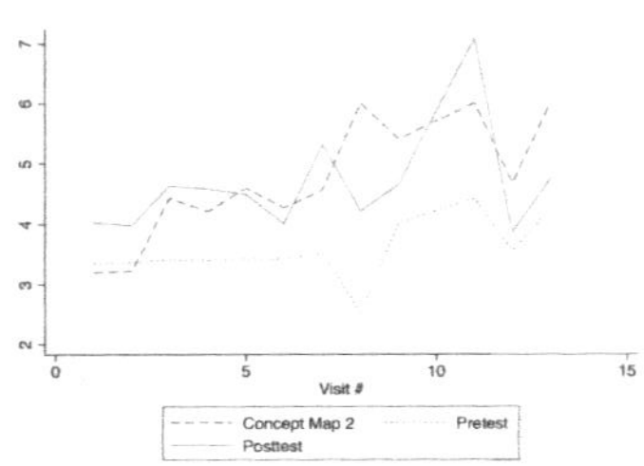

Figure 8: Averages of scores by visit numbers

Again, only the previous concept map score [$\beta = 0.55$, p <0.001] and time spent on the simulation [$\beta = 0.17$, p <0.001] were significant, and the regression model does not fit the data very well, with an R-squared value of 0.32. Descriptive statistics for this simulation can be found in Figure 5. It is interesting that this model explains such a low amount of variance since the concept maps offer a fairly close transfer of knowledge gained from the simulations.

Looking at changes in activity based on visit number, we find that students spend less time on average each time the revisit a simulation (Figure 6). In addition, only about half of students visit the simulation three or more times. Looking at Figure 7, we see that students do not restart the simulation, use the slider button, or "Watch" rays with any regularity after visit 2. However, students do continue to examine what happens after adding and decreasing greenhouse gases. The next concept map asks students to map the relationship between greenhouse gases and temperature using a map of how energy transforms. We see from Figure 7 that students may be focused on gaining specific pieces of information to help them construct their concept map during later visits to the simulation; students do not spend as much time or log as many actions during later visits.

Looking at Figure 8, we see that scores on the second concept map generally increase with number of visits. Score on the posttest also increases, but the relationship between number of visits and score is not as clear on the posttest. Interestingly, students who score higher on the pretest seem to revisit the simulations more often, suggesting that there may be a difference between how low and high prior knowledge students interact with the simulation.

Limitations and Future Work

Since students are expected to learn during each activity included in our curriculum, assessing all student interactions over time may be better done using a hidden Markov model. Future research may compare our engineered features to those generated using a deep neural network. This work also begins to examine differences between low and high prior knowledge students, but more work needs to be done. Examining why and when students revisit simulations is also a possibility for future research using a combination of NetLogo action log data and WISE action log data. One specific way to examine this data could also be in the context of spaced practice. Insight into how students revise their understanding of complex topics using the simulations would be important to developing automated guidance for simulations.

References

[1] Conati, C., Fratamico, L., Kardan, S., and Roll, I. Comparing representations for learner models in interactive simulations. In *Artificial Intelligence in Education*, Springer (2015), 74–83.
[2] Kardan, S., Roll, I., and Conati, C. The usefulness of log based clustering in a complex simulation environment. In *Intelligent Tutoring Systems*, Springer (2014), 168–177.
[3] Linn, M., and Eylon, B. *Science learning and instruction: Taking advantage of technology to promote knowledge integration.* Routledge, 2011.
[4] NRC. Inquiry. the national science education standards, 2000.
[5] Wilensky, U., and Reisman, K. Thinking like a wolf, a sheep, or a firefly: Learning biology through constructing and testing computational theoriesan embodied modeling approach. *Cognition and instruction 24*, 2 (2006), 171–209.

A Constructionist Toolkit for Learning Elementary Web Development at Scale

Meen Chul Kim
Drexel University
Philadelphia, PA 19104 USA
meenchul.kim@drexel.edu

Sukrit Chhabra
Drexel University
Philadelphia, PA 19104 USA
sukrit.chhabra@gmail.com

Thomas H. Park
Drexel University
Philadelphia, PA 19104 USA
park@drexel.edu

Andrea Forte
Drexel University
Philadelphia, PA 19104 USA
aforte@drexel.edu

Brian Lee
Drexel University
Philadelphia, PA 19104 USA
bl389@drexel.edu

L@S 2016, April 25-26, 2016, Edinburgh, Scotland, UK.
ACM 978-1-4503-3726-7/16/04.
http://dx.doi.org/10.1145/2876034.2893411

Abstract
We describe the design rationale and principles of a web authoring tool for beginner web developers called Snowball. We explain how this constructionist toolkit exposes content creators to computational features of web pages, enabling them to create meaningful artifacts while they move from content creation to basic coding. Finally, we discuss how we are instrumenting learning analytics in Snowball.

Author Keywords
Computing education at scale; constructionism; informal learning; web development

ACM Classification Keywords
K.3.2. Computers and education: Computer and information science education

Introduction
Constructionist approaches to learning emphasize the creation of personally meaningful artifacts as a powerful learning experience [2], but scaling such an approach to computing education in a systematic way is challenging. Constructionist learning can be chaotic and difficult to measure: creating artifacts that are intimate and personally meaningful generally means learners create dissimilar projects that require acquiring different skills and overcoming unique challenges in the

process. Moreover, it is difficult to design toolkits for creating computational artifacts that are understandable and appealing to large numbers of people without the structure offered by traditional courses and MOOCs. We have designed such a toolkit called Snowball for journalists and bloggers. Snowball is a WordPress plugin that supports the creation of sophisticated web articles while gradually exposing content creators to some of the computation underlying the articles they build. We have also instrumented Snowball to collect data about when people use features that support engagement with code and are in the initial stages of deployment and data collection.

Design of Snowball

Targeted learners and technological platform

Snowball is targeted towards journalists and journalism students because many are interested in creating sophisticated web content, but lack the motivation or means to learn how to do so. With the goal of integrating learning experiences within their existing practices rather than through isolated interventions, we designed Snowball as an open source WordPress plugin. In an analysis of content management system (CMS) usage at 100 major market and 100 college newspapers in North America, we identified WordPress as the most widespread CMS at 11% among the major newspaper websites and 68% for college newspapers.

Designing a constructionist toolkit

Constructionist projects facilitate making both personal and epistemological connections to domains of learning [2]. From a constructionist perspective, learners might be able to use a WYSIWYG web editor to make something personally meaningful and may become excited about their creations, but the experience can lack epistemological connections to computing as a discipline. Snowball was designed to ensure that people could both create compelling web projects and begin to explore computation. Snowball aims to provide a stepping stone to the more advanced stage of coding [3] by providing a development environment that is accessible to non-programmers, but allows them inspect and tinker with the underlying code.

Building articles with blocks

Constructionists have developed visual programming languages like Scratch [4] that support the easy creation of computer applications. We have similarly designed Snowball to support the composition of articles by combining multiple blocks (Figure 1). Snowball is differentiated from existing block-based programming languages by the following. First, it integrates with the existing tools and practices of our target learners. Second, blocks in Snowball serve to scaffold higher-level code patterns like interactive data widgets and social networking services rather than programming constructs like loops and conditionals.

Blocks provide scaffolding for a variety of content types, including basic content (*e.g.*, text, images, pull quotes, HTML), media (*e.g.*, YouTube video, SoundCloud audio, Google Maps), and data visualizations (*e.g.*, scatter plot, choropleth map). A graphical interface is available to populate each block's content and most pertinent styles, and preview the resulting output. The code inspector can also be activated to reveal the underlying HTML, CSS, and JavaScript (Figure 2), where the CSS can be modified to further customize the block. Additionally, an HTML block type is available for users to create fully custom blocks.

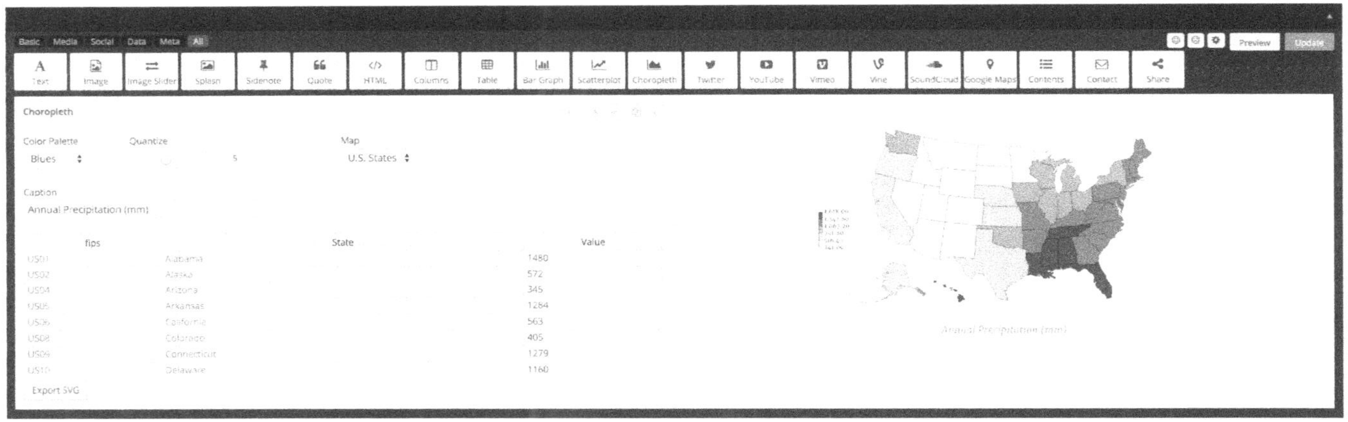

Figure 1. Embedding of a Choropleth block, with graphical inputs on the left and a live preview on the right. Additional blocks can be added to the article by clicking the buttons at the top.

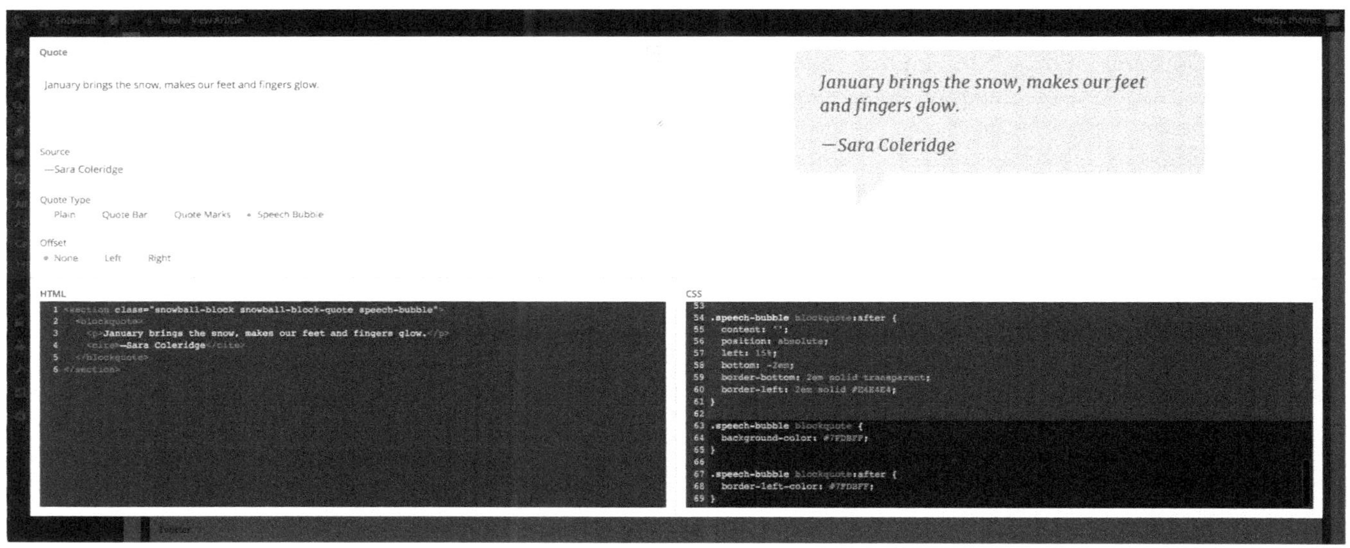

Figure 2. The code view of a Quotes block, used to inspect and modify the underlying HTML and CSS code.

Instrumenting for learning analytics
In constructionist environments, the complexity of computational artifacts and learning outcomes can vary considerably from individual to individual, particularly "in the wild," creating a challenge for constructionist approaches to be applied at scale. Recent work has addressed this issue by defining situated aspects of learning and applying quantitative techniques to the assessment of informal learning progress [1, 5]. Our work with Snowball takes a similar approach.

Research questions

Constructionism assumes individual learners construct their own mental models based on their experiences solving problems as they pursue their own project goals. Accordingly, not only what they learn but also how they learn differs. Therefore, we focus on measuring and analyzing two aspects of learning: 1) sophistication of the computational artifacts learners create, and 2) pathways of learning. The following research questions frame our investigation: 1) How can the knowledge state of learners be modeled during their early engagements with code through web development? 2) What patterns of learning occur as they learn to create more sophisticated computational artifacts?

Methods

As a block-based programming environment, the use of blocks in Snowball and the tinkering of underlying code can be used to infer how learners progress from initial to more complex understandings of web authoring [1, 5]. To answer our research questions, we consider the following analytical strategies. First, we aim to understand a user's learning process as a temporal change of block usage. We assume that a wider and faster use of blocks may be an indicator of learning to use the toolkit. As they become more proficient and meet the limitations of the blocks, we anticipate engagement in the direct modification of HTML and CSS. Our next goal is to capture critical pathways of learning. We expect to explore patterns of learning among users, using clustering approaches to discover groups of Snowball users that share similar learning behaviors.

Data collection

Upon the installation of Snowball, a user agrees to our collection of their activity while using the tool. We are logging user events in Snowball, as well as accompanying metadata such as user name, blog name and URL, used blocks, actions, timestamp, and publication status. Through this data, we aim to track and analyze how learners move from initial stages of content development to deeper engagements with code.

Acknowledgment
This work is supported by NSF grant 1339344.

References
[1] Fields, D.A., Giang, M., and Kafai, Y. Programing in the wild: Trends in youth computational participation in the online Scratch community. In *Proc. WiPSCE 2014*, ACM Press (2014), 2-11.

[2] Papert, S., and Harel, I. *Situating constructionism*. in Harel, I., and Paper, S. eds. Constructionism, Ablex Publishing Corp., New York, 1991, 1-11.

[3] Park, T.H., and Wiedenbeck, S. Learning web development: Challenges at an earlier stage of computing education. In *Proc. ICER 2011*, ACM Press (2011), 125-132.

[4] Resnick, M., et al. Scratch: Programming for all. *Communications of the ACM 52*, 11 (2009), 60-67.

[5] Yang, S., et al. Uncovering trajectories of informal learning in large online communities of creators. In *Proc. L@S 2015*, ACM Press (2015), 131-140.

Using Android Wear for Avoiding Procrastination Behaviours in MOOCs

Cristóbal Romero
University of Cordoba
Computer Science Department
Cordoba, Spain
cromero@uco.es

Jose Antonio Espino
University of Cordoba
Computer Science Department
Cordoba, Spain
i82espaj@uco.es

Rebeca Cerezo
University of Oviedo
Psychology Department
Oviedo, Spain
cerezorebeca@uniovi.es

Manuel Bermudez
University of Cordoba
Social Science Department
Cordoba, Spain
l62bevam@uco.es

L@S 2016, April 25-26, 2016, Edinburgh, Scotland UK
ACM 978-1-4503-3726-7/16/04.
http://dx.doi.org/10.1145/2876034.2893412

Abstract
This paper introduces a new feature for instructors to communicate with their MOOC learners via SmartWatches in a different way to the traditional e-mails in order to try to avoiding procrastination. We have developed an Android Wear-based SmartWatches application designed for receiving notifications from MOOCs, and a specific section in Google Course Builder interface that allows instructors to configure and send the messages to each user registered in the course. We have evaluated the implementation of our proposal in an Introduction to Philosophy MOOC. The number and percentage of students who did assessments on time, together with their comments in a satisfaction questionnaire present very promising results.

Author Keywords
MOOC; Android Wear; SmartWatches; Notifications; Procrastination.

Introduction
Procrastination refers to the delay of initiation or timely completion of a task. Some studies [1] have shown that procrastinators show poor achievement and feel a compulsion to dropout frequently throughout a course. Furthermore, the consequences of procrastination in e-learning are considered more damaging on achievement than procrastination in traditional

Figure 1. Notification about the availability of Chapter 1 of the course.

classrooms. Procrastination in MOOC causes worse outcomes [2] due to its massiveness and difficulty in the communication between one instructor and thousands of students from all over the world. In order to solve this problem we suggest to use the new available Android Wearable technology with MOOC. Android Wear is a version of Android OS designed for SmartWatches and other Wearables that is mainly based on notifications and vibrations to inform users of important messages. Furthermore, our wrists are much more sensitive than other areas of the body that are usually in contact with SmartPhones [3] such as the outer thighs, upper arms, chest, etc. Some authors [4] have also identified some points about how Education can benefit with Android Wear: to get real time notifications about classes and exams, to plan daily study routines during class, etc. In this paper, we suggest that Android Wearable can help the instructor communicate more effectively with students than using e-mails.

Developed Applications

On the one hand, we have used Google Course Builder (GCB) framework for developing our MOOC because it allows Google APIs and technologies compatible with Android Wear to be easily used. We have developed and integrated a new section on the instructor interface in GCB named "Announcement". You must be a course instructor or administrator in order to access to this interface for configuring the messages to the students: the title of the message, the date in which it is sent, the body of the message and whether we also want to send the message by e-mail. We have used Google Cloud Messaging (GCM) and Google Group technologies in order to send notifications to Android devices and/or traditional e-mails respectively. On the other hand, we have developed a Wear application named adGCB (avisos desde GCB) and uploaded it to the Android Market[1]. Its purpose is to show a notification card on the SmartWatch screen together with a sound alert as soon as a new message from the MOOC is received (see Figure 1).

Experiments

We have performed an experiment using a GCB MOOC about Introduction to the Philosophy[2]. The course consisted of 7 units with YouTube video lectures as visual lessons and one final quiz as assessment for each unit. The course had 1059 students registered 136 of which installed the Android Wear application. The objective of this experiment has been to observe whether the use of our Wear application could contribute to help overcome procrastination behaviours (on delivery time of assignments). Regarding the sample used in the experiment, the students registered (N = 1059) were categorized into two different groups: Group 1 or students with Android Wear (n=136) and Group 2 students without Android Wear (n=923). We calculated the number of students who completed each assignment on time on a basis weekly basis (see Table 1). Group 1 students received the course notifications about the assignments' deadlines to their SmartWatches and e-mails, and Group 2 students only by e-mail. The message of the notification indicated that they had until the end of the current week to complete the assessment.

[1] https://play.google.com/store/apps/details?id=com.arjonasoftware.adgcb&hl=es

[2] http://www.uco.es/mooc/filosoque

Course Units	Group 1	Group 2
Registered/Installed	136	923
Assessment 1	107	250
Assessment 2	93	167
Assessment 3	89	137
Assessment 4	86	106
Assessment 5	76	78
Assessment 6	79	77
Assessment 7	86	113

Table 1. Number of students who completed each course assessment on time.

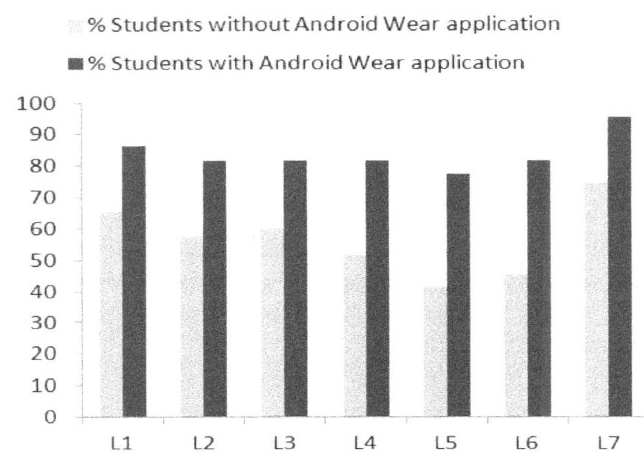

Figure 2. Percentage of students who completed each course assessment on time.

As seen in Figure 2, Group 1 (students with Wear Application) had a higher percentage of students who completed all the assessments on time than the Group 2 (student without Wear Application). Even in assessments 5 and 6 the number of students who completed them on time was almost equal or even higher in the Group 1 than the Group 2 even though this group is made up of a smaller number of students (see Table 1).

Finally, the students who installed the Android Wear application (Group 1) were asked to complete a satisfaction survey at the end of the course. It was composed of 5 items, 3 quantitative questions answered in a 6 point Likert scale (1 - not at all; 6 - very much) and 2 qualitative open questions:

- **Q1:** Do you prefer to receive only emails for important notifications?
- **Q2:** Do you prefer to receive also notifications to your SmartWatch?
- **Q3:** Did you like the SmartWatch application?
- **Q4:** Indicate what advantages you think the SmartWatch application has.
- **Q5:** Indicate what disadvantages you think the SmartWatch application has.

Statistic	Q1	Q2	Q3
Mean	3.1	4.7	4.3
SD	1.5	1.2	1.3
Mode	4	6	6

Table 2. Satisfaction survey statistics for Q1, Q2 and Q3.

The results of Q1-Q3 are displayed in Table 2 (Mean value, Standard Deviation and Mode). As can be seen, the students preferred to receive notification by both, e-mail and SmartWatch (Q2), through the application rather than only by emails, with a difference of more than 1.5 points. The average satisfaction with the application is good but the most remarkable result is that the most frequent answer (Mode) to Q3 was the highest score in the Likert scale (6) when students were asked if they had liked the application. Regarding the two open questions (Q4 and Q5), valuable information can be extracted to guide the future improvement of the application and its implementation. In general, most of the answers to the weak points of the application (Q5) were related to easily fixable technical issues. Some examples are: *"Seeing a large message on my smartwatch is not practical"* and *"The interface is very simple and could be more interactive, with more options"*. However, when the students answer to the strengths (Q4), their answers were more centred in relevant aspects for their learning process. Some examples are: *"Following the course is more stimulating" and "I like the immediacy of notifications"*.

Conclusions

Although this is an initial study of our Android Wear-based SmartWatches application, it has shown promising results. On the one hand, the percentage of students that completed the course assessments on time was higher for those who used the application. It could be explained because the notifications could be acting like an external aid to empower the self-regulation necessary to succeed in e-learning environments [5] and avoid procrastination. However, behaviours such as cramming or submissions that barely meet the deadline are also procrastinating behaviour, but were not considered in this study. On the other hand, the student's satisfaction seems to be high with the application. Users' satisfaction has been traditionally difficult to measure but is undeniably important for the efficacy of an implemented action. In this sense, one of the limitations of this study is that the satisfaction was not measured in both groups, nor referring to the general course. For that reason, improving the design of the evaluation is one the goals for future studies and to test our Android Wear application with more students. We would like to use a better experimental method using control and experimental groups in which a half of students with SmartWatch were randomly assigned to control group. We would like also to compare different messaging techniques in terms of content, frequency, and types of message for testing what are the most effective. Finally, we want to improve the functionality of the Application, and to make it available to others MOOC platforms.

Acknowledgements

This research is supported by projects of the Spanish Ministry of Science and Technology TIN2014-55252-P, EDU2014-57571-P, the Innovative Teaching project of the UCO 2014-12-1004 and the GRUPIN14-053.

References

1. Michinov, N., Brunot, S., Le Bohec, O., Juhel, J., Delaval, M. Procrastination, participation, and performance in online learning environments. Computers & Education 56, 1 (2011), 243-252.
2. Diver, P., Martinez, I. MOOCs as a massive research laboratory: opportunities and challenges. Distance Education 36, 1 (2015) 5-25.
3. Karuei, I., Foley-Fisher, Z., Koch, S., MacKenzie, R., El-Zohairy, M., and MacLean, K. E. Vibration Perception in Mobile Contexts. Graphics Interface, Ottawa, Canada, (2010) 28-29.
4. Google's Android Wear: How it is going to Innovate Education. http://www.edtechboard.com/googles-android-wear-how-it-is-going-to-innovate/
5. Cerezo, R., Alvarez, D., Sanchez-Santillan, M., Nuñez Pérez, J.C. New Technologies for learning assessment in virtual learning environments at higher education. Innovación Educativa en la Educación Superior (2013) 77-96.

Beyond Traditional Metrics: Using Automated Log Coding to Understand 21st Century Learning Online

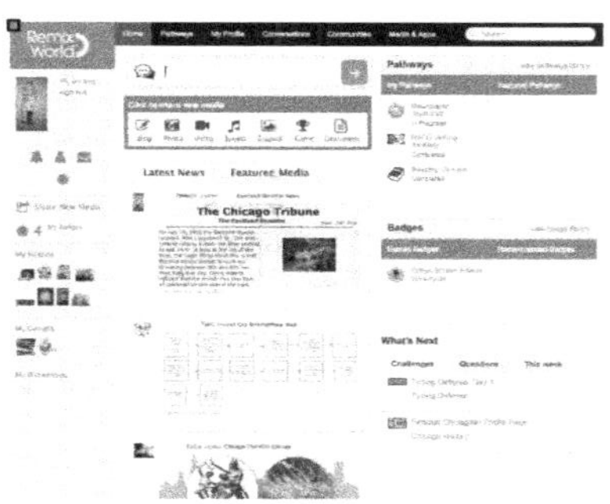

Figure 1. iRemix online social learning network for youth and adult educators.

Denise Nacu
DePaul University
243 South Wabash Avenue
Chicago, IL 60604 USA
dnacu@cdm.depaul.edu

Michael Schutzenhofer
DePaul University
2219 North Kenmore Ave
Chicago, IL 60614 USA
mschutz1@depaul.edu

Caitlin K. Martin
Digital Youth Network
14 East Jackson
Chicago, IL 60604 USA
cmartin@digitalyouthnetwork.com

Nichole Pinkard
Associate Professor
DePaul University
243 South Wabash Avenue
Chicago, IL 60604 USA
npinkard@cdm.depaul.edu

L@S 2016, April 25-26, 2016, Edinburgh, Scotland UK
ACM 978-1-4503-3726-7/16/04.
http://dx.doi.org/10.1145/2876034.2893413

Abstract

While log analysis in massively open online courses and other online learning environments has mainly focused on traditional measures, such as completion rates and views of course content, research is responding to calls for analytic frameworks that are more reflective of social learning models. We introduce a generalizable approach to automatically code log data that highlights educator support roles and student actions that are consistent with recent conceptualizations of 21st century learning, such as creative production, self-directed learning, and social learning. Here, we describe details of a log-coding framework that builds from prior mixed method studies of the use of iRemix, an online social learning network, by middle school youth and adult educators in blended learning contexts.

Author Keywords

Log analysis; educational data mining; online learning; teaching roles; 21st century learning

21st Century Learning Activities
Creative Production. Understanding and using appropriate media, elaborating and refining ideas and work, creating new and worthwhile ideas, developing media literacy and technological fluency and confidence through production and participation. *Related skills:* • **Developing Identity.** Ex., creating and editing user profiles. • **Creation and Sharing**. Ex., creating, editing, and posting creative work.
Self-directed Learning. Reflecting on learning experiences and processes, personalizing learning by making connections with individual interests and goals, taking initiative, being a lifelong learner, developing self-direction, making decisions, seeking out information. *Related skills:* • **Exploration.** Ex., looking at potential activities, using resources. • **Reflection.** Ex., Reviewing own work and progress.
Social Learning. Communicating and collaborating around work and ideas, being open to new ideas and perspectives, teaching and learning from others. *Related skills:* • **Communication.** Ex., Commenting on work, sending messages, and participating in debates. • **Observation and Connection.** Ex., Viewing and participating in groups.

Table 1. 21st century learning activities afforded in online social learning networks.

Introduction
Log analysis in massively open online courses (MOOCs) and other online learning environments has mostly focused on metrics that are aligned with traditional, lecture-based instructional models such as reporting findings related to course completion rates, viewing of course content, and grades received (e.g., [4], [9]). Several researchers have pointed out the inadequacy of these approaches and have called for conceptualization of new analytics that are more relevant to social learning models that emphasize personalization, collaboration on projects, and learning as a process of identity development as opposed to only accumulating content knowledge [3], [8]. Within informal learning contexts such as afterschool programs, less traditional outcomes have been documented that are critical to the 21st century skill-set, including managing information; directing learning pathways; collaborating on projects, discussion and critique around common artifacts; and building collective intelligence [1], [4].

Recent efforts to automatically code content from student and educator communication in online learning environments (e.g., discussion forums) have provided a promising start for improving feedback, promoting active participation, and fostering collaborative learning communities [5], [7], [10]. These efforts, such as gathering data on how often students revise their work [5], provide a richer perspective of student actions and learning processes than those obtained from traditional metrics. Despite these content exploration methodologies and growing interest in using networked online learning systems to foster 21st century skills, there is scant knowledge about how to find evidence of such learning using logs generated by users in systems such as MOOCs and other online learning networks.

We respond to this research gap by building a coding framework that can be used to inform system design, educator practice, and theory about online teaching and learning. This study aims to 1) develop a generalizable coding framework to support interpretation of student and educator logged actions that reflect 21st century learning, and 2) use these coding frameworks, metadata, and logged user actions to visualize and discover patterns to better understand learning and teaching online. Here, we describe our method of coding logs in the data-preprocessing phase. This type of coding framework is needed to reveal patterns of 21st century learning in systems such as MOOCs as well as smaller scale online learning environments.

Research Context
This work is part of a three-year study examining interactions among youth and adults in online social learning networks that lead to 21st century learning outcomes. Focusing on middle school youth, we have been engaged in design and research in both formal classrooms (English/Language Arts and History) and informal after school contexts (girl's electronics and wearable computing program) using iRemix (Figure 1), a closed social network that supports interaction among peers and adult educators around the creation, sharing, and communication of digital artifacts. In this context, users are on the system regularly (at least weekly) for extended periods of time (from six months to over two years), resulting in extensive logged activity by a stable user base of 141 youth and 16 adult educators. To generate our coding method and processing for this work, we looked at user activity over a 26-month period, totaling 203k actions. To help understand and validate our coding and interpretations of log data, we are triangulating with detailed qualitative data from the

Educator Learning Support Roles
Audience. View what youth are doing online
Encourager. Encourage youth about work or participation
Evaluator. Provide grades, ratings, badges, or other formal assessments
Friend. Exhibit personal approachability/ friendship/ mentorship including social posts, off-topic conversation
Instructor. Directly teach a concept or skill or provide an assignment. Provide prompts and/or feedback to further student thinking or work
Learning Broker. Connect youth with learning opportunities (e.g., people, activities, institutions, etc.)
Model. Share own creative work/process
Monitor. Impose or suggest rules of behavior online
Promoter. Showcase youth participant work
Resource Provider. Provide learning resources (how-to guides, links, embedded media, etc.)

Table 2. Educator online learning support roles.

learning environment, including classroom observations, and educator and student interviews.

Theoretical Framework

Our coding framework highlights both student and educator actions to describe learning interactions online. We build on previous work that has defined capacities and dispositions critical for learners in the 21st century [1], [4], prior studies of youth-educator interactions and roles played to support the development of such dispositions [1], [7], and analysis of common features of online social learning networks. Along with related skills supported in iRemix, Table 1 describes three strands of learning activities that are afforded in online social learning networks: *creative production*, *self-directed learning*, and *social learning*. For example, youth use the *message* and *debate forum* features to communicate with others. Although each activity has different implications in terms of the scope of the audience, both are evidence of social interaction online. Table 2 identifies key roles that educators play to support learners in developing these 21st century skills (see [7]). Like the student actions, the adult learning support roles are aligned with common social network features found in iRemix. For example, educators can play the *Audience* role by viewing individual youth artifacts and profile pages. They can play the *Encourager* role by submitting a status update that congratulates the entire group, commenting, or using reaction tags on an artifact.

Data Preparation and Coding Method

To prepare a target dataset for data mining and pattern analysis, we process a database of Actions from iRemix. Based on variables in the Action logs that indicate *who* performed *what type* of action *to whom* (if applicable), we derive *Actor*, *Action*, and *Recipient*. Together, data from these variables define a unique type of log to which we apply an interpretive code based on analysis of either *Student* actions or *Educator* actions. Thus, a set of coding rules use *Actor*, *Action*, and *Recipient* data to automatically generate the target dataset.

Coding Student Actions

For each student log (*Actor* = Student), the *Action* and *Recipient* data generates an interpretive code that makes student log data easily understandable to aid exploration by researchers and other stakeholders (see Table 3 for a sample of values for student logs). Table 4 shows a sample of how the interpretive codes link to the higher-level 21st century learning actions.

Action	Recipient	Code
View a video	Peer	ViewWorkOfOthers
View a video	Self	ReviewOwnWork
Create a video	N/A	Create
Comment on a video	Peer	Communicate
Edit a blog post	Self	EditOwnWork

Table 3. Sample coding of student logs (Actor = Student)

Coding Educator Actions

For each educator log (*Actor* = {teacher, mentor, ...}), *Action* and *Recipient* data generates a learning support role code. Some actions cannot be coded automatically since the coding rules do not consider or interpret the related content (e.g., the text of a comment). In those cases, the code applied is *Hand*, indicating that it requires manual interpretation. Our prior research has used hand coding [7], and future work will explore the use of text mining to enable automated coding. A sample of coding educator logs is shown in Table 5.

Student Action Codes and 21st Century Skills
ViewResources → Work Independently (Self-Directed learning)
ReviewOwnWork →Reflection (Self-Directed learning)
Create → Creation and Sharing (Creative Production)
Communicate → Communication (Social Learning)
EditOwnWork → Creation and Sharing (Creative Production)

Table 4. Student action codes and their alignment to 21st century skills.

Action	Recipient	Code
Viewed a video	Student	Audience
Commented on a video	Student	Hand
Rated a video	Student	Evaluator

Table 5. Sample coding of educator logs (Actor = Educator)

Significance

The coding method presented here responds to the need for metrics that provide a richer picture of interactions in MOOCs and online social networks. By revealing types of actions that reflect models of 21st century learning, the coding framework helps to make these kinds of activities and interactions more visible to inform our understanding of online learning and the design of these environments. The ability to automatically code log data is a necessary first step to enable knowledge discovery using clustering and data mining techniques for a smaller scale system like iRemix, but also for larger scale learning systems and MOOCs. And, by coding actions with attention to user interactions (capturing actor, action, and recipient), we also lay the groundwork for robust analysis of social connections among participants. Future work will use coded log data for pattern analysis and data mining of iRemix data. We also aim to validate our framework by comparing log data to external assessments (e.g. [2], [5]), and explore application of this framework to log analysis of other online learning systems.

Acknowledgements

This work is based on work supported by the National Science Foundation (1325004).

References

1. Barron, B., Gomez, K., Pinkard, N., Martin, C.K. 2014. *Digital Youth Network: Cultivating Digital Media Citizenship in Urban Communities*. MIT Press, Cambridge, MA.
2. Care, E., Griffin, P., Scoular, C., Awwal, N., & Zoanetti, N. (2015). Collaborative problem solving tasks. In P. Griffin and E. Care (Eds.). *Assessment and teaching of 21st century skills: Methods and approach*. Educational Assessment in an Information Age. Dordrecht, Springer: 85-104.
3. Eisenberg, M., & Fischer, G. 2014. MOOCs: A perspective from the learning sciences. *Proc.ICLS 2014*.
4. Ho, A. D., Reich, J., Nesterko, S. O., Seaton, D. T., Mullaney, T., Waldo, J., & Chuang, I. 2014. HarvardX and MITx: The first year of open online courses (HarvardX and MITx Working Paper No. 1).
5. Koenig, J. A. (Ed.) 2011. *Assessing 21st century skills: Summary of a workshop*. National Academies Press, Washington, DC.
6. Kulkarni, C., Bernstein, M. S., & Klemmer, S. 2015. PeerStudio: Rapid Peer Feedback Emphasizes Revision and Improves Performance. In *Proc. ACM L@S 2015*, 75-84.
7. Nacu, D., Pinkard, N., Martin C., & Gray, T. 2014. *Analyzing educators' online interactions: a framework of online learning support roles.* Learning, Media and Technology, DOI: 10.1080/17439884.2015.975722
8. Pea, R. 2013. Learning Sciences and Learning Analytics: Time for a Marriage. *EDUCAUSE Learning Initiative, February* (Vol. 5).
9. Perna, L., Ruby, A., Boruch, R., Wang, N., Scull, J., Evans, C., & Ahmad, S. 2013. The life cycle of a million MOOC users. *MOOC Research Initiative Conf.*
10. Skrypnyk, O., Joksimović, S., Kovanović, V., Gašević, D., & Dawson, S. 2015. Roles of course facilitators, learners, and technology in the flow of information of a cMOOC. *Br. J. Educ. Technol. Spec. Issue MOOCs*.

A Framework for Topic Generation and Labeling from MOOC Discussions

Thushari Atapattu
Katrina Falkner
School of Computer Science
University of Adelaide
Adelaide, Australia
{firstname.lastname}@adelaide.edu.au

Abstract
This study proposes a standardised open framework to automatically generate and *label* discussion topics from Massive Open Online Courses (MOOCs). The proposed framework expects to overcome the issues experienced by MOOC participants and teaching staff in locating and navigating their information needs effectively. We analysed two MOOCs – *Machine Learning* and *Statistics: Making Sense of Data* offered during 2013 and obtained statistically significant results for automated *topic labeling*. However, more experiments with additional MOOCs from different MOOC platforms are necessary to generalise our findings.

L@S 2016, April 25-26, 2016, Edinburgh, Scotland UK
ACM 978-1-4503-3726-7/16/04.
http://dx.doi.org/10.1145/2876034.2893414

Author Keywords
MOOC, discussion forums, topic modeling, LDA, Naïve Bayes, Learning Analytics

Introduction
Discussion forums or communities form a significant component of many MOOCs, particularly within the connectivist MOOC model (cMOOCs) [1]. Due to the massive amount of discussion data generated within MOOCs, it is challenging for participants to effectively locate and navigate their information need unassisted. Similarly, the workload required to manage the magnitude of existing discussions, along with the fact that discussions may develop around any course topic at any point in time, makes it difficult for teaching staff to effectively focus their attention and support learners. In order to address this problem at large scale, we propose a framework to identify *key* discussion topics, supporting a topic-wise organisation of discussion contents.

Background

Topic analysis of MOOC *discussion content* using existing topic models (e.g. LDA, Structural topic model) has been explored in some recent works [2, 3]. However, these existing works are limited in their usage to end-user applications (e.g. visualisation, recommender systems) due to their inability to provide *topic labels* for generated topics without human intervention [2-4]. Topic analysis from other text sources such as document collections rely on external resources for topic labeling. Ramage et al. [5] propose a labeled LDA using supervised learning techniques trained with a corpus of tagged web pages. Lau et al. [6] introduce an automated topic labeling approach by querying the web to obtain candidate labels from titles of Wikipedia articles. Magatti et al. [7] utilise Google directory hierarchy to obtain candidate labels. This approach is only applicable to a hierarchical topic model and relies on a pre-existing ontology. While initial works in automated topic labeling have promise, a new mechanism is necessary in order to cope with the scale present in a MOOC and the dynamic and diverse nature of discussion contents.

Topic Analysis & Labeling

The framework proposed in this paper builds upon existing topic models, introducing a novel solution for *automated topic labeling* at scale (Figure 1). Topic modeling is an unsupervised approach to discover hidden thematic structures in large text corpora [8]. This work utilise Latent Dirichlet Allocation [8], the state of the art in topic modeling.

The aim of topic labeling is to generate a set of candidate labels and develop a ranking mechanism to determine the most relevant and meaningful label for unlabeled topics extracted from a text corpora (i.e. discussion forums in this work). This work incorporates titles of lectures introduced by the lecturers within their lecture materials (e.g. video transcripts and lecture slides) to obtain candidate topic labels for discussion topics.

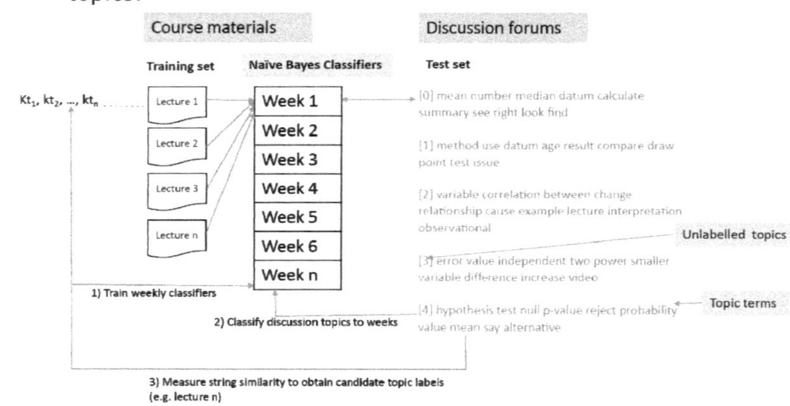

Figure 1. Overview of topic labeling process

Given the dynamic nature and scale present in MOOC discussions, it is likely that a large number of topics will be generated, proportional to the number of discussion threads. Due to this scale, direct comparison of each topic across the corpora of lecture materials to obtain candidate labels is a highly inefficient approach. Further, due to the self-paced nature of most MOOCs, discussion can be generated at any point in time related to any course content. Therefore, it is not practical to rely on candidate labels generated at the commencement of the course from early discussions, as these are unlikely to be suitable as the course progresses.

Course	Users*	Threads	Lecture-related threads
ML	6368	5449	972
STAT	2313	1145	392

*Anonymous users are counted as 1 unit

Table 1. Statistics of selected courses

Course	Thread*	Post	Comment
ML	972	3670	1778
STAT	392	1643	882

*Thread is a combination of thread title, corresponding posts and comments

Table 2. Statistics of *lecture-related* discussions

Topic	Topic terms
1	Function cost gradient descent minimum theta square point error algorithm
2	Class boundary point decision positive classification probability svm example line
3	Layer network neural output input hidden node unit weight image
4	Learning algorithm machine learn problem datum example system unsupervised result
5	Matrix pca inverse vector pinv dimension octave loop svd datum

Table 3. Sample topics (unlabeled) from ML course

In order to address this problem, we introduce text classifiers (i.e. Naïve Bayes) to narrow the focus of topic labeling to a subset of the course contents organised by weeks. We build text classifiers for each week, using the contents from course materials (i.e. top 50 key terms) of a given week in the 'positive' class and the key terms from course materials of remaining weeks in the 'negative' class (Figure 1(1)). Then, candidate topic labels are generated by measuring the similarity between topic terms of discussions and key terms extracted from course materials of the corresponding week/s. In order to summarise course materials as a set of key terms, we use state the art term extraction algorithms including basic term frequency and Chi-squared algorithm [9]. We also reused authors' previous work in extracting key terms from lecture slides [10]. The generated set of candidate labels are ranked based on the similarity scores between discussion content and course content.

Methodology

Data

This work utilises Coursera discussion forum data from the MOOCs offered during 2013. For this study, we selected two MOOCs offered in English and none self-paced: *Machine Learning* (ML) course (Stanford University – 10 weeks) and *Statistics – Making sense of data* (STAT) course (University of Toronto – 8 weeks) (Table 1). This work primarily focuses on lecture-related discussions for the analysis (Table 2).

Research question: *How can we leverage the learner-generated discourse from discussion forum contents to better identify key topics of interest?*

Method

The topic analysis approach involves pre-processing of discussion contents including removal of non-textual contents, stop words, language detection and translation to English, and lemmatisation. We utilise existing JavaScript implementation of LDA (jsLDA[1]) and obtains 40 and 25 topics from ML and STAT courses respectively (Table 3). To overcome the brevity of discussion posts when applying common topic models, we merge all posts and comments belonging to a single thread. The topics generated from topic models are used as testing data for text classifiers to classify the discussion topics into weeks while contents of course materials (weekly-basis) are used as training data (Figure 1). Our manual topic labeling task involves 3 volunteer domain experts for each course. These experts are senior academic staff or post-doctoral researchers from the Computer Science school of University of Adelaide. The task of each expert is to examine the given topics and rank the suggested candidate labels. The ranks are defined as *most related label to the given topic (rank-1), reasonably related label to the given topic (rank-2),* and *least related to the given topic (rank-3)*. Human annotators also had the option to mention when the generated labels are *not related* or more than one label are equally likely ranked.

Results and Discussion

We have calculated the Spearman's ranking correlation coefficient (r_s) between the ranks generated by machine and human (Table 4). Assuming that the rankings are performed independently across the different participants since each individual obtained

[1] http://mimno.infosci.cornell.edu/jsLDA/index.html

Course	H1	H2	H3	Mean (SD)
ML	0.575	0.612	0.637	0.608 (0.03)
STAT	0.705	0.669	0.525	0.633 (0.09)

*H1, H2, H3 denotes the human expert involved in each course

Table 4. Spearman ranking correlation between machine and human topic labeling

Course	H1-H2	H1-H3	H2-H3	Mean (SD)
ML	0.702	0.525	0.675	0.634 (0.09)
STAT	0.506	0.573	0.653	0.577 (0.07)

*Human annotator pairs denote different individuals in each course

Table 5. Inter-rater agreement (Kappa)

randomly arranged list of candidate labels, the results show a positive ranking correlation ($p < 0.01$) for both courses. Our classifiers also performed well for almost all weeks with a macroaveraged F-measure of 0.946 and 0.926 (10-folds cross-validation) for ML and STAT courses respectively. We calculated the inter-rater agreement using Cohen's Kappa between annotators and mean is obtained per course (Table 5). According to Table 5, our inter-rater agreement is low when one rater suggested a rank for a given topic label while other left it blank when they find it uncertain. Additionally, topics terms generated from specific examples, category headings or similar candidate labels suggested from both main lecture and tutorials primarily influenced the agreement between raters. Due to these issues, some annotators suggested to revisit the manual labeling procedure by providing texts of de-identifiable threads as a supplementary.

Conclusion and Future Works

This initial work establishes a step towards introducing labeled topic analysis approach to be utilised in end-user applications (e.g. visualisation tools, recommendation systems) within the MOOC context. With the longstanding goal of assisting in personalised learning at large scale through a 'topic-wise organisation' of discussion contents, we plan to extend this work to effectively navigate large quantities of discussions, recommending the similar threads on the same topic. Our findings of promising preliminary results provide benefits to the learning at scale research community through an open framework to be used to analyse discussions of MOOCs. We are extending our experiments with further MOOCs from different disciplines and MOOC platforms (e.g. edX, Coursebuilder) in order to generalise our findings for arbitrary courses. Additionally, we are expanding our focus on contents from *assessment-related* discussions.

Acknowledgement

The authors would like to acknowledge Google Inc. for supporting this project through the 'Google MOOC Focused Research Award Scheme'.

References

[1] Seimens, G. MOOCs are really a platform. *EleanSpace,* (2002).

[2] Ezan-Can, A., et al. Unsupervised modeling for understanding MOOC discussion forums: a learning analytics approach. In *Proc. LAK 2015.*

[3] Reich, J., et al. Computer Assisted Reading and Discovery for Student Generated Text in Massive Open Online Courses. *Learning Analytics, (2015).*

[4] Joksimović, S., et al. What do cMOOC participants talk about in social media?: a topic analysis of discourse in a cMOOC. In *Proc. LAK 2015.*

[5] Ramage, D., et al. Labeled LDA: a supervised topic model for credit attribution in multi-labeled corpora. In *Proc. EMNLP 2009.*

[6] Lau, J. H., et al. Automatic labelling of topic models. In *Proc. ACL 2011.*

[7] Magatti, D., et al. Automatic labeling of topics. In *Proc. ISDA 2009.*

[8] Blei, D. M., et al. Latent Dirichlet Allocation. *Machine Learning Research, 2003.*

[9] Matsuo, Y. and M. Ishizuka. Keyword extraction from a single document using word co-occurrence statistical information. *Artificial Intelligence Tools, (2004).*

[10] Atapattu, T., et al. Acquisition of triples of knowledge from lecture notes: A natural language processing approach, In *Proc. EDM, 2014.*

A Preliminary Look at MOOC-associated Facebook Groups: Prevalence, Geographic Representation, and Homophily

Anna Kasunic
Jessica Hammer
Robert Kraut
Carnegie Mellon University
Pittsburgh, PA 15213, USA
akasunic@andrew.cmu.edu
hammer@cs.cmu.edu
robert.kraut@cmu.edu

Michael Massimi
Facebook
Menlo Park, CA, 94025
mmassimi@fb.com

Amy Ogan
Carnegie Mellon University
Pittsburgh, PA 15213, USA
aeo@andrew.cmu.edu

L@S 2016, April 25-26, 2016, Edinburgh, Scotland UK
ACM 978-1-4503-3726-7/16/04.
http://dx.doi.org/10.1145/2876034.2893415

Abstract
Although xMOOCs are not designed to directly engage students via social media platforms, some students in these courses join MOOC-associated Facebook groups. This study explores the prevalence of Facebook groups associated with courses from MITx and HarvardX, the geographic distribution of students in such groups as compared to the courses at large, and the extent to which such groups are location and/or language homophilous. Results suggests that a non-trivial number of MOOC students engage in Facebook groups, that learners from a number of non-U.S. locations are disproportionately likely to participate in such groups, and that the groups display both location and language homophily. These findings have implications for how MOOCs and social media platforms can support learners from non-English speaking contexts.

Author Keywords
Massive Open Online Courses; MOOCs; Facebook; Social Media; Homophily

ACM Classification Keywords
H.5.3 Group and Organization Interfaces

	Total
Courses	27
Courses with at least one associated group	20
Number of groups	233
Total participants	29,684
Avg size	127.4
Median size	12
St. Dev	533.9
SIQ range	28.5

Table 1: Summary, MOOC-associated Facebook groups

	Total
Total learners in subset	361,388
Forum participants	6,734
As % of total enrollment	*1.9%*
FB participants	19,035
As % of total enrollment	*5.3%*

Table 2: Facebook and forum participation, considering only the subset of courses for which forum data is available.

Introduction

Unlike the original cMOOCs (connectivist massive open online courses), the widely known xMOOCs popularized by sites like edX typically do not formally integrate social networking services (SNS) like Twitter and Facebook [8]. Recent research suggests that social media platforms may be a viable context for enriching learning experiences [3], and cMOOC studies have found positive learning impacts of SNS integration, e.g. [1,2], but because xMOOC are content-driven, not connectivist or social-centric, research on xMOOCs has focused on the use of course forums rather than SNS (e.g. [5,9]). Given high rates of global participation in SNS [7], we posit that SNS may already play a role in xMOOC learning, particularly for those whose first language is not the same as that of the course. This study investigates three research questions: 1) How prevalent are Facebook groups associated with MOOC courses? 2) What is the geographic distribution of MOOC-associated Facebook group members vs all MOOC learners? 3) To what extent are MOOC-associated Facebook groups location and/or language homophilous? Findings from this work provide insight into how xMOOC learners worldwide already use social media platforms to connect with one another and supplement their learning, which in turn has research and design implications for future MOOCs and SNS.

Data Sources

Both HarvardX and MITx provide public access to individual-level, de-identified clickstream and large-scale survey data from their first year of courses (Fall 2012-Spring 2013) [6]. HarvardX has also released a separate aggregate-level dataset for years one and two (Fall 2012-Spring 2014) of HarvardX courses [4], which excludes forum data. We use the most comprehensive, recent dataset available, defaulting to the aggregate-level HarvardX data for years one and two, and MITx year one data. All courses in the dataset are introductory science/technology and arts /humanities xMOOCs. The research team also collaborated with Facebook to obtain aggregate-level information about Facebook groups associated with MOOC courses. Facebook employees constructed database queries based on course numbers and names in the MITx-HarvardX dataset, and manually reviewed query results to confirm their validity. Unless otherwise noted, we only considered Facebook groups for MITx and HarvardX courses with start dates during the course sessions (before May 2013 and May 2014, respectively), to mitigate potential overestimation issues. We ran the query in July of 2015, omitting all 0, null, and 1-member Facebook groups from the analysis.

Findings

RQ1: How prevalent are MOOC Facebook groups?

As Table 1 shows, about 74% of the courses in our dataset (20/27 total courses) have at least one associated Facebook group. Some courses had multiple associated groups; a HarvardX introductory CS course held the maximum of 99 distinct groups. Group membership was highly right-skewed, with a median size of 12 but an average size of about 127; the largest group had 7,492 members. The number of participants in Facebook groups was equivalent to 2.2% of the total HarvardX-MITx enrollment. Given that MOOC courses often see attrition rates hovering around 90% of total enrollment, such a figure is not trivial. As shown in Table 2, we can also see that for the subset of six MITx and two HarvardX courses for which forum data is available, more individuals joined Facebook groups than posted in official course forums, representing a

	FB groups	MOOCs
US*+	3.6K 20.5%	460K 36.9%
IN*	3.7K 20.5%	142.5K 11.4%
EG*	1.4K 7.6%	15.5K 1.2%
PK*	1.2K 6.6%	18.2K 1.5%
CO*	.68K 3.8%	11.8K 0.9%
BZ*	.98 K 5.5%	39.8K 3.2%
CN*+	.27 K 1.5%	43.4K 3.5%
GR	0.6K 3.3%	16.1K 1.3%
PH*	0.5K 3.0%	14.9K 1.2%
BG*	0.4K 2.2%	6.1K 0.5%

Table 3: Top 10 differences in FB group participants and MOOC learner proportions (descending), by country. *Denotes significance at the 99% confidence level. +Denotes higher representation in FB groups. Countries listed above are as follows: India (IN), United States (US), Egypt (EG), Pakistan (PK), Brazil (BZ), Colombia (CO), Canada (CN), Greece (GR), Philippines (PH), Bangladesh (BG).

higher percentage of the total number of MOOC course enrollees. These preliminary results therefore suggest that the ability to connect with peers on social media may be more appealing than traditional course forums. By analyzing group titles and descriptions, we additionally found that the number of "unofficial," student-led groups far outweighed the number of official instructor-led groups: In our sample of 233 groups, MITx courses only had one official Facebook group with 1,042 members, and HarvardX courses had four groups, with 4,398 total members. Eighty MITx groups (15,279 members) and 148 HarvardX groups (8,965 members) were unofficial. Student-led groups co-existed with instructor-led groups for these courses, suggesting that learners may join student-led and instructor-led Facebook group for different reasons.

RQ2: How geographically representative are MOOC-associated Facebook groups?
We compared the proportion of learners by country in MOOC courses and MOOC-associated Facebook groups. On an aggregate level, chi-square tests revealed statistically significant differences in country distributions between Facebook groups and MOOC courses, with p-values well below 0.01 when examining data for MITx and HarvardX both separately and in aggregate. We also examined differences in proportions on a country-by-country level. For 9 of the 10 countries with the largest differences in relative proportions, differences were significant at the 99% confidence level. Table 3 reports the results of 2-tailed z-tests for the difference between two independent proportions for these 10 countries. In some cases, the magnitude of the differences is quite large. For example, students from India accounted for 20.5% of the Facebook group users, but only 11.4% of the MOOC learners; conversely, US learners accounted for only 20.2% of Facebook learners, but 36.9% of the MOOC learners. This suggests Facebook groups may especially appeal to learners of specific, non-U.S. countries.

RQ3: To what extent are MOOC-associated Facebook groups location and/or language homophilous?
Finally, we investigated whether MOOC learners joined Facebook groups by location or language. We found that over half (64.4%) of the Facebook groups in our dataset, accounting for about 15.7% of the individuals across all groups, were location and/or language homophilous (150 groups and 4,671 participants, respectively); all were student-led. We arrived at these totals using both title/description and Facebook-generated data, excluding overlap between the two measures. We first examined each title and description manually to determine if the group was language and/or country specific (e.g., Harvard Intro CS-Bangladesh). Table 4 depicts the breakdown of these groups. We secondly used Facebook-generated data about the location of group members, considering groups where learners from a single country made up over 70% of the membership to be location homophilous. Although there was considerable overlap with groups with language/location-specific titles, 72 groups (719 members) showed homophily in membership not reflected in the title or description, suggesting that location-homophilous MOOC-related groups may arise even where the original intent of the group is not specifically to encourage location- or language- homophilous interactions.

Implications, Limitations and Future Work
Our current findings indicate that 1) surprisingly, membership in course-associated Facebook groups may

	# groups	# total members
LOCATION		
India	7	571
"Arab nations"*	1	260
Indonesia	2	132
Egypt	3	74
Portugal	2	69
LANGUAGE		
Spanish	19	1643
Portuguese	9	720
Arabic	2	78
Span. + Portuguese	1	52
Hungarian	1	4

Table 4: Top 5 countries/region and language-specific groups, by total membership. *As specified in title/description.

be more common than official forum participation, 2) certain non-English speaking countries are more highly represented in Facebook groups than in the courses at large, and 3) in many cases learners themselves are creating these groups to connect with other learners of specific languages and location. These findings lead us to propose that SNS provide course developers with a productive avenue to better support MOOC learners, particularly global learners. For example, operating services like peer-matching directly through existing SNS, may help both global learners seeking language-homophilous learning groups, and any learners who feel more comfortable in informal rather than formal learning settings.

These findings also demonstrate the importance of further investigation into the use of SNS in xMOOCs. In this study, we were unable to include data about deactivated Facebook users, nor could we verify if or when participants in the Facebook groups had joined the official MOOC courses. In addition to addressing such limitations, future research in this area should explore specific activities within SNS groups, such as the extent to which MOOC learners are forming lasting relationships with one another on Facebook.

Acknowledgements
We thank Google for sponsoring Anna Kasunic's graduate student research.

References
1. Carlos Alario-Hoyos, Mar Perez-Sanagustin, Carlos Delgado-Kloos, Hugo Parada G., and Mario Munoz-Organero. 2014. Delving into participants' profiles and use of social tools in MOOCs. *IEEE Transactions on Learning Technologies*: 8 pages. http://doi.org/10.1109/TLT.2014.2311807
2. Pavani Cherukuru, Anil Agarwal, Krishna Chandramouli, and Ebroul Izquierdo. 2014. Learner Centric Enhancement Towards Socio Moodle. In *IACEE 14th World Conference on Continuing Engineering Education*, Stanford University, Vol 15, Paper 116, 6 pages.
3. Christine Greenhow and Cathy Lewin. 2015. Social media and education: reconceptualizing the boundaries of formal and informal learning. *Learning, Media and Technology*: 1–25. http://doi.org/10.1080/17439884.2015.1064954
4. HarvardX. 2015. HarvardX Insights. Retrieved September 9, 2015 from http://harvardx.harvard.edu/harvardx-insights
5. Jonathan Huang, Anirban Dasgupta, Arpita Ghosh, Jane Manning, and Marc Sanders. 2014. Superposter behavior in MOOC forums. In *Proceedings of the first ACM conference on Learning @ scale conference* – (L@S '14), ACM Press, 117–126. http://doi.org/10.1145/2556325.2566249
6. MITx and HarvardX. 2015. MITx and HarvardX Dataverse. Retrieved August 9, 2015 from https://dataverse.harvard.edu/dataverse/mxhx
7. Pew Research Center's Global Attitudes Project. Social Networking Popular Across Globe. 2012. Retrieved January 10, 2015 from http://www.pewglobal.org/2012/12/12/social-networking-popular-across-globe/.
8. George Siemens. 2013. Massive Open Online Courses: Innovation in Education? *Open Educational Resources: Innovation, Research and Practice.* Athabasca University: 5-16.
9. Diyi Yang, Mario Piergallini, Iris Howley, and Carolyn Rose. 2014. Forum Thread Recommendation for Massive Open Online Courses. In *Proceedings of the 7th International Conference on Educational Data Mining*, 257–260.

Structured Knowledge Tracing Models for Student Assessment on Coursera

Zhuo Wang
School of EECS
Peking University
Beijing, 100871, China
wangzhuo@pku.edu.cn

Zhiting Hu
School of Computer Science
Carnegie Mellon University
Pittsburgh, PA 15213
zhitingh@cs.cmu.edu

Jile Zhu
School of EECS
Peking University
Beijing, 100871, China
zhujile0918@pku.edu.cn

Ming Zhang
School of EECS
Peking University
Beijing, 100871, China
mzhang@net.pku.edu.cn

Xiang Li
School of EECS
Peking University
Beijing, 100871, China
lixiang.eecs@pku.edu.cn

L@S 2016, April 25–26, 2016, Edinburgh, UK.
ACM 978-1-4503-3726-7/16/04.
http://dx.doi.org/10.1145/2876034.2893416

Abstract
Massive Open Online Courses (MOOCs) provide an effective learning platform with various high-quality educational materials accessible to learners from all over the world. However, current MOOCs lack personalized learning guidance and intelligent assessment for individuals. Though a few recent attempts have been made to trace students' knowledge states by adapting the popular Bayesian Knowledge Tracing (BKT) model, they have largely ignored the rich structures and correlations among knowledge components (KCs) within a course. This paper proposes to model both the hierarchical and the temporal properties of the knowledge states in order to improve the modeling accuracy. Based on the content organization characteristics on the Coursera MOOC platform, we provide a well-defined KC model, and develop Multi-Grained-BKT and Historical-BKT to capture the above features effectively. Experiments on a Coursera course dataset show our approach significantly improves over previous vanilla BKT models on predicting students' quiz performance.

Author Keywords
Knowledge Tracing, MOOCs, Student Assessment, Student Modeling, Hierarchical and Temporal Knowledge Tracing; MOOCs; Student Assessment; Student Modeling; Hierarchical and Temporal

Parameter	Explanation
p(L_0)	Learned: initial knowledge states
p(T)	Transition: the probability of learning the knowledge component
p(G)	Guess: the probability of guessing correctly in the unlearned state
p(S)	Slip: the probability of answering incorrectly in the learned state

Table 1: All the four parameters in basic BKT.

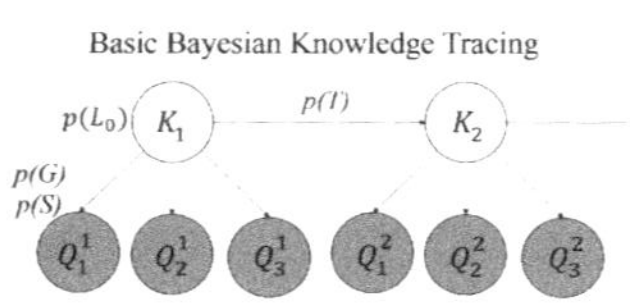

Figure 1: Basic BKT: a time slice represents a quiz submission and there are multiple questions in a single time slice. Node K_t represents the student's knowledge state at time t and node Q_k^t represents the student's response for question k at time t.

Introduction

MOOCs as an effective learning platform provide abundant high-quality learning resources. With the increasing prevalence, however, it becomes impossible for instructors to track individual learners' knowledge states and provide personalized learning guidance. An automatic and accurate student assessment model can be useful for both instructors and learners. For example, it can provide overall feedback to instructors and suggest the need for further explanations; and infer the weakness of students and recommend appropriate learning materials.

Extensive advances have been made on student assessment. The BKT model [1] is among the most popular techniques, especially in the intelligent tutoring systems where knowledge is manually categorized into fine-grained KCs by experts. Despite its impressive success, application of BKT on MOOCs is limited due to the lack of explicit KC definition. A few recent work has attempted to retrofit BKT: e.g., Pardos et al. adapted BKT to edX [1] by assuming questions in quizzes as KCs [3]. However, these simple extensions largely fail to model the rich structures and correlations among KCs within a MOOC, and thus can lead to suboptimal performance. This paper addresses the above issues on Coursera [2], one of the most popular MOOC platforms. We leverage the resource organization characteristics where each chapter of a course consists of multiple lecture videos, based on which we provide a well-defined KC model, and further develop two novel knowledge tracing methods, Multi-Grained-BKT and Historical-BKT, to model the distinct yet closely-related fine-grained KCs for each coarse-grained KC, and capture the correlations between multiple quiz submissions, respectively. Both methods significantly outperform previous vanilla BKT models on a dataset collected from a Coursera course. To the best of our knowledge, we are the first to model both the hierarchical (i.e., multi-grained) and the temporal (i.e., historical) properties of knowledge states for accurate student assessment. Our method can be helpful for integrating adaptive learning systems and designing personalized study plans on MOOCs.

[1] https://www.edx.org/
[2] https://www.coursera.org/

Methodology

Basic Bayesian Knowledge Tracing Model

Knowledge tracing was proposed based on mastery learning where knowledge is composed of KCs. The notion was then introduced into intelligent tutoring [1]. BKT is a hidden Markov model (HMM), as shown in Figure 1, where student's knowledge states are represented by a series of binary variables K. There are four key parameters in BKT (Table 1), namely, prior knowledge, probability of learning, guessing, and slipping. And we have:

$$p(Q_k^t = 1) = p(L_t)(1 - p(S)) + (1 - p(L_t))p(G)$$
$$p(L_t = 0) = p(L_{t-1}) + (1 - p(L_t))p(T)$$

The parameters are learnt from data through the expectation-maximization (EM) algorithm. BKT is widely used in the context of intelligent tutoring systems, where KCs have been designed in detail by domain experts, and each question is labelled with a specific KC.

Knowledge Organization on Coursera

In order to trace knowledge states on MOOCs using BKT, we first notice that Coursera (and most other MOOC platforms) allows multiple submissions for a quiz and we regard each submission as a time slice. Moreover, Coursera allows several variations for a question so that questions are different between sequential trials for the same quiz. In fact, students are encouraged to do quizzes again and again to master relevant knowledge.

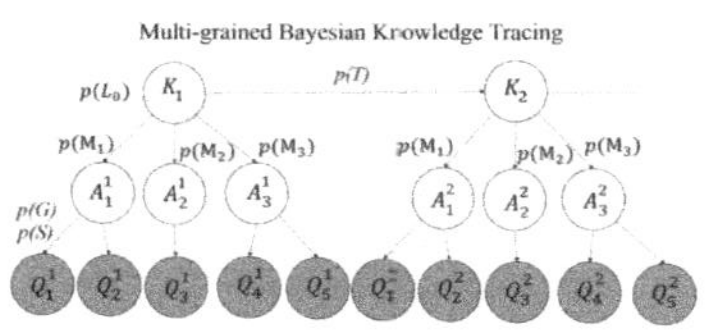

Figure 2: Multi-Grained-BKT: there are multiple fine-grained KCs for a coarse-grained KC with one or more questions. Node A_k^t represents the knowledge state of fine-grained KC k at time t. $p(M_k)$ represents the probability of mastering fine-grained KC k when the overall KC has been mastered.

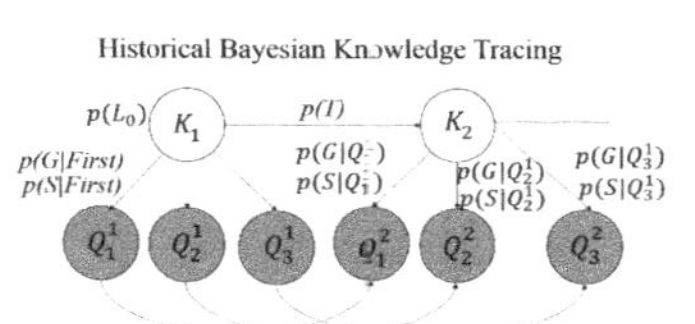

Figure 3: Historical-BKT: The response depends not only on the KC, but also on the previous question response. That is, $p(G)$ and $p(S)$ parameters of node Q_k^t depend on node Q_k^{t-1}

Compared to the mastering learning context, on MOOCs there is no explicit KC definition. A straightforward solution is to regard a whole chapter as a KC, because each chapter is about a specific topic. We call the baseline BKT model based on this definition as *Coarse-BKT*. However, such a KC definition is too coarse and it is hard to model student's knowledge states precisely.

An alternative way to enable fine-grained tracing is to make use of the characteristics of the knowledge organization on MOOCs where each chapter usually consists of several lecture videos and each video, often in a few minutes, focuses on a specific yet complete topic. We can thus see the content covered by each video as a KC. We denote the second baseline, which applies the Basic BKT on the fine-grained KC definition, as *Fine-BKT*.

Such a KC definition has several advantages: 1) MOOCs usually provide abundant materials for lecture videos, e.g., slides and in-video quizzes. This makes KCs well-defined and interpretable, as compared to clustering-based methods [2]; 2) Computers can handle KCs through natural language processing techniques automatically using texts like subtitles and forum posts. This paper asked two teaching assistants who had designed the quizzes to do the labelling for accuracy.

Multi-Grained-BKT

However, Fine-BKT ignores the fact that KCs in a chapter are closely related to each other. To address this issue, we come up with a novel method called *Multi-Grained-BKT*, in which we still regard the whole chapter as an overall coarse-grained KC and the content covered by each lecture video as one of its fine-grained KC.

Figure 2 shows Multi-Grained-BKT has an additional layer of "fine-grained KCs". When a student masters a coarse-grained KC, there is a probability of mastering one of its fine-grained KCs, modelled by $p(M_k)$. Otherwise, he/she cannot master any of its fine-grained KCs, i.e.,

$$p(A_k^t = 0) = p(L_t)(1 - p(M_k)) + (1 - p(L_t))$$

The parameter $p(M_k)$ models the difficulty of mastering a specific fine-grained KC. We pre-specify its value as the average correct rate of relevant questions:

$$p(M_k) = \frac{\#\{correct\ responses\ for\ fine-grained\ KC\ k\}}{\#\{all\ responses\ for\ fine-grained\ KC\ k\}}$$

We thus control the model complexity to four free parameters as before, and use EM algorithm to estimate the parameters and predict quiz submission results.

Historical-BKT

As mentioned, each submission is regarded as a time slice, and Coursera allows variations for a question in sequential trials. However, these questions are still closely related, usually about the same problem with different operational data or different multiple choice options. To make use of this characteristic, we propose a novel method called *Historical-BKT* (Figure 3). The probability of guessing and slipping will depend on the previous question response. Intuitively, if previous response is correct $p(G)$ tends to be larger and $p(S)$ smaller. We thus have:

$$p(Q_k^t = 1) = p(L_t)(1 - p(S|Q_k^{t-1})) + (1 - p(L_t))p(G|Q_k^{t-1})$$

As there are three different states for responses in the previous submission (i.e., Correct, Incorrect, and Not existing), this model has eight parameters in total.

Experiment

Setup

Our data is from the Data Structures and Algorithms course held by Peking Univ. on Coursera in fall, 2013. It

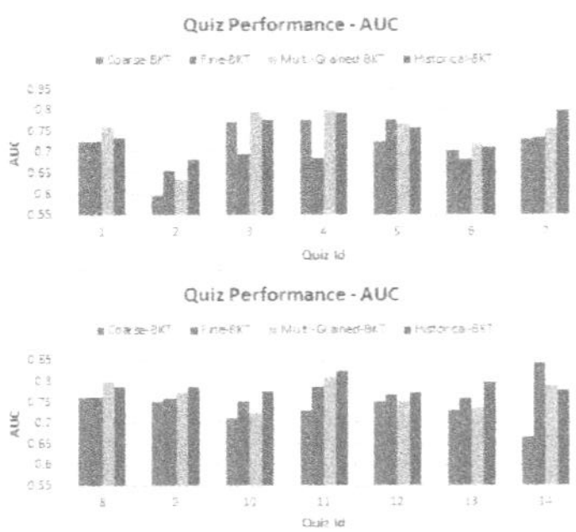

Figure 4: Cross-validated AUC results of the four models on all 14 quizzes. Multi-Grained-BKT and Historical-BKT achieve higher AUC in most quizzes.

Model	Coarse	Fine	Multi-Grained	Historical
Average AUC	0.7233	0.7415	0.7584	0.7695
P-value to Coarse-BKT	—	0.3110	0.0015	0.0003

Table 2: The average AUC results on all 14 quizzes and the p-values of t-tests between Coarse-BKT and the other three.

	Previous Wrong	Previous Correct	First Submission
p(G)	0.3099	0.5687	0.5178
p(S)	0.3211	0.0578	0.1683

Figure 5: Parameter analysis for Historical-BKT shows that $p(G|PreviousCorrect) >$ $p(G|PreviousWrong)$ and $p(S|PreviousCorrect) <$ $p(S|PreviousWrong)$

was a 14 week-long online course with learning materials published in each week as a chapter. Weekly quizzes consist of an average of 7.43 questions. There are 13,170 students registered for this course. We selected those who had submitted quizzes, and got a dataset of 1,077 students and 6,583 submissions. The KC labels of quiz questions were acquired from the teacher assistants.

We compare all four models on predicting students' question responses in the last submission with a 5-fold cross-validation at student level. [3] We use the area under the curve (AUC) as the metric, which is widely-used in binary classification. We enumerate all pairings of correct and incorrect responses and the AUC is simply the percentage of the pairings where the correct responses get higher predictive probability over the incorrect responses.

Result

Figure 4 shows the AUC results of the four models on all the 14 quizzes, and Table 2 lists the two-tailed paired t-tests to evaluate the significance of the performance difference. The AUC of Fine-BKT is not significantly different from that of Coarse-BKT, showing that merely using the fine-grained KC is not sufficient. In contrast, Multi-Grained-BKT achieves an improvement of 0.0351 over Coarse-BKT (p-value=0.0015). The reason is that Multi-Grained-BKT models the hierarchical structure of KCs in different granularities, and is able to capture the relatedness between fine-grained KCs in the same chapter.

Historical-BKT, which captures the relations between multiple quiz submissions, performs as well as the Multi-Grained-BKT (p-value=0.1801) and achieves a significant improvement of 0.0462 over Coarse-BKT (p-value=0.0003). Figure 5 shows that students are more likely to response correctly if their answer was already correct in the previous submission.

Conclusion and Future Work

This paper has provided a new KC definition on MOOCs and developed two knowledge tracing methods, Multi-Grained-BKT and Historical-BKT, to model the hierarchical KCs and capture the correlations between quiz submissions, respectively. Both methods greatly improved over the vanilla BKT. We note that our methods rely on those features common to popular MOOC platforms (e.g., Coursera and edX), e.g., allowing multiple quiz submissions with slight question variations. This ensures the applicability of our methods on these platforms.

There are several directions worth further investigation in the future. A complicated question in a quiz can be related to multiple KCs. Our methods can be improved to deal with the one-to-many mapping. Besides, a more powerful BKT can be considered to incorporate the rich behavior data in MOOCs (e.g., logs of watching videos).

Acknowledgements

This paper is partially supported by the National Natural Science Foundation of China (NSFC Grant Numbers 61272343 and 61472006) as well as the National Basic Research Program (973 Program No. 2014CB340405).

References

[1] Corbett, A. T., and Anderson, J. R. Knowledge tracing: Modelling the acquisition of procedural knowledge. *User Modeling and User-Adapted Interaction 4*, 4 (1995), 253–278.

[2] Matsuda, N., Furukawa, T., Bier, N., and Faloutsos, C. Machine beats experts: Automatic discovery of skill models for data-driven online course refinement. In *Educational Data Mining* (2015), 101–108.

[3] Pardos, Z., Bergner, Y., Seaton, D., and Pritchard, D. Adapting Bayesian knowledge tracing to a Massive Open Online Course in edX. In *Educational Data Mining* (2013), 137–144.

Predicting Students' Standardized Test Scores Using Online Homework

Mingyu Feng
SRI International
333 Ravenswood Ave
Menlo Park, CA 94025 USA
mingyu.feng@sri.com

Jeremy Roschelle
SRI International
333 Ravenswood Ave
Menlo Park, CA 94025 USA
Jeremy.roschelle@sri.com

Abstract
How students do homework has been underresearched relative to classroom learning because it is more difficult to collect data on students' homework behaviors. Presumably, such data would have implications for students' achievement. To understand how students do homework and how homework performance and behaviors relate to end-of-year standardized test scores, we analyzed the system logs from an online homework support platform used by more than 1,500 seventh-grade students in Maine.

Author Keywords
Online math homework; log analysis, prediction

L@S 2016, April 25-26, 2016, Edinburgh, Scotland UK
ACM 978-1-4503-3726-7/16/04.
http://dx.doi.org/10.1145/2876034.2893417

ACM Classification Keywords
K.3.1 Computers and Education: Computer Uses in Education–Computer-assisted instruction

Introduction
Homework is a well-established practice in schools and has been stable since the mid-1980s [10, 12]. Yet public controversy has arisen from time to time about homework's impact on learning [e.g., 2, 11] and whether it is worthwhile [1]. Research has also addressed the role and practices of homework and its relationship with student learning, especially in mathematics [3-5, 8, 9, 13, 14, 15, 16].

Relative to classroom learning, however, homework has been underresearched because it is difficult to collect objective data (as opposed to self-reported data) on homework behaviors. Little is known about when students do homework, how long it takes them to complete it, how much time they spend on problems, and whether and where they struggle. As educational technologies such as Khan Academy, ALEKS, and IXL.com have gained wider use in schools and in the home, the opportunity exists to better leverage homework for learning and also better understand homework practices from the data collected through computer systems.

Design of the Maine Online Homework Efficacy Study

The Maine Online Homework Efficacy Study was funded by the Institute of Education Sciences, U.S. Department of Education. The study had a school-level, delayed-treatment, randomized experimental design. Implementation of Use of ASSISTments was staggered by cohort. During the 2012–15 school years, 44 schools in Maine joined the study in two cohorts. Each school stayed in the study for two consecutive years. Within each cohort, half the schools were randomly assigned to the treatment condition and half to the control condition. A total of 87 seventh-grade math teachers in the treatment schools used ASSISTments to assign and review homework. They were expected to assign approximately 25 minutes of homework in ASSISTments for a minimum of three nights per week. The specific days of assignment were determined by the teachers.

SRI International, with the University of Maine and Worcester Polytechnic Institute, conducted a large-scale efficacy study in 44 schools in Maine. The objective was to test the hypothesis that the ASSISTments homework support platform improves student mathematics outcomes. Teachers choose (or add) homework items in ASSISTments, and students complete the items online. Students receive immediate feedback on the correctness of their answers, hints messages, or help decomposing multistep problems into parts. Teachers receive reports with such information as the percentage of items students got correct on their nightly assignment and common errors among groups of students. Teachers are encouraged to use the information for more targeted homework reviews and to more generally adapt or differentiate their teaching. We've analyzed the outcome data from the study and found a significant treatment effect (effect size = .27).

Feng et al. [6] had established the assessment validity of ASSISTments using data on how students performed and interacted with the system during class time to predict their end-of-year state test scores. In the research reported here, we replicated that approach to explore the relationship between students' ASSISTments use on homework outside the classroom and their performance on a summative standardized test.

Data Source

The data were math homework log data from ASSISTments, TerraNova test scaled scores (range 400–900), and performance levels (1–5) of 1,555 seventh-grade students from Maine. The ASSISTments system collects data on student log-in, problems solved, problem-solving attempts, requests for help, response from the online tutor, and assignment completion status. All the actions are time stamped. TerraNova is a standardized paper test and was given to all students in control and treatment groups so as to have a common end-of-year measure. The test was nationally norm referenced, and both the scaled score and performance levels for each student were reported.

Analysis of Homework Log Data

We constructed metrics that represented students' use, performance, and behaviors in ASSISTments and calculated their correlation with students' scaled scores from the TerraNova test (Table 1). Among the features, *p*_count is a measure of intensity of use, and perc_avg and *p*_time_avg are performance measures. The remaining features captured students' behaviors: help-seeking (hint_avg and bhint_avg), frequency of attempts, time taken to respond to a problem on the first try, and whether homework was completed on time, late, or left unfinished (completed_perc, incomplete_perc, and late_perc). We found that perc_avg positively and strongly correlated with the scaled score (.479). We observed a weak negative relationship ($.2 < r < .4$) between TerraNova scaled scores and the behavioral variables hint_avg, bhint_avg, attempt_avg, and resp_time_avg.

Metrics	Description	Cor.
*p*_count	Total number of problems completed	.226
perc_avg	Avg % correct across assignments	.479
*p*_time_avg	Avg numbers of times needed to complete a problem	-.055
hint_avg	Avg number of hint requests per problem	-.340

Group	Avg *p*_count	*t*/*p*
I	620	I vs. II: $t = -9.55$, $p < .001$;
II	919	
III	1,097	II vs. III: $t = -2.31$, $p = .02$

Table 2. Number of problems completed by groups

Metrics	Description	Cor.
bhint_avg	Avg number of bottom-out hint (revealing answer) requests	-.353
attempt_avg	Avg number of attempts	-.242
resp_time_avg	Avg response time	-.307
completed_perc	% of assignments completed on time	.214
late_perc	% of assignments completed but late	-.160
incomplete_perc	% of assignments started but not completed	-.153

Table 1. Data features and their correlation with students' scaled scores from the TerraNova test

We then split the students into three groups based on their performance on the TerraNova test: I, performance levels 1 or 2; II, levels 3 or 4; and III, level 5. There was a significant difference in the *p*_count among the three groups (see Table 2). Similar trends were evident across the three groups for other features. For example, students at a higher performance level finished more assignments on time, used a significantly fewer bottom-out hints, and had significantly fewer incomplete assignments.

After the exploratory analysis, we built a series of predictive models (Table 3) using students' TerraNova scores as the dependent variable and various combinations of the homework features as predictors (after they were normalized) and used R^2 and the Bayesian Information Criterion (BIC) to compare models. We started with a baseline linear regression model with no predictors (model.0), added perc_avg (model.1), and then added all other features in Table 1 as independent variables. We used a two-direction stepwise model training and variable selection process, using BIC as the selection criterion (model.2).

Of all the models, model.3 had the lowest BIC and the highest R^2, 0.41. It was a two-level mixed-effects model, including perc_avg, resp_time_avg, and *p*_count (the selected variables from model.2) as fixed effects and a school-level random effect. This suggested that students doing more homework problems in less time would have better achievement outcomes.

Models	Independent V.	BIC	R^2
model.0	None	15184	0
model.1	perc_avg	14817	0.22
model.2	perc_avg + p_count + resp_time	14743	0.26
model.3	variables in model.2 as fixed effects + school level random effect	**14489**	0.41
model.4	All features as fixed effects + school level random effect	14511	0.41

Table 3. Predictive models, BICs and R^2

Conclusion and Future Work

The predictive model using student homework logs from an online support system did not show results as impressive as those reported [6] when classroom use data were used to predict end-of-year standardized test scores ($R^2 = 0.73$). Yet considering that homework (a) takes only a limited percentage of time in students' overall learning, (b) is much more distributed and casual than classroom practice, and (c) is largely self-monitored and student controlled, we believe this work contributes to our understanding of how students do homework and thus can help teachers and students better leverage it to improve learning outcomes. We foresee that using technology to drive homework improvement is an important opportunity for learning at scale. An immediate next step following this work is to examine whether a relationship exists between students' use of ASSISTments for homework and any change in their performance on summative standardized tests, controlling for their incoming knowledge.

Given that we have identified variables linked to student performance, adaptations could be made so that ASSISTments better supports students. For example, detectors could be built in to sense and alert teachers to changes in homework completion patterns or high rates of bottom-out hints. Teachers could then provide interventions to promote more effective use of ASSISTments for homework support.

References

[1] Abramian, A. Fourth-grade twins, one with homework, one without. The Motherlode blog. *New York Times* (2015).

[2] Bennett, S. and Kalish, N. *The Case Against Homework: How Homework Is Hurting Our Children and What We Can Do About It*. Crown Publishers, New York, NY, USA, 2006.

[3] Cooper, H., Robinson, J.C. and Patall, E.A. Does homework improve academic achievement? A synthesis of research, 1987-2003. *Review of Educational Research, 76* (2006), 1–62.

[4] Cooper, H. *The Battle Over Homework* (3rd Ed.). Corwin Press, Thousand Oaks, CA, USA, 2007.

[5] Eren, O. and Henderson, D. Are we wasting our children's time by giving them more homework? *Economics of Education Review*, *30*, 5 (2011), 950-961.

[6] Feng, M., Heffernan, N.T. and Koedinger, K.R. Addressing the assessment challenge in an online system that tutors as it assesses. *User Modeling and User-Adapted Interaction*, *19*, 3 (2009), 243-266.

[7] Feng, M., Roschelle, R., Murphy, R. and Heffernan, N. Using analytics for improving implementation fidelity in a large scale efficacy trial. In *Proc. ICLS 2014,* International Society of the Learning Sciences (2014), 527-534.

[8] Fernández-Alonso, R., Suárez-Álvarez, J. and Muñiz, J. Adolescents' homework performance in mathematics and science: Personal factors and teaching practices. *Journal of Educational Psychology,* March 16 (2015).

[9] Galloway, M. K. and Pope, D. Hazardous homework? The relationship between homework, goal orientation, and well-being in adolescence. *Encounter*, 20 (2007), 25–31.

[10] Gill, B. and Schlossman S. A nation at rest: The American way of homework. *Educational Evaluation and Policy Analysis*, *25*, 3 (2003).

[11] Kohn, A. *The Homework Myth: Why Our Kids Get Too Much of a Bad Thing*. Da Capo Press, Cambridge, MA, USA, 2006.

[12] Loveless, T. *The Brown Center Report on American Education*. The Brookings Institution, Washington, DC, USA, 2014.

[13] Maltese, A.V., Robert, H.T. and Fan, X. When is homework worth the time? Evaluating the association between homework and achievement in high school science and math. *The High School Journal*, October/November (2012), 52-72.

[14] Marzano, R. J. and Pickering, D. J. The case for and against homework. *Educational Leadership*, *64* (2007), 74–79.

[15] Trautwein, Ulrich, et al. Do homework assignments enhance achievement? A multilevel analysis in 7th-grade mathematics. *Contemporary Educational Psychology*, 27.1 (2002), 26-50.

[16] Trautwein, U. The homework-achievement relation reconsidered: Differentiating homework time, homework frequency, and homework effort. *Learning and Instruction*, *17* (2007), 372–388.

Predicting Students' Performance: Incremental Interaction Classifiers

Miguel Sanchez-Santillan
Department of Computer Science
University of Oviedo
UO167275@uniovi.es

MPuerto Paule-Ruiz
Department of Computer Science
University of Oviedo
paule@uniovi.es

Rebeca Cerezo
Department of Psychology
University of Oviedo
cerezorebeca@uniovi.es

JCarlos Nuñez
Department of Psychology
University of Oviedo
jcarlosn@uniovi.es

L@S 2016, April 25-26, 2016, Edinburgh, Scotland UK
ACM 978-1-4503-3726-7/16/04.
http://dx.doi.org/10.1145/2876034.2893418

Abstract
One of the Educational Data Mining (EDM) main aims is to predict the final student´s performance, analyzing their behavior in the Learning Management Systems (LMSs). Many studies make use of different classifiers to reach this goal, using the total interaction of the students. In this work we study if it is possible to build more accurate classification models in order to predict the output, analyzing the interaction in an incremental way. We study the data gathered for two years with three kinds of classifying algorithms and we compare the total interaction models with the incremental interaction models.

Author Keywords
Educational Data Mining; eLearning; Classifiers

Introduction
Currently the LMS store the students´ interaction in databases or log files. The analysis of this interaction through Data Mining techniques allows us a better understanding of the students´ behavior in the LMS. EDM is a discipline that studies and develops methods to reach such goals [1].

Moodle created variables

Time Lesson. Minutes spent in lesson.

Time Quiz. Minutes spent in quiz.

Time Forum. Minutes spent in forum.

Days Lesson. The days that go by since block is unlocked until the student consults the lesson for the first time.

Days Quiz. Days until student consults the quiz for the first time.

Days Finish Quiz. Days until student sends the quiz for the first time.

Days Forum. Days until student checks the forum for the first time.

Days Post. Days until student writes in the forum for the first time.

Relevant Actions. Number of log's entries generated by the student.

Time spent. The days that go by since the students make the first interaction until they carry out the last interaction.

As a matter of fact, one of the EDM particular goals is to predict the students´ final performance [2] using classifiers. Such classifiers analyze the whole data to create accurate models for every possible result.

During the past few years researchers have carried out diverse studies about how to create classification models which will enable us to predict or improve the students´ performance. [3-5]. Using them means a great support for teachers, as they can be used as indicators of the students´ behavior in the LMS [6].

Generally speaking, these studies classification models are built using the total interaction that students generate through the LMS. However, inasmuch as the course year moves forward, the students' participation in the LMSs tends towards steep drop-offs and highly unequal patterns of participation [7].

Henceforth, in this work we study if it is possible to obtain more accurate classification models through the analysis of the students' interaction in an incremental way.

Case Study

We have used Moodle to create a training program which is divided in 11 blocks. Each week a new block is unlocked for 15 days and students must carry out three basic tasks to complete each part: read a lesson, complete a quiz and add a post in the forum.

We gathered the students' interaction in two different years; 2012 (N= 111 students) and 2013 (N= 84 students). The structure and procedure have been the same in both cases.

Data

We created a combination for every year and every block with the collected students' interaction. Therefore, the datasheet drawn from the last block represents the total students' interaction in the training program. Moreover, we generated another 11 datasheets with the total of the sample. As a whole, we got 33 different datasheets.

We have made use of 11 variables in our study. From Moodle's log we generated 10 variables for each block, as shown in the sidebar. We discretized students' final grade as "FAIL" and "PASS". Grades below 5 were labeled as "FAIL" meanwhile grades with a value of 5 or higher were labeled as "PASS".

We use WEKA in order to analyze the datasheets using three different algorithms; JRIP (a RIPPER implementation [8], J48 (an open source Java implementation of the C4.5 [9]) and Bayesian Network [10]. We chose these algorithms because the classification models that they provide are built in a different way; classification rules, decision trees and neural networks, respectively. Results have been tested through cross-validation with 10 folds.

2012 course results

Total of Blocks	JRIP	J48	BayesNet
1	75.67%	73.87%	77.47%
2	74.77%	72.97%	77.47%
3	79.27%	77.47%	79.27%
4	81.98%	75.67%	81.08%
5	75.57%	77.47%	79.27%
6	77.47%	75.67%	80.18%
7	76.57%	76.57%	77.47%

Total of Blocks	JRIP	J48	BayesNet
8	74.77%	74.77%	79.27%
9	77.47%	78.37%	79.27%
10	78.37%	78.37%	79.27%
11	76.57%	78.37%	78.37%

Table 1. Classifiers accuracy results for each incremental model using 2012 course datasheet.

As shown in Table 1, the classification of the total interaction with JRIP is overcome by models 3, 4, 6, 9 and 10. As regards to the algorithm J48 any model classifies better than the total model. To finish with, the results obtained by BayesNet are even further off. The total model is surpassed by the models 3, 4, 5, 6, 8, 9 and 10.

2013 course results

Total of Blocks	JRIP	J48	BayesNet
1	61.90%	70.23%	64.28%
2	61.90%	61.90%	65.47%
3	63.09%	61.90%	65.47%
4	63.09%	60.71%	65.47%
5	60.71%	57.14%	65.47%
6	61.90%	57.14%	65.47%
7	63.09%	60.71%	65.47%
8	70.23%	60.71%	64.28%
9	66.66%	59.52%	64.28%
10	61.90%	64.38%	67.85%
11	65.47%	64.28%	65.47%

Table 2. Classifiers accuracy results for each incremental model using 2013 course datasheet.

As shown in Table 2, the classification of the total interaction with JRIP is overcome by models 8 and 9. As regards to the algorithm J48 only models 1 and 10 surpass the total model. To finish with, the results obtained by BayesNet show that the total model is surpassed by the model 10.

2012 and 2013 datasheets merged

Total of Blocks	JRIP	J48	BayesNet
1	70.25%	66.15%	70.76%
2	67.69%	67.18%	71.79%
3	68.71%	71.28%	70.25%
4	68.71%	70.25%	68.71%
5	68.71%	70.76%	70.25%
6	71.79%	66.15%	69.23%
7	68.71%	70.76%	67.17%
8	70.25%	67.18%	66.15%
9	70.76%	72.82%	67.17%
10	65.64%	66.66%	69.23%
11	68.71%	66.66%	67.69%

Table 3. Classifiers accuracy results for each incremental model using 2012 and 2013 courses datasheets merged.

As shown in Table 3, the classification of the total interaction with JRIP is overcome by models 1, 6, 8 and 9. As regards to the algorithm J48 the total model is surpassed by the models 2, 3, 4, 5, 7, 8 and 9. To finish with, the results obtained by BayesNet show that the total model is surpassed by the models 1, 2, 3, 4, 5, 6 and 10.

Discussion and future work

Just as the results show, it is possible to obtain better classification models using an incremental interaction. Employing this kind of incremental models will be useful to improve the feedback that teachers get in respect of the students' performance. Nonetheless, this case study is based on a course already structured in different blocks, and so it will be needed to test the accuracy of incremental models in different cases. For instance in those courses in which the interaction is not only limited by time intervals, being this way the students able to access, more or less freely, to the different resources.

We have employed three different algorithms to test the generation of the models, nevertheless we are going to explore more algorithms and we are going to design a system that will automate the process of models generation with the maximum number of possible algorithms.

Acknowledgements

This work has been funded by the Department of Science and Innovation (Spain) under the National Program for Research, Development and Innovation: EDU2014-57571-P. We have also received funds from the European Union, through the European Regional Development Funds (ERDF); and the Principality of Asturias, through its Science, Technology and Innovation Plan (grant GRUPIN14-100 and GRUPIN14-053).

References

[1] Baker, R. S., & Yacef, K. (2009). The state of educational data mining in 2009: A review and future visions. JEDM-Journal of Educational Data Mining, 1(1), 3-17.

[2] Romero, C., & Ventura, S. (2010). Educational data mining: a review of the state of the art. Systems, Man, and Cybernetics, Part C: Applications and Reviews, IEEE Transactions on, 40(6), 601-618.

[3] Romero, C., López, M. I., Luna, J. M., & Ventura, S. (2013). Predicting students' final performance from participation in on-line discussion forums.Computers & Education, 68, 458-472.

[4] Ahmed, A. B. E. D., & Elaraby, I. S. (2014). Data Mining: A prediction for Student's Performance Using Classification Method. World Journal of Computer Application and Technology, 2(2), 43-47.

[5] Bunkar, K., Singh, U. K., Pandya, B., & Bunkar, R. (2012). Data mining: Prediction for performance improvement of graduate students using classification. In WOCN Conference (pp. 1-5). IEEE.

[6] Ranjan, J., Khalil, S. (2008). Conceptual Framework of Data Mining Process in Management Education in India: An Institutional Perspective. In Information Technology Journal, 7, 1, 16-23.

[7] Clow, D. (2013). MOOCs and the funnel of participation. In LAK Conference (pp. 185-189). ACM.

[8] Cohen WW (1995). Fast effective rule induction. In: Proceedings of the 12th International Conference on Machine Learning. pp. 115-123.

[9] S. F. Chen, Z. Q. Chen, Artificial intelligence in knowledge engineering [M]. Nanjing: Nanjing University Press, 1997.

[10] R.R. Bouckaert. Bayesian Belief Networks: from Construction to Inference. Ph.D. thesis, University of Utrecht, 1995.

Learning at Scale: Using an Evidence Hub To Make Sense of What We Know

Rebecca Ferguson
The Open University
Milton Keynes, MK7 6AA, UK
Rebecca.ferguson@open.ac.uk

L@S 2016, April 25-26, 2016, Edinburgh, Scotland, UK
ACM 978-1-4503-3726-7/16/04.
http://dx.doi.org/10.1145/2876034.2893419

Abstract
The large datasets produced by learning at scale, and the need for ways of dealing with high learner/educator ratios, mean that MOOCs and related environments are frequently used for the deployment and development of learning analytics. Despite the current proliferation of analytics, there is as yet relatively little hard evidence of their effectiveness. The Evidence Hub developed by the Learning Analytics Community Exchange (LACE) provides a way of collating and filtering the available evidence in order to support the use of analytics and to target future studies to fill the gaps in our knowledge.

Author Keywords
Ethics; evidence; Evidence Hub; learning; learning analytics; teaching

Introduction
The past decade has seen an explosion in the numbers of people learning at scale. Early MOOCs reported course registrations similar to those for the formal courses at some large universities, in the hundreds or low thousands (2). The largest MOOCs are now reporting hundreds of thousands of registrations (4). Except in courses that position 'teacher as learner as teacher' (6), these courses necessarily have an extremely high student/teacher ratio. New tools and strategies are therefore needed to support learners when educators cannot do so on a one-to-one basis.

LACE Evidence Hub propositions

1. Learning analytics improve learning outcomes.

2. Learning analytics improve learning support and teaching, including retention, completion and progression.

3. Learning analytics are taken up and used widely, including deployment at scale.

4. Learning analytics are used in an ethical way.

evidence.laceproject.eu

Learning analytics 'is the measurement, collection, analysis and reporting of data about learners and their contexts, for purposes of understanding and optimizing learning and the environments in which it occurs' (7). The massive online qualities of learning at scale mean that this sector is well suited to the use of analytics. The vision is that analytics will provide 'a new model for college and university leaders to improve teaching, learning, organizational efficiency, and decision-making and, as a consequence, serve as a foundation for systemic change' (5).

However, learning analytics has only been developing as a field for a few years (the first international LAK conference was held in 2011). Although researchers and practitioners can draw on established bodies of work in areas such as educational data mining and business analytics, much work is still in its early stages. Many publications in the area therefore focus on concepts, pilots, promising work and small-scale trials.

This is appropriate and understandable for a new research field, but can prove frustrating for people who are developing learning at scale. With hundreds of thousands of learners in need of support, developers and educators do not necessarily have enough free time to trawl through the literature in search of the hard evidence and analysis that could provide them with the help and guidance that they need.

Filtering the Literature

The need to filter this large body of literature has been addressed by the international Society for Learning Analytics Research (SoLAR) and its members in several ways. The first of these is the development of numerous literature reviews (for example, 1). These are typically aimed at researchers in the field rather than at educators in search of guidance.

The LAK Dataset 'makes publicly available machine-readable versions of research sources from the Learning Analytics and Educational Data Mining communities, where the main goal is to facilitate research, analysis and smart explorative applications' (3). This is a rich and valuable resource for developers in the field but is not easily accessible to readers.

On the SoLAR website, the 'Info Hub' brings together and tags publications, research and events. At the time of writing, it included links to 43 papers, videos, slide-sets and other relevant resources. It provides a useful introduction, but only for those with time to view and read a wide range of resources.

LACE Evidence Hub

The European-funded Learning Analytics Community Exchange (LACE) project is in the process of developing an Evidence Hub that will enable users to search and filter the available evidence. It is designed to be equally useful to researchers and practitioners, and does not presuppose any previous experience of the area.

The Hub centres on four propositions (see sidebar). Each piece of evidence added to the Hub is classified as for or against (or, less frequently, neutral) in relation to one of these propositions. Users can therefore search for evidence that learning analytics improve learning outcomes – or for examples of cases where they have clearly not improved learning outcomes.

The Hub can be searched using different dimensions. Each piece of evidence is also classified in terms of whether it relates to schools (compulsory education, universities (post-compulsory education), workplace learning or informal learning. It is also related to a geographical location. Where possible, this shows where the research was carried out; if this is not possible, it shows where the lead author is based.

The metadata associated with individual pieces of evidence mean that the Hub can be visualized and interrogated in a variety of ways. Its Search facility supports search by keyword, as well as enabling users to focus on a specific country or sector of interest. Once a search has been run, summaries of the evidence can be viewed. Each summary contains a link to the original evidence, which is not stored in the Hub.

Depending on the needs of the user, these summaries can be accessed in different ways. Country maps show the balance of negative and positive evidence in different countries. The Evidence Map provides a different view of the world that can be searched by proposition, polarity and/or sector, or title keywords. The Evidence Flow diagram shows how much evidence in the Hub relates to each proposition, how much originates in each sector of education, and how much is positive, negative and neutral/mixed.

The main purpose of the Evidence Hub is to help users navigate and make sense of evidence. However, in this fast-developing field, users also need to be able to find out about work under development or currently being piloted. This is particularly the case in the workplace learning sector, where little published evidence is currently available. The LACE consortium has therefore added a Projects section to the Hub as a way of investigating where work is currently being carried out. Project entries include a title, description, country and relevant tags. They can be visualised using a project map.

Once evidence has been located, a plug-in provides mouse-over text that provides an explanation of acronyms. For example, 'MOOC' is explained as 'massive open online course'. The list of acronyms can be expanded as new ones are introduced to the Hub.

Evidence can be exported once it has been located – the CleanPrint plug-in enables download in rich text, PDF or a variety of other formats. These can either be saved to cloud-sharing services such as Dropbox and Google Drive or printed directly.

Additions to the Hub can be publicised using the 'WP to Twitter plug-in'. This automatically tweets 'New evidence: #title# #url#'. This template can be amended to include elements such as author, tag or category – or authors can choose their own structure.

Evidence in the Hub

At the time of writing, there are 70 entries in the Evidence Hub, as well as numerous projects. The Hub contains a balance of entries from Europe and North America and from Schools and Universities. This demonstrates that contributors to the Hub have not restricted their focus to any one geographic area or education sector. With no benchmark for comparison, it is not possible to determine if this is truly representative. However, this does appear to reflect the impression among learning analytics stakeholders that there is much more research in the schools and universities sectors than other sectors.

In general, the Hub contains mostly positive (69%, N=48) or mixed (19%, N=13) reports. The majority of evidence reported on the site in respect to learning is classed as positive, yet the picture in respect to the impact on teaching is more mixed. Reports about the uptake of learning analytics are mostly positive whilst there are as yet only six entries relating to ethical use of analytics.

Using and Developing the Hub

In recent months, the LACE project has worked with SoLAR to align the Evidence Hub with the submission process for LAK conferences. Everyone who submitted a research paper to LAK16 (co-located with this conference) was asked to fill in fields indicating how their work related to the Hub's four propositions. Now that final versions of LAK16 papers have been submitted, authors will be contacted and all relevant papers will be added to the Hub. This process will be repeated in future years.

The LACE Evidence Hub is therefore a resource that will be of increasing interest to those working in, and researching, learning at scale. This work-in-progress paper not only serves as an introduction to this resource but also provides a call to action, asking all those who attend Learning at Scale 2016 to contribute their own evidence to the project.

Acknowledgements

The LACE Evidence Hub is powered by WordPress and based on the OER Research Hub developed by Rob Farrow and Martin Hawksey in the Institute of Educational Technology at The Open University as part of a project funded by the Hewlett Foundation. The European Commission Seventh Framework Programme funds the LACE project: grant number 619424.

References

1. Shane Dawson, Dragan Gašević, George Siemens and Srecko Joksimovic. 2014. Current state and future trends: a citation analysis of the learning analytics field. *Proceedings of LAK 14* (Indianapolis, IN, USA), ACM, 231-240.
2. Rita Kop. 2011. The challenges to connectivist learning on open online networks: learning experiences during a massive open online course. *IRRODL* 12, 3.
3. LAK Dataset and Challenge. Retrieved January 14, 2016 from http://lak.linkededucation.org/
4. Chris Parr. 'Biggest-ever' MOOC starts on FutureLearn. 2015. Retrieved Jan 14, 2016 from www.timeshighereducation.com/news/biggest-ever-mooc-starts-on-futurelearn/2020257.article
5. Phil Long and George Siemens. 2011. Penetrating the fog: analytics in learning and education. *Educause Review* 46, 5, 31-40
6. Alexander McAuley, Bonnie Stewart, George Siemens and Dave Cormier. *The MOOC model for digital practice*. 2010. Retrieved January 14, 2016 from http://davecormier.com/edblog/wp-content/uploads/MOOC_Final.pdf
7. George Siemens, Dragan Gašević, Caroline Haythornthwaite, Shane Dawson, Simon Buckingham Shum, Rebecca Ferguson, Erik Duval, Katrien Verbert and Ryan Baker. *Open Learning Analytics: An Integrated and Modularized Platform*. SOLAR. 2011. Retrieved January 14, 2016 from solaresearch.org/OpenLearningAnalytics.pdf

Elice: An online CS Education Platform to Understand How Students Learn Programming

Suin Kim
School of Computing
KAIST
Daejeon, South Korea
suin.kim@kaist.ac.kr

Jungkook Park
School of Computing
KAIST
Daejeon, South Korea
pjknkda@kaist.ac.kr

Jae Won Kim
School of Computing
KAIST
Daejeon, South Korea
jaewonk@kaist.ac.kr

Alice Oh
School of Computing
KAIST
Daejeon, South Korea
alice.oh@kaist.edu

L@S 2016, April 25–26, 2016, Edinburgh, UK.
ACM 978-1-4503-3726-7/16/04.
http://dx.doi.org/10.1145/2876034.2893420

Abstract
We present **Elice**[1], an online CS (computer science) education platform, and **Elivate**, a system for taking student learning data from Elice and infers their progress through an educational taxonomy tailored for programming education. Elice captures detailed student learning activities, such as the intermediate revisions of code as students make progress toward completing their programming exercises. With those data, Elivate recognizes each student's progression through an education taxonomy which organizes intermediate stages of learning such that the taxonomy can be used to evaluate student progress as well as to design and improve course materials and structure. With more than 240,000 intermediate source codes generated by 1,000 students, we demonstrate the practicality of the Elice and Elivate. We present case studies that confirm that categorizing student actions into the different steps of the taxonomy results in better understanding of the effect of TA's assist and student's performance.

Author Keywords
Online education; online programming; social learning; collaborative learning; computer science education

[1] https://www.elice.io

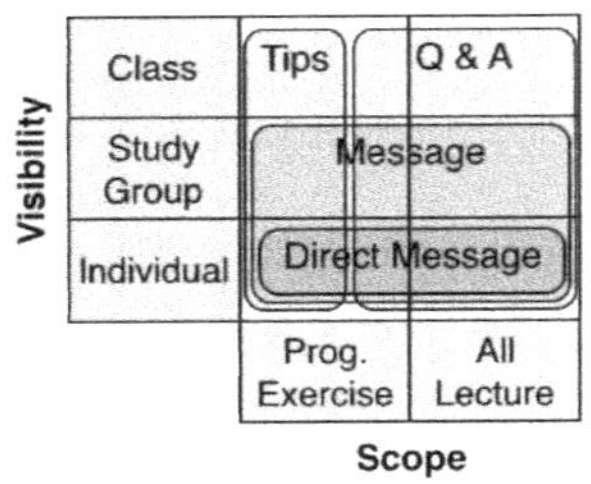

Figure 1: Three channels of sharing the knowledge.

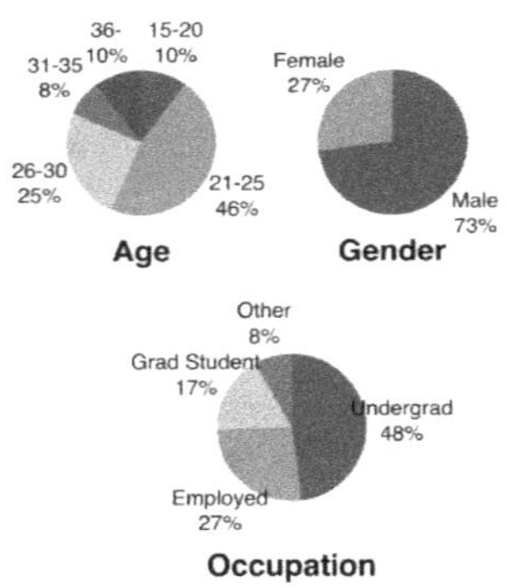

Figure 2: Demographics of the students enrolled in Elice for the machine learning online summer camp.

Introduction

With well-designed technologies, the domain of CS education is quite appropriate for systematic development and research about understanding student progress and assisting learning for individual students in large offline or online classes. In this paper, we present Elice, a Web-based platform, which integrates the three important aspects of analyzing and supporting CS education: 1) collecting and analyzing all actions of the students in doing the programming exercises, 2) mapping students' intermediate steps to an educational taxonomy to understand their progress, and 3) enabling students and TAs to interact using chat, forum, and tips features. We connect the automatic analysis of student progress and online tutoring with a learning taxonomy [2]. For each programming exercise, we map the students' actions to each of the steps in the taxonomy, such that they can be analyzed to infer the students' learning progress in more detail than just completion of the exercise. This allows TAs to help the students to move up (i.e., Elivate) through the learning taxonomy to achieve the maximum attainment.

Elice: An Online CS Education Platform

Elice is an online social CS education platform that supports online programming and collaborative learning. In Elice, students watch lecture videos and work on programming exercises in a Web browser. Elice enables collaborative and social learning with peers, teaching assistants (TAs), and lectures through multiple feedback channels.

Online Programming
We designed online programming to maximize the actual programming experience for students. Elice lets students skip the development environment setups by using a pre-defined container. Each student's code submission is compiled in the pre-defined development container, and the output is displayed back in the student's browser. During this compilation process, all of the student's data including the input data, the submitted code and the output are stored in Elice. When students submit their code for grading, a test script runs and shows grades to students in real-time. Elice allows students to submit their code multiple times for grading and even after receiving full credit for the programming exercises.

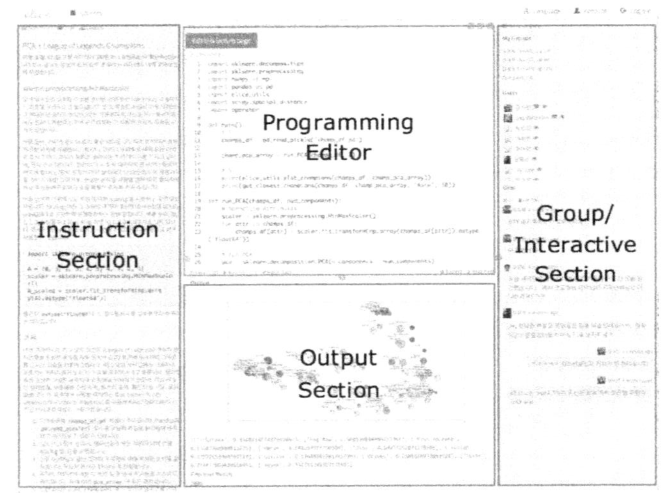

Figure 3: Elice Web-based programming platform. Current screen shows the exercise and result of the PCA algorithm.

Collaborative Learning
We have designed three channels of social interaction that facilitate collaborative learning among peers, TAs and lecturers (Figure 1). These channels support varying time spans of collaboration, from instant to delayed, and have

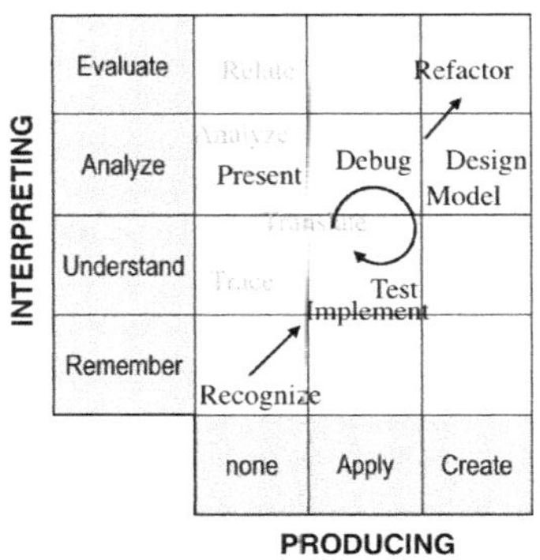

Figure 4: Fuller's CS-specific educational taxonomy.

Step	Meaning
Recognize	Read a lecture material
Design & Model	Devise a solution structure
Imple-ment	Translate the solution to code
Test & Debug	Apply the set of test cases;detect and correct flaws
Refactor	Try to get a better answer after achieving full credit
Present	Share tips and provide answers

Table 1: 6 steps of learning process for programming exercises in Elice

different scope and visibility. In Elice, a class includes all students, TAs and lecturers who are registered in the same online course. Students in the same class may be assigned to a group consisting of two or more students.

Machine Learning Online Summer Camp
In August 2015, we recruited students for an online summer camp to learn about basic machine learning algorithms. The initial registration was about 4,000 students, and we selected around 1,000 of them. Then, we randomly assigned these students to 30 TA Groups with 10 students each, 31 No-TA Groups with 10, 20, or 30 students each, and the rest worked individually (No-Group). TA-Group had ten students each and one TA who logged in two assigned days in a week for 1.5 hours to guide the students during these online office hours. Students in No-TA-Group had no assigned TA, and No-Group took the course individually and had no access to the chats. Demographics of the students are shown in Figure 2. Each week included short introductory lecture videos for machine learning algorithms and eight to ten programming exercises, in total 35 programming exercises for four weeks.

Elivate: Identifying the Learning Process

In education research, a widely-cited educational taxonomy by Bloom [1] organizes the "higher order thinking skills" from simple to complex. This taxonomy can be used by a lecturer to define the objectives of a course, as well as evaluate the learning stages of a learner. In this paper, we adopt Fuller et al.'s definition of educational taxonomy [2], specifically tailored for computer science programming education (Figure 4). Fuller's taxonomy was developed based on the findings that there are semi-independent abilities in learning to program, ability to understand and to produce. Using 12 problem-solving activities from [2], we re-define six steps of learning process, shown in Table 1.

Mapping student activities to programming education taxonomy
We map between student activities that can be detected and logged using Elice and the stages in the two-dimensional programming education taxonomy. Recognize can be easily detected by checking if the user reads the lecture material. Implement and Test & Debug correspond to each code submission, and we detect using student's code and input data. Refactor is the most advanced stage, and any code submission after getting a 100% score falls into this category. Present involves the activity of sharing, which can be done through three channels: chat, tips, and board.

Case Studies

Using the data collected from Elice, we analyze two important questions from the perspective of educational research.

Case 1: Overview – The 3 levels of TA assistance
Our study incorporates three levels of feedback for students in the three groupings: TA-Group, No-TA-Group, and No-Group. When we look at the distribution of the stages in the educational taxonomy (Figure 5), the difference is quite clear. Average students in TA-Group made significantly more code submissions compared to No-TA-Group and No-Group students ($p < 0.001$). Also, it is notable that Refactor, the most advanced stage in the computer science education taxonomy, is the highest achieved from students in TA-Group. This implies that higher levels of assistance help student to "traverse the learning process" to maximum attainment.

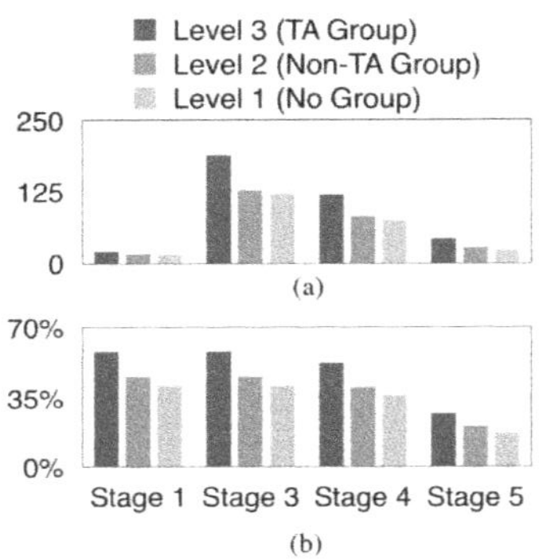

Figure 5: Code submissions from students receiving different levels of assistance. (a) Count of learning activities. (b) Average percentage of users achieved the learning stage.

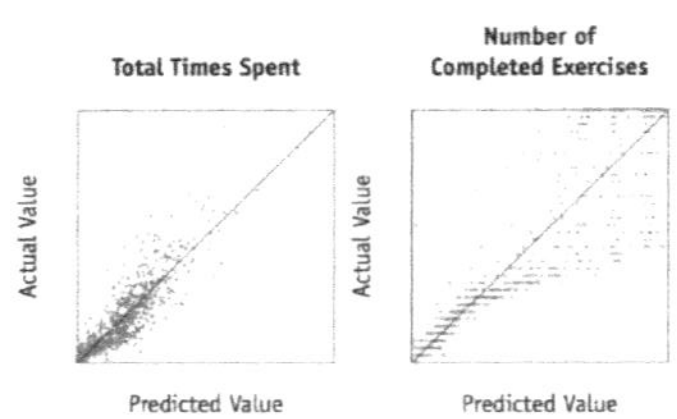

Figure 6: Prediction of the two final performance statistics using student's learning progress from the first two weeks. Pearson's r values are 0.914 an 0.905, respectively.

Case 2: Iterative transitions in the learning process
Starting from the Recognize process, by reading a lecture material, a student internally Design & Models the structure of the solution. After then, during the Implementation stage the student translates the design into source code. Test reveals the error of the code, so the student Debugs by patching the design structure of the solution. Then Implementation and Test & Debug occur iteratively. After analyzing submissions from 214 students who completed the course, we found that students in TA-Group, on average, significantly have higher number of iterations while solving the programming exercises (Figure 5).

Case 3: Predicting student's learning performance
Predicting whether a student will complete the class including all exercises is important for online classes. An early prediction may enable early personalized feedback to motivate and assist students who may be having difficulties. In this case study, we predict two variables: (i) total time spent and (ii) number of completed exercises. We trained a simple linear regression with OLS to predict two variables using the features of student's learning process at first two weeks. With Pearson's r value for total times spent and number of solved exercises are 0.914 and 0.915, additional correlation analysis verifies that the proposed taxonomy-related features show higher correlation score compared to conventional features (Figure 6).

Discussion and Future Work

The number of students taking CS courses is rapidly increasing. In order to support ever-growing number of students, it is essential to provide online programming environment and find the status of students for appropriate guidance and feedback. Our online social CS education platform, Elice, allows students to start programming immediately in their Web browser and collaborate with peers and TAs when they struggle. All of these student's data, including interactive activities to intermediate code submissions, are collected in Elice. From the collected data, we have identified the effect of assistance and the six steps of learning process in CS education. Such findings confirm that the important role of TAs when it comes to learning experience even in online setting. Therefore, in order to support the large number of students with limited number of TAs, it is vital to increase the efficiency of TAs. The six steps of learning process defined in our study help TAs identify the status of students quickly and increase the productivity of TAs.

We need to explore better means of helping students to move on to the next stage in the learning taxonomy. One possible method could be pushing appropriate tips or hints to students if the system finds that students are struggling or spending too much time in each stage.

Acknowledgements

This work was supported by Institute for Information & communications Technology Promotion(IITP) grant funded by the Korea government(MSIP) (No.10041313, UX-oriented Mobile SW Platform).

References

[1] Bloom, B. S., and Engelhart, M. D. *Taxonomy of Educational Objectives: The Classification of Educational Goals*. David McKay, 1969.

[2] Fuller, U., Johnson, C. G., Ahoniemi, T., Cukierman, D., Hernán-Losada, I., Jackova, J., Lahtinen, E., Lewis, T. L., Thompson, D. M., Riedesel, C., et al. Developing a computer science-specific learning taxonomy. In *ACM SIGCSE Bulletin*, ACM (2007).

Work in Progress: Student Behaviors Using Feedback in a Blended Physics Undergraduate Classroom

Jennifer DeBoer
Purdue University
701 W Stadium Ave, ARMS 1311
West Lafayette, IN 47907 USA
deboerj@purdue.edu

Lori Breslow
MIT
77 Massachusetts AVE. E62-336
Cambridge, MA 02139
lrb@mit.edu

Abstract
Two major benefits of Massive Open Online Course platforms are their collection of fine grain data on student interactions with the course website and their capacity to give students immediate feedback on their work. We study the patterns of students' usage of immediate feedback in an undergraduate physics course that uses blended learning, and we present informative aggre-gate descriptives from this 474-student class. We find that overall student study strategies mirror those in "traditional" courses, that students strategically use the auto-checking feature of the platform, and that they extensively use the other content resources available to them on the platform. Several of these findings support educational research that has not had the benefit of the data MOOC platforms give us access to. Better understanding of how students engage with blended learning will aid residential instructors in tailoring in-class time and providing their students with recommendations for approaches to studying.

L@S 2016, April 25–26, 2016, Edinburgh, UK.
ACM 978-1-4503-3726-7/16/04.
DOI: http://dx.doi.org/10.1145/2876034.2893421

Author Keywords
MOOC platforms; blended learning; immediate feedback

ACM Classification Keywords
K.3.1 Computer Uses in Education: CAI

Introduction
Researchers in digital learning and analytics are just beginning to be able to guide instructors in how to maximize blended learning. Studies in blended learning [1], [2] have yielded mixed results so that best practices have yet to be identified with confidence.

Variable	Ave	Med	Min/ Max
Total # of hours in problem-solving sessions	27	26	6 / 59
# of problems not attempted	1.16	0	0 / 17
Average time (hrs) between 1st check and due time for each attempted problem	69	64	5 / 216
Average time (hrs) between last check and due time for each attempted problem	58	53	3 / 192
Average time (hrs) between first and last check for each attempted problem with >1 check	13	11	0.07 / 61
# problem - solving sessions	20.98	20	5/ 49
Average interval (days) between problem-solving sessions	4	4	2/ 13

Table 1. Informative descriptives highlighted in this WiP paper. All variables are averaged across students (noted where averaging across problems/sessions).

Background and Conceptual Framework

We use data gathered from an introductory physics course, "Classical Mechanics," offered at MIT in fall 2014. This class, which is the first in a two-course physics sequence required of all undergraduates, has been taught in a blended learning format since 2003 [3]. Known as Technology Enabled Active Learning (TEAL), the course combines short lectures with desktop experiments and in-class problem solving [3]. Although students had access to extensive materials on the course website, in 2014, online assessments, powered by the edX learning platform (www.edx.org), were added. One of the most popular capabilities of the online assessment is the "checkable answer feature" (CAF), which immediately indicates to the students whether their answer is correct or incorrect [4]. The course instructors and researchers believed this capability would particularly benefit student learning given research into feedback [5], [6] and time on task [7], [8]. Data collected for this study has helped to confirm this hypothesis as well as to support those earlier studies.

Data

In this work-in-progress, we focus on the usage behaviors of students whom we observe via the MITx platform. Student behaviors are recorded by logging every time a student "clicks" on a link on the course website, which could include navigation to a content resource or submission of an answer to the CAF. We have time-stamped logs from September 1st to December 31st, 2014, during which time students' interactions with the course website resulted in more than 30 million interactive events, constituting more than 8 GB of raw log data.

Students were assigned weekly problem sets as homework; 2 problems were submitted completely online and 4 to 6 were handed in. For the 22 online problems, as soon as students received a "correct" check via the CAF for that problem, they were awarded the points. For the 63 written homework problems that were distributed online, students could check interim steps via the CAF, but they were required to write out all of their work and submit it on paper. In this study, we focus on interactions with the 22 purely online problems. Our logs include the sequence of incorrect and correct answers students submitted for every one of the problems the students attempted.

Methods

We provide basic descriptive statistics in this paper as the first step in our analyses. Our goal is to better understand the aggregate picture of student behaviors using the CAF. We therefore illustrate both measures of central tendency and spread, noting that some of the distributions of student online behaviors are somewhat skewed. This reflects the extreme levels of skew observed in solely online MOOCs [9]. Because we have log data, we provide aggregate estimates for all 474 students enrolled in the fall 2014 course. We measure student behaviors on 30 different metrics, such as number of total checks, the average time interval between CAF checks for a given problem, and the total time spent watching videos during a problem solving session.

Findings

We found that emergent results could be grouped into three main areas of insight: findings related to the "big picture" of students' macro strategic behaviors working on the online problems, findings related to students'

Variable	Ave	Med	Min/ Max
Average # incorrect checks for each problem	4.69	4.00	0.23/ 36.73
Fraction of attempted problems where first try correct *	0.19	0.16	0.00/ 0.69
Fraction of attempted problems where last try correct	0.83	0.88	0.00/ 0.90
Average # correct checks for each problem	0.92	0.95	0.05/ 1.77
Average time (hrs) between 1st & 2nd check for each attempted problem	3	1	0.01/ 20
# weeks with overlap between problems	5.78	6	0/ 9
Average length (min) of sessions	77	76	2/ 107
Proportion of incorrect checks with other activities after	0.03	0.02	0.00/ 0.18

Table 2. Informative descriptives highlighted in this WiP paper. All variables are averaged across students (noted where averaging across problems/sessions).

*weighted by problem difficulty

"micro scale" problem solving and checking behaviors, and findings related to the resources that students used to a greater or lesser extent while solving online problems.

"Big picture" student behaviors

On average, students spent about 27 hours engaged in problem solving sessions working on the online homework problems (Table 1). Given the 22 online problems over the course of the semester, this is a rough average of about 74 minutes on each problem. This meets traditional homework expectations for the course (MIT Bulletin; 8.01 listed as 3-2-7; see http://student.mit.edu/catalog/m8a.html).

On average, students started the online problems three days before they were due (μ = 69 hours), and, on average, they made the last check on the online problems about 2 ½ days before they were due (μ = 58 hours). On average, students had nearly 21 problem solving sessions over the 15 weeks of the class, with an average of four days between problem solving sessions. Overall, we found that students approached the online component of their problem sets in a manner similar to traditional homework assignments.

Student micro scale checking behaviors

The detailed individual clickstream data allow us to see the ways in which students engaged in answer checking via the immediate feedback feature. Across all of the online homework problems, students had an average of nearly 5 incorrect answers per problem (μ = 4.69). After weighting the problems by difficulty, we see that, across problems, about 20% of the attempted problems were checked as correct on the first try (μ = 19%), and about 92% of the checks for any attempted problems were correct (μ = 92%).

On average, students took about 3 hours between the first and second check for a given problem, if they checked a second time. However, if we average across all of the problem checks instead of just the first two, it appears as though the first and second check are necessarily farther apart—the average time interval between checks for the same problem is approximately 4 minutes. Although some students take much less time between checks (e.g., they might have quickly changed a response to reflect a possible algebraic mistake) and some take much more (e.g., they might have talked to other students), most do take enough time to use the feedback and reflect before resubmitting.

Since the average overlap time is 12 hours from the first check of the second problem to the last check of the first, it seems as if students were working back and forth between problems strategically. If we look across students, there was an average of 6 weeks (about half the semester) when there was overlapping time back and forth between the online problems (μ = 5.78 weeks).

The average problem-solving session was 1.25 hrs. (μ = 77 min.); those sessions happened, on average, every 4 days. This is much less than what deliberate practice research gives for experts' level of work (~4 hrs./day) [10].

Resource usage

Most students did use the variety of online content resources they were provided, although, on average,

Variable	Ave	Med	Min/ Max
Average time (min) viewing videos in each session	18	0	0/ 180
Average time (min) viewing e-text in each session	49	29	0/ 360
Average time (min) viewing class PDF notes in each session	18	6	0/ 240
Average time (min) viewing problem-solving session notes	7	0	0/ 120

Table 3. Informative descriptives highlighted in this WiP paper. All variables are averaged across students (noted where averaging across problems/sessions).

they used them at low levels. Interestingly, students looked at other resources after getting an incorrect check only 3% of the time. During any given problem solving session, students spent an average of 49 minutes browsing the e-textbook, 18 minutes watching videos, 8 minutes looking at PDF notes of in-class problems, and 7 minutes looking at problem-solving session notes.

Discussion

From this study, we see that students in a blended college/university physics course behave in ways that mirror our sense of how they work in traditional courses. For example, we see variation in when students start their homework, that they don't finish it in one sitting, and that they work back and forth between problems. However, in the fall 2014 version of the course, we see students making frequent use of the instant feedback from the "checkable answer feature." We know that in traditional courses, students use other resources to do their homework, but we can now see what they are using and for how long.

Acknowledgements

The authors gratefully acknowledge the support and collaboration of the Classical Mechanics instructional team. We would like to acknowledge the hard work of Dr. Cindy Chen on the data management and analysis described here. We would also like to acknowledge the contributions of undergraduate researcher Xingyu Zhou. This material is based upon work supported in part MIT's Office of Digital Learning and in part by the National Science Foundation (NSF) under #1454558. Any opinions, findings, and conclusions or recommendations expressed here are those of the authors and do not necessarily reflect the views of NSF.

References

[1] K. A. Lack, "Current status of research on online learning in postsecondary education," Ithaka, Mar. 2013.

[2] Y. Zhao and L. Breslow, 2013. "Literature Review on Hybrid/Blended Learning." TLL Working Papers.

[3] Y. J. Dori and J. Belcher, "How does technology-enabled active learning affect undergraduate students' understanding of electromagnetism concepts?," *J. Learn. Sci.*, vol. 14, no. 2, pp. 243–279, 2005.

[4] S. Rayyan and J. Belcher, "8.02 TEAL+x: Students say 'Yes' to MITx in 8.02 TEAL," *MIT Fac. Newsl.*, vol. XXVII, no. 2, Nov. 2014.

[5] J. Hattie and H. Timperley, "The Power of Feedback," *Rev. Educ. Res.*, vol. 77, no. 1, pp. 81–112, Mar. 2007.

[6] V. J. Shute, "Focus on formative feedback," *Rev. Educ. Res.*, vol. 78, no. 1, pp. 153–189, 2008.

[7] N. Karweit, "Time-on-task reconsidered: synthesis of research on time and learning," *Educ. Leadersh.*, vol. 41, no. 8, pp. 32–35, 1984.

[8] J. B. Carroll, "A model of school learning," *Teach. Coll. Rec.*, vol. 64, no. 8, pp. 723–731, 1963.

[9] A. D. Ho, I. Chuang, J. Reich, C. A. Coleman, J. Whitehill, C. G. Northcutt, J. J. Williams, J. D. Hansen, G. Lopez, and R. Petersen, "HarvardX and MITx: Two Years of Open Online Courses Fall 2012-Summer 2014," Social Science Research Network, Rochester, NY, SSRN Scholarly Paper ID 2586847, Mar. 2015.

[10] K. A. Ericsson and N. Charness, "Expert performance: its structure and acquisition," *Am. Psychol.*, vol. 49, no. 8, pp. 725–747, 1994.

Macro Data for Micro Learning: Developing the FUN! Tool for Automated Assessment of Learning

Taylor Martin
O'Reilly Media
Sebastopol, CA, USA 95472
tmartin@oreilly.com

Sarah Brasiel
Utah State University
Logan, UT, USA 84322
sarah.brasiel@usu.edu

Soojeong Jeong
Utah State University
Logan, UT, USA 84322
sadsjs@gmail.com

Kevin Close
Utah State University
Logan, UT, USA 84322
kevin.j.close@gmail.com

Kevin Lawanto
Utah State University
Logan, UT, USA 84322
kevin.lawanto@aggiemail.usu.edu

Phil Janisciewcz
Agile Dynamics
pjanisiewicz@gmail.com

L@S 2016, April 25-26, 2016, Edinburgh, Scotland UK
ACM 978-1-4503-3726-7/16/04.
http://dx.doi.org/10.1145/2876034.2893422

Abstract

Digital learning environments are becoming more common for students to engage in during and outside of school. With the immense amount of data now available from these environments, researchers need tools to process, manage, and analyze the data. Current methods used by many education researchers are inefficient; however, without data science experience tools used in other professions are not accessible. In this paper, we share about a tool we created called the Functional Understanding Navigator! (FUN! Tool). We have used this tool for different research projects which has allowed us the opportunity to (1) organize our workflow process from start to finish, (2) record log data of all of our analyses, and (3) provide a platform to share our analyses with others through GitHub. This paper extends and improves existing work in educational data mining and learning analytics.

Author Keywords

Micro learning; Digital learning environments; Educational data mining; Assessment

Design goals for the FUN! tool

1. To create easily reproducible analyses
2. To create easily reusable analyses (for different data sets)
3. To record details about every procedure
4. To be able to adapt a wide variety of data
5. To scale well as data sets become larger
6. To be a model automated analysis tool for education researchers

Background

Our work is informed by research in Educational data mining (EDM) and learning analytics (LA). Researchers [4] have discussed the analysis of learning events at the level of log data to understand learning that is ubiquitous, heterogeneous, and complex. For example, such research has shown a relationship between engagement and learning, and the prevalence of specific affective states [1] through the use of automated detection techniques and data mining. This fine-grained detection allowed the discovery of a relationship between frustration and confusion, and learning [1,6]. Beyond detection, this work is important because engagement has been shown to be predictive of significant long-term education outcomes [6,8].
Another example of research in EDM/LA that has informed our research is [9] to understand learning from game play in a reliable and meaningful way using "stealth assessment." There are other tools being used for real time streaming data [2,3] that show promise for adding to our understanding in education data science. Unfortunately, while the field of education data mining supplies methodologies for analyzing these data, the analytic techniques are often difficult for researchers without advanced data science experience.
In addition, we have experienced the challenge of conducting complex analyses for multiple projects in an inefficient manner repeating similar processes with each new data set for different projects. We have also suffered from the consequences of either lack of documentation or incomplete documentation of research analysis processes. This inefficiency is compounded with the rotation of graduate and affiliated researchers on projects.
These challenges led us to consult with our data scientist to explore domain engineering with reusable software [7]. This approach takes a domain and analyzes the based function and processes and attempts to automate them. One researcher [5] identified three steps in this process: (1) identification of reusable entities, (2) abstraction or generalization, and (3) classification and cataloging for further reuse. Using a similar approach we believed that there were processes that we repeated for multiple projects that could be automated and abstracted so that they could be used for similar projects. We also saw how these processes could be shared with others on our research team as well as more broadly through workshops and other dissemination opportunities.

Design FUN! Tool

We created the FUN! tool because we anticipated that researchers, who have access to an increasing amount of data from digital learning environments, would benefit from a tool to help manage and analyze all of this data. We hope the tool is flexible enough to be used with a variety of data sets and research questions, but easy enough to use, that a researcher (or team member) would only need an intermediate amount of programming experience to repurpose the tool.
Research questions drive every analysis process, but some elements of the analysis process (such as cleaning data and reporting results) can be repeated regardless of which research questions are driving the analysis. The FUN! tool automates the elements of the analysis that are repetitive and also makes the other elements (such as adapting to different data sources, applying different analysis techniques, and reporting results in a variety of ways) simple to change. The FUN! tool is essentially an engine that automatically moves data through a workflow process which is

How to use the FUN! tool
To access the open source FUN! tool, researchers should follow these steps:
1. Download python 3 from https://www.python.org/downloads/. Windows: Download pyyaml from http://pyyaml.org/download/pyyaml/PyYAML-3.11.zip. Run "py -3 setup.py --without-libyaml install"
2. Windows: Open the command prompt; run "py -3 –m install funtool". Mac: Open the terminal; run "pip3 install funtool"
3.Windows: Run "py -3 –m install funtool_scratch_processes." Mac: Run "pip3 install funtool_scratch_processes"
4. Download the example analysis template at https://github.com/activelearninglab/funtool-analysis and clone the funtool-analysis to your desktop.
5.Download the Userguide for the FUN! tool from https://github.com/activelearninglab. Follow the directions in the Userguide.

divided into four parts: adaptors, selectors, measures, and reporters
Data are adapted from a raw form into something usable by adaptors, selected based on various measures, analyzed, and reported to the user. (see Figure 1).

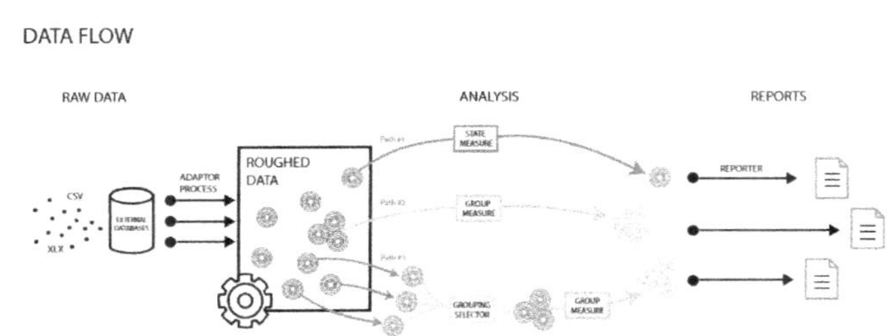

Figure 1. Diagram showing how data ideally flows through the FUN! tool.

Though the data appear to travel on a single path through the FUN! tool, the processes (see Table 1) can feed between each other in a non-linear pathway depending on the complexity and stage of analysis.

Process	Definition
Adaptors	Transform datum from source into a useful form for the engine
Grouping Selector	Creates groups of states
Analysis Selector	Always internal to the measure process, creates an analysis
State Measures	Creates a measure on a state
Group Measures	Creates a measure on a group
Reporters	Outputs information (could be intermediate or end results)

Table 1: FUN! Tool Processes

For example, researchers dealing with new data may not know what measures to apply or what analyses to run. In this case, the data may be adapted, selected, measured, then re-selected, and re-measured before being analyzed and reported. The processes themselves are run by the engine of the FUN! tool.

Preliminary Results and Conclusions
We created FUN! tool and applied our initial version of it to three real project data sets from several different digital learning environments (e.g., Scratch). We then found that the FUN! tool allowed us to (1) organize our workflow process from start to finish, (2) record log data of all of our analyses, and (3) provide a platform to share our analyses with others through GitHub.
Although automated analysis tools, like the FUN! tool, are already being used in the business sector (see Spark, Oozie, Hamake), the FUN! tool is part of the first generation of tools to anticipate and address the challenges that will come with the incoming data deluge in education [10,11].
In fact, the FUN! tool is deliberately open source so that others in the community, researchers, educators, or otherwise, can continue to adapt the tool as data sources change and data analysis techniques advance. The FUN! tool is not designed to be a final product that addresses every need, but rather a first generation tool that models, not only a useful tool, but also a high quality data framework for those interested in analyzing educational data. Data sources change, but the approach for how to handle the data analysis process stays, more or less, the same. Features, such as logging each step and separating concerns, are key elements for a responsible and efficient data analysis process. When these elements are compromised, the analysis process often becomes convoluted which can

undermine the validity of the results. Researchers should spend their time defining complex and robust measures to apply to data, not worrying about how to clean, analyze, and report them.

Furthermore, researchers should not consider the FUN! tool to be a cure-all to their data afflictions. The FUN! tool is best used with quality data that already has the capacity to answer the desired research questions (e.g., timestamps are necessary for temporal analyses). Researchers should develop a relationship with the developer of the data source to make sure the data is rich enough for their research and be prepared to translate event data into state data if necessary. The FUN! tool is best used in conjunction with rich data and quality data scientist support.

Acknowledgements

This material is based upon work supported by the National Science Foundation (Grant IIS-1319938). Any opinion, findings, and conclusions or recommendations expressed in this material are those of the authors and do not necessarily reflect the views of the National Science Foundation.

References

1. Baker, R. S., D'Mello, S. K., Rodrigo, M. M. T., & Graesser, A. C. 2010. Better to be frustrated than bored: The incidence, persistence, and impact of learners' cognitive–affective states during interactions with three different computer-based learning environments. *International Journal of Human-Computer Studies, 68*(4), 223-241.
2. Dumbill, E. 2013. Making sense of Big Data. *Big Data*, 1(1): 1-2.
3. Hare, J. 2014. Bring it on, Big Data: Beyond the Hype. *Big Data*, 2(2): 73-75.
4. Martin, T., & Sherin, B. 2013. Learning analytics and computational techniques for detecting and evaluating patterns in learning: An Introduction to the special issue. *Journal of the Learning Sciences, 22*(4), 511-520.
5. McCain, R. 1985. "Reusable Software Component Construction: A Product Oriented Paradigm", In Proceedings of the 5th AIAA/ACM/NASA/IEEE Computers in Aerospace Conference, Long Beach, CA, 125--135, October 21-23.
6. Pardos, Z. A., Baker, R. S., San Pedro, M., Gowda, S. M., & Gowda, S. M. 2014. Affective States and State Tests: Investigating How Affect and Engagement during the School Year Predict End-of-Year Learning Outcomes. *Journal of Learning Analytics, 1*(1), 107-128.
7. Prieto-Díaz, R. 1990. Domain analysis: An introduction. *ACM SIGSOFT Software Engineering Notes, 15*(2), 47-54.
8. San Pedro, M. O. Z., Baker, R. S., Bowers, A. J., & Heffernan, N. T. 2013. Predicting college enrollment from student interaction with an intelligent tutoring system in middle school. In Proceedings of the 6th international conference on educational data mining (pp. 177-184).
9. Shute, V. J. 2011. Stealth assessment in computer-based games to support learning. In S. Tobias, & J. D. Fletcher (Eds.), *Computer games and instruction* (pp. 503–524). Charlotte, NC: Information Age.
10. Stenerson, M. E., Salmon, A., Berland, M., & Squire, K. 2014, October. Adage: an open API for data collection in educational games. In Proceedings of the first ACM SIGCHI annual symposium on Computer-human interaction in play (pp. 437-438). ACM.
11. Werner, L., McDowell, C., & Denner, J. 2013. A first step in learning analytics: pre-processing low-level Alice logging data of middle school students. *JEDM-Journal of Educational Data Mining*, *5*(2), 11-37.

PEER Support In MOOCs: The Role Of Social Presence

Kwamena Appiah-Kubi
School of Computer Science
University of Lincoln
Brayford Pool
Lincoln, UK
LN6 7TS
kappiahkubi@lincoln.ac.uk

Duncan Rowland
School of Computer Science
University of Lincoln
Brayford Pool
Lincoln, UK
LN6 7TS
drowland@lincoln.ac.uk

L@S 2016, April 25-26, 2016, Edinburgh, Scotland UK
ACM 978-1-4503-3726-7/16/04.
http://dx.doi.org/10.1145/2876034.2893423.

Abstract
MOOCs by their design are able to reach several thousands of participants with very few instructors creating, delivering and facilitating the content. Participants interact with each other usually with text based asynchronous discussion forums built into the MOOC platform. The purpose of this research is to explore the role of social presence in facilitating peer support among a large community of learners.

Author Keywords
MOOC; Social Interaction; Group Cohesion; Social Presence; Community of Inquiry.

Introduction & Motivation
Online learning platforms, MOOCs being no exception, mostly employ the use of text based asynchronous discussion forums to facilitate discourse and interactions among students. Participants are able to share their views and thoughts on lessons as well as seek assistance with tasks and quizzes from other participants [7]. With usually thousands of participants trying to interact, the factors that influence learning and collaboration such as learner motivation, isolation, course design, and social interaction [12, 15] may very well be compounded under these circumstances [5, 9]. The large volume of data generated in MOOCs from logs of click activity on the platform and learners'

Figure 1: Elements of the Community of Inquiry, from [4]

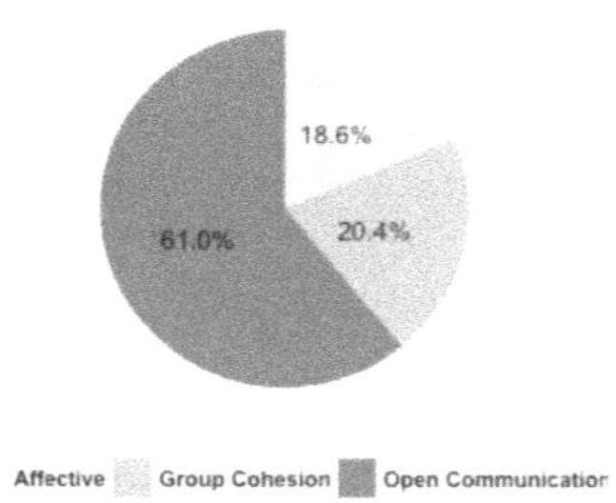

Figure 2: Distribution of Social Presence categories

interactions in the forum do not lend themselves easily to qualitative-based methods [6, 2] which are better suited to provide insight into the human nature of the interactions of participants, their learning, motivations and values [10, 2].

Data & Methods

This paper reports on historical data from a 2014 MOOC hosted by Stanford University's on the OpenEdx platform. More than twenty six thousand participants registered for the course. Majority of the participants were the USA accounting for 25% of registered participants, with India, China and the UK accounting for 8%, 5% and 4% respectively. About three thousand eight hundred posts and comments were generated over the duration of the course. It is worth noting that the dataset had been thoroughly scrubbed by the Stanford team to remove any identifying information of participants prior to making it available to investigators.

Qualitative-based methods, such as content analysis, applied to the forum posts can reveal attitudes and behavior of participants as well as characteristics of their interactions [2, 10]. This is relevant as the increased number of participants may amplify or dilute factors that influence learning and engagement that have previously been investigated in traditional or formal online learning environments. The next section identifies a qualitative based framework developed for the purpose of identifying factors necessary for a successful online learning experience.

Community of Inquiry Framework

Developed by Garrison, Anderson and Archer in the early 2000s to investigate the challenges they were facing with a newly deployed online graduate program [13] the Community of Inquiry framework defines a set of characteristics for researchers investigating online learning as an environment for "worthwhile educational experience" [4]. It comprises three core elements: "Cognitive Presence", "Social Presence" and "Teaching Presence", which interact to facilitate the online learning experience [**Figure 1**]. The framework is based on social constructivist principles with the premise that knowledge is created through interactions with others, that is to say knowledge creation is a social activity [16, 3].

Social presence establishes an environment that fosters interaction that leads to a sense of community among participants. Previous studies have posited that Social Presence facilitates the learning process via the interactions and community established [4, 8, 1]. Tu and McIsaac observed positive correlations between Social Presence and factors of interaction such as participants' willingness and frequency of interaction [14]. Social Presence is important in an online learning environment as it facilitates the collaboration, and participation in knowledge construction [4].

Preliminary Work

A total of 2187 posts were created between the first and eighth weeks of the course. Of these 596 had at least one reply. These posts with at least one comment and their associated comments were selected. The forum thread, that is each post with its ensuing replies, was reconstructed to create a coherent flow of interaction. The selected data was loaded into the NVivo qualitative analysis software package to be coded using the revised Social Presence coding scheme by Shea et al [11] to explore the Social Presence

	%
Phatic & Greetings	55.4
Vocatives	29.8
Addresses Group	12.5
Course Reflection	2.3
Social Sharing	0

Table 1: Group Cohesion (n=601)

	%
Self-disclosure	44.5
Unconventional expressions	18.8
Expressing Emotions	15.9
Expressing Value	12.7
Use of Humour	8.1

Table 1: Affective (n=528)

	%
Continuing a thread	47.6
Asking questions	24.8
Expressing agreement	12.1
Complementing	8.2
Personal advice	3.5
Expressing disagreement	1.9
Referring others' msg	1.2
Quoting others' msg	0.8

Table 3: Open Comm. (n=2622)

behaviours of participants in the discussions. Aggregate distribution of indicators is shown in **Figure 2**. Open communication category, comprising indicators such as "Quoting from others' message", "Complementing, expressing appreciation", and "Expressing disagreement", was used most frequently. It appears indicators from Group Cohesion and Affective categories are similarly used on a week-by-week basis as well as show in **Figure 3**.

Social sharing, an indicator which captures interactions such as commemorating a colleagues' birthday or other such life events was hardly expressed in the dataset under investigation. If "Continuing a thread" which is the act of reply to a post was eliminated, "Asking questions" comes out on top as the most used indicator by frequency, followed by "Phatic, Salutations and Greetings" and "Expressing Agreement". "Self-disclosure", which categorizes personal details given by posters usually to add extra context when asking questions or replying to another learner's post, features prominently within the "Affective" indicators category. Taken together, this may highlight these interactions as utilitarian oriented rather than community building.

Discussion & Future Work

This preliminary work has explored forum interactions though the Social Presence lens of the Community of Inquiry framework. We observe "Open Communication" as the predominant interaction behavior, and from this initial investigation it may appear interactions within this forum may be utilitarian. Further analysis will delve deeper to explore if this is truly so. Closely following this is investigating how peer support is enacted. Using Teaching Presence from the Community of Inquiry framework, what roles or behaviours are exhibited by participants that can be classified as peer support? Is there a relationship between these behaviours and Social Presence?

An exploration of the development and evolution of a MOOC's social climate may yield an understanding of participants' interaction patterns as a reflection of their sense of belonging to a group of learners and how this relates to their learning outcomes. A better understanding of how the social atmosphere develops and evolves within this large transient group could better provide insights into the design of online courses for this unique context.

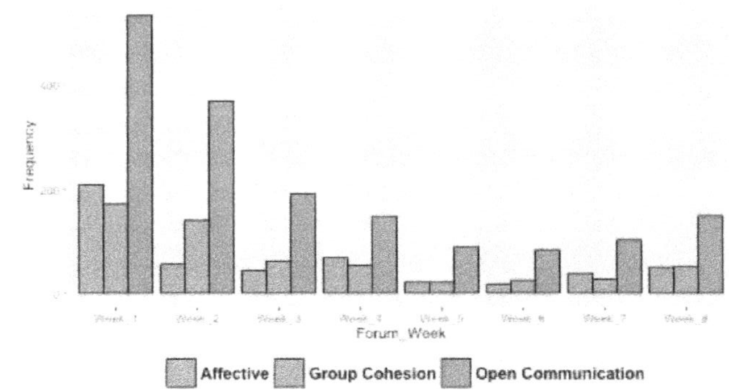

Figure 3: Weekly breakdown of Social Presence indicators categories

Acknowledgements

We are thankful to the *Stanford Center for Advanced Research through Online Learning* for providing access to the MOOC dataset.

References

1. Caspi, A., & Blau, I. 2008. Social presence in online discussion groups: Testing three conceptions and

their relations to perceived learning. Social Psychology of Education, 11(3), 323–346

2. Fournier, H., Kop, R., & Durand, G. 2014. Challenges to Research in MOOCs. MERLOT Journal of Online Learning and Teaching, 10(1), 1–15.
3. Garrison, D. R. & Anderson T. 2011. E-learning in the 21st century: A framework for research and practice. Taylor & Francis.
4. Garrison, D. R., Anderson, T., & Archer, W. 2000. Critical inquiry in a text-based environment: Computer conferencing in higher education. The Internet and higher education, 2,2: 87-105
5. Gasevic, D., Kovanovic, V., Joksimovic, S., & Siemens, G. 2014. Where is research on massive open online courses headed? A data analysis of the MOOC Research Initiative. The International Review Of Research In Open And Distributed Learning, 15(5).
6. Gillani, N. (2013). Learner Communications in Massively Open Online Courses
7. Graham, Charles R., and Melanie Misanchuk. Computer-Mediated Learning Groups. (2005): in Encyclopedia of information Science and technology, 1:5. 502-507.
8. Molinari, D. L. 2004. The role of social comments in problem-solving groups in an online class. The American Journal of Distance Education, 18,2: 89-101.
9. Rosé, C. P., Carlson, R., Yang, D., Wen, M., Resnick, L., Goldman, P., & Sherer, J. 2014. Social factors that contribute to attrition in MOOCs. In Proceedings of L@S '14 (pp. 197–198). New York, New York, USA: ACM Press.
10. Rotman, D., He, Y., Preece, J., & Druin, A. 2013. Understanding large scale online environments with qualitative methods. doi:10.9776/13155.
11. Shea, P., Hayes, S., Vickers, J., Gozza-Cohen, M., Uzuner, S., Mehta, R., Valchova, A. and Rangan, P., 2010. A re-examination of the community of inquiry framework: Social network and content analysis. The Internet and Higher Education, 13(1), pp.10-21.
12. Sun, P.-C., Tsai, R. J., Finger, G., Chen, Y.-Y., & Yeh, D. 2008. What drives a successful e-Learning? An empirical investigation of the critical factors influencing learner satisfaction. Computers & Education, 50(4), 1183–1202.
13. Swan, K., & Ice, P. (2010). The community of inquiry framework ten years later: Introduction to the special issue. Internet and Higher Education, 13(1-2), 1–4.
14. Tu, C. H., & McIsaac, M. 2002. The relationship of social presence and interaction in online classes. The American journal of distance education, 16, 3: 131-150
15. Willging, P. A., & Johnson, S. D. 2009. Factors that influence students' decision to dropout of online courses. Journal of Asynchronous Learning Network, 13(3), 115–127.
16. Zehra, A., Arbaugh, J. B., Cleveland-Innes, M., Garrison, D. R., Richardson, J. C., & Swan, K. 2009. A Response to the Review of the Community of Inquiry Framework Learning Processes vs. Learning Outcomes. Journal of Distance Education, 23:2, 123–136

Peer Reviewing Short Answers using Comparative Judgement

Pushkar Kolhe
Georgia Institute of Technology
801 Atlantic Drive,
Atlanta, GA 30332, USA
pushkar@cc.gatech.edu

Dr. Michael L. Littman
Brown University
115 Waterman St.
Providence, RI 02912, USA
mlittman@cs.brown.edu

Dr. Charles L. Isbell
Georgia Institute of Technology,
801 Atlantic Drive,
Atlanta, GA 30332, USA
isbell@cc.gatech.edu

L@S 2016, April 25–26, 2016, Edinburgh, UK.
ACM 978-1-4503-3726-7/16/04.
http://dx.doi.org/10.1145/2876034.2893424

Abstract
We propose a comparative judgement scheme for grading short answer questions in an online class. The scheme works by asking students to answer short answer questions. Then a multiple choice question is created whose choices are the answers given by students. We show that we can formulate a probabilistic graphical model for this scheme which lets us infer each students proficiency for answering and grading questions.

Introduction
Asking questions in a class is an important element in keeping students engaged. In an online class this is usually done with multiple choice questions or answers that can be easily graded. However for some topics it is essential to ask open ended short answer questions. Online classes don't often have these type of questions because it is hard to give timely feedback on them. We propose a new scheme that uses comparative judgment to give feedback for such questions.

Our method can be used to completely automate grading of short answer questions. An adaptive comparative judgement scheme can generally be used to rank short answers. Our method allows this scheme to grade these answers as correct or wrong. Just like adaptive comparative judgement schemes our method does not suffer from grader bias. Our method also allows us to recognize ambiguous answers and refer them to an expert.

Related Work

There has been significant work in the peer grading literature. For example, [3, 1, 4] have shown various approaches for peer grading short essay questions. Our work extends their work by using the new approach explained below.

Our work is related to the Completely Automated Public Turing test that is used to tell Computers and Humans Apart (reCAPTCHA) system [5]. It is a challenge response system used online to determine whether a user is a human or a computer. In it, users are asked to translate images into words. The reCAPTCHA system specifically challenges the user with two images. In its most simplest instantiation the system knows the translation of an image but does not know the translation of the other image. When the user answers the challenge, the system verifies if the user was indeed a human or not from the known translation. The other answer is then directly used as a label to translate the other image. The reliability of the translation increases when several users translate this image with the same label.

In the same vein, our questions are True/False questions (but they could be simple short answer questions too). Students provide a label and an explanation when they answer this question. These answers are then converted to a multiple choice questions by combining answers of atleast two students. Then we challenge the students to choose correct answers. We use this grading to determine two things: proficiency of the student at grading and correctness of the answer.

Problem Formulation

Every student u has some proficiency and every question v has a hardness parameter associated with it. Simply put, if the student's proficiency is higher than the question's hardness, there is a good chance that the student answers the question correctly. In any given exam the student is asked a series of True/False questions and a series of Multiple Choice questions. In the multiple choice questions, the choices are answers given by other students. Our models assume the existence of the following parameters which are either observed or latent variable which we wish to estimate.

- Grader Proficiency: Every student who is participating in the exam has a reliability score associated with them. There are two types of reliabilities - one for **generating** a correct answer and the other for **recognizing** a correct answer.
- Question Hardness: Every question has a hardness parameter associated with it.
- Answer Correctness: Every answer is labeled by the student. This parameter shows the probability that the grade was correct.
- Observed Answer Grades: Finally this is the observed grade for an answer.

Computing the posterior is non-trivial since all the variables are correlated with each other. That is why we use an approximate inference technique like Gibbs sampling.

Creating Multiple Choice Questions

As we have shown in Figure 1 student's answers are converted to multiple choice questions. When we run or Gibbs

Figure 1: The figure shows an example question as it can appear to two different students. In the first case the student is going to provide an answer to the question. In the second case, the student is shown two answers and asked to choose correct answers.

sampler we get confidences associated with the correctness of every answer's grading. If our confidence is low on a particular answer, we can get more information by posing it for grading to a highly proficient student. A systematic approach is used here so that we can improve confidence in our grading with the minimum number of times we pose a multiple choice question.

We can pair up an answer of high confidence with an answer of low confidence. If the grader grades the high confidence answer correctly, we can be assured that will also grade the other answer correctly.

If we know that the grader is highly proficient in grading, we can pose answers with low confidence values to them. Since we have confidence over their grading, we can be assured that they will grade the answers correctly.

Grading through multiple choice questions is used to improve our estimates on the answer correctness. We run our Gibbs sampler again after a student solves the multiple choice questions posed to them.

Conclusion

We showed a new approach to model the peer grading problem. In this model we have two reliability parameters for the students: one for their proficiency in answering questions and the second for grading. Also our formulation does not ask the student grader to grade with a numerical value, so it removes grader bias.

Our experiments show that with Gibbs Sampling we can estimate these parameters very reliably. Also as the number of students in a class increase, the reliability improves.

Discussion

Polar Grading

In linguistics, a question with a binary choice is known as a polar question. We call our grading *polar grading* because we ask the students to tell us if an answer is correct or wrong. We don't ask them to give a numerical grade. We assume that students are better at making a polar choice than making a qualitative judgment to determine a numerical score. There has been some study in the linguistics area towards this question. Some studies show how children respond to a yes-no question as opposed to an open ended wh-question [2]. We would like to perform similar experiments in the context of peer grading.

Student Ranking

As teachers we have to give grades to our students. A grade is usually a measure of how much the student proficiency in the class material. Usually these are determined by the score the students scores in the exams, that is, the sum of the scores of the *true grade* in this exam.

However if a grade is a measure of the student proficiency, then in our scheme two parameters that could relate to this are the reliability parameters - *reliability of generation* and *reliability of recognition*. In fact, one can argue that good students can answer hard questions and good students can grade hard questions. In a way Teaching Assistants (TAs) are the best students of their class.

If we had to rank students, traditionally we have used true grades. But there is a case to consider the reliability parameters for ranking too. Which of these parameters best represents the actual student proficiency is an open question. Answering it will be a part of our future work in this subject.

REFERENCES

1. Edward F Gehringer. 2001. Electronic peer review and peer grading in computer-science courses. *ACM SIGCSE Bulletin* 33, 1 (2001), 139–143.
2. Carole Peterson, Craig Dowden, and Jennifer Tobin. 1999. Interviewing preschoolers: Comparisons of yes/no and wh-questions. *Law and Human Behavior* 23, 5 (1999), 539.
3. Chris Piech, Jonathan Huang, Zhenghao Chen, Chuong Do, Andrew Ng, and Daphne Koller. 2013. Tuned models of peer assessment in MOOCs. *arXiv preprint arXiv:1307.2579* (2013).
4. Karthik Raman and Thorsten Joachims. 2014. Methods for ordinal peer grading. In *Proceedings of the 20th ACM SIGKDD international conference on Knowledge discovery and data mining*. ACM, 1037–1046.
5. Luis Von Ahn, Benjamin Maurer, Colin McMillen, David Abraham, and Manuel Blum. 2008. recaptcha: Human-based character recognition via web security measures. *Science* 321, 5895 (2008), 1465–1468.

Assessing Problem-Solving Process at Scale

Shuchi Grover
SRI International
Menlo Park, CA 94025 USA
shuchi.grover@sri.com

Marie Bienkowski
SRI International
Menlo Park, CA 94025 USA
marie.bienkowski@sri.com

John Niekrasz
SRI International
San Diego, CA 92131 USA
niekrasz@ai.sri.com

Matthias Hauswirth
University of Lugano
CH-6904 Lugano, Switzerland
matthias.hauswirth@usi.ch

L@S 2016, April 25-26, 2016, Edinburgh, Scotland UK
ACM 978-1-4503-3726-7/16/04.
http://dx.doi.org/10.1145/2876034.2893425

Abstract
Authentic problem solving tasks in digital environments are often open-ended with ill-defined pathways to a goal state. Scaffolds and formative feedback during this process help learners develop the requisite skills and understanding, but require assessing the problem-solving process. This paper describes a hybrid approach to assessing process at scale in the context of the use of computational thinking practices during programming. Our approach combines hypothesis-driven analysis, using an evidence-centered design framework, with discovery-driven data analytics. We report on work-in-progress involving novices and expert programmers working on Blockly games.

Author Keywords
Problem solving; evidence-centered design; assessment, programming process, K-12 computing.

Introduction
New K-12 STEM curricula emphasize inquiry- and design-driven pedagogies that have students solve authentic problems often in digital environments involving games, simulations, and/or programming. Such problem solving tasks can be open-ended with ill-defined pathways to a goal state, and require the application of complex problem solving skills and disciplinary concepts. Learners therefore need scaffolds

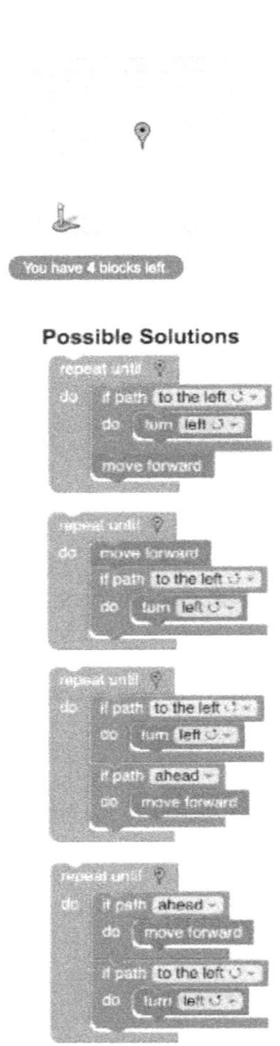

Figure 1: Maze Level 6 and possible solutions.

and formative feedback on the cognitive aspects of the problem solving process they may be struggling with.

To deliver the needed supports at scale, researchers capture and analyze log data to model student knowledge, misconceptions, and process to a solution. Recent efforts are exploring educational data mining and learning analytics (EDM/LA) approaches to model learning pathways in exploratory learning pedagogies (vs. structured ones where student actions are constrained), including science simulations and programming [e.g. 1, 3, 5]. Research in the context of widely used block-based introductory programming environments is still largely uncharted territory, however, and with computer science and programming expanding in K-12, we see an opportunity to investigate important "computational thinking practices" (CTP) such as task decomposition, debugging, and iterative refinement. We expect that our approach and findings will have broad applicability in studying STEM problem solving and design activities.

Approach

We combine quantitative and qualitative approaches as well as a hybrid hypothesis- and discovery-driven strategy to understand what patterns of behavior in logs from block-based programming environments provide evidence of learners' skill level and use of CTP. Our hypothesis-driven approach requires that we define, a priori, patterns to look for in data as evidence of CTP; these patterns are derived from applying Evidence Centered Design (ECD), a principled method for modeling domains for assessment purposes that is especially useful for hard-to-assess practices [2]. ECD provides the structure to connect constructs with observable behaviors that can serve as models and measure patterns of learner actions to provide evidence of those practices. ECD is thus complementary with the analytics from discovery-driven approaches that use EDM/LA methods [2]. We envision using our manually built ECD evidence models to tag log files with semantically meaningful labels and then use EDM/LA to build scalable evidence models using log data of strategies for solving the problem (as in [4]). Manual annotation is thus used only for the purposes of creating robust models for detecting CTP that will eventually be employed to power real-time analytics.

Such an approach enables us to explore data from smaller datasets, look at datasets from different types of tasks, and guide the iterative refinement of hypothesis generation and confirmation [4] about actions and the CTP for which they provide evidence. By intentionally placing learners into task situations that evoke CTP "patterns," such as breaking a problem into subparts or building out a program through iterative refinement, we can identify possible distinguishing features that are patterns in the log data.

Method

We are working with the open-source Blockly Games that teach novices introductory programming constructs using sequences of puzzles (and versions of which have been used in Code.org's popular "Hour of Code" activities). These are of increasing problem solving difficulty and have a well-defined endpoint indicating success, but different possible paths to the successful terminating state (Figure 1). Users solve a puzzle using blocks in a programming workspace, and can see the immediate results by clicking "run." To log process data, we instrumented two games that stress CTP: Maze, that teaches foundational constructs of

Table 1. Examples of Observables for CTP skill— Problem Decomposition in Maze Level 5 & Pond Level 5

Maze Level 5 Each of the two legs of the path requires a different treatment, but each treatment has more than one block. If students test the first subpart in isolation, this indicates they might have broken down the problem.

Pond Level 5 Task: This opponent is also too far away to use the cannon. But you are too weak to survive a collision. Swim towards the opponent while your horizontal location is less than than 50. Then 'stop' and use the cannon.

Pond Level 5 Solution: Requires the duck to first swim until the target is within range, stop, and then shoot. Do data logs suggest a breakdown into 3 discrete subparts through interim testing and debugging?

sequence, loops, and conditionals; and Pond that uses predefined functions requiring parameters and requires CTP strategies at Level 5 & up that include iterative refinement and problem decomposition.

Data logged for our initial phase included program snapshots in XML each time "run" was pressed, timestamp, and game level. We also recorded the screen as the subject worked on each puzzle to get a complete picture of users' actions. This yielded insight into user actions between consecutive "runs" since our early instrumentation was coarse-grained. In the initial phase we gathered data from 25 subjects varying on gender, age (between 11 and 50), and self-reported programming expertise.

Two-pronged Analyses

The discovery-driven component of our analysis, based upon automated pattern recognition methods, started with a method for transforming logged XML program states into abstract syntax trees (ASTs) (Figure 2, next page). The AST format supports a succinct and meaningful comparison of program snapshots. Next, we developed a set of "feature extractors." Each feature extractor examines and summarizes a unique, automatically discernible characteristic of the program or the subject's programming activity. Initially, we have focused on developing extractors that we expect to be informative for identifying higher-level programming practices. Feature examples include: the number of times a subject clicks "run," replacement of a numeric function parameter, or addition/deletion of control-flow blocks. These elementary descriptors (features) are the basis of our statistical analysis, and ground our study of what constitutes higher-level structures and activities (as coded in our manual analysis).

Concurrently, we performed a detailed manual analysis of each of the puzzles. By watching Camtasia® screen captures, we also listed out attributes of each task such as possible solutions, typical approaches to solving the problem, possible novice misconceptions that could interfere with solving the task, and disciplinary knowledge and skills. We then mapped them to observables in the levels of Maze and Pond (Table 1).

Preliminary Findings

Data-driven analyses alone of log data reveal evidence that the time taken to solve a level predicts skill level with ~63% accuracy, as does the time taken between runs (~55% accuracy). An increased presence of control and looping structures is positively correlated with level of programmer experience. However, these are coarse measures and require further development. Completing a full set of features will allow us to conduct experiments geared toward inferring features' relationships to meaningful CTP. For example, we will identify minimal sets of features that are predictive of a target CTP, or induce clusters of features by looking at their co-occurrence. Manual analyses can serve as ground truth in such a study, and the inferred correlations can be compared to hypothesized ones.

From the qualitative analyses, we have seen initial evidence of strategies: (1) basic iterative refinement, when subjects test different numeric parameters for angles or distances in the *Pond* game; (2) breaking down a problem into sub-problems and recombining the partial solutions into an overall solution; and (3) testing and debugging. However, we found that our initial sample is too small for developing robust models so we have collected a classroom sample from 111 7th and 8th graders: 58 subjects using Maze, 63 using Pond.

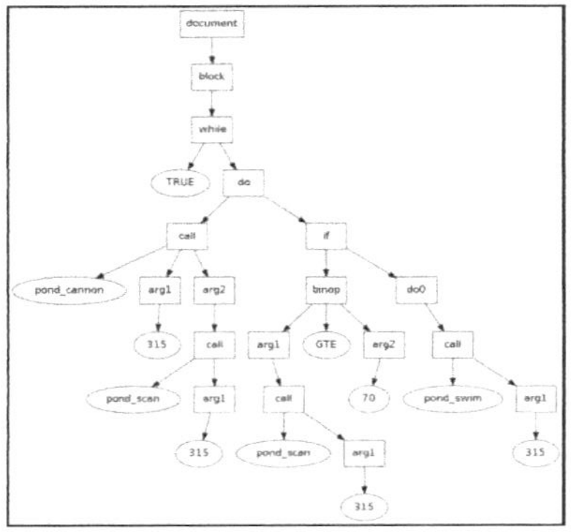

Figure 2: Interim solution to Pond Level 7 as an Abstract Syntax Tree

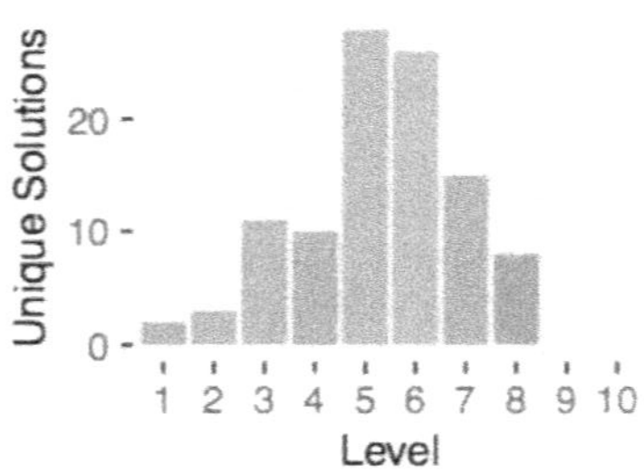

Figure 3: # of Unique Solutions for Pond

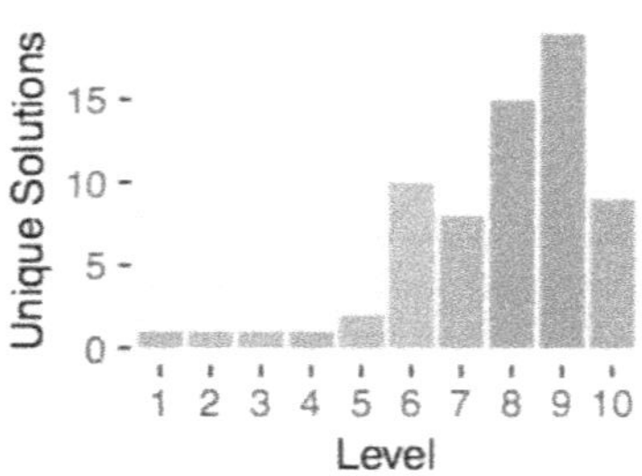

Figure 4: # of Unique Solutions for Maze

Figures 3 and 4 show the number of solutions for each of the games' levels, which increase in difficulty with each subsequent level.

Next Steps & Conclusions

To address the issues of volume and the grain size of log data in our initial phase of this study we have expanded our instrumentation to capture every user action in the workspace for a finer-grained view and developed a server-based implementation of the instrumented software (http://blocklygames.sri.com) for larger scale *data we are still currently capturing in classrooms*. We anticipate the next phase of analyses will provide more insights into problem solving process.

To study program growth and refinement, we have also expanded our manual task analysis to identify key features of the solution *state.* Then, our larger scale of data capture will support the use of statistical pattern recognition methods to learn models for automating this higher-level analysis. More precisely, the feature-based representation mentioned above will serve as input to machine-trained models that predict the presence of the high-level structures, which will be manually coded and serve as the training data for prediction targets in supervised machine learning experiments. Automated labeling of these sequences will enable detection of productive program growth as an indicator of a strategic application of CTP within, for example, formative programming learning environments. It will also help detect unproductive persistence (where the distance does not change significantly over several "runs"). Lastly, we plan to build more generalizable models for CTP such as problem decomposition through analyzing large numbers of data logs of the same task.

Our initial work provides direction for the next phase of this ongoing work: to build detectors of specific CTPs. Our approach also provides guidance for building detectors in STEM contexts especially where inquiry-based tasks have been modeled using frameworks such as ECD. Such detectors could be deployed in online environments for automating assessment and providing formative feedback during the problem-solving process.

Acknowledgements

We acknowledge the contributions of Dr. Grit Denker, Dr. Ed Chow, and Rukman Senanayake at SRI.

References

1. Blikstein, P., Worsley, M., Piech, C., Sahami, M., Cooper, S., & Koller, D. 2014. Programming pluralism: Using learning analytics to detect patterns in the learning of computer programming. *Journal of Learning Sciences, 23*(4), 561-599.
2. Mislevy, R. J., Behrens, J. T., Dicerbo, K. E., & Levy, R. 2012. Design and discovery in educational assessment: Evidence-centered design, psychometrics, and educational data mining. *JEDM, 4*(1), 11-48.
3. Piech, C., Sahami, M., Huang, J., & Guibas, L. 2015. Autonomously Generating Hints by Inferring Problem Solving Policies. In *Proc. of the 2nd ACM Conference on Learning@Scale*. 195-204.
4. Rupp, A. A., Levy, R., Dicerbo, K. E., Sweet, S., Crawford, A. V., Caliço, T., et al. 2012. Putting ECD into Practice: The Interplay of Theory and Data in Evidence Models within a Digital Learning Environment. *JEDM, 4*(1), 49–110.
5. Segedy, J. R., Loretz, K. M., & Biswas, G. 2013. Model-driven assessment of learners in open-ended learning environments. In *Proceedings of the 3rd Annual Conference on Learning Analytics and Knowledge (LAK '13)*. ACM, 202-204.

Designing for Open Learning: Design Principles and Scalability Affordances in Practice

Olga Firssova
Francis Brouns
Marco Kalz
Welten Institute
Open University of the Netherlands
Valkenburgerweg 177
6419 AT Heerlen
Olga.Firssova@ou.nl
Francis.Brouns@ou.nl
Marco.Kalz@ou.nl

L@S 2016, April 25-26, 2016, Edinburgh, Scotland Uk
ACM 978-1-4503-3726-7/16/04.
http://dx.doi.org/10.1145/2876034.2893426

Abstract
This work-in-progress paper elaborates on a gradually evolving approach to design of open learning and the design principles used by the Open University of the Netherlands in short open courses - online masterclasses and in Massive Open Online Courses – delivered in the learning environment of the Open University and in the experimental multilingual MOOC aggregator EMMA as part of a European project. As the paper will demonstrate, these principles can be seen as building blocks of open scalable design of active and engaging learning.

Author Keywords
Open online learning; MOOCs; design principles; active learning; scalability.

Introduction
Massive open online courses or MOOCs present a specific case in online learning. The promise of *openness* implies inclusiveness, in other words, accepting learners of diverse knowledge levels and backgrounds with potentially equally varying goals, interests and intentions regarding MOOC participation [5]. *Massiveness* refers to the fact that a course can host large numbers of participants. Attributes *open* and

In a Massive Open Online Course all are welcome, yet, it is not known how many will turn up, whether they will stay or not, what they will actually do once they turn up and choose to stay and how to support them in their learning.

massive point to a new situation from the organizational and pedagogical perspectives as well. Providing meaningful learning experiences to potentially large yet unknown and not clearly defined learner populations is a challenging task. Fitting instructional design solutions that can be both scalable and effective from the point of view of deep and engaging learning are not at hand [2].

This proof of concept paper presents several instantiations of an approach to open online education realized recently by the Open University of the Netherlands in MOOCs produced as part of a European project EMMA. This approach explicitly connects design principles for active and engaging learning with the notions of openness and scalability.

Open online academic level learning offered by the Dutch Open University targets professionals as lifelong learners [4]. Learning tasks are based on state-of the-art in the domain, have relevance for the professional practice and follow the principles of active and engaging distance learning [7, 10]. Offering such tasks in the online learning environment is seen as a stimulus for interaction of learners with each other and with the course content. Feedback can be provided by different actors and technologies [3, 6].

One particular type of open learning at the Open University are *online masterclasses*, designed as one week-long interactive learning events [4, 8] with a fixed structure. Each event starts with a limited number of introductory warming-up activities to be followed by an interactive live video session with a subject matter expert, some follow-up learning tasks that can be based on readings on the topic, asynchronous discussion assignments and another live session presenting new domain-specific research to end the event.

In the live sessions subject matter experts make use of and refer to the contributions of the participants posted during introductory activities, respond to questions and involve the audience in further discussions. These sessions are recorded and integrated in the course learning environment for those who have missed the live session but are still invited to contribute to discussions in the asynchronous mode. Thus, experts create an opportunity to interact with the learners both in real time and asynchronously.

In alignment with the notion of open learning, learners have full control of the extent of engagement with the course and its components. To enhance active participation, they are offered assignments and readings that are embedded in and relevant for the professional practice. Participants are stimulated to share their experiences with others and thus to contribute to the course.

Design principles crystallized and refined in the masterclasses were used to develop MOOCs. These principles are:

- Combining fixed course structure and flexibility enabled by live video interaction between experts and participants.
- Providing individualized feedback to participants as Questions & Answers parts of the live sessions and asynchronous forums in the form of one-to-many responses.
- Offering learning activities that are relevant for the professional practice of the participants, that they can use in their practice, like artefacts, analyses or designs.
- Re-use of materials such as video-recordings, units of instruction and assignments from previously held

events (i.e., online masterclasses) or regular Open University courses.

One of the MOOCs integrated a series of thematically connected online masterclasses with theoretical course design. Short reflection assignments linked these masterclasses to the MOOC core to broaden the offer of relevant content for the MOOC participants and increase the amount of meaningful exchanges between a broader group of learners involved in different learning trajectories. Although an absolute majority of participants of this MOOC remained non-contributors, a comment in the discussion board indicates that non-contributors are not necessarily non-learners: "*I was only reading and would like to thank all those who contributes. I learn and enjoy this experience*".

In another MOOC group formation was introduced to increase the level of interaction between participants. Participants were encouraged to share contributions and provide feedback to each other in dedicated group spaces. The level of individual participation differed substantially per group, however, the overall activity level in this MOOC increased substantially [8].

Participation of the Open University in the EMMA project allowed to further develop and test this approach. The focus of the EMMA project is on providing European learners access to MOOCs in multiple European languages through a single platform, and thus promoting cross-cultural and multilingual learning (http://platform.europeanmoocs.eu).

One of the projects' objectives is to test replicability of MOOCs across learning platforms and get deeper insights in the principle of re-use of viable instructional models and designs for MOOC design. Therefore, the two Open University MOOCs described above were replicated in the EMMA environment and delivered in Dutch and English. Thereafter, a MOOC on a new topic was designed and delivered in EMMA based on the lessons learned from the first EMMA experiences.

In EMMA MOOCs were delivered as bilingual courses, open for both Dutch and English speaking participants. Subtitles in both languages were provided to the video recordings of interactive sessions from the original MOOCs. In both MOOCs the course content and the navigation were adjusted to the platform and the interaction flow was adjusted to fit the communication functionality in EMMA. No groups were formed in EMMA. Additionally learning analytics were introduced to assist both learner and teacher [9].

Important lessons from the first implementation of the MOOCs in EMMA were as follows:

- Automatic subtitling and translation services proved an effective tool for delivery of the MOOC content in two languages. However, substantial effort in revision of transcription proved necessary [1].
- Recordings of interactive video sessions had to be adjusted for re-use in a new MOOC as they proved to be overloaded with the references to the original interactions with the audience. For participants in the new MOOC, it was difficult to understand the message and use the video to learn.

In design of a new MOOC in EMMA, re-use of recordings was combined with contextualizing. Short explanations about the origin of the recording were embedded in learning tasks together with questions or dedicated assignments. Furthermore, time frames were added to the fragments relevant for the task in order to allow efficient use. To stimulate interaction between participants other than in the content-embedded format, social media use was integrated by use of a closed Facebook group and a twitter hashtag. While the course was designed as a sequence of meaningful learning tasks, each task constituted a meaningful entity so that MOOC participants in EMMA could have a meaningful learning experience independent of the amount of time investment in learning activities. Last but not least, a synchronous interactive video session was offered in addition to videos based on re-used recordings of video sessions with topic experts.

A second run of the new EMMA MOOC is scheduled that will account for participants' personal requests and interested by the delivery of additional topics and interactive live events in both MOOC languages. The use of participant preferences and direct requests in MOOC design presents a further stimulus of interactivity of MOOC as a form of open course delivery.

In sum, development of open learning can be seen as a chain of design iterations through which active learning principles undergo continuous testing and evaluation in practice. Ample use of video is combined with the search for formats effective in terms of learner-expert interaction as well as cost-effective. Re-use of materials, including video, organizing feedback as one-to-many communication, exploring affordances of social media as learning support manifest themselves as building blocks of open scalable learning design.

Acknowledgements

This project has received funding from the European Union's Competitiveness and Innovation Framework Programme under grant agreement no 621030.

References

1. Brouns, F., Serrano Martínez-Santos, N., Civera, J., Kalz, M., & Juan, A. (2015). Supporting language diversity of European MOOCs with the EMMA platform. In M. Lebrun, M. Ebner, I. de Waard, & M. Gaebel (Eds.), *Proceedings of the Third European MOOCs Stakeholder Summit* (pp. 157-165). May, 18-20, 2015, Mons, Belgium.
2. Ferguson, R., & Sharples, M. (2014). Innovative pedagogy at massive scale: Teaching and learning in MOOCs. In *Open Learning and Teaching in Educational Communities* (pp. 98-111). Springer.
3. Hermans, H., Kalz, M., & Koper, R. (2014). Toward a learner-centered system for adult learning. *Campus-Wide Information Systems*, 31(1), 2–13.
4. Kalz, M., & Specht, M. (2013). If MOOCS are the answer, did we ask the right questions? Implications for the design of large-scale online-courses. Maastricht School of Management.
5. Kalz, M., Kreijns, K., Walhout, J., Castaño-Munoz, J., Espasa, A., & Tovar, E. (2015). Establishing a European cross-provider data collection about open online courses. *International Review of Research in Open and Distributed Learning*, 16(6), 62-77.
6. Laurillard, D., (2002). Rethinking University Teaching. A conversational framework for the effective use of learning technologies. London: Routledge
7. Merrill, M. D. (2002). First principles of instruction. *Educational Technology Research and Development*, 50(3), 43-59
8. Rubens, W., Kalz, M., & Koper, R. (2014). Improving the learning design of massive open online courses. *The Turkish Online Journal of Educational Technology*, 13(4), 71-80
9. Tammets, K., & Brouns, F. (2014). Learning analytics approach of EMMA project. LADS14, Graz, Austria. Available at http://www.laceproject.eu/wp-content/uploads/2014/07/LADS_TammetsBrouns.pdf
10. Van Merriënboer, J., & Kirschner, P. (2012). Ten Steps to Complex Learning. Mahwah, N.J.,: Lawrence Erlbaum Associates

Towards Cross-domain MOOC Forum Post Classification

Aneesha Bakharia
Queensland University of Technology
Brisbane, Australia
aneesha.bakharia@gmail.com

L@S 2016, April 25-26, 2016, Edinburgh, Scotland UK
ACM 978-1-4503-3726-7/16/04.
http://dx.doi.org/10.1145/2876034.2893427

Abstract
Preliminary research is presented on the generalisability of confusion, urgency and sentiment classifiers for MOOC forum posts. The Stanford MOOCPosts data set is used to train classifiers with forum posts from individual courses and validate these classifiers on MOOC forum posts from other domain areas. While low cross-domain classification accuracy is achieved, the experiment highlights the need for transfer learning and domain adaptation algorithms; and provides insight into the types of algorithms required within an educational context.

Author Keywords
Classification, Forum, MOOC, Domain Adaptation.

ACM Classification Keywords
H.2.8. [Database Applications]: Data Mining

Introduction
Forum post classification, if performed in real time has the ability to provide valuable insight to instructors moderating and planning interventions within MOOC forums. The grand vision is to provide instructors with dashboards to easily evaluate student confusion, urgency and sentiment [5], more advanced collaborative learning classification schemes and Community of Inquiry [3] models. Current research has

Additional Experiment Details

Preprocessing: The urgency, confusion and sentiment classifications contained likert scale values which were converted to a binary Yes/No categorization with values over 4 indicating the presence of a category. Forum posts were tokenised with tf-idf applied to the bag-of-words matrix. Only simple unigram features were included.

Machine Learning Algorithms: The Naïve Bayes, Support Vector Machine (using both the RBF and Linear), AdaBoost and Random Forest classification algorithms were initially evaluated using 10-fold cross validation with the results for the 3 best performing algorithms included due to space constraints. The Support Vector Machine parameters were tuned using cross-validated grid search (C=1 and gamma=1).

focused on training and testing classification models within a specific domain or course. In order to achieve real-time classification for unseen data in new domain areas, transfer learning and domain adaptation algorithms will need to be used. The preliminary research presented in this paper, evaluates cross-domain MOOC classification accuracy for confusion, urgency and sentiment. The findings are used to direct future research into the selection of appropriate transfer learning and domain adaptation algorithms to improve cross-domain classification performance.

Experiment Design

The Stanford MOOCPosts data set [4], made available upon successfully fulfilling application requirements was used in the experiment. The MOOCPosts data set contains approximately 30,000 forum posts from MOOCs within the Humanities, Medicine and Education domain areas. Courses from each domain area with the largest amount of forum posts were selected for evaluation. Table 1 includes the list of courses, the total number of posts in the forums and the relative size of each category evaluated in the experiment. The forum post classification was performed by human coders and the website [4] contains additional information on the coding process and the creation of the gold standard data set. Only the urgency, confusion and sentiment classifications were used in this experiment.

Classification accuracy for each category (i.e., confusion, urgency and sentiment) within each of the 3 courses was first evaluated with multiple machine learning algorithms namely the Naïve Bayes, Support Vector Machine (RBF kernel) and Random Forest algorithms using 10-fold cross validation. The algorithm that achieved the highest average accuracy was then used to build classification models for each course and category, which was evaluated against held out data from the other two courses.

		Confusion		Urgency		Sentiment	
Dataset	**Size**	**Yes**	**No**	**Yes**	**No**	**Pos**	**Neg**
Education How to Learn Math (DS 1)	9879	3164	6715	461	9418	8189	1690
Medicine Sci Write Fall2013 (DS 2)	5184	4703	481	1870	3314	3907	1277
Humanities Science Stat Learning Winter 2014 (DS 3)	3030	2540	490	977	2053	2834	196

Table 1: Forum post classification counts for courses from the Stanford MOOCPosts data set selected for evaluation.

Table 3 includes the cross-domain MOOC accuracy where a model in trained on the forum posts from a single course and then validated with unseen forum posts from the other two courses.

The cross-domain performance varies across categories. The sentiment cross-domain MOOC classifiers achieve the best performance (the lowest accuracy being 0.62) while the urgency and confusion classifiers are unable to produce consistent generalisable performance for MOOC courses from a different domain. The lowest accuracy is achieved for confusion classification (i.e., 0.25).

Analysis and Discussion

Only the average classification accuracy calculated from 10-fold cross validation for each algorithm is provided in Table 2. For all the classifications, an accuracy of over 0.7 was achieved, which illustrated that with only simple unigram features a good model, was able to be learnt for the individual MOOC course.

The best performing algorithm was the Support Vector Machine using a RBF kernel, which was then selected to build models for the cross-MOOC classification evaluation. The average accuracy from the classifier that achieved the highest result for a category has been made bold in Table 2.

	Confusion			**Urgency**			**Sentiment**		
Dataset	Naïve Bayes	SVM (RBF)	Random Forest	Naïve Bayes	SVM (RBF)	Random Forest	Naïve Bayes	SVM (RBF)	Random Forest
DS 1	0.68	0.71	**0.72**	**0.95**	**0.95**	**0.95**	0.84	**0.85**	0.84
DS 2	0.88	**0.90**	**0.90**	0.70	**0.75**	0.74	0.80	**0.81**	0.79
DS 3	0.79	**0.85**	0.83	**0.83**	0.70	0.72	0.91	**0.93**	**0.93**

Table 2: Average classifier accuracy from 10-fold cross validation for confusion, urgency and sentiment classification.

	Education EDUC115N How to Learn Math (DS 1)			Medicine Sci Write Fall2013 (DS 2)			Humanities Science Stat Learning Winter 2014 (DS 3)		
	Confusion	Urgency	Sentiment	Confusion	Urgency	Sentiment	Confusion	Urgency	Sentiment
DS 1				0.25	0.62	0.68	0.28	0.66	0.81
DS 2	0.33	0.76	0.74				0.76	0.57	0.78
DS 3	0.33	0.86	0.82	0.86	0.59	0.74			

Table 3: Classification accuracy for cross-domain MOOC forum posts.

Category	Top features
Confusion	base, log, size, solved, explanation, eta_1, helped, modified, logical, set, design, frequentist, joined, protect, clarifying, variable, predictors, r_
Urgency	thank, does, advance, video, confused, chapter, error, download, great, validation, downloaded, cross, certificate, understand, missing, wondering, tell, supposed, wrong, unable
Sentiment	sigh, annoying, unenroll, hell, browser, bummer, geez, navigation, chrome, exhausting, voice, spring, browsers, country, declared, shame, shocking, screen, connection

Table 4: Top features for each category selected using the chi-squared statistic for Science Stat Learning Winter 2014 (DS 3).

Many transfer learning and domain adaptation algorithms [1] [2] have been proposed that allow classification algorithms to achieve improved performance when applied to other domain areas particularly for sentiment classification (e.g., applying a model trained on movie reviews to book reviews). In order to select algorithms for use in an educational context, an understanding of why low accuracy is achieved for confusion and urgency classification is required. Table 4 includes the top words for each category within the DS 3 course (the features for the other 2 courses are omitted due to space restrictions), selected using the chi-squared statistic. Feature selection with chi-squared statistic removes features that are most likely to be independent and irrelevant for the classification.

Inspection of the top features (words) in each category, revealed the reason for low performing cross-domain classification results. The top features for confusion and sentiment are highly related to the context in which the confusion or sentiment was expressed. In particular confusion included words for the concepts that were found to be confusing while urgency was associated with technology issues that students may have required an urgent response for.

The next steps for the research include conducting a literature review to find algorithms that are able to exclude domain specific words or find related pivot words in cross-domain datasets. A domain adaptation technique known as structural correspondence learning is an example of an algorithm that leverages pivot features [2].

Conclusions and Future Directions

In this paper, I was able to illustrate that while good cross-validated classifier performance for confusion, urgency and sentiment detection in MOOC forums is able to be achieved, that these results do not generalise well when applied to MOOC forum posts originating from other domain areas. Future research will involve evaluating transfer learning and domain adaptation algorithms that are able to address issues associated with MOOC content specific features (i.e., words). It is hoped that this early research will trigger further sharing of human coded data sets for supervised machine learning evaluation.

References

1. John Blitzer, Mark Dredze, Fernando Pereira, et al. Biographies, bollywood, boom-boxes and blenders: Domain adaptation for sentiment classification. In *ACL*, volume 7, pages 440–447, 2007.
2. John Blitzer, Ryan McDonald and Fernando Pereira. Domain adaptation with structural correspondence learning. In the *Proceedings of the Proceedings of the 2006 conference on empirical methods in natural language processing*, pages 120–128. ACL, 2006.
3. Vitomir Kovanovic, Dragan Gasevic, and Marek Hatala. Learning analytics for communities of inquiry. *Journal of Learning Analytics*, 1(3):195–198, 2014.
4. The Stanford MOOCPosts Data Set. Retrieved January 15, 2016 from http://datastage.stanford.edu/StanfordMoocPosts/.
5. Miaomiao Wen, Diyi Yang, and Carolyn Rose. Sentiment analysis in mooc discussion forums: What does it tell us? In *Educational Data Mining 2014*, 2014.

Scaling up Online Question Answering via Similar Question Retrieval

Chase Geigle
University of Illinois at
Urbana-Champaign
201 N Goodwin Ave
Urbana, IL 61801
geigle1@illinois.edu

ChengXiang Zhai
University of Illinois at
Urbana-Champaign
201 N Goodwin Ave
Urbana, IL 61801
czhai@illinois.edu

L@S 2016, April 25-26, 2016, Edinburgh, Scotland UK
ACM 978-1-4503-3726-7/16/04.
http://dx.doi.org/10.1145/2876034.2893428

Abstract
Faced with growing class sizes and the dawn of the MOOC, educators are in need of tools to help them cope with the growing number of questions asked in large classes since manually answering all the questions in a timely manner is infeasible. In this paper, we propose to exploit historical question/answer data accumulated for the same or similar classes as a basis for automatically answering previously asked questions via the use of information retrieval techniques. We further propose to leverage resolved questions to create test collections for quantitative evaluation of a question retrieval algorithm without requiring additional human effort. Using this evaluation methodology, we study the effectiveness of state of the art retrieval techniques for this special retrieval task, and perform error analysis to inform future directions.

Author Keywords
Community question answering; information retrieval

ACM Classification Keywords
H.3.3 [Information Search and Retrieval]: Information filtering

Introduction
The need for automatic educational systems continues to rise in recent years, motivated by sustained growth of

Original question:
How to access a work in a dictionary
How do you access the value (word) in dict in anagram?

Original answer:
Just like you would access anything in a std::map... dict[key], or dict.find(key)
Or are you asking what the key should be? (That's part of the assignment.)

Proposed 1. 12992.txt 37.4169
You could do it like that, but it's probably better practice to use find, and then compare it against end. You can then use the return value of find to extract the value, if they key was in the map. Using [] will actually create the entry in the map if the key wasn't already in it.
In either case, it does indeed return a reference to the vector which contains the anagrams associated with an "anagram key".

Proposed 2. 13197.txt 27.1635
dict[key] will return you a reference to the value associated with key. It's slightly problematic in a const function though since operator[] will create a default value for the key if the key wasn't already in the map. If you want to avoid this you should use find, which is described on the lab page and can also be found here: http://www.cplusplus.com/reference/...

Figure 1: A successful output from the system

class sizes with a lack of a proportional increase in faculty/staff. In such large classes it becomes nearly impossible to promptly answer student questions.

Thus, an interesting question is whether we can develop an intelligent system to automatically answer student questions. In this paper, we propose to exploit historical question/answer data of a course (obtained via an online Q&A platform, e.g. Piazza[1] or a university's LMS) as a basis for automatically answering those questions that have already been asked via the use of information retrieval techniques to retrieve similar or related questions from past data. Our proposal raises an interesting new research question that we believe has not yet been addressed in the research community: can such datasets of past question/answer pairs from a course be leveraged to create a system that can learn how to answer new questions in a future offering?

Below we present our preliminary work on addressing this question, including the formulation of the problem as an information retrieval problem, the feasibility of using a standard retrieval algorithm to solve this problem, and how we address the challenge of evaluating such a retrieval algorithm by using resolved questions to create test collections for quantitative evaluation of question retrieval algorithms without requiring additional human effort. Using the proposed evaluation methodology, we study the effectiveness of state of the art retrieval techniques for this special retrieval task, and perform error analysis to inform future directions.

Automated Q&A using Information Retrieval

Formally, our computation problem is the following information retrieval problem: given a database of past question/answer pairs $\mathbf{D}_c = \{(\mathbf{q}_1, \mathbf{a}_1), \ldots, (\mathbf{q}_n, \mathbf{a}_n)\}$ for a particular course c and a new question $\mathbf{q}_e$ asked in course c, find the most relevant answers in $\mathbf{D}_c$ to the unseen question $\mathbf{q}_e$. We treat both questions $\mathbf{q}$ and answers $\mathbf{a}$ as purely unstructured text documents. Thus, this can be seen as an instance of the traditional document relevance ranking problem from information retrieval, where $\mathbf{q}_e$ is the query and each $(\mathbf{q}_i, \mathbf{a}_i)$ is a document.

[1] https://piazza.com

This problem formulation allows us to apply many existing information retrieval algorithms (such as the state-of-the-art vector space model ranking function Okapi BM25 [2]) directly to solve our problem and support automated question answering. These methods generally rely on keyword matching between the query and documents. They mainly differ in how they choose to do ranking in this scenario. For similar question retrieval methods, we will leverage *only* the question text $\mathbf{q}_i$ for each document as its representation during ranking, under the assumption that similar questions should have similar answers. After the database $\mathbf{D}_c$ has been ranked via question similarity to the query, the list's contents are replaced with each $\mathbf{q}_i$'s corresponding $\mathbf{a}_i$ and returned to the user as our result.

Evaluation Methodology

A standard practice in information retrieval evaluation is to follow the Cranfield evaluation methodology and create a test set that can be reused to compare different algorithms or examine the effectiveness of a component in an algorithm [3]. The basic idea is to create a set of sample documents, a set of sample queries, and a set of relevance judgments about which documents should be retrieved for each query. This allows us to generate an ideal ranking of documents for each query. We can then compare a system's ranking with the ideal ranking and use a measure to quantify the deviation of the system ranking from the ideal one.

Original question: RandomNNS Test Failing
So I'm confused on why I'm failing the RandomNNS test. What does that test entail at a high level? I'm passing the constructor test, but am I missing any edge cases in my find nearest neighbor? I'm also missing the PrimaryColorsMosaic test and the RandomMosaic one. Edge cases I cover (not necessarily in that order, but overall, it passes all the monad tests we were given):
- Left index = right index
- finding the leaf node first
- Replacing the current best with the other best that we found in the other subtree
- replacing the current best with the current node as we recurse up
Thanks.

Original answer:
Well just based on the short description you've wrote, you don't want to check every subtree otherwise you will fail the mines test. Also have you consider the case where the left index > right index?

Proposed 1. 6775.txt 82.119
Sounds perfect to me. :)

Proposed 2. 1686.txt 79.8583
Sounds great!

Proposed 3. 6765.txt 75.3043
this was resolved

Figure 2: An example "failure" output from the system

In our case, the past question answer archive can naturally serve as our document set. We can also collect the questions asked by the students. However, creating relevance judgments requires much manual work since it requires examining all the documents in the collection for each query to assess the relevance. To solve this problem, we propose an automatic form of relevance judgment that takes advantage of the structure of our problem. Intuitively, retrieved answers should be similar (textually) to the "gold standard" answer that a question eventually receives. This can give us a form of "psuedo-relevance": an answer's relevance to the query $\mathbf{q}_e$ can be approximated by its similarity to the corresponding answer in the test dataset $\mathbf{a}_e$. Formally, we can say $\widetilde{rel}(\mathbf{q}_e, \mathbf{a}_i) = score(\mathbf{a}_e, \mathbf{a}_i)$ where $score(\mathbf{a}_e, \mathbf{a}_i)$ is the similarity of the gold standard answer to the proposed answer using a retrieval function—BM25 in our case—treating $\mathbf{a}_e$ as a query and $\mathbf{a}_i$ as a document to be scored.

It is important to notice here that a "psuedo-relevance" judgment is not a binary judgment: it is a real number. Furthermore, it is not necessarily directly comparable between different queries (as the similarity functions used for ranking are not guaranteed to be symmetric). We thus need some mechanism for normalization on a per-query basis as well as an evaluation function that can utilize non-binary relevance judgments. Fortunately, normalized discounted cumulative gain (NDCG) is a common retrieval evaluation function that satisfies these properties [2], so we can directly apply it to our use case by replacing the traditionally user-supplied relevance score with $\widetilde{rel}(\mathbf{q}_e, \mathbf{a}_i)$ and obtain an NDCG score for each query in our test set $\mathbf{E}_c$.

Experiments

We utilized a large set of question/answer pairs fetched from the course Piazza for many past offerings of a undergraduate data structures course offered in a computer science department. We leveraged six semesters from fall 2011 through spring 2014, giving us a total of 14,018 question/answer pairs. From this, we kept only questions that were tagged through the Piazza software as being related to an assignment, lab, or examination and were at least 8 characters in length. In total, we arrived at 11,175 question/answer pairs in $\mathbf{D}_c$ after filtering. Our test dataset was obtained from another offering of the same computer science course (fall 2014) and was filtered similarly. This gave us an evaluation dataset $\mathbf{E}_c$ consisting of 2,110 question/answer pairs. The questions in $\mathbf{E}_c$ were used as queries against $\mathbf{D}_c$ for evaluation purposes. For our initial experiments, we leveraged BM25 for performing our similar question retrieval as well as providing our pseudo-relevance score. We used the META toolkit[2] at version 1.2 for our search engine implementation with its default tokenizer, stemmer, stopword list, and BM25 parameters.

Evaluation using this data set shows that the BM25 retrieval function gives an average NDCG@5 across all 2,110 queries of 0.226. This means that the ranking deviates quite a bit from the ideal ranking generated using the pseudo-relevance judgment, suggesting much room for further improvement. This evaluation method can be easily used to compare different retrieval algorithms and help understand how to improve a retrieval algorithm for this task. In the future, we will experiment with more advanced retrieval algorithms to better understand what makes an effective model for this retrieval task.

We also provide some subjective analysis. In figure 1, it is clear that the system's top proposed answers are indeed relevant to the question based on the gold standard answer provided. However, the narrative surrounding them is not always correct anymore. The second proposed answer is

[2] https://meta-toolkit.org

Original question:
MergeSort backwards
From what I can guess from the autograder, I am failing the backwards test for mergesort. However, all of my backwards tests work for each function, which mergesort calls. I believe I have implemented mergesort correctly, so I'm not sure how I should go about debugging this.

Original answer:
What do you mean by "all of your backwards tests work" (do you mean that the autograder's tests pass, or do you mean you've tested it yourself)? What test cases have you tried?

Proposed 1. 12582.txt 69.7938
Try this...after you mergesort a list, call reverse on it and see if it reverse correctly.

Proposed 2. 12369.txt 50.1041
I don't think your mergesort is the problem. Have you taken a close look at your merge?

Proposed 3. 806.txt 47.8744
You probably have an error with your prev pointers that is causing an infinite loop, eg something pointing to itself.

Proposed 4. 5847.txt 45.8111
Valgrind?

Proposed 5. 8193.txt 45.6453
Be extra careful with your pointers. It's hard to say exactly what you could be doing wrong since your error is so... vague/common.
I strongly suggest drawing pictures to help you figure out exactly what's going on. For instance, do you know where 10->next is pointing when your program finishes? That'd be as good a place to start as any. (looks like it might be NULL currently) Also be sure to keep track of your head/tail. Losing those would never be good.

Figure 3: An example of a successful output from the system, but a poor one from our NDCG evaluation

actually slightly better than the first, but has a significantly worse similarity score. This suggests benefit in trying to synthesize answers [4].

Next, we look at a failure case for our system (figure 2). Three short and irrelevant answers were at the top of our ranked list, all with fairly similar scores. While question synthesis would not help us at all due to the lack of content, this suggests that our ranking function might need to penalize short answers and bias the ranking towards questions that have long, more detailed, answers.

Finally, we can see an instance of the shortcomings of our empirical NDCG@5 evaluation. In figure 3, each of the proposed answers is a reasonable debugging step for the assignment, but they share almost nothing in common with the gold standard answer. Thus, while our proposed empirical evaluation may be a reasonable heuristic, it cannot replace human judgments.

Conclusions and Future Work

In this work, we proposed scaling up question answering in massive online discussion forums for large classes via similar question retrieval. Such a strategy can be regarded as using a student's question to automatically trigger a search over the past question answer archive for the same or similar courses to retrieve relevant questions with answers. A very attractive advantage of the proposed strategy is that as more and more data accumulates through the repeated offerings of the course, the likelihood of being able to retrieve a relevant question/answer increases as well (leveraging the benefit of our own "big data").

We proposed a new way to automatically construct a test set by leveraging the known answers to questions in the archive and adapted the NDCG measure for quantifying ranking accuracy. We constructed a data set using the forum data from a computer science course and experimented with a state of the art basic retrieval function (BM25) and found that it has a "pseudo-relevance" NDCG@5 of 0.226 on our data set, indicating much room for further improvement. Qualitative analysis of some of the retrieval results show that the prototype system can provide some useful results to the students (figures 1, 3), but still fails in some cases (figure 2).

Obvious future directions include incorporating more complex retrieval models [1, 5, 4] to improve our system's retrieval quality as well as exploring answer synthesis models [4]. Question metadata (e.g. tags) may also be useful. Finally, we should also obtain relevance judgments for our dataset to more fairly evaluate our system empirically.

Acknowledgments

This material is based upon work supported by the NSF GRFP under Grant Number DGE-1144245.

References

1. J. Jeon, W. B. Croft, and J. H. Lee. 2005. Finding Similar Questions in Large Question and Answer Archives. In *CIKM*. 84–90.
2. C. D. Manning, P. Raghavan, and H. Schütze. 2008. *Introduction to Information Retrieval*. Cambridge University Press, New York, NY, USA.
3. M. Sanderson. 2010. Test Collection Based Evaluation of Information Retrieval Systems. *Foundations and Trends in Information Retrieval* 4, 4 (2010), 247–375.
4. A. Shtok, G. Dror, Y. Maarek, and I. Szpektor. 2012. Learning from the Past: Answering New Questions with Past Answers. In *WWW*. 759–768.
5. X. Xue, J. Jeon, and W. B. Croft. 2008. Retrieval Models for Question and Answer Archives. In *SIGIR*. 475–482.

Challenge and Potential of Fine Grain, Cross-Institutional Learning Data

Alan Dix
Talis
48 Frederick Street
Birmingham, UK, B1 3HN
and
HCI Centre
School of Computer Science
University of Birmingham
Edgbaston
Birmingham, UK, B15 2TT

ajd@talis.com

http://alandix.com/academic/papers/LS2016/

L@S 2016, April 25-26, 2016, Edinburgh, Scotland UK
ACM 978-1-4503-3726-7/16/04.
http://dx.doi.org/10.1145/2876034.2893429

Abstract
While MOOCs and other forms of large-scale learning are of growing importance, the vast majority of tertiary students still study in traditional face-to-face settings. This paper examines some of the challenges in attempting to apply the benefits of large-scale learning to these settings, building on a growing repository of cross-institutional data.

Author Keywords
learning analytics; education technology; reading lists; MOOCs; OER; linked data.

Introduction
Can the benefits of scale work for traditional face-to-face institutions or smaller distance classes as well as MOOCs and similar environments? While large-scale courses can attract tens of thousands of students, the majority of the nearly 100 million new tertiary student enrolments worldwide [9] are in traditional face-to-face settings and most of the rest in much smaller distance courses. This is large-scale by any definition, but especially vast in terms of heterogeneity.

The number of tertiary students is expected to grow from around 180 million to 260 million by 2025 ([3] as reported in [6]). Even if many are in large-scale courses (which is unlikely), it is clear that we need to

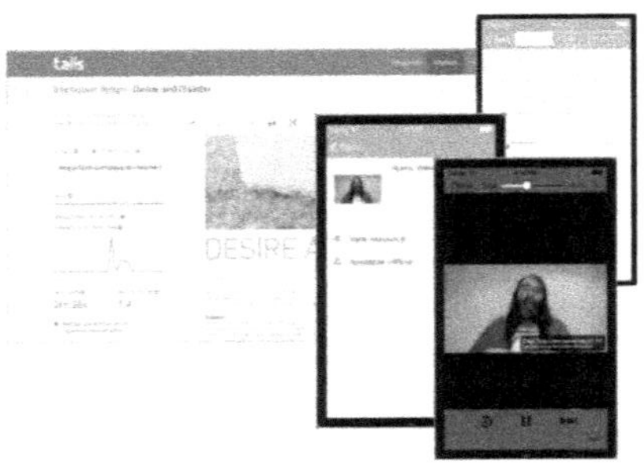

Figure 1. Universal media player, web and mobile version.

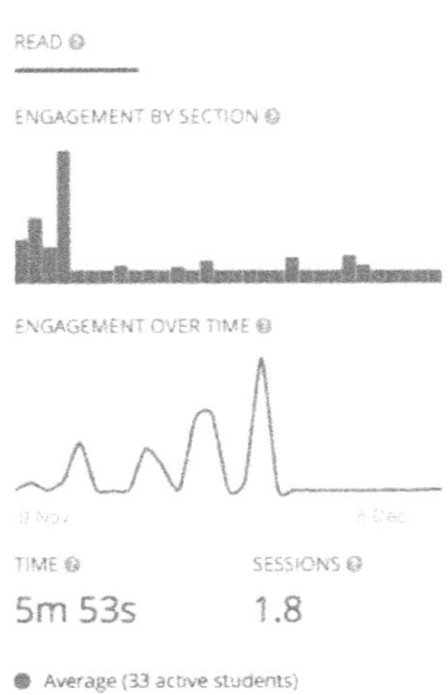

Figure 2. Document learning analytics

use the lessons learnt from large-scale learning to benefit the hundreds of millions in traditional settings.

Potential

Talis provides teaching and learning software for higher education including a reading list management module used by 86 institutions in 8 countries, including over 50% of UK universities. Currently, Talis serves nearly half a million lists with over twenty million references.

While the number of students covered by these is tiny compared to the world statistics, it is large enough to start to consider the potential for using the techniques of large-scale data. For example, it would be possible to offer textbook recommendations to educators based on usage data from other similar educators.

In addition, Talis is developing a universal media player currently under pilot in a project called Lighthouse (fig. 1). This player allows fine-grained tutor and student annotation of videos, PDF documents, etc., and also usage tracking at the level of page views within a PDF or sections within a video, not simply click-through (fig. 2). That is as well as a large volume of students, there will be highly detailed information available about each. In principle this could allow, for example, sharing of annotations between students studying the same material in different institutions, allowing new forms of peer interaction.

Challenges

However, despite the clear potential of this combination of large and fine scale, there are challenges in leveraging this volume of data to aid individual academics and students.

- *Heterogeneity of courses* – There are many different kinds of courses both within institutions and between, as well as very different teaching styles. In addition, individuals differ markedly.
- *Individuality* – In step-by-step programmed instruction, progress is easy to measure, but things are far more complex where teaching is less constrained and when individuals' patterns of reading/viewing media vary.
- *Cross-institutional issues* – When looking at data across institutions heterogeneity is increased, and additional factors arise, not least connected with privacy and ownership.

MOOCs avoid many of these challenges. By having a large number of students addressing the same material provided by the same organization it is possible to perform large-scale analysis on relatively homogeneous data and also more easily enable pedagogic elements such as peer learning.

We now look at each challenge in a little more detail.

Heterogeneity of courses

This is an issue within a single institution with many different kinds of material from lab-based work to reading focused topics, but in addition institutions vary.

Looking simply at reading list length, these range from over a thousand items for a single module to some with just a core textbook and a few additional resources. It would be tempting to see this in terms of broad subject areas such as humanities (long list) vs. sciences (core textbook). However, this would be simplistic because

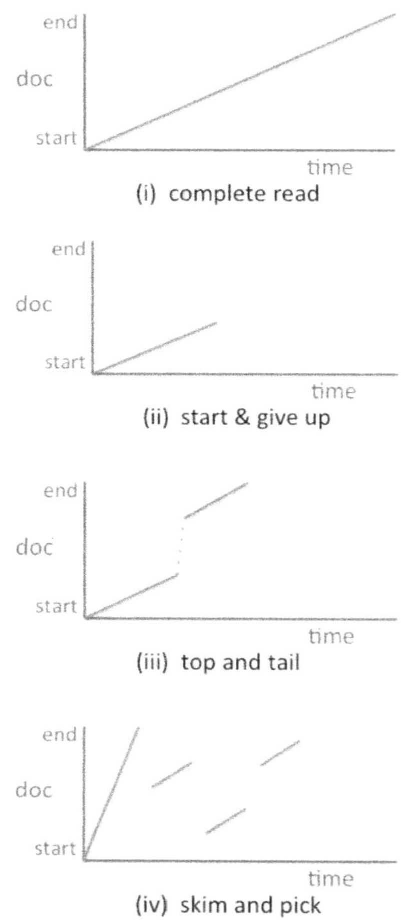

Figure 3. Patterns of document access (N.B. possible examples, not based on data analysis)

of variations within areas (e.g. a creative writing course may be 'hands on' rather than reading based) and radically different ways of teaching the same topic (e.g. theory-then-apply vs. problem-based learning). More content-based approaches are needed.

The Open University (OU) analysed module content in terms of seven kinds of activities (assimilative, finding information, communication, productive, experiential, interactive, assessment) and then looked at the relative proportions of these and created clusters [8]. The clusters turned out not to be subject based, but rather related to different teaching styles: constructivist, assessment-driven, balanced-variety, and social constructivist. Having done this they were then able to correlate these with student experience measures.

This OU analysis seems to require an initial hand categorization of activities; however, we envisage that similar analysis may be possible based on content alone, especially given different kinds of content (video, article, book, quiz).

Individuality

While the content of MOOCs is identical for large numbers of students, the students themselves vary; of course this is even more challenging when combined with heterogeneity of courses. Learning styles, of multiple kinds, have become a minor education 'industry'. While there is evidence of differences, empirical evidence of clear pedagogic value is still scant compared to other individual factors [2].

There are successful examples grouping/clustering students automatically. P2PU (Peer-to-Peer University) have used simple user profiling (principally time zone) to organize students into smaller groups [5], and Purdue 'Signals' is based on a combination of historical student data and in-course behaviour [1].

Fine-grained behavioural data offers more potential for understanding individual behaviour, but is also correspondingly more complex. The engagement graph in figure 2 shows that although a few students have read all the document, many have just read the first part; this was used by the tutor to suggest to students that even if they skip the middle of the document they should read the last section [4].

However, aggregation inevitably hides individual differences. While it would be possible to view each individual, it would also be useful to be able to classify student reading behaviours, rather like the OU have done for their modules. We have not done this yet, but fig. 3 shows the kinds of reading patterns we might expect to see.

Cross-institutional issues

Perhaps most difficult are the challenges faced because data arises from multiple institutions. This complicates both the preceding challenges, but also adds issues of privacy and ownership.

Talis encourages customers to make reading lists available with open data licences and the reading list software makes the data available in RDF linked data format, providing the beginnings of an 'education graph' linking resources across institutions [7].

However, this is content only; student usage, progress, etc., is confidential and private to the institution.

There would be potential benefits to institutions if suitably anonymised student data were combined, analysed, and the results fed back to improve individual student experience. However, not all institutions may wish to share such data out of concern for privacy of students or perceived value of the data. Furthermore, the balance of control and ownership between the institution and the student may vary depending on each institutions' policies, student agreements, and national laws. These legal and ethical problems almost certainly outweigh technical challenges.

Summary

This paper has discussed a number of challenges if large-scale learning benefits are to be brought to bear on traditional face-to-face institutions. These have been driven by the particular data available and systems developed at Talis, and our work on addressing the challenges, but the lessons are likely to apply equally to providers of VLEs and other widely used educational software.

References

1. Arnold, K. and Pistilli, M. 2012. Course signals at Purdue: using learning analytics to increase student success. In *Proc. of the 2nd International Conference on Learning Analytics and Knowledge (LAK '12)*. ACM, NY, USA, 267-270. doi:10.1145/2330601.2330666
2. Coffield, F., Moseley, D., Hall, E. and Ecclestone, K. (2004) *Learning Styles and Pedagogy in post-16 learning: a systematic and critical review*. London: Learning and Skills Research Centre http://www.lsneducation.org.uk/research/reports/
3. Davis , D. and Mackintosh, B. (eds). *Making a Difference: Australian International Education*. UNSW Press (2012)
4. Dix, A. More than one way to flip a class: learning analytics for mixed models of learning. *APT 2015*, Greenwich, 7th July 2015. http://alandix.com/academic/papers/apt2015-more-than-one-way/
5. Ewald, C. (2013). *The Mechanical MOOC – Behind the Machine*. P2PU, 15th Jan. 2013. http://info.p2pu.org/2013/01/15/the-mechanical-mooc-behind-the-machine/
6. Gibney, E. A Different World. *Times Higher Education*, January 31, 2013. https://www.timeshighereducation.com/features/a-different-world/2001128.article
7. Heath, T., Singer, R., Shabir, N., Clarke, C., and Leavesley, J. Assembling and Applying an Education Graph based on Learning Resources in Universities. *Proc. of the 2nd International Workshop on Learning and Education with the Web of Data (LiLe-2012)*, 2012. http://ceur-ws.org/Vol-840/
8. Rienties, B. Leveraging the full value of learning analytics: The power of learning design. (keynote) *LACE SoLAR Flare 2015*, OU, Milton Keynes, UK (2015). http://www.slideshare.net/laceproject/leveraging-the-full-value-of-learning-analytics-the-power-of-learning-design
9. UNESCO. *Education: Gross enrolment ratio by level of education*, UNESCO Institute of Statistics (accessed 7/1/2016) http://data.uis.unesco.org/index.aspx?queryid=142

Open-DLAs: An Open Dashboard for Learning Analytics

Ruth Cobos
University Autónoma of Madrid,
Spain
Ruth.cobos@uam.es

Ángel Lareo
University Autónoma of Madrid,
Spain
Angel.Lareo@uam.es

Silvia Gil
University Autónoma of Madrid,
Spain
Sylvia.Gil@uam.es

Francisco A. Vargas
University Autónoma of Madrid,
Spain
Fra.Vargas@estudiante.uam.es

L@S 2016, April 25–26, 2016, Edinburgh, UK.
ACM 978-1-4503-3726-7/16/04.
http://dx.doi.org/10.1145/2876034.2893430

Abstract
In this paper a learning analytics dashboard for MOOCs is proposed. It visualises the progress of learners' activity taking into account navigation, social interactions and interaction with educational resources. This approach was tested with the MOOCs created by the University Autonóma of Madrid (Spain) in the edX platform. Nowadays, the dashboard is being improved taking into account the received feedback from MOOCs instructors and assistants. Finally, a new version is presented to work along with edX and Open edX.

Author Keywords
MOOCs; Learning Analytics; Dashboard

ACM Classification Keywords
H.5.m. Information interfaces and presentation (e.g., HCI): Miscellaneous

Introduction
MOOCs (Massive Open Online Courses) are freely accessible courses delivered online for a massive set of students. Currently, MOOCs are valuable resources for getting information and learning on the Internet [4,14]. Effort and knowledge are being entrusted on them by the most prestigious universities in the world. These universities are using and developing new didactic methods and tools for education in a public and

The first MOOCs of UAM are delivered twice. First delivery started on the 24th of February in 2015, and the second one on the 6th October 2015. These courses are:

- Android301x: Programming with Android
- Quijote501x: History of Spain
- QuiOrg101x: Organic Chemistry
- TxEtj201x: Ethical issues in Organ Transplantation

Their detailed description: https://www.edx.org/school/uamx.

Next MOOCs of UAM are delivered on 1st March 2016:

- Equidad801x: Quality education for all
- Idealismo501x: Philosophical idealism
- Renal701x: Kidney Pathophysiology
- SegAlim201x: Food Security in the European Union Law

widespread format. As a result, millions of people are increasingly involved in exploring and learning new subjects.

However, the development of high-quality MOOCs requires a great effort from the people and institutions involved on it. For example, Open-access implies a high diversity of students, which makes much more complex the process of managing and evaluating them.

As a result, those who run MOOCs face the need to develop new ways to analyse and evaluate the learning processes. Learning analytics are a set of mathematical and visualization tools that use data collected from the MOOCs platform in order to allow measuring and understanding the learning conditions [3,5,11]. The goal of using learning analytics is to design and implement more effective learning experiences. These learning analytics are normally grouped at dashboards [10].

Some research works have demonstrated the utility of social network analysis (SNA) for this task [1,2]. Moreover, important research works show evidences of different student activity patterns from their interactions with educational resources as videos in MOOCs [7,9,13].

Therefore, this effort requires learning instruments that allows measuring and understanding the learning conditions [12] and such measures improve current courses and their future deliveries but they can also influence the teaching methods of formal education programs. In order to go deep in these tools and measures is necessary to define and appropriate the concept of learning analytics by each institution.

Besides that, we need easy-to-use platforms that allow instructors and teaching assistants to visualize and analyse student interactions.

We presented here a work-in-progress learning analytics dashboard, which is being developed by University Autónoma of Madrid (UAM. Spain), and in use with data collected from the MOOCs generated by UAM for edX Consortium.

Related Works

Some of the most known MOOC platforms already offer learning analytics visualizations. For instance, in the case of Open edX this service is provided by the edX Insights tool, however, its installation is troublesome (https://open.edx.org/).

Due to this lack, some groups of different institutions have developed learning analytics tools for Open edX. For instance, on the one hand, a group from the University Carlos III of Madrid (Spain) developed a learning analytics module named ANALYSE (http://www.it.uc3m.es/pedmume/ANALYSE/). And on the other hand, the University of Queensland (Australia) offers a modular system for managing MOOC research data, which is called MOOCczar (https://github.com/UQ-UQx/MOOCczar).

In the case of FutureLearn platform (https://www.futurelearn.com), University of Southampton offers a learning analytics dashboard; the UoS Dashboard, which was developed under Shiny, an R based framework and R Studio [8]. This dashboard looks at the student progress from two key perspectives: learners' social interactions and learners' performance.

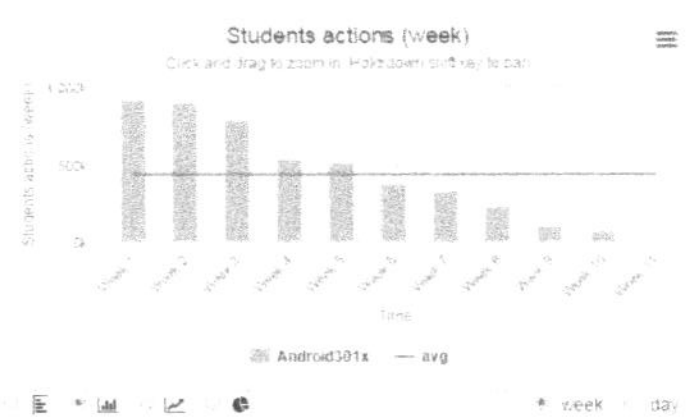

Figure 1: A sample of how OPEN-DLAs presents activity data from students.

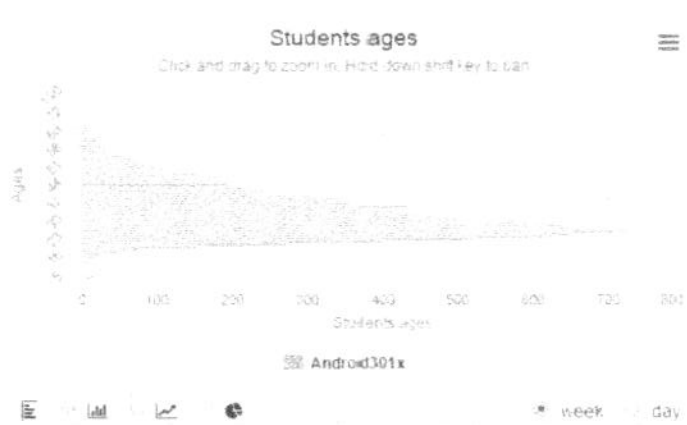

Figure 2: Another sample chart, showing a different layout (at the bottom side the layout can be modified)

Charts can be dynamically repainted by selecting a part of them, focusing on the selected fragment.

It is possible to download each chart in several formats, such as: csv file, pdf document or jpeg image.

The proposed approach: Open-DLAs

The mentioned edX Insights tool is constantly being improved by the edX Consortium. However, the University Autónoma of Madrid (UAM, http://www.uam.es) had the need to provide detailed learning analytics visualization to their Faculty during the year 2015, when the institution launched their first four MOOCs at edX, therefore a learning analytics dashboard was created by UAM called Open-DLAs [6].

Open-DLAs visualizes the progress of learners' activity per MOOC in the following sections: i) their participation in the discussions or forums, ii) their navigation among the educational resources, iii) their interactions with the videos and iv) their results or performance.

Each mentioned section provide the needed information in a sparse way. Each section is composed by a group a graphs, which can be maximized, minimized and moved to another space in the page. Moreover, each graph has the possibility of showing de information in different graph types, such as: bar chart, line chart, etc.

Nowadays, this dashboard is being improved taking into account the feedback provided by the Faculty of the mentioned MOOCs [6]. The new dashboard version would support not only edX courses, but also courses on Open edX platform. Database access would be enhanced due to a direct query system, which reduces the parsing and pre-processing made by the web administrator.

This new dashboard version is being projected as a native module to Open edX page, so the instructors and teaching assistants will not have the necessity of switch between platforms to access the analytics data. For the edX courses, since the platform doesn't allow direct connections to the database nor web site modifications, a replica database server needs to be deployed using periodically collected data dumps, in order to access seamlessly from the web application through an API.

In order to achieve full compatibility with the current platforms for data dump collection (via Amazon S3 service) and web service (via Python-based framework Django), is being intended to develop the new platform in Django, using official AWS SDK for Python (Boto3) instead of current operating system dependent scripts. Additional scripts in JavaScript are currently in use and should be refactored to work with the new platform.

Conclusions

We proposed a learning analytics dashboard, Open-DLAs, which have been tested in 2 deliveries of four MOOCs generated by the University Autónoma of Madrid (UAM) in the edX platform, providing relevant data visualization and analytics. It has assisted instructors during the MOOCs, who expressed their satisfaction for the given insights. However, as showed in this paper, their features are still being improved.

Acknowledgements

This work was possible thanks to UAMx Office. This work was partially supported by the University Autónoma of Madrid (Spain) and by the Spanish National Plan of R+D, project number TIN2014-52129-R and by the Autonomous Community of Madrid, e-Madrid project, number project S2013/ICE-2715.

References

1. Peter J Carrington, John Scott, and Stanley

Wasserman. 2005. Peter J. Carrington, John Scott and Stanley Wasserman, eds., Models and Methods in Social Network Analysis. Methods, October.

2. Iván Claros, Ruth Cobos, and César A Collazos. 2015. An Approach Based on Social Network Analysis Applied to a Collaborative Learning Experience. IEEE Transactions on Learning Technologies, (pp): 1–8. http://doi.org/10.1109/TLT.2015.2453979
3. Adam Cooper and others. 2012. What is analytics? Definition and essential characteristics. CETIS Analytics Series 1, 5: 1–10.
4. Pierre Dillenbourg, Armando Fox, Claude Kirchner, John Mitchell, and Martin Wirsing. 2014. Massive Open Online Courses: Current State and Perspectives. *Dagstuhl Manifestos*, *4*, 1: 1-27.
5. Rebecca Ferguson. 2012. Learning analytics: drivers, developments and challenges. International Journal of Technology Enhanced Learning 4, 5/6: 304–317.
6. Laura Garcia. (2015) Learning Analytics in On Line Educational Environments. Final Project. University Autónoma of Madrid. Supervisor: Ruth Cobos.
7. Juho Kim, Philip J Guo, Daniel T Seaton, Piotr Mitros, Krzysztof Z Gajos, Robert C Miller. 2014. Understanding in-video dropouts and interaction peaks in online lecture videos. In Proceedings of the first ACM conference on Learning@ scale conference: 31-40. ACM.
8. Manuel León, Ruth Cobos, Kate Dickens, Susan White, Hugh, Davis, H. Visualising the MOOC experience: a dynamic MOOC dashboard built through institutional collaboration. European MOOC Stakeholder Summit 2016 (eMOOCs 2016), Graz, Austria. 22-24 Febrero, 2016. pp. 461-470.
9. Nan Li, Lukasz Kidzinski, Patrick Jermann, and Pierre Dillenbourg. 2015. Characterising MOOC Video Behaviours with Video Interaction Styles: What do they tell? Proceedings of the 10th European Conference on Technology Enhanced Learning.
10. Kowen Pauwels, Tim Ambler, Bruce H. Clark, et al, "Dashboards as a Service: Why, What, How, and What Research Is Needed?," Journal of Service Research: JSR, 12, 2009
11. George Siemens and Ryan S. J. D. Baker. 2012. Learning analytics and educational data mining. Proceedings of the 2nd International Conference on Learning Analytics and Knowledge - LAK '12: 252. http://doi.org/10.1145/2330601.2330661
12. George Siemens and Phil Long. 2011. Penetrating the Fog: Analytics in Learning and Education. EDUCAUSE Review 46: 30–32.
13. Ahmed Yousef and Mohamed Chatti. 2014. Video-based learning :A critical analysis of the research published in 2003-2013 and future visions. eLmL 2014: The Sixth International Conference on Mobile, Hybrid and On-line Learning, 112–119.
14. Ahmed Yousef, Mohamed Amine Chatti, Ulrik Schroeder, Marold Wosnitza, and Harald Jakobs. 2015. The State of MOOCs from 2008 to 2014: A Critical Analysis and Future Visions. In Computer Supported Education. Springer, 305–327.

Profiling MOOC Course Returners: How Does Student Behavior Change Between Two Course Enrollments?

Vitomir Kovanović
School of Informatics,
University of Edinburgh
Edinburgh, United Kingdom
v.kovanovic@ed.ac.uk

James Owers
School of Informatics,
University of Edinburgh
Edinburgh, United Kingdom
james.owers@ed.ac.uk

Srećko Joksimović
Moray House School of Education,
University of Edinburgh
Edinburgh, United Kingdom
s.joksimovic@ed.ac.uk

Anne-Marie Scott
Information Services,
University of Edinburgh
Edinburgh, United Kingdom
anne-marie.scott@ed.ac.uk

Dragan Gašević
Moray House School of Education
and School of Informatics,
University of Edinburgh
Edinburgh, United Kingdom
dgasevic@acm.org

Amy Woodgate
Information Services,
University of Edinburgh
Edinburgh, United Kingdom
amy.woodgate@ed.ac.uk

L@S 2016, April 25-26, 2016, Edinburgh, Scotland UK.
ACM 978-1-4503-3726-7/16/04.
http://dx.doi.org/10.1145/2876034.2893431

Abstract
Massive Open Online Courses represent a fertile ground for examining student behavior. However, due to their openness MOOC attract a diverse body of students, for the most part, unknown to the course instructors. However, a certain number of students enroll in the same course multiple times, and there are records of their previous learning activities which might provide some useful information to course organizers before the start of the course. In this study, we examined how student behavior changes between subsequent course offerings. We identified profiles of returning students and also interesting changes in their behavior between two enrollments to the same course. Results and their implications are further discussed.

Author Keywords
MOOCs; Clustering; Learning Analytics; Student Behavior; Self-regulated learning; Educational technology use;

ACM Classification Keywords
H.3.3 Information Search and Retrieval: Clustering; K.3.1 Computer Uses in Education: Distance learning; I.6.4 Model Validation and Analysis; I.6.5 Model Development; I.5.3 Clustering;

#	Course	Offers
1	Artificial Intelligence Planning	1, 2, 3
2	Animal Behavior and Welfare	1, 2
3	AstroTech: The Science and Technology behind Astronomical Discovery	1, 2
4	Astrobiology and the Search for Extraterrestrial Life	1, 2
5	The Clinical Psychology of Children and Young People	1, 2
6	Critical Thinking in Global Challenges	1, 2, 3
7	E-learning and Digital Cultures	1, 2, 3
8	EDIVET: Do you have what it takes to be a veterinarian?	1, 2
9	Equine Nutrition	1, 2, 3
10	Introduction to Philosophy	1, 2, 3, 4
11	Warhol	1, 2

Table 1: Courses used in this study.

Introduction

One of the important characteristics of Massive Open Online Courses (MOOCs) is their complete openness to students with different learning goals, motivations, and backgrounds [2]. As such, instructors have typically very little or no information who students who enrolled in their courses are. Typically, the primary sources of information about registered students are MOOC platform demographics and pre-course surveys which are often filled out by only a small subset of all course registrants.

Besides demographic and survey data, another valuable source of information about students enrolling a particular MOOC could be obtained from their previous enrollments. With the growing number of MOOCs offered and with their multiple instances, it became common to have the same students enrolled in different MOOCs from the same institution and even enrolled to different offerings of the same course. This data could provide valuable information about students before the start of the course and can help course designers and instructors to better cater their online courses to the target population.

Not only can data from previous course offerings be used to improve course offerings, but it can also be used to study learning similarly to the repeated measurement experiments. As the selection of MOOC participants is out of the instructor's control, analysis of the data from several offerings of the same course can provide some insight into the choices student make regarding the use of the available resources, tools, and affordances.

Research Questions

Given the potentials of the MOOC data to understand learning behavior and choices about the use of available resources, tools, and technologies, we examined MOOC trace data from the students who enrolled in the same course at least twice. The primary research questions addressed in this paper are:

RQ1: *What are common behavioral profiles of students who enroll MOOCs multiple times?* This question is the first step in our analysis and it allows for examining whether there are any particular forms of MOOC engagement by the students who enroll in the same courses multiple times.

RQ2: *How do students change their behavior between subsequent offerings of the same course?* This follow-up question is a natural extension to our first question and focuses on student self-regulation of learning. Do students change something in their behavior between two offerings or they simply continue with the same form of participation as they did the first time?

Method

Dataset

The data for this study comes from the 28 offerings of the 11 different MOOCs offered by the University of Edinburgh on the Coursera platform (Table 1). In our analysis, we examined only data about students' first and second enrollment. That is, we did not analyze students who enrolled only once, and we also excluded any subsequent (i.e., third or fourth) enrollments. In total, we had 26,025 double course enrollment records (52,050 course enrollment records).

Variable	Description
Days	No. of days active
Sub.	No. of submitted assignments
Wiki	No. of wiki page views
Disc.	No. of discussion views
Posts	No. of discussion messages written
Quiz.	No. of quizzes attempted
Quiz. Uni.	No. of different quizzes attempted
Vid. Uni.	No. of different videos watched
Vid.	No. of videos watched

Table 2: Clustering variables.

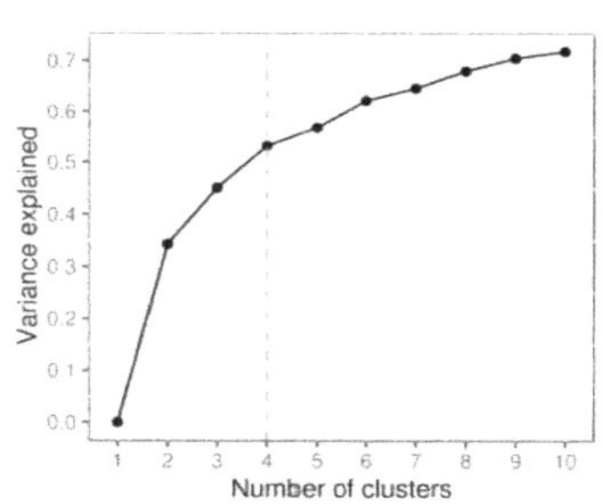

Figure 1: Variance explained by a given number of clusters

Analysis procedure
To answer our research questions, we conducted a cluster analysis of the 52,050 enrollment records using the variables listed in Table 2. As overall student activity in each course was slightly different, we first performed unitization with zero minimum (i.e., x-min/range) per each course offering, along with a z-score normalization on the whole corpus. That way we ensured that 1) specifics of each course (and each course offering) were taken into account for scaling each classification variable, and 2) all variables were on the same scale to ensure the equal importance of variables. Given that there is also a large number of students who only enrolled in courses (and have not accessed them afterward), we removed those records from our subsequent cluster analysis and assigned them a predefined "Enroll Only" cluster.

We performed K-means clustering using Lloyd's algorithm (with ten restarts and a maximum of 300 iterations) for values of K between 2 and 10 and the evaluated the percentage of variance explained by the different clustering solutions (Figure 1). We selected the K-means algorithm as the size of our dataset (52,050) was too large for analysis using some of the more sophisticated classification techniques that involve pairwise distance matrix. Finally, after identifying student clusters, we examined a transition graph between students' first and second enrollment to see what the most common cluster transitions are.

Results and Discussion

Clustering
Our results and scree plot analysis (Figure 1) revealed four clusters of student behavior in our dataset, in addition to our "Enroll Only" cluster of students who did not exhibit any course activity. In total, we identified five clusters of the behavior of returning students. The cluster centers are shown in Figure 2 while their relative sizes are shown in Table 3. These results are aligned with the previous work on online courses [3] and MOOCs [1] that showed similar disproportions between highly active and inactive students. The identified clusters (Figure 2) reveal that the largest part (85% of all enrolled students) have no or have very little course activities. Around 10% of the students focused primarily on viewing video lectures, while 4.1% of students were highly engaged and, besides watching videos, also utilized quizzes and engaged in homework assignments. Finally, less than 1% of student put an emphasis on online discussions, while being less engaged with video lectures. This cluster of students also stayed longest active in courses.

Cluster transitions
To investigate how student behavior changes between subsequent course enrollments, we constructed a directed state transition graph (Figure 3) which shows what percentage of first enrollment cluster members transferred to other clusters (or remained within the same cluster). The majority of students from all the clusters except the "Social" cluster either just enrolled in a course or had very low level of engagement. A certain number of students who utilized both video lectures and quizzes during their first enrollment either retained the same level of engagement or focused primarily on video lectures in the second course enrollment. These two patterns are likely driven by the goal of obtaining course certificate or brushing up on a particular course topic. Finally, the most interesting finding is related to the students from the "Social" cluster who had the highest level of participation in

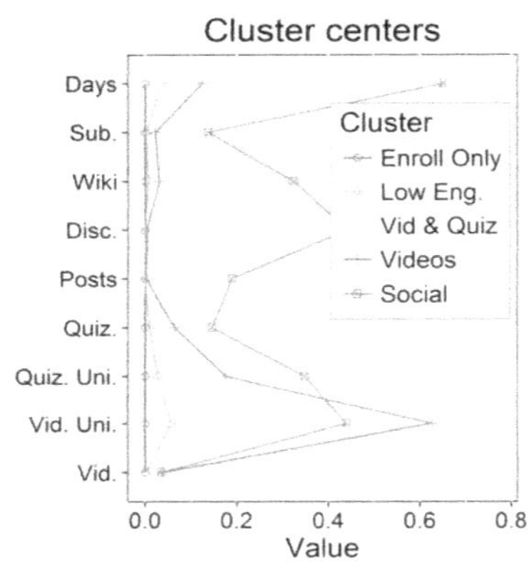

Figure 2: Cluster centers

Cluster	Students	%
Enroll Only (E)	22,932	44.1
Low Engagement (LE)	21,776	41.8
Videos & Quizzes (VQ)	2,120	4.1
Videos (V)	5,128	9.9
Social (S)	94	0.2

Table 3: Cluster sizes.

		Second enrollment				
		E	LE	VQ	V	S
First enrollment	E	.65	.28	.03	.04	.00
	LE	.43	.45	.04	.08	.00
	VQ	.35	.37	.16	.11	.00
	V	.35	.42	.08	.14	.00
	S	.21	.26	.11	.14	.28

Table 4: Cluster transitions as percentage of first enrollments.

online discussions and also most days spent in the course. While a certain number of students became disengaged in the next offer of the course, a large chunk of them (28%) kept their level of participation, signaling the goal of engaging with other learners rather than the prescribed course content.

Implications and Future Work

There are several practical implications of our findings. First, as a majority of students who were not active (or had low levels of activity) in their first enrollment were likely to stay inactive, course instructors might consider targeting those particular students with a certain set of instructional interventions which would increase their levels of participation. Similarly, students who exhibited high levels of activity in the first offer might be targeted with interventions that would encourage them to participate more in the discussions, or with interventions related to particularly challenging course content (as indicated by their quiz and assignment scores in the previous enrollment). Finally, through identification of socially engaged students, instructors might identify suitable community teaching assistants which could be then better supported by the instructional team.

Although our analysis provides interesting insights, there are still many potential areas for the future research. In particular, understanding the relationship between course participation and answers to pre-course surveys and certificate earning in the first enrollment. By answering of these important questions, we aim to enable instructors to better cater their online courses to the prospective students, and also to better understand MOOC learning in general.

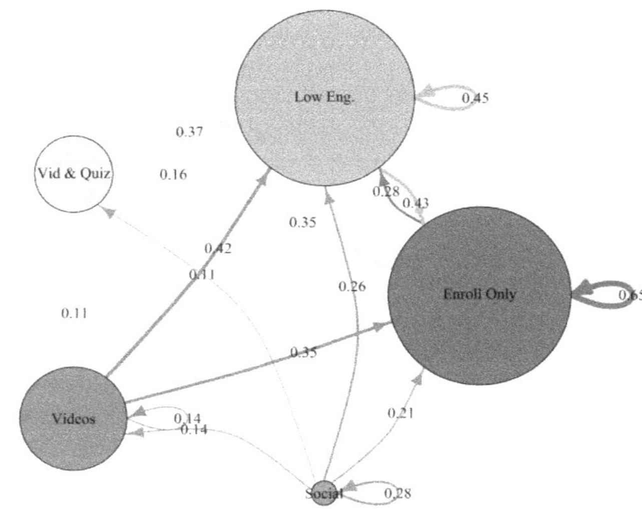

Figure 3: Cluster transition graph. Sizes of nodes represent the number of students while edge labels represent percentage of source cluster transitioning to the destination cluster

References

1. Doug Clow. 2013. MOOCs and the Funnel of Participation. *Proceedings of the Third International Conference on Learning Analytics and Knowledge*, ACM, 185–189.
2. R.F.a Kizilcec and E.b Schneider. 2015. Motivation as a lens to understand online learners: Toward data-driven design with the OLEI scale. *ACM Transactions on Computer-Human Interaction* 22, 2.
3. Vitomir Kovanović, Dragan Gašević, Srećko Joksimović, Marek Hatala, and Olusola Adesope. 2015. Analytics of communities of inquiry: Effects of learning technology use on cognitive presence in asynchronous online discussions. *The Internet and Higher Education* 27: 74–89.

Making the Production of Learning at Scale more Open and Flexible

Tina Papathoma
The Open University
Milton Keynes, MK7 6AA, UK
Tina.Papathoma@open.ac.uk

Angela Coe
The Open University
Milton Keynes, MK7 6AA, UK
Angela.Coe@open.ac.uk

Rebecca Ferguson
The Open University
Milton Keynes, MK7 6AA, UK
Rebecca.Ferguson@open.ac.uk

Allison Littlejohn
The Open University
Milton Keynes, MK7 6AA, UK
Allison.Littlejohn@open.ac.uk

L@S 2016, April 25-26, 2016, Edinburgh, Scotland, UK.
ACM 978-1-4503-3726-7/16/04.
http://dx.doi.org/10.1145/2876034.2893432

Abstract
Professional learning is a critical component of the ongoing improvement, innovation and adoption of new practices that support learning at scale. In this context, educators must learn how to apply digital technologies and work effectively in digital networks. This study examines how higher education professionals adapted their practice to enable more open and flexible work processes. A case study carried out using Activity Theory showed that teams involved in the development of a module all need access to a range of expertise both practical and academic. At each stage, they need to be clear about the learning outcomes of the module, the responsibilities of each team and its constraints. Teams need to be willing to agree ways to shift those constraints in order to develop a module effectively.

Author Keywords
Online Courses; Professional Learning; Activity Theory; Innovation; Case Study

Background
The rapid changes in society and working life that have taken place during the past few decades have increased interest in workplace learning and made lifelong learning and learning in the workplace a necessity for organisations, nations and individuals [1]. Rapid learning needs to take place in new environments such

Community	Roles
5 'Academic' members **(Module team)**	Writing module content
1 Module Chair **(Module team)**	Guiding academics & liaising with LTS
1 Curriculum manager **(Module team)**	Project management of academics ,liaising with different sections of the community
4 'Learning and Teaching Solutions' (LTS) members	Implementing innovative ways of supporting module production
3 Management members	Ensuring everyone remains on schedule

Table 1. Roles of the community

as learning at scale, not only through intentional formal training [2] such as workshops but also through learning on the job, which may not be recognised as 'learning'. Different types of knowledge require different types of learning.

'Integrative Pedagogy' provides a way of bringing together key elements of learning and the development of expertise [3]. It consists of four tightly integrated elements: theoretical knowledge (formal), practical knowledge (tacit), regulative knowledge (individuals decide how they learn) and sociocultural knowledge. The last three types of knowledge are not explicit. Learning is embodied in the development of better practices and skills as well as in the creation of social and material innovations nurtured by progressive problem solving and the intention to integrate conceptual understanding with problem solving [1].

This study explores how the professional practice of educators changes when using innovative tools to adapt the process of authoring an online module. The study's research questions relate to professionals' use of digital tools in online education, the importance of learning on the job, and integrative pedagogy.

- How does the professional practice of a module team at a university change when module production becomes more open and allows flexibility?
- What are the enablers and the barriers to those changes?

Methodology

A case study was conducted within an Open University (OU) module team. The team deals with learning at scale, using systems that are structured to deal with thousands of learners and hundreds of educators, so change usually takes time. The aim of the study was to explore and trial new ways of producing module content (i.e. course content) and examine how the professional practice of a team changes when there is more flexibility in ways of working together with access to innovative tools for module design. A case study design was used because it enabled researchers to answer explanatory questions about contemporary events without manipulating behaviour [4].

The unit of analysis for the study was the activity system of a community of people (see Table 1) contributing towards an advanced level (equivalent to final-year undergraduate) Science Module requiring 600 study hours. This case was chosen because the conventional method of module production had been disrupted, prompting the professionals to change their practice. They authored content directly on an open online platform, whereas the previous practice had been to use a word processor and then pass content to colleagues for multiple editing phases.

The study used the terms of Activity Theory (AT) in order to identify and analyse changes in practice associated with the production of the online module. According to AT, human activities are complex, socially situated phenomena. A key idea is that activities are outcome-oriented and driven by project goals and motives related to past experience. There may be multiple motives within an activity system as subjects negotiate the relationship of their motives with the emergent motives of the community. Such differing motives produce tensions in the activity system [5].

Past	Present
Linear, Asynchronous, Fragmented , Individual process	Dynamic, Synchronous, Transparent, Collaborative process
Limited view of module development	Holistic view
Ideas forgotten	Ideas captured
Deadlines lost	Work grows dynamically
Academics were more passive	Academics were active
Management found process difficult to monitor	Management could monitor the process more easily

Table 2. Changes in Practice

The components and relationships of the activity system represent the situation in which members (**subjects** i.e. the module team) work on an **object** (i.e. module production) or problem space, transforming it into an **outcome** (i.e. change of professional practice) using **tools** (i.e. open platform). The tool-mediated action may be constrained or enabled by implicit and explicit **rules** (i.e. university regulations and faculty guidelines related to university standards) and the broader social context (**community** i.e. the teams represented in Table 1.) within which the activity takes place. **Labour** (i.e. the tasks of the module team) is divided among the community members (**roles**).

Sample

As shown in Table 1, the module team of this study consisted of the Academics, the Module Chair and the Curriculum manager. The focus is on this team because the module team, and especially the academics within it, had taken more central roles in the module production and this changed the activity of the system and the motives not only of the module team but also of the rest of the community.

Three groups (academics, management, 'Learning and Teaching Solutions' group) and two individuals – the Module Chair (lead academic) and Curriculum Manager – made up different sections of the Activity Systems' community and were interviewed in order to identify the changes in the motives of each team in their setting. There was a focus on how action is mediated with the use of new tools. The study followed the ethical guidelines of the British Educational Research Association (BERA).

Analysis

Thematic analysis [6] was used to identify the components and relationships of the 'activity system' community. The transcribed text of interviews was coded using codes from the activity system – object, tools, rules and division of labour. Emergent themes were added to these, including 'roles' of the community (subtly related to division of labour) and 'tensions' between roles and rules of the activity system. NVivo was used to study how interviewees talked about the changes in practice associated with the new models of production, with an emphasis on aspects that enabled or hindered these changes.

This analysis revealed changes in professional practice between conventional module development (past) and the new process (present). These are summarised in Table 2. Enablers and barriers to changes in practice are summarised in Table 3.

Discussion

The change of practice was an evolutionary process for the module team. It gave them opportunities to learn on the job, rather than through formal training, and to gain skills quickly.

The study provided insights into improved practices that could be used by teams developing learning at scale using new tools and approaches. Meeting new challenges helped community members to develop collaborative skills. The open platform that the teams used, provoked tensions between the Academic grouping and the LTS grouping, because historically LTS had had more control of the final product than the Academics and the new roles on the platform were not clearly defined.

Enablers to change
-Efficient, less time-consuming process -Production timeline as a form of currency -Affective impact of freedom from systematic constraints (rules). Rules changed- from 'system control' to 'people control' -The open platform enhanced creativity
Barriers to change
-Negative impact of LTS role change & disagreement on end product & demotivation -Achievement of change of practice overlooked -Process still termed 'module production'& entrenches cultural expectations -Tensions negotiated within single teams - Trust broke down when project timeline changed & teams went back to previous practice -ownership of innovation unclear

Table 3. Enablers & Barriers

Using the terms of activity theory, the study found that a community needs to have access to a range of expertise associated with the object in order to reach the outcome. The outcome, the division of labour and the rules should all be clearly defined. The community needs to be prepared to change or amend the rules during the activity in order to reach an effective outcome.

In other words, teams contributing to the development of a course or module need to have access to a variety of practical and academic expertise. They should also be clear about the learning goals of the module, the responsibilities of each team, and its constraints. Teams need to work together on ways to deal with constraints in order to reach an effective outcome. This is challenging, because practices involving huge systems, structured to deal with large numbers of learners and educators take time to change.

Conclusion

Higher education is changing as it increasingly uses digital technologies to provide courses and therefore professionals in this area need to change their practice. This initial exploratory case study provides insights that can benefit teams who need to change their practice and work more flexibly in order to develop learning at scale. In particular, it identifies a need to define and make clear to everyone the intended outcome of module development, the division of labour and the constraints on the process. The findings of the study will inform further research into learning at scale and the ways in which large numbers of people can collaborate to create online courses and shift their practice from a face-to-face to an online environment.

Acknowledgments

We thank Doug Clow who provided helpful comments on versions of this document. We also thank Sam Smidt, Anne Jelfs, Sarah Bridgman and all the interviewees.

References

1. Päivi Tynjälä. 2008. Perspectives into Learning at the Workplace. *Educational Research* Review, 3:130–154.
2. Michael Eraut, Wendy Hirsh. 2007. *The Significance of Workplace Learning for Individuals, Groups and Organisations*. Skope Monographs, Oxford.
3. Päivi Tynjälä, David Gijbels. 2012. Changing World: Changing Pedagogy. In *Transitions and Transformations in Learning and Education,* Päivi Tynjälä, Marja-Leena Stenström, Marjatta Saarnivaara (Eds). Springer, 205–222.
4. Robert K. Yin. 2003. *Case Study Research: Design and Methods* 3rd ed., Sage Publications, Newbury Park.
5. Yrjö Engeström. 2005. Knotworking to create collaborative intentionality capital in fluid organizational fields. In *Collaborative Capital: Creating Intangible Value.* Michael M. Beyerlein, Susan T. Beyerlein, Frances A. Kennedy (Eds.) Elsevier, Amsterdam, 307–336.
6. Victoria Braun, Virginia Clarke 2006. Using thematic analysis in psychology. *Qualitative Research in Psychology*, 3,2: 77–101

Browser Language Preferences as a Metric for Identifying ESL Speakers in MOOCs

Judith Uchidiuno
HCI Institute
Carnegie Mellon University
Pittsburgh, PA 15213 USA
jio@cs.cmu.edu

Evelyn Yarzebinski
HCI Institute
Carnegie Mellon University
Pittsburgh, PA 15213 USA
eey2@cs.cmu.edu

Amy Ogan
HCI Institute
Carnegie Mellon University
Pittsburgh, PA 15213 USA
aeo@andrew.cmu.edu

Jessica Hammer
HCI Institute
Carnegie Mellon University
Pittsburgh, PA 15213 USA
hammerj@cs.cmu.edu

Kenneth R. Koedinger
HCI Institute
Carnegie Mellon University
Pittsburgh, PA 15213 USA
koedinger@cs.cmu.edu

L@S 2016, April 25-26, 2016, Edinburgh, Scotland UK
ACM 978-1-4503-3726-7/16/04.
http://dx.doi.org/10.1145/2876034.2893433

Abstract
Open access and low cost make Massively Open Online Courses (MOOCs) an attractive learning platform for students all over the world. However, the majority of MOOCs are deployed in English, which can pose an accessibility problem for students with English as a Second Language (ESL). In order to design appropriate interventions for ESL speakers, it is important to correctly identify these students using a method that is scalable to the high number of MOOC enrollees. Our findings suggest that a new metric, browser language preference, may be better than the commonly-used IP address for inferring whether or not a student is ESL.

Author Keywords
Foreign Language Students; MOOC Accessibility

Introduction
Massively Open Online Courses (MOOCs) are revolutionizing higher education by making college-level courses available to anyone in the world with an internet connection. This open access is proving successful – the average MOOC has about 43,000 students enrolled [3] with a vast percentage of these enrollees from non-English speaking countries [2]. Given the international audience that MOOCs attract, there is a potential accessibility issue for students with

English as a Second Language (ESL), as the majority of MOOC courses are offered in the English language[1].

Many interventions are possible to support ESL students in MOOCs, such as contextual dictionary support, closed captioning, and connecting them with language-diverse peers. However, in order to deploy these interventions, we must be able to reliably identify ESL students at scale. Current practice is to assume learners speak the dominant language in the country indicated by the IP address from which they access the MOOC [2,4,6]. While this method can identify many ESL speakers correctly, it will misidentify ESL speakers who currently live in English speaking countries – in the US alone, over 20% of the population speaks a language other than English at home [5]. This metric also misidentifies English-proficient students who live in non-English speaking countries.

There is another readily available metric to infer a student's language abilities – all popular web browsers allow individuals to set the languages in which they prefer to view their web pages. This metric is based on students' personal preferences rather than simply their location, yet does not require self-report or access to survey responses which learners may not return. To evaluate the potential of this metric, we analyzed video interaction logs of students enrolled in an MOOC deployed on the Coursera platform. Based on prior literature showing ESL students' relative difficulty comprehending spoken English [1], we expect that these students will interact differently with MOOC videos compared to native English speakers; we expect that they will experience more difficulty with videos, as demonstrated by increased pausing and replaying. We analyze the video interaction behavior for native English speaking and ESL students as identified by IP address, and again for native English speaking and ESL students as identified by browser language preference. We then evaluate which metric better captures the expected differences in video interaction behavior between English-native and ESL learners.

Empirical Evaluation and Results

We analyzed video interaction logs of 905 students who enrolled in and completed a 12-week Psychology MOOC course. We analyzed the number of times they pressed the play and pause buttons, changed the speed of the video ("rate change"), and the number of times their video stalled as a result of buffering and bandwidth issues ("stall"), across all videos in the course. Similar to [4], we determined if students were categorized as English speakers (by IP) if their IP address was associated with a country where English is spoken[2]. Otherwise, the student was categorized as ESL. To determine students' ESL status by browser language, students were categorized as English speakers if their most-preferred browser language was English, and as ESL if it was any other language.

We determined the students' ESL status using each of the two metrics, and analyzed the results using our expectation of finding behavioral differences in video use between English-native and ESL learners to evaluate the goodness of these metrics. Of the 905 students, 34.97% were flagged as ESL by their browser language preference, while 38.64% were flagged as ESL based on their IP address. The ESL status for 77.5% of students matched across both metrics.

[1] https://www.mooc-list.com /languages

[2] https://www.cia.gov/library/publications/the-world-factbook/fields/2098.html

	English N=473; 67.4%	ESL N=228; 33.1%
Avg. Play Count	151.05	183.55
Avg. Pause Count	134.12	181.57

Table 1. Average play/pause count when ESL status based on IP and Browser match; 77.5% of total N

	English N=120; 59%	ESL N=84; 41%
Avg. Play Count	132.03	253.71
Avg. Pause Count	111.59	236.04

Table 2. Average play/pause count when IP_ESL ≠ Browser_ESL, showing ESL based on browser; 22.5% of total N

Figure 1 shows a comparison of the video feature use (play, pause, rate change, and stall) of English speaking to ESL students when categorized by their IP address. A one-way ANOVA was run to determine if there were significant differences in the behavior of the students between the two groups.

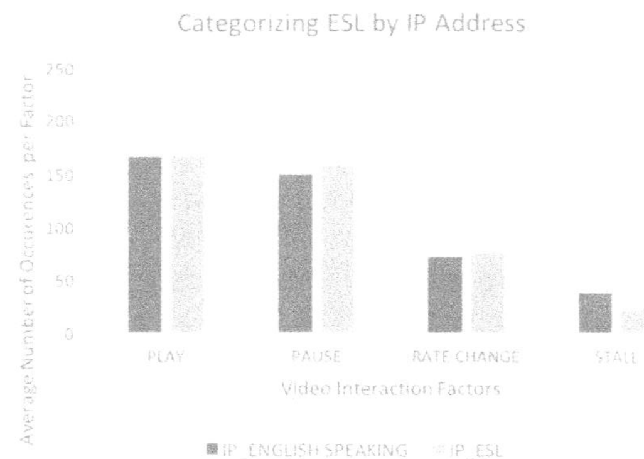

Figure 1: Average Number of Occurrences of Video Interaction Features with ESL Metric of IP Address

Our results show that there were no significant differences in the play count (F(1)=0.001, p=0.975), pause count (F(1)=0.127, p=0.722), rate change count (F(1)=0.107, p=0.744), and stall count (F(1)=2.009, p=0.157). In other words, when students' ESL status was determined based on IP address, there were no significant differences in the video interaction behavior of English speaking students, and foreign language students.

Figure 2 shows the same factors with ESL status determined by browser language preference. Results of a one-way ANOVA shows that ESL students are pressing the play button (F(1)=6.406, p=0.0115), and the pause button (F(1)=8.191, p=0.00431) significantly more than English speaking students, as expected from prior literature. There were no significant differences observed on the rate change count (F(1)=0.089, p=0.765) or the stall count (F(1)=0.773, p=0.379). In other words, when ESL status was determined by the browser language preference, those identified as ESL students are more likely to interact differently with MOOC videos (increased pausing and replaying) than those identified as English-speaking students. It is important to note that since there was no significant difference in stall count, these effects are not a result of bandwidth or buffering issues.

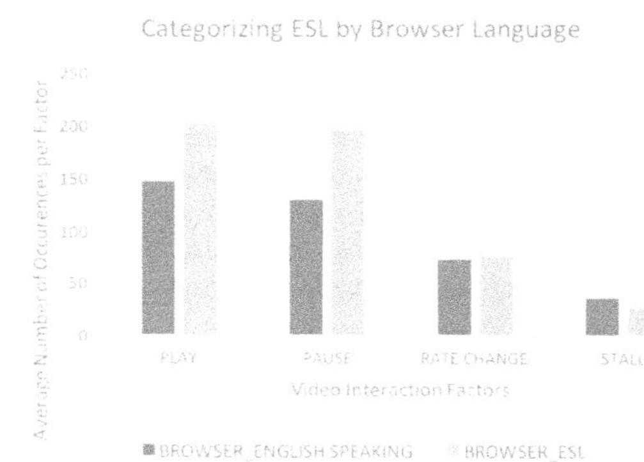

Figure 2: Avg. Number of Occurrences of Video Interaction Features with ESL Metric of Browser Language Preference

Table 1 shows the average play/pause count for the 77.5% of the cases where both metrics (IP and browser) matched in identifying students as ESL or English speaking. The average play/pause count is similar to the results shown in Figure 2 – ESL students are pressing play and pause more than English speaking students. Table 2 shows the play/pause count for the 22.5% of cases where the students' browser language and IP address differ, displayed by browser classification; it, too, is consistent with the results in Figure 2, with ESL students pressing pause and play more. This means that with the inverse classification, by IP address, students identified as English speaking pause and replay more than students identified as ESL. When browser language and IP address data conflict, inferring students' language abilities based on their browser preferences appears to identify English-speaking and ESL students better than classifying by IP address.

Conclusion

In our research study, we assessed the use of two metrics for ESL identification by evaluating video interactions of students in a MOOC course. We show that when ESL students are identified using the popular method of IP address tracking, their video interaction behaviors are very similar to English-speaking students, which does not support well-established research findings that foreign language students struggle significantly with comprehending spoken language. Our findings show instead that inferring students' language abilities from their web browser language preferences more accurately predicts their video usage, a proxy for ESL status. Although there may be some students who set English as their preferred language (even if they are not a native speaker), they may already be proficient enough to not need additional language support. We believe this finding will more quickly and accurately classify ESL and native English speakers, and will allow MOOC providers to design and accurately deliver more appropriate interventions for each group.

Acknowledgements

We thank Google for their support in this and related research through a Google Focus Award.

References

1. Anna Ching-Shyang Chang and John Read. 2006. The Effects of Listening Support on the Listening Performance of EFL Learners. *TESOL Quarterly* 40, 2: 375–397.
2. Jennifer DeBoer, Glenda S. Stump, Daniel Seaton, and Lori Breslow. 2013. Diversity in MOOC students' backgrounds and behaviors in relationship to performance in 6.002 x. *Proceedings of the Sixth Learning International Networks Consortium Conference.*
3. Gregory Ferenstein. Study: Massive Online Courses Enroll An Average Of 43,000 Students, 10% Completion. *TechCrunch*. http://social.techcrunch.com/2014/03/03/study-massive-online-courses-enroll-an-average-of-43000-students-10-completion/
4. Philip J. Guo and Katharina Reinecke. Demographic Differences in How Students Navigate Through MOOCs. *L@S 2014, March 4–5, 2014.*
5. US Census Bureau Public Information Office. New Census Bureau Report Analyzes Nation's Linguistic Diversity - American Community Survey (ACS) - Newsroom - U.S. Census Bureau. https://www.census.gov/newsroom/releases/archives/american_community_survey_acs/cb10-cn58.html
6. Daniel T. Seaton, Sergiy Nesterko, Tommy Mullaney, Justin Reich, Andrew Ho, and Isaac Chuang. 2014. Characterizing video use in the catalogue of MITx MOOCs. *Proceedings of the European MOOC Stakeholders Summit. Lausan: PAU Education*: 140–146.

An Investigation of the Effects of Online Test Strategy on Students' Learning Behaviors

Tzu Chi Yang
Academia Sinica
No 128, Academia Road, Section 2
Nankang, Taipei 115, Taiwan
tcyang.academic@gmail.com

Dai Ling Shih
National Taiwan University
No 1, Roosevelt Road, Section 4
Taipei City 106, Taiwan.
clementine249@msn.com

Meng Chang Chen
Academia Sinica
No 128, Academia Road, Section 2
Nankang, Taipei 115, Taiwan
mcc@iis.sinica.edu.tw

L@S 2016, April 25–26, 2016, Edinburgh, UK.
ACM 978-1-4503-3726-7/16/04.
DOI: http://dx.doi.org/10.1145/2876034.2893434

Abstract
Online tests have been identified as a core learning activity. Unlike conventional online tests, which cannot completely reflect students' learning status, two-tier tests not only consider students' answers, but also take into account reasons for their answers. Thus, research into a two-tier test had mushroomed but few studies examined why the two-tier test approach was effective. To this end, we conducted an empirical study, where a lag sequential analysis was used to analyze behavior patterns. The results indicated students with the two-tier test demonstrated different behaviors which develop "breadth to depth" and "depth to breadth" strategies.

Author Keywords
Learning Behavior; Online Test; Lag Sequential Analysis

Introduction
In past decades, the importance of online test has been well recognized. Most of the online test is presented with multiple-choice questions (MCQ), which are easy to conduct. However, it is not sufficient to use the multiple-choice questions only to diagnose students' learning problems. For example, Researcher [1] highlighted that university students were able to select correct answers but they often did not know why they were doing what they were doing. The multiple-choice questions might not reflect the actually learning status

Two-tier test: The two-tier test consists of a set of two-level multiple choice questions. The first tier assesses students' descriptive or factual knowledge of the phenomenon to be assessed while the second tier investigates the reasons for their choices made in the first tier.

Lag Sequential Analysis: The LSA was firstly introduced by Bakeman and Gottman [5], which showed the effectiveness of the LSA in discovering human behaviors.

Significant level of LSA: The z-score value of each sequence was calculated to determine whether the continuity of each one reached the level of significance and a z-value greater than +1.96 indicates that a sequence reaches the level of significance ($p<0.05$)

of the students. To this end, researchers (e.g., [2]) attempted to make some improvement and they recognized that such improvement should not only emphasize on a student's progress of reasoning for answering questions, but also should keep efficiency of multiple-choice questions. In this vein, a two-tier test (2T) strategy was proposed. The two-tier test approach is widely employed in educational settings, e.g. [3]. However, previous studies mainly emphasize on the outcomes of using the two-tier test. Paucity of research investigates why the two-tier test offers such benefits. Thus, there is a need to conduct comprehensive investigation to examine the students' learning process in such online test environment. With this regard, the Lag Sequential Analysis (LSA) has been recognized as a promising approach, which can examine sequential relationships between each learning behavior based on a statistical theory. Recently, an increasing number of studies have applied the LSA to analyze behavior happening in educational settings, e.g., [4]. In this vein, the LSA was applied to analyze how learners with a 2T test environment and those with a conventional MCQ test environment behave differently. In summary, the study presented in this paper aims to provide a deep understanding of the influences of the two-tier test. To achieve this aim, the research question is investigated in this study is that how students with a two-tier test and those with a conventional MCQ test behave differently. To answer this research question, we developed an online test system, the effectiveness of which was evaluated by conducting an empirical study. In the empirical study, a LSA was applied to analyze students' learning behaviors recorded in a log-file.

DEVELOPMENT OF AN ONLINE TEST SYSTEM

The web-based learning system system accommodates two kinds of test: (1) conventional multiple-choice questions selected from the test item bank; and (2) a two-tier test, in which every test item had three or four choices in the first tier, followed by three or four reasons for each choice in the second tier. Figure 1 and Figure 2 show an example of a MCQ test item and that of a two-tier test item, respectively. Moreover, the system provides a list of recommended topics for students to review based on their weaknesses while the system provides students with learning materials synchronized with those delivered in lectures based on their learning status.

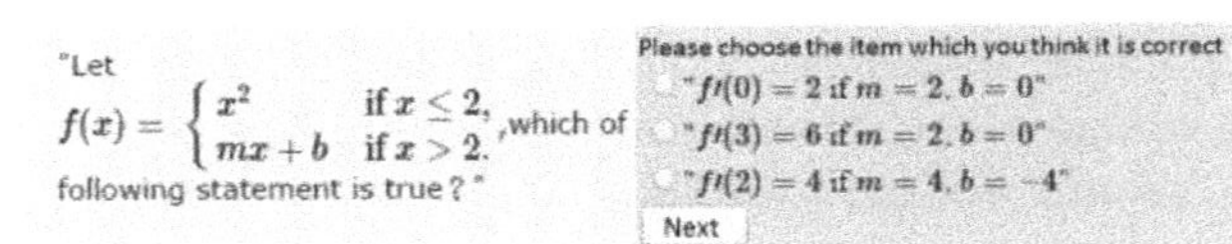

Figure 1: An example of a conventional MCQ test item.

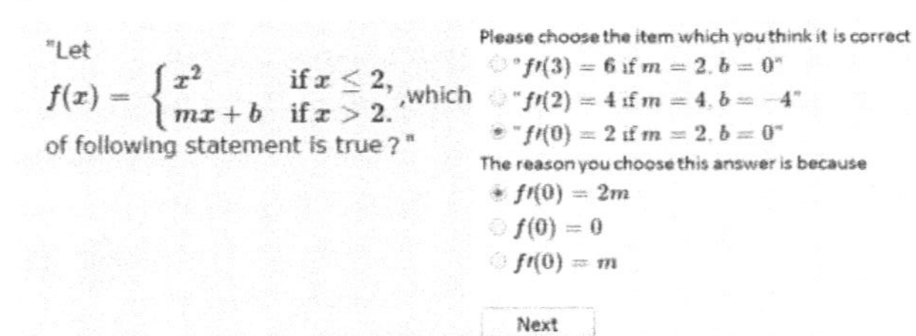

Figure 2: An example of a two-tier test item.

EXPERIMENT DESIGN

We conducted an empirical study, where students' learning processing data (i.e., log-file) were collected. The pre-test and post-test were designed to assess the

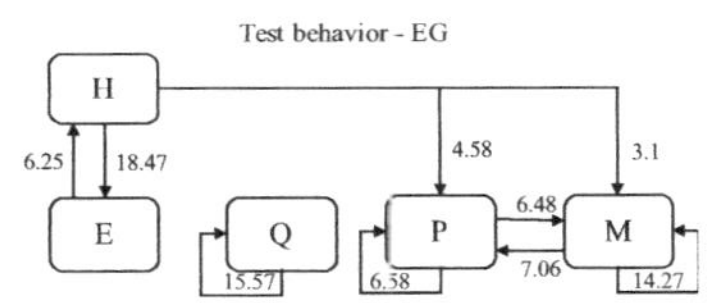

Figure 3: The behavioral transition diagram of taking test of the EG

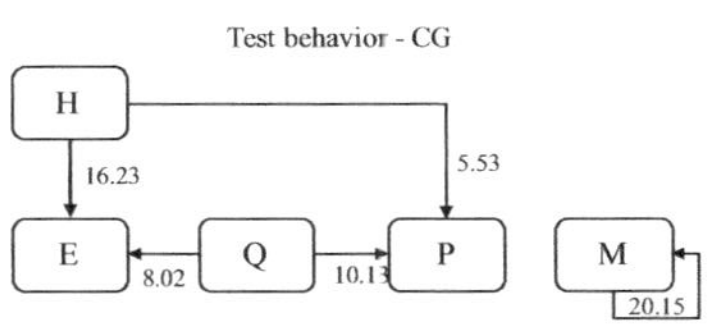

Figure 4: The behavioral transition diagram of taking test of the CG

participants' learning achievement both before and after using the proposed learning system. A total of 43 university students participated in this experiment. They were randomly divided into an experiment group (EG) with N=22 and a control group (CG) with N=21. Both groups were asked to take regular tests via the system after each lecture was delivered. They would interact with the system at least once per week. The students in the EG used the 2T while those in the control group used the MCQ test. After taking tests, both groups were given correct answers and explanations for the rationale of the correct answers. Besides, they were allowed to browse the same learning materials and take the same test again. The learning activity was conducted for six weeks for both groups and their interactions were recorded in a log database.

Behavior	Codes	Description
Login	H	To login into the system
Take a regular test	E	To take a test related to current lecture
Retake a same test	Q	To retake the latest test
Take a unit test	P	To retake a test which they took before
Take a summary test	M	To take a test that includes every topic they learnt.

Table 1: Coding schema of online test behaviors

RESULTS AND DISCUSSION

The learning achievement of the EG and that of the CG were compared with an ANCOVA, where the pre-test score was considered as the covariant. The result shows that the EG significantly performed better than the CG (F=4.79). Furthermore, the effect size (Cohen's d) is 0.56, which suggests that the proposed 2T test has medium effects on the learning achievement. Accordingly, we investigate how students with the 2T and those with the MCQ test behave differently. To deal with this issue, a LSA was applied to analyze students' behavior patterns.

Different behaviors

The individual behavior of the 43 participants was coded using the coding scheme, which included five kinds of codes (Table 1). According to the rationale of the LSA. The EG and CG also demonstrated some different behaviors. The CG demonstrated significant behavior sequences (Figure 3), i.e., Q→E indicated that the CG often took the regular test after repeating to take the same test. The Q→P showed that they also tended to take the unit test after repeating to take the same test. Such behavior patterns implied that the CG tended to take various types of test, including the regular tests and unit tests. The results might be due to the fact that the CG considered tests as a kind of practice. On the contrary, the EG showed different behavior sequences (Figure 4), i.e., Q→Q and P→P. The behavior sequence Q→Q indicated that the EG often focused on taking tests within a same scope and the behavior sequence P→P revealed that they were also keen to repeatedly take a unit test within a specific topic. Such findings suggested that the EG tended to focus on a single type of test, instead of taking multiple tests. Such result may suggested that the EG would like to review what they had learnt and confirmed if they had a clear understanding of the subject content so they repeated to take the same test. In addition, the behavior pattern M↔P, which revealed EG has a two way behavior sequence on taking summary test unit test. The behavior sequence M→P showed that they often took the unit test immediately after taking the summary test. On the other hand, the behavior sequence P→M indicated that students tended to take the summary test after he/she took a unit test. The former refers to a "breadth to depth" strategy while the latter refers to a "depth to breadth" strategy. In other words, the EG took two types of strategy. However, either the "breadth to depth" strategy or the "depth to breadth" strategy was not happened for the CG. The aforementioned results suggest that the EG had a good plan to undertake the online tests. They use the online tests not only to practice what they have learnt, but also to diagnose their learning problems and address their weaknesses. This may be explain why EG tended to take the summary test immediately (H→M).

CONCLUSION

As the aforementioned, this study investigates "how students with a two-tier test and those with a conventional MCQ test behave differently". To answer the research question, the learning achievement, sequential behavior patterns are considered. Regarding learning achievement, our results show that students' achievement is improved. Regarding behavior patterns, the findings from this study revealed that the students with the two-tier test approach and those with the conventional MCQ test showed some similar behavior but there were some differences between them. An interesting finding is that the EG developed the "breadth to depth" and "depth to breadth" strategies while such strategies were not discovered in the CG. With regard to methodology, this study analyzed the experimental data with a LSA approach. Such approach is useful to investigate what behave students learning (e.g., learning behavior patterns). However, it was a relatively small study. Further work needs to be undertaken with a larger sample to provide additional evidence.

Acknowledgment

The authors would like to thank the Ministry of Science and Technology of the Republic of China, Taiwan, for financial support (MOST104-2221-E-001-007-MY3)

References

1. Sealey, V. 2014. A framework for characterizing student understanding of Riemann sums and definite integrals. *The Journal of Mathematical Behavior* 33: 230-245.

2. Treagust, D. F. 1988. Development and use of diagnostic tests to evaluate students' misconceptions in science. *International Journal of Science Education* 10, 2: 159-169.

3. Peşman, H., and Eryılmaz, A. 2010. Development of a Three-Tier Test to Assess Misconceptions About Simple Electric Circuits. *The Journal of Educational Research* 103, 3: 208-222.

4. Lin, P. C., Hou, H. T., Wu, S. Y. and Chang. K. E. 2014. Exploring College Students' Cognitive Processing Patterns during a Collaborative Problem-solving Teaching Activity Integrating Facebook Discussion and Simulation Tools. *The Internet and Higher Education* 33: 51-56.

5. Bakeman, R., and Gottman, J. M. 1997. *Observing interaction: An introduction to sequential analysis. (2nd ed.).* Cambridge University Press, UK.

TAPS: A MOSS Extension for Detecting Software Plagiarism at Scale

Dana Sheahen
Georgia Institute of Technology
Atlanta, GA, USA
danasheahen@gatech.edu

David Joyner
Georgia Institute of Technology
Atlanta, GA, USA
david.joyner@gatech.edu

L@S 2016, April 25-26, 2016, Edinburgh, Scotland UK.
ACM 978-1-4503-3726-7/16/04.
http://dx.doi.org/10.1145/2876034.2893435

Abstract
Cheating in computer science classes can damage the reputation of institutions and their students. It is therefore essential to routinely authenticate student submissions with available software plagiarism detection algorithms such as Measure of Software Similarity (MOSS). Scaling this task for large classes where assignments are repeated each semester adds complexity and increases the instructor workload. The MOSS Tool for Addressing Plagiarism at Scale (MOSS-TAPS), organizes the MOSS submission task in courses that repeat coding assignments. In a recent use-case in the Online Master of Science in Computer Science (OMSCS) program at the Georgia Institute of Technology, the instructor time spent was reduced from 50 hours to only 10 minutes using the managed submission tool design presented here. MOSS-TAPS provides persistent configuration, supports a mixture of software languages and file organizations, and is implemented in pure Java for cross-platform compatibility.

Author Keywords
Software plagiarism; MOSS; cheating; academic integrity.

Introduction

Plagiarism in computer science classes can damage the reputation of institutions and their students. It is a problem that must be addressed by instructors to preserve the integrity of awarded class credit, particularly for an accredited degree program such as the Online Master of Science in Computer Science (OMSCS) program at Georgia Tech. However, as the number of students increases and as classes and assignments are repeated from semester to semester, more assignments must be cross-checked with an ever-increasing pool of previous submissions using available software plagiarism detection algorithms such as Measure of Software Similarity (MOSS) [1]. Even if the rate of plagiarism remains constant, detection at a larger scale becomes unwieldy without persistent workflow plans and straightforward management tools.

The MOSS Tool for Addressing Plagiarism at Scale (MOSS-TAPS) repackages and organizes submissions for plagiarism detection for courses that repeat a coding design assignment from semester to semester.

Need

Why check for software plagiarism?

Cheating in computer science classes in the form of software plagiarism exists at an estimated incidence rate of 10% or more [2] per assignment. It is therefore essential to routinely authenticate software submissions from students to expose dishonesty, deter future problems, and to assure students that their honest efforts are not undermined by students that copy previous solutions.

Classes in the OMSCS at Georgia Tech have the same concerns in this regard as any on-campus program, with the added complication of a larger scale, i.e. more students, more assignments to check, more combinations to cross-check.

Challenge

Current tools

MOSS-TAPS specifically submits assignments to MOSS, one of the most effective software plagiarism detection algorithms available [4] [5], and currently offered as a free (for non-commercial use) web service executed on Stanford University servers. To test for software plagiarism using MOSS, an instructor submits a batch of individual student code directories, also called the corpus, to MOSS servers using a PERL script provided by MOSS, and receives, as a result, pairwise similarity percentages and counts via a web page. The results must then be analyzed and "suspicious pairs" reviewed individually. MOSS provides ordering of the results by highest similarity (most suspicious), with additional links for each pair to color-coded webpages for review.

Use-case example

A recent example of the challenges faced in this process occurred in the CS7637 Knowledge Based Artificial Intelligence (KBAI) course at Georgia Tech [3]. The class includes three or four open-ended coding projects that students must complete. The online version of the class averages 200-400 students; 1400 students have taken the course through spring 2016, with an 80% completion rate.

As the pool of past participants increases, so does the pool of correct solutions. In order to fully check for plagiarism in a current class, it is necessary to compare not only the current submissions against each other, but

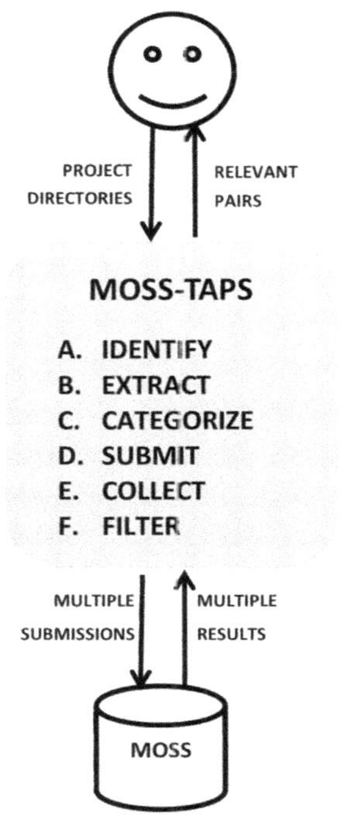

Figure 1: MOSS-TAPS provides management of multiple language submissions, arbitrary directory depths, multiple project iteration submissions, and results filtering.

all previous assignment submissions against the current submissions.

In the summer 2015 KBAI class, its third iteration, the submission management problem became quite cumbersome as 400 current projects were checked against each other as well as 500 previous ones. In particular, the instructor identified the following challenges to the process:

- Mixed Languages: This particular class allows student choice of Python or Java implementations, so all of these assignments required separation by the instructor before submission to MOSS.
- File Management: The student online submission scheme included zip files and multiple depths of directories that had to be expanded and normalized by the instructor before submission to MOSS.
- Filtering: The projects were checked against previous semester projects, but the matches found among previous projects needed to be manually ignored. Additionally, the projects were checked against previous assignments that the projects built upon within the semester, but matches to the same student needed to be manually ignored.
- Cross-platform: The PERL script provided for MOSS did not work on a Windows machine and had to be submitted with Linux. An available Windows version was unable to handle the number of files required.

Design Solution

The design approach to solving these challenges is to require the instructor to store each past project collection in one directory ("Corpus") and each current semester project in another ("Current"). The tool is responsible for finding the actual source code files under each student's submission, organizing and submitting the files to MOSS, and filtering the results so that only relevant comparisons are viewed.

Configuration and Mixed Language Support
The basic MOSS submission requires the user to specify a software language, MOSS user ID, and some optional parameters. MOSS-TAPS addresses these configuration setups persistently through default settings and a configuration file. In addition, MOSS-TAPS allows a mixture of software language submissions for a single project. This supports the case where a software coding assignment allows students to choose which language he/she wishes to use for implementation.

File Management of Submissions
MOSS-TAPS supports a file structure that includes unique student directories of any depth located immediately under a project directories. MOSS-TAPS searches each student directory for relevant source files, unzips any compressed files or directories, and packs the files for submission. This removes the necessity of manually putting all the nested, same-language, packaged files from a complex project in a single directory or requiring a particular directory structure arrangement from students.

Filtering
The result provided by MOSS is an ordered list of comparison pair links presented on a webpage. MOSS-TAPS filters the list on the webpage to exclude comparisons within previous projects and between a student and his or her own previous assignments. The results are provided as comma delimited files for each of the software languages identified.

Cross-Platform Support

The basic MOSS script is guaranteed to work in UNIX, but not necessarily on other platforms. The MOSS site provides links to a number of unofficial open source 3rd party alternatives for socket management of the MOSS server protocol. One such is MOJI [6], an unofficial Java client for MOSS. MOSS-TAPS incorporates MOJI to interface with the MOSS server. MOJI and MOSS-TAPS are pure Java, and provide cross-platform support.

Results

In the summer 2015 KBAI class example provided above, the instructor spent 50 hours organizing, submitting, and filtering the class assignments for the purpose of software plagiarism detection. For the fall 2015 iteration of the class, the instructor spent only 10 minutes on the submission process with this tool design, even though an additional semester's previous results were added to the corpus. The time savings and ease of submission gained ensure that this necessary step in the instructor's grading workflow can be incorporated smoothly even with large numbers of assignments.

Open Source and Future Enhancements

MOSS-TAPS was inspired and designed to solve particular use-cases for classes at the Georgia Institute of Technology. There are a number of enhancements and additional use-cases that can be built on and expanded from MOSS-TAPS going forward. MOSS-TAPS is a true Work-in-Progress and is provided as an open source solution hosted publicly on GitHub at https://github.com/danainschool/moss-taps .

Acknowledgements

This work was completed in a class offered in the Georgia Tech OMSCS program, supported by the Georgia Tech College of Computing, Udacity, Inc., Georgia Tech Professional Education, and AT&T. We are grateful to all members of these organizations that played critical roles in developing this program and allowing this research to take place. We would like to thank Education Technology mentor Ken Brooks for his continued support and encouragement in this endeavor as well.

References

1. Alex Aiken. 2014. Moss - A System for Detecting Software Plagiarism. Retrieved January 8, 2016 from https://theory.stanford.edu/~aiken/moss/
2. Charlie Daly and Jane Horgan. 2005. Patterns of plagiarism. *SIGCSE Bull.* 37, 1 (February 2005), 383-387.
3. Ashok Goel and David Joyner. 2014. CS7637: Knowledge-Based AI:Cognitive Systems [Online Course]. Retrieved January 8, 2016 from https://www.udacity.com/course/knowledge-based-ai-cognitive-systems--ud409
4. T. Lancaster and F. Culwin. 2004. A comparison of source code plagiarism detection engines. *Computer Science Education*, 14, 2, 101-112.
5. Divya Luke, Divya P.S., Sony Johnson, and Elizabeth Varghese. 2014. Software Plagiarism Detection Techniques: A Comparative Study. International Journal of Computer Science and Information Technologies. *International Journal of Computer Science and Information Technologies.* 5020-5024.
6. Bjoern Zielke. 2014. MOJI unofficial Java client for Moss [gitHub]. Retrieved January 8, 2016 from https://github.com/nordicway/moji

A Queueing Network Model for Spaced Repetition

Siddharth Reddy
Dept. of Computer Science,
Cornell University
Ithaca, NY 14850, USA
sgr45@cornell.edu

Igor Labutov
Dept. of Electrical and
Computer Engineering, Cornell
University
Ithaca, NY 14850, USA
iil4@cornell.edu

Siddhartha Banerjee
School of Operations Research
and Information Engineering,
Cornell University
Ithaca, NY 14850, USA
sbanerjee@cornell.edu

L@S 2016, April 25–26, 2016, Edinburgh, UK.
ACM 978-1-4503-3726-7/16/04.
http://dx.doi.org/10.1145/2876034.2893436

Abstract
Flashcards are a popular study tool for exploiting the spacing effect – the phenomenon in which periodic, spaced review of educational content improves long-term retention. The Leitner system is a simple heuristic algorithm for scheduling reviews such that forgotten items are reviewed more frequently than recalled items. We propose a formalization of the Leitner system as a queueing network model, and formulate optimal review scheduling as a throughput-maximization problem. Through simulations and theoretical analysis, we find that the Leitner Queue Network (LQN) model has desirable properties and gives insight into general principles for spaced repetition.

Author Keywords
Spaced Repetition; Flashcard Scheduling

Introduction
The ability to retain a large number of new ideas in memory is an essential component of human learning. In recent times, there has been a growing body of work that attempts to 'engineer' this process – creating tools that enhance the learning process by building on the scientific understanding of human memory. Flashcards are one such tool that use the idea of *spaced repetition* to overcome the human 'forgetting curve'. Though they have been

around for a while in the physical form, a new generation of spaced repetition software such as SuperMemo [9], Anki [4], and Mnemosyne [1] allow a much greater degree of control and monitoring of the process. As these software applications grow popular, there is a need for formal models for reasoning about and optimizing their operations. In this work, we use ideas from queueing theory to develop such a formal model for one of the simplest and most popular spaced repetition systems: the Leitner system.

Related Work

The exponential forgetting curve, which was first studied by Ebbinghaus in 1885 [3], models the probability of recalling an item as a function of the time elapsed since previous review and memory 'strength'. The exact nature of how strength evolves as a function of the number of reviews, length of review intervals, etc. is not clear, though a general *spacing effect* in which spaced reviews lead to greater strength than massed reviews (cramming) has been observed [2]. Recent studies have proposed more sophisticated probabilistic models of learning and forgetting [8, 6]. In our queueing model, we assume the exponential forgetting curve and a simple model of memory strength.

Novikoff et al. have proposed a theoretical framework for spaced repetition [7] that assumes strict spacing constraints and considers items to be identical. They propose deterministic algorithms for satisfying different spacing constraints, and examine the rate at which new items can be presented to different types of students using these algorithms. We improve upon their ideas by posing the throughput-maximization problem as an optimization problem that incorporates the user's review frequency budget and non-identical item difficulties.

Memory Model

The probability of a student recalling an item is as follows.

$$\mathbb{P}[\text{recall}] = \exp\left(-\theta \cdot d/s\right)$$

where θ is the item difficulty, d is time elapsed since previous review, and s is memory strength. In the queueing model, we will assume that memory strength s is equal to the position of the deck that the item is currently in. We have performed preliminary experiments on large-scale log data from the popular Mnemosyne spaced repetition software that validate this probabilistic model of memory.

Queueing Network Model

Leitner System

The Leitner system is a heuristic for prioritizing items for review. After the user sees an item for the first time, it enters the system at deck 1. Each deck is a first-in-first-out queue, and when the user requests an item to review, the system randomly chooses a deck i, and shows the user the item at the top of deck i. If the user forgets the item, it is added to the bottom of deck $i-1$. If the user recalls the item, it is added to the bottom of deck $i+1$. The key idea is that when the system randomly chooses a deck, it places more weight on lower decks than higher decks, so the user spends more time working on new and difficult items, and less time on items that are almost mastered. A user might work on items from deck 1 every day, deck 2 every other day, deck 3 every week, deck 4 every month, etc. One of our main contributions is a principled method for selecting deck review frequencies to maximize the rate at which items are mastered while respecting the user's review budget.

Leitner Queue Network

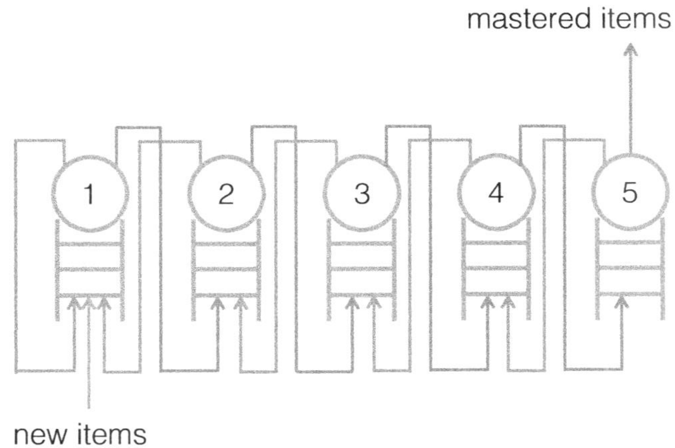

Figure 1: A diagram depicting the routing of items between queues in the network model (where the number of queues is $n = 5$). Green arrows indicate transitions that occur when an item is recalled, and red arrows indicate transitions for forgotten items.

Consider a network of n inter-connected M/M/1 queues [5], as in Figure 1. New items arrive into deck 1 according to a Poisson process with rate λ_{ext}. The routing probability matrix is P, where $P_{ij} = \mathbb{P}[\text{recall} \mid s = i, \cdot]$ when $i < n \wedge j = i + 1$, $P_{ij} = 1 - \mathbb{P}[\text{recall} \mid s = i, \cdot]$ when $(i > 1 \wedge j = i - 1) \vee i = j = 1$, and $P_{ij} = 0$ otherwise.

Items exit the system from deck n with probability $\mathbb{P}[\text{recall} \mid s = n, \cdot]$. The service rate for deck i is indicated by μ_i, and the user's work rate budget (e.g., the maximum number of items the user can review per day) is given by U. This network of queues is a *Jackson network*, and can be treated as a continuous-time Markov chain. Thus, we can characterize the steady state of the system using flow-balance equations and queue length stability conditions. We are interested in finding μ_i that maximize the steady-state throughput of the system such that the budget constraint $\sum_{i=1}^{n} \mu_i \leq U$ is satisfied. Formally, we must solve the following *static planning problem*.

$$
\begin{array}{lll}
\text{maximize} & \lambda_{ext} & \\
\text{subject to} & \sum_{i=1}^{n} \mu_i \leq U & \\
 & \lambda_{ext} + P_{11}\lambda_1 + P_{21}\lambda_2 = \lambda_1 & \\
 & P_{12}\lambda_1 + P_{32}\lambda_3 = \lambda_2 & \\
 & \vdots & \\
 & P_{n-1,n}\lambda_{n-1} + P_{nn}\lambda_n = \lambda_n & \\
 & \mu_i, \lambda_i \geq 0 & \forall i \\
 & \lambda_i < \mu_i & \forall i
\end{array}
$$

We can use an application of Jensen's inequality and the closed-form expected delay in a Jackson network to turn this into a tractable nonlinear optimization problem, and use a solver (e.g., IP-OPT) to find the optimal deck review rates μ_i^*. The algorithm for selecting the next item to present to the user is simple: sample deck i with probability $\frac{\mu_i}{\sum_{i=1}^{n} \mu_i}$, and select the item at the top of the sampled deck.

The vanilla model assumes a global item difficulty θ. We can easily extend the model to handle item-specific difficulties θ_i by creating parallel copies of the queueing system for different discretized difficulties, and enforcing joint budget constraint on the parallel systems.

Experiments

Exploring throughput-optimal review policies, we observe several intuitive results (e.g., the user should review lower decks more frequently than higher decks), as well as the following non-obvious results: (1) expected delay between consecutive reviews *increases* as an item moves up through the system – this is desirable behavior, since there is support in the experimental psychology literature for expanding intervals between repetitions [2]; (2) for small item difficulty, the user should spend a roughly uniform amount of time on each deck, but for large item difficulty, the user should spend more time on lower decks than higher decks; (3) maximum throughput λ_{ext}^* seems to be a convex function of review budget U, which implies *increasing* returns to user effort.

We simulated the queueing system and verified that a phase transition occurs when the arrival rate of new items exceeds the maximum throughput predicted by the Leitner Queue Network model: throughput decreases sharply for arrival rates greater than the predicted threshold.

Conclusion

We have proposed the first formalization of the Leitner system, which can be used to help spaced repetition software developers and users calibrate review schedules to achieve learning goals under a budget. Simple topological properties of our queueing network model lead to desirable properties in review schedules (e.g., expanding delays between reviews), and the model can be easily extended to handle realistic scenarios (e.g., non-identical item difficulties). Jupyter notebooks for running our experiments – as well as a full paper describing recent results – are available online at http://siddharth.io/leitnerq.

Acknowledgements

This work was funded in part by the Cornell Presidential Research Scholars Program, and a grant from the John Templeton Foundation provided through the Metaknowledge Network at the University of Chicago.

References

[1] The mnemosyne project. http://mnemosyne-proj.org, 2006.

[2] Cepeda, N. J., Pashler, H., Vul, E., Wixted, J. T., and Rohrer, D. Distributed practice in verbal recall tasks: A review and quantitative synthesis. *Psychological bulletin 132*, 3 (2006), 354.

[3] Ebbinghaus, H. *Memory: A contribution to experimental psychology*. No. 3. University Microfilms, 1913.

[4] Elmes, D. Anki. http://ankisrs.net, 2015.

[5] Kendall, D. G. Stochastic processes occurring in the theory of queues and their analysis by the method of the imbedded markov chain. *The Annals of Mathematical Statistics* (1953), 338–354.

[6] Lindsey, R. V., Shroyer, J. D., Pashler, H., and Mozer, M. C. Improving students' long-term knowledge retention through personalized review. *Psychological science 25*, 3 (2014), 639–647.

[7] Novikoff, T. P., Kleinberg, J. M., and Strogatz, S. H. Education of a model student. *Proceedings of the National Academy of Sciences 109*, 6 (2012), 1868–1873.

[8] Pashler, H., Cepeda, N., Lindsey, R. V., Vul, E., and Mozer, M. C. Predicting the optimal spacing of study: A multiscale context model of memory. In *Advances in neural information processing systems* (2009), 1321–1329.

[9] Wozniak, P., and Gorzelanczyk, E. J. Optimization of repetition spacing in the practice of learning. *Acta neurobiologiae experimentalis 54* (1994), 59–59.

Promoting Student Engagement in MOOCs

Jiye Baek
Boston University
595 Commonwealth Avenue,
Boston, MA 02215
jiyebaek@bu.edu

Jesse Shore
Boston University
595 Commonwealth Avenue,
Boston, MA 02215
jccs@bu.edu

Abstract
MOOCs offer valuable learning experiences to students from all around the world. In addition to providing filmed lectures, readings, and problem sets, many MOOCs allow students to ask and answer questions about course materials with each other through interactive user forums. However, in current MOOCs, only 3 to 5 percent of those students interact in the user forum (Breslow 2013, Rosé et al. 2014) and more than 90 percent of students stop attending the course altogether (Jordan 2014). According to prior studies, this low level of social engagement in MOOCs may lead to student attrition and low performance (Ren et al. 2007). Hence, a natural question that arises then is, how can we promote interaction among students in MOOC discussion forums in order to reduce students' attrition and raise their performance? In this paper, we conduct a field experiment on the edX platform to identify factors that promote student engagement in MOOC discussion forums. Researchers have discovered that the number of people interacting in one online location (e.g. group, community or virtual classroom size) is a key characteristic mediating user engagement (Butler et. al 2014), and most prior works have shown that users in a smaller size group participate more per person. However, contrary to prior research, our results show that the students in larger size cohorts interact more per person and that this greater interaction in turn increases student retention and performance.

L@S 2016, April 25–26, 2016, Edinburgh, UK.
ACM 978-1-4503-3726-7/16/04.
DOI: http://dx.doi.org/10.1145/2876034.2893437

Introduction
Massive Open Online Courses (MOOCs) have been growing rapidly in recent years and offer valuable learning experiences to students. Nevertheless, despite all the potential, MOOCs are suffering from extremely high attrition rates where more than 90% of students drop out of the course. (Jordan 2014). In addition to the high attrition rates, MOOCs are also suffering from low interaction and participation rate in the discussion forum. For example, only 3-5% of users interact in the current MOOCs (Breslow 2013, Rosé et al. 2014). Why do so many people not interact with each other and drop out of MOOCs and how can we solve this?

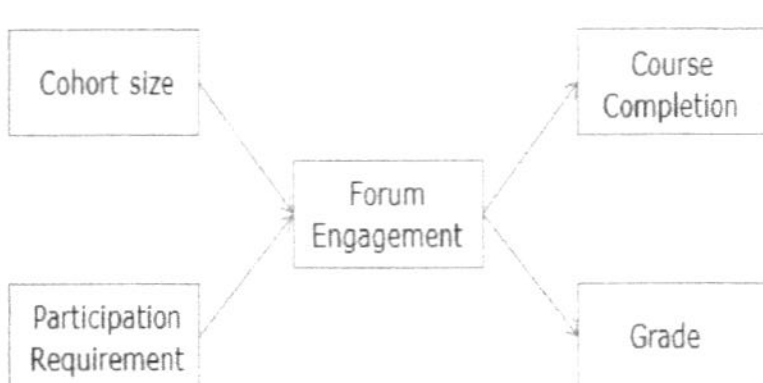

Figure 1. Abstract mental model

Online communities rely on member interaction to generate community sustainability by increasing member retention (Levine and Moreland 1998; Ren et al. 2007). Over the past few years, researchers have discovered that group size (the number of people interacting in one online location) is one of the key characteristics mediating the sustainability of online communities such as Q & A sites or online learning sites (Butler et. al 2014). However, there exist theoretical debates on how large the group size should be for better social interaction and member retention.

One stream of research has shown that for members' continued interaction, the group should be small enough to provide manageable communications (Wasko and Faraj 2005). Known as "social loafing" (Latane et al., 1979) or the "bystander effect" (Darley and Latane, 1968), prior research has shown that in limited group size, members tend to contribute more time and energy to interact with others because they feel responsibility to provide desired benefits to the group and this will increase member retention (Butler 2001). Despite the large amount of evidence on this stream of research, most studies were conducted on the context of task team, where there is a common goal to achieve. However, online discussion community, such as MOOC's discussion forum, normally does not have explicit common goal. Members of discussion community rather have common interest and share the knowledge through communication hence, further investigation is needed in this context.

Resource-based theory explains better about this online discussion community context. It suggests that, whether traditional or online, social groups are sustainable by retaining members only if they have access to enough resources that allow them to provide benefits for their members (Butler 2001). When group members are a primary source of resources as in discussion community, the size of a group indicates resource availability and the number of possible interactions rather increases exponentially with the group size. However, not only there is little empirical evidence on this, but also, according to Butler (2001), these positive effects of size expected to have a greater effect on member attraction, while member's continued social engagement might be more affected by the problems such as free-riding or social loafing.

Here, we seek to reconcile these differing perspectives with a study of a field experiment on a real course on a MOOC platform. In this experiment, we test the effect of different cohort sizes on students' engagement in MOOC discussion forums, and in turn, on student retention and grade. In addition to the cohort size, we also test the effect of an expressed participation requirement of participation on students' engagement, on which not many MOOCs or online communities are applying but most offline-classrooms have been applied (see figure 1).

Method

We conduct a 2x2 over 1x3 design (as table 1) field experiment in Boston University's 'Sabermetrics 101' course offered on edX which has been started on July 7th (2015) and run for 10 weeks. One week before it started, the course had an enrollment of 6,000 students. With these students, we design 3-way treatment on cohort size (125 vs. 500 vs. 2,000) and 2-way treatments of whether or not forum participation is a requirement. 6,000 students were randomly assigned into these 5 treatment groups as in table 1. Every student who enrolled after the one week before the course starts went into one default cohort.

	Group "S" 125 people/cohort (small: "classroom")	**Group "M"** 500 people/cohort (medium:"community")	**Group "L"** 2000 people/cohort (large: "crowd")
Group "A" Forum participation **NOT** a requirement	Group SA 8 cohorts (n=1000)	Group MA 2 cohorts (n=1000)	Group LA 1 cohort (n=2000)
Group "B" Forum participation **IS** a requirement	Group SB 8 cohorts (n=1000)	Group MB 2 cohorts (n=1000)	NA

Table 1. Experirnent design

Throughout the course, students receive prompts reminding them of their discussion cohort size and participation requirement condition via email and message on the courseware page. In a treatment group where the participation is a requirement, students are notified that the instructor will be requiring students to post to the discussion forum as part of their grade while students in non-treatment group do not get those instructions.

As a result, each student is in one and only one cohort. Once the course begins, on the discussion page, each student can only see his or her own cohort-specific discussion forum. This cohort-specific discussion forum is only for students' in-cohort discussion and they cannot see other cohorts' discussion pages at all even though the students know that there exists other cohorts. Additionally, to provide students with a consistent experience throughout the course run, we do not change a student's cohort after the course begins, so we can interpret the results clearly. All cohorts have access to the same course materials.

There are three dependent variables in our model as in figure 1; forum engagement, grade and course completion rate. In this study, forum engagement was calculated by the number of posts including questions and comments that a student had been made. Grade is an average grade of assignment, quiz and final exam. Course completion rate is the number of completed quizzes and assignments divided by the total number of quizzes and assignments. We also conduct the online survey on the final exam day. However, the response rate was extremely low (11% for those who ever used discussion forum).

Results and Discussion

Students are nested within cohorts, so there is variability not only between individual students but also between cohorts. Therefore, our analysis is primarily via random effects models.

Effect of cohort size (small, medium and large) on DVs
Surprisingly, the students in the larger cohorts show higher forum engagement per person controlling for verified status, whether verified or audited, gender and college graduation status. The odds of posting (forum engagement) in medium size cohorts (size of 500 cohorts) and small size cohorts (size of 125 cohorts) are 0.65 (***) times and 0.57 (***) times what they are in the large size cohorts (size of 2000 cohorts). The odds of posting in the small size cohorts are 0.87(***) times what they are in the medium size cohorts. The forum engagement has a positive effect on grade and course completion while we don't see any direct effect of cohort size on grade and course completion.

These results contradict prior organizational and educational research (Blatchford and Mortimore, 1994; Finn et al., 2003) that the people in a smaller group interact and make contribution more per person and achieve higher performance. In our study, the larger size cohort rather induces more students' continued engagement on the discussion forum. This suggests that MOOCs platforms may work like crowdsourcing site such as Github, Quora or TopCoder – where crowd matters because large number of users coming from diverse backgrounds, bringing to bear different experiences – are going to offer a greater variety and depth of resources for the problem-solving process (Kozinets et al., 2008; Boudreau and Lakhani, 2013).

Then, how does this MOOCs discussion forum different from other online communities, hence, the results contradict the prior research on group size? In the survey, students in larger cohorts answered that they felt more comfortable to write on the forum. This may due to the characteristics of a learning platform where students feel less embarrassment to ask question when they can observe many others doing the same thing. Less embarrassment makes students more comfortable to write on the forum, in turns, let them participate more. However, for the survey results, we need to consider that the response rate was extremely low.

Effect of participation requirement on DVs
For the participation requirement's effect, we can see a positive effect of participation requirement on forum engagement and the forum engagement has a positive effect on grade and course completion. Participation requirement also has a direct effect on grade and completion rate controlling for the cohort size.

Other results
Additionally, students who had active intentions to complete the course (verified track) achieved higher forum engagement, grade and completion rate than those who had not. Also, the students who did well in the course are people who took the course for their own enrichment after they've graduated from college. Gender had no effects.

In summary, in this study, we showed that it is possible to increase interaction among students by the design choices. Students in larger cohorts interact more per person in MOOCs platform, in turns, increase retention and performance. In addition, students who are required to participate also interact more per person in MOOCs platform, in turns, increase retention and performance. This study provides initial understanding of student engagement in MOOCs platform.

References

1. Blatchford, P., & Mortimore, P. (1994). The issue of class size for young children in schools: what can we learn from research?. *Oxford Review of Education*, 20(4), 411-428.
2. Boudreau, K. J., & Lakhani, K. R. (2013). Using the crowd as an innovation partner. *Harvard business review*, 91(4), 60-69.
3. Breslow, L., Pritchard, D. E., DeBoer, J., Stump, G. S., Ho, A. D., & Seaton, D. T. (2013). Studying learning in the worldwide classroom: Research into edX's first MOOC. *Research & Practice in Assessment*, *8*(1), 13-25.
4. Butler, B. S. (2001). Membership size, communication activity, and sustainability: A resource-based model of online social structures. *Information systems research*, 12(4), 346-362.
5. Butler, B. S., Bateman, P. J., Gray, P. H., & Diamant, E. I. (2014). An attraction-selection-attrition theory of online community size and resilience. *Mis Quarterly*, 38(3), 699-728.
6. Darley, J. M., & Latane, B. (1968). Bystander intervention in emergencies: diffusion of responsibility. *Journal of personality and social psychology*, 8(4p1), 377.
7. Finn, J. D., Pannozzo, G. M., & Achilles, C. M. (2003). The "why's" of class size: Student behavior in small classes. *Review of Educational Research*, 73(3), 321-368
8. Jordan, K. (2014). Initial trends in enrolment and completion of massive open online courses. *The International Review Of Research In Open And Distributed Learning,* 15(1).
9. Kozinets, R. V., Hemetsberger, A., & Schau, H. J. (2008). The wisdom of consumer crowds collective innovation in the age of networked marketing.*Journal of Macromarketing*, 28(4), 339-354.
10. Latane, B., Williams, K., & Harkins, S. (1979). Many hands make light the work: The causes and consequences of social loafing. *Journal of personality and social psychology*, 37(6), 822.
11. Levine, J. M., and R. L. Moreland 1998 'Small groups' in The handbook of social psychology. D. T. Gilbert, S. T. Fiske and G. Lindzey (eds). 415–469. Boston: McGraw-Hill.
12. Ren, Y., Kraut, R., & Kiesler, S. (2007). Applying common identity and bond theory to design of online communities. *Organization studies*, 28(3), 377-408.
13. Rosé, C. P., Carlson, R., Yang, D., Wen, M., Resnick, L., Goldman, P., & Sherer, J. (2014, March). Social factors that contribute to attrition in moocs. In *Proceedings of the first ACM conference on Learning@ scale conference* (pp. 197-198). ACM.
14. Wasko, M. M., & Faraj, S. (2005). Why should I share? Examining social capital and knowledge contribution in electronic networks of practice. *MIS quarterly*, 35-57

Exploring the Effects of Lightweight Social Incentives on Learner Performance in MOOCs

Katherine Brady
Vanderbilt University
Electrical Engineering and Computer Science
katherine.a.brady@vanderbilt.edu

Douglas Fisher
Vanderbilt University
Electrical Engineering and Computer Science
douglas.h.fisher@vanderbilt.edu

Gayathri Narasimham
Vanderbilt University
Vanderbilt Institute for Digital Learning
gayathri.narasimham@vanderbilt.edu

L@S 2016, April 25–26, 2016, Edinburgh, UK.
ACM 978-1-4503-3726-7/16/04.
http://dx.doi.org/10.1145/2876034.2893438

Abstract
We are exploring the effects of social incentives and motivation on learner performance in a massive open online course. In the preliminary study that we report here, we asked learners if they wanted to be considered for a community TAship in a subsequent offering of the course, if they finished in the top 20% of those who completed the current course instance. We prompted students near the beginning of the course and in the middle of the course. This prompt appears to have had a significant, albeit small effect on learner completion when given early in the course. The prompt had no significant effect when given later in the course. We also discuss our plans to follow-up this study.

Author Keywords
Incentives, Completion, Community TAs

ACM Classification Keywords
K.3.1 [Computer Uses in Education]: Distance learning

Introduction
Massive open online classes (MOOCs) have high drop out rates. Wilkowski et al. (2014) found, in one MOOC, that only 25% of students who claimed they wanted to earn a certificate actually earned one. [4].

Examining MOOC attrition rates, Clow noted that the steep decline in participation mirrored that found on social media websites [1]. This steep drop off is well known in marketing circles as "The Funnel of Participation". Clow hypothesised that the open nature of MOOCs – the ease of entry and the ease of exiting – which is similar to social media, was largely to blame. He noted that courses for online universities, presumably somewhere between traditional classrooms and MOOCs in terms of openness, have higher attrition rates than traditional classes but lower drop-out rates than MOOCs. These findings are also consistent with Clow's hypothesis that attrition and ease of exit/entry are linked.

There is evidence that the ease of exiting a MOOC can be curtailed by introducing more social accountability. An analysis of student motivation surveys across several courses by Kizilcec and Schneider in 2015 found that having a friend take the course was more predictive of earning a certificate than wanting a certificate at the beginning of the course [2]. Yang et al. had a similar finding in 2013. They examined the forums to observe the drop-out patterns of all students (not just those who respond to surveys). They found that students who became engaged with other students in forums performed better in a MOOC than those who did not [5].

This leaves us with the challenge of introducing social accountability for all students. Krause and Williams found that retention in a MOOC was improved by making the course more game like. Adding the social element of competing against other students further increased retention [3]. Our study examines whether similar results can be achieved without redesigning the entire course.

Method

We hypothesised that students would do better if they were given a social motivation. Our case study was the third offering of an introductory programming MOOC (Introduction to Programming with MATLAB by Ledeczi, Fitzpatrick, and Tairas; Vanderbilt University). In all offerings, this course had active volunteers called community TAs. These volunteers were often thanked profusely for their contributions on the forums. They clearly had high social status. Moreover, in the post course survey for the first offering, many students indicated interest in becoming community TAs for future offerings.

We constructed the following message to send to students in two experimental groups of the third offering.

> If you complete this course in the top 20% of those who complete, would you like to be considered for a Community TAship in a subsequent offering of the course? Your response to this question is optional, and your response, if any, will have no effect on your score in the course.

The experiment included all students who signed up for the third offering at least a day before the first assignment was due. For the first round of the experiment, we partitioned students into two equal size groups. Each group received equal numbers of signature track students. The experimental group (n=7257) received an email with the message above on the day before the first assignment was due. They were given a link to respond to the question on the Coursera platform.

After the deadlines for the first two assignments passed, we ran a second round of the experiment. Students from the first control group (n=7258), who had completed both assignments (n=593) were divided evenly into experimental and control groups. A diagram showing the groups for the two experiments is shown in figure 1.

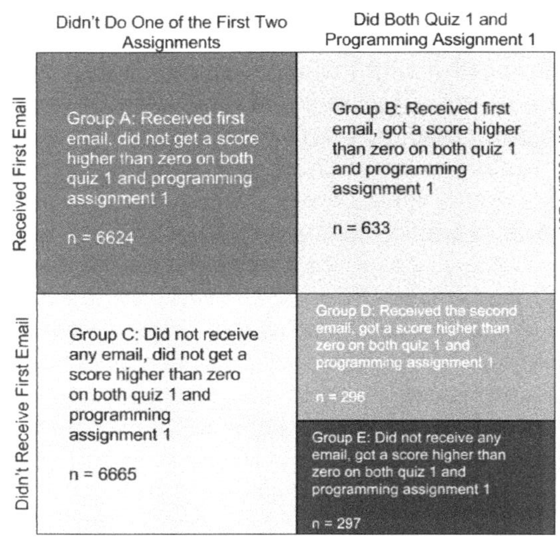

Figure 1: A diagram of how students were broken into control and experimental groups.

After both the initial email and the second email, we assessed the participation levels of each group on each subsequent assignment of the course's third offering.

Results

We found that the first email had a slight, but significant positive impact on completion of the final assignment (p=0.057). It had no significant impact on completion of any of the earlier assignments. This surprised us since we had assumed any impact would be concentrated in the assignments immediately following the email. The results for the first experiment can be seen in figure 2. In retrospect, this effect on the final assignment could be the result of gradual attrition among students, but at a slower rate for those who were prompted than for those who were not prompted, with the result that a significant difference in completion rates only manifests in the final assignment. An alternative analysis might look at the slope of attrition rates in the two conditions, asking whether there is a significant difference in slopes.

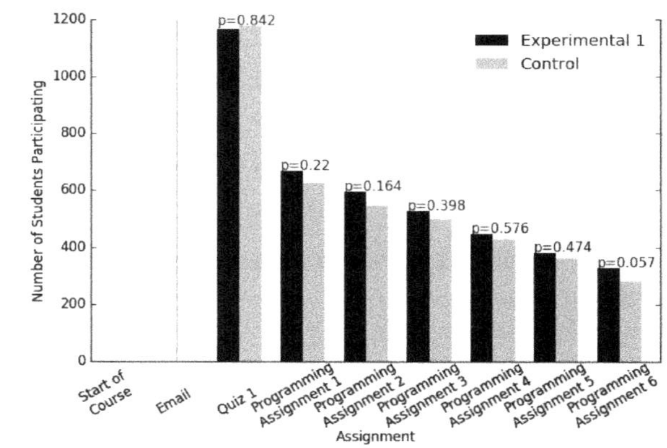

Figure 2: The number of students who participated in each assignment. This is a comparison of students who received the first email to students who did not. These groups correspond to the rows in fig 1. The p values are shown above each bar.

The difference in participation was not significant for any of the assignments in the second experiment. It could be that interventions later in a course have a smaller impact than those earlier in the course. Perhaps more exactly, the intervention has a larger effect on those who are "on the fence" than those who are already committed to finishing or unable to for "hard" external reasons. We hypothesize that the second prompt might have had more impact if it included students who had done only one of the first two assignments, as these students would be more likely to be "fence-sitters". More generally, we will want to characterize different populations of learners, from "committed" to less committed, and look at effects on these different populations.

There are some other smaller points of note. Recall that students who received the email prompt were asked, but not required, to follow a link to indicate interest in a Community TAship. There were no significant differences between students who followed the link to the survey and those who did not. For a larger sample, we may find a difference as following the link may indicate how much an incentive our email prompt is to different learners. In addition, because the email prompt pointed to a survey on the course platform where learners could indicate their interest in a Community TAship, there were some students who did not receive the email and found the survey after completing the course. We hope to make our survey harder to stumble upon in future experiments. This was not a population included in our analysis. It was small (n=90) relative to the size of the experimental and control groups.

Having issued the prompt for interest in a Community TAship, we are defining a vetting process to select among those who finished in the top 20% and said they were interested, in preparation for the fourth course offering.

Conclusion and Future Work

Our work thus far is quite preliminary, providing evidence that encouraging students to have a social goal does have a slight positive impact on participation if given early in the course. This impact is quite small compared to the effects reported by Krause and Williams but our intervention was much easier to implement.

In the future we plan to examine whether in prompting students even earlier (i.e. before the course starts) shows a larger effect than we saw here, and additionally identifying different populations of learners for which particular possibilities, notably the possibility of a Community TAship, are in fact incentives (or not). Additionally we will look into some other interventions that can be easily added to existing courses.

References

[1] Clow, D. MOOCs and the funnel of participation. *Proceedings of the Third International Conference on Learning Analytics and Knowledge - LAK '13* (2013), 185.

[2] Kizilcec, R. F., and Schneider, E. Motivation as a lens to understand online learners: Toward data-driven design with the OLEI scale. *ACM Transactions on Computer-Human Interaction 22*, 2 (2015), 1–24.

[3] Krause, M., and Williams, J. J. A Playful Game Changer : Fostering Student Retention in Online Education with Social Gamification. In *Learning at Scale* (2015), 95–102.

[4] Wilkowski, J., Deutsch, A., and Russell, D. Student skill and goal achievement in the mapping with google MOOC. *ACM conference on Learning @ scale conference* (2014), 3–10.

[5] Yang, D., Sinha, T., Adamson, D., and Rose, C. Turn on, Tune in, Drop out: Anticipating student dropouts in Massive Open Online Courses. *Proceedings of the NIPS Workshop on Data Driven Education* (2013), 1–8.

Supporting Peer Instruction with Evidence-Based Online Instructional Templates

Tricia J. Ngoon
The Design Lab
Department of Cognitive Science
University of California, San Diego
La Jolla, CA 92092 USA
tngoon@ucsd.edu

Alexander Gamero-Garrido
Department of Computer
Science & Engineering
Center for Applied Internet Data
Analysis
University of California, San Diego
La Jolla, CA 92092 USA
agamerog@eng.ucsd.edu

Scott Klemmer
The Design Lab
Department of Cognitive Science
Department of Computer
Science & Engineering
University of California, San Diego
La Jolla, CA 92092 USA
srk@eng.ucsd.edu

L@S 2016, April 25-26, 2016, Edinburgh, Scotland UK
ACM 978-1-4503-3726-7/16/04.
http://dx.doi.org/10.1145/2876034.2893439

Abstract
This work examines whether templates designed from principles of multimedia learning design, and learning sciences research, can support peer instruction in creating more effective educational content on the web. Initial results show that the structure and guidelines within these templates can help novices produce meaningful learning content while improving the overall learning experience. This experiment provides insights into how to design and implement structured outlines online for web users to share learning content, and potentially shift researchers' focus to more learner-centered online education.

Author Keywords
online education; peer learning; peer instruction; templates; learning

Introduction
As Massive Open Online Courses (MOOCs) grow in both quality and popularity, the issue of scale remains at large with the sheer size of large-scale courses and resources required, hindering instructors in their ability to provide individual attention to students [8]. However, harnessing peer instruction for peers to teach and learn from each other is a promising solution to the challenges that large-scale online learning presents. Multimedia learning environments are of interest in supporting peer instruction, but much of the research in this area has been more instructor-focused than peer-

focused. This research seeks to understand whether templates designed based on learning sciences principles can help create a better online learning experience for novice "tutors" and "learners."

We hypothesize that tutors who use templates will be better able to create effective and organized educational content. We further hypothesize that learners who learn from template presentations will demonstrate greater learning gains, compared to learners who learn from non-template presentations. This paper introduces theory behind our hypotheses, our experimental paradigm, and initial results.

Related Work

Templates have been a useful approach in increasing faculty adoption of online learning practices. Hoffman and Ritchie [3] developed a workshop with templates that incorporate principles of connecting learning content, applying it, and reflecting upon it in asynchronous online learning environments to help faculty better organize their curriculum. While instructional templates have been useful in structuring of online content, the research done in this realm has been geared towards professional instructors. Further, these instructional templates are often designed to accommodate for an entire online course, illustrating a more instructor-centered focus.

One related project in templates for novices is the "Wallet Project" from the Institute of Design at Stanford University [1], which consists of an activity to guide design students through an entire design process, using templates and a facilitator's guide for instructors. These templates help students ideate, iterate, and collaborate on their projects. Similarly, our template is designed to facilitate novice tutors through the instructional process to create effective educational content online.

Template Design

To explore how to better support peer instruction online, we designed a template for novice tutors that incorporates guidelines based on Lohr's [4] principles for instructional interface design:

- Organization of elements into a meaningful hierarchy of learning tasks.
- Organize the sections into a coherent whole.

To accomplish the implementation of these principles, elements derived from learning sciences evidence were built into the template. These include: learning goals, external representations, and guided activities. Figure 1 shows the overall outline of the template.

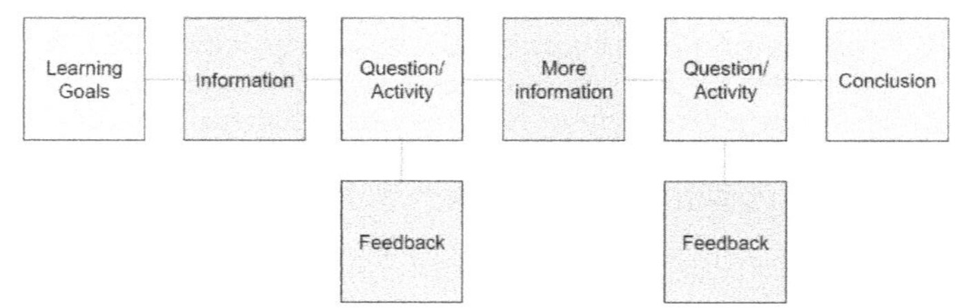

Figure 1. Overall outline of the template. The learning goals and conclusion serve to create a coherent whole of the learning activities and information in between.

Learning Goals

Learning goals, or mastery goals, give learners a frame of reference prior to beginning a learning activity, which has positive consequences on learning gains [2]. By instructing tutors to state learning goals both at the beginning and at the end of their presentation (as a conclusion), our template attends to both design principles in giving learners a clear hierarchy of tasks

a)

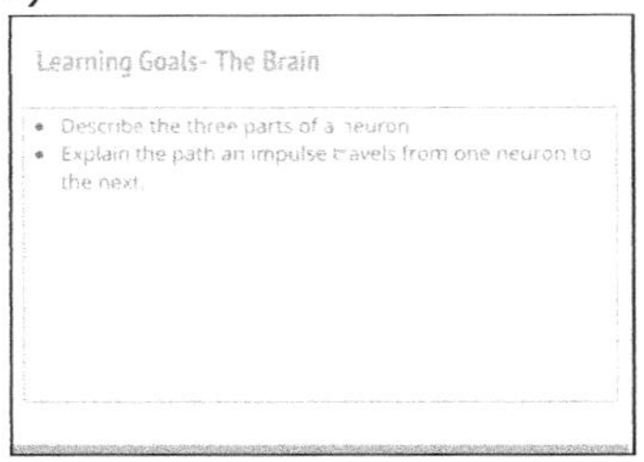

b)

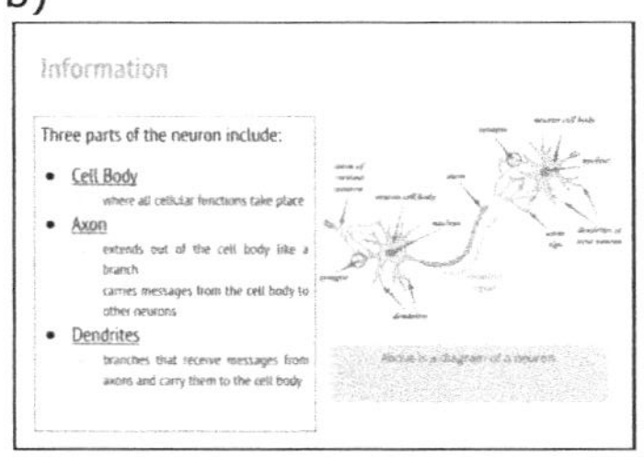

c)

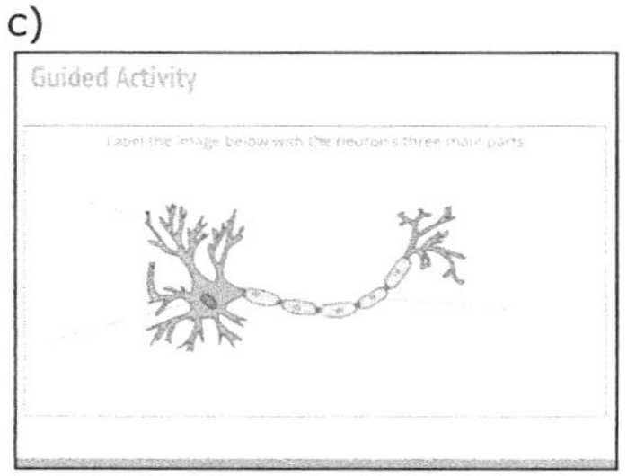

Figure 2. Example of a Learning Goal slide (a), External Representation (b), and Guided Activity (c) created by a template tutor.

and placing the entire context into a coherent whole (Figure 2a).

External Representations
External representations are pictorial depictions of verbal or textual information. Relevant external representations displayed in conjunction with textual information have been shown to improve learner outcomes, particularly when displayed in synchrony [6]. Our template gives tutors guidelines on how to well integrate external representations with text, breaking the information into meaningful sections (Figure 2b).

Guided Activity
The guided activity principle suggests that people can learn better when content includes interactivity, which facilitates engagement and encourages greater reflection [5]. Our template's guided activities instruct tutors to create questions and activities to engage the learner with the presented material and provide feedback to help the learner better comprehend and apply the information (Figure 2c).

The Experiment
Participants were assigned as either tutors or learners. Tutors were asked to create an educational presentation in Google Slides using either our designed template or with a blank presentation template. The presentation was to be based on an introductory passage on "The Central Nervous System" (adapted from [7]).

We then randomly assigned tutor presentations to learners. Control learners saw presentations created by control tutors while template learners saw presentations created by template tutors. After going through the presentation, learners were directed to a separate web article and instructed to identify some details from the article as a distractor task. Learners were then given a six-question quiz on the information they learned in the presentation. After taking the quiz, learners were given a questionnaire to evaluate their enjoyment of the learning experience.

Participants
75 adult participants completed participation in this study and were recruited from Usertesting.com. All participants resided in the United States and were required to have a native or bilingual fluency level in speaking and reading English.

25 participants were assigned as tutors (mean age=22.48). 13 tutors (11 female) were placed in our control condition, and the other 12 (10 female) tutors created presentations with the designed template in our template condition.

50 participants (mean age=27.61) were assigned as learners, allowing each tutor's presentation to be seen by two learners. 26 learners (12 female) saw presentations created by tutors in the control condition while 24 learners (11 female) saw presentations created by tutors in the template condition. All learners had two or fewer high school or college courses in basic biology.

Results
A two-sample Kolmogorov-Smirnov (K-S) test revealed a significant difference in the distribution of the two groups (D-stat=0.25, D-crit=0.19). Template learner performance was more normally distributed with a positive skew, and control learner performance was more evenly distributed (Figure 3). This skew suggests that learning gains for template learners were more consistent for template learners than for control learners. We believe that the positive skew of scores could be due to greater variance in quality of the control presentations compared to the template presentations. Thus, these results show the potential of guided templates in supporting peers with minimal teaching experience in creating effective educational content to share on the web.

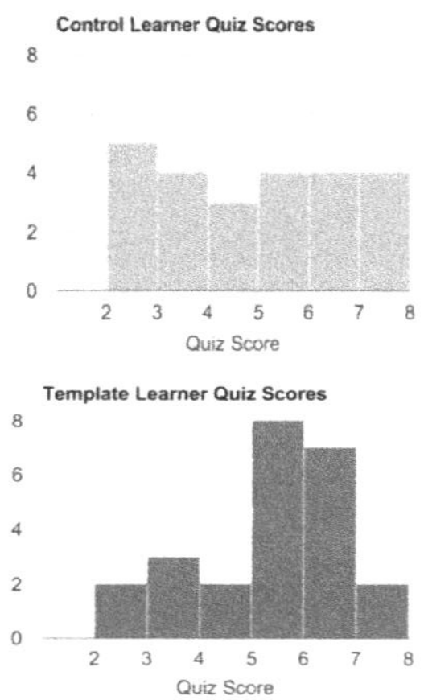

Figure 3. Histograms for quiz scores for control (top) and template (bottom) learners.

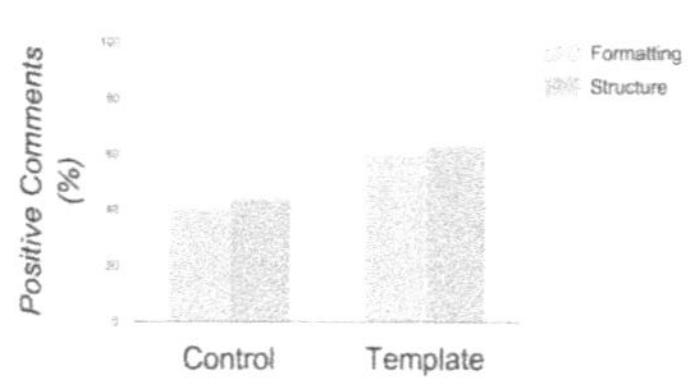

Figure 4. A larger percentage of template learners reported positive comments towards the formatting and structure of their assigned presentation than control learners.

We also examined learners' reported experience with the structure and formatting of all presentations. Template learners reported more positive views towards both presentation formatting and structure (60.0% and 66.2%, respectively) compared to control learners (40.9% and 44.7%, respectively) (Figure 4).

Future Directions & Conclusions

Future work will examine what type of guidance provided in the template is most beneficial for tutors. Another area of future work is understanding what design principles should be applied in order to make more flexible, general purpose teaching templates. The ultimate goal for this research will be to implement such templates and outlines in online education courses or platforms to allow peers to share educational content with each other.

Based on our findings, web presentation templates are helpful in guiding novice tutors in making content, and they improve both the quality of experience and learning outcomes of online learners. Our work explored how peer instruction can be harnessed through templates that provide structure and guidance for novices, allowing them to create effective educational content on the web. Further, we provided initial evidence showing how such templates could be implemented into online learning sites.

By providing better support for novices to create educational content online, we can further shift the focus of online education from instructor-focused learning to learner-centered learning.

Acknowledgements

We thank UserTesting for providing us with a platform to recruit and run participants through this experiment. We also thank our colleagues in the Design Lab at UCSD, particularly Ailie Fraser, for their support and guidance in this work. Research by author Gamero-Garrido is based upon work supported by the National Science Foundation under Grant No. CSE-1422240.

References

[1] Both, T. The Wallet Project. *Institute of Design at Stanford*.

[2] Pintrich, P.P.R., De Groot, E.V., Motivational and self-regulated learning components of classroom academic performance. *Journal of educational psychology 82*, 1 (1990), 33–40.

[3] Hoffman, B., and Ritchie, D. Teaching and Learning Online: Tools, Templates, and Training. *Society for Information Technology & Teacher Education International Conference* (1998), 119–123.

[4] Lohr, L.L. Designing the instructional interface. *Computers in Human Behavior 16*, 2 (2000), 161–182.

[5] Moreno, R., and Mayer, R. Interactive Multimodal Learning Environments. *Educational Psychology Review 19*, 3 (2007), 309–326.

[6] Schwonke, R., Berthold, K., and Renkl, A. How multiple external representations are used and how they can be made more useful. *Applied Cognitive Psychology 23*, 9 (2009), 1227–1243.

[7] Van Meter, P. Drawing construction as a strategy for learning from text. *Journal of Educational Psychology 93*, 1 (2001), 129–140.

[8] Yuan, L., and Powell, S. MOOCs and Open Education: Implications for Higher Education. *Cetis* (2013), 19.

Learning about Teaching in Low-Resource Indian Contexts

Aditya Vishwanath
Georgia Institute of Technology
Atlanta, GA, USA
adityavishwanath@gatech.edu

Arkadeep Kumar
Georgia Institute of Technology
Atlanta, GA, USA
arkadeepkumar@gatech.edu

Neha Kumar
Georgia Institute of Technology
Atlanta, GA, USA
neha.kumar@gatech.edu

Abstract
Online learning environments are being deployed globally to offer learning opportunities to diverse student communities. We propose the deployment of such an environment in low-resource after-school settings across India. We draw on preliminary research conducted in summer 2015 that leveraged existing ties with an NGO working across 35 after-school classrooms. Our larger goal is to (1) support tutors in curating and distributing learning content to students, (2) engage students in a mobile, networked learning environment where they can share and collaborate, and (3) evaluate the feasibility of online learning environments for low-resource contexts. In this submission, our focus is on the first component.

L@S 2016, April 25-26, 2016, Edinburgh, Scotland UK
ACM 978-1-4503-3726-7/16/04.
http://dx.doi.org/10.1145/2876034.2893440

Author Keywords
ICTD; HCI; learning; India

ACM Classification Keywords
H.5.0 [Information Interfaces and Presentation]: General.

Introduction
Learning environments in developing world contexts have been too under-resourced (and thus under-explored) for feasible technology initiatives, but growing penetration of mobile technologies and internet connectivity drives us to explore the potential of state-of-the-art and relatively low cost technologies to enhance learning experiences for low-resource contexts.

We aim to address two problems with our research. First, there is an access problem. Students and tutors in low-resource settings have limited access to learning/teaching. Second, there is an immense opportunity to address a learning problem as well. The quality of teaching can occasionally be sub-par – this is a part-time job for the tutors, they are compensated little for their efforts, they may be ill-equipped as teachers, and the students must learn alongside peers across a spectrum of ages and backgrounds. The first problem is more straightforwardly addressed by technology. As for the second, we aim to enhance pedagogical intent and capacity of functional learning environments, as recommended in [2]. Our primary and immediate goal is to integrate low-cost technology in low-resource learning environments to address an access problem. Our secondary, longer term goal is to address a learning problem, improving learning outcomes *at scale* through engaged, situated interactions with tutors and other students. Our research questions are thus as follows:

1. Teaching: Can tutors constrained for time and money benefit from an online learning platform? Do they value having access to varied educational content online? Can they successfully adapt their teaching style to integrate online learning?

2. Learning: Do students engage and adapt easily to online learning? What aspects of online sharing and collaboration do they value? Do they show measurable improvement in learning outcomes?

3. Feasibility: Can existing and relatively low-cost technology be leveraged to enhance the learning experience for students and tutors in low-resource environments? What implications might this have for testing larger-scale MOOC-style learning environments for rural users?

In answering these research questions, our project aims to incorporate the inputs of various stakeholders in this space, including children, tutors, and NGO volunteers, while designing the online learning experience. We stress that, for our initiative to be sustainable, active participation of the users (particularly that of the teachers/tutors) is critical to ensure a successful deployment.

Research Plan

There are multiple components to the system that we aim to build. First, we need a comprehensive assessment of the educational content currently being used by teachers in low-resource Indian settings. For this, we conducted an exhaustive survey of content providers that we describe the highlights of below. We also conducted interviews with teachers to assess their expertise with digital pedagogical content and their receptivity to a platform such as the one we intend to provide. This exercise would aid our second goal of providing content that the teachers can curate from a repository given to them. Third, we will build our learning environment and, fourth, we will generate curricula for a directed research study.

In terms of work done so far - in [1] we published findings from the needs assessment we conducted last summer at three target classrooms. We deployed a tablet (Android) application for Math learning and iterated on its design during a six-week study. We found that tablet applications were appropriate and feasible learning and assessment tools, opened up avenues for personalized learning, led to improved learning outcomes (as assessed by the tutors), and allowed for the consideration of different kinds of learning content (e.g. Math and English, which students in Tamil Nadu have been found to be weakest in [9]). These findings and subsequent discussions with the NGO and tutors motivated us towards proposing and deploying a holistic model that integrates mobile technologies and curated media into an online learning community of students.

We next describe the highlights from our survey of Indian content providers (and electronic learning services) and our interviews with teachers.

Surveying Content Providers
We surveyed 40 web-based content providers and attempted to identify and compare their key features. The highlights of our survey are given below.

A large number of online content providers are not in the open source domain and most services and packages provided, such as practice problem sets and lecture videos, are paid services. This can potentially prevent us from curating content, since a large chunk of the content is under a privately held license. Additionally, most of the content that we surveyed was directed at high school students, either focusing on grades 9 to 12 or on competitive examinations for universities.

We found a substantial repository of learning content in the open source domain as well. A lot of the content is aligned with the Indian education system. Many content providers provide software and hardware solutions, such as learning platforms and tablets/laptops respectively, packaged with their online learning content. We name a few notable web-based learning tools that we surveyed.

The Educomp Smart School Program [3] is a novel and comprehensive learning package that includes a complete digital repository of classroom learning content, bundled with learning and lesson plans, simulations, assessments, and virtual laboratories. This Smart School Project also contains an "English Mentor", which is an English language tutor tool that simulates an English language learning course in an Indian accent, using suitable examples for a student studying in an Indian setting.

Nytra is an augmented reality application offered by the MBD Group [4] that works with Nytra textbooks to create augmented reality animations alongside course textual material. The application animates images and illustrations in the book with voiceovers and videos to increase student engagement while reading. The MBD Group also provides apps for kindergarten learning, in an assortment of rhymes in English and Hindi. Its goal is to create a blend of traditional rhymes and modern learning techniques, accompanied with music and animations.

Among other providers, there was Magic Pathshala [5], which provided students with a large open source repository of organized and categorized Math and English content, sorted by skills and grades. WybeeTab [6], produced by CarveNiche Technologies, is a comprehensive tablet-based learning platform and content provider that stores all content remotely so that the entire system works offline.

Interviewing Teachers
We sought a deeper understanding of the experiences of teachers/tutors for our proposed online learning community. These teachers taught in schools in peri-urban Kolkata and low-income, urban Mumbai. Their experiences with the digital content they had been using and their comfort level in their previous uses of digital media/devices gave crucial feedback for our

design process, helping to identify how the technology could be improved.

Talking with teachers/tutors and NGO volunteers from different parts of India and across different socio-economically situated after-school centers/schools, we were told that children are more engaged when digital media (visual pictures/videos) are used to explain concepts. Another common theme that emerged was that students were far more enthusiastic than their teachers when it came to embracing the idea of an online learning community. The teachers' reasons ranged from content not being in a language they are comfortable with (regional languages like Marathi/Bengali) to the content not having a "local flavor", to not having enough training to use emerging technologies and digital media. These are concerns we plan to address in the online platform we design.

Future Work

Having conducted an elaborate and rigorous needs assessment, our goal moving forward is to compile a repository and allow teachers to curate lesson plans from this repository. We also intend to test the robustness and effectiveness that such a platform can offer in acutely resource-constrained regions. Deploying our platform in three disparate contexts – rural Tamil Nadu, peri-urban Kolkata, and urban slums in Mumbai – will also allow us to compare the impact across different communities.

References

[1] Aditya Vishwanath and Neha Kumar. 2015. Designing for a Rural Online Learning Community. In*Proceedings of the 2015 Annual Symposium on Computing for Development* (DEV '15). ACM, New York, NY, USA, 73-74.

[2] Toyama, K. - There are no technology shortcuts to good education: 2011. http://edutechdebate.org/ict-in-schools/there-are-no-technology-shortcuts-to-good-education/. Accessed: 2016-01-14.

[3] Educomp Smart School: 2015. http://educomp.com/content/educomp-smart-school. Accessed: 2016-01-14.

[4] MBD Group E-Learning: 2015. http://mbdgroup.com/Digital-Learning.html. Accessed: 2016-01-14.

[5] Magic Pathshala: 2013. http://www.magicpathshala.com/. Accessed: 2016-01-14.

[6] WybeeTab: 2014. http://carveniche.com/wybee.html/. Accessed: 2016-01-14.

[7] Heimerl, K., et al. "Local, sustainable, small-scale cellular networks." (ICTD '13)

[8] Gaver, B., Dunne, T., and Pacenti, E. "Design: cultural probes." Interactions 6.1 (1999): 21-29.

[9] ASER Annual Status of Education Report: 2014. http://img.asercentre.org/docs/Publications/ASER%20Reports/ASER%202014/fullaser2014mainreport_1.pdf. Accessed: 2016-01-15.

Modeling Student Scheduling Preferences in a Computer-Based Testing Facility

Matthew West
Mechanical Science and Engineering
University of Illinois at Urbana-Champaign
Urbana, IL 61801, USA
mwest@illinois.edu

Craig Zilles
Computer Science
University of Illinois at Urbana-Champaign
Urbana, IL 61801, USA
zilles@illinois.edu

L@S'16, April 25–26, 2016, Edinburgh, Scotland.
Copyright © 2016 ACM ISBN/14/04...$15.00.
DOI string from ACM form confirmation

Abstract
When undergraduate students are allowed to choose a time slot in which to take an exam from a large number of options (e.g., 40), the students exhibit strong preferences among the times. We found that students can be effectively modelled using *constrained discrete choice theory* to quantify these preferences from their observed behavior. The resulting models are suitable for load balancing when scheduling multiple concurrent exams and for capacity planning given a set schedule.

Author Keywords
student modeling; asynchronous exams; discrete choice theory; capacity planning; computerized testing

ACM Classification Keywords
I.6.5 [Simulation and Modeling]: Model Development; H.1.2 [Information Systems]: User/Machine Systems

Introduction
The Computer-Based Testing Facility (CBTF) [4] at the University of Illinois at Urbana-Champaign (UIUC) is a testing facility that allows students to self-schedule time slots for mid-term and final exams using the PrairieLearn [3] online problem-solving system.

In Fall 2015 the CBTF conducted about 2000 exams per

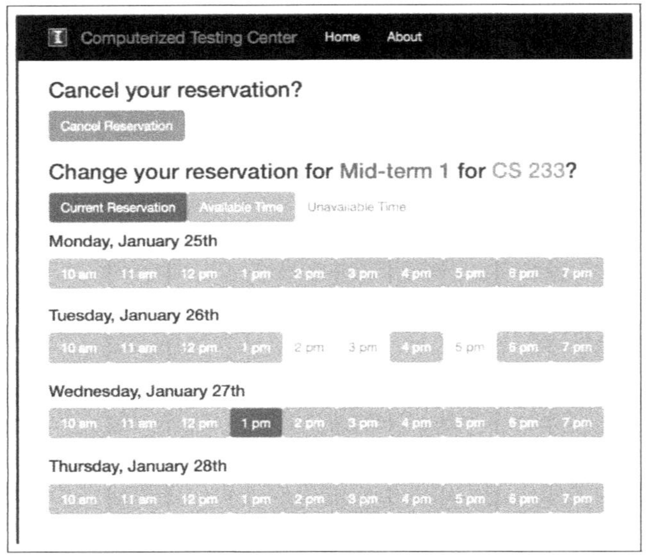

Figure 1: The student exam sign-up interface for the CBTF (Computer-Based Testing Facility).

week with 9 different large-enrollment courses scheduling an average of 6 total distinct exams per week. Each exam has a block of 3 to 5 days during which students are free to schedule their individual exam time. Exams start on the hour, typically 10am to 10pm daily, giving about 30 to 60 possible time slots that a student can choose from for each exam. However, the testing facility can only accommodate 45 students simultaneously, so there are significant constraints on student choice. Scheduling is handled via a self-service online system (the *CBTF Scheduler*) where students can sign up for any time slot that currently has seats available, and they are also able to delete or reschedule their future reservations. Figure 1 shows the student scheduling interface.

For planning purposes it is desirable to have a predictive model of student preferences and scheduling behavior. For example, different exams need to be spaced out over the course of a week to balance load across the days, and usage needs to be forecast so that more proctors can be scheduled during busy periods. Data from Fall 2015 shows strong and consistent patterns in student scheduling preferences and behavior, indicating that predictive models should exist.

Constrained discrete choice models

To model student choices of time slots, we use the framework of *discrete choice theory* [2] from economics, which models choices that people make from a set of discrete alternatives. In particular, we use discrete choice models *with capacity constraints* [1], because each time slot in the CBTF can only accommodate a maximum of 45 students simultaneously.

We use n to index *decisions*, which are students choosing time slots, i to index time *slots*, h to index the *hour-in-week* of a time slot, and r to be the number of *days remaining* within the period of a given exam. Using these variables, we define four binary arrays:

$a_{ni} \in \{0,1\}$ is whether slot i was available for decision n

$y_{ni} \in \{0,1\}$ is whether slot i was chosen for decision n

$x_{ih} \in \{0,1\}$ is whether slot i is at hour-in-week h

$w_{nir} \in \{0,1\}$ is whether slot i for decision n has r days remaining in the exam period.

The desirability of time slot i for the student making decision n is modeled by its *utility* V_{ni}. We will model this by assuming the utility of a time slot depends on which hour in the week it falls (that is, the hour of day and the day in week) and also how many days are remaining in the exam period. We expect that students will prefer certain hours and days (e.g., they might prefer late afternoon on weekdays) and that they will prefer to do exams close to the end of each exam period. Our model is described by parameters β_h and λ_r as follows:

$$\begin{aligned} V_{ni} &= \text{utility of slot } i \text{ for decision } n \\ &= \sum_{h=1}^{N_\text{h}} \beta_h x_{ih} + \sum_{r=1}^{N_\text{r}} \lambda_r w_{nir} \\ \beta_h &= \text{utility of hour-in-week } h \\ \lambda_r &= \text{utility of } r \text{ remaining days in the exam period.} \end{aligned}$$

Constrained discrete choice theory uses random utility models [2] to derive the probability p_{ni} that decision n chooses slot i to be:

$$p_{ni} = \frac{a_{ni} e^{V_{ni}}}{\sum_{j=1}^{N_\text{i}} a_{nj} e^{V_{nj}}}.$$

Given a set of actual choices in the array y_{ni}, we can determine the best-fit model parameters β_h^* and λ_r^* using maximum-likelihood estimation. This gives:

$$\begin{aligned} L &= \text{log-likelihood of the set of actual choices} \\ &= \sum_{n=1}^{N_\text{n}} \sum_{i=1}^{N_\text{i}} y_{ni} \log p_{ni} \\ \beta^*, \lambda^* &= \operatorname*{argmax}_{\beta,\lambda} L(\beta, \lambda). \end{aligned}$$

Results

Using data from the CBTF at UIUC in Fall 2015 we found the maximum likelihood parameters shown in Figures 2 and 3. These parameters show that students prefer Thursdays and Fridays (but not Friday evenings), they prefer

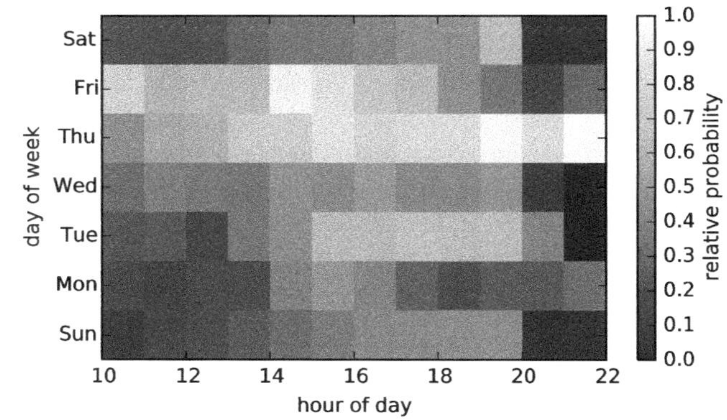

Figure 2: The relative probability (proportional to $\exp \beta_h^*$) of a student choosing a time slot as a function of the hour-in-week h.

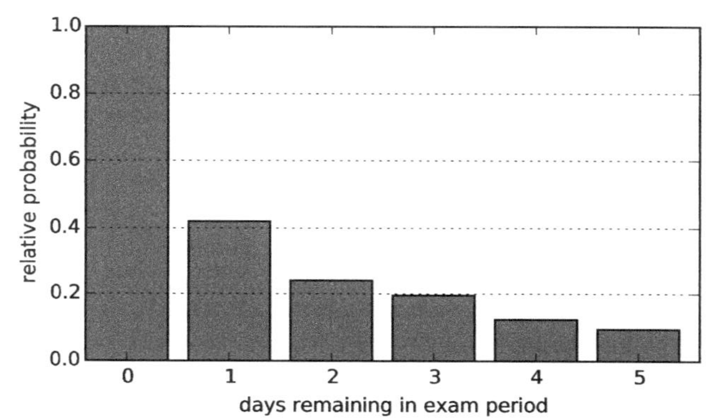

Figure 3: The relative probability (proportional to $\exp \lambda_r^*$) of a student choosing a time slot as a function of days remaining r.

	Model	Uniform
Median absolute error	3.7%	9.6%
Mean absolute error	7.2%	14.5%
Root mean square error	11.8%	21.3%

Table 1: Prediction errors from the discrete choice model ("Model") and a naive uniform prediction ("Uniform"). Errors are given as percentages of maximum capacity (45 students). The model-based predictions have about half the error of the uniform.

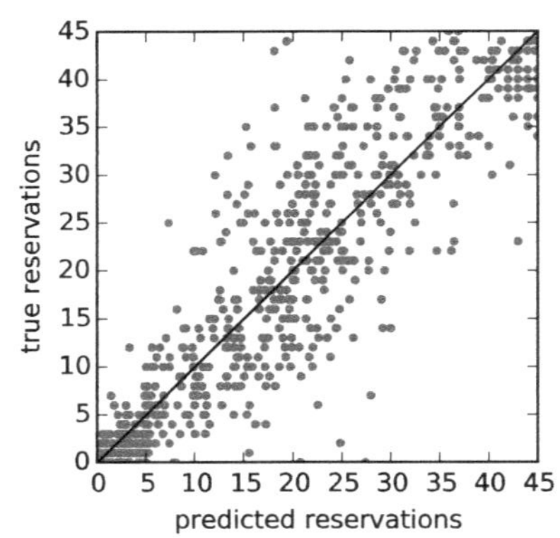

Figure 4: The predicted number of reservations per time slot using the discrete choice model, versus the true numbers. The 45° black line represents a perfect predictor.

afternoon time slots, and they very much prefer to do the exam on the last possible day.

The predicted versus true number of students per time slot are shown in Figure 4, which have errors as shown in Table 1. The discrete choice model generally performs well, with well under 10% mean absolute error in the number of students who choose any given time slot.

Conclusions and future work

We fitted a constrained discrete choice model for student scheduling preferences in a Computer-Based Testing Facility (CBTF) and found that the model predicted time slot usages with a mean absolute error of 7.2%, indicating that it is a practical model for planning purposes. Future work includes full cross-validation studies and extensions to per-course parameters and per-student modeling.

Acknowledgements

MW acknowledges support from NSF DUE-1347722.

REFERENCES

1. A. de Palma, N. Picard, and P. Waddell. 2007. Discrete choice models with capacity constraints: An empirical analysis of the housing market of the greater Paris region. *Journal of Urban Economics* 62, 2 (2007), 204–230. DOI: http://dx.doi.org/10.1016/j.jue.2007.02.007
2. K. E. Train. 2009. *Discrete Choice Methods with Simulation* (second ed.). Cambridge University Press.
3. M. West, C. Zilles, and G. Herman. 2015. PrairieLearn: Mastery-based Online Problem Solving with Adaptive Scoring and Recommendations Driven by Machine Learning. In *Proceedings of the American Society for Engineering Education (ASEE) 2015 Annual Conference*. DOI: http://dx.doi.org/10.18260/p.24575
4. C. Zilles, R. T. Deloatch, J. Bailey, B. B. Khattar, W. Fagen, C. Heeren, D Mussulman, and M. West. 2015. Computerized Testing: A Vision and Initial Experiences. In *Proceedings of the American Society for Engineering Education (ASEE) 2015 Annual Conference*. DOI: http://dx.doi.org/10.18260/p.23726

Bringing Non-programmer Authoring of Intelligent Tutors to MOOCs

Vincent Aleven
aleven@cs.cmu.edu
Human-Computer Interaction Institute
Carnegie Mellon University

Ryan Baker
Baker2@tc.columbia.edu
Human Development
Teachers College
Columbia University

Yuan Wang
Elle.wang@columbia.edu
Human Development
Teachers College
Columbia University

Jonathan Sewall
sewall@cs.cmu.edu
Human-Computer Interaction Institute
Carnegie Mellon University

Octav Popescu
octav@cmu.edu
Human-Computer Interaction Institute
Carnegie Mellon University

L@S 2016, April 25-26, 2016, Edinburgh, Scotland Uk
ACM 978-1-4503-3726-7/16/04.
http://dx.doi.org/10.1145/2876034.2893442

Abstract
Learning-by-doing in MOOCs may be enhanced by embedding intelligent tutoring systems (ITSs). ITSs support learning-by-doing by guiding learners through complex practice problems while adapting to differences among learners. We extended the Cognitive Tutor Authoring Tools (CTAT), a widely-used non-programmer tool kit for building intelligent tutors, so that CTAT-built tutors can be embedded in MOOCs and e-learning platforms. We demonstrated the technical feasibility of this integration by adding simple CTAT-built tutors to an edX MOOC, "Big Data in Education." To the best of our knowledge, this integration is the first occasion that material created through an open-access non-programmer authoring tool for full-fledged ITS has been integrated in a MOOC. The work offers examples of key steps that may be useful in other ITS-MOOC integration efforts, together with reflections on strengths, weaknesses, and future possibilities.

Author Keywords
Intelligent tutoring systems, ITSs, MOOCs, Interoperability, Feasibility study, Log data analysis

ACM Classification Keywords
K.3.1 Computer Uses in Education*:* Distance learning

CTAT Example-tracing Tutor Features

- Provide custom-designed problem-solving interfaces that break down complex problems
- Provide step-by-step guidance within problems, not just end-of-problem feedback
- Support immediate and delayed feedback on steps
- Provide on-demand hints that give guidance
- Can follow students with respect to multiple different solution paths through problems, regardless of which path the student pursues
- Track individual student's knowledge growth in terms of fine-grained knowledge components
- Select problems adaptively, on an individual basis, so students practice un-mastered knowledge components until they master the targeted knowledge

Introduction

A recent study suggests that, in MOOCs, learning-by-doing has a stronger influence on learning outcomes than learning by reading or by watching [5]. MOOCs have previously supported learning-by-doing for example by posing questions with feedback and assignments with peer grading.

By contrast, intelligent tutoring systems (ITS) support learning-by-doing through practice on sets of complex problems. They break problems into steps, provide step-level guidance within problems, monitor individuals' knowledge growth, and adaptively select problems. There is substantial evidence that ITS can enhance student learning, compared to other methods of instruction [6][8][11][13][15]. Although at least one MOOC has incorporated an ITS [12] and others have incorporated ITS-like elements (e.g., [9][10][14]), we are not aware of prior integration into a MOOC platform of a full-fledged ITS, created with an openly available dedicated ITS authoring tool.

It makes sense therefore to investigate whether and how ITS and MOOCs can be synergistic. Given that ITS and MOOCs have evolved separately, they first need to be technically integrated. This technical integration is not straightforward, however. In this paper, we present a pilot study that tested the feasibility of this integration in the context of the edX MOOC "Big Data in Education". We focus on example-tracing tutors [1], a type of tutoring system that can be built without programming, using dedicated authoring tools.

CTAT: Non-Programmer Authoring of Tutors

The Cognitive Tutor Authoring Tools (CTAT) support the authoring of example-tracing tutors using a variety of end-user programming techniques: drag-and-drop interface building, programming by demonstration, graph editing, formula writing, and template-based mass production [2]. CTAT example-tracing tutors support key ITS behavior (see sidebar). CTAT is integrated with the Tutorshop, a web-based learning management system (LMS) we created for tutor use in classrooms. This tutor development environment has been used by roughly 650 authors for many dozens of research projects [2]. 44,000 students have used CTAT-built tutors, mostly in classrooms, at all levels of education, from elementary school through college.

We recently completed the technical integration of CTAT/Tutorshop and edX [3] by: (a) Reimplementing the "tutor engine" (which provides within-problem guidance) in Javascript, (b) implementing the Learning Tools Interoperability (LTI; [7]) Provider interface in the Tutorshop. This implementation enables us to integrate CTAT tutors in edX or any other LTI-compliant learning management system.

Pilot Study

Using CTAT, we created 8 tutored activities, each with 8-13 steps, for use in the edX MOOC "Big Data in Education" (Figure 1). The tutors provide support for assignments in which students analyze data sets using standard tools such as RapidMiner to, for example, build prediction models using different classification algorithms and validation schemes. The tutors provided brief instructions for each subtask to be carried out in RapidMiner, provided feedback when the subtask had been completed and the result entered into the tutor, provided hints upon the student's request, and revealed instructions for the next subtask when the previous had been completed. Although this tutoring behavior is simple, it was appropriate for the given assignments.

Creating an example-tracing tutor in CTAT

1. Create problem-solving interface An author creates problem-solving interfaces for the targeted problem types, which break the problem into steps. They can be built through a Flash or Java IDE, or by writing code in HTML.

2. Create a behavior graph The author then demonstrates, on the problem-solving interface, solution paths that students might reasonably take, which CTAT's Behavior Recorder records in a *behavior graph*. She generalizes the behavior graph with formulas and other means so it represents an appropriately broad range of student behavior.

3. Prepare graph for tutoring The author attaches hints, feedback messages, and knowledge component labels to the graph.

At student run time, the tutor uses the graph to interpret and guide students' problem-solving behavior, and to track students' knowledge growth.

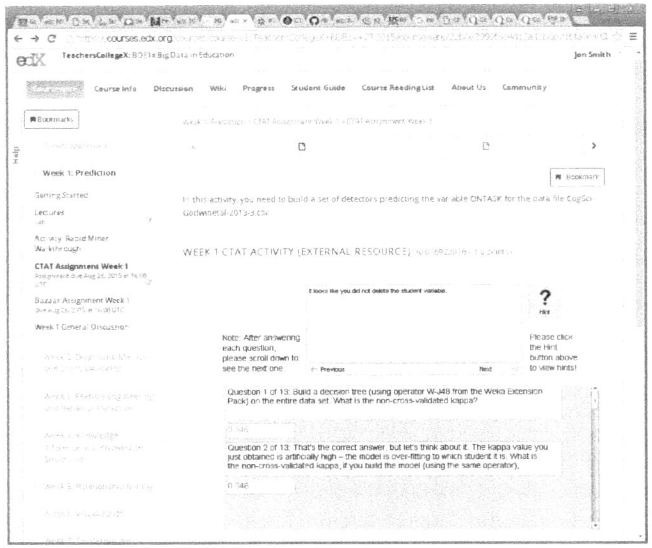

Figure 1: CTAT tutor in edX MOOC "Big Data in Education"

As is the case for all CTAT tutors, all student-tutor interactions were logged to DataShop [4], a large online repository of educational technology data sets, together with tools for analysis. The analysis that follows is based on exports from DataShop data. Of the 10,358 students who enrolled in the course, 559 started the first tutor activity and 86 started the last. The moderate hint and error frequencies (Figure 2; chart generated by DataShop) suggest that these assignments were appropriately challenging and that the tutor provided useful guidance to many students.

ITS log data and tools like DataShop play an increasingly important role in iteratively refining tutors [4]. For example, they help tutor authors identify common errors so that they can extend their tutor to give specific feedback when these errors occur. Also,

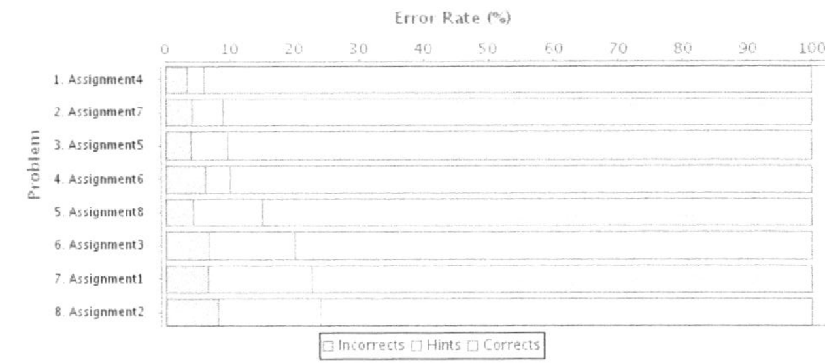

Figure 2: DataShop report displaying error rate (red) and hint use (yellow) on the tutor activities

authors can use log data to analyze what is most challenging for students and to refine the tutor's underlying knowledge component model, which can help make the tutor more effective or efficient [1].

Discussion

Our study demonstrates the technical feasibility of embedding example-tracing tutors in MOOCs. Any example-tracing tutor built with CTAT can now be embedded in any LTI-compliant MOOC or e-learning platform. The work thus brings non-programmer authoring of one class of ITSs to MOOCs. To the best of our knowledge, it represents the first integration of a MOOC and a full-blown ITS created with a free ITS authoring tool (http://ctat.pact.cs.cmu.edu). Although the tutors used in this study were rather simple, the integration supports all adaptive tutoring behaviors of CTAT tutors. The same means of integration (i.e., engineering the tutor so that it can run as a self-contained learning object in a browser; making it compatible so that an LTI-compliant LMS can launch it) could be used for other MOOCs and with other ITSs. There are some limitations, however. First, instead of launching the tutors from a separate server, it would be

ITS in edX Course "Big Data in Education"

- Eight CTAT tutors, a new one assigned each successive week
- Each tutor included 8-13 steps, some requiring analysis with tools such as RapidMiner
- Course certification required completing 70% of tutored activities
- 10,358 students enrolled, 114 received a certificate of completion
- 559 students started the first tutor assignment, 86 started the last tutor assignment (the 8th)

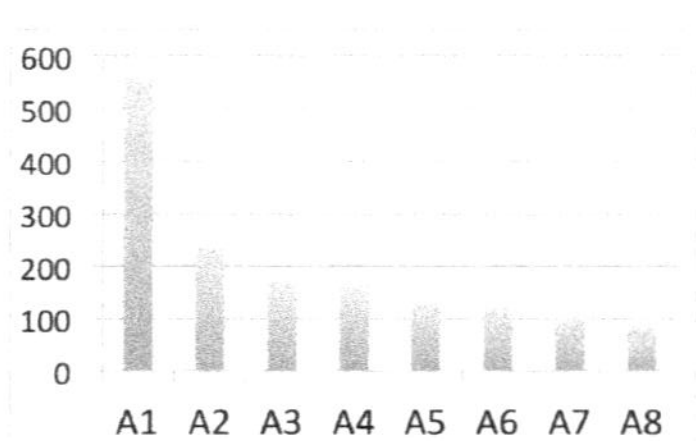

Figure 3: Number of students who started each tutor problem

preferable to host them on the edX site itself. We are working toward achieving this goal via use of edX XBlocks, but this integration would be an edX-only solution, unlike the LTI integration. Second, the LTI 1.1 standard limits the amount of data about student performance that the tutor can pass to the edX LMS, although this limitation may be loosened in LTI 2.0.

We see this work as expanding the options for learning-by-doing in MOOCs and for applying the one-on-one coaching of ITS at scale, where detailed, individualized guidance can be hard to provide. Further, it opens the door for addressing research questions on how typical MOOC activities and ITSs can best be combined and whether students learn better as a result. A key idea – not novel, but we are not aware of any implementation – is to share a student model across the ITS and the other MOOC elements. This integration could enhance the capabilities for adaptivity in both. For example, the tutor's adaptive behaviors could depend on what videos the student has watched and how well she did on quizzes embedded in those videos. Conversely, the system may recommend videos that help with content with which the student struggled in the tutor.

References

[1] Aleven, V. and Koedinger, K.R. 2013. Knowledge component approaches to learner modeling. In *Design recommendations for adaptive intelligent tutoring systems,* Army Research Lab., Orlando, FL, 165-182.

[2] Aleven, V., McLaren, B.M., Sewall, J., van Velsen, M., et al 2016. Example-Tracing tutors: Intelligent tutor development for non-programmers. *International Journal of AI in Education.* 26, 1.

[3] Aleven, V., et al 2015. The beginning of a beautiful friendship? Intelligent tutoring systems and MOOCs. *Proc. AIED 2015,* 525-528.

[4] Koedinger, K.R., Baker, R.S.J.d., Cunningham, K., Skogsholm, A., et al 2010. A data repository for the EDM community: The PSLC Datashop. In *Handbook of Ed Data Mining,* CRC Press, Boca Raton, FL, 43-55.

[5] Koedinger K.R., Kim J., Jia J.Z., McLaughlin E.A., Bier N.L. 2015. Learning is not a spectator sport: Doing is better than watching for learning from a MOOC. *Proc. Learning at Scale 2015,* 111-120.

[6] Kulik, J.A. and Fletcher, J.D. 2015. Effectiveness of intelligent tutoring systems. *Rev. Ed. Res.*

[7] https://www.imsglobal.org/activity/learning-tools-interoperability

[8] Ma, W., Adesope, O.O., Nesbit, J.C., and Liu, Q. 2014. Intelligent tutoring systems and learning outcomes: A meta-analysis. *Journal of Educational Psychology.* 106, 4, 901.

[9] Mitros P. and Sun F. 2014 Creating educational resources at scale. *Proc. ICALT 2014,* 16-18.

[10] https://www.oppia.org/

[11] Pane, J.F., Griffin, B.A., McCaffrey, D.F., and Karam, R. 2014. Effectiveness of Cognitive Tutor Algebra I at scale. *Educational Evaluation and Policy Analysis* 36, 2, 127-144.

[12] https://schoolyourself.org/

[13] Steenbergen-Hu, S. and Cooper, H. 2014. A meta-analysis of the effectiveness of intelligent tutoring systems on college students' academic learning. *Journal of Educational. Psychology.* 106, 2, 331-347.

[14] Strader, R. 2015 OLI and edX Collaborate on New Feedback Mechanisms for Learners. Open edX blog. https://open.edx.org/blog/oli-and-edx-collaborate-new-feedback-mechanisms-learners

[15] VanLehn, K. 2011. The relative effectiveness of human tutoring, intelligent tutoring systems, and other tutoring systems. *Educational. Psychologist.* 46, 4, 197-221.

Automatically Learning to Teach to the Learning Objectives

Rika Antonova
Carnegie Mellon University
Pittsburgh PA USA
rantonov@andrew.cmu.edu

Min Hyung Lee
Carnegie Mellon University
Pittsburgh PA USA
mhlee1116@gmail.com

Joe Runde
Carnegie Mellon University
Pittsburgh PA USA
jrunde@andrew.cmu.edu

Emma Brunskill
Carnegie Mellon University
Pittsburgh PA USA
ebrun@cs.cmu.edu

Abstract

We seek to automatically identify which items to include in a set of curriculum, and how to adaptively select these items, in order to maximize student performance on some specified set of learning objectives. Our experimental results with a histogram tutoring system suggest that Bayesian Optimization can quickly (with only a small amount of student data) find good parameters, and may help instructors identify misalignment between their course, and their desired learning objectives.

L@S 2016, April 25-26, 2016, Edinburgh, Scotland UK
ACM 978-1-4503-3726-7/16/04.
http://dx.doi.org/10.1145/2876034.2893443

Author Keywords

Automated instructional design; machine learning.

ACM Classification Keywords

H.5.m. Information interfaces and presentation (e.g., HCI): Miscellaneous.

Introduction

Educators want to provide the best learning experience for their students, but there are many ways to create pedagogical content (videos, quizzes, etc), sequence content, and provide personalized support and feedback. Instructors frequently have learning objectives for a course: a list of capabilities the student should have after taking the course. Therefore, a natural way to measure the course effectiveness is to evaluate how well students reach a specified input set of learning objectives, and to adjust the course to improve how well students achieve these objectives. It is well known that changing the content and the way in which material is taught can make an enormous difference to the effectiveness and efficiency in which students learn. For example, creating a blended statistics learning class led to the same final scores in half the time as a traditional statistics in person class [5].

However, which content to change and how to sequence or select content to improve learning is still a challenge. Existing approaches to addressing this often involve researchers performing extensive data analysis to identify places where the existing models or curriculum can be revised in order to improve student learning (see e.g. [2]). Another common approach is to use standard experimental design to compare multiple ways to teach the material, but such work typically requires a very large number of subjects to explore many conditions.

Fortunately in trying to find the best way to teach some material, we may not need to fully quantify the effectiveness of all possible approaches (as is typical in experimental design). This motivates recent machine learning approaches such as using multi-armed bandits optimization to identify the best of a finite set of teaching conditions, or treating the problem as function optimization using Bayesian optimization (BO) to find the maxima of a latent function that describes how adjusting the (continuous) parameters that prescribe how to teach impacts student outcomes in cognitive task learning [4].

Our work builds on this second line of work, but makes several important additional contributions. First, prior work has considered optimizing only fixed instructional policies that are independent of student performance [4] (e.g. optimizing fixed sequence of practicing vocabulary words which does not depend on how students are performing). However, it is well known that it is often beneficial to select the pedagogical material based on how the student is doing. Given this, in our work we consider optimizing over adaptive instructional policies. A second key contribution is to automatically identify when the current curriculum and/or method of teaching is inadequate for obtaining the desired input learning objectives. Our experimental results with a histogram teaching tutoring system demonstrate this, and highlight the opportunity for systems that can proactively assist instructors to focus their attention on which parts of the course (material or ordering) should be revised. This has the potential of greatly accelerating the rate at which classes can be improved, without requiring substantially more (instructional or experimental) resources.

Bayesian Optimization for Instruction

In our work we seek to automatically identify which items to include in a set of curriculum, and how to adaptively select these items, in order to maximize student performance on some specified set of learning objectives. In many situations instructors desire not just effective, but efficient pedagogical approaches. Therefore, the evaluation criteria for a particular way of teaching may combine multiple measures.

We can view this general challenge as an instance of finding the parameter values (indicating a set of items to chose, how to teach) that maximize a function value (student performance on learning objectives when taught using an automated policy with the specified parameters). Of course, in general there are a huge number of possible parameter values to try. Bayesian optimization is a popular machine learning approach for finding the optimal value of a function when evaluating the function at a particular set of parameters is costly, and we wish to minimize the number of parameters tried to find the optimal function value. This is certainly true in education, where each function evaluation corresponds to providing one (or more) real students with a particular instructional curriculum or approach to selecting that curriculum, and measuring the resulting outcome value (effectiveness/efficiency).

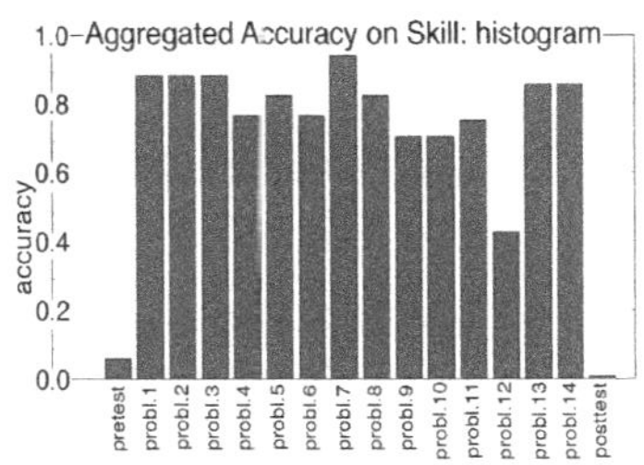

Figure 1: This figure displays the pretest performance and then student performance on each of the sequence of 14 problems, followed by their post test performance. Performance is measured by average accuracy. Note that there seems to be no steady increase in performance, and the pre and post test performance are both less than 10%. This potentially indicates instructional material not suitable for the learning objective.

Histogram Tutor & Preliminary Experiment

As a first step towards this general aim, we used Bayesian Optimization to optimize how to adaptively select activities in an online histogram tutor. Histograms are frequently used to convey information but there is good evidence that many students find understanding histograms challenging. Indeed even after instruction students may lack basic concepts such as what the axes of a histogram represent [3].

Our histogram tutor consists of activities/questions for 8 different skills considered core knowledge about histograms and/or common misconceptions [3]. These skills represent our learning objectives for students. We also created a test based closely on assessment items previously made to evaluate some of these skills [3]. Note that the BO approach can be applied much more broadly to tutors without skill labels on activities.

Bayesian Knowledge Tracing (BKT) is a popular 4-parameter model of student learning [1]. A simple approach for mastery teaching adds a fifth threshold parameter: halt teaching a skill when the BKT estimate of the probability that the student has mastered the skill exceeds the threshold. However, without student data it is unclear how to set the parameters of a BKT mastery teaching policy. Even given data, existing approaches tend to use maximum likelihood methods to fit the BKT parameters and then hand set the threshold parameter. However, BKT only approximately models student learning, and it may be beneficial to directly optimize all 5 mastery parameters.

For each skill, we seek to directly find the 5-parameter BKT policy $\boldsymbol{\pi}$ that maximizes the function value $f(\boldsymbol{\pi})$,

$$f(\boldsymbol{\pi}) = \frac{p_{\boldsymbol{\pi},s} + \mathbb{I}(p_{\boldsymbol{\pi}} \geq 0.7)}{\sqrt{l_{\boldsymbol{\pi},s} + 1}}$$

where $p_{\boldsymbol{\pi},s}$ is the normalized post test score for this given skill, $p_{\boldsymbol{\pi}}$ is the normalized post test score over all skills (with *0.7* as desired passing score), and $l_{\boldsymbol{\pi},s}$ is the number of practice problems given to the student for this skill (subscript $\boldsymbol{\pi}$ means following policy $\boldsymbol{\pi}$). This objective encourages policies where the student quickly does well broadly and on this skill.

We use BO to efficiently search over the space of policies for each skill. When a new student starts to use our tutor, we first use BO with the popular expected improvement acquisition function to identify a good next set of policy parameters to try for each skill. These parameters define a mastery policy that is used to teach a student and determine when to halt and present the student with the post test. Given the student's result on the post test, we compute the above $f(\boldsymbol{\pi})$ value that is used by BO to select a (potentially new) set of parameters $\boldsymbol{\pi}$ to try for the next student.

As an initial exploration, we used this approach to teach a sequence of 30 subjects that were recruited through Amazon turk. In between each subject BO was used to automatically identify the next set of parameters to use. Subjects were compensated for their time, and were prescreened such that subjects who already appeared to understand histograms were not included.

We then took the best policy parameters $\boldsymbol{\pi}_{bst}$ identified after 30 subjects, and tested performance of this policy on 10 new subjects. We were interested in the average performance of $\boldsymbol{\pi}_{bst}$ for two reasons. First, $\boldsymbol{\pi}_{bst}$ is expected to yield best performance so far (in contrast to parameters BO chooses at each step/student that could be exploratory). Second, student post test scores can be quite noisy (on a small set of problems), and averaging multiple scores gives us a better estimate of the expected f. We compared the average objective values to a simple but reasonable baseline we tried with 19 subjects: provide all available content on each skill. We had the same or better objective value for each skill compared to the baseline policy. This suggests that BO can be a beneficial tool for quickly identifying how best to sequence activities to achieve a desired objective.

Interestingly, the final policies identified as yielding the best expected objective gave zero practice problems for 6 of the 8 skills. One possibility is that our objective function may not represent our true desired intent — for example, it may over penalize an increase in the number of practice opportunities. From this perspective, algorithmic optimization of teaching may be a useful tool for helping reveal potential gaps between instructor's stated learning goals and objectives for the class, and what they may actually hope to achieve. A second possible explanation for our tutor learning not to teach certain skills is that the available curriculum for these skills does not improve post test scores — providing an important indication of misalignment between the teaching materials and the stated goals. To investigate this possibility, we examined if there was a positive trend between the number of practice items provided and student learning. Figure 1 shows one of the skills where there was not: both pretest and post test scores are low, even though student performance is consistently quite high on all tutor practice opportunities, without any significant trend upwards. This suggests that the material available is not well aligned with the desired learning objective as measured in the assessment item. Therefore, this data-driven optimization can also quickly help to identify key limitations of the existing curriculum (or, class of methods for teaching it) in terms of achieving the instructor's goals. The instructor can then source or invent new materials, or identify alternate approaches for teaching, in order to help students better and more efficiently accomplish the desired learning objectives.

Conclusion

We have shared a preliminary investigation into using Bayesian Optimization to automatically find the adaptive instructional policy parameters designed to optimize a given input teaching objective. Our results suggest that BO can quickly (within a small number of students) find good parameters, and can be used as a tool to help instructors identify misalignment between their present curriculum and approaches to sequencing that material, and their desired learning objectives.

Acknowledgements

We appreciate the support from a Google joint research grant and ONR grant N00014-16-1-2241.

References

1. A. Corbett and J. Anderson. 1994. Knowledge Tracing: Modeling the acquisition of procedural knowledge. *User Model User Inter* 4 (4): 253-278.
2. K.Koedinger, J. Stamper, E. McLaughlin and T. Nixon. 2013. Using data-driven discovery of better student models to improve student learning. *Proc of AI Educ* 421-430.
3. J. Kaplan, J. Gabrosek, P. Curtiss, and C. Malone. 2014. Investigating student understanding of histograms. *J Stat Educ* 22, 2
4. R. Lindsay, M. Mozer, W. Huggins and H. Pashler. 2013. Optimizing Instructional Policies. *Proc of Neural Info Proc Sys* 2778-2786.
5. M. Lovett, O. Meyeter and C. Thille. 2008. Measuring the effectiveness of the OLI statistics course in accelerating student learning. *J Interactive Media in Educ* 1: Art-13.

Deep Neural Networks and How They Apply to Sequential Education Data

Steven Tang
UC Berkeley
Tolman Hall
Berkeley, CA 94720
steventang@berkeley.edu

Joshua C. Peterson
UC Berkeley
Tolman Hall
Berkeley, CA 94720
jpeterson@berkeley.edu

Zachary A. Pardos
UC Berkeley
4641 Tolman Hall
Berkeley, CA 94720
zp@berkeley.edu

L@S 2016, April 25-26, 2016, Edinburgh, Scotland Uk
ACM 978-1-4503-3726-7/16/04.
http://dx.doi.org/10.1145/2876034.2893444

Abstract
Modern deep neural networks have achieved impressive results in a variety of automated tasks, such as text generation, grammar learning, and speech recognition. This paper discusses how education research might leverage recurrent neural network architectures in two small case studies. Specifically, we train a two-layer Long Short-Term Memory (LSTM) network on two distinct forms of education data: (1) essays written by students in a summative environment, and (2) MOOC clickstream data. Without any features specified beforehand, the network attempts to learn the underlying structure of the input sequences. After training, the model can be used generatively to produce new sequences with the same underlying patterns exhibited by the input distribution. These early explorations demonstrate the potential for applying deep learning techniques to large education data sets.

Author Keywords
Educational Data Mining; Deep Learning; Long Short-Term Memory.

ACM Classification Keywords
K.3.2 [Computers and Education]: Computer and Information Science Education.

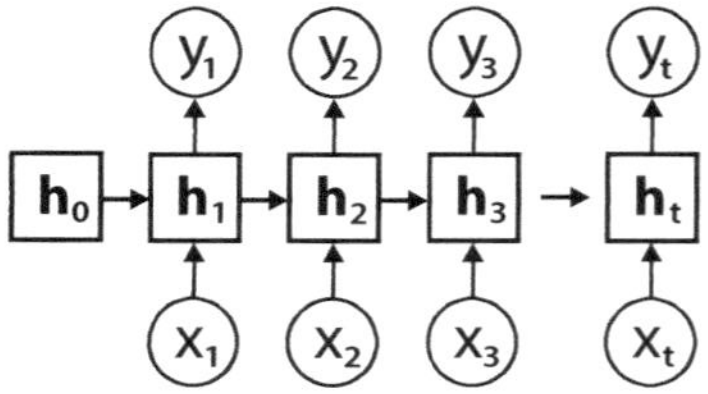

Figure 1: Simple recurrent neural network

Deep Learning & Education

In recent years, deep learning techniques have dramatically improved on previous state-of-the-art results in many fields. As a result, some educational researchers have recently begun to apply deep learning techniques to improve student modeling. As one example, [4] represented the Knowledge Tracing problem using Recursive Neural Networks (RNNs) to model student learning and achieve improved predictive capability over Bayesian Knowledge Tracing models [1]. The authors noted that a key advantage of using deep learning models was that they do not require human expert annotations and can take advantage of any student input that can be vectorized.

In this work-in-progress paper, we leverage a standard Long Short-Term Memory neural network model to explore two different contexts within education: writing samples from students in summative environment and clickstream activity within a Massive Open Online Course (MOOC). The use of a single model and architecture highlights the flexibility and broad applicability of deep recurrent neural networks to large, sequential student data.

Recurrent Neural Networks & LSTMs

Recurrent neural networks (RNNs) are a family of networks that can connect neurons over time, allowing for input sequences of arbitrary length. Crucially, RNNs incorporate a high dimensional, continuous latent state. This representation allows RNNs to use information from the past to impact a prediction at a later point in time. A popular variant of the RNN is the Long Short-Term Memory [3] architecture, which is thought to help recurrent networks train more effectively through the addition of gates that learn when to retain information in the latent state and when to clear or "forget" that information, allowing for meaningful long-term interactions to persist. Figure 1 shows a diagram of a simple recurrent neural network.

$$\boldsymbol{h}_t = tanh(\boldsymbol{W}_x \boldsymbol{x}_t + \boldsymbol{W}_h \boldsymbol{h}_{t-1} + \boldsymbol{b}_h) \quad (1)$$
$$\boldsymbol{y}_t = \sigma(\boldsymbol{W}_y \boldsymbol{h}_t + \boldsymbol{b}_y) \quad (2)$$

The RNN model is parameterized by an input weight matrix $\boldsymbol{W}_x$, recurrent weight matrix $\boldsymbol{W}_h$, initial state $\boldsymbol{h}_0$, and output matrix $\boldsymbol{W}_y$. $\boldsymbol{b}_h$ and $\boldsymbol{b}_y$ are biases for latent and output units, respectively.

LSTMs add additional gating parameters that are explicitly learned in order to determine when to clear and when to augment the latent state with useful information. Each hidden state h_i is instead replaced by an LSTM cell unit, which contains additional gating parameters. As a result of these gates, LSTMs have been found to train more effectively than simple RNNs. The update equations for an LSTM are:

$$\boldsymbol{f}_t = \sigma(\boldsymbol{W}_{fx} \boldsymbol{x}_t + \boldsymbol{W}_{fh} \boldsymbol{h}_{t-1} + \boldsymbol{b}_f) \quad (3)$$
$$\boldsymbol{i}_t = \sigma(\boldsymbol{W}_{ix} \boldsymbol{x}_t + \boldsymbol{W}_{ih} \boldsymbol{h}_{t-1} + \boldsymbol{b}_i) \quad (4)$$
$$\tilde{\boldsymbol{C}}_t = tanh(\boldsymbol{W}_{Cx} \boldsymbol{x}_t + \boldsymbol{W}_{Ch} \boldsymbol{h}_{t-1} + \boldsymbol{b}_C) \quad (5)$$
$$\boldsymbol{C}_t = \boldsymbol{f}_t * \boldsymbol{C}_{t-1} + \boldsymbol{i}_t * \tilde{\boldsymbol{C}}_t \quad (6)$$
$$\boldsymbol{o}_t = \sigma(\boldsymbol{W}_{ox} \boldsymbol{x}_t + \boldsymbol{W}_{oh} \boldsymbol{h}_{t-1} + \boldsymbol{b}_o) \quad (7)$$
$$\boldsymbol{h}_t = \boldsymbol{o}_t * tanh(\boldsymbol{C}_t) \quad (8)$$

Figure 2 shows the anatomy of a cell, where the numbers in the figure correspond to the previously mentioned update equations for the LSTM. $\boldsymbol{f}_t$, $\boldsymbol{i}_t$, and $\boldsymbol{o}_t$ represent the gating mechanisms used by the LSTM to determine "forgetting" data from the previous cell state, what to "input" into the new cell state, and what to output from the cell state. $\boldsymbol{C}_t$ represents the latent cell state for which information is removed from and added to as new inputs are fed into the LSTM. $\tilde{\boldsymbol{C}}_t$ represents an intermediary new candidate cell state that is gated to update the next cell state. The model

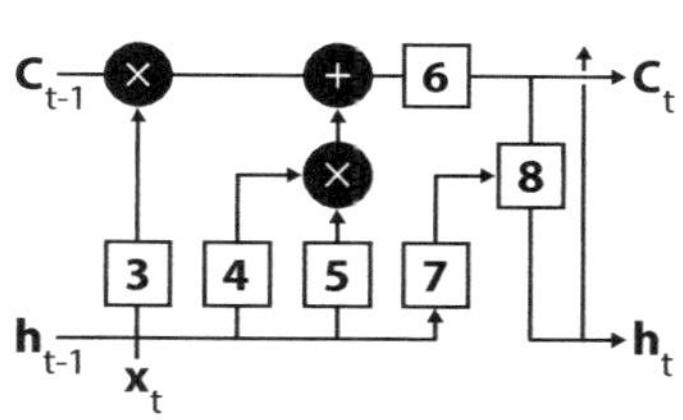

Figure 2: An LSTM cell, where the numbers correspond to previously mentioned update equations

used in this paper consisted of two LSTM layers with 128 hidden nodes each.

LSTM on Student Essays

LSTMs have been used in many language modeling applications in recent years. Such models applied to student essay corpora can potentially be used to tutor students by providing automated word suggestions based on what has already been written in the context of a given writing prompt. The ideal tutoring system would make suggestions that are both grade-appropriate and prompt-specific. The data for the student essays [5] came from a publicly held competition initiated on Kaggle, a platform for machine learning competitions. We were interested in generating "good" student writing at this grade level, only considering essays which were scored highly (top third of graded essays) from a particular prompt. This "good quality" data set included 472 essays, with an average of 541 words per essay. Twenty-three essays were used as a hold-out set for validation, while the rest were used for training. There was a total of 7485 unique words in the entire set.

Essay Results

In the essay case, the LSTM was successful in generating samples of text that emulate the underlying structure of the data. To ask the model to generate text, one simply needs to start with a "seed" context, and the LSTM will then produce predictions for the next word in the sequence. For the sake of example, we randomly sampled a seed of 10 words (not necessarily at the start of a sentence or essay) from an actual student essay: "hit the ball. Correctly. Tennis also increase your" and asked the model to generate 20 new predictions. The model produced: "way to get out from the computer. The computer is a great way to communicate. If you ..." Although this English sounds choppy at first glance, the LSTM has picked up elements of structure in English relative to the data it has been trained on, which consists of middle school level writing and a particular prompt. It is also important to remember that the LSTM starts with absolutely no knowledge of English, and simply learns both long- and short-term relationships between words from the training data. These results were expected given the success of these methods in other research contexts surrounding languages [2].

Like any neural network machine learning architecture, these methods greatly run the risk of overfitting to the training data, especially in the present case since our training set was quite small. One metric that can evaluate the generalizability of the model is accuracy on a held out validation set. In this case, "accuracy" refers to predicting the next word given some context. At the start of training, accuracy on a validation set of essays starts at .05, which means the model is simply guessing the most common word, which in this case is a period. After 150 iterations of training, the model has learned to predict words other than periods based on the previous context. During training, prediction accuracy on the held out set peaked at .21. Thus, out of 7485 possible words to choose from, the model is predicting the next word a student will write with 21% confidence.

LSTM on MOOC streams

Constructing a model to predict student actions has the potential to augment automated recommendation systems, so that the MOOC system might be able to automatically suggest a resource to go to when a learner is struggling. Indeed, previous work has shown that relatively simple topical N-gram models based on clickstream logs can capture student activity patterns associated with success in a course [6]. We applied the same LSTM architecture from the previous section to student clickstream data from a BerkeleyX MOOC from Spring 2013. There were 27 dis-

Event	Count
Problem view	4877414
Page view	3114154
Video play	2488490
Page close	1878973
Video pause	1531153
Problem check	1370943
Forum view inline	703938
Seq goto	415883
Problem save	171160
Wiki view	136020
Problem show answer	114745
Seq next	78672
Forum view inline	76836
Seq prev	20428
Forum search	19580
Forum upvote	13512
Forum reply	11350
Forum view user profile	5639
Forum create	4414
Forum view followed threads	4180
Forum follow	1583
Forum update	1314
Forum unvote	1234
Forum unfollow	442
Forum delete	355

Figure 3: Logged student action types from all students

tinct student actions logged, which are shown in figure 3. Note that this figure includes log data from all students enrolled in the MOOC, not just those who ended up certified. The MOOC was a 5-week course with a midterm and a final. We chose to train on student action data from students who were considered "certified" by the end of the course, which primarily reflects passing grades on the homework assignments, midterm, and final. There were a total of 8094 distinct learners in the data set, with an average of 1595 actions per learner.

MOOC Results

In the MOOC case, the LSTM was unable to learn beyond predicting better than the majority class for samples of student actions. This result shows that the granularity at which the student action data was fed into the model did not have an underlying pattern governing the actions that was consistently predictive across different students. The next steps in applying our LSTM model to student clickstream data will aim to improve the granularity of the student action sequence data by including more specific information about each action, such as an indication of which problem or unit the learner is accessing, with the goal of uncovering an underlying pattern that generalizes across students to predict which specific learning objects a student will interact with next. Future work applying this model is currently underway and has improved prediction beyond baseline.

Conclusion

This work-in-progress paper detailed preliminary results in applying deep recurrent neural network models to two sets of education data. Future work will attempt to extend and augment these models with the hope of creating tutoring systems that can generate helpful recommendations to students based on their previous actions and choices. Recurrent neural networks and other deep learning techniques are impressively finding insights in many fields when it comes to large sets of often uncategorized data, and there are clear applications where education and learning can be improved, specifically where large amounts of student actions have already been collected.

Acknowledgement

This work was supported by a grant from the National Science Foundation (IIS: BIGDATA 1547055).

References

[1] Albert T Corbett and John R Anderson. 1994. Knowledge tracing: Modeling the acquisition of procedural knowledge. *User modeling and user-adapted interaction* 4, 4 (1994), 253–278.

[2] Alex Graves. 2013. Generating Sequences With Recurrent Neural Networks. *CoRR* abs/1308.0850 (2013). http://arxiv.org/abs/1308.0850

[3] Sepp Hochreiter and Jürgen Schmidhuber. 1997. Long short-term memory. *Neural computation* 9, 8 (1997), 1735–1780.

[4] Chris Piech, Jonathan Bassen, Jonathan Huang, Surya Ganguli, Mehran Sahami, Leonidas J Guibas, and Jascha Sohl-Dickstein. 2015. Deep Knowledge Tracing. In *Advances in Neural Information Processing Systems*. 505–513.

[5] Mark D. Shermis. 2014. State-of-the-art automated essay scoring: Competition, results, and future directions from a United States demonstration. *Assessing Writing* 20 (2014), 53 – 76.

[6] Miaomiao Wen and Carolyn Penstein Rosé. 2014. Identifying latent study habits by mining learner behavior patterns in massive open online courses. In *Proceedings of the 23rd ACM International Conference on Information and Knowledge Management*. ACM, 1983–1986.

Thesis Writer (TW) – Tapping Scale Effects in Academic Writing Instruction

Christian Rapp
Zurich Univ. of Applied Sciences
St. Georgenplatz 2
Winterthur, 8400
Switzerland
rapp@zhaw.ch

Otto Kruse
Zurich Univ. of Applied Sciences
Theaterstrasse 17
Winterthur, 8400
Switzerland
kreo@zhaw.ch

L@S 2016, April 25-26, 2016, Edinburgh, Scotland, UK.
ACM 978-1-4503-3726-7/16/04.
http://dx.doi.org/10.1145/2876034.2893400

Abstract
Writing a thesis is no less challenging a task for students, than for organizations who instruct and tutor thesis writing at higher education institutions. Annually within just our departments, 1000 undergraduates face the task of writing a thesis. Increasing student numbers and stagnating resources pose management problems, as well as constant threats to the quality of instruction. In reaction to this, we started exploring how instruction and supervision of thesis writers and related administrative tasks could be electronically supported, allowing for scale effects.

A learning environment named Thesis Writer (TW) was developed, and piloted during the fall of 2015. TW supports individual writing and collaboration between writers, peers, tutors, and supervisors. This web-based software runs in common web browsers, independently of the operating system.

In this paper we highlight the core functions of TW and address such uses in which scale effects can be realized. Conference attendees can use and test the system including real-time collaboration, in either English or German, and discuss experiences made and data collected during the pilot by 300 BA students.

Author Keywords
Academic writing; Technology enhanced learning; research-based learning; learning to write

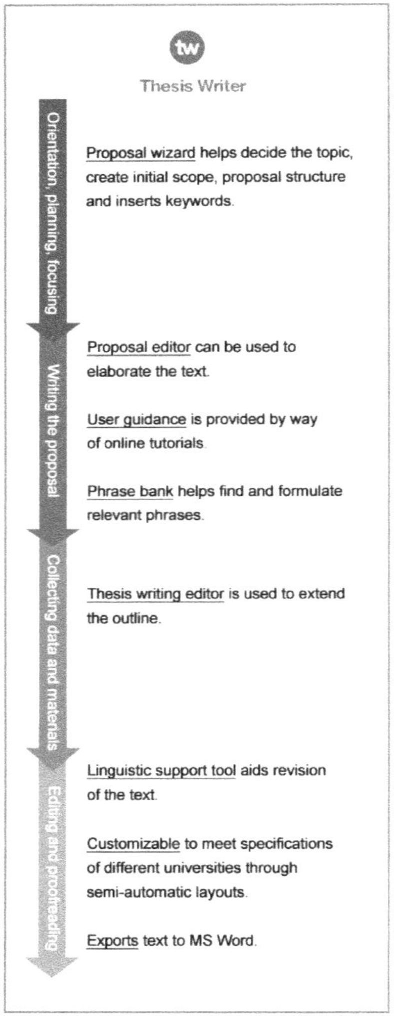

Core functions provided by TW

TW provides support to students in the areas of: (1) Orientation, planning and focusing; (2) Proposal writing; (3) Text production; (4) Collaboration and coordination between students and HE institution (tutors, instructors, study program directors).

Figure 1: How *Thesis Writer* supports students during each stage of academic writing.

(1) TW aids thesis writing through a variety of tools and tutorials, guiding students through the writing process from initial idea to completed thesis. The flexible structure provided fits most academic and scholarly papers. TW is also adaptable to different disciplines. (2) A proposal wizard guides students step-by-step through the proposal writing process. (3) New tools facilitate the formulation process by integrating large discipline-specific corpora from which users can derive linguistic support through an integrated open source corpus analysis tool. (4) TW allows real-time co-creation of texts for proposals or theses written collaboratively. A feedback function (for commenting) is currently being implemented to allow for peer-/tutor/supervisor feedback. Building Communities of Practices is supported via an integrated Moodle Forum. Coordination processes are supported as institutions often set parameters for thesis writing (evaluation criteria, citation, style guides etc.). TW acts as a portal and single point of reference for resources, standards and regulations related to thesis writing and allows for one (institution) to many (students) communication.

Scaling effect realization of TW

In the area of (1) orientation, planning and focusing, TW provides guidance through tutorials and instructional videos which can be used by an infinite number of users in a mode of autonomous learning. The hierarchical structure of the instruction supports writers exactly at the moment they need it and thereby reducing writer insecurity at all stages of the process. (2) The proposal wizard ensures that students adhere to predefined structures, meet set expectations, and enhances comparability among huge numbers of theses. (3) Instructing and learning the conventional aspects of the formulation process is often a daunting and time-consuming task. The corpus search tools allow for individualized queries about various linguistic items to support first-/second-language writers. (4) Collaborative processes among peers, students, and tutors have the potential to reduce guidance and supervision provided by instructors. Acting as a single point of information and providing one-to-many communication, administrative aspects related to thesis writing and grading can be optimized.

Conclusion

TW aims at increased efficiency in academic writing instruction through the unburdening of instructors from routine tasks, facilitating students' self-directed learning, and the supporting of administrative processes. Initial pilot results are encouraging, although issues still need to be resolved and tests applied to different audiences. Available in English and German, targeting both undergraduate and postgraduate levels, as well as multidisciplinary adaptability, creates limitless end-user potential.

e-Tutor – Scaling Staff Development in the Area of e-Learning Competences

Christian Rapp
Zurich Univ. of Applied Sciences
St. Georgenplatz 2
Winterthur, 8400
Switzerland
rapp@zhaw.ch

Yasemin Gülbahar
Ankara University
Gölbaşı Yerleşkesi
Ankara, 06110
Turkey
gulbahar@ankara.edu.tr

L@S 2016, April 25-26, 2016, Edinburgh, Scotland Uk
ACM 978-1-4503-3726-7/16/04.
http://dx.doi.org/10.1145/2876034.2893401

Abstract
Faculty development in the area of emerging technologies is demanding and resource intensive. This increases when aiming to qualify instructors to support their teaching virtually, e.g. in blended- and distance learning environments. Most elements of instructional design, delivery, and assessment require rethinking for technology integration. It is also a challenge to develop a sound instructional design model and corresponding teaching materials for courses aimed at developing the necessary skills and competences among staff. With "*e-Tutor*" a corresponding certificate course was developed at Ankara University, Turkey, a country for which, due to its geographical size and population, e-Learning is now highly popular. Under a project funded by the Swiss National Science Foundation, the course was translated into English, Russian, and Ukrainian, and then made accessible as an Open Educational Resource under Creative Commons Licence. Delivered in Turkish since 2011 with 350 participants, the course has also been successfully conducted with 300 participants from 11 countries in English, and with 320 participants in Ukrainian. This paper will briefly introduce the course design and its resources, before addressing to what extent it allows for scaling effects in staff development.

Author Keywords
e-learning; e-competences; faculty development; e-tutoring; train-the-trainer

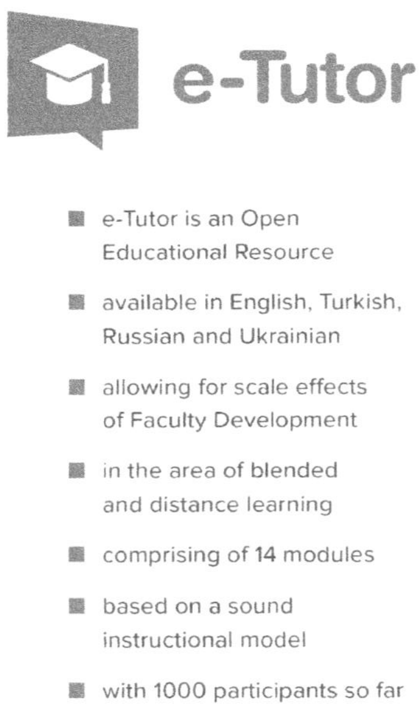

Figure 1: Key facts of e-Tutor

Design and content of e-Tutor

e-Tutor is conceptualised for a train-the-trainer and learn-by-doing approach – we deem it helpful that future e-tutors experience and learn as being online learners first, before becoming online instructors. This provides first-hand experiences of the potential and problems of online learning, considered a valuable basis for their future online course design and conduct. Therefore, the course is conducted completely online. The attendants are expected to work problem-based, i.e. to design and develop a course they aim to conduct online in the future, and to perform all necessary tasks to develop all the materials during the course. For the assignments, from module to module, each required task is set and artefacts evaluated; ensuring each participant exits the course with a sound theoretical background, valuable experience, plus their own instructional materials ready for deployment.

e-Tutor is comprised of 14 modules, with Moodle used as the Learning Management System, each covering a different aspect of teaching online considered the must-have competencies of online instructors. Each module uses a wide range of materials to ensure engagement of learners: handouts, narrated presentations, narrated videos, audios, interactive activities, e-portfolio artefacts and other Web resources. *e-Tutor* provides support to students in the areas of: (1) Fundamentals of e-Learning; (2) Online Learning Theories; (3) Learning and Content Management Systems; (4) Virtual Classrooms Management; (5) Online Instructional Design; (6) Online Instructional Methods; (7) Copyright, Digital Rights Management (DRM) and Plagiarism; (8) e-Assessment; (9) Graphical Design; (10) Creating Effective Visuals; (11) Multimedia Content Development; (12) Creating Interactive Applications; (13) Social Media and Emerging Technologies; and (14) Quality Control.

Scaling effect realization of e-Tutor

So far we conducted *e-Tutor* either in 14 week semesters at one hour per week, or in a condensed form over seven weeks with 2 hours a week. In the first case one instructor can conduct the course; in the second case two are advisable. Conducting the course is scalable, only limited by the technology used (so far Adobe Connect and Big Blue Button) and we found up to 150 participants easily manageable, allowing for a certain degree of interaction. Assessment and feedback provision is not scalable, but course instructors can be supported by other, perhaps less expensive, tutors.

Further scaling effects can be realized when *e-Tutor* is utilized in the train-the-trainer approach. Within the framework of an Eastern European project (2012-2015) funded by the Swiss National Science Foundation, we responded to the challenge that many universities in Eastern Ukraine, due to crisis/war, had to vacate their facilities and rapidly switch from classroom teaching presence to virtual environments. Suitable faculty (200 active users) from affected universities were selected and trained using *e-Tutor* in the fall of 2015. These trainees are now training their fellow colleagues with the Ukrainian version of *e-Tutor*.

Conclusion

e-Tutor, as an Open Educational Resource available in four languages, has so far been used to train around 1,000 faculty members. It allows for flexible and relatively inexpensive faculty development in the area of online course design and conduct.

A Demonstration of ANALYSE: A Learning Analytics Tool for Open edX

Héctor J. Pijeira Díaz
Universidad Carlos III de Madrid
Av. Universidad, 30, 28911
Leganés (Madrid) Spain
100075697@alumnos.uc3m.es

Pedro J. Muñoz-Merino
Universidad Carlos III de Madrid
Av. Universidad, 30, 28911
Leganés (Madrid) Spain
pedmume@it.uc3m.es

Javier Santofimia Ruiz
Universidad Carlos III de Madrid
Av. Universidad, 30, 28911
Leganés (Madrid) Spain
100060449@alumnos.uc3m.es

Carlos Delgado Kloos
Universidad Carlos III de Madrid
Av. Universidad, 30, 28911
Leganés (Madrid) Spain
cdk@it.uc3m.es

José A. Ruipérez-Valiente
Universidad Carlos III de Madrid
IMDEA Networks Institute
Leganés (Madrid) Spain
jruipere@it.uc3m.es

L@S 2016, April 25-26, 2016, Edinburgh, Scotland Uk.

http://dx.doi.org/10.1145/2876034.2893402

Abstract
Education is being powered by technology in many ways. One of the main advantages is making use of data to improve the learning process. The massive open online course (MOOC) phenomenon became viral some years ago, and with it many different platforms emerged. However most of them are proprietary solutions (i.e. Coursera, Udacity) and cannot be used by interested stakeholders. At the moment Open edX is placed as the primary open source application to support MOOCs. The community using Open edX is growing at a fast pace with many interested institutions. Nevertheless, the learning analytics support of Open edX is still in its first steps. In this paper we present an overview and demonstration of ANALYSE, an open source learning analytics tool for Open edX. ANALYSE includes currently 12 new visualizations that can be used by both instructors and students.

Author Keywords
Learning Analytics, Open edX, Visualizations, MOOCs

Introduction
Open edX is currently one of the main possibilities to use as an open source platform to deliver MOOCs or other online courses. Recent reports [2] indicated that at the moment there are more than 150 sites running Open edX

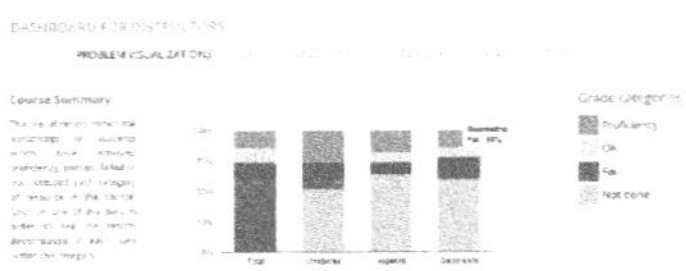

Figure 1: Dashboard for instructors with *Course Summary* visualization for the entire class, where the instructor can find the results for each section and problem of the course.

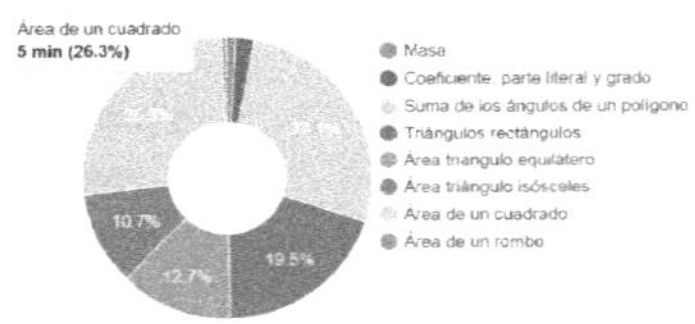

Figure 2: Example of *Video Time Distribution* visualization which shows the amount of time invested in each video for the selected student.

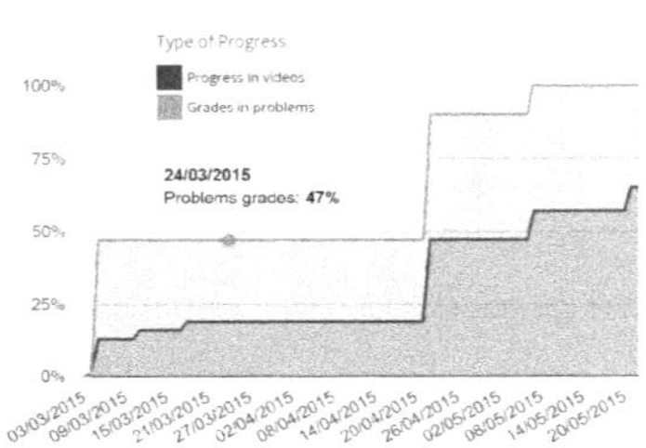

Figure 3: *Problem and Video Progression* visualization for a specific student, where he/she can learn about his/her progress in the course day by day.

with more than 1500 courses. However, the learning analytics support is still very scarce for a platform that is having such a high impact. One of the initiatives from edX in this direction is Insights, but at the moment it might not fulfil all the requisites for instructors, and is not available for students self-awareness. At Universidad Carlos III of Madrid, we have developed our own learning analytics platform for Open edX, which is called ANALYSE[1] and is open source[2]. For the aforementioned reasons, we believe that many institutions and researchers can be interested in ANALYSE.

Overview of ANALYSE

Technologies and Architecture
ANALYSE has been designed to be a Django app within the learning management system of Open edX. We have used mainly the same technologies as Open edX, such as Django, Python, Celery for scheduling jobs and we use Google Charts for the visualizations.

Metrics about the Learning Process
Currently ANALYSE contains 12 new metrics that were not present by default in Open edX. All these metrics are calculated for each student in a course but we also provide aggregates of the entire class. We have grouped these metrics in three sections. Related to the interaction of students with exercises, with videos, and more generally related to course activity. We can see some examples of these metrics in Figures 1, 2, 3.

Visualization Dashboard
We have implemented a visualization dashboard to display all the metrics. This dashboard is accessible by both students and instructors, however, while instructors are able to watch information about all students and course aggregates, students can access only their own data. We believe that ANALYSE visualization dashboard can be used for several purposes, for example to monitor students individually, to detect problems in resources, or for self-awareness. Another specific example is the use of ANALYSE to detect problems in videos [1], i.e. to see which parts of the videos are reviewed more often.

[1]http://www.it.uc3m.es/pedmume/ANALYSE/
[2]https://github.com/jruiperezv/ANALYSE

Demonstration Outline
The attendants to the conference will be able to interact with ANALYSE within an Open edX instance with data from real students. They can explore the different visualizations and case studies proposed by the authors of the work.

Acknowledgements

This work has been supported by the "eMadrid" project (Regional Government of Madrid) under grant S2013/ICE-2715 and "RESET" project under grant RESET TIN2014-53199-C3-1-R

References

[1] Pijeira, H. J., Santofimia, J., Ruipérez-Valiente, J. A., Muñoz-Merino, P. J., and Delgado Kloos, C. Using Video Visualizations in Open edX to Understand Learning Interactions of Students. In *10th European Conference on Technology Enhanced Learning, EC-TEL 2015, Toledo, Spain* (2015), 522–525.

[2] Porter, B., Haseltine, M., and Batchelder, N. The state of Open edX. In *The Open edX Conference 2015* (2015).

Beetle-Grow: An Effective Intelligent Tutoring System to Support Conceptual Change

Elaine Farrow
University of Edinburgh
School of Informatics
10 Crichton Street
Edinburgh, EH8 9AB, UK
elaine.farrow@ed.ac.uk

Johanna D. Moore
University of Edinburgh
School of Informatics
10 Crichton Street
Edinburgh, EH8 9AB, UK
j.moore@ed.ac.uk

L@S 2016, April 25–26, 2016, Edinburgh, Scotland, UK.
ACM 978-1-4503-3726-7/16/04.
http://dx.doi.org/10.1145/2876034.2893403

Abstract

We will demonstrate the BEETLE-GROW intelligent tutoring system, which combines active experimentation, self-explanation, and formative feedback using natural language interaction. It runs in a standard web browser and has a fresh, engaging design. The underlying back-end system has previously been shown to be highly effective in teaching basic electricity and electronics concepts.

BEETLE-GROW has been designed to capture student interaction and indicators of learning in a form suitable for data mining, and to support future work on building tools for interactive tutoring that improve after experiencing interaction with students, as human tutors do.

We are interested in partnering with teachers and other education researchers to carry out large-scale user trials with BEETLE-GROW in the classroom and remotely.

Author Keywords

intelligent tutoring; natural language; interaction data; conceptual learning; physics; electronics

Description of Demonstration

Our demonstration will showcase the BEETLE-GROW intelligent tutoring system [3]. Student interaction data (Figure 1) and other indicators of learning are logged in a format suitable for data mining and as training data for

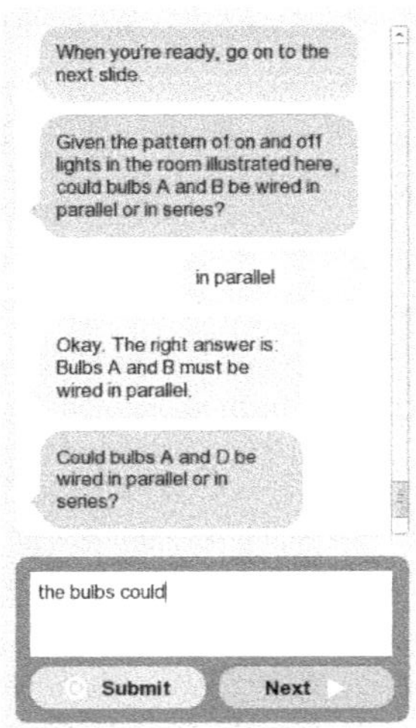

Figure 1: Students use natural language to answer questions in a familiar 'chat'-style interface.

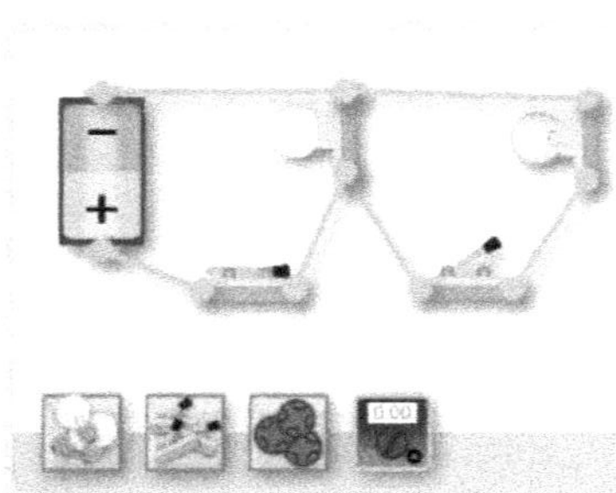

Figure 2: The interactive circuit workbench allows learners to experiment freely.

machine learning. The system can be accessed through a standard web browser and is designed for large-scale data collection, while also delivering a valuable learning experience in its own right.

The curriculum used in Beetle-Grow implements the conceptual change instructional approach [1] in the context of a simulated circuit workbench (Figure 2). This approach encourages students to think deeply about the phenomena that they observe and to attempt to infer the underlying explanatory principles in the domain. User studies have shown it to be highly effective, producing significant pre- to post-test learning gains [2].

Our demonstration will work through example exercises from the curriculum that illustrate the conceptual change approach. These examples include (a) using voltage to find a fault in a simple series circuit, (b) understanding the behavior of bulbs in a parallel circuit with multiple switches, and (c) a more complex exercise involving deducing possible wiring arrangements from observed behavior in the real world (Figure 3). We will also describe and discuss the student answers and indicators of learning collected in the online learning environment.

We will use a laptop computer for our demonstration and an external screen for display if possible. Attendees will also be encouraged to try out Beetle-Grow on their own mobile devices. It can be accessed at http://beetle-grow.inf.ed.ac.uk.

Acknowledgments

We thank the US Office of Naval Research for their financial support under Award number N000141410733, and our colleagues Myroslava Dzikovska, Mary Hutchison, and Edmund Farrow.

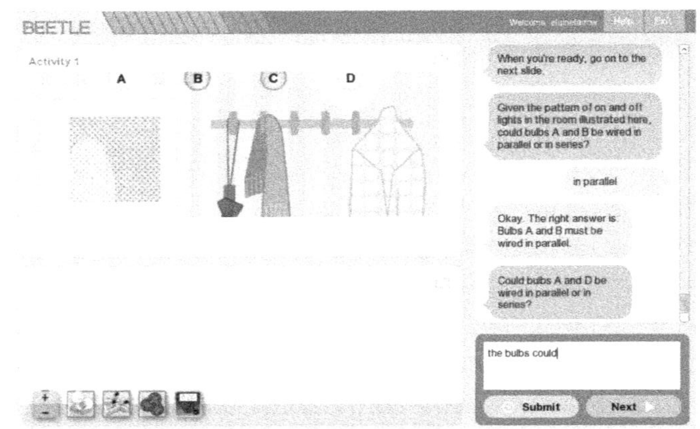

Figure 3: The browser-based user interface uses industry standard technologies: HTML5, CSS3, JavaScript, and the Play Framework, an open source web programming framework.

References

[1] Duit, R., and Treagust, D. F. Conceptual change: A powerful framework for improving science teaching and learning. *International Journal of Science Education 25*, 6 (2003), 671–688.

[2] Dzikovska, M., Steinhauser, N., Farrow, E., Moore, J., and Campbell, G. Beetle II: Deep natural language understanding and automatic feedback generation for intelligent tutoring in basic electricity and electronics. *International Journal of Artificial Intelligence in Education 24*, 3 (9 2014), 284–332.

[3] Farrow, E., Dzikovska, M. O., and Moore, J. D. Beetle-Grow: An effective intelligent tutoring system for data collection. In *Proceedings of the Third (2016) ACM Conference on Learning @ Scale*, L@S '16, ACM (New York, NY, USA, 2016).

Studying Learning at Scale with the ASSISTments TestBed

Korinn S. Ostrow
Worcester Polytechnic Institute
Worcester, MA 01609, USA
ksostrow@wpi.edu

Neil T. Heffernan
Worcester Polytechnic Institute
Worcester, MA 01609, USA
nth@wpi.edu

Abstract
An interactive demonstration on how to design and implement randomized controlled experiments at scale within the ASSISTments TestBed, a new collaborative for educational research funded by the National Science Foundation (NSF). The Assessment of Learning infrastructure (ALI), a unique data retrieval and analysis tool, is also demonstrated.

Author Keywords
ASSISTments TestBed, Randomized Controlled Experimentation at Scale, Authentic Learning Environments, Assessment of Learning Infrastructure.

L@S 2016, April 25-26, 2016, Edinburgh, Scotland UK
ACM 978-1-4503-3726-7/16/04.
http://dx.doi.org/10.1145/2876034.2893404

ACM Classification Keywords
K.3.1 Computer Uses in Education; H.5.2 User Interfaces – Training, help, and documentation.

Introduction
This demonstration serves as an interactive tutorial highlighting the ease with which researchers can conduct educational experiments at scale using the ASSISTments TestBed [3]. The TestBed is a unique collaborative funded by an NSF SI2 grant [1] that allows researchers to design controlled experiments with student level randomization and to implement them at scale by leveraging ASSISTments' pre-existing content and user population. ASSISTments, a popular online learning platform, has over 50,000 student users per year and offers an authentic learning environment in which researchers can observe the effects of learning interventions within online learning [2]. This demonstration will also offer a hands-on trial of the Assessment of Learning Infrastructure (ALI), a new data retrieval and analysis tool to be introduced at the Learning Analytics & Knowledge Conference [4].

Intellectual Merit of the TestBed
Prior to recent advances in learning technologies, conducting educational research at scale was tumultuous. Research carried high costs, was restricted by teacher-level randomization, and was often obtrustive to natural learning processes. However,

Features of the ASSISTments TestBed

Funded: The TestBed is funded by an NSF SI2 Grant [1], meaning low (or no) out of pocket costs for researchers.

IRB: ASSISTments' IRB allows for research designs qualifying as 'normal instructional practice.' Researchers simply need approval from their IRB to access anonymized data.

Simple UI: ASSISTments offers content authoring tools that are easy to use and do not require complex programming knowledge [2].

Collaborative Laboratory: The TestBed brings researchers together with students and teachers to study effective learning interventions while iteratively improving ASSISTments content and the user experience.

Data Retrieval: The Assessment of Learning Infrastructure (ALI), a state of the art data retrieval and analysis tool, streamlines data cleaning and analysis [4].

online learning platforms like ASSISTments offer authentic learning environments in which students receive immediate feedback on classwork or homework while teachers enhance their lessons through robust data driven reports. Built around the benefits inherent to the ASSISTments platform, the new ASSISTments TestBed [3] revolutionizes educational research by making it simple for researchers to design and implement low cost, high power, randomized controlled experiments that are unobtrusive to student learning.

Demonstration Details

Researchers from around the world already successfully use the ASSISTments TestBed to study educational interventions at scale. Through this demonstration, we hope to expand the benefits of this infrastructure to a broader research community. This demonstration will cover the following points in an interactive fashion:

- An overview of ASSISTments and its importance to the TestBed.
- Highlights from studies currently running in the TestBed, outlining the 5-stage research process (Figure 1).

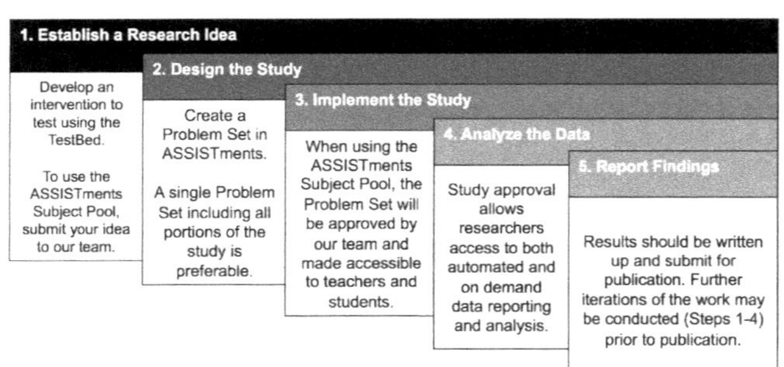

Figure 1: The five stages of conducting research within the ASSISTments TestBed.

- Introduction to accessing ASSISTments' subject pool and implementing a study.
- Hands-on session building and altering content within ASSISTments.
- Hands-on design and implementation of a simple study, with demonstration participants as subjects.
- Hands-on introduction to ALI, a unique tool for automated data retrieval and analysis [4].

Researchers will leave this demonstration with an understanding of how to use the ASSISTments TestBed to study learning at scale.

Acknowledgements

We acknowledge funding from the NSF (1440753, 1252297, 1109483, 1316736, 1535428, & 1031398), the U.S. Dept. of Ed. (R305A120125, R305C100024, & P200A120238), and ONR's "STEM Grand Challenges."

References

1. Heffernan, N. (2014). SI2-SSE: Adding Research Accounts to the ASSISTments Platform: Helping Researchers Do Randomized Controlled Studies with Thousands of Students. (NSF #1440753). http://goo.gl/lv2Ndi
2. Heffernan, N. & Heffernan, C. (2014). The ASSISTments Ecosystem: Building a Platform that Brings Scientists and Teachers Together for Minimally Invasive Research on Human Learning and Teaching. *Int J of AIED. 24(4), pp.* 470-497.
3. Ostrow, K. & Heffernan, C. (2015). ASSISTments TestBed Resource Guide. https://goo.gl/9GHuiS
4. Ostrow, K., Selent, D., Wang, Y., Van Inwegen, E., Heffernan, N., & Williams, J.J. (In Press). The Assessment of Learning Infrastructure (ALI): The Theory, Practice, and Scalability of Automated Assessment. To be included in the Proceedings of the 6th *Int Conf on LAK*.

Instructor Dashboards In EdX

Colin Fredericks
Harvard University
125 Mt. Auburn Street 4th Floor
Cambridge, MA 02139 USA
Colin_Fredericks@harvard.edu

Glenn Lopez
Harvard University
125 Mt. Auburn Street 4th Floor
Cambridge, MA 02139 USA
Glenn_Lopez@harvard.edu

Victor Shnayder
EdX
141 Portland Street
Cambridge, MA 02139 USA
victor@edx.org

Saif Rayyan
MIT
Bldg. 8-310
77 Massachusetts Avenue
Cambridge, MA 02139 USA
srayyan@mit.edu

Daniel Seaton
Harvard University
125 Mt. Auburn Street 4th Floor
Cambridge, MA 02139 USA
dseaton@gmail.com

L@S 2016, April 25–26, 2016, Edinburgh, UK.
ACM 978-1-4503-3726-7/16/04.
http://dx.doi.org/10.1145/2876034.2893405

Abstract
Staff from edX, MIT, and Harvard will present two instructor dashboards for edX MOOCs. Current workflows will be described, from parsing and displaying data to using dashboards for course revision. A major focus will be lessons learned in the first two years of deployment.

Author Keywords
mooc; dashboard; edx; analytics; instructor

Introduction
Course dashboards in edX provide aggregated student data and simple research results to instructional teams. This demonstration walks through the process of designing, deploying, and using dashboards, from the viewpoints of programmers, data scientists, course authors, and institutional researchers.

Dashboards
Two different dashboards are available for use with edX: the Insights dashboard, available to all users of the edX and Open edX platforms, which is accessible from within the platforms, and an MIT/Harvard collaboration called XAnalytics, which is available to course teams and institutional researchers at each institution, and is being adopted by other institutions as well. Both dashboards are open-source.

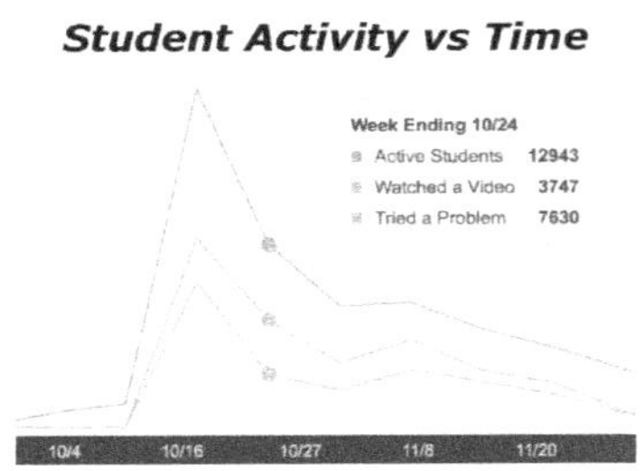

Fig. 1: Using dashboard data to identify which components are engaging students.

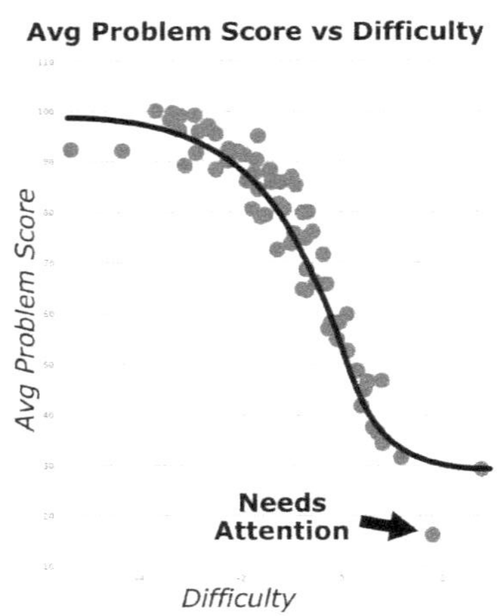

Fig. 2: Using dashboard data to identify assessments that need revision.

Three major groups use these dashboards: course leads, professors, and administrators. The choice of what data to display and how to display it was made in close consultation with these users.

Within a particular constituency, there can be substantial differences in user requirements. Discussion at the demonstration will include how these differences are handled in the two systems. For example, the needs of MOOC teachers differ greatly from the needs of on-campus teachers. In a face-to-face course where online materials are used to provide homework or additional resources, advising and assessing individual students is a major priority. Consequently, there is a greater need for up-to-the-minute information. Figure 1, from the Insights dashboard, shows how dashboard data can identify which components of the course are most engaging to the students. Conversely, MOOC instructors do not have the time or ability to address thousands of students individually. Dashboard data is instead used to guide iterative course development in a months-long cycle. Figure 2, from XAnalytics, shows how graphs of IRT-derived data can point out individual assessment items that need attention.

Many MOOC instructors also find demographic and geographical breakdowns to be very motivating. Both XAnalytics and Insights provide this information in aggregate form.

Future Developments

The future evolution of these dashboards will be a major focus of our discussion at our demonstration. We encourage L@S attendees to join in the conversation about how to handle novel and difficult sources of data.

In particular, both XAnalytics and Insights plan to group student data by demographics, performance, and other factors. We expect that these reports will be very valuable in reaching traditionally under-served groups of students. The XAnalytics team hopes to add the ability to handle custom survey questions (from sources such as Qualtrics), while the Insights team is considering how to handle the filtering of engaged and disengaged students.

Discussion forum data is also an acknowledged blind spot for both dashboards, and a complex task for computer-driven analytics. Both teams are considering how best to approach these difficult items, and we welcome input.

Demonstration

Both the Insights and XAnalytics dashboards will be demonstrated using real, anonymized student data from live courses. Both the instructor-facing side and the data chain will be shown.

Acknowledgements

The close collaboration between researchers at Harvard and MIT has been a boon for the development of the XAnalytics dashboards. Likewise, the deep involvement both institutions have with edX has helped to shape and drive the Insights dashboards. We are thankful for the community of research that has been created in Cambridge and Boston around online learning, and for the generosity of the individuals and institutions who help us improve education for the world.

Elivate: A Real-Time Assistant for Students and Lecturers as Part of an Online CS Education Platform

Suin Kim
School of Computing
KAIST
Daejeon, South Korea
suin.kim@kaist.ac.kr

Jungkook Park
School of Computing
KAIST
Daejeon, South Korea
pjknkda@kaist.ac.kr

Jae Won Kim
School of Computing
KAIST
Daejeon, South Korea
jaewonk@kaist.ac.kr

Alice Oh
School of Computing
KAIST
Daejeon, South Korea
alice.oh@kaist.edu

L@S 2016, April 25–26, 2016, Edinburgh, UK.
ACM 978-1-4503-3726-7/16/04.
http://dx.doi.org/10.1145/2876034.2893406

Abstract
We present Elice[1], an online CS (computer science) education platform, and **Elivate**, a system for (i) taking student learning data from Elice, (ii) inferring their progress through an educational taxonomy tailored for programming education, and (iii) generating the real-time assistance for students and lecturers. Online courses suffer from high average attrition rates, and early prediction can enable early personalized feedback to motivate and assist students who may be having difficulties. Elice captures detailed student learning activities including intermediate revisions of code as students make progress toward completing their programming exercises and timestamps of student logins and submissions. Elivate then takes those data to analyze each student's progress and estimate the time to completion. In doing so, Elivate uses a learning taxonomy and automatic clustering of source code revisions. Using more than 240,000 code revisions generated by 1,000 students, we demonstrate how Elivate processes large-scale student data and generates appropriate real-time feedback for students.

Demonstration
A major problem in online education is the high attrition rate which can be reduced by early feedback and one-on-one assistance for students experiencing problems.

[1]https://www.elice.io

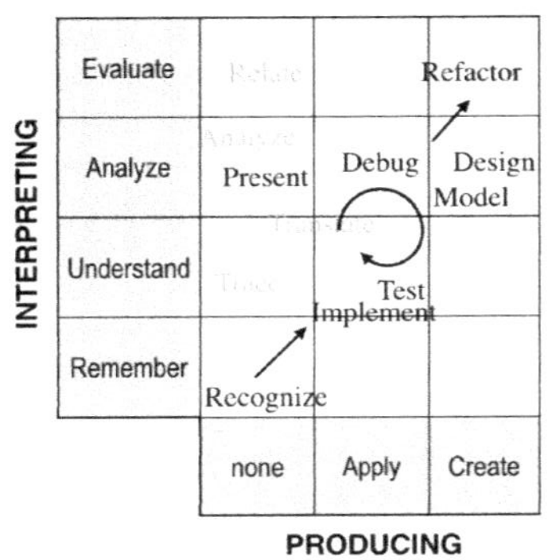

Figure 1: 6 stages of learning, from Fuller's CS-specific educational taxonomy.

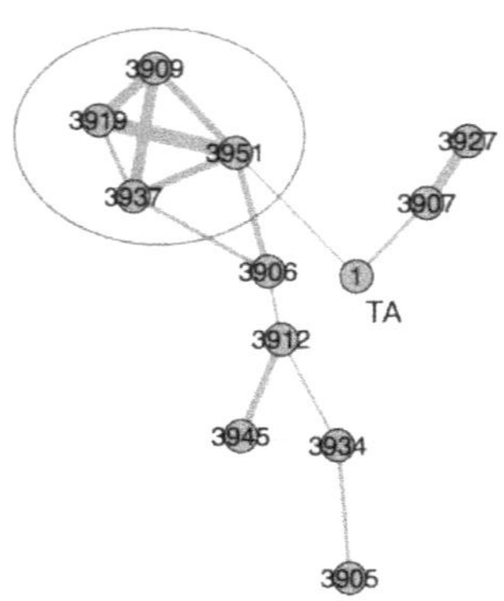

Figure 2: Part of the plagiarism network detected from KAIST Fall 2015 data structures course.

We demonstrate Elice, an online CS education platform with the goal to (i) identify the students who need assistance and (ii) reduce the teaching assistant (TA)'s time from redundant tasks. This way, we can scale CS education using our online education platform.

Student's Progress Using the Educational Taxonomy
From the educational taxonomy, we re-define the six steps of learning stages of solving a programming exercise in Elice (Figure 1; recognize, design & model, implement, test & debug, refactor, present). For each students intermediate code submission, Elivate can identify students current stage of learning and report to TA. With those reports, TAs can summarize each students individual characteristics. Using each student behavior in the initial two weeks, we can predict the student's final outcome at the end of 6 weeks (r=0.91).

Estimated Time to Completion
With more than 240,000 code submissions, we clustered student's intermediate revision snapshots to generate the state transition network for each programming exercise, so that every code revision is assigned to one of the states. The state starts with each student in the "skeleton" state (the initial code skeleton given to students), and they progress probabilistically between the states, eventually reaching the final state of "100%". As students submit more code revisions, the state network is automatically updated. Using this network, we can effectively predict each student's time to complete the exercise. Using Elivate, TAs can quickly identify students who need assistance, even before they proactively ask for help.

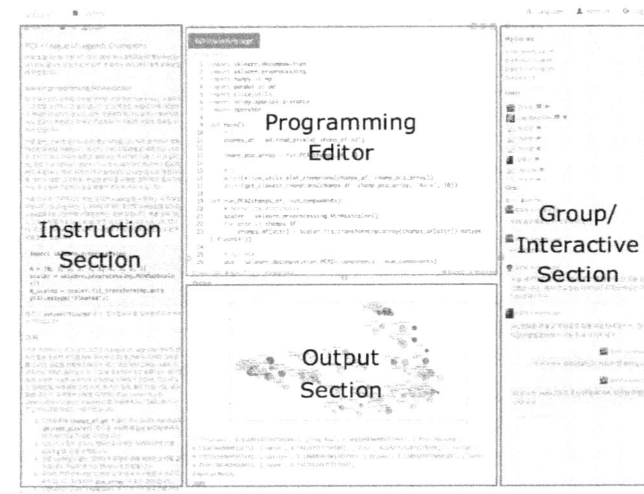

Figure 3: Elice Web-based programming platform. Current screen shows the exercise and result of the PCA algorithm.

Automated Grading and Plagiarism Detection
Surveys show that one of the most time-consuming tasks for TAs is grading. To save them time from such redundant and repeated task, we designed Elice to accept predefined test cases that run on the given skeleton code to allow automatic grading. In addition, we integrate a plagiarism detection module, thus TAs get notification of potential copying behavior of source code that may require further inspection.

Acknowledgements
This work was supported by Institute for Information & communications Technology Promotion(IITP) grant funded by the Korea government(MSIP) (No. B0101-15-0307, Basic Software Research in Human-level Lifelong Machine Learning (Machine Learning Center))

Effective Pedagogy at Scale – Social Learning and Citizen Inquiry

Mike Sharples
Institute of Educational Technology,
The Open University
Milton Keynes, England
mike.sharples@open.ac.uk

ABSTRACT

For the past four years The Open University has published annual Innovating Pedagogy reports. Our aim has been to shift the focus of horizon scanning for education away from novel technologies towards new forms of teaching, learning and assessment for an interactive world, to guide teachers and policy makers in productive innovation. In the most recent report, from over thirty pedagogies, ranging from bricolage to stealth assessment, we have identified six overarching themes, of scale, connectivity, reflection, extension, embodiment, and personalisation [8]. Delivering education at massive scale has been the headline innovation of the past four years. This success begs the question of "which pedagogies can work successfully at scale?".

Sports coaching is an example of teaching that does not scale. It involves monitoring and diagnosis of an individual's performance, based on holistic observation of body movements, followed by personal tutoring and posture adjustments. Any of these elements might be deployed at scale (for example, diagnostic learning analytics [10], or AI-based personal tutoring [4] but in combination they require the physical presence of a human coach.

The major xMOOC platforms were initially based on an instructivist pedagogy of a repeated cycle of inform and test. This has the benefit of being relatively impervious to scale. A lecture can be presented to 200 students in a theatre or to 20,000 viewers online with similar impact. Delivered on personal computers, instructivist pedagogy offers elements of personalisation, by providing adaptive feedback on quiz answers and alternative routes through the content.

But what pedagogies improve with scale? We start with the Network Effect [5]. This states that, for some highly networked systems, the value of the system increases with the number of people using it. A telephone network becomes increasingly valuable as more people join, extending opportunities for communication. By analogy, if learners can be enabled to form networks, then the more who take part, the more varied and diverse their interactions. The Network Effect was originally formulated to describe data connections. However, learners engage in meaningful communication rather than transfer of data and they gain value from the personal relevance of their communications [2]. We should look for education systems based on scalable networks for learning [3].

The FutureLearn platform was initially developed from a pedagogy of conversational learning [6]. Conversation Theory [7] is a cybernetic theory of how people, individually and collectively, come to know. Learning is described in terms of conversations between different systems of knowledge. Conversation Theory does not make a fundamental distinction between people and interactive systems such as computers, so it can be applied equally to human teachers and learners, computer-based instruction, or learning support systems such as MOOCs. It has similarities to connectivist learning but predates it by some 40 years and is based on collaborative negotiation of meaning in relation to structured content, rather than occurring within "nebulous environments of shifting core elements" [9].

Conversation Theory predicts that if the educational system can be structured to promote active and reflective conversation, then the more people who engage, bringing diverse knowledge, the more effective the process of learning. Some early design decisions for FutureLearn included building the platform around 'pedagogic Lego bricks' each with a distinct pedagogy, linking free-flowing conversations to each element of content, supporting structured reflective discussions, and implementing a conversational process of peer review. The implementation of conversational learning on FutureLearn has been largely successful. On average, 36% of learners engage in social interaction on the platform. The largest course, *Understanding IELTS*, from The British Council had 270,000 learners, with just one video attracting 56,000 comments and responses. The scale of learner interaction led to an unexpected problem of managing the profusion of comments and reducing the tendency of learners, and educators, to feel overwhelmed by the volume of learner-originated content. Techniques from social networking, including liking, following, profiling and roles have been introduced, resulting in an emerging pedagogy of 'social networked learning at massive scale'.

L@S 2016, April 25–26, 2016, Edinburgh, UK.
ACM 978-1-4503-3726-7/16/04.
http://dx.doi.org/10.1145/2876034.2896321

Learning as conversation is not the only pedagogy that can improve with scale. In general, candidates for scalable pedagogy should integrate well-designed learning resources with contributions from learners that are *timely* (offering learning resources when needed), *relevant* (being appropriately helpful), *contextual* (from a diversity of locations and cultures) and *engaging* (making learning interesting). For example, StackExchange (stackexchange.com) draws on its 5 million users to provide timely and relevant answers to queries. The iSpot platform (www.ispotnature.org) employs a combination of timeliness (through its mobile app to post pictures of nature), relevance (with a system of reputation management to reward appropriate identifications of species), contextuality (from location-based observations), and engagement (with user-contributed images of wildlife).

Massive-scale learning needs to be visualised and orchestrated, through 'social operators' [1] such as filtering content and grouping learners, to lessen the sense of being overwhelmed and to support educators in identifying teaching issues and opportunities. There are also opportunities to implement new methods of assessment, such as peer-assisted dynamic assessment where each learner is paired with an appropriate peer to overcome a specific learning problem.

At The Open University we are exploring the scalability and sustainability of pedagogies. Recent work has investigated Citizen Inquiry, which combines inquiry-led learning with citizen science. The nQuire-it platform (www.nquire-it.org) allows members of the public to propose and post science 'missions' then recruit participants and share findings. While nQuire-it and iSpot show possibilities of scaling inquiry-led learning, issues to be resolved include how to recruit participants to crowd-sourced investigations and how to facilitate the site to ensure sustainability.

Innovative pedagogy at massive scale offers many promises, including engaging people in global learning projects, gaining insights into cultural and national perspectives and conducting large-scale evaluations of methods of teaching, learning and assessment.

Biography

Mike Sharples is Professor of Educational Technology in the Institute of Educational Technology at The Open University, UK. He also has a post as Academic Lead for the FutureLearn company. His research involves human-centred design of new technologies and environments for learning. He inaugurated the mLearn conference series and was Founding President of the International Association for Mobile Learning. He is Associate Editor in Chief of IEEE Transactions on Learning Technologies. He is author of over 300 papers in the areas of educational technology, science education, human-centred design of personal technologies, artificial intelligence and cognitive science.

REFERENCES

1. Dillenbourg, P. (2015). *Orchestration Graphs: Modeling Scalable Education.* Lausannne, Switzerland: EPFL Press.
2. Downes, S. (2007). *The Personal Network Effect.* Blog posting, 4th November 2007. Accessed online, 17th February, 2016, at http://halfanhour.blogspot.co.uk/2007/11/personal-network-effect.html.
3. Ferguson, R. & Sharples, M. (2014). Innovative pedagogy at massive scale: Teaching and learning in MOOCs. In C. Rensing, S. de Freitas, T. Ley & P. J. Muñoz- Merino (Eds.) *Open Learning and Teaching in Educational Communities, proceedings of 9th European Conference on Technology Enhanced Learning (EC-TEL 2014)*, Graz, Austria, September 16-19. Heidelberg: Springer, pp. 98-111.
4. Graesser, A. C., Conley, M. W. & Olney, A. (2012). Intelligent tutoring systems. In K.R. Harris, S. Graham, T. Urdan, A.G. Bus, S. Major, H.L. Swanson (eds.), *APA educational psychology handbook, Vol 3: Application to learning and teaching.* Washington, DC, US: American Psychological Association, pp. 451-473.
5. Katz, M.L. & Shapiro, C. (1994). Systems competition and network effects. *The Journal of Economic Perspectives.*8(2), 93-115.
6. Laurillard, D. (2002). *Rethinking University Teaching: A Framework for the Effective Use of Learning Technologies*, 2nd edition. London: Routledge Falmer.
7. Pask, G. (1976). *Conversation Theory: Applications in Education and Epistemology.* Amsterdam and New York: Elsevier.
8. Sharples, M., Adams, A., Alozie, N., Ferguson, R., FitzGerald, E., Gaved, M., McAndrew, P., Means, B., Remold, J., Rienties, B., Roschelle, J., Vogt, K., Whitelock, D. & Yarnall, L. (2015). *Innovating Pedagogy 2015: Open University Innovation Report 4.* Milton Keynes: The Open University.
9. Siemens, G. (2005). Connectivism: A learning theory for the digital age. International Journal of Instructional Technology and Distance Learning, 2(1). Available online at http://www.itdl.org/Journal/Jan_05/article01.htm .
10. Vatrapu, R, Teplovs, C., Fujita, N., & Bull, S. (2011). Towards visual analytics for teachers' dynamic diagnostic pedagogical decision-making. In P. Long, G.Siemens, G. Conole, D. Gasevic (eds.), *Proceedings of the 1st International Conference on Learning Analytics and Knowledge.* New York: Association for Computing Machinery, p. 93-98.

A Data-Driven Approach for Inferring Student Proficiency from Game Activity Logs

Mohammad H. Falakmasir[⋆,#] **José P. González-Brenes**[⋆] **Geoffrey J. Gordon**[§] **Kristen E. DiCerbo**[⋆]

[⋆]School Research
Pearson
{jose.gonzalez-brenes,
kristen.dicerbo}@pearson.com

[#]Intelligent Systems Program
University of Pittsburgh
falakmasir@pitt.edu

[§]Machine Learning
Carnegie Mellon University
ggordon@cs.cmu.edu

ABSTRACT
Student assessments are important because they allow collecting evidence about learning. However, time spent on evaluating students may be otherwise used for instructional activities. Computer-based learning platforms provide the opportunity for unobtrusively gathering students' digital learning footprints. This data can be used to track learning progress and make inference about student competencies. We present a novel data analysis pipeline, Student Proficiency Inferrer from Game data (SPRING), that allows modeling game playing behavior in educational games. Unlike prior work, SPRING is a fully data-driven method that does not require costly domain knowledge engineering. Moreover, it produces a simple interpretable model that not only fits the data but also predicts learning outcomes. We validate our framework using data collected from students playing 11 educational mini-games. Our results suggest that SPRING can predict math assessments accurately on withheld test data (Correlation=0.55, Spearman ρ=0.51).

Author Keywords
Educational Games, Student Modeling, Stealth Assessment

1. INTRODUCTION
Educational assessments are important because they collect evidence about whether instructional goals are achieved or not. Unfortunately, the process of administering assessments is usually disconnected from the instructional environment, and it is often disruptive to the learning experience. In many developed countries, students now find themselves spending increasing amounts of time preparing for and taking tests instead of learning [11]. For example, a survey of the current state of testing in the United States of America revealed that students are taking an average of 113 standardized tests between pre-K and high school [12]. For these reasons, it is not surprising that both politicians and the general population have been weighing in on the question of whether students are being tested too much [12].

L@S 2016, April 25–26, 2016, Edinburgh, UK.

DOI: http://dx.doi.org/10.1145/2876034.2876038

Learning and succeeding are not easily measured by solving constrained tasks and answering verbal or multiple-choice questions. Advancements in educational measurements allow us to diagnose student competencies more accurately and effectively at various levels during the course of learning. According to Evidence Centered Design (ECD) [16], the goal of assessment is to characterize the evidence regarding claims one wants to make about the competencies of individuals or groups of students. The assessment process involves identifying, organizing, or creating activities for students so that we may observe that evidence. An alternative to traditional summative assessment (e.g, exams) is to use data collected from computer-based learning environments. This data can be used for invisible (or stealth) assessment [22]. One of the advantages of invisible assessment is to blur the distinction between assessment and learning.

Analyzing log data collected from students playing educational games is a promising way to perform invisible assessment. Studying the sequence of actions in an educational game provides incremental evidence about mastery of specific skills and allows us to infer what students know at any point in time. Prior studies have also reported that invisible assessment may reduce test anxiety while not sacrificing validity and reliability of the results [21]. Unfortunately, engineering a system that interprets log data is costly and time-consuming. For example, Shute et al. [22, 23] relied extensively on domain expertise to define a *Competency Model* in the form of a Bayesian Network to describe the set of knowledge and skills involved in the learning environment. They also conducted feature engineering on the performance data to build an *Evidence Model* that expresses how student interactions with the system constitute evidence about competency model variables.

In this paper, we propose *Student PRoficiency INferrer from Game data* (SPRING), a novel data analysis pipeline that models game playing behavior. Our motivation is that invisible assessment from game data may become more accurate and cheaper to implement if the domain knowledge engineering could be automated by a data-driven process. Our experiments suggest that SPRING is able to capture student differences and provide features that can be used to predict student proficiency. The rest of this paper is organized as follows: § 2 describes the specific challenges that make game data difficult to analyze; § 3 details the SPRING algorithm; § 4 evaluates the SPRING algorithm with student data; § 5 relates to prior work; § 6 provides concluding remarks.

2. SLOT AND FILLER DATA

Game data is often logged in a format that we call a *slot and filler*. In Table 1, we show a simplified example of a real educational game log that uses slot and filler structure. The Event Name column lists a number action or events that have been logged. For each event, there is a set of slots (properties) that further describe the event. Each filler represents a property value of the slot. In the context of this paper, we assume that each slot takes exactly one filler. For example, a `Move Object` event that represents the learner moving an object on the screen may have x and y coordinates as slots and the target position in two-dimensional space $(361, 82)$ as the fillers.

Id	User Id	Event Name	Event Data
1	ABC	Game Start	{ }
2	ABC	Move Object	{X:363,Y:82}
3	ABC	Move Object	{X:361,Y:54}
4	ABC	Open Toolbox	{}
5	ABC	Activate Tool	{tool:gluumi}
6	ABC	Use Gluumi	{sizeGluedTo:8,sizeNew:9}
...			

Table 1: An example fragment of a log from an educational game.

Analyzing slot and filler data is difficult. Some general-purpose predictive models (like logistic regression or decision trees) that are used in off-the-shelf data mining packages, such as Weka [8], use a vector representation of features as input. A vector representation requires mapping of observations onto a fixed number of features. It is not obvious how to best map the sequence of events (with slot and filler modifiers) into feature vectors. Feature vectors need to be of a predetermined dimension, and a game log may have a variable number of events and slots.

Machine learning algorithms that are able to work with data that is not represented as feature vectors include kernel methods and graphical models. Popular general-purpose graphical models, such as Hidden Markov Models (HMM), allow structure learning from sequential data with a variable number of events. However, these models usually require input observations with the same number of dimensions for each time step. It is not clear how to transform observations when the number of slots can vary for different events. For example, in Table 1, the `Move Object` requires 2 slots, while the `Game Start` has no slots. On the other hand, *ad hoc* graphical models have been proposed for mining specific games. However, these graphical models were tailored by subject matter experts and do not generalize across different games [20].

SPRING models slot and filler data for educational games when domain knowledge is too expensive or cumbersome to collect. To learn a SPRING model, we need (i) logs from students playing educational games, (ii) and their results in traditional assessments. SPRING transforms the slot and filler data to sequences that can be modeled with Hidden Markov Models. It then extracts features from the sequences and uses them in a regression model to predict the score of the traditional assessment. After this, SPRING is able to predict assessment performance of students by just observing their game activity as described by their slot and filler log.

3. SPRING ALGORITHM

SPRING is designed to capture the sequential decision-making process of students in a way that is representative of their mastery with minimum reliance on expert knowledge. Our data analysis pipeline receives raw data of student interactions in slot and filler format and extracts features to build a model that predicts post-test scores from game playing data. SPRING assumes that an event is always described with the same set of slots. For example, an event such as `Move Object` always would be described with x and y slots.

Procedure 1 The SPRING algorithm

Input: : A log file $\mathbf{L_{g,s,t}}$ of events (with slot and fillers) for each game g and student s (indexed by time t), results from a student assessment y_s, number of performance clusters K, number of latent states H.

for each game g **do**
  $\mathbf{D_{g,s,t}} \leftarrow$ Discretize_Fillers($\mathbf{L_{g,s,t}}$)
  $\langle s, c \rangle \leftarrow$ Cluster_Students(y_s, K) } Discretization
  for each student performance group c **do**
    $\mathbf{D_c} \leftarrow \mathbf{D_{g,s,t}}$ where $s \in \langle s, c \rangle$
    $\theta_{g,c} \leftarrow$ Learn_HMM($\mathbf{D_c}, H$) } Sequence Model
for each sequence d in $\mathbf{D_{g,s}}$ **do**
  $\phi_{g,s} \leftarrow$ Extract_Features($d, \theta_{g,c}$)
Learn a model that predicts y_s from $\phi_{g,s}$ } Feature Vector Model

Procedure 1 describes the three main steps of our pipeline: discretization, sequence modeling, and feature vector modeling. The discretization step transforms filler observations into multinomial indicators that are used as evidence for learning. The sequence modeling step learns a representation from data in the form of a Hidden Markov Model for high- and low-performing students. The feature vector modeling step uses the likelihood of student sequences in each game level as a feature to predict the post-test results. We now explain the different steps in detail.

3.1 Discretization

We now describe how we discretize the slot and fillers (§ 3.1.1) and the student performance (§ 3.1.2).

3.1.1 Slot-Filler Discretization

Consider the `Move Object` event from Table 1. We wish to transform the different possible fillers into discrete units. Figure 1a shows a screenshot of a minigame that generates `Move Object` events. The purpose of this game is for learners to move ice cubes from the mountain top onto the two designated areas to prevent the Yeti from crossing the wall. Figure 1b shows a scatterplot of the x and y fillers aggregating across 77 students.

Procedure 2 describes the method we use to discretize fillers for each game. The input is time-ordered student interactions

(a) Screenshot of game level 2, *None Shall Pass!*

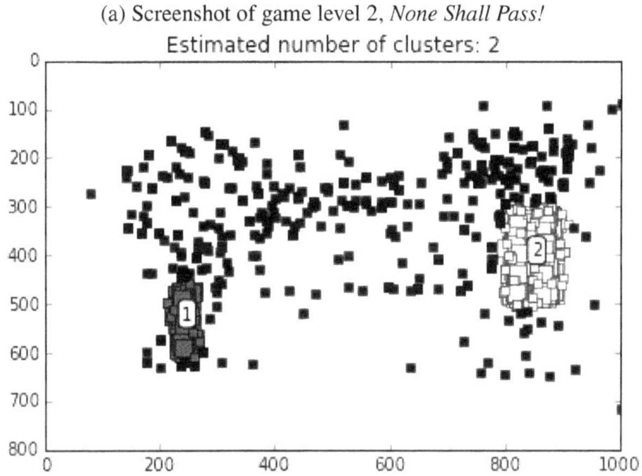

(b) Clusters found using DBSCAN method. We transform each movement action into corresponding cluster id during the discretization step.

Figure 1: Analysis of the `Move Object` slots and fillers from the *None Shall Pass!* mini game.

in slot-and-filler format for a single game g. The purpose is to transform the fillers of an event into discrete (multinomial) observations appropriate for sequence modeling. For this, we use an unsupervised clustering algorithm for the fillers of each event. For example, in Figure 1b, we show three clusters: cluster one and two (red and yellow respectively) that represent frequent movements, and cluster zero (black) that represents "outlier" movements. We speculate that the outlier group is a result of either technical glitches in the gaming environment or student misconceptions. To build discrete events we use the concatenation of event and cluster labels as an observation in the sequence modeling phase. For example, instead of modeling from an infinite domain like "`Move Object` $\langle x:363, y:83\rangle$", we use a number of discrete observations like "`Move Object Cluster 1`".

The specific clustering algorithm we used in our experiments is DBSCAN [6]. In preliminary experiments, we tried other unsupervised methods, but we found DBSCAN easier to use because it can find arbitrarily shaped clusters and does not require one to specify the number of clusters in advance. The time complexity of DBSCAN is $O(n \log n)$ (n = the number of

Procedure 2 The filler discretization step of SPRING

Input: : $L_{g,s,t}$, sequence of slot-and-filler observations in game level g

procedure DISCRETIZE_FILLERS($\mathbf{L_{g,s,t}}$)
  $\mathbf{Z} \leftarrow$ enumerate_slots($\mathbf{L_{g,s,t}}$)
  for each event z **do**
    $\mathbf{F_z} \leftarrow$ get_fillers($\mathbf{L_{g,s,t}}$)
    $\langle \mathbf{F_z}$, clustersIDs $\rangle \leftarrow$ Cluster($\mathbf{F_z}$)
    model $\leftarrow$ learn_classifier($\mathbf{F_z}$, clustersIDs)

  for each student s' **do**
    for each time step t' **do**
      if $z ==$ slot($L_{g,s',t'}$) **then**
        $\hat{f} \leftarrow$ model.predict(filler($L_{g,s',t'}$))
        $d \leftarrow$ concat(z, $\hat{f}$)
        $\mathbf{D_{g,s',t'}} \leftarrow d$
  return $\mathbf{D}_{g,s,t}$

data points) and there are recent parallelized implementations that are scalable [4, 17].

Clustering algorithms like DBSCAN often can only discretize observations in the training dataset, and would not generalize to unseen fillers. To work around this limitation, we trained a classifier for transforming any filler into a cluster label. In particular, we used a K-Nearest Neighbor (K-NN, K=5) classifier because similar to DBSCAN, it uses Euclidean distance as a similarity metric. The classifier is trained to identify a cluster label using the fillers as predictors. The K-NN classifier might not be the best choice for fillers in the outlier cluster. However, our preliminary experiments using cross-validation showed that it has enough discriminative power to distinguish the outlier fillers from other clusters.

3.1.2 Student Performance Clustering

We use assessment data to group students according to their performance. For this, we simply divide students into two groups by comparing their score to the median score of the population: students who score below or equal to the median are assigned to the low-performing group and the students who received a post-test score higher than the median in the high-performing group.

We did not consider other more sophisticated clustering techniques. Due to the small number of students in our dataset, particularly in the later game levels, we only use two clusters and do not tune the number of performance groups. We hypothesize that students in the two performance groups play the game differently. Our sequence modeling phase should be able to capture these differences by learning the interaction patterns of each group in different game levels.

3.2 Sequence Modeling

Once we have transformed the slot-and-filler structure into sequences of discrete observations, we can start looking for sequential patterns among different performance groups in each game level. Hidden Markov Models are a popular statistical tool for analyzing sequential patterns. We can model the sequence of student actions as observations, and infer a set of unobserved (latent) states. In this context, the states describe the process that generated the observations, along with statistical patterns that can describe and distinguish those states.

Learning the "best" value for the number of states (H) is a difficult problem in practice. There has been considerable prior work on this problem that used penalized likelihoods [18], Monte-Carlo cross-validation [24], and mixtures of HMMs [25]. We used the Hierarchical Dirichlet Process HMM (HDP-HMM) [7], which allows state spaces of unknown size to be learned from data. HDP-HMM defines a *hierarchical Dirichlet process* prior on transition matrices over countably infinite state spaces and is able to make a principled choice of how many states it needs based on the complexity of its training data. For details on training methods please refer to [7].

In summary, we used the output of the discretization step (2D array of multinomial observations) and trained two HDP-HMMs, one for high-performing and the other for low-performing students in each game level. The two models can be considered as a stochastic representation of the sequence of actions and we can use them to infer the likelihood of any arbitrary sequence as a feature for the regression step.

3.3 Feature Vector Modeling

For each of the game levels g, the HMM parameters of the high performing group $\theta_{g,\text{high}}$, or the low-performing group $\theta_{g,\text{low}}$ can be used to determine the likelihood of a sequence. Consider the sequence of discretized observations for a student s. The likelihood of the sequence given the high-performing HMM is:

$$l_{g,s,\text{high}} = p(\text{event}_1, \text{event}_2, \dots \text{event}_n | \theta_{g,\text{high}}) \tag{1}$$

This likelihood can be estimated efficiently with an algorithm called the Forward-Backward algorithm. For each student s in each game level g, we calculate the difference ($d_{s,g}$) between the log-likelihood of observing the sequence of actions given the two models. To scale the values between -1 and 1, we use a function called hyperbolic tangent:

$$d_{g,s} = tanh[K * (l_{g,s,\text{high}} - l_{g,s,\text{low}})] \tag{2}$$

If one HMM fits the data much better than the other, the value of $d_{s,g}$ is closer to -1 or 1. On the other hand, when the likelihoods are similar, the value of is close to zero. The parameter K represents the scaling factor. Larger values for K result in output distribution that is closer to +1 and -1 in the case of clear difference. We experimented with different K values across game levels and picked K=100.

We use the transformed log-likelihood differences in each game level as features of a linear regression model that predicts the post-test scores:

$$\hat{y}_s(\beta) = \sum_g \beta_g \cdot d_{g,s} + \beta_0 \tag{3}$$

Figure 2: A screenshot of hint provided in game level 11, "You Kraken Me Up!", in Alice in AreaLand. Students should combine four squares into a column and create three copies of the column to cover the designated area and prevent the octopus from attacking Alice while she crosses the bridge.

Here, $\hat{y}_s(\beta)$ is the predicted post-test score, and β_0 is an intercept for the model.

We learn the regression parameters using data:

$$\beta^* = \underset{\beta}{\operatorname{argmin}} ||y_s - \hat{y}_s(\beta)||_2 + \lambda \cdot ||\beta||_1 \tag{4}$$

Here, y_s is the true score of the student. To avoid over-fitting, we experiment with different regularization methods, but only report LASSO [26] as it worked best in our preliminary comparisons. For our experiments, we optimize the parameters of the model using a 5-fold cross-validation on our development set.

4. EMPIRICAL EVALUATION

We use data collected from an educational game called *Alice in AreaLand* to evaluate SPRING. This game is developed for research purposes as a part of Pearson Insight Learning System[1]. It focuses on teaching and assessing geometric measurement, specifically the understanding of area, among 6th-grade students. The game targets three main stages in the development of area: 1) area unit iteration, 2) use of unit squares to measure area, and 3) use of composites to measure area. The current version has 12 game levels. A simple student scenario involves covering a 2D area with smaller unit squares placed end-to-end in a non-overlapping fashion, combining the single squares into rows or columns, and then determining the number of rows or columns needed. Figure 2 shows a screenshot of one game level.

Throughout the game, Alice is accompanied by Flat Cat – an assistant character who provides feedback and scaffolding to the player at the beginning of each game level and upon request when students push a hint button (represented by two magnifiers at the bottom center of Figure 2). Earlier game

[1] http://researchnetwork.pearson.com/learning-science/insight-learning-system

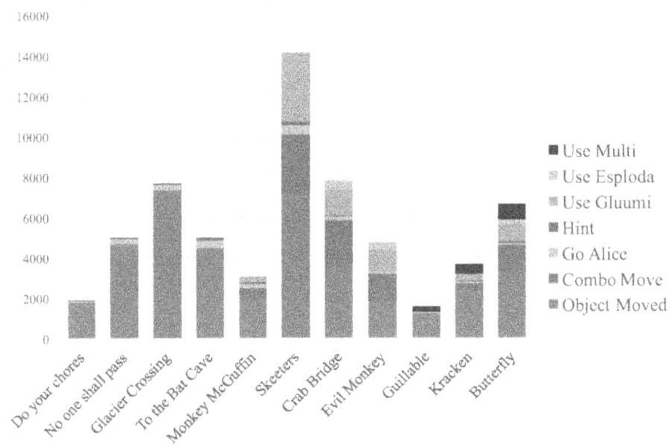

Figure 3: Frequency of Events in Each Game Level

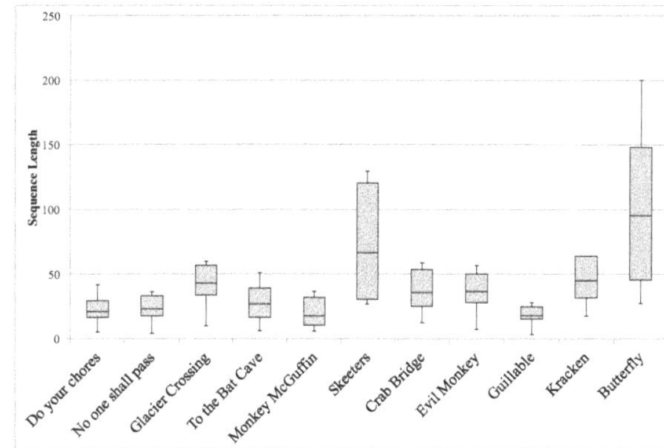

Figure 4: Boxplot of sequence length in each game level

levels are designed for students to learn about area unit iteration and usually require them to cover a number of predefined areas with unit squares (not necessarily in a non-overlapping fashion).

By advancing through game levels, students are presented with three tools: *Gluumi* for combining unit squares by gluing them together; *Multy*, for making copies of different objects; and *Esploda* for breaking compound shapes into single units. There is no limit for completing a game level regarding time or number of actions students may execute. The students press the *Go Alice* button (bottom left corner of Figure 2) if they deem their performance to be satisfactory for *Alice* to proceed. Based on the covered area and the arrangement of the tiles, they either advance to the next level or receive feedback and stay at the same level. Beginning levels only involve simple concepts, and they get more complicated while the student progresses.

4.1 Dataset

Our dataset consists of time-stamped interactions of 129 students in 11 game levels. We do not use the data from one of the game levels due to technical issues. For 77 students, we also have post-test scores from a paper-based exam with 20 questions in the 3 skills of geometric measurement as described above. The post-test scores range from 0 to 18 (out of 20) with the mean of 7.81 and standard deviation of 4.36.

In total, there are 88,458 events recorded in the dataset from 1,510 game sessions, meaning that students tried some of the game levels multiple times. Based on the ECD framework, beginning levels only involve the area unit iteration skill and other skills and related tools are gradually added to the later game levels. Figure 3 shows the frequency of different events in each game level. As depicted in Figure 3, the student interaction with the system in all game levels is dominated by movements. Figure 4 shows a boxplot for the sequence length in each game level.

We only use the interactions of students who participated in the post-test (77 students) in our data analysis pipeline. Our dataset includes the records of multiple attempts (sequence of actions) students made to solve each game level. Students may struggle with a game level on the first attempt and change their answers multiple times to find the solution. Different attempts are a rich data source for studying students' change of performance over time. However, we decided to only incorporate the first attempt in each game level in our analysis because SPRING only accepts one sequence of action per game level for each student. Figure 4 shows the boxplot of sequence length in each game level.

4.2 Experimental Setup

We divide students into two groups, one (80%) for training and development purposes, and the other (20%) for test and verification. In the discretization phase, we transform the log data from slot-and-filler structures for each game level into sequences of multinomial variables that can be used as evidence for learning for each student. In the sequence modeling phase, we use the multinomial sequences of students in the development set (80%) to train two HMMs that represent high- and low-performing students. In the feature vector modeling phase, we use the likelihood of students' sequences in order to build a regression model that is predictive of the post-test results. Finally, we test the regression model on the held-out set (20%) and report the results.

4.3 Quantitative Results

We evaluate two implementations of SPRING, each of them using two ($K = 2$) HMMs for each game level as described previously– one for high-performing students and one for low-performing students:

- SPRING ($H = 1$) uses an HMM with only one hidden state, a model with no memory (no temporal information). This model evaluates the effect of our discretization step since it only considers the distribution of the discretized observations in a sequence to distinguish between high- and low-performing students (as in Gaussian Mixture Model).
- SPRING (H^*) learns the best number of states for each game level based on the training examples using a Hierarchical Dirichlet Process [7].

Additionally, we evaluate two baseline methods:

- Success / Failure: A regression model with eleven binary features. Each feature represents whether a student successfully passed each of the 11 different mini-games on the first attempt.
- Sequence Length: A regression model that uses the normalized sequence lengths in each game level.

Table 2 summarizes our results. We use each method to predict the students the assessment score of the students in the test set. We compare the predictions to true scores using popular evaluation metrics: Pearson product-moment correlation coefficient (R), Spearman rank correlation ρ, mean absolute error (MAE) and root mean squared error (RMSE). The best-performing model according to all of the metrics is SPRING H^*.

Predictive Features	R	ρ	MAE	RMSE
Sequence Length (Normal)	0.15	0.35	2.93	3.61
Success / Failure	0.02	0.16	3.21	4.08
SPRING ($K = 2, H = 1$)	0.17	0.25	3.60	3.10
SPRING ($K = 2, H^*$)	**0.55**	**0.51**	**2.84**	**3.35**

Table 2: The results of predicting post-test scores using three different feature sets.

The baselines and SPRING have a positive correlation with the true values. However, the correlation is statistically significant only for SPRING H^* (one-sided t-test: $r = 0.55$, $n = 15$, and $p < 0.05$). This suggests that the predicted scores of SPRING H^* are positively correlated with the true assessment scores.

We also calculate the absolute difference between the true and predicted post-test scores for all of the students based on each model. We use a paired one-sided t-test (n=15) to judge the significance of improvement over the baselines. We cannot reject the null hypothesis that the baselines are as good or better than SPRING ($p = 0.20$ over the Success/Failure baseline and $p = 0.26$ over the Sequence Length baseline).

Our results suggest that even though there is a significant and positive correlation between the true and SPRING's predicted post-test scores, the improvement in terms of MAE may not be significant. We notice that changes in correlation are more drastic than changes in MAE. For example, in Table 2 a 0.4 improvement in correlation over the first baseline resulted in only a change of 0.09 and improvement in MAE. It is unclear which evaluation metric is better for our application. A possible explanation of why the MAE is not significant is that our dataset is too small. Our held-out set contains only 15 students and a few of them achieved poor performance results in the post-test while successfully finishing most of the game levels. Future research could investigate how to evaluate invisible assessment systems, as well as replicate our results with larger datasets to see if the observed trend continues.

A limitation of our approach is that our student performance clustering phase uses the post-test scores (independent variable) to divide students into high- and low-performance groups.

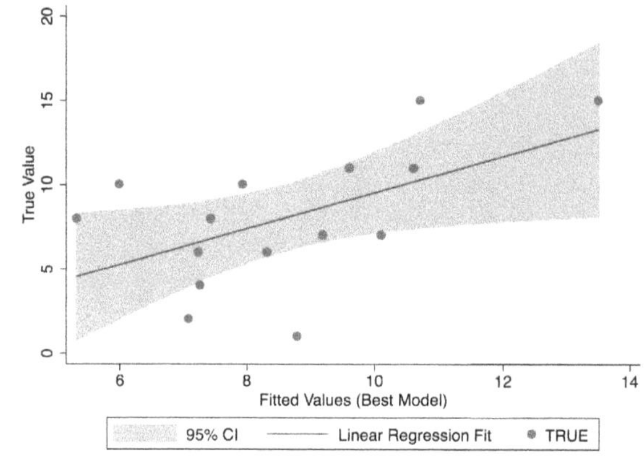

Figure 5: Results of predicting the post-test scores of the held-out set along with the regression line and 95% interval.

In order to avoid using information from the independent variable to calculate the features of our regression model, we are using an 80%-20% split to validate the results instead of for example using a 10-fold cross validation. This design decision, while necessary, reduces the sample size further.

Figure 5 compares the true post-test scores against the predicted values. The regression line is calculated using LASSO and the 95% confidence interval is plotted. The regression model also provides us with an insight into how important each game level is in distinguishing between high- and low-performing students.

Table 3 shows the weights of each game level in the best performing model. As it is shown in the table, game level 11 (*You Kraken Me Up!* – screenshot Figure 2), has the highest weight in the regression model. This supports that the difference between the sequence of student interactions in this game level has the highest factor in distinguishing between high- and low-performing students.

The difference in predictive performance between game levels is likely related to game design. Some game levels are designed to introduce game tools and techniques while others are created to present choices to players aligned with math proficiency. We believe the source of difference is mainly due to the fact that finding the solution to later game levels requires mastery in all three major subskills targeted by the game design.

Game Level	**Weight**
You Kraken Me Up!	1.686
Skeeterz	1.059
Evil Monkeys	1.053
To the Bat Cave	0.855
None Shall Pass	0.417
...	

Table 3: Weights of each game level in the best performing model.

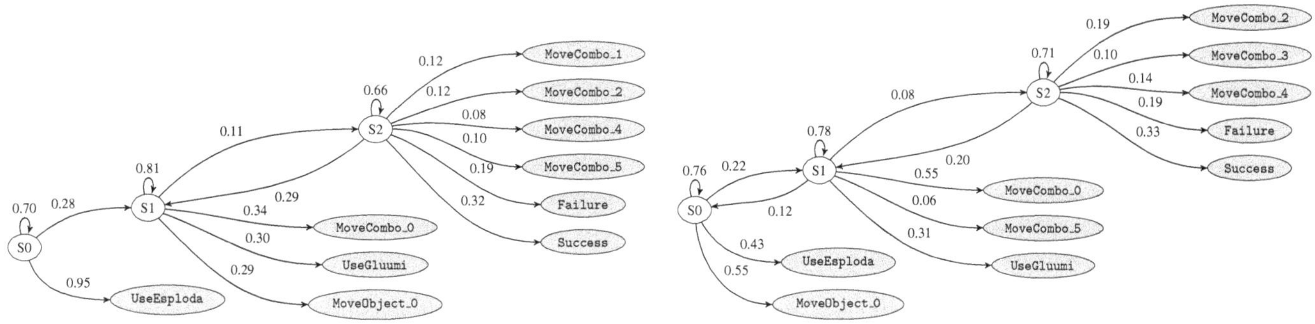

(a) High performing students (b) Low performing students

Figure 6: Transition diagram learned from data of students playing one of the games

4.4 Discussion of Interpretability

Predicting post-test scores is not the only motivation for designing the pipeline. We are also looking for an interpretable model that can give us insight into how students interact with the system and identify patterns that are suggestive of learning. Figure 6 shows the difference between two HMMs learned for one of the game levels. In this game level in the initial state, students are presented with composite objects and they have to use the `Esploda` tool to convert them into single unit objects. Then, they have to use the `Gluumi` tools to convert the single unit objects into composite objects that fit the designated area. And finally, they have to move the composite object they have created into the designated area. For comparison purposes, we are showing a three-state HMM for both high- and low-performing students and removed the edges that had a probability below 0.05.

Figure 6a represents the HMM for high-performing students. The three latent states, S_{0-2} can be interpreted as sequential steps that students took for solving this problem. As illustrated in Figure 6a, high-performing students follow the expected path of using the `Esploda` tool in S_0, using the `Gluumi` tool in S_1, and then moving the composite objects into the designated areas `MoveCombo_ClusterID` until they successfully finish the game. On the other hand, low-performing students (Figure 6b) do not necessarily follow the expected path and the probability of moving an object into the outlier cluster (`MoveObject_0 and MoveCombo_0`) is also higher across states for low-performing students.

5. RELATION TO PRIOR WORK

The potential of computer games for educational purposes has been of interest since nearly the beginning of video games. Unlike video games, which focus on creating an entertaining experience for the user, educational games require principles and strategies that engage students while maximizing their learning gain. However, games have produced mixed learning outcomes in the classroom [10, 15] and studying student interactions is a crucial step toward understanding their learning process and improving the game environment in the future.

There have been numerous attempts by the educational research community to develop analytic methods and build predictive models based on the data from educational games. For example, *Rumble Blocks* [3] is a physics educational game designed to teach basic concepts of structural stability and balance to children in grades K-3 (ages 5-8 years old). Harpstead et al. [9] learned a two-dimensional context-free grammar (CFG) from student interactions within the game and used a modified version of CYK algorithm to parse and extract conceptual features from student solutions. They used the features and performed cluster analysis of student solutions to measure how many follow the designers' envisioned path. While the CFG framework offers a promising method to learn features from game activity logs, we are particularly interested in a model that can represent the sequence of interactions and not the characteristics of final submission.

Crystal Island [20] is an educational 3D game environment for learning microbiology in middle school. Rowe and Lester [19] used a hand-authored dynamic Bayesian network (DBN) to model student knowledge in four broad components: narrative, content, strategy, and solution knowledge. They handpicked a set of observable actions that can serve as evidence of the student's underlying knowledge in each category and defined the parameters of the model in terms of conditional probability tables for each of the network nodes (observable and latent). They used observations from 116 eighth-graders interacting with the game environment in 50-minute sessions. In order to evaluate the model, they experimented with different threshold levels to discriminate between mastered and un-mastered knowledge components and used the final estimate of student knowledge in each category (mastered vs. un-mastered) to predict their post-test results. The DBN framework is an example of extensive domain authoring that we are trying to avoid by using data-driven methods.

One way to avoid extensive domain authoring is to use the state-action graph of the game environment. States are different configurations of the game environment and actions represent different ways students can interact with the game in each state. For example, *Refraction* [1] is another educational game for learning about fractions by splitting laser beams into fractional amounts to target spaceships and avoid asteroids. Liu et al. [14] created an ensemble algorithm that combines elements of Markov models, player heuristic search, and collaborative filtering techniques with state-space clustering in order to predict player movements on the last game level based on the history of movements in previous game levels. Lee et al. [13] extended the former framework by building a state-action graph and using feature selection techniques to reduce the number of features for each state. To ensure extensibility, they also tested the framework on another game, *DragonBox*, and reported improvement over [14]. While the state-action graph of the game environment offers a potential for micro-level analysis of student interactions, we are particularly interested in patterns that are representative of student proficiency.

Quantum Spectre is a more complex puzzle-style educational game designed for high school students to learn about optics. Eagle et al. [5] used interaction networks (IN) to visualize and derive insight into students' problem-solving behavior and common misconceptions. They used data from 195 students in 15 classes and created the full IN of every state and possible actions for each game level. Next, they used clustering to reduce the state-action space into a high-level visualization of how students progress through the puzzle and classify each student interaction into four categories: correct, placement error, rotation error, and puzzle error. Finally, they picked a smaller set of students (n=10) and used a linear regression model for predicting their post-test results. The results show a direct negative relationship between science-related gameplay errors and the post-test scores. Constructing the full interaction network for each game level can easily become intractable for complex games such as *Alice in AreaLand*. Moreover, integrating results from multiple game levels is not straightforward since each game level has its own state-action graph and further engineering is required to extract features that are generalizable across game levels.

6. CONCLUSIONS AND FUTURE WORK

Educational games are an interesting source of data that provide evidence of complex cognitive behavior. In this study, we propose a novel data-driven method, SPRING, for student modeling in educational games. Modeling student behavior is a promising research direction with applications for game designers, educators, and even policy makers.

Unlike prior work in invisible assessment, we do not use domain knowledge to design features that relate gameplay behavior with student performance. Instead, we explore the effectiveness of data-driven methods for student modeling in educational games. We evaluate our models quantitatively in terms of how well it can predict student assessments. To demonstrate the effectiveness of our framework, we predict the post-test scores of students using a regression model. The parameters of the regression model quantify how much an educational game is useful in distinguishing between high- and low-performing students. We suggest that SPRING is an interpretable model, and it may provide insight into how students learn.

There are many possible directions for future work. On a lower level, we can integrate the discretization and sequence modeling step by employing Hidden Markov Models that accept slot and filler sequences as input. On a higher level, instead of dividing students into two groups (high- and low-performing), we can use the HMM to cluster students [2, 25] into more groups that might be more representative of different approaches students follow to solve each game level. We can also replace our regression model with a more powerful ensemble method that considers different subskills in order to integrate features of each game level to predict the post-test scores. Future work could address the assumptions of our method. For example, SPRING assumes that events are always described with the same set of slots and each slot can only accept one filler.

Even though we only evaluated SPRING using data from a single game, the algorithm may be useful for similar gaming environments that use slot-and-filler structures to log student interactions with the system. We are optimistic that our approach may be useful to make assessment less intrusive and better embedded to classroom education.

7. REFERENCES

1. Erik Andersen, Yun-En Liu, Ethan Apter, François Boucher-Genesse, and Zoran Popović. 2010. Gameplay analysis through state projection. In *Proceedings of the fifth international conference on the foundations of digital games*. ACM, 1–8.
2. Manuele Bicego, Vittorio Murino, and Mário AT Figueiredo. 2003. Similarity-based clustering of sequences using hidden Markov models. In *Machine learning and data mining in pattern recognition*. Springer, 86–95.
3. Michael G Christel, Scott M Stevens, Bryan S Maher, Sean Brice, Matt Champer, Luke Jayapalan, Qiaosi Chen, Jing Jin, Daniel Hausmann, Nora Bastida, and others. 2012. RumbleBlocks: Teaching science concepts to young children through a Unity game. In *Computer Games (CGAMES), 2012 17th International Conference on*. IEEE, 162–166.
4. Bi-Ru Dai, I Lin, and others. 2012. Efficient map/reduce-based dbscan algorithm with optimized data partition. In *Cloud Computing (CLOUD), 2012 IEEE 5th International Conference on*. IEEE, 59–66.
5. Michael Eagle, Elizabeth Rowe, Drew Hicks, Rebecca Brown, Tiffany Barnes, Jodi Asbell-Clarke, and Teon Edwards. 2015. Measuring Implicit Science Learning with Networks of Player-Game Interactions. In *Proceedings of the 2015 Annual Symposium on Computer-Human Interaction in Play*. ACM, 499–504.
6. Martin Ester, Hans-Peter Kriegel, Jörg Sander, and Xiaowei Xu. 1996. A density-based algorithm for discovering clusters in large spatial databases with noise.. In *Kdd*, Vol. 96. 226–231.
7. Emily B Fox, Erik B Sudderth, Michael I Jordan, and Alan S Willsky. 2008. An HDP-HMM for systems with state persistence. In *Proceedings of the 25th international conference on Machine learning*. ACM, 312–319.
8. Mark Hall, Eibe Frank, Geoffrey Holmes, Bernhard Pfahringer, Peter Reutemann, and Ian H Witten. 2009.

The WEKA data mining software: an update. *ACM SIGKDD explorations newsletter* 11, 1 (2009), 10–18.

9. Erik Harpstead, Christopher J MacLellan, Kenneth R Koedinger, Vincent Aleven, Steven P Dow, and Brad Myers. 2013a. Investigating the solution space of an open-ended educational game using conceptual feature extraction. (2013).
10. Erik Harpstead, Brad A Myers, and Vincent Aleven. 2013b. In search of learning: facilitating data analysis in educational games. In *Proceedings of the SIGCHI conference on human factors in computing systems.* ACM, 79–88.
11. Peter Hofman, Bryan Goodwin, and Stuart Kahl. 2015. Re-Balancing Assessment: Placing Formative and Performance Assessment at the Heart of Learning and Accountability. (2015).
12. M Lazarín. 2014. Testing overload in America's schools. *Center for American Progress. Retrieved from www.americanprogress.org/issues/education/report/2014/10/16/99073/testing-overload-in-americas-schools* (2014).
13. Seong Jae Lee, Yun-En Liu, and Zoran Popovic. 2014. Learning Individual Behavior in an Educational Game: A Data-Driven Approach. In *Educational Data Mining 2014.*
14. Yun-En Liu, Travis Mandel, Eric Butler, Erik Andersen, Eleanor O'Rourke, Emma Brunskill, and Zoran Popovic. 2013. Predicting player moves in an educational game: A hybrid approach. In *Educational Data Mining 2013.*
15. Merrilea J Mayo. 2009. Video games: A route to large-scale STEM education? *Science* 323, 5910 (2009), 79–82.
16. Robert J Mislevy, John T Behrens, Kristen E Dicerbo, and Roy Levy. 2012. Design and discovery in educational assessment: evidence-centered design, psychometrics, and educational data mining. *JEDM-Journal of Educational Data Mining* 4, 1 (2012), 11–48.
17. Mostofa Patwary, Diana Palsetia, Ankit Agrawal, Wei-keng Liao, Fredrik Manne, and Alok Choudhary. 2012. A new scalable parallel DBSCAN algorithm using the disjoint-set data structure. In *High Performance Computing, Networking, Storage and Analysis (SC), 2012 International Conference for.* IEEE, 1–11.
18. Lawrence R Rabiner, CH Lee, BH Juang, and JG Wilpon. 1989. HMM clustering for connected word recognition. In *Acoustics, Speech, and Signal Processing, 1989. ICASSP-89., 1989 International Conference on.* IEEE, 405–408.
19. Jonathan P Rowe and James C Lester. 2010. Modeling User Knowledge with Dynamic Bayesian Networks in Interactive Narrative Environments.. In *AIIDE.*
20. Jonathan P Rowe, Lucy R Shores, Bradford W Mott, and James C Lester. 2010. Integrating learning and engagement in narrative-centered learning environments. In *Intelligent Tutoring Systems.* Springer, 166–177.
21. Valerie J Shute, Eric G Hansen, and Russell G Almond. 2008. You can't fatten a hog by weighing it-Or can you? Evaluating an assessment for learning system called ACED. *International Journal of Artificial Intelligence in Education* 18, 4 (2008), 289.
22. Valerie Jean Shute and Matthew Ventura. 2013. *Stealth assessment: Measuring and supporting learning in video games.* MIT Press.
23. Valerie J Shute, Matthew Ventura, Malcolm Bauer, and Diego Zapata-Rivera. 2009. Melding the power of serious games and embedded assessment to monitor and foster learning. *Serious games: Mechanisms and effects* 2 (2009), 295–321.
24. Padhraic Smyth. 1996. Clustering Using Monte Carlo Cross-Validation.. In *KDD.* 126–133.
25. Padhraic Smyth and others. 1997. Clustering sequences with hidden Markov models. *Advances in neural information processing systems* (1997), 648–654.
26. Robert Tibshirani. 1996. Regression shrinkage and selection via the lasso. *Journal of the Royal Statistical Society. Series B (Methodological)* (1996), 267–288.

An Exploration of Automated Grading of Complex Assignments

Chase Geigle, ChengXiang Zhai, Duncan Ferguson
University of Illinois at Urbana-Champaign
{geigle1,czhai,dcf}@illinois.edu

ABSTRACT
Automated grading is essential for scaling up learning. In this paper, we conduct the first systematic study of how to automate grading of a complex assignment using a medical case assessment as a test case. We propose to solve this problem using a supervised learning approach and introduce three general complementary types of feature representations of such complex assignments for use in supervised learning. We first show with empirical experiments that it is feasible to automate grading of such assignments provided that the instructor can grade a number of examples. We further study how to integrate an automated grader with human grading and propose to frame the problem as learning to rank assignments to exploit pairwise preference judgments and use NDPM as a measure for evaluation of the accuracy of ranking. We then propose a sequential pairwise online active learning strategy to minimize the effort of human grading and optimize the collaboration of human graders and an automated grader. Experiment results show that this strategy is indeed effective and can substantially reduce human effort as compared with randomly sampling assignments for manual grading.

Author Keywords
Automatic grading; ordinal regression; supervised learning; learning to rank; active learning; text mining

INTRODUCTION
Information Technologies have been transforming education dramatically recently, leading to the rapid growth of Massive Open Online Courses (MOOCs), which have not only made education more affordable and scalable, but also have huge potential to enable more effective personalized learning. Automatic grading technology has been a key component enabling the success of MOOCs. Unfortunately, the current technology for automatic grading is mostly limited to multiple-choice questions, short answers [3, 16, 20, 26, 22], and simple essay scoring [2], which makes it quite challenging for the current MOOCs to provide sophisticated assignments for teaching complex concepts or skills (e.g., critical thinking skills) since they cannot be easily graded in a scalable way. A solution currently adopted to bypass this difficulty is to use the calibrated peer review [2, 30, 24]. While there are encouraging findings about peer assessment and methods proposed to improve it [14, 24], there are still systematic problems with this approach: discrepancy between peer and instructor ratings, variation in ratings over time by the same peer rater, inconsistency across exercises for rating two works of similar quality, differences in rater stringency, and random fluctuation of ratings of the same work under varied conditions [30]. Preliminary data from a recent attempt to use this technique with veterinary students has also shown that peer reviews have a distinct positive bias (vide infra) relative to an expert instructor analysis [9]. Thus, it is important to develop more powerful automatic grading technology that can be applied to more sophisticated exercises than those provided by the current MOOCs, which are necessary in many education scenarios.

To automate grading of such a complex assignment, a natural idea is to use supervised machine learning to learn from graded examples for automatically assigning grades to ungraded assignments. As in other machine learning applications, the general idea here is that if we can extract those features from the assignments that can indicate the quality of an assignment, a machine learning program would be able to pick up the patterns of the features that can distinguish high-quality work from low-quality work from a sample of graded assignments (i.e., "training data"), thus potentially assigning a grade automatically to an ungraded assignment.

Although this idea is natural and appealing, there are many challenges and questions that we must address before we can effectively deploy such a technology in a real education environment, and a main goal of this paper is to take a first step toward systematically addressing these questions.

1. **Feasibility:** How feasible is it to use machine learning to automate grading of a complex assignment? What general features can we extract from assignments for automated grading? How effective are the state of the art machine learning approaches for automated grading? Are they sufficiently effective to be immediately useful in practice?

2. **Problem Formulation and Evaluation:** How should we formulate the grading problem as a machine learning problem? There are at least two options. One is to frame it as a classification problem with the goal of classifying an assignment into one of the finite number of pre-defined grade levels based on a rubric. The other is to frame it as a

L@S 2016, April 25 - 26, 2016, Edinburgh, Scotland UK

ACM 978-1-4503-3726-7/16/04 $15.00
DOI: http://dx.doi.org/10.1145/2876034.2876049

ranking problem where the goal is to rank the assignments based on the quality without necessarily assigning a specific grade—human graders can then go through the ranked list to segment the assignments into different grade levels. How should we design evaluation metrics to measure the quality of the results of automated grading?

3. **Integration of Automated Grading and Human Grading:** How exactly should such an automated grader be integrated with instructor or TA grading? A more general question is: how can we optimize the collaboration of an imperfect automated grader with more reliable human graders? Intuitively, the optimization depends on a trade-off between the quality/reliability of grading and the amount of human effort required. But given an expected amount of human effort, what is the best way to have the automated grader to assist a person in grading? What is the best way to have a human grader help train the machine-learning based automated grader?

While some of these questions have been studied for non-complex assignments, most of them are open new questions that have not been addressed in the existing work (see Section 2 for a detailed discussion of related work). In this paper, we will systematically study these questions using a particular type of complex assignment that requires sophisticated critical thinking skills, i.e., medical case assessment. This kind of assignment is very important for medical professional education. By studying how to automate grading for medical assessment assignments, we can potentially enable medical professional education to scale up—a much needed effort. Not teaching clinicians about clinical uncertainty has been referred to as "the greatest deficiency of medical education throughout the twentieth century" [7, 11]. However, implementing an instruction plan with an online education system at large scale to teach clinical uncertainty in decision making raises many significant challenges that must be solved, particularly challenges in automatic evaluation of the case studies completed by the students, which we address in this paper by leveraging information retrieval and machine learning techniques.

To study the feasibility questions, we propose a general methodology for designing three complementary types of feature representations of such complex assignments, including token features, similarity features, and selection features, and experiment with these features using ordinal regression for predicting the grade levels in multiple dimensions of rubrics. The token features are based on the term tokens extracted from an assignment and they offer the most general representation and are robust in practice. The similarity features are to capture the similarity between an assignment and the solution provided by an instructor; the intuition is that the higher the similarity is, the higher the grade should be. Finally, the selection features are to quantify the accuracy of the selection of relevant parts in a case description based on how well the selected parts match the solutions (e.g., choosing to run the right lab tests in a clinical case). While it is generally beneficial to manually design assignment-specific features, such features cannot be generalized to work on other assignments; in this paper, we focus on studying *general* features that can be *automatically computed* on any semi-structured complex assignment, and aim at understanding their effectiveness.

A practical challenge in studying our problem is the lack of a large set of graded assignments which is needed both for training a machine learning program and for validating the results of automated grading. This is partly due to the fact that grading such assignments takes much human effort: the very reason why we need to study automated grading for such assignments. In our experiments, we used a data set of 107 student submissions for one medical case assessment assignment that is available to us. While the data set is small, we are able to observe statistically significant differences in our experiments, thus it still allows us to draw meaningful conclusions about different approaches to automated grading.

Our study with this data set shows that it is feasible to automate grading of a complex assignment such as a medical case assessment using standard machine learning approaches and the proposed three kinds of general features provided the instructor can grade a small number of examples, but the grading accuracy on different rubric categories varies substantially.

The results of our feasibility study reveal that there is a great deal of variation in the grades given by instructors due to the inevitable subjectivity of the rubrics. This suggests that it might be less effort and more reliable for an instructor to make pairwise judgments between a pair of assignments as opposed to assigning an exact numerical or letter grade. Working on such pairwise preference judgments also makes it easy to integrate non-expert judgments (such as peer grading) that might not be reliable in the exact grades assigned but may include relatively reliable preference judgments. Moreover, working on pairwise preferences naturally "eliminates" the need for normalizing numerical grades which might be biased (e.g., some graders may be overly generous).

Given that we will attempt to obtain pairwise preferences as training examples, it follows that we should frame the problem of automated grading as to rank the ungraded assignments, as opposed to predict the exact grade of an assignment. The ranking would be in descending order of quality (in any rubric dimension or overall quality with consideration of multiple dimensions), and a human grader can then easily segment the list into any desired grade levels. In comparison with predicting exact grades, such a ranking formulation also offers a natural way to engage humans in validating and finalizing the grades. For evaluation, although retrieval measures such as Mean Average Precision (MAP) or normalized Discounted Cumulative Gain (nDCG) are commonly used for evaluating a ranked list, we suggest that the Normalized Distance-based Performance Measure (NDPM) [31] is a better measure for our ranking problem since it can better handle the many inevitable ties that occur in our case.

In practice, an automated grader must be integrated with a human grader so as to minimize the overall effort of the human grader while ensuring a certain level of grading accuracy. There is an inherent trade-off here since to increase the grading accuracy we would like to have as many training examples (i.e., manually graded assignments) as possible, which, however, would incur more human effort. To optimize human-machine collaboration and enable a flexible trade-off between human effort and grading accuracy, we propose the following sequential training process based on active machine learning: *(1)* a human grader first grades a small number of assignments as the initial training set (this could be either numeric or letter grades, or pairwise judgments); *(2)* the machine would learn from the initial set, and identify the next "best" example (i.e., assignment) to label and present it for human to grade (where "best" here means that the example is most valuable to help the automated grader improve its accuracy); *(3)* a human would grade the nominated example to increase the size of the training set by one; *(4)* the machine would learn from the augmented training set and repeatedly present a new example for the human to grade until it reaches a desired level of accuracy, at which point, the process stops and the human grader would segment the final ranked list to generate grades for all the assignments. Our experiment results show that this online active learning process is much more effective than batch training.

RELATED WORK

To the best of our knowledge, no previous work has studied how to automatically grade a complex assignment such as a medical case assessment. However, our work is related to multiple lines of existing work, which we briefly review below.

Automated grading has been explored mostly for constrained question types where the correct answer has a certain, well known form. Programming assignments, for example, have long been a target for automatic grading [10, 12] as their very medium can easily be leveraged for providing "yes" or "no" feedback with respect to programmatic correctness. For specific assignment types, more sophisticated techniques like edit-distance of canonical representations has been explored [1]. Recent efforts have focused on providing feedback to students about their programs by leveraging structural similarities in the code itself to allow feedback to be provided to many assignments at once that share particular features [23, 25].

In this vein, clustering-based techniques have been applied to tools designed to help instructors manually grade short-answer MOOC assignments at scale by allowing them to assign grades to entire clusters of students at once [3]. Hierarchical clustering methods were applied in this work to allow the instructor to "drill down" as far as he/she would like to assign grades and feedback to students. Their method, PowerGrading, can be regarded as optimizing the collaboration of humans and machines heuristically, but the approach does not take advantage of supervised learning from graded examples of instructors, which we explore. Furthermore, if a cluster is poorly formed, the grading error can be serious no matter how an instructor optimizes the grade assignment to a cluster.

Mitros et. al. [21] give a brief overview of different strategies for grading and proposed a heuristic workflow to optimize the collaboration of assessors in consideration of different costs associated with different graders. However, it does not address the question of how to optimize the recommendation of assignments for graders to grade in order to maximize the effectiveness of the machine learning component of their framework, a goal we seek to achieve in this paper. We could deploy our technology in their framework by modifying the threshold strategy (e.g., for cutoffs on a ranked list). Both of these methods [3, 21] only explored the short-answer question space, leaving semi-automated grading of more complex assignment outputs (like the outline-form case assessments we study here) unexplored.

Another approach would be to attempt to predict the grades explicitly. One branch of work in this direction based on information extraction techniques focuses on matching expected patterns in the answer; Many methods require the manual construction of these patterns [20, 16], while others attempt to learn them from large training datasets [26]. In either case, the methods require strong supervision support to be effective. Other works take an unsupervised text-similarity approach and compare the student answers with a gold standard answer using a wide variety of similarity functions [22].

Grading of long-form student answers has also been explored [2]. In CARMELTC [27] a combination of topic modeling and text classification approaches are taken to score student essays. The system attempts to determine which "key components" have been mentioned in each essay and uses this information to suggest to students what components they may be missing. Approaches that purely use document similarity metrics [8] or purely supervised classifiers [15] have been used for grading as well, but the rubrics are not as complex as those required for medical case assessment.

The task of predicting categorical labels with an implicit ranking (ordinal variables, often the result of surveys on a Likert scale) is often solved via ordinal regression methods [19]; our work adds yet another application of ordinal regression to the many already explored. Using machine learning for optimizing ranking has been extensively in information retrieval [18]; our work explores an interesting novel application of online active learning to automated grading where we are interested in minimizing the training sample to label while maximizing the ranking accuracy over a finite number of known test cases.

MEDICAL CASE ASSIGNMENT

Complex assignments inevitably vary across courses. As a first step toward studying how to automate grading of such assignments, we use a medical case assignment in the veterinary medicine domain for our study. At a high level, such an assignment represents a typical type of analysis assignment where the students are given a case description with both an unstructured text description as well as some structured data (e.g., lab test results), and are asked to perform an analysis of the case. The analysis generally involves 1) selecting relevant content from the case description, which can be selected from both the text part and the structured data, 2) answering questions with short textual answers, and 3) writing assessments in natural language text.

More specifically, the case exercises were developed using the WhenKnowingMatters (WKM) web-based case formulation software[1] which facilitates development and exchange of text-based cases while allowing students to objectify their

[1] http://www.whenknowingmatters.com

analysis	2.6355 ± 0.7660
answers	3.0280 ± 0.7668
application	2.8692 ± 0.5651
clarity	3.3832 ± 0.9437
quality	3.1121 ± 0.9795
questions	2.8224 ± 0.6810

Table 1. Mean and standard deviation of ranks in each of the rubric dimensions we study.

observations from a case and manipulate them in an outline format around a suggested scaffold provided by the instructor. The student's analysis is then rendered into a structured text format to facilitate automatic grading.

Due to the lack of automated grading tools, the assignments are currently graded manually. An assessment rubric designed prior to instruction was used by the instructor to evaluate student performance on a subjective, 5-point scale (listed here in increasing order): novice, beginner, competent, proficient, and expert. Rubric categories were related to elements of critical thinking and communication: *(1)* **Questions:** developing relevant refining (or clarifying) questions to answer based upon an honest assessment of current knowledge base; *(2)* **Answers:** approach to seeking answers to developed questions; literature search, etc.; *(3)* **Quality:** judgment of quality of information; awareness and application of standards of a discipline, bias detection including appropriate humility to detect one's own potential bias, application of statistical concepts; *(4)* **Analysis:** analysis of an argument; *(5)* **Clarity:** clarity and communication of thought; conciseness, grammar, spelling, elocution; and *(6)* **Application:** application and understanding of appropriate disciplinary content.

For our experiments, we used a data set consisting of $n = 107$ student submissions for one medical case analysis assignment in a veterinary medicine course at UIUC. Each was graded according to the rubric detailed above. We report the mean rank and standard deviation for each of these six labels in Table 1; where 1 corresponds to novice and 5 to expert. The instructor also created a "gold standard" assessment for the assignment case, which is available for the automated grading tool to use. We wish we could use a much larger data set, but the size of the data set is limited by the amount of manual work needed for grading, which is precisely our motivation for studying how to automate grading.

Figure 1 shows an example of a very simple case and a typical student answer. In the case description, the student can see a text description of the case and a number of lab test results in the form of structured data. The student assessment is seen to be a semi-structured text with indented structures based on a scaffold provided by the instructor. Multiple tags indicate different kinds of answers, including, e.g., selected content from the original case description, selected lab tests (both are "observations"), and text input by the student reflecting his/her assessment (called "analysis").

Because of the complexity, automated grading of such an assignment is very challenging. First, due to variations across different assignments, it is almost impossible to learn from the grading results of one assignment to automate grading of another (often called "transfer learning"), even though such an "inter-assignment" automated grading is ideal. We thus focus on a more realistic setting of attempting to automate the grading after the instructor has already graded some assignments, which we may refer to as "intra-assignment" automated grading, which, strictly speaking, is actually semi-automatic grading. Our goal is thus to study whether and how we can leverage machine learning to learn from the graded assignments to reduce the grading burden on an instructor, either by directly predicting grades or by providing a ranking as a scaffolding for assigning grades.

FEASIBILITY OF AUTOMATED GRADIING

In this section, we discuss and study the feasibility of using machine learning methods, particularly supervised learning, for automating the grading of complex assignments. We first present the general idea of supervised learning, then propose a general methodology for designing three complementary types of features for representing assignments, which are needed for supervised learning, and finally present experiment results.

Supervised Learning

In supervised learning, a model is built to predict the outcome (or label) of a new data example based on previous examples it has seen before (called the training data). Thus a natural way to use supervised learning for grading is to have a human (e.g., instructor) to grade a set of assignments to be used as training data to learn a model to predict the grade of each ungraded assignment. A critical component of this infrastructure is the decomposition of examples into feature vectors—this decomposition enables the use of algorithms for learning functions from these vectors to the output labels desired. Typically, these feature vectors are either binary or real-valued, and are often (but not always) in a high-dimensional space. The performance of the learned function is directly tied to the features used in the vector representation of the examples—poor features result in low predictive capability due to the algorithm being unable to find meaningful patterns in the examples. As such, these features are a critical component of any supervised learning approach. With a properly defined set of features that are capable of capturing the salient patterns in the training examples, the task can be given to any of a number of state-of-the-art algorithms for learning appropriate predictive functions that can be applied to yet-unseen data (the test data). Another factor affecting the accuracy of prediction is the number of training examples, with more training examples leading to higher accuracy. However, since creating training examples generally requires manual work, we tend to have only a limited number of training examples to work with. How to define general features that we can automatically compute based on a complex assignment and how to minimize manual effort in creating training examples are two major questions that we study in this paper.

Defining Features of a Student Assignment

The performance of a supervised learning approach is highly dependent on the effectiveness of the features fed into the learning program. Thus a main technical challenge we need

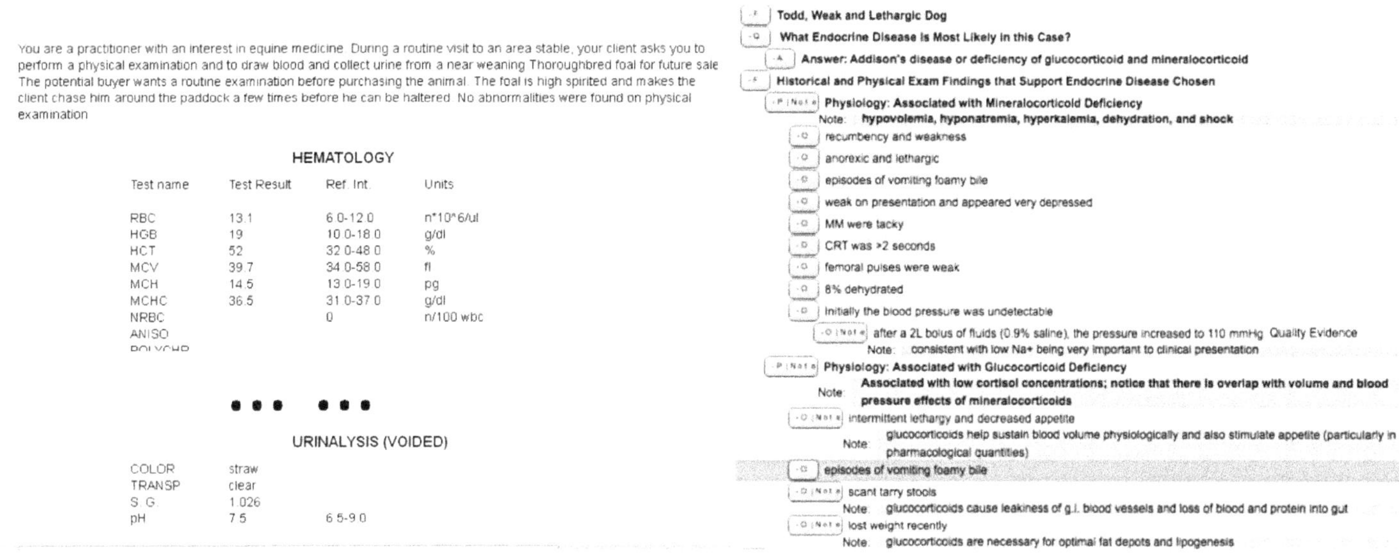

Figure 1. An example of a case description (left) and a reference assessment (right). Assessment bullets are labeled: "F" is part of the instructor provided framework, "Q" is a question posed by the instructor, and "P" is a physiological point made by the student.

to solve is how to design effective features for representing an assignment.

To address this challenge, we propose a general framework for defining features for complex assignments such as the one we explore in this paper. The features we propose are general in nature and thus should be applicable to any assignment that is presented in a text-based, semi-structured response form. We describe a set of feature classes and evaluate the performance of these features on an example autograding task to evaluate their predictive capacity. Our framework consists first of constructing a "view" of an assignment and then defining features based on this view. The view chosen for the assignment is critical in that it changes the way we may naturally describe it and thus leads to the definition of distinct classes of features distinguished by the view taken to derive them. We will explore features by progressively taking views that make stronger assignment design assumptions: while the features are still general, each view progressively narrows the space of possible student response types.

The first class of features, which we call **token features**, are generated by taking a view of the student response consistent with the traditional "bag of words" approach common in information retrieval contexts [18]. In this view a document is decomposed into a vector of count data that indicates the frequency of words within the document. Two features are thus natural. The first type of feature would indicate the number of occurrences of a given word in a student submission (and is thus real-valued), and the second would indicate the presence or absence of a word (and is thus binary-valued). These features would both create a high-dimensional representation of the student submission, and are motivated by an attempt to capture the difference in vocabulary between assignments. This is often enough to capture whether the correct ideas are mentioned without requiring extensive computation (features from this class are trivial to compute for every student submission), though more discriminative units such as n-grams (a sequence of n words) may also be easily used to replace single words if necessary. Document classification techniques typically operate in this kind of space.

The second class of features, which we call **similarity features**, are generated by characterizing a student submission by the "distance" from a gold standard (e.g., an assignment submission generated by the instructor). With this view, features can be derived that strongly utilize the structure of the assignment (e.g., how closely does the outline structure of the student assignment match the outline structure of the instructor assignment?) as well as features that loosely utilize or completely ignore the structure of the assignment. Examples of features that loosely utilize the assignment structure would be the similarity of certain outline bullet types with the gold standard bullet types of the same category. A bullet type in our examples could be "observation" (indicating something selected from the assignment text directly) or "analysis" (indicating original thoughts from the student). These features require the assignment to be structured in such a way that this information is easily extracted, but do not look so closely at the overall structure of the outline itself. Ignoring the structure of the assignment, features can be generated that indicate the overall similarity with the gold standard. Document clustering techniques typically operate in this kind of space, as well as retrieval functions in search systems [18].

The third class of features, which we call **selection features**, are generated by measuring concrete statistics about the selection of bullet points compared to a gold standard. In some sense, these are similar to the similarity features, but they differ in that they make a stronger assumption about the assignment structure—namely, that students are producing the exact same text that should occur in a similar section of the gold standard. Examples of selection features would be precision (what fraction of the bullets selected by the student also appear in the gold standard?) and recall (what fraction of bullets selected in the gold standard were also selected by the student?) [18].

analysis	0.5642 ± 0.0733
answers	0.5491 ± 0.0634
application	0.3321 ± 0.0580
clarity	0.7604 ± 0.0659
quality	0.7868 ± 0.0810
questions	0.4321 ± 0.0640

Table 2. Difficulty of grading each rubric dimension, characterized by MAE of a SVOR model learned on 50% of the data. 10 randomized experiments were run; reported is the average and standard deviation.

Ordinal Regression for Grade Prediction

Because of the ordinal nature of our grade labels (categorical with an implicit ranking), it is natural to apply ordinal regression techniques to our automated grading setup. In particular, we will utilize support vector ordinal regression (SVOR) [5], a generalization of the popular support vector machine (SVM) [6] for classification to the case of ordinal labels in the study of feasibility of grade prediction.

Experiment Results

We now present the results of ordinal regression on our medical assignment data set to assess the effectiveness of the proposed features and examine how effective such a state of the art learning method is for solving the grading problem.

We first explored using only the most general of our feature types—token features—to attempt to understand the differences in grading difficulty across our different rubric dimensions. Frequency-based token features were extracted: we used the META toolkit[2] at version 1.1 with its default tokenizer, stemmer, and stopword list. For regression, we used a modified version of LIBSVM[3] for ordinal regression [17].

In an actual grading scenario, the instructor would manually grade a certain number of the submissions, learn the regression function from these labeled examples, and then apply the learned model to the remaining unlabeled examples. To simulate this, we ran the following experiments: for each rubric dimension, we took the collection of student documents and randomly split it into two groups (the training and test sets) each containing 50% of the data[4]. A function is learned based on the labeled training set which is then used to label the examples in the test set. We compute the **mean absolute error** (MAE), defined as

$$MAE = \frac{1}{n}\sum_{i=1}^{n} |r(f(x_i)) - r(y_i)|$$

where $f(x_i)$ is the predicted label of the example x_i, $r(\cdot)$ is the rank of a given label, and y_i is the gold standard label for the example x_i. This experiment is repeated for ten different randomized splits, and we report the average and standard deviation of the test set MAE in Table 2.

We can observe that the rubric labels with the least variation are the easiest to predict (e.g., "application" and "questions"), whereas rubric dimensions with higher data variance (e.g., "quality") are more difficult.

The Impact of Different Feature Types

Moving beyond simple token features, we extracted both similarity and selection features from our assignments and incorporated them incrementally into our model to measure the predictive capacity of different feature types.

Our token features were generated using the same process detailed previously (frequency-based features extracted using the META toolkit). Our similarity features (compared against an instructor-generated assignment submission) were overall similarity, similarity of only "observation" bullets, and similarity of only "analysis" bullets. These were computed using the Okapi BM25 similarity function often used in information retrieval as a scoring function [18], treating the instructor submission as a query and the student submissions as documents to be scored. Finally, our selection features were precision and recall [18] of the selected lab data in the student case analysis when compared against the instructor's assignment.

We investigate the predictive capacity of these features by exploring the improvement of the model when predicting our most challenging labels ("quality" and "clarity"). We ran ten separate experiments with different randomized training sets consisting of 50% of the data when using different feature combinations to represent the student submissions. We again report the average and standard deviation of the MAE on the test set across the ten runs. To further explore whether the regression method is truly capturing patterns relevant for grading, we compare its MAE against the MAE obtained by using a naïve baseline: compute the most frequent label in the training data, and then assign this label to all examples in the test set. Intuitively, this is a very reasonable baseline when comparing MAE—if the labels are normally distributed, picking the most frequent one will ensure an absolute error of zero for the majority of the examples—while simultaneously being unhelpful for discriminative grading (which the regression method hopes to capture). Our results are summarized in Tables 3 and 4.

We see that for the "quality" dimension, the model is able to successfully learn generalizable patterns in our features to predict the label with errors that are statistically significantly less than the baseline method. In general, the token features dominate the performance, but it would seem as though the similarity and selection features have lower variability in the MAE. Again, this result suggests that there are likely gains to be had by utilizing a more sophisticated feature selection method to remove some of the noise introduced by extraneous token features.

However, the "clarity" label shows us that the problem is far from being solved in a general sense. Here, we see that our method consistently fails to beat the baseline method, with the winning method being seemingly random. This indicates that the features we have selected thus far are more tailored toward discrimination along certain dimensions of the grading rubric than others. More work must be placed into developing features that truly capture the "clarity" dimension to allow

[2] https://meta-toolkit.org

[3] http://www.work.caltech.edu/~htlin/program/libsvm/

[4] We do not use something like 10-fold cross validation due to the small size of the available labeled data to ensure that the training and test sets can be as representative of the actual data as possible.

	Baseline	SVOR
sim (3)	0.9358 ± 0.0882	$\mathbf{0.8811 \pm 0.0940}$
sim + sel (5)	0.9566 ± 0.1677	$\mathbf{0.8642 \pm 0.0325}$
toks (2646)	0.9075 ± 0.0789	$\mathbf{0.7660 \pm 0.0910}^{\dagger}$
all (2651)	0.9792 ± 0.1568	$\mathbf{0.7566 \pm 0.0738}^{\dagger}$

†: statistically signifigant using an unpaired t-test with $p \leq 0.05$.

Table 3. Effectiveness (in terms of MAE) of incorporating additional features in grade prediction for "quality" dimensions using SVOR methods compared to the mode-assigning baseline. Number of features is given in parenthesis.

	Baseline	SVOR
sim (3)	0.7906 ± 0.0771	$\mathbf{0.7830 \pm 0.0836}$
sim + sel (5)	$\mathbf{0.7623 \pm 0.0649}$	0.7811 ± 0.0561
toks (2646)	0.7528 ± 0.0550	$\mathbf{0.7415 \pm 0.0597}$
all (2651)	$\mathbf{0.7189 \pm 0.0617}$	0.7226 ± 0.0527

Table 4. Similar experiment to Table 3, but for "clarity" dimension.

the model to extract the patterns the instructor observes when grading along this dimension.

What this demonstrates is that automatic grading of complex assignments is currently feasible, but perhaps only in a limited fashion. Careful feature generation is required, but in some cases a model can be learned to effectively grade assignments. We suspect that significant gains in grading performance can be obtained in other dimensions with better features.

AUTOMATED GRADING AS RANKING ASSIGNMENTS

Some of the results from our feasibility study using ordinal regression raise the question whether framing the problem of automated grading as ordinal regression is appropriate. Indeed, as we will discuss, it appears to be more advantageous to frame the problem as one of ranking the ungraded assignments, which a human grader can segment into desired grade levels.

Specifically, as we observed in Tables 3 and 4, outright prediction of an ordinal grade can be very challenging due to the highly concentrated nature of the dataset labels (see Table 1). The vast majority of grade information available for the grade prediction task is centered around the mean, leaving very little information in the tails for a supervised learner to extract patterns from. (In some cases, for example, there are as few as one example for the highest and lowest ordinal grade values). The result is noisy output that may be inappropriate for using directly. However, it is worth noting that ordinal grade prediction is a hard problem, even for humans: a previous study suggests disagreement rates around 44% for short answer grading [22]. We suspect that this only becomes larger as assignments become more complex and difficult to grade, which makes the task of outright label prediction much more difficult for the machine as well.

Thus an alternative, and more reasonable approach may be to produce a ranked list of assignments from best to worst. Annotators are typically more consistent at providing judgments of the form "is *a* better than *b*?" than "on a scale from 1–5, how good is *a*?" [4], so it is reasonable to suspect that a machine learning model could achieve better results when trained using such pairwise judgments. If a system can provide a good ranking of assignments, an instructor simply needs to assign "cutoff" points in this ranking to determine grades. This simplifies the learning problem from attempting to predict an ordinal label for a specific assignment to assigning a ranking to a set of assignments. This is a well studied area in information retrieval called "learning to rank" [13, 18], and there are a wide variety of methods available that one can use to learn a ranking function for documents given a set of features.

One particular method that we will explore is a pairwise solution called a Ranking SVM [13], where the problem of learning to create ranked lists is decomposed into the problem of determining preferences for pairs of items (i.e., whether a should appear before b). A traditional SVM model is learned on this decomposition, and its weight vector is used to define a retrieval function that is the dot product with a document's feature vector.

Before we explore the efficacy of such an approach, however, we must first redefine some measure by which we can measure performance. Because the system is no longer predicting a rating for each assignment, we cannot use MAE as before.

Evaluating Ranking-based Grading Systems

Our goal is to produce a ranking of student assignments that is consistent with instructor evaluation. One way of framing this problem is to compare the ranking produced by the system to the ranking produced by the instructor (which we'll call the "reference ranking"). A system's ranking can then be evaluated using some measure of correlation between the two rankings. We note a preference for metrics that take into account the *entire* ranked list—this contrasts with most of the preferred measures in information retrieval evaluation which typically place heavier emphasis on the top-ranked elements. While this makes sense in a search context, our goal is to produce an exhaustive ranking of the assignments, so we focus on these types of measures.

Measures for rank correlation are plentiful. Perhaps the most commonly used metrics are Kendall's τ or Spearman's ρ (which have been found to be highly correlated in practice [29]; thus, we present only one for illustration). Kendall's τ can be formulated as

$$\tau = \frac{n_c - n_d}{\frac{1}{2}n(n-1)},$$

where n_c is the number of *concordant pairs*, and n_d is the number of *discordant pairs*, and n is the number of items ranked. To compute n_c and n_d, one considers all pairs (x_i, y_i) and (x_j, y_j) (that is, pairs of tuples) of assigned rankings in the system ranking X and the reference ranking Y (the denominator is simply the number of such pairs). A pair is *concordant* if the ordering of the items i and j in X and Y is consistent—in other words, if $(x_i < x_j) \wedge (y_i < y_j)$ or $(x_i > x_j) \wedge (y_i > y_j)$. A pair is *discordant* if the ordering of items in the two lists is inconsistent—in other words, if $(x_i < x_j) \wedge (y_i > y_j)$ or $(x_i > x_j) \wedge (y_i < y_j)$. This is then a correlation measure, with values bounded in $[-1, 1]$, with 1 indicating a perfect correlation and -1 indicating inverse correlation.

One of the assumptions Kendall's τ makes is that there are no ties in ranks. However, in a realistic grading scenario based on rubrics we expect many ties. Fortunately, there is a variation of Kendall's τ, denoted as τ_b, that accounts for ties in the rankings. This is formulated as

$$\tau_b = \frac{n_c - n_d}{\sqrt{(n_c + n_d + t_x)(n_c + n_d + t_y)}}$$

where t_x is the number of pairs that were tied on *only* their ranking from X, and t_y is the number of pairs that were tied on *only* their ranking from Y.

This may, at first glance then, seem like a good measure to use, but it is not without its problems. Despite taking into account ties in the rankings, it may still penalize a system for re-ordering items that were tied in the reference ranking—in other words, we may be penalized for not correctly identifying elements who are tied in the reference ranking. Consider a simple example: suppose the ranking proposed by a system is $X = (1,2,3,4,5,6)$ but the reference ranking is $Y = (1,1,2,2,3,4)$. Intuitively, the system made no real mistakes in that no pair where the reference ranking asserted an is in the wrong order in X. However, we'll see that $\tau_b \approx 0.9309$, indicating that the system did not achieve perfect correlation.

To address this issue, Yao [31] proposed the normalized distance-based performance measure (NDPM), which computes a distance between two rankings that is insensitive to a system's reordering of tied elements in the reference ranking. NDPM is computed as

$$NDPM = \frac{2n_d + t_x}{2(n_c + n_d + t_x)}.$$

This can also be described as the distance between the system ranking and the reference ranking divided by the maximum achievable distance any ranking could have from the reference ranking. Thus, a value of 0.3 would indicate that the system ranking was 30% of the distance away from the reference ranking than the reverse of the reference ranking. Since this is a normalized *distance* measure, a value of 0 would indicate a perfect ranking. Indeed, if we compute NDPM for the example rankings above, we achieve this result. Thus, we feel that NDPM is perhaps the most appropriate measure for evaluating automatic grading systems that produce an ordering of assignments as their output.

EFFICIENTLY UTILIZING HUMAN JUDGMENTS WITH ACTIVE LEARNING

As in all supervised learning approaches, the accuracy of the automated grader based on learning to rank. depends on the quantity and quality of the training examples available for the learner to use. Ideally, we would like human graders to provide as many graded examples as possible, but this would reduce the benefit of an automated grader. Indeed, if a human grader completes grading all the assignments, there would be no need for the automated grader! However, if there are insufficient training examples to learn from, the automated grader migh have a low accuracy, which would further require more human effort on "post-editing" the grading results of the automated grader. Thus there is clearly a complicated tradeoff between the effort of manual grading and the utility of the trained grader that may have to be empirically optimized in an application-specific way.

However, it is very clear that if we ask human graders to grade a certain amount of assignments, we would like the graded assignments to be as useful to the automated grader as possible. Just randomly selecting a sample of assignments for manual grading is not the best way. A natural solution to this problem is to employ active learning to allow the machine learning model to guide the instructor in providing the supervision to make the most effective use of his/her effort.

Building on these observations, we thus propose the following "pairwise active learning to rank" model for automatic grading, which will employ the following process where k_1 is a parameter that can be empirically set: *(1)* Ask the instructor for comparative judgments on k_1 pairs of assignments, *(2)* Learn a model using a learning-to-rank approach on the available pairwise judgments, *(3)* Apply the model to all remaining unjudged pairs, *(4)* Select an unjudged pair to present to the instructor for judgment, and *(5)* Go to step *(2)*. Instantiations of this general approach will differ mainly in steps *(2)* and *(4)*.

To study whether our proposed active learning approach better utilizes human judgments during the grading process, we performed the following experiment. We took our assignments and assigned each a "composite score", computed as the average of their ordinal score for each of the six rubric dimensions. Our task is then to learn a ranking that is consistent with the ranking produced by these composite scores while simultaneously *minimizing instructor effort* in labeling.

We first transform the $n = 107$ assignments into $\frac{1}{2}n(n-1) = 5671$ assignment *pairs* (x_i, x_j) with corresponding labels $y_{ij} \in \{+1, -1\}$ indicating whether x_i should be ranked above or below x_j in the ranking. Ties were broken arbitrarily by assignment id. The supervision given by the instructor is then to indicate a preference for ranking x_i relative to x_j.

Following the process laid out in the beginning of the section, we first start with $k_1 = 10$ random pairs selected from the transformed data and ask for labels from the instructor. We then learn the model, compute the NDPM for the ranking produced by the model for all n assignments, and then ask for additional supervision by selecting the unlabeled assignment pair whose distance from the decision boundary for the model is lowest (this is a known, simple approach to uncertainty sampling [28]) and repeat the training/evaluation loop. Our particular model choice was a linear SVM provided through the META toolkit.

We compare this active learning scenario with a random learning baseline, which is the exact same process as above, but instead of selecting the most uncertain pair in the unlabeled data we select one uniformly at random. This will allow us to see whether the uncertainty sampling approach is truly helping to guide the learning process to make more efficient supervision choices or not.

Our results are summarized in Figure 2. Recall that a NDPM value of 0.3 indicates that a system ranking was 30% of the maximal achievable distance away from the reference ranking. We can see that even at a small fraction of all of the assignment pairs, the active learning approach (blue line) is able to achieve better NDPM than simply learning at random (red line). This

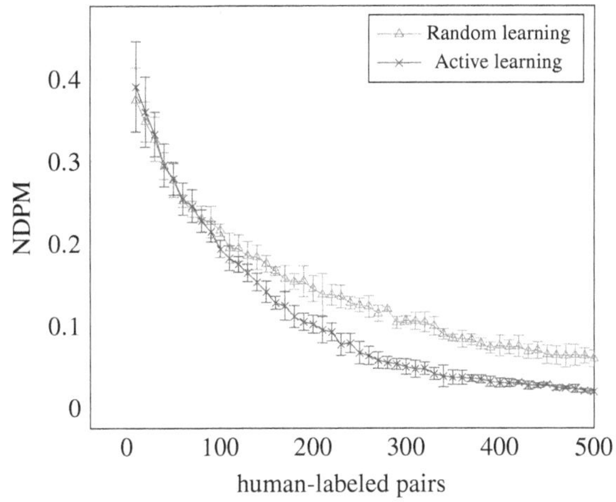

Figure 2. A comparison between a randomized learning solution and an active learning solution to the grading-as-ranking problem. Reported is the average NDPM (lower is better) over 5 runs, with error bars indicating one standard deviation.

is consistent with our hypothesis that active learning as part of an automatic grading system can make more effective use of an instructor's time than a purely passive supervised approach.

How much instructor effort goes in to judging 200 assignment pairs? This may initially seem like a lot, but each pair is not labeled in isolation—labeling many pairs will inevitably include assignments that have already been seen before. These familiar assignments make providing a pairwise judgment faster than it would be if done "cold". In general, it is also reasonable to assume that the effort involved in simply saying whether assignment *a* is better than assignment *b* is lower than having to consult a rubric to assign an actual point (or letter) value. It is important, however, to ensure that providing a pairwise judgment takes as little effort as possible relative to assigning a numeric or letter grade. An interesting future direction is then to design an interactive system that attempts to further drive the cost of providing judgments down.

DISCUSSION AND FUTURE WORK

In the previous experiments we formulated the automated grading problem as a ranking problem, and introduced a rank distance measure (NDPM) as a form of evaluating the quality of a ranked list generated by an automated (or semi-automated, in our case) system. Under a ranking-based problem formulation, we argue that this is the most sensible metric for evaluating the ranking accuracy relative to a gold standard.

However, the value of NDPM cannot be easily compared with the values of existing metrics (such as MAE) that have been traditionally used in evaluating automated grading systems in the past. There is a need to evaluate a ranked list from the perspective of its impact on the eventual grades assigned to student work. Unfortunately, how to evaluate the utility of a ranked list appropriately remains a challenge partly due to the difficulty in choosing the cutoffs, which may depend on the desired tradeoff that an instructor wants (e.g., a desired distribution of grades in different brackets). In practice, we envision that the instructor would visit points in the ranked list and choose cutoffs based on the tradeoff between the different types of grading errors. Exploring grade cutoff assignment strategies remains an important future direction, and our framework coupled with such a cutoff strategy would enable evaluation based on the traditional grade prediction task.

While we believe the results here show that the methods employed are feasible for grading complex assignments, more work remains to be done to understand just how well our system performs relative to human judgments. Future work should explore this by measuring human consensus in grading these complex assignments, similar to what has done for short answers [22]. Furthermore, we only investigated very simplistic features—such as the bag-of-words model—which are very general but not very sophisticated. Exploring the feature space further to find more sophisticated features that perform well in practice and are more tailored to the goals of medical case assessments remains as future work.

Another major limitation of our study is the limited size of the data set. This is partly due to the fact that such complex assignments currently can only be graded by human graders. In the future, we hope to deploy our automated grading tools to help scale up such courses to enable more students to participate, which in turn, would help collecting more data for further verification of our observations and conclusions.

Finally, a crucial direction that remains unexplored is feedback: how could such a system give more detailed feedback to students beyond just their ordinal rating along a rubric dimension? Currently, peer grading approaches have an advantage in this sense, as your peers can suggest to you corrections or point out specific mistakes that you made. It is worth investigating whether or not we can generate "explanatory reports" of grading results when using a supervised learning approach.

CONCLUSIONS

Automated grading of complex assignments is necessary for scaling up learning without compromising effectiveness of learning. Using a data set of medical case assessment assignments, we conducted the first systematic study of how to leverage machine learning to automate grading of such a complex assignment. Our study has led to several contributions.

First, we have experimentally shown the feasibility of using supervised learning techniques for automated grading of medical case assignments under certain conditions provided that the instructor can manually label a number of the assignments to serve as a training set. In particular, an ordinal regression method can be applied to the data with results that consistently outperform the majority-label baseline in terms of MAE.

Second, we proposed a general framework for the development of three complementary types of representative features for student submissions (i.e., token features, similarity features, and selection features) —while we applied these features to our specific task of medical case analysis grading, these feature types (and generation framework) are general and should apply to the grading of any complex assignment.

Third, we proposed to frame the problem of automated grading as a ranking problem, which can more naturally assist human graders to validate and finalize grades of ungraded assignments and learn from pairwise preference judgments that can be potentially created more reliably by human graders including through peer grading. We also suggested NDPM as potentially a better measure for this ranking task than other measures due to its superiority in handling many tied cases.

Finally, we proposed an iterative procedure of online active learning to rank to efficiently utilize human judgments, and thus optimizing the collaboration between human graders and the automated grader. Experiment results confirm the efficiency of this procedure which can substantially save human effort as compared with randomly choosing sample assignments for humans to grade.

ACKNOWLEDGMENTS

This material is based upon work supported by the National Science Foundation Graduate Research Fellowship Program under Grant Number DGE-1144245.

REFERENCES

1. R. Alur, L. D'Antoni, S. Gulwani, D. Kini, and M. Viswanathan. 2013. Automated Grading of DFA Constructions *(IJCAI)*. 1976–1982.
2. S. P. Balfour. 2013. Assessing writing in MOOCs: Automated essay scoring and calibrated peer review. *Research and Practice in Assessment* 8, 1 (2013), 40–48.
3. M. Brooks, S. Basu, C. Jacobs, and L. Vanderwende. 2014. Divide and Correct: Using Clusters to Grade Short Answers at Scale. In *ACM L@S*. 89–98.
4. C. Callison-Burch, C. Fordyce, P. Koehn, C. Monz, and J. Schroeder. 2007. (Meta-) Evaluation of Machine Translation. In *WMT*. 136–158.
5. W. Chu and S. S. Keerthi. 2007. Support Vector Ordinal Regression. *Neural Comput.* 19, 3 (2007), 792–815.
6. C. Cortes and V. Vapnik. 1995. Support-Vector Networks. *Mach. Learn.* 20, 3 (1995), 273–297.
7. B. Djulbegovic. 2004. Lifting the fog of uncertainty from the practice of medicine. *British Medical Journal* 329, 7480 (2004), 1419–1420A.
8. R. M. Duwairi. 2006. A Framework for the Computerized Assessment of University Student Essays. *Comput. Hum. Behav.* 22, 3 (2006), 381–388.
9. DC Ferguson, LK McNeil, EM Mills, and JE Ehlers. 2014. International efforts to encourage critical clinical thinking (CCT) skills in veterinary students.. In *Veterinary Educational Collaborative biannual meeting, Ames, IA.* (abstract).
10. G. E. Forsythe and N. Wirth. 1965. Automatic Grading Programs. *Commun. ACM* 8, 5 (1965), 275–278.
11. E. Gambrill. 2006. *Critical Thinking in Clinical Practice: Improving the Quality of Judgments and Decisions* (2nd ed.). Wiley and Sons. 648 pages.
12. M. T. Helmick. 2007. Interface-based Programming Assignments and Automatic Grading of Java Programs. In *SIGCSE*. 63–67.
13. T. Joachims. 2002. Optimizing Search Engines Using Clickthrough Data. In *KDD*. 133–142.
14. C. Kulkarni, K. P. Wei, H. Le, D. Chia, K. Papadopoulos, J. Cheng, D. Koller, and S. R. Klemmer. 2013. Peer and Self Assessment in Massive Online Classes. *ACM Trans. Comput.-Hum. Interact.* 20, 6 (2013), 33:1–33:31.
15. L. S. Larkey. 1998. Automatic Essay Grading Using Text Categorization Techniques. In *SIGIR*. 90–95.
16. C. Leacock and M. Chodorow. 2003. C-rater: Automated Scoring of Short-Answer Questions. *Computers and the Humanities* 37, 4 (2003), pp. 389–405.
17. L. Li and H. Lin. 2007. Ordinal Regression by Extended Binary Classification. In *NIPS*. MIT Press, 865–872.
18. C. D. Manning, P. Raghavan, and H. Schütze. 2008. *Introduction to Information Retrieval*. Cambridge University Press, New York, NY, USA.
19. P. McCullagh. 1980. *Regression models for ordinal data.*
20. T. Mitchell, T. Russell, P. Broomhead, and N. Aldridge. 2002. Towards robust computerised marking of free-text responses. In *ICAAC*.
21. P. Mitros, V. Paruchuri, J. Rogosic, and D. Huang. 2013. An Integrated Framework for the Grading of Freeform Responses. In *MIT LINC*.
22. M. Mohler and R. Mihalcea. 2009. Text-to-text Semantic Similarity for Automatic Short Answer Grading. In *EACL*. 567–575.
23. A. Nguyen, C. Piech, J. Huang, and L. Guibas. 2014. Codewebs: Scalable Homework Search for Massive Open Online Programming Courses. In *WWW*. 491–502.
24. C. Piech, J. Huang, Z. Chen, C. Do, A. Ng, and D. Koller. 2013. Tuned Models of Peer Assessment in MOOCs. In *EDM*.
25. C. Piech, J. Huang, A. Nguyen, M. Phulsuksombati, M. Sahami, and L. J. Guibas. 2015. Learning Program Embeddings to Propagate Feedback on Student Code. In *ICML*. 1093–1102.
26. S. G. Pulman and J. Z. Sukkarieh. 2005. Automatic Short Answer Marking. In *BEA*. ACL, 9–16.
27. C. P. Rosé, A. Roque, D. Bhembe, and K. Vanlehn. 2003. A Hybrid Text Classification Approach for Analysis of Student Essays. In *BEA*. ACL, 68–75.
28. B. Settles. 2012. Active Learning. *Synthesis Lectures on Artificial Intelligence and Machine Learning* 6, 1 (2012), 1–114.
29. G. Shani and A. Gunawardana. 2011. *Evaluating Recommendation Systems*. Springer, Chapter 8.
30. H. Suen. 2014. Peer assessment for massive open online courses (MOOCs). *The International Review of Research in Open and Distance Learning* 15, 3 (2014).
31. Y. Y. Yao. 1995. Measuring Retrieval Effectiveness Based on User Preference of Documents. *J. Am. Soc. Inf. Sci.* 46, 2 (1995), 133–145.

Fuzz Testing Projects in Massive Courses

Sumukh Sridhara
UC Berkeley
sumukh@berkeley.edu

Brian Hou
UC Berkeley
brian.hou@berkeley.edu

Jeffrey Lu
UC Berkeley
jeffreylu017@gmail.com

John DeNero
UC Berkeley
denero@berkeley.edu

ABSTRACT
Scaffolded projects with automated feedback are core instructional components of many massive courses. In subjects that include programming, feedback is typically provided by test cases constructed manually by the instructor. This paper explores the effectiveness of *fuzz testing*, a randomized technique for verifying the behavior of programs. In particular, we apply fuzz testing to identify when a student's solution differs in behavior from a reference implementation by randomly exploring the space of legal inputs to a program. Fuzz testing serves as a useful complement to manually constructed tests. Instructors can concentrate on designing targeted tests that focus attention on specific issues while using fuzz testing for comprehensive error checking. In the first project of a 1,400-student introductory computer science course, fuzz testing caught errors that were missed by a suite of targeted test cases for more than 48% of students. As a result, the students dedicated substantially more effort to mastering the nuances of the assignment.

Author Keywords
automated assessment; behavioral analytics; online learning

INTRODUCTION
Assignments that provide automated feedback to students are a core instructional tool in many massive courses [8, 18]. In technical subjects that involve programming, such as computer science and data science, assignments often ask students to implement a program according to a specification. Feedback is generated automatically by an *autograder*, a program that executes test cases against a student's implementation [12, 6, 13]. The test suite is typically constructed manually by the course instructors, with some tests distributed to students and some tests held out for assessment. This paper describes how *fuzz testing* [15] can complement manually constructed test cases to improve the feedback provided to students.

Fuzz testing involves randomly generating inputs to a program and then verifying some property of the output or program behavior. For example, this technique is often applied to find inputs on which a program will crash. In the context of large-scale education, randomized testing can be used by an autograder to verify that the output generated by a student's submission to a programming assignment matches the output produced by a reference implementation created by the instructor [19]. This paper describes the conditions necessary for fuzz testing to be used for autograding, as well as an array of options for distributing fuzz tests to students without exposing the instructor's reference implementation.

Programming assignments and automated feedback are often the primary mechanisms by which massive courses encourage students to explore the technical details of a subject. In such settings, test cases provide two complementary services to students. *Targeted test suites* highlight particular known points of confusion, often using simple inputs for which the correct output can be generated easily by hand. *Comprehensive test suites* attempt to detect all deviations from the specification. Targeted tests are helpful in providing preliminary feedback to students, while comprehensive tests encourage students to continue working on the assignment until it is completed correctly. When a comprehensive test suite fails to detect an error, the student may stop attempting to improve her or his submission. As a result, the student may inadvertently miss the learning opportunity of identifying and correcting the error.

To explore the impact of fuzz testing, we studied the behavior of students in a large on-campus CS 1 course with 1,400 enrolled students, CS 61A at UC Berkeley[1]. We focused on their first substantial programming project, which students completed either alone or in pairs. The most challenging question in the project asked students to write a function that simulates playing a dice game. Students were provided with both a manually constructed suite of targeted test cases and a fuzz test. Our autograder recorded each partial solution submitted for testing, so we were able to study students' progress through the problem.

We found that adding a fuzz test dramatically increased the number of incorrect solutions identified. More than 48% of students created and tested a partial solution that passed the targeted test suite, but still contained a logical error identified by the fuzz test. Many random inputs were required to detect these errors; 6% of the errors we found were not discovered until more than 500 random inputs were explored.

[1] `cs61a.org`.

L@S 2016, April 25–26, 2016, Edinburgh, UK.

ACM 978-1-4503-3726-7/16/04 ...$15.00.
http://dx.doi.org/10.1145/2876034.2876050

Fuzz tests are easy to construct and distribute using the strategies we describe in this paper. They proved to be an effective complement to manually created tests even for a basic assignment: the first project in a CS 1 course. Our study of how students behave in a large-scale class provides compelling evidence that fuzz testing should be included regularly in autograded programming assignments.

AUTOGRADING

For many successful massive open online courses (MOOCs), programming projects are distributed with autograders that provide comprehensive feedback about the correctness of a student's implementation. These projects are not primarily used for assessment, but rather to maximize the instructional value of completing the assignment [4]. All students are encouraged to revise their project submissions until they are correct, and in the process they are exposed to important concepts from the course. Many popular programming-based MOOCs include comprehensive autograders, such as *Algorithms*[2], *Coding the Matrix*[3], *Foundations of Computer Graphics*[4], *Machine Learning*[5], and many others.

Several design issues arise in the construction of autograders that are relevant to the use of fuzz testing as described in this paper.

Test Distribution

Autograder tests can be distributed with a project or applied by an instructional server when an assignment is submitted. The advantages of distributing tests with a project are that they can be run offline, the computation required to execute the tests is distributed to students' machines, and students who do not want to share their progress with instructors due to privacy concerns still have access to test cases. However, one challenge of distributing tests to students is that they cannot include a solution to the project without potentially exposing that solution to the student.

Assessment

Not all test suites distributed with programming projects are designed to be comprehensive. Indeed, a common practice in programming-based courses is to withhold certain test cases for assessment. Students are sometimes encouraged to generate their own test cases to verify their implementations before submitting their work. These alternatives to comprehensive testing are certainly a proper fit for certain courses, but in this paper we focus on tests distributed to students that are intended to provide comprehensive evaluations of correct program behavior.

Targeted Tests

When designing the test suite of an autograder, it can be valuable to consider more than just comprehensive test coverage; instructors may also seek to provide guidance that properly matches each stage of a student's development process. We call any test case that isolates a particular issue a *targeted test*. Targeted tests complement comprehensive tests by focusing students' attention on particular details within a large program. These tests are often designed to make students think about certain edge cases that they may overlook in a first pass through an implementation.

Fully quantifying the value of targeted tests is beyond the scope of this paper, but in constructing our evaluation of fuzz testing we also discovered some evidence that targeted tests are a valuable complement to comprehensive tests. In the Spring 2015 offering of CS 61A, students were provided only with comprehensive tests for the question we describe later in the paper. In the Fall 2015 offering, they were provided with both targeted tests and comprehensive tests. When provided no targeted tests (Spring 2015), the median time between starting this question and passing at least one test case was 55 minutes. When provided targeted tests (Fall 2015), the median time to passing at least one test case was greatly reduced to 14 minutes. Targeted tests provide timely positive feedback that students are making progress in the correct direction.

Summary

Although the space of possible autograder designs is large, we focus on the particular setting in which a test suite is distributed to students with the project. The test suite includes both targeted tests to focus attention on key issues and comprehensive tests that attempt to detect all deviations from the assignment specification. The purpose of fuzz testing is to improve comprehensive tests while simplifying their development.

FUZZ TESTING

Fuzz testing—testing the behavior of a program on many random inputs—was first described as a technique to discover errors in mature UNIX tools [15]. Generating random inputs was sufficient at that time to crash 25-33% of core utility programs from various distributions of UNIX. This original paper aptly remarked that fuzz testing is best viewed as a complementary technique to conventional testing in which specific inputs are chosen manually by a programmer. A variety of work has improved and extended the original idea of fuzz testing, e.g. [7, 14]; randomized fuzz testing is now standard practice in software engineering [3]. The relative value of random testing is typically high compared to its implementation cost [11, 16]. Creating fuzz tests is often far less effort-intensive than designing tests manually.

Application

Fuzz tests are commonly used to assess the security of a program given some randomized inputs [5, 10]. During execution, the program state is monitored to ensure that security constraints are maintained. In common usage, fuzz tests watch for a specific behavior (such as a buffer overflow or program crash), often ignoring the actual output of the program. The correct output for a random input is often unknown, because no reference implementation exists for most

[2] `www.coursera.org/course/algs4partI`
[3] `www.coursera.org/course/matrix`
[4] `courses.edx.org/courses/BerkeleyX/CS_184.1x`
[5] `www.coursera.org/learn/machine-learning`

programs being tested in this way. By contrast, when applying fuzz testing to programming projects, a reference implementation (the instructor solution) often exists. With a reference implementation, we can apply fuzz testing to student submissions to test for correctness.

Creating and Distributing Fuzz Tests

Any program can be fuzz tested for correctness as long as the behavior of the program for a space of inputs is uniquely defined by the assignment specification. The behavior of the reference implementation must be deterministic, and the specification of the implementation must precisely resolve any possible sources of non-determinism (such as breaking ties in a maximization).

To fuzz test student code, the autograder must programmatically feed random input into the student's program. Since the input domain for the program is known, an instructor can easily generate valid inputs. Existing work on fuzz testing tools provides a variety of strategies for the generation for complex inputs [9, 2, 20].

These inputs alone help verify that the program does not crash on valid inputs, but do not verify correctness of the program. Instead, some mechanism must provide access to the correct response for a random test according to the reference implementation, but without distributing the reference to students.

Our solution is to generate one set of random fuzz tests using a fixed random seed. The same set of tests is distributed to all students, ensuring fair and consistent autograder responses across multiple autograder runs, while maintaining the simplicity of randomly generated tests. We compute the correct response for each test according to the reference implementation to obtain the expected fuzz test output. The following options describe methods in which this expected output can be distributed.

1. **Raw Output.** This approach provides students with the reference implementation's raw output for each fuzz test input. The reference output is compared to the output generated by the student's program. Since each run of the autograder tests the same inputs, it is possible for students to hard-code their implementation to pass the fuzz test, without fully completing the assignment.

2. **Obfuscated Output.** Obfuscating the random inputs and outputs is one method to discourage students from hard-coding their answer to match the correct fuzz test outputs. Students are only informed whether their implementation passes or fails a sequence of fuzz tests, with no further information.

   To implement this behavior, students are given the encrypted output of the instructor solution, rather than the raw output. The encrypted output can be computed using a one-way hash function H that combines all fuzz test outputs for the instructor solution, $fuzz(solution)$, and produces a hash $h_{correct} = H(fuzz(solution))$. A student's implementation is correct if their hash $H(fuzz(student))$ matches $h_{correct}$.

3. **Traces.** If the internal state of the student's code can be inspected by the autograder, it is possible to provide even more detailed feedback to the student. Specifically, the autograder can not only state that a specific fuzz test failed, but rather exactly when the internal state differed from the reference state. This level of detail requires that tests include a serialized list of all program states in the trace. This additional information allows fuzz tests to pinpoint the places in which a student's implementation deviates from the reference, as with a targeted test, without requiring careful test generation from the instructor.

4. **Hidden.** It is also possible to keep the fuzz tests hidden from student view, instead choosing to apply fuzz tests as a way to assess student progress and identify frequent errors. Instructors can use these data to alter their assignments accordingly. If desired, the instructors can publish the most common errors as well as test cases that highlight these errors. Knowing the most common incorrect outputs allows instructors to determine common bugs and more effectively address student questions either in-person or online. This information becomes more important in massive classes as the observed set of unique incorrect implementations grows large.

5. **Final Assessment.** Fuzz tests are useful for assessing the correctness of submitted assignments, even if the fuzz tests are never distributed to students. Using fuzz tests for assessment saves the effort of constructing new tests for each course offering. In some courses, test cases that are used to assign a student's grade are never released to students, even after scores are assigned, in part due to the effort required to generate new test cases for future course offerings. However, when students are not provided with the inputs that caused their program to fail, they lose the opportunity to understand why they were penalized. Communicating fuzz tests to students does not compromise the set of hidden tests available for future course offerings.

IMPLEMENTATION

We explored the use of fuzz testing in an autograder by adding a fuzz test to an existing manually created test suite of the first project in a CS 1 course. We distributed the fuzz test using the *Obfuscated Output* method described in the previous section.

The Game of Hog

The first project in our CS 1 class is implementing a simulator for the game of Hog [17]. In Hog, two players alternate turns trying to be the first to end a turn with at least 100 total points. On each turn, the current player chooses some number of dice to roll, up to 10. That player's score for the turn is the sum of the dice outcomes. There are some additional rules to make the game more exciting to play and challenging to implement.

We used a fuzz test to verify student implementations of the game's main simulation loop, the fifth of ten questions in the project. This main loop updates the players' scores after each roll of the dice. CS 1 students find this question challenging to implement because they must use iteration to simulate each turn of the game, modify multiple variables, and apply functions that were implemented in previous parts of

Students Attempting Project	1,392
Students Attempting Target Question	1,355
Students Completing Project	1,331
Code Snapshots	486,482
Average Snapshots Per Student	349
Incorrect Attempts at Target Question	48,079
Snapshots with Fuzz Test Errors	22,375

Figure 1. Collected Dataset

the project. Our students commonly struggle with off-by-one errors where they simulate an additional turn after the game should have ended, infinite loops where their games never end as a result of forgetting to modify variables, or incorrect score updates.

The number of possible inputs to this function is extremely large because each player can roll a number of dice between 0 and 10 for all 10^4 game states, creating at least 10^{10} unique inputs to define the players' strategies.[6] Attempting to verify the correctness of a student implementation by enumerating all legal inputs is infeasible. However, fuzz tests are an easy way to augment hand-designed test cases to provide better coverage of the input space. In our implementation, the random input dictated both players' strategies and all dice outcomes.

Autograder Interface

Project source files are distributed with a suite of test cases and an open-source autograder called OK[7]. Students use OK to run correctness tests on their implementation after unlocking conceptual questions [1]. Every question has several instructor-designed test cases to provide students with targeted feedback on the correctness of their solution. Students are strongly encouraged to correct their solutions to pass all test cases before progressing to the next question.

Students can run the provided tests on a particular question as often they would like. Each time students run the tests, a snapshot of their code, as well as metadata about which question they are working on and the number of tests that their solution passes, is sent to the OK server. These snapshots allow us to continuously monitor student progress, which we have used to develop a large dataset of in-progress work, as seen in Figure 1.

After running OK on a particular question, students receive feedback on the correctness of their program. When students fail a test case, OK displays the test that triggered the failure, the expected value, and the student's returned value. This interface provides students with enough information to start debugging their error. Once their solution passes all tests for a question, students know it is safe to proceed to the next question.

Figure 2 (Fall 2015) and Figure 3 (Spring 2015) show how often students ran the autograder to check their solutions for each question of Hog in two separate offerings of the course.

[6]If a random sequence of dice outcomes is included in the input as well, the space of possible inputs grows much larger still.

[7]`okpy.org`

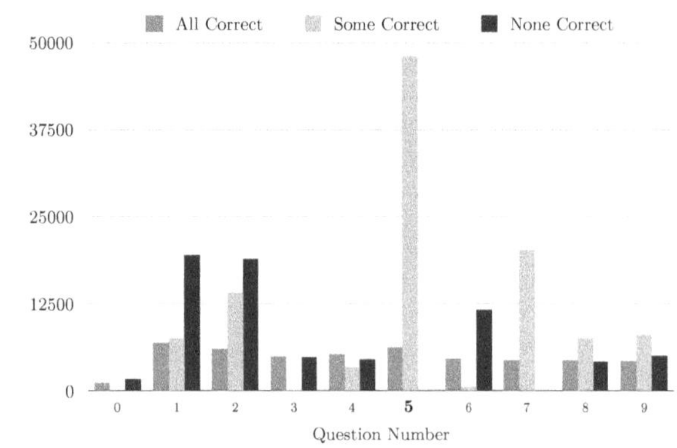

Figure 2. The distribution of attempts on each question of Hog. In the Fall 2015 offering of the course, we provided both targeted tests and fuzz tests for Question 5.

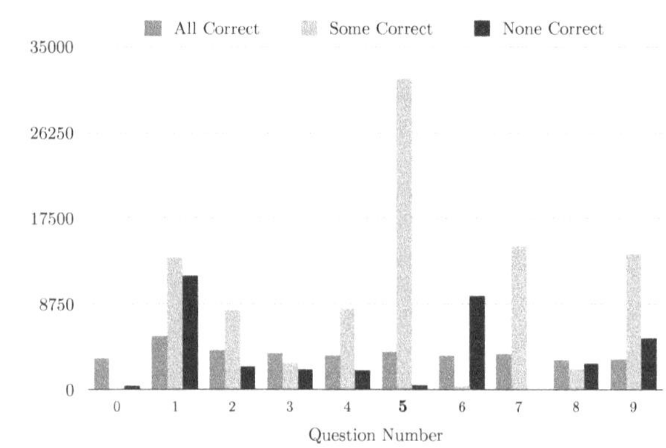

Figure 3. The distribution of attempts on each question of Hog. In the Spring 2015 offering of the course, we provided only a few manually designed fuzz tests for Question 5. This offering had approximately 30% fewer students than Fall 2015, so the vertical axis has been scaled accordingly.

For each question, we classify each attempt to pass the autograder into three scenarios: no test cases passed ("None Correct"), some test cases passed ("Some Correct"), and all test cases passed ("All Correct"). The question that we have targeted for fuzz testing is Question 5. It is the most challenging question on the project and therefore requires a large number of autograder runs before passing all tests. In our project, a question refers to a subtask of the project that has tests for correctness.

Student Experience

We investigated student experience of the fuzz test by observing the number of questions asked about the fuzz test on the class forum. The online Q&A forum, called Piazza, allows students to ask questions of their peers and instructors. The median response time for public posts about the project was 27 minutes for peer responses and 37 minutes for an instructor response.

Our choice to obfuscate the output of the fuzz test significantly increased the amount of time required for the instructors to assist a student with a question about the fuzz test, both in office hours and on Piazza. Due to the obfuscated output, students' only recourse for help if they were failing the fuzz test was to share their code in office hours or make a private post with their code attached for instructors to view. There were 86 such private posts (which is about 1 post for every 8 students who failed the fuzz test). The median time for a response from an instructor to these posts was 2.3 hours due to the difficulty of identifying the student's error in the large space of potential errors identified by the fuzz test.

In a midterm survey with 1,245 responses, 575 students (46%) reported spending at least one hour trying to debug errors caught by the fuzz test; 19% reported spending more than four hours. 346 students (28%) responded that they did not fail the fuzz test or did not remember the fuzz test.

EVALUATION

We first quantified how fuzz testing complemented our manually constructed test cases by measuring the number of students who passed all of our manually constructed test cases but failed the fuzz tests.

Student Fuzz Test Design

We designed a fuzz test that simulates 100 games of Hog. Before distributing the project, we randomly generated 100 fuzz test inputs and evaluated the staff solution on each of these inputs. We computed a hash from the 100 staff solution outputs, which we then distributed to students along with the targeted tests.

Usage Pattern

For the question that we analyzed, students were provided with a sequence of 9 targeted tests, as well as the fuzz test described above, which was executed only after the students passed the previous 9 tests.

This analysis excludes students who opted out of uploading progress as well as those who worked on the project without running the provided tests.

Fuzz Test Evaluation

To analyze the effects of additional fuzz tests on detecting student errors, we developed a larger fuzz test than the one distributed to students originally. We randomly generated 1,000 test inputs. We graded all snapshots in which students modified the originally provided code for the target question, resulting in a total of 173,468 snapshots of student code.

For each snapshot, we evaluated the student code on all 1,000 fuzz test inputs, producing a vector of 1,000 student outputs. We assumed that if two snapshots produced the same output vector, they contained the same logical errors. The snapshots that we examined manually all validated this assumption.

Figure 4 shows the frequency of the most common logical errors. Each bar represents one response vector, ordered from most to least common. The figure shows that the 10 most common logical errors account for 41% of snapshots with errors. The 50 most common errors account for 71% of snapshots. Figure 5 describes the logical errors that resulted in the ten most common errors. However, a long tail of student errors account for a small but significant number of snapshots. In total, the fuzz test discovered 1,235 distinct errors.

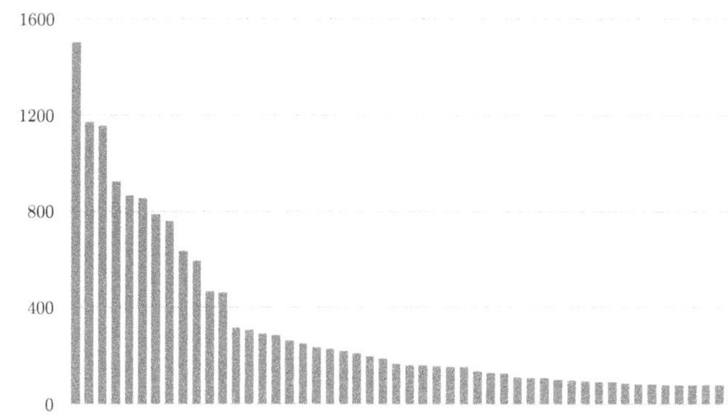

Figure 4. The 50 most common errors revealed by the fuzz test followed by a long tail of 1,185 other errors (not shown). Each bar represents the frequency of one output vector. We assumed that if two snapshots produced the same output vector, they contained the same logical errors.

Rank	Snapshots	Logical Error
1	1,502	Did not modify returned variables
2	1,171	Incorrectly determined tens digit for numbers larger than 100
3	1,156	Incorrectly determined tens digit for single-digit numbers
4	925	Did not switch player after turns
5	867	Classified 2 as a nonprime number
6	854	Stopped after two turns
7	789	Did not apply a rule in some cases
8	759	Did not implement a rule
9	637	Stopped after one turn
10	594	Gave all points to one player

Figure 5. The 10 most common errors revealed by the fuzz test.

This large number of unique errors is consistent with previous work in applying fuzz tests to evaluate open-ended programming questions: A system that used a fixed error model to identify the differences between student and reference implementations could only find a difference conforming to the model in 65% of cases, indicating a large space of possible logical errors [19].

In a massive course, fuzz tests can identify groups of students that have the same logical error, even when that error is quite rare. Finding these groups can be helpful to the students by connecting them with each other and helpful to instructors who can attempt to assist all of them at once.

Infrastructure

To analyze data from fuzz tests at this scale, we created an autograding infrastructure that dynamically adjusts capacity based on demand. During our use, it was capable of testing more than 5,000 submissions per minute (each running a fuzz test with 1,000 inputs). This throughput can be used to generate quick analysis of student progress for instructors.

1. **Results Database.** We use a cluster of three virtual machines running *Redis* (a key-value datastore) to store the results.

2. **Job Queue.** Each of the 173,468 student code snapshots is inserted into a job queue that is also backed by the Redis cluster.
3. **Grading Containers.** All of the grading happens inside of a *Docker* container that is sandboxed from the host machine and has all of the dependencies to grade the project pre-installed.
4. **Grading Servers.** Virtual Machines run 10 workers that each grab snapshots from the job queue, launch grading containers, and communicate the results to the results database. Grading is a CPU intensive operation which requires relatively powerful virtual machines. We reduce costs by 70% through the usage of Preemptible Instances that may be terminated at any time. This an acceptable tradeoff because any lost work is easily recomputable.
5. **Autoscaling.** Google Compute Engine was configured to automatically adjust the number of grading servers based on average CPU load of the existing servers. This results in the system rapidly creating many grading servers, each of which results in 10 new workers. Once grading was completed, the machines were automatically terminated to reduce costs.

The job took about three hours to complete and utilized approximately fifty distinct virtual machines. The total cost of the grading servers was $7.53, showing that fuzz testing is logistically feasible for grading in massive classes, despite the distributed infrastructure required for fast analysis.

Results

After analyzing the in-progress work of students, we discovered that 656 students (48.4% of students who attempted the question) were able to write code that passed the 9 manually constructed tests, but still contained a logical error identified by the fuzz test. Without this feedback from the fuzz test, half of the course would have progressed with incorrect implementations.

Figure 6 shows the distribution of attempts made by students in this group before finally passing the provided fuzz test. The median time for a student to resolve an error revealed in a fuzz test was 3.4 hours. This time stands in stark contrast to the median time of 18 minutes to resolve errors revealed in targeted tests. We attribute this difference to both the comprehensiveness of fuzz tests at finding errors (seen in Figure 4) as well as the obfuscation of the fuzz test output provided to students.

In Figure 7, we analyze how additional fuzz test inputs help detect additional bugs. First, all snapshots are tested with 1,000 inputs. Snapshots that produce a different output vector than the reference solution are labeled as incorrect. Then, we determine how many incorrect snapshots match the reference solution for the first k fuzz tests inputs. When only one fuzz test input is considered ($k = 1$) against 22,375 snapshots with an incorrect implementation, only 16,010 (71.6%) are identified as containing a logical error. The fuzz test that we provided to students only contained 100 inputs. Figure 7 shows that this was insufficient to catch all student errors. The

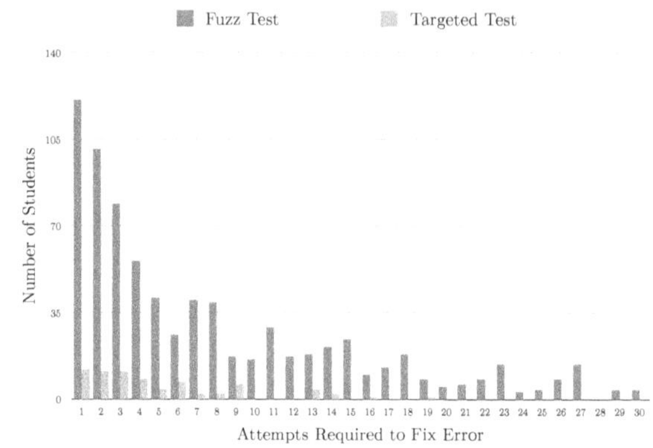

Figure 6. Distribution of attempts required by students to resolve errors for each test type

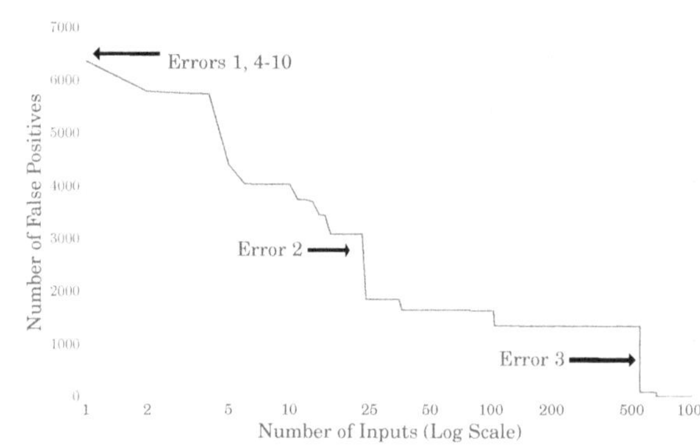

Figure 7. As the number of fuzz test inputs increases, more snapshots are revealed to have errors. The sharp drops are labeled with the error from Figure 5 that was caught by that test input.

first 100 fuzz tests only caught 92.7% of snapshots with errors. Therefore, some students were given full credit without a correct solution.

In addition, Figure 7 shows that some fuzz test inputs are more useful for detecting errors than others. For example, inputs 105 to 545 were unable to detect many more errors than the first 104 inputs alone. However, input 546 tested a rare scenario where students were asked to find the tens digit for a three-digit number, rather than a two-digit number. Because the fuzz test inputs are randomly sampled from the space of inputs, these uncommon scenarios may not be tested until a large number of inputs are randomly generated.

CONCLUSION

Fuzz testing student submissions by comparing their output on random inputs to the output of a reference implementation is both easy to implement and effective for comprehensive testing. When combined with targeted tests that are manually constructed to identify common issues, test suites can enhance the instructional value of programming projects by guiding students to correct implementations. Our empirical evaluation exposed some surprising results: fuzz testing identified errors that were missed by hand-crafted tests in almost half of student implementations. A small number of random inputs was insufficient for identifying errors; many submissions matched the reference for hundreds of random inputs before diverging. The number of unique errors that arose in the one programming problem we studied was enormous: 1,235 unique errors among 1,355 students. With such a variety of possible issues that may arise in programming problems in a large course, fuzz testing should be considered an essential tool for providing automated feedback at scale.

Acknowledgements

This work was supported by a Google Research Cloud Credits Award.

REFERENCES

1. Basu, S., Wu, A., Hou, B., and DeNero, J. Problems before solutions: Automated problem clarification at scale. In *Proceedings of the Second (2015) ACM Conference on Learning@ Scale*, ACM (2015), 205–213.
2. Becker, S., Abdelnur, H., Obes, J. L., State, R., and Festor, O. Improving fuzz testing using game theory. In *Network and System Security (NSS), 2010 4th International Conference on*, IEEE (2010), 263–268.
3. Bounimova, E., Godefroid, P., and Molnar, D. Billions and billions of constraints: Whitebox fuzz testing in production. In *Proceedings of the 2013 International Conference on Software Engineering*, ICSE '13, IEEE Press (Piscataway, NJ, USA, 2013), 122–131.
4. DeNero, J., and Klein, D. Teaching introductory artificial intelligence with pac-man. In *Proceedings of the Symposium on Educational Advances in Artificial Intelligence* (2010).
5. Dormann, W., and Plakosh, D. Vulnerability detection in activex controls through automated fuzz testing. *Unpublished working paper* (2008).
6. Edwards, S. H., and Perez-Quinones, M. A. Web-cat: automatically grading programming assignments. In *ACM SIGCSE Bulletin*, vol. 40, ACM (2008), 328–328.
7. Forrester, J. E., and Miller, B. P. An empirical study of the robustness of windows nt applications using random testing. In *Proceedings of the 4th Conference on USENIX Windows Systems Symposium - Volume 4*, WSS'00, USENIX Association (Berkeley, CA, USA, 2000), 6–6.
8. Glassman, E. L., Singh, R., and Miller, R. C. Feature engineering for clustering student solutions. In *Proceedings of the First ACM Conference on Learning @ Scale Conference*, L@S '14, ACM (New York, NY, USA, 2014), 171–172.
9. Godefroid, P., Kiezun, A., and Levin, M. Y. Grammar-based whitebox fuzzing. In *Proceedings of the 29th ACM SIGPLAN Conference on Programming Language Design and Implementation*, PLDI '08, ACM (New York, NY, USA, 2008), 206–215.
10. Godefroid, P., Levin, M. Y., Molnar, D. A., et al. Automated whitebox fuzz testing. In *NDSS*, vol. 8 (2008), 151–166.
11. Hamlet, D., and Taylor, R. Partition testing does not inspire confidence (program testing). *IEEE Trans. Softw. Eng. 16*, 12 (Dec. 1990), 1402–1411.
12. Hollingsworth, J. Automatic graders for programming classes. *Commun. ACM 3*, 10 (Oct. 1960), 528–529.
13. Ihantola, P., Ahoniemi, T., Karavirta, V., and Seppälä, O. Review of recent systems for automatic assessment of programming assignments. In *Proceedings of the 10th Koli Calling International Conference on Computing Education Research*, Koli Calling '10, ACM (New York, NY, USA, 2010), 86–93.
14. Miller, B. P., Cooksey, G., and Moore, F. An empirical study of the robustness of macos applications using random testing. In *Proceedings of the 1st International Workshop on Random Testing*, RT '06, ACM (New York, NY, USA, 2006), 46–54.
15. Miller, B. P., Fredriksen, L., and So, B. An empirical study of the reliability of unix utilities. *Commun. ACM 33*, 12 (Dec. 1990), 32–44.
16. Pacheco, C., Lahiri, S. K., Ernst, M. D., and Ball, T. Feedback-directed random test generation. In *Proceedings of the 29th International Conference on Software Engineering*, ICSE '07, IEEE Computer Society (Washington, DC, USA, 2007), 75–84.
17. Parlante, N., Zelenski, J., Dodds, Z., Vonnegut, W., Malan, D. J., Murtagh, T. P., Neller, T. W., Sherriff, M., and Zingaro, D. Nifty assignments. In *Proceedings of the 41st ACM Technical Symposium on Computer Science Education*, SIGCSE '10, ACM (New York, NY, USA, 2010), 478–479.
18. Piech, C., Sahami, M., Huang, J., and Guibas, L. Autonomously generating hints by inferring problem solving policies. In *Proceedings of the Second (2015) ACM Conference on Learning @ Scale*, L@S '15, ACM (New York, NY, USA, 2015), 195–204.
19. Singh, R., Gulwani, S., and Solar-Lezama, A. Automated feedback generation for introductory programming assignments. In *Proceedings of the 34th ACM SIGPLAN Conference on Programming Language Design and Implementation*, PLDI '13, ACM (New York, NY, USA, 2013), 15–26.
20. Tsankov, P., Dashti, M. T., and Basin, D. Secfuzz: Fuzz-testing security protocols. In *Proceedings of the 7th International Workshop on Automation of Software Test*, AST '12, IEEE Press (Piscataway, NJ, USA, 2012), 1–7.

Peer Grading in a Course on Algorithms and Data Structures: Machine Learning Algorithms do not Improve over Simple Baselines

Mehdi S. M. Sajjadi
Max Planck Institute for Intelligent Systems*
Spemannstr. 38
72076 Tübingen
msajjadi@tuebingen.mpg.de

Morteza Alamgir
University of Hamburg
Vogt-Kölln-Str. 30
22527 Hamburg
alamgir@informatik.uni-hamburg.de

Ulrike von Luxburg
University of Tübingen*
Sand 14
72076 Tübingen
luxburg@informatik.uni-tuebingen.de

ABSTRACT
Peer grading is the process of students reviewing each others' work, such as homework submissions, and has lately become a popular mechanism used in massive open online courses (MOOCs). Intrigued by this idea, we used it in a course on algorithms and data structures at the University of Hamburg. Throughout the whole semester, students repeatedly handed in submissions to exercises, which were then evaluated both by teaching assistants and by a peer grading mechanism, yielding a large dataset of teacher and peer grades. We applied different statistical and machine learning methods to aggregate the peer grades in order to come up with accurate final grades for the submissions (supervised and unsupervised, methods based on numeric scores and ordinal rankings). Surprisingly, none of them improves over the baseline of using the mean peer grade as the final grade. We discuss a number of possible explanations for these results and present a thorough analysis of the generated dataset.

Author Keywords
machine learning; peer grading; peer assessment; peer review; L@S; ordinal analysis; rank aggregation.

INTRODUCTION
Peer grading refers to a process where students grade the work of their co-students based on a scoring rubric provided by the instructor. While it has been experimented with in the past (see [7]), it has become increasingly popular in the context of MOOCs, where thousands of students hand in homework that has to be graded (e.g., [2]). Similar to other crowd-sourcing scenarios, the hope is that even though students may not be perfect graders, it might be possible to come up with a *fair* or *accurate* final grade for each submitted homework by aggregating many such imperfect grades. The challenge of finding good aggregation algorithms has been taken up by the machine learning community and a number of suggestions have been made in the literature (e.g., [4, 9, 5, 6, 1, 10, 8]). The bottom line of these papers is that statistical models or machine learning algorithms are successful at solving this task.

Intrigued by its idea and potential, we used peer grading in an undergraduate course in computer science at the University of Hamburg: the course on algorithms and data structures (AD). Throughout one semester, students solved 6 exercise sheets with 2-5 exercises each. 6 Teaching assistants (TAs) graded all submissions in the traditional way, but at the same time we applied peer grading on the same set of submissions. The data generated during the whole semester has been made publicly available, the link can be found on our homepages. We refer to it as *AD data* below. At the end of the semester, we applied various algorithms to aggregate the peer grades and to analyze our data. Contrary to other researchers we found that none of these methods show a satisfactory improvement over a simple baseline. We will discuss a number of possible explanations for these results and analyze sources of problems that prevent more sophisticated methods to succeed.

OUR SETUP
For our peer grading experiment we selected the course on algorithms and data structures at the Department of Computer Science, University of Hamburg in the winter term 2014/15. The course is compulsory for all bachelor students in computer science and had 219 active participants in total. We had 6 TAs grade all homework in the traditional way. Roughly once every two weeks, students received an exercise sheet as homework, resulting in 6 sheets with 19 individual exercises in total. The exercises consisted of puzzles on algorithms or proofs about algorithmic properties. For example, the students were asked to apply a given algorithm by hand on a small input or they were asked to design an algorithm to solve a particular problem. In each exercise, students could collect a certain number of points. Getting at least 50% of all homework points in the semester was a necessary requirement to pass the course. Exercises were solved and submitted by groups of up to three students. This semester we had a total of 79 groups. For each

*This work was carried out while the authors were still at the University of Hamburg.

L@S 2016, April 25–26, 2016, Edinburgh, UK.

ACM 978-1-4503-3726-7/16/04 ...$15.00.
http://dx.doi.org/10.1145/2876034.2876036

individual exercise, every group handed in their submission via an online system (we used a modification of the moodle open source platform[1]). After the submission deadline, a sample solution together with assessment criteria was posted online by the course instructor. We tried to describe all possible correct solutions to the exercises, point out pitfalls or common errors and discuss details about the grading procedure. Grading took place simultaneously in the following three different ways.

(i) Self grading. The students were asked to read and understand the sample solution and then grade their own submission first. While they solved exercises in groups of three, the self grading took place individually, resulting in 3 self grades per submission.

(ii) Peer grading. Each student graded 2 randomly selected submissions of other groups, resulting in about 6 peer grades per submission. Grading was double-blind.

(iii) TA grading. All submissions were furthermore randomly assigned to and graded by one of the 6 TAs.

In two exercise sheets, we experimented with slightly altered settings. In one case, we increased the number of peer grades by each reviewer from 2 to 5, which results in about 15 peer grades for each submission. On another exercise sheet, we applied ordinal peer grading: Instead of assigning every submission an absolute grade, we gave each student a total of 5 peer submissions and asked them to only rank these submissions from worst to best.

In order to ensure that the students take their peer grading duties seriously, we made a reasonable peer grading performance a mandatory requirement to pass the course: students were required to participate in the peer grading of at least 5 exercise sheets, and we announced that sloppy grading behavior would not be tolerated. Moreover, the peer grades contributed to the final grades for the submissions with a weight of 20% (with the other 80% being the respective TA grade). An anonymous questionnaire at the end of the semester revealed that about half the students liked the concept of peer grading, had the impression that it helped them deepen their understanding, and would like to repeat it in another course. The other half of the students did not like it, mainly because it had taken too much of their time.

ALGORITHMS FOR ESTIMATING TRUE GRADES

From a statistical or machine learning point of view, the most interesting questions in the context of peer grading are the following.

(i) Unsupervised setting. In the complete absence of TA or instructor grades, is it possible to take several "imperfect" peer grades and to aggregate them into a "fair" or "accurate" final grade for each submission? MOOCs traditionally have this setting.

(ii) Supervised setting In a setting where partial grading is available by an instructor, is it possible to predict or recover the instructor's grades based on aggregated peer grades? If instead of a single instructor, partial grading is performed by several TAs, is it possible to predict missing grades in the quality of TA grades or even better? This is a realistic scenario in large university courses.

(iii) Adversarial setting Is it possible to come up with a grading scheme that is robust against adversarial behavior of individuals (such as students deliberately giving everyone very high grades or trying to downgrade others) or adversarial attacks of groups of students (such as a cartel of students that act together in order to fool the grading procedure)?

Our work focuses on the first two questions. Let us introduce some notation. Over the course of the semester, students solved and graded several exercises. Fix one exercise and suppose that submissions $s_1, s_2, \ldots$ to this exercise have been handed in by the students. Consider a set of graders $g_1, g_2, \ldots$. By $\text{score}(s,g)$ we denote the score given to submission s by grader g. In the unsupervised scenario, we do not have any data on what the "true" score of each submission should be. Instead, the standard approach is to simply *define* the true score $\text{score}(s, true)$ as the population average over the scores of *all* potential graders. As we only observe the scores of few graders in practice, the goal of an unsupervised algorithm is to correct for inaccuracies that are introduced by the actual grading procedure. In the supervised setting the true score may be given by the instructor or TAs. The goal of supervised peer grading algorithms is to give an estimate $\text{score}(s, estimated)$ of the true scores for all submissions based on the set of the given peer grades.

Depending on whether the focus is on the absolute values of the scores or just on the ranking of the submissions, the model performance is evaluated using different error functions. We use the L_2 error to compare the absolute score values and the Kendall-τ error to compare the rankings induced by the scores. The Kendall-τ error between two rankings counts the number of pairs of items for which the ranking order is inversed. For each pair of items an error of 0 is given for agreement, 1 for inversion, and an error of 0.5 if exactly one of the rankings gives both items the same rank. The final Kendall-τ error is the mean over the errors for all possible pairs.

Unsupervised models

Mean and **Median**. We simply estimate the true score of a submission by taking the mean (resp. median) of all peer grades for this submission. These algorithms serve as baseline.

Unsupervised-single-task (UST). Following [4], we make some model-based assumptions. Fix a single exercise. We assume that the true scores of all submissions to this exercise are normally distributed as $\mathcal{N}(\mu_{score}, \sigma^2_{score})$. Each grader g has an inherent $\text{bias}(g)$ and a certain $\text{reliability}(g)$. The intuition is that the bias models the tendency of a grader to generally give high scores or to be very strict, whereas the reliability accounts for the variance in the grading performance. Formally, if a submission s has a true $\text{score}(s, true)$, then the grade reported by g is normally distributed as

$$\mathcal{N}\Big(\text{score}(s,true) + \text{bias}(g), 1/\text{reliability}(g)\Big).$$

As the actual true score is not known, it is replaced by the current estimate $\text{score}(s, estimated)$ in practice. The bias of

[1] https://moodle.org/

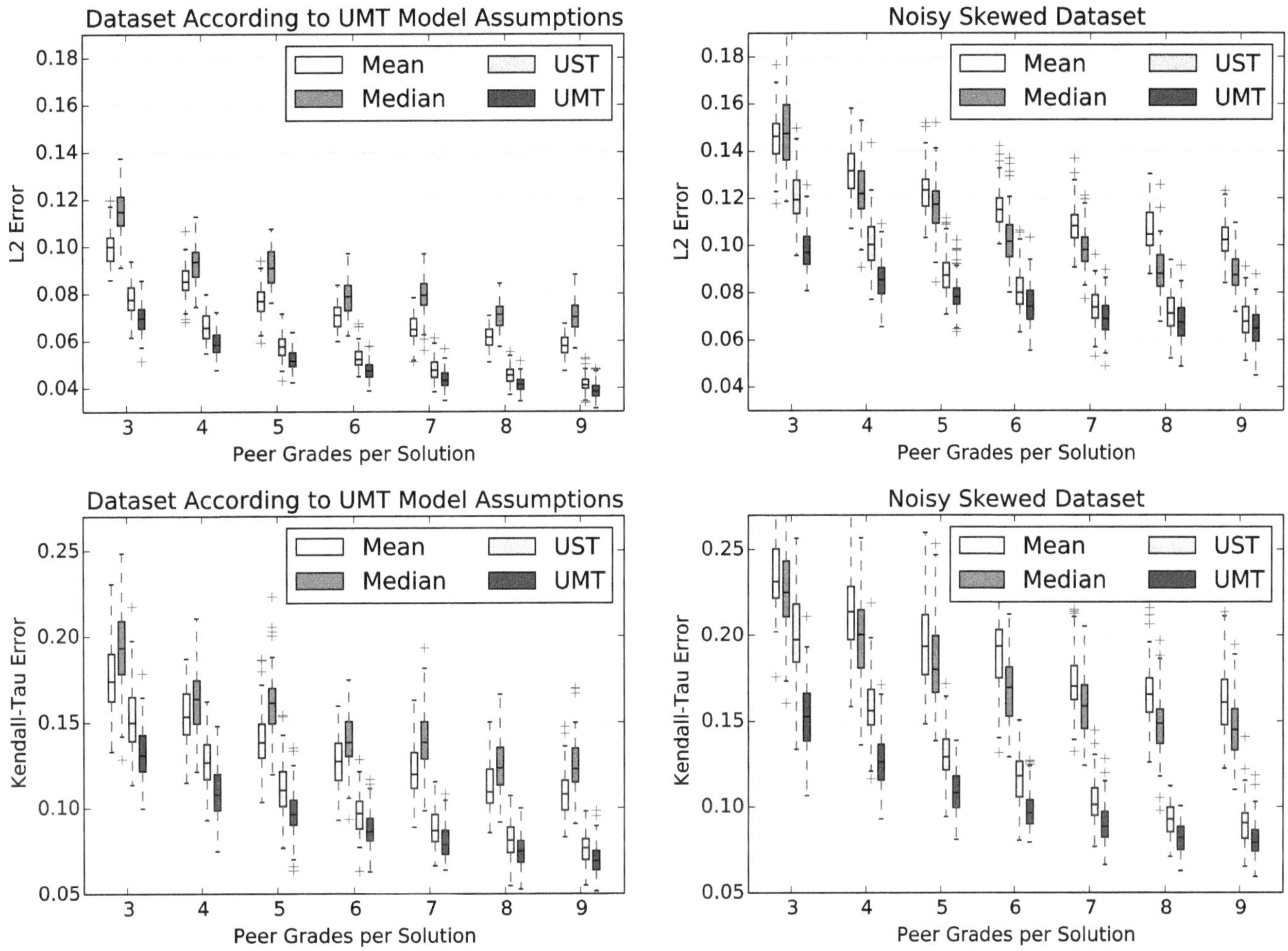

Figure 1. Fitting UST and UMT on artificial data (100 submissions, 100 graders, 5 exercises). The panels show the L_2 and Kendall-τ errors of the estimated grades with respect to the actual underlying true grades. The box plots show the distribution over the errors of 100 independently generated datasets while the number of peer grades per submission increases along the x-axis. Left: Dataset generated according to UMT's model assumptions with reasonably realistic hyperparameters (true scores generated with $\mathcal{N}(1/2, 1/6^2)$, bias $\mathcal{N}(0, 1/8^2)$ and reliability $\Gamma(3, 1/30)$). Right: Skewed true score distribution according to Weibull$(3/2, 1/3)$ and additionally, 20 graders always draw scores uniformly at random while bias and reliability for the remaining 80 graders is modeled as before.

all graders is distributed as $\mathcal{N}(0, \sigma_{bias}^2)$ and the reliability is Gamma-distributed as $\Gamma(\alpha, \beta)$. The hyperparameters μ_{score}, σ_{score}, σ_{bias}, α, β can be used to control the weight of bias and reliability estimation as well as the strength of regularization. The goal is to fit the model to the observed data and to learn the parameters bias(g), reliability(g) and score$(s, estimated)$. For this purpose we use the EM algorithm, which [4] found to give results similar to those obtained by more elaborate Gibbs sampling procedures.

Unsupervised-multiple-tasks (UMT). In our course, each student graded a total of about 57 different submissions for 19 exercises over the whole semester. While the UST model just learns from one exercise at a time, the UMT model learns the parameters jointly over all exercises. UMT's basic assumption that the bias and reliability of a grader are inherent attributes and do not vary over different exercises could lead to more accurate estimates as there is much more data to work with.

Evaluating UST and UMT on artificial data confirms the finding in [4] that such models do a remarkable job at recovering the true underlying score, see Figure 1 for an illustration. As more grades per submission are added, UST performs almost as well as UMT and they both beat simple algorithms such as mean and median by far. For example, UMT only needs 4 grades per submission to reach the error rates of the mean algorithm with 9 peer grades as seen in the left figures. In particular, the models even work reasonably well on artificial data with a model mismatch, i.e. data that has not been generated according to the model assumptions.

Ordinal models. It has been suggested that instead of collecting numeric grades for each submission (cardinal peer grading), it might be more reliable to ask each student to only *rank* a set of submissions. Using those partial rankings of each reviewer, the purpose of the ordinal algorithms is to generate an overall ranking of all submissions and to assign them cardinal rankings following a certain score distribution.

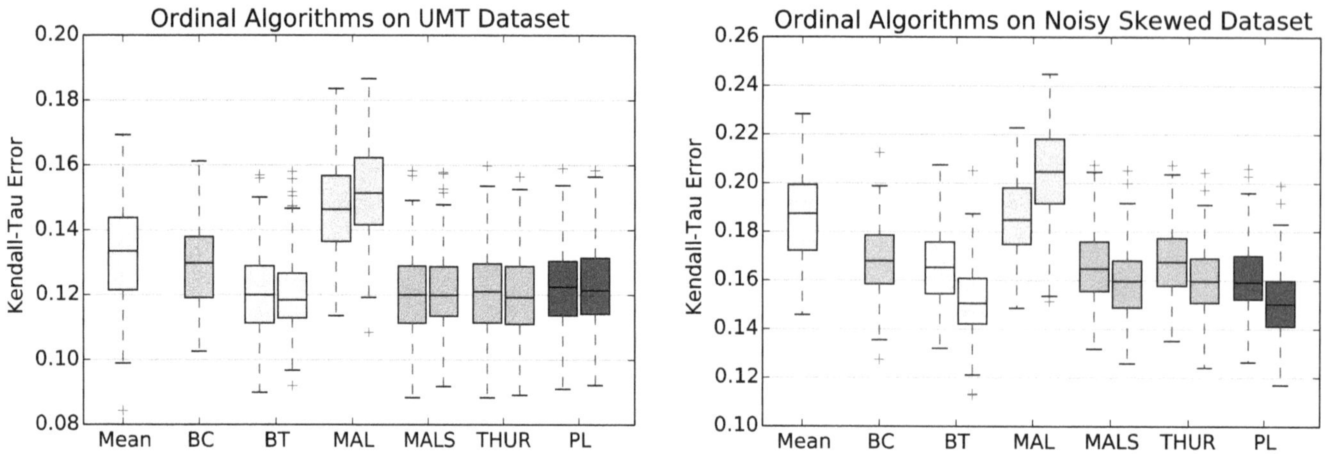

Figure 2. Fitting the ordinal algorithms on artificial data (100 submissions, 100 graders, 1 exercise, 6 peer grades per submission) according to UMT model assumptions (left) and on the noisy skewed dataset (right) as in Figure 1. The two bars for BC, MAL, MALS, THUR and PL show the performance without (left bar) and with (right bar) reliability estimation.

A very simple algorithm for this purpose is **Borda Count (BC)**. Given a ranked set of submissions $s_0 < \ldots < s_k$ by a reviewer (where $k+1$ is the number of reported grades by each reviewer), the algorithm gives submission s_i the score i that is the number of submissions that were ranked lower than s_i. The sums of these scores for each submission determine the overall BC score. A number of more elaborate models have been described for this purpose in [5]: **Mallows (MAL)** and **scored Mallows (MALS)**, **Bradley-Terry (BT)**, **Thurstone (THUR)** and **Plackett-Luce (PL)**.

We will focus here on the BT model, which assumes that the likelihood of switching the ranking of a pair of submissions depends on the distance of their true scores and on the reliability of the grader:

$$P(\text{score}(s_1,true) > \text{score}(s_2,true))$$
$$= \frac{1}{1+\exp(-\text{reliability}(g)\cdot(\text{score}(s_1,g)-\text{score}(s_2,g)))}$$

The scores and reliabilities are then estimated using an alternating stochastic gradient descent algorithm. The performance of the ordinal algorithms in comparison to the Mean baseline on artificial datasets is shown in Figure 2. Note that the Mean baseline is computed on the actual grades as opposed to the ordinal models that only have access to the rankings. Nonetheless, all ordinal models but MAL beat the Mean algorithm. The reliability estimation only shows improvements in the right figure, which is unsurprising, as ordinal grading implicitly applies a threshold for inaccuracies in the reported grades: while it is likely that a reviewer misses the true cardinal grade, getting just the order right is much easier, so the effects of the reliability estimation are only visible here when a large portion of the reviewers is reporting random grades. Increasing the magnitude of the bias values for the reviewers decreases the performance of the Mean algorithm while that only has a negligible effect on the ordinal models (not shown in the figure).

Supervised models

In the supervised models, the goal is to learn to use the peer grades to predict the true grades as given by an instructor. In our case, we take the grades provided by the TAs as ground truth. We consider the following two approaches.

Supervised-naive (SN). As baseline we use the following naive algorithm. For all exercises, the submissions are split into a training set and a test set. We use the TA grades as ground truth for the training sets to estimate the overall student grader biases. With those bias estimates, we compute the bias-corrected mean scores. Denote the submissions that student g graded over the whole course in the training set by $s_1,\ldots,s_n$. Taking the TA grades as true scores, we calculate the overall bias for the student as

$$\text{bias}(g) = \frac{1}{n}\sum_{i=1}^{n}\text{score}(s_i,g)-\text{score}(s_i,true).$$

On the test set, let $g_1,\ldots,g_k$ be all students who graded submission s. The bias-corrected mean score is then given as

$$\text{score}(s,estimated) = \frac{1}{k}\sum_{j=1}^{k}\text{score}(s,g_j)-\text{bias}(g_j).$$

Supervised-multiple-tasks (SMT). Another approach is to incorporate the TA grades directly into the UMT model. For some subset of the submissions, the respective TA grades are put into the model like any other peer grade, but the TA reliabilities are set to a high constant. This automatically corrects the student reviewer biases towards the TA grades and also gives higher reliabilities to students that grade similar to the TAs. To see how much this improves the overall accuracy, the error is only computed on submissions whose TA grades are unknown to the model.

Linking the data

While all introduced models estimate the scores, bias and reliability in a very direct way, more accurate results might be obtained by linking up the data in other ways. For example,

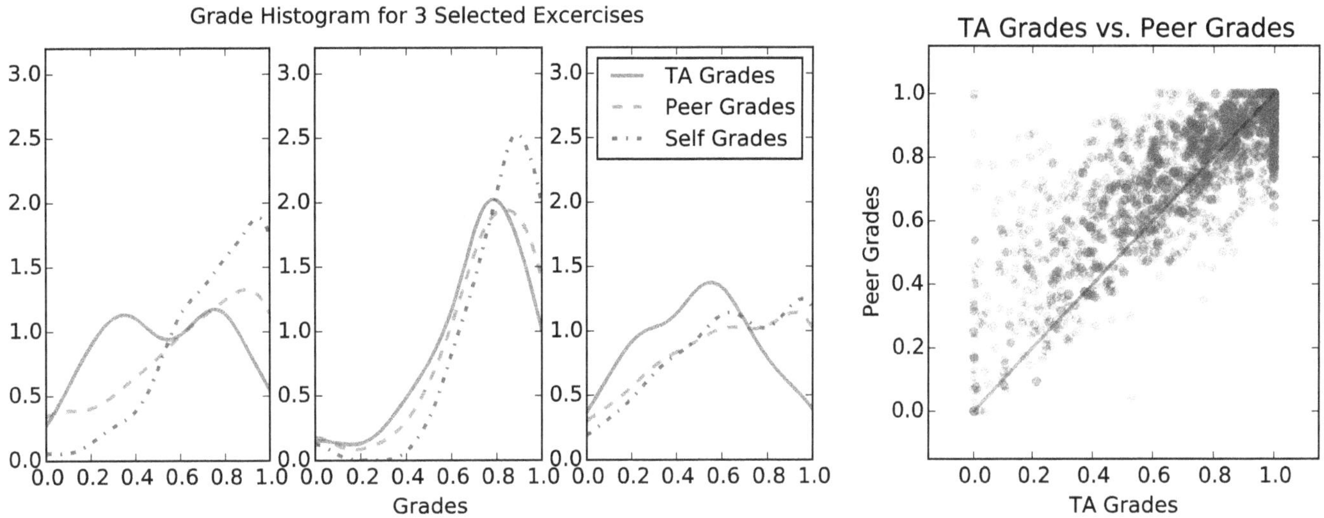

Figure 3. TA grades compared to mean peer grades. Left: Smoothed and rescaled score histograms for three selected exercises. Right: Overview of all submissions and their grades. Each circle depicts one submission with its position indicating the TA score and mean peer grade (jitter added to avoid clustering due to different scales). If the TAs and students fully agreed on the scores, all circles would lie on the indicated diagonal.

it stands to reason that students with higher grades on their own homework submissions are likely to be more reliable at grading than students with lower grades. One may even take it a step further by making the homework scores dependent on their grading reliability in order to motivate them to put more effort into the peer grading. Another example is that better performing students might have higher standards when grading other submissions, effectively resulting in a negative bias.

Assuming the data shows strong correlations in this regard, there are several ways to incorporate these additional ties into the model. A very simple approach is fitting a linear function between the own homework scores to the bias/reliability and to use that in the computation of the final grades. Using UMT, one can also build a hybrid model by scaling the estimated reliability with the output of the linear function that takes the own score as input. Such approaches have been shown to improve the model accuracy, see e.g. [4, 3]. We will study these correlations in our dataset and analyze whether they can be used to improve the score estimates.

OUR DATASET AND ITS ANALYSIS

AD data: first observations

We will begin with an overview over the raw data. To be able to compare performances across different exercises, we rescale the scores of each exercise to lie in the interval $[0,1]$. A different standardization of shifting and rescaling the scores to have mean 0 and variance 1 (z-scores) leads to very similar results. To get a first impression of our data, consider the plots on the left in Figure 3. In each panel, the figure shows histograms of scores for a particular exercise. These already show a number of interesting points. Not very surprisingly, we see that self grades are often higher than peer grades, which in turn tend to be higher than the grades given by the TAs. For some of the exercises, it looks like the peer grade histograms are "shifted versions" of the TA histograms but this is not always the case. To the contrary, sometimes the overall characteristics and shapes of the histograms are quite different. In general the scores do not seem to be normally distributed. The first obvious reason is that the scores are bounded to a fixed interval which can lead to several artifacts. The score distributions are often skewed, for example when the exercise was easy and many students got full marks for their submission. In many cases the score distribution is clearly bi- or multi-modal: this can arise if a large number of students solved only part of the exercise whereas others solved it completely.

A second aspect illustrated in Figure 3 (right) visualizes the relationship between TA grades and peer grades for individual submissions. While the tendency of peer grades generally being higher than the TA grades is again evident here, we can also see quite a number of submissions that received a score of 0 by TAs but moderate to large scores by peers. Looking into the corresponding submissions reveals that a typical reason is a wrong solution to the exercise where many reviewers miss the error and give full marks instead. We can also see in the figure that there is a large number of submissions with full TA grades but slightly lower peer grades. This happens because it is simply unlikely for all 6 peer grades to be full scores and a single lower grade will drag down the mean value.

On a more abstract level, the figure reveals that the "sources of error" for a grader are not only a bias due to different taste or different levels of strictness as suggested in the probabilistic models, but also a serious lack of understanding or information. This is problematic for statistical algorithms: if a submission gets high scores by most peer graders, there is no way to know whether this is really justified because the given solution is correct or whether the reason is that all peer graders have overlooked a crucial mistake in the submission. On the other hand, it is hard to detect cases of otherwise reliable graders getting a score completely wrong, in particular in the realistic scenario where only few grades are given for each submission.

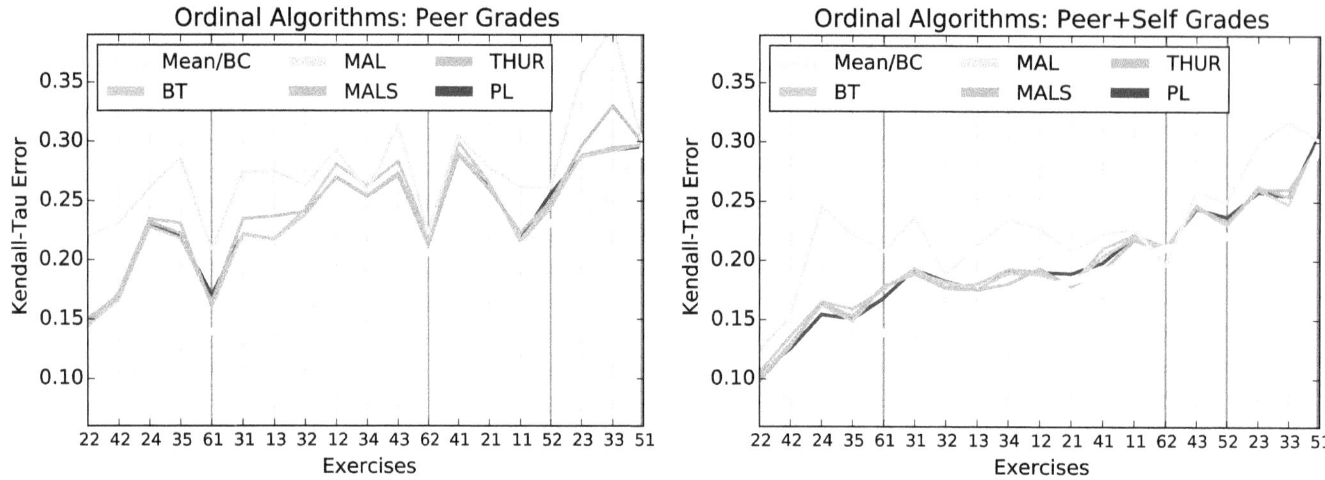

Figure 4. Comparing the performance of the ordinal models without reliability estimation on the AD dataset with the mean algorithm as baseline. The exercises on the x-axis are sorted by the error of the mean algorithm. In exercises 61 and 62 (green), each student reported 5 instead of 2 peer grades. Exercises 51 and 52 (red) were graded ordinally, so the BC algorithm is used as a baseline instead of the mean.

Fitting the models to the data

We analyze our data using the introduced models. In the unsupervised scenario, we simply take all grades, fit the models, and estimate a "true score". Note that in the unsupervised setting, we cannot optimize the model to fit any ground truth (such as the TA grades). If the histogram of peer grades is shifted with respect to the TA grades[2], there is no way for an unsupervised model to correct for this. Hence, comparing the estimated true scores to TA scores by any loss function that compares the scores directly, such as the L_2 error, might be dominated by the overall bias shift. To cover for this, we use the Kendall-τ rank correlation as a second error measure.

The hyperparameters of the models are chosen as follows. The parameters μ_{score}, σ^2_{score} and σ^2_{bias} for UST and UMT only control the strength of regularization and were found to have little to no impact on the overall accuracy. The reliability parameters α and β control whether the model gives all students a similar reliability or fits them to a large variety of reliability values. In our evaluations, we use the sample mean and variance of the given peer grades for each exercise to set μ_{score} and σ^2_{score} and fix the remaining hyperparameters at $\sigma^2_{bias} = 1/36$, $\alpha = 3$ and $\beta = 1/30$. For BT, we again use the sample mean and variance as priors and choose $\alpha = 10$, $\beta = 2$ for the reliability. Note that in the exercise sheet where we applied the pure ordinal setting, students only report rankings of submissions, so sample mean and variance are unknown there. In that case, the parameters can be chosen arbitrarily to control the distribution of the resulting scores.

Analysis of unsupervised models

We will begin with a comparison of the **ordinal algorithms** (For this section, the implementation provided by [5] was used.) A plot of the algorithm performance on each individual exercise is shown in Figure 4. In our case study we usually collected numeric grades – only their induced rankings are fed into the ordinal algorithms. For that reason, we again use the Mean algorithm as baseline. Exercises 51 and 52 are an exception to that, as we collected the grades in an ordinal fashion there, so we use the simple BC algorithm as baseline for those two exercises. With the exception of Mallow's model, all ordinal algorithms perform very similarly. In particular, using only the peer grades they all perform worse than the mean algorithm by a significant margin. The difference is smaller when the peer and self grades are combined, as there are significantly more pairwise comparisons in this dataset which helps the ordinal models. Adding the reliability estimation to the models curiously increased the Kendall-τ errors in most exercises by 0.01-0.03 (not shown in the figure). On the exercises 61 and 62, we asked each student to grade 5 other submissions instead of 2. The effect is visible on the peer grades, as the performance of the ordinal algorithms is substantially better on those tasks, strengthening the point that ordinal models inherently need more grades to match the performance of cardinal algorithms.

As a further experiment, we collected the grades in an ordinal fashion in exercises 51 and 52. Much to our surprise, the embarrassingly simple approach of the BC algorithm yields no worse results than the rankings of the more complex ordinal algorithms on exercise 51 and even beats them on exercise 52. This could imply that more complicated models are not needed for ordinal peer grading. Additionally, we can see that the performance of the ordinal algorithms on exercises 51 and 52 is rather bad in general. One reason for this might be the grading behavior of the students in ordinal tasks. Many students reported that they made less of an effort for ordinal peer grading than for cardinal peer grading because they considered it easier to quickly come up with a ranking than to report absolute grades. We believe that this might be a serious drawback of collecting peer grades in an ordinal fashion. If students do not look at the details of a submission, it is unlikely that the overall grading performance improves over cardinal grading.

Figure 5 shows the results of the **cardinal models** on our AD dataset along with BT representing the ordinal models.

[2]See e.g. in the third panel of Figure 3 (left).

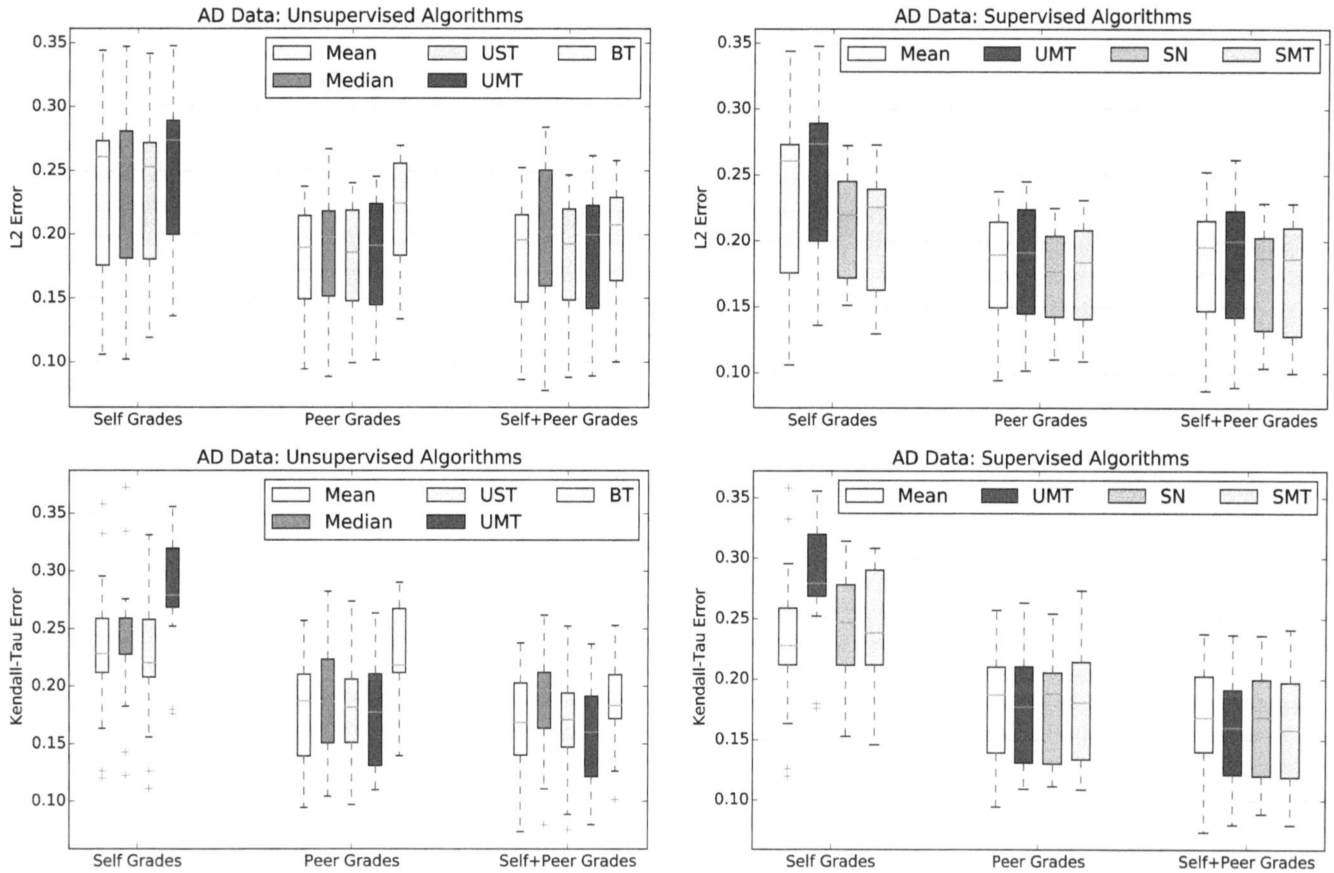

Figure 5. Fitting cardinal models to our AD data. The box plots show the L_2 errors (top) and Kendall-τ errors (bottom) with respect to the TA grades of each exercise over the whole semester. In each panel, the three groups refer to the data that was used to fit the models: the 3 self grades only, the 6 peer grades, or both together.

Note that BT cannot be run exclusively on the self assessment grades, as each student only graded one submission which does not imply any ranking. As opposed to the results on the artificial data in Figure 1 where the model-based approaches clearly outperform the baseline, we can now see that UST and UMT provide no improvement over the simple mean. This finding is disappointing and contradictory to the results in the literature. We will discuss possible explanations for this behavior in the following section.

Why do the models provide no improvements over mean?

Amount of data. We have about 6 peer grades and 3 self grades per submission, collected over 19 exercises. Each student submitted around 57 grades in total. The results on artificial datasets as well as other studies on peer grading suggest that this should be enough to get a reasonably reliable estimate. A lack of data is not the problem here.

Model assumptions mismatch. As seen above, our data usually does not satisfy the model assumptions (normal distributions, etc). However, experiments with artificial data whose distributions do not agree with the model assumptions show that the model typically still works reasonably well. We do not believe that the model mismatch is the major source of the problem.

Model fitting. We set the hyperparameters as described above, though in our experiments, we found that the models are not sensitive to the choice of the hyperparameters. The actual model fitting was done with the EM algorithm. [4] reported that the results of the EM algorithm are almost equal to the ones of Gibbs sampling. Furthermore, simulations with a number of different artificial datasets resulted in consistent estimates for the score, bias and reliability values.

TAs as baseline. We evaluate our errors against the TA grades, that is we consider the scores or orderings given by the TA grades as ground truth. However, these grades have been given by 6 different TAs, so the variance within these grades might make them unsuitable to serve as ground truth (in the extreme case, if we compared against random grades, then none of the models would outperform the others). We first study this effect with artificial experiments. Consider the setting in Figure 1, but we now add noise to the true grades before computing the errors (we use Gaussian noise with standard deviation 0.05). The results can be seen in Figure 6 (right). They still look similar to the original results in Figure 1, just the overall performance worsened slightly due to the noise. In particular, the UST and UMT models still considerably outperform the mean estimate. This is even the case if we use an unrealistically large standard deviation for the noise, say 0.2.

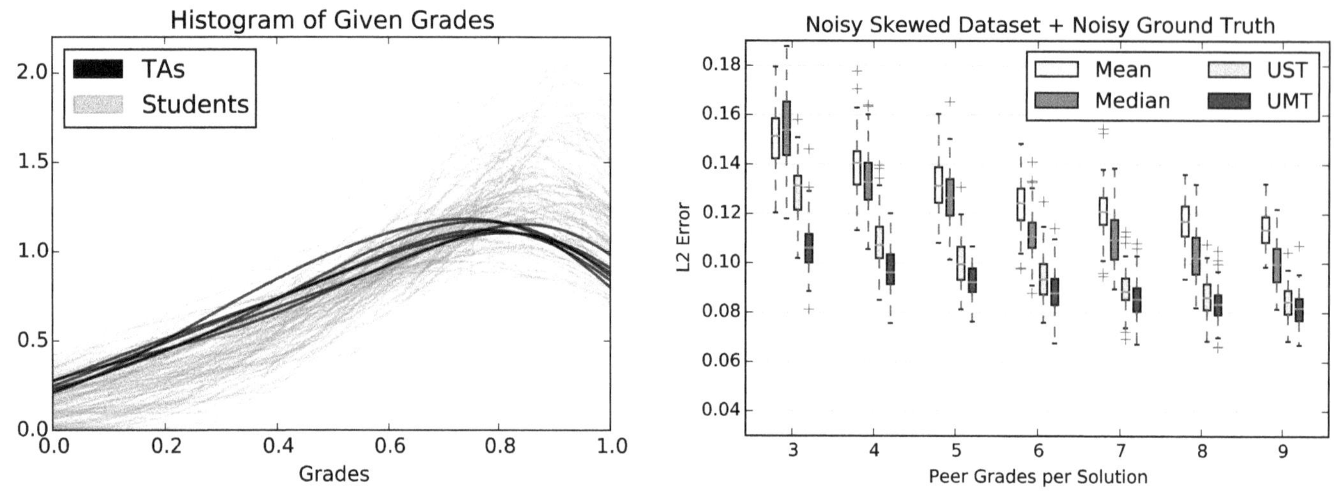

Figure 6. Analyzing the effect of using several TAs as baseline. Left: Smoothed histograms of all given grades by the TAs and students. Right: Box plots in the same setting as in Figure 5 (top right), but with white noise added for the evaluation step to simulate the effect of using several TAs: errors were computed against noisy true grades (independent Gaussian noise $\mathcal{N}(0, 0.05^2)$).

As a next step, we look at our actual data to evaluate the consistency among the TA grades in comparison to the consistency among the peer grades. Due to constraints during data collection, we did not have the possibility to conduct an extensive experiment to compare the grading performance of the TAs with each other. Instead, we consider the following evaluations. We first compare the average reported grade of the TAs to the average grades given by the student reviewers. As can be seen in Figure 7 (left), the TAs have a very low bias amongst each other, in particular it is much lower than the biases amongst the students. Next, we look at the overall histograms of all given grades by each TA, see Figure 6 (left). There is little variance amongst the TA histograms, in particular compared to the variance in the peer histograms. All in all it looks like the TAs grade reasonably consistently, so we believe that the use of different TA grades as ground truth cannot be the major reason for the lack of improvement of the probabilistic models over the simple baseline.

Bias vs. reliability. As seen in Figure 7 (mid, right), the overall biases are not very large, only few exceed an absolute value of $|0.1|$. On the other hand, the variance in reporting grades is quite high. More than half the students reported grades that deviate from the mean peer grades with a standard deviation of at least 0.14 (a variance of roughly 0.02). To gain some intuition on the values, note that a student who theoretically always reported the same score 0.72 for all submissions (the overall mean peer grade on all exercises together) would end up with a variance of 0.05.

It was reported by [4] that more than 90% of UST's improvements are due to the fact that the model-based approaches correct for the bias, an effect that we also confirmed on artificial data. However, in our AD data, the errors induced by low reliabilities dominate the errors due to bias. This may be part of the reason why the models do not perform well here.

Sources of grading error. As discussed above, reasons for differences in grading behavior are not only that people have "different tastes" or are "differently strict". Rather, it is often the case that graders make serious errors due to lack of information or lack of understanding in the topic. This problem is bound to come up when using peer grading in a course such as algorithms and data structures and might be much less of an issue when grading is used to evaluate project reports [5] or design questions [2].

To check whether the model-based algorithms improve if we just use "easy-to-grade" exercises, we selected a number of exercises where the errors were low, indicating that the students had no difficulties in grading the submissions. We found that even in this scenario, the model-based algorithms do not perform better than the mean. This may be due to the fact that in easy-to-grade exercises, the mean algorithm does a good enough job at eliminating the different biases or reliabilities, so there is not much room left for improvements. Similarly, if we just train on "difficult-to-grade" exercises, we do not find an improvement of model-based algorithms compared to the mean. The reason is that in this scenario, the errors are dominated by the submissions that are graded totally wrong by a large number of students, so none of the algorithms can do a good job.

Unmotivated students. One might suspect that some proportion of students tried to get away with minimal effort and produced grades that are pretty much random. However, looking closely into the data reveals that we only had a very small number of these students, so the models should succeed at giving them low reliabilities and lead to a better performance.

Analysis of supervised models

Considering the results for the supervised learning models in Figure 5, we see a similarly disappointing picture: the supervised models do not improve over the simple mean estimator. While the Kendall-τ errors do not change much compared to the unsupervised models, the variance in L_2 errors over different tasks gets smaller. This is an effect of calculating the student reviewer bias values against the TA grades which

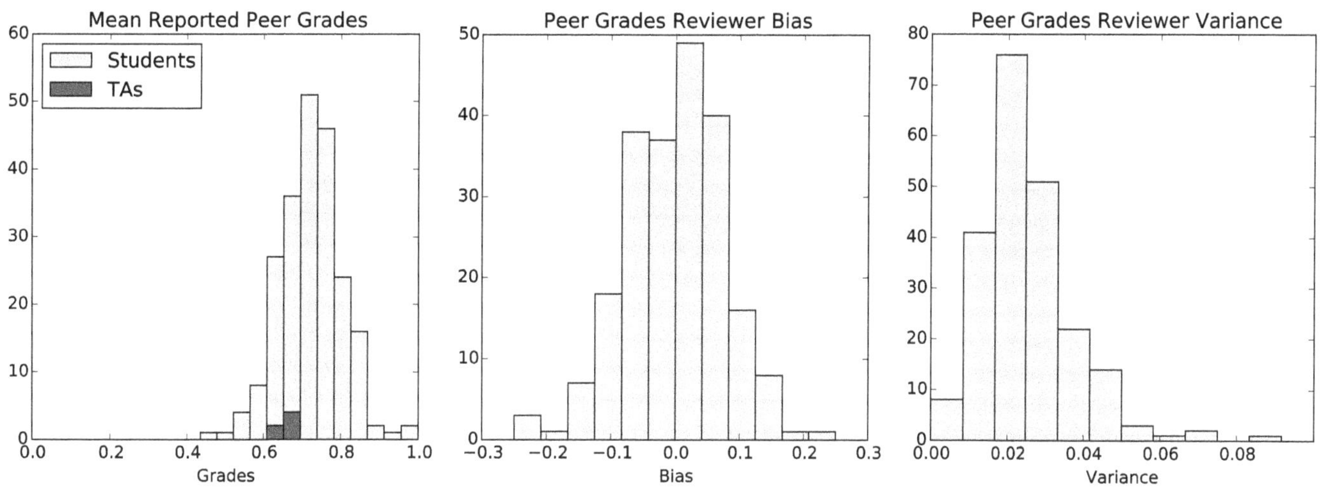

Figure 7. Left: Histogram depicting the mean of all peer grades that each student (and TA) reported over the course of the semester. Mid, right: For each student and all exercises, the deviations of the student's reported grade from the mean of all other grades for the same submissions are calculated. The sample mean of those deviations is the reviewer bias while the sample variance is similar to the inverse of the reliability in the UST and UMT models.

improves the overall error in tasks that have a very high error and overfits in tasks that were graded well by most students in the first place. All in all, supervision does not seem to have a significantly positive effect on the performance of our algorithms.

Analysis of further correlations in the data

To see whether we can meaningfully improve the performance of the models, we first check the correlation between the mean homework performance and the overall bias or mean deviation of the students' reported grades compared to the TA grades. For bias, we use the same formula as in the SN model. The mean deviation for a student g is likewise calculated on all reported grades $s_1, \ldots, s_k$ over the whole course in relation to the TA grades $\text{score}(s, true)$ as

$$\frac{1}{k}\sum_{i=1}^{k} |(\text{score}(s_i, g) - \text{bias}(g)) - \text{score}(s_i, true)|.$$

The homework performance and the bias of the students are only weakly correlated with an r-value[3] of -0.22, i.e. students with higher grades on their own submissions tend to report lower grades. However, this is not due to better students being stricter or having higher standards but rather because better students are more likely to find flaws in the submissions and therefore report lower grades on average. While the former would necessitate a correction, this would punish students for doing a good job at finding large mistakes and results in a worse overall performance concerning grade accuracy.

The correlation between the mean deviation and the homework grades is even weaker at an r-value of only -0.10, indicating a marginally higher agreement between well performing students and the TAs. A possible explanation for the low correlations is the fact that students handed in submissions in groups which means that the scores of each student do not necessarily reflect their knowledge on the topic. A more personal measure is given by the exam that was written at the end of the course. First, we note that the exam grades and the mean homework grade for the students are correlated with an r-value of 0.28, a rather low value. Taking the exam grades instead of the mean homework grade, the correlation with the bias is now slightly higher at $r = -0.26$ while the mean deviation is correlated with the exam grades at $r = -0.28$ which is much stronger than the correlation with the homework scores.

We incorporate the exam grades as a measure of reliability into the model using both mentioned approaches. To use the exam grades directly as the (constant) reliability for each student in the UMT model, we simply scale them to lie in the range $[0, 150]$, resulting in a distribution similar to the Gamma-distribution for the estimated reliability in UMT. For the second approach, we estimate the reliability as usual in UMT but then multiply these values with the normalized exam grades (exam grade divided by mean exam grade). Both approaches yield similar results that are only marginally better than UMT. It seems that using the exam grade for the reliability compensates for some of the error that UMT introduces but still fails to significantly improve over a simple mean.

CONCLUSIONS

We have mixed feelings towards peer grading after evaluating all the data collected in our algorithms and data structures course. The positive point of view is that even though peer grades tend to be more optimistic than TA grades, the size of this effect is not very large. The peer grades give a reasonably informed picture of the true grades. For this reason, using simple estimates such as the mean grade is competitive to more elaborate model-based algorithms. From an application point of view this finding is helpful: an easy to understand mechanism such as a simple mean is more acceptable to students than a complicated model when it comes to generating their final grades.

[3]Pearson product-moment correlation coefficient.

From a statistical or machine learning point of view, our results are somewhat disappointing. None of the models we tested outperforms the simple mean estimator on our data. Our general feeling is that it will be very difficult to come up with algorithms that do a much better job in this particular setting. The reasons for this difficulty might be the heterogeneity of the score distributions of different exercises, the high variance among graders and the different and rather unpredictable sources of grading errors ("lack of understanding" rather than a "slightly different taste"). It seems very hard to model all these aspects unless one has a much larger amount of grades per submission. However, the peer grading setup does not allow us to simply scale up the number of grades per submission, because students are not willing to invest even more time into this process. Finally, let us mention that our negative findings may be special to a course such as algorithms and data structures. Peer grading could be more successful for tasks where grading is a matter of taste rather than of understanding.

As opposed to other papers in the literature, we could not confirm the hypothesis that collecting grades in an ordinal rather than in a cardinal fashion leads to improved estimates. To the contrary, the students themselves reported that they tend to be more sloppy when being asked to provide ordinal grades, so we are somewhat pessimistic about ordinal grading in general.

The data set generated by our class as well as a moodle plugin that supports peer grading in a group-based scenario as used in the AD course have been been made publicly available on our homepages.

Acknowledgments

This work has been supported by the German Federal Ministry of Education and Research (01PL12033, Universitätskolleg/TP 16 Lehrlabor at Universität Hamburg), the German Research Foundation (LU1718/1) and the Institutional Strategy of the University of Tübingen (Deutsche Forschungsgemeinschaft, ZUK 63). The authors alone are responsible for the content of this publication.

REFERENCES

1. J. Dıez, O. Luaces, A. Alonso-Betanzos, A. Troncoso, and A. Bahamonde. 2013. Peer assessment in MOOCs using preference learning via matrix factorization. In *NIPS Workshop on Data Driven Education.*
2. C. Kulkarni, K. P. Wei, H. Le, D. Chia, K. Papadopoulos, J. Cheng, D. Koller, and S. R. Klemmer. 2015. Peer and self assessment in massive online classes. In *Design Thinking Research.* 131–168.
3. F. Mi and D.-Y. Yeung. 2015. Probabilistic graphical models for boosting cardinal and ordinal peer grading in MOOCs. In *29th AAAI Conference on Artificial Intelligence.*
4. C. Piech, J. Huang, Z. Chen, C. Do, A. Ng, and D. Koller. 2013. Tuned models of peer assessment in MOOCs. In *International Conference on Educational Data Mining.*
5. K. Raman and T. Joachims. 2014. Methods for ordinal peer grading. In *International Conference on Knowledge Discovery and Data Mining (SIGKDD).* 1037–1046.
6. N. B. Shah, J. K. Bradley, A. Parekh, M. Wainwright, and K. Ramchandran. 2013. A case for ordinal peer-evaluation in MOOCs. In *NIPS Workshop on Data Driven Education.*
7. K. Topping. 1998. Peer assessment between students in colleges and universities. In *Review of Educational Research,* Vol. 68. 249–276.
8. M. Venanzi, J. Guiver, G. Kazai, P. Kohli, and M. Shokouhi. 2014. Community-based bayesian aggregation models for crowdsourcing. In *Proceedings of the 23rd International Conference on World Wide Web.* 155–164.
9. A. Vozniuk, A. Holzer, and D. Gillet. 2014. Peer assessment based on ratings in a social media course. In *International Conference on Learning Analytics And Knowledge.* 133–137.
10. T. Walsh. 2014. The PeerRank method for peer assessment. In *European Conference on Artificial Intelligence.*

AXIS: Generating Explanations at Scale with Learnersourcing and Machine Learning

Joseph Jay Williams[1] Juho Kim[2] Anna Rafferty[3] Samuel Maldonado[4]
Krzysztof Z. Gajos[1] Walter S. Lasecki[5] Neil Heffernan[4]

[1]Harvard University
Cambridge, MA
joseph_jay_williams@harvard.edu, kgajos@eecs.harvard.edu

[2]Stanford University & KAIST
Stanford, CA
juhokim@cs.kaist.ac.kr

[3]Carleton College
Northfield, MN
arafferty@carleton.edu

[4]WPI
Worcester, PA
{sjmaldonado,nth}@wpi.edu

[5]Computer Science & Engineering
University of Michigan, Ann Arbor
wlasecki@umich.edu

ABSTRACT
While explanations may help people learn by providing information about why an answer is correct, many problems on online platforms lack high-quality explanations. This paper presents AXIS (Adaptive eXplanation Improvement System), a system for obtaining explanations. AXIS asks learners to generate, revise, and evaluate explanations as they solve a problem, and then uses machine learning to dynamically determine which explanation to present to a future learner, based on previous learners' collective input. Results from a case study deployment and a randomized experiment demonstrate that AXIS elicits and identifies explanations that learners find helpful. Providing explanations from AXIS also objectively enhanced learning, when compared to the default practice where learners solved problems and received answers without explanations. The rated quality and learning benefit of AXIS explanations did not differ from explanations generated by an experienced instructor.

CCS Concepts
•Human-centered computing → Human computer interaction (HCI); •Applied computing → Education; Computer-assisted instruction; Interactive learning environments; Collaborative learning; •Computing methodologies → Sequential decision making;

Author Keywords
Explanation; learning at scale; crowdsourcing; learnersourcing; machine learning; adaptive learning.

INTRODUCTION
Explanations go beyond facts to provide understanding and help people identify principles that generalize to new problems [18, 21]. For example, students learning math frequently memorize how to apply rote procedures to solve problems [8]. With only superficial changes to how problems are described (e.g., which side of the equation the variable x appears on) students may misapply procedures and make mistakes. They cannot draw on conceptual descriptions (explanations) of *why* a procedure works in order to generalize to a broader suite of problems. This problem is exacerbated in online learning and MOOCs, where rapid feedback on answers allows people to game the system [3] and to try many answers until they get it right, without understanding why it is right. Some existing platforms such as intelligent tutoring systems present explanations to learners, which has been shown to enhance learning [1].

However, generating high quality explanations for why those answers are correct is significantly more difficult than providing answers [10]. Instructors have limited time and resources to generate quality explanations for all the problems they create. This means that online learners typically attempt problems and get answers without additional explanations. Even when instructors handcraft explanations — like explanations of how to solve math problems on Khan Academy [khanacademy.org] or ASSISTments [assistments.org] — it is rare for these to be revised over time. This is problematic if an initial explanation suffers from an *expert blind spot* which limits recognition of how students will misunderstand explanations [20]. Online platforms run the risk of scaling the negative effect of poor explanations to thousands of learners.

The challenge we address is how to develop a scalable mechanism to generate and improve explanations for online learning materials. To offload the explanation generation effort from busy instructors or amateur content creators, we turn to learners. Learners are a viable crowd for generating explanations, because they are *experts* in typical misconceptions, directly experiencing the effect of gaps in their knowledge. However, asking individual learners to generate explanations for others is unlikely to be reliable unless one can determine which explanations are most helpful, as many learner-generated explanations may be superficial or even incorrect.

L@S 2016, April 25 - 26, 2016, Edinburgh, Scotland Uk.

ACM 978-1-4503-3726-7/16/04...$15.00.
DOI: http://dx.doi.org/10.1145/2876034.2876042

In this paper, we present AXIS (Adaptive eXplanation Improvement System), a system that dynamically improves explanations over time as a byproduct of learners' collective interactions with the content. AXIS does this by adding and iteratively refining explanations via a combination of learner prompts to crowdsource explanations and machine learning to choose effective ones. Learners contribute by reporting their level of knowledge, evaluating the quality of explanations generated by others, and adding or refining explanations. Upon analyzing the learner-provided information, machine learning algorithms sift through the changing pool of explanations to identify those that are consistently judged to have highest quality, as rated by learners. The system seamlessly introduces improved versions of explanations to future learners as more learner contributions become available, without requiring manual revision or republication cycles by the instructor. All of these system components are not only designed to improve explanations, but are designed to integrate into learners' interactions with the problems by prompting them to reflect on the information being presented [8, 25].

To evaluate our approach, we recruited 150 participants online from Mechanical Turk and asked them to solve math problems using AXIS. We discuss the design of AXIS and how it was deployed to collect and evaluate explanations. To evaluate the quality of the explanations AXIS collects and the selection policy it discovers, we also report results from a randomized controlled experiment with an independent group of 524 participants. The experiment is designed to measure how the AXIS explanations and policy are judged by learners, and whether they impact learning.

While there were poor explanations generated by learners, the evaluation showed that AXIS was able to identify explanations that many learners rated as helpful. These explanations were also demonstrated to improve learning over the default practice, in which learners simply solve problems and receive unexplained answers. The explanations learnersourced by AXIS even approached those by experienced instructors in terms of perceived benefit and objective learning gains.

Our approach shifts the effort required to create useful learning materials from instructors to the community of learners. It helps both expert instructors, whose time is scarce, and non-expert instructors not trained in formulating effective explanations. Both can use systems like AXIS to generate explanations for instructional materials by leveraging crowds of learners. Additionally, AXIS leverages learners' collective insight into the problem-solving process to help future learners, even when instructor resources are not available, such as in settings where explanations are generated on-the-fly by end users in live sessions [15].

Specifically, this work contributes:

- AXIS, a prototype semi-automated system that instructional designers can add to online problems for which no explanation exists. AXIS engages learners to generate, revise, and evaluate explanations, and provides quality explanations to future learners.
- Results from a study showing that AXIS elicits quality explanations and discovers effective policies for deciding which explanations to provide to learners. We report evidence that people who are solving problems learn more when explanations from AXIS are provided, and that AXIS-curated explanations are as effective for learning as explanations written by an instructor.
- An approach that combines crowdsourcing and machine learning to leverage learners' organic interactions with content, which in turn enhance future learners' experience.

RELATED WORK

AXIS uses crowdsourcing from learners (*learnersourcing*, [11]) to elicit explanations, and machine learning to differentiate among these explanations and determine which are most helpful. We briefly overview other educational systems that have used crowdsourcing and provide background for our machine learning approach.

Crowdsourcing Systems for Education

Prior learnersourcing systems build on successes in designing systems for human computation that satisfy the dual objectives of helping users learn while simultaneously getting useful work done. For example, to provide real-time captions for deaf and hard of hearing users, Lasecki *et al.* ask learners in a classroom to collaboratively caption what they hear using Scribe [16]. Recent work in Massive Open Online Courses (MOOCs) mines traces of MOOC learners' interactions with video to adaptively alter the video interface to highlight sections other students have paid attention to [12]. More active learnersourcing is observed in Crowdy, which embeds prompts for learners to summarize subgoals in sections of an instructional video. While giving learners a useful learning exercise, the system converts the learnersourced summary labels into a browsable text outline for the video [23]. AXIS contributes a novel application to this growing body of research by focusing on learnersourcing explanations that are applicable to a variety of online learning contexts.

Machine Learning for Exploration & Exploitation

Reinforcement learning is a common machine learning technique for situations in which a system must determine which of several actions is best and information about the actions' effectiveness is gathered only by trying an action and observing the results. It has been used successfully in educational applications, including modeling student knowledge [5] and automatically generating hints [4]. Most relevant to AXIS is a subset of reinforcement learning problems known as multi-armed bandit problems, which have been examined in education for choosing sequences of teaching actions [9] and automated experimentation in educational games [17]. Multi-armed bandits are increasingly used in large-scale randomized A/B experimentation by technology companies [13]. This paper frames explanation generation as a multi-armed bandit problem in a large-scale experimentation setting.

In multi-armed bandit problems, the system repeatedly faces a choice of which action to take and seeks to maximize the total cumulative reward over many repetitions of the choice. In such a problem, there is generally a fixed set of actions (arms), and typically, the system maintains an estimate of the expected reward from taking each action. At each timestep, the system chooses one action and observes the reward from taking that action; over time, the system learns which actions are more effective and thus can earn larger rewards. The key challenge in this type of problem is to balance exploiting the information that has already been gained about the effectiveness of each action and exploring actions where the estimates about their value are still relatively uncertain. For example, imagine a bandit problem with three actions. If each action has only been selected once, with observed rewards of 4, 5, and 6, it probably does not make sense to then only choose the third action at all remaining timesteps. The rewards for each action may be variable, and it could be the case that exploring the first or second actions by choosing them several more times would reveal that they actually produce higher rewards than the third action, on average.

A number of approaches have been proposed for how to select an action at a given timestep based on the evidence observed in the previous timesteps (e.g. [2], [7]). Most approaches combine information about the current estimated expected value of an action and the uncertainty of that estimate, as measured by the variability in observed rewards and the number of times that the action has been selected. Existing methods have been evaluated both theoretically and empirically, with theoretical results [2] making guarantees about asymptotic performance and empirical results helping to illustrate performance given real-world scenarios [7]. In AXIS, we formulate the selection of an explanation as a multi-armed bandit problem where the actions to choose from are explanations generated by learners, and the reward for taking the action of presenting an explanation is the learner's rating of its helpfulness.

AXIS OVERVIEW

Design Goals. While sites like Khan Academy hire hundreds of teachers to produce explanations for their problems, many instructors create online learning materials with far fewer resources. AXIS is aimed at helping these instructors, who often lack the time or experience to create high quality explanations for all of their content but do have access to a large pool of learners. The goal of AXIS is to take a problem and its answer, and then to construct explanations for how to solve this problem, by leveraging the interactions of many learners who solve this problem. AXIS crowdsources production and evaluation of explanations to learners and uses machine learning to analyze this data to identify and deploy the effective explanations.

Core System Components. The two key AXIS components are (1) the learnersourcing interface and (2) the explanation selection policy. The learnersourcing interface collects learning data from learners and their evaluations of explanations, and elicits the generation of new explanations from future learners. The explanation selection policy is used to decide which candidate explanation to present to a new learner. This policy is continually updated based on learners' interactions with the system. The system chooses explanations to present to learners, while the learnersourcing interface prompts them to

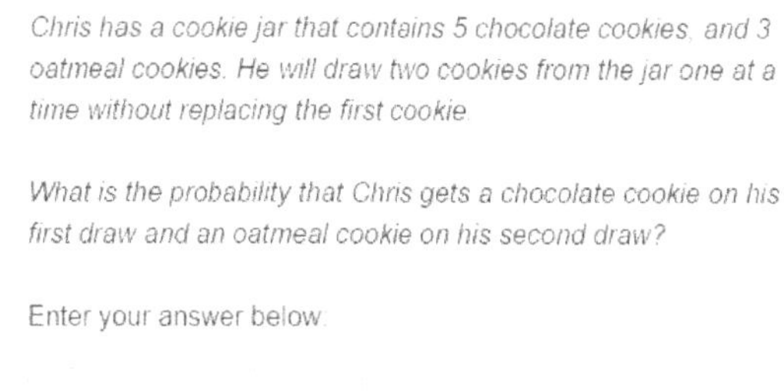

Figure 1. Example of a math problem users might be solving.

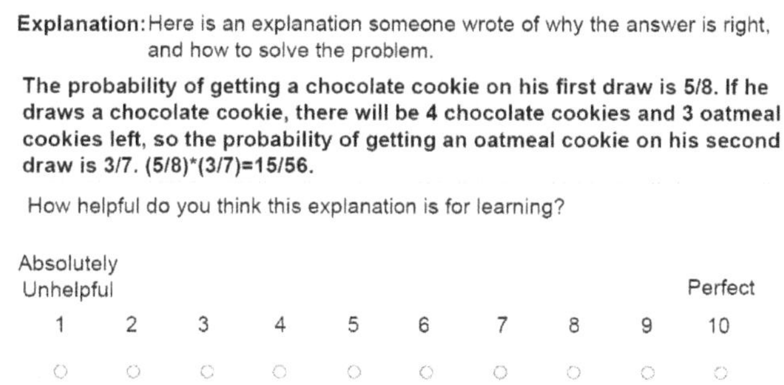

Figure 2. Presentation of explanation to user for learning & rating.

rate the explanations. A multi-armed bandit algorithm is used to statistically analyze these ratings and update the explanation selection policy. This allows the system to perpetually add new explanations, while dynamically learning which explanations to present, without needing human intervention.

Learnersourcing Interface

A dual goal guides the design of the learnersourcing interface: supporting learners through behavioral science and instructional wisdom, while simultaneously acquiring useful input for computational processes that continually improve the system. Figure 2 shows an example of how the Learnersourcing Interface presents an explanation to a learner of how to solve a problem, *and* prompts them to rate how helpful the explanation is for learning. This data is provided to algorithms in the AXIS backend and used to change which explanations are delivered to future learners. The learnersourcing interface also displays questions that prompt learners to write self-explanations, which existing cognitive and learning sciences research has shown is beneficial for constructing knowledge [1, 8, 25]. At the same time, learners' explanations can be useful to other learners, if they are added to the system pool.

Explanation Selection Policy

AXIS provides learners with explanations of how to solve problems. Soliciting explanations from learners addresses the problem of scalable creation of explanations for a large and potentially growing database of activities. But it introduces a new challenge: how can we reliably determine which explanations are effective for helping new users, without instructional designers expending significant time vetting contributions? We address this challenge by formulating the problem of selecting explanations as a multi-armed bandit problem.

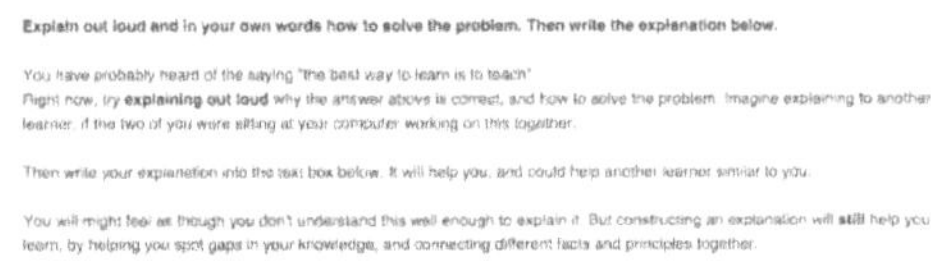

Figure 3. Self-explanation prompt for learner to write an explanation for why the given answer to a math problem is correct.

Multi-armed bandit problems require a system to repeatedly select an action, and to learn which action is most effective, based on observing the non-deterministic results. This is exactly the scenario that AXIS faces: each problem can be viewed as a different multi-armed bandit. When a new user is introduced to a problem, the system must choose which explanation to show to the user. The explanations are thus different action choices. After the explanation has been given to the user, we must measure how effective it was; this is the observed reward in the bandit formulation. In the case of an educational system, this might correspond to having users provide feedback on how much the explanation helped them learn. Other reward signals can be used, and in our future directions we consider accuracy on subsequent problems. In the current system deployment, the algorithm aimed to optimize for learners' ratings of the helpfulness of an explanation because it is a direct function of the actions AXIS is deciding between: which learnersourced explanation to present. Although we seek explanations that teach well enough that the learner gets the next problem correct, this variable is noisy and influenced by many variables outside system control.

By framing explanation selection as a multi-armed bandit problem, we can draw on the existing literature for an algorithm that addresses the problem of exploitation (presenting explanations that have been observed to be relatively effective) versus exploration (experimenting with different explanations to gain more evidence about their effectiveness). We use Thompson sampling, a Bayesian algorithm that has been shown to have near-optimal regret bounds and performs well on practical problems [7]. Other bandit algorithms may also have been effective, but Thompson sampling has advantages for future work with instructors, because it facilitates interpretable representations of the system's beliefs at any point in time. We can intuitively capture both estimates about explanations' effectiveness and the algorithm's uncertainty about those estimates.

Like most bandit algorithms, Thompson sampling provides a dynamic policy for choosing which explanation to give a new user, and an algorithm for incorporating new information to update this policy based on observing the reward after an explanation has been selected. Thompson sampling stores an estimated distribution for the reward for each explanation. This distribution indicates both the expected reward from choosing a particular explanation, and how variable the reward is. Both of these aspects can impact what action we wish to select. The parameters of each distribution are initially set based on a prior, which intuitively indicates our beliefs about the effectiveness of explanations that have not yet been presented to any users, and then are updated based on the likelihood of the observed evidence.

AXIS's beliefs about the value of each explanation are represented using a Beta distribution. The prior for this distribution is also a Beta distribution, and the likelihood is a Bernoulli distribution. The posterior is then proportional to the product of the prior and the likelihood, with the likelihood updated after each reward observation; this update is easy to implement because the Beta and Bernoulli distributions are conjugate. In AXIS, explanations are added by learnersourcing. AXIS uses a filtering mechanism, only adding explanations to the system pool when: the explanation is above a minimum character length, the explainer displays above average knowledge about how to solve this type of problem, and the explainer rates her explanation as likely to be helpful to other learners. Explanations that meet these criteria are added as new arms to the bandit for the problem. The prior distribution for their reward or expected rating follows a Beta(19, 1) distribution, which expresses beliefs analogous to having seen the explanation get rated a 9 and a 10. Intuitively, this distribution reflects a great deal of optimism about how helpful new explanations will be – the expected rating is 9.5 out of 10. But at the same time the prior will be rapidly updated, as these highly optimistic beliefs are based on the equivalent of just two observations. This prior encourages the algorithms to collect data about new explanations, as discussed below.

After an explanation has been chosen and displayed to the user, we use the user's rating of its effectiveness (shown in Figure 2 as the observed reward. In order to allow the same infrastructure to be used for a binary reward signal as for the rating reward signal, we treat each action as adding 10 total observations of a Bernoulli variable. The number of successes is the user's rating of the explanation's effectiveness (on a 10-point scale where 10 is maximally helpful), and the number of failures is ten minus the number of successes. The update to a posterior that is $\text{Beta}(x, y)$ is simply $\text{Beta}(x + \text{number of new successes}, y + \text{number of new failures})$.

As an example, consider a learnersourced explanation that has been rated as five out of ten by each of the first two subsequent learners who viewed the explanation. While the initial expected rating for this explanation was high, due to the $\text{Beta}(19, 1)$ prior, this distribution also has significant uncertainty. This means that ratings by even a few learners have a large influence on this expected rating. To incorporate these two ratings of five out of ten, the Beta distribution is updated as described above, resulting in $\text{Beta}(29, 11)$ as the posterior distribution. The expected rating indicated by this distribution is only 7.25. Thus, the prior indicates a high expected rating early on, encouraging the algorithm to use the explanation, but the uncertainty in the prior means that collected explanations quickly dominate the expected value of the posterior.

So far, we have described how Thompson sampling represents the observed data about each explanation and how this representation is updated based on new observations. The final component of Thompson sampling is its policy: how to select an appropriate explanation for a new user. Thompson sampling selects the explanation that satisfies $\text{argmax}_{e \in \text{explanations}} E[reward|\theta_e] p(\theta_e|D)$, where D is the set of observed data and θ_e is the parameters of the Beta distribution for this explanation. That is, it chooses the explanation that has highest expected value, taking into account the uncertainty we have about the distribution of rewards from this explanation. This corresponds to selecting each explanation in proportion to the probability that it is the best explanation, given the priors and observed data. Implemented via highly efficient sampling, such a policy balances exploration and exploitation by incorporating uncertainty about the underlying distribution.

The probabilistic policies for multi-armed bandits have several advantages over more obvious methods, like presenting the highest rated explanation. Apparently simpler methods raise many questions. For example, if AXIS used ranking, how many good ratings would a new learnersourced explanation have to receive for AXIS to identify it as the current best? Instead of choosing an arbitrary heuristic (5? 10?), this question can be answered in a principled way by capturing uncertainty in the probability distributions used in Thompson Sampling. These allow AXIS to encode beliefs about how noisy learner ratings are, by defining the likelihood of broad versus narrow ranges of ratings. Does the risk of showing students a poor explanation outweigh the value of getting an explanation that is 10% better than the best? Multi-armed bandits provide an extensively studied formal model for answering questions about balancing exploitation–giving explanations known to help– against exploration– trying out new explanations that may turn out to be bad or good.

Implementation

Our goal in designing AXIS was for intelligent web apps to be easily duplicated and shared to enable end-user programing [19] for online educational resources like websites, lessons, problems, and quizzes. User groups like instructors rarely manage servers and write code, value support in automating some features of instruction, and wish to maintain discretion and control over learning materials. Our mashup integration for implementing systems like AXIS combines (more or less) freely available web resources that bridge easy-to-use features like WYSIWYG with underlying programming languages and flexible APIs. The interface for presenting and collecting information was created using Qualtrics, an advanced survey software that most universities have an unlimited license to. The machine learning algorithm was written, hosted and deployed using the Apps Script functionality in Google Spreadsheets. Code using Javascript libraries received data from the Qualtrics API every time a learner interacted with the AXIS front-end, made this data available for display and manipulation in a Google Spreadsheet, implemented Thompson Sampling to analyze the data and update the policy after each user, and sent instructions via the Qualtrics API as to which explanations to present. A key consideration in the choice of these resources, despite their many technical limitations, was availability to end-users. The combination of Qualtrics and Google Spreadsheets/Apps Script allows those without programming knowledge to obtain, host, modify, deploy, and share customized intelligent educational agents that run machine learning algorithms on request. Access to the resources we've created can be requested via `http://tiny.cc/useaxis`.

AXIS CASE STUDY: GENERATING EXPLANATIONS FOR SOLVING MATH PROBLEMS

We deployed and tested AXIS in the context of providing explanations to learners solving math problems. The target user in our case study was an online instructional designer overseeing online math problems for ASSISTments [`assistments.org`], a math platform similar to Khan Academy. This platform has a content library of over 500 math problems, hundreds of which do not have explanations. The instructional designer wanted a way to generate explanations to present to learners, but she had not had much success in relying on work-study undergraduate students to do so. We identified four math problems that she had already written explanations for, as it would allow us all to see how close the output of AXIS could get to explanations she had already created. The problems covered algebra, expressions, and probability, at a level appropriate to both middle schoolers and adults. Before implementing AXIS with students in classrooms, she wanted to see evidence that AXIS could successfully cull explanations from untrained people.

The next section explains how we implemented and deployed AXIS with 150 study participants solving the four math problems. Our evaluation was done in two stages: in the first stage, we describe the explanations AXIS collects and how the policy changes over time; in the second stage, we report results from a randomized experiment. This experiment investigates recruits an independent group of participants to investigate how their perceptions and success in learning are influenced by different components of the AXIS explanation pool and policy.

Methods: AXIS Implementation & Deployment

Participants

The deployment case study was conducted with 150 people residing in the US who were recruited online to participate in an education research study, via Amazon Mechanical Turk. Each task paid \$3.50 for the 40 minute study. 150 participants roughly matches the number of students learning a math topic at a typical middle school, and the size of a large introductory university course.

Understanding these 150 participants' baseline level of knowledge is useful for interpreting results from AXIS. Participants gave a subjective rating of their relevant school and work experience for solving each problem, as a percentile of the general population. 25.0% of participants rated themselves as being in the bottom quartile (0th to 25th percentile), 41.7% in the second quartile, 28.6% in the third quartile, and only 4.7% rated themselves in the top quartile (75th-100th percentile).

An objective measure of learning was also available from whether their answers to the problems were correct or incorrect. 13.3% of participants had accuracy between 0 and 0.25, 20.0% accuracy of 0.25–0.50, 19.1% accuracy of 0.50–0.75, and 47.5% accuracy of 0.75–1.00.

Additional demographic information was not collected, although it should be in future research. We anticipate that the trends will match typical distributions on Amazon Mechanical Turk. For example, [6] found that the population of workers on MTurk is similar to the general US population, albeit

	Explanation	Explanation Rating
Learner Explanation AXIS Discarded via Filtering Rule	It is three over seven because after the chocolate cookie has been removed there are 7 cookies in the jar, leaving 3 oatmeal cookies remaining.	5.2
Early Stage AXIS	go based on the amount of cookies that are available and run a trial until the chocolate cookie is picked out, then do the same for oatmeal	4.2
Later Stage AXIS	When you have 8 cookies in the jar and 5 are chocolate you have a 5/8 chance of the cookie you draw being chocolate. When there are 7 cookies in the jar and 3 are oatmeal you have a 3/7 chance of drawing the oatmeal cookie. To get the overall probability you need to multiply 5/8 by 3/7 which results in overall probability of 15/56	6.8
Written by Instructional Designer	The total number of cookies in the jar is 8. Since there are 5 chocolate cookies the probability that Chris gets an chocolate cookie is 5/8 Since Chris removed 1 cookie from the jar and did not replace it or put it back there are now 7 cookies in the jar. So, the probability that Chris gets an oatmeal cookie from the jar is 3/7 5/8 x 3/7 = 15/56 So, the probability of Chris getting a chocolate cookie on the first draw, and an oatmeal cookie on the second draw is 15/56 Type in 15/56	7.7

Figure 4. Examples of explanations for one of the problems that AXIS was deployed for. After deployment, we conducted an independent evaluation study with new users to evaluate explanations from AXIS and other sources. The explanations were included in the evaluation study, and the mean helpfulness ratings are shown in the second row.

slightly younger (M = 32.3), more educated (M = 14.9 years of education), and more female (60.1%).

Procedure and System Configuration
All participants worked on the four math problems in a random order. For each problem, after entering an answer, they were told the correct answer. AXIS would then displayed an explanation for why the answer was right (chosen by the explanation selection policy) and/or a prompt for learners to explain to themselves why the answer was right. Figure 3 shows this prompt, which emphasized the value of explaining as a way to help the learner to understand more deeply. At first the explanation pool was empty, so learners would instead see only the self-explanation prompt. We defined an *AXIS Filtering Rule* to automatically discard explanations that were unlikely to be helpful to others. Specifically, AXIS added a learner's explanation to the explanation pool only if it was longer than 60 characters, the learner rated herself as having above average knowledge of how to solve problems like the current one, and the learner rated the likelihood of the explanation helping another learner as higher than 6, on a scale from 1 (Zero Chance) to 10 (Absolutely Likely). Once added to a problem's explanation pool, the explanation would be probabilistically selected for presentation to future learners working on the problem, based on how highly it had been rated whenever presented. A separate explanation pool and policy was maintained for the explanations in each of the four problems.

Results: Description of AXIS Explanation and Policy

Adding Learnersourced Explanations to the Pool
By interacting with AXIS, 150 learners generated between 60 and 72 explanations for each of the four problems. The AXIS Filtering Rule added 12, 9, 12, and 12 of the learner-sourced explanations to the pools for the 4 problems. Figure 4 illustrates the explanations that learners generated, and how AXIS processed them. The *Discarded using Filtering Rule* explanation generated by a learner was discarded because it did not meet the AXIS Filtering Rule. The *Early Stage AXIS* explanation was added to the pool via the filtering rule, but analysis of its ratings by the selection policy resulted in its probabilistic phasing out – continually decreasing probability of being sampled for a new learner. In contrast, the selection policy has identified the *Later Stage AXIS* explanation as one of the highest rated, with a higher probability of being sampled for users. For comparison is the explanation our ASSISTments instructional designer wrote for this problem. The Explanation Rating column provides mean helpfulness ratings that were collected in the experiment we conducted to evaluate AXIS.

Dynamic Evolution of AXIS Policy
Once explanations are collected from the learnersourcing interface, AXIS automatically analyzes each new learner's ratings of how helpful an explanation was for learning, and immediately updates the probabilistic policy for which explanations should be presented to the next learner. As an illustration, we examine the policy for one of the four problems, the Compound-Probability problem. Figure 5 shows two snapshots of how this policy dynamically varied as more learners used the system. The policy for this problem can be represented as a probability distribution over the ten explanations AXIS selected for presentation. Figure 5 shows the AXIS probabilistic policy for determining which explanation would be seen by the 76th learner (after the first 75 learners) and the policy for the 151st learner (after all 150 AXIS learners).

This illustrates a challenge with evaluating the explanations while the AXIS system is changing dynamically. To evaluate the AXIS explanations and policies we randomized their presentation to a new group of 524 people, collecting ratings of explanations, along with subjective and objective measures of whether these explanations influenced learning.

EVALUATION OF AXIS EXPLANATIONS AND POLICY
To evaluate whether the AXIS system was able to collect and identify *useful* explanations from learners, it is necessary to determine if AXIS successfully picks explanations that are helpful to future learners and discards ones that are not. Our experiment compared the quality of the explanations selected by AXIS to explanations AXIS filtered out and discarded, and to the original explanations that the ASSISTments instructional designer had written for the problems. An ambitious secondary goal of the experiment was to investigate whether these learnersourced explanations could impact learning.

Methods

Participants
The randomized experiment recruited 524 new people to participate in a HIT posted on Amazon Mechanical Turk. Each HIT paid $3.50 for the 40 minute study.

Procedure
The study consisted of a learning phase in which participants solved the four problems and provided ratings for explanations,

	AXIS Index for Explanation	1	2	3	4	5	6	7	8	9	10
AXIS Policy for Presenting Explanations: Probability of each explanation being presented.	Policy for 76th learner (after 75 learners)	0.36	0.34	0.31	0	0	0	0	0	0	0
	Policy for learner 151 (after 150 learners)	0.1	0.1	0.09	0.1	0.09	0.1	0.1	0.09	0.11	0.11
Outcomes of AXIS Policy	Explanation Rating	3.97	3.85	5.36	7.97	5.5	6.97	8.53	8.16	3.21	7.29
	Increase in Perceived Skill at Solving Problems (on a 1 to 10 scale)	-0.63	-0.91	-0.28	0.55	-0.06	0.47	0.81	1.71	-1.71	0.29
	Learning Gains	-0.01	0.06	0.16	0.02	-0.10	-0.01	0.03	0.27	-0.04	-0.04

Figure 5. AXIS Policy for the explanation pool for one of the four problems. The policy's probability distribution over the ten explanations that were added to the pool during deployment is shown after 75 learners (row 2) and after 150 learners (row 3).

followed by an assessment phase where they had to solve twelve problems without being given any feedback.

Learning Phase. In this phase, participants were randomly assigned to a number of different conditions, in order to evaluate a wide range of explanations. One condition was solving *Problems with answers only*, standard practice for many online problems without explanations. The other conditions all included explanations that were displayed after seeing the correct answer to a problem. For any one of the four problems, participants were randomly assigned to one of many conditions. They could see one of the explanations from the AXIS pool for that problem, an explanation that was *Filtered out by AXIS* and not presented, or an original explanation *Written by Instructional Designer* at ASSISTments. This provided two important comparisons to AXIS explanations and policy; a lower bound in the form of explanations AXIS filtered out and did not present, and an upper bound in the form of the high quality explanations written by the original instructor.

Participants were prompted to rate how helpful these explanations were for learning, on a scale from 1 (Not Helpful At All) to 10 (Extremely Helpful). Moreover, participants were asked to indicate how likely they were to solve future problems like the one they were working with. They made this rating on a scale from 1 (Zero Chance) to 10 (Absolutely Certain). By comparing these ratings before and after learners received different explanations, we had a more direct measure of the impact of different explanations on people's learning.

Assessment Phase. The ideal outcome for the learnersourced explanations is impact on objective behavioral measures of learning, especially *transfer* of knowledge to novel problems. The learning phase was followed by problems designed to assess whether participants learned from particular explanations. For each of the four original problems, there was an *isomorphic* problem where only the numbers and surface details (e.g., names in an expression) were changed. To measure *transfer* of the knowledge gained from explanations, participants were provided with two problems that were novel but tested the same topic as the original problem (e.g., compound probability, using variables in algebraic expressions).

Results: Usefulness of Explanations for Learners

Figure 6 shows data about the effects of providing explanations while people solved math problems. These diverse measures ranged over rating explanations, subjective judgments about solving future problems, and objective measures of accuracy on novel problems. To investigate the benefits of explanations from AXIS, we used randomized comparisons to explanations (or lack thereof) from a range of sources. Participants were randomly assigned to see: No explanation (original problems), AXIS explanations, learner explanations discarded by AXIS filtering rule, or explanations written by the instructional designer. All our reported analyses used linear mixed–effect models, including a fixed factor representing which explanations were provided. This factor had a significant effect in all analyses conducted, all *ps* < 0.05. Problem type (since four different probability and algebra problems were used) was a within-subjects variable that was incorporated as a random effect. All statistics reported in this section concern pairwise comparisons conducted within the mixed-effects model, unless otherwise stated.

To evaluate the effectiveness of the AXIS policy at a particular point in time, we must consider both how good each explanation is, and how likely it the explanation is to be shown under the current policy. The evaluation experiment randomized presentation of every explanation in the AXIS pool to learners, to assess its impact on their behavior and their perceptions of its helpfulness. For example, to quantify the overall *helpfulness* of AXIS at timestep 150, we compute a weighted average of the helpfulness of all the explanations in the pool at that time, where the weights were determined by the probabilistic policy. This builds on the approach in [7] for assessing the quality of a bandit's policy. We also computed measures of the benefits of the AXIS explanation pool and policy after 75 learners (*AXIS-75*), a subset of the AXIS explanation pool and policy after 150 learners (*AXIS-150*). This data is shown in Figure 6 to provide a qualitative snapshot of how AXIS was changing over time.

Rated Quality of AXIS Explanations

The learnersourced explanations AXIS presented were rated as significantly more helpful for learning than the explanations removed by the filtering rule ($M = 6.83$ vs. 6.03, $SE = 0.28$, $p < 0.01$).This provides evidence for a reliable improvement over learnersourced explanations that were not screened and optimized by AXIS.

Increase in Perceived Skill at Solving Problems

For each problem in the learning phase, participants were asked to rate how likely it was that they could solve problems like it without any help. They responded on a scale from 1 (Zero Chance) to 10 (Absolutely Certain). After attempting the problem, seeing the answer, and (depending on condition)

	Discarded Learner Explanations (removed by AXIS Filtering Rule)	AXIS 75: Presented by AXIS after interacting with 75 learners	AXIS 150: Presented by AXIS after interacting with 75 learners	Instructional Designer's Explanations	Practice Problems Only (No Explanations)
Explanation Rating (1-Unhelpful to 10-Excellent)	6.03 (3.01)	6.57 (2.84)	6.83 (2.45)	7.30 (2.45)	---
Increase in Perceived Likelihood of Solving Problem (1 – 10 Scale)	0.69 (2.78)	0.57 (2.66)	0.71 (2.71)	0.48 (2.51)	-0.01 (2.30)
Accuracy Increase in Solving Problems	0.02 (0.47)	0.12 (0.44)	0.12 (0.46)	0.09 (0.47)	0.03 (0.48)
Accuracy Increase: Problems Isomorphic to Study	0.19 (0.60)	0.23 (0.52)	0.23 (0.55)	0.17 (0.57)	0.16 (0.58)
Accuracy Increase: Transfer Problems	-0.06 (0.49)	0.06 (0.48)	0.07 (0.50)	0.05 (0.51)	-0.04 (0.51)

Figure 6. Data from evaluation experiment about effects of different (or no) explanations, reflected in means for: Subjective Rating of Explanation helpfulness for learning; increase in Self-Reported Skill at solving problems; and increase in objective Accuracy in solving problems.

interacting with explanations, the next page showed them the problem and asked them to make the judgment again about their likelihood of solving it. We analyzed the increase from before to after the problem as a measure of how much different explanations resulted in learners perceiving that they would be better able to solve future problems. Figure 6 shows these values in the third row.

Learners who received the AXIS-150 explanations were more likely to experience increases in their expectation that they could solve future problems, when compared to those learners simply practicing problems without explanations. ($M = 0.71$ vs. -0.01, $SE = 0.13$, $p < 0.001$). There was no significant difference in learners' beliefs about being better able to solve problems, whether they received the AXIS explanations or those written by the ASSISTments instructional designer ($M = 0.71$ vs 0.48, $SE = 0.23$, $p = 0.14$).

Learning Gains in Accurately Solving Problems

The most ambitious test of AXIS is whether it provides explanations to learners that measurably increase their success in solving problems. Participants might report that explanations from other learners were helpful, and even feel a sense of understanding and capacity for solving problems. But these explanations could still fail to produce any actual learning or lasting acquisition of knowledge. Participants' accuracy in solving the four problems in the learning phase was used as a baseline of knowledge, and Figure 6 shows the overall increase in accuracy from the learning to assessment phase, as a result of receiving AXIS explanations, explanations from other sources, or no explanations.

In fact, AXIS explanations did not merely have subjective benefits. Participants were significantly more likely to solve future problems after receiving AXIS explanations, when compared to practicing of problems. A pairwise comparison within the mixed-effect model revealed a significant increase in accuracy from the initial problems to the assessment problems, $M =$ 12% versus just 2.7%, $SE = 0.027$, $p < 0.05$.

Of course, it might seem obvious in hindsight that providing *any* explanation will increase learning and success on future problems. However, this was not the case. The learnersourced explanations AXIS discarded did not provide any learning benefits beyond normal practice of math problems ($M = 2\%$ vs 3%, $p = 0.86$). Simply providing explanations was not sufficient to support learning, and these explanations were significantly less beneficial for learning than explanations delivered by the AXIS policy ($M = 12\%$ vs. 2%, $SE = 0.04$, $p < 0.029$).

The AXIS explanations also increased success in solving novel transfer problems that required going beyond the explicit information in the explanation (differences of 9-12%, $SE = 0.03$, 0.04, $p < 0.01$). Overall, it was encouraging that there were no significant differences between learnersourced explanations curated by AXIS, and the explanations written by the ASSISTments instructional designer herself (all $ps > 0.30$).

QUALITATIVE RESULTS

Instructional Designer's Perspective

Our hope is that AXIS makes it easy for instructors to add a plugin to problems and educational content that will build a pool of explanations, and automatically learn which ones to present. We conducted a 30 minute semi-structured interview with the instructional designer at ASSISTments to show her several of the AXIS explanations. She said that the top-rated AXIS learnersourced explanations were comparable to the explanations she had written, and were of sufficient quality to deploy to the middle school students currently using ASSISTments. She admitted a natural preference for the explanations she herself had written, but believed the quality was sufficiently similar to the AXIS learnersourced explanations, that the best test to discriminate them would be actually comparing their effect on student learning. She was surprised but pleased that the learning benefits were comparable in our evaluation experiment. She also commented on how the AXIS plugin could be used more generally than explanations for math problems, since textual explanations can fit on any webpage in a course, or take the form of motivational messages and tips for learning.

Currently we are building a Learning Technologies Interoperability (LTI)–compliant connector that would allow AXIS to be embedded within ASSISTments and all LTI–compliant MOOC platforms and on-campus Learning Management Systems. This currently includes Coursera, EdX, Moodle, and Canvas.

Moreover, while AXIS does not require manual intervention by instructors for the system to run, it is designed to enable an instructor to interact with the explanation pool and algorithm at any point, through examining data or looking at explanations in the Google Spreadsheet. By typing into cells of the Google Spreadsheet, instructors can freeze and override AXIS's policy changes, or set the policy manually. For future research we will explore using interactive machine learning to allow instructors to work cooperatively with AXIS by adding their own explanations, and adjusting weights for explanations according to their opinion, by typing different prior probabilities. AXIS could also be used in conjunction with systems for automatic generation of educational content beyond explanations, such as hints [4].

Learner's Perspective

The reciprocity of help might encourage learners to participate in learnersourcing explanations, even when individual benefits are not apparent at the time of contribution. By providing explanations that help future learners, learners know they will sometimes benefit from explanations previous learners have provided for them. In addition, we took a step further to qualitatively explore direct benefits to learners in our deployment. After using the system they answered an online form with open-ended questions about what they thought of the learning activities, how they felt about writing explanations, and what they found helpful for learning. Some learners candidly stated that explaining wasn't helpful, or that they did not bother to explain: "I didn't write explanations because I don't think I could get it down on paper."

A substantial number acknowledged the challenge in writing explanations ("While it can sometimes be a bit frustrating") but were pleasantly surprised by the value: "It lets you really understand the logic behind it so you are more able to solve similar problems," and "Talking it out really helps. I will try and use that strategy for other problems besides math."

DISCUSSION AND LIMITATIONS

While AXIS and its evaluation showed some initial promise in generating explanations, there are limitations to the current system and the evaluation methods. AXIS focuses on presenting a single best explanation to all learners, agnostic to their level of knowledge and preference. Personalization of different explanations to different profiles of learners was not explored. Future versions of AXIS could use the learnersourcing interface to elicit information that could be used to personalize delivery of explanations across learners– like study preferences or current state of confusion. AXIS could then implement Thompson Sampling for *contextual* multi-armed bandits, in which the reward of an action depends on a context vector of side information [14]. The reward of an explanation would therefore depend on a set of variables about the user. A second limitation was that our participants were paid crowd workers on Mechanical Turk. While these workers share more demographic features with online learners than convenience samples in typical laboratory studies, future deployments will embed AXIS within platforms like ASSISTments and edX to help authentic students, who may be less (or more) motivated.

There are clear limitations to having AXIS optimize for a reward signal like learners' subjective ratings of explanation quality. We chose to have AXIS select explanations based on their ratings rather than accuracy on subsequent problems because: it was continuous rather than binary, immediately available, and arguably less influenced by factors extraneous to the explanation. However, an extensive literature reveals learners' failures in metacognitive awareness of what they do and do not know, such as the *illusion of explanatory depth* [22] reveal people's great surprise at their erroneous assumptions about being able to provide detailed explanations. While this version is limited to explanation rating, a general strength of AXIS is that it allows instructors to set variables that the multi-armed bandit takes actions to optimize. Future work can explore reward variables like performance on quizzes, continued persistence, or even attitudes towards learning, by varying which versions of explanations and other educational content are presented. The underlying approach AXIS takes in using machine learning to do automatic and real-time optimization of educational content should also be generalized beyond its current application to explanations for solving problems.

The current results do not shed light on many design choices, like knowing when sufficiently many explanations have been collected. Future research can investigate these and other issues, like which filtering rules should be used to add explanations to the pool. This paper had the narrower aim of describing the first implementation of the AXIS system, and evaluating whether it was even effective with the small samples of 75–150 that are typical in larger university courses, and K12 classes.

We chose to separate the evaluation from the deployment phase to provide a rigorous assessment of AXIS performance even when limited to a crowd of 75–150 learners. This allowed for greater statistical power, increasing from 150 participants in deployment to 524 in evaluation. Even with 524 participants, any individual explanation from AXIS was only seen by an average of 30 people. The evaluation study also included additional extensive measures of learning that would have been onerous in the system deployment. However, when thousands of participants are easily available, future system deployments can build on the current work to integrate deployment for practical use with *in vivo* evaluation.

CONCLUSION AND FUTURE WORK

Generating explanations for a large number of online learning materials requires significant time and effort from instructors. In this paper, we present an alternative model that engages learners to help generate and refine explanations. AXIS combines techniques from crowdsourcing and machine learning to achieve this goal. In an experiment with math problems, AXIS successfully led learners to produce quality explanations that helped improve the learning of future users.

While we focused on explanations to math problems in this paper, our approach can generalize to producing and improving explanations for other types of online learning content: adding *why* information to how-to instructions that teach procedural skills, adding more illustrative examples in a learning material, or clarifying task instructions on online workplaces (e.g., Mechanical Turk) to improve worker understanding and success. Any instructor or researcher can register interest in collaboration or access to AXIS via `http://tiny.cc/useaxis`, or build adaptive online resources using the *MOOClet* formalism [24] we used to implement AXIS.

REFERENCES

1. Vincent AWMM Aleven and Kenneth R Koedinger. 2002. An effective metacognitive strategy: Learning by doing and explaining with a computer-based Cognitive Tutor. *Cognitive science* 26, 2 (2002), 147–179.
2. Peter Auer, Nicolo Cesa-Bianchi, and Paul Fischer. 2002. Finite-time analysis of the multiarmed bandit problem. *Machine learning* 47, 2-3 (2002), 235–256.
3. Ryan Shaun Baker, Albert T Corbett, Kenneth R Koedinger, and Angela Z Wagner. 2004. Off-task behavior in the cognitive tutor classroom: when students game the system. In *Proceedings of the SIGCHI conference on Human factors in computing systems*. ACM, 383–390.
4. Tiffany Barnes and John Stamper. 2008. Toward automatic hint generation for logic proof tutoring using historical student data. In *Intelligent Tutoring Systems*. Springer, 373–382.
5. Joseph E Beck and Beverly Park Woolf. 2000. High-level student modeling with machine learning. In *Intelligent tutoring systems*. Springer, 584–593.
6. Adam J Berinsky, Gregory A Huber, and Gabriel S Lenz. 2012. Evaluating online labor markets for experimental research: Amazon. com's Mechanical Turk. *Political Analysis* 20, 3 (2012), 351–368.
7. Olivier Chapelle and Lihong Li. 2011. An empirical evaluation of thompson sampling. In *Advances in neural information processing systems*. 2249–2257.
8. Michelene TH Chi, Miriam Bassok, Matthew W Lewis, Peter Reimann, and Robert Glaser. 1989. Self-explanations: How students study and use examples in learning to solve problems. *Cognitive science* 13, 2 (1989), 145–182.
9. Benjamin Clement, Pierre-Yves Oudeyer, Didier Roy, and Manuel Lopes. 2014. Online optimization of teaching sequences with multi-armed bandits. In *Educational Data Mining 2014*.
10. Arthur C Graesser, Patrick Chipman, Brian C Haynes, and Andrew Olney. 2005. AutoTutor: An intelligent tutoring system with mixed-initiative dialogue. *Education, IEEE Transactions on* 48, 4 (2005), 612–618.
11. Juho Kim. 2015. *Learnersourcing: Improving Learning with Collective Learner Activity*. Ph.D. Dissertation. Massachusetts Institute of Technology.
12. Juho Kim, Philip J. Guo, Carrie J. Cai, Shang-Wen (Daniel) Li, Krzysztof Z. Gajos, and Robert C. Miller. 2014. Data-driven Interaction Techniques for Improving Navigation of Educational Videos. In *Proceedings of the 27th Annual ACM Symposium on User Interface Software and Technology (UIST '14)*. 563–572.
13. Ron Kohavi, Roger Longbotham, Dan Sommerfield, and Randal M Henne. 2009. Controlled experiments on the web: survey and practical guide. *Data mining and knowledge discovery* 18, 1 (2009), 140–181.
14. John Langford and Tong Zhang. 2008. The epoch-greedy algorithm for multi-armed bandits with side information. In *Advances in neural information processing systems*. 817–824.
15. Walter S. Lasecki, Juho Kim, Nick Rafter, Onkur Sen, Jeffrey P. Bigham, and Michael S. Bernstein. 2015. Apparition: Crowdsourced User Interfaces That Come to Life As You Sketch Them. In *Proceedings of the 33rd Annual ACM Conference on Human Factors in Computing Systems (CHI '15)*. ACM, New York, NY, USA, 1925–1934.
16. Walter S. Lasecki, Christopher Miller, Adam Sadilek, Andrew Abumoussa, Donato Borrello, Raja Kushalnagar, and Jeffrey Bigham. 2012. Real-time Captioning by Groups of Non-experts. In *Proceedings of the 25th Annual ACM Symposium on User Interface Software and Technology (UIST '12)*. ACM, New York, NY, USA, 23–34.
17. Yun-En Liu, Travis Mandel, Emma Brunskill, and Zoran Popovic. 2014. Trading Off Scientific Knowledge and User Learning with Multi-Armed Bandits. In *Educational Data Mining 2014*.
18. Tania Lombrozo. 2006. The structure and function of explanations. *Trends in cognitive sciences* 10, 10 (2006), 464–470.
19. Brad A Myers. 1995. User interface software tools. *ACM Transactions on Computer-Human Interaction (TOCHI)* 2, 1 (1995), 64–103.
20. Mitchell J Nathan, Kenneth R Koedinger, and Martha W Alibali. 2001. Expert blind spot: When content knowledge eclipses pedagogical content knowledge. In *Proceedings of the Third International Conference on Cognitive Science*. Citeseer, 644–648.
21. Alexander Renkl. 1997. Learning from worked-out examples: A study on individual differences. *Cognitive science* 21, 1 (1997), 1–29.
22. Leonid Rozenblit and Frank Keil. 2002. The misunderstood limits of folk science: An illusion of explanatory depth. *Cognitive Science* 26, 5 (2002), 521–562.
23. Sarah Weir, Juho Kim, Krzysztof Z. Gajos, and Robert C. Miller. 2015. Learnersourcing Subgoal Labels for How-to Videos. In *Proceedings of the 18th ACM Conference on Computer Supported Cooperative Work & Social Computing (CSCW '15)*. 405–416.
24. Joseph J. Williams, Na Li, Juho Kim, Jacob Whitehill, Samuel Maldonado, Mykola Pechenizkiy, Larry Chu, and Neil Heffernan. 2014. The MOOClet Framework: Improving Online Education through Experimentation and Personalization of Modules. *Social Science Research Network Working Paper Series* (Nov. 2014). http://ssrn.com/abstract=2523265
25. Joseph J Williams and Tania Lombrozo. 2010. The role of explanation in discovery and generalization: evidence from category learning. *Cognitive Science* 34, 5 (2010), 776–806.

Improving the Peer Assessment Experience on MOOC Platforms

Thomas Staubitz, Dominic Petrick, Matthias Bauer, Jan Renz, Christoph Meinel
Hasso Plattner Institute, Potsdam, Germany
{thomas.staubitz, matthias.bauer, jan.renz, christoph.meinel}@hpi.de
dominic.petrick@student.hpi.de

ABSTRACT
Massive Open Online Courses (MOOCs) have revolutionized higher education by offering university-like courses for a large amount of learners via the Internet. The paper at hand takes a closer look on peer assessment as a tool for delivering individualized feedback and engaging assignments to MOOC participants. Benefits, such as scalability for MOOCs and higher order learning, and challenges, such as grading accuracy and rogue reviewers, are described. Common practices and the state-of-the-art to counteract challenges are highlighted. Based on this research, the paper at hand describes a peer assessment workflow and its implementation on the openHPI and openSAP MOOC platforms. This workflow combines the best practices of existing peer assessment tools and introduces some small but crucial improvements.

Author Keywords
MOOC; Online Learning; Peer Assessment; Assessment.

INTRODUCTION
MOOCs can have tens of thousands of participants, which is why assignments are often offered in machine-gradable formats. However, machine-grading of hardly quantifiable criteria, e.g. elegance, style, and creativity, is difficult or next to impossible. Additionally, individualized feedback is an integral part of education, but can not be delivered by using automated assessments [30].

Peer assessment (PA) is employed in today's MOOCs as an attempt to tackle these issues. This method allows participants to receive personalized feedback and to engage in challenges that go beyond the capabilities of automatic machine-grading by allowing the participants to grade and comment each other's work [30].

While PA seems to be an ideal tool for MOOCs to bring complex assignments and feedback to participants, the various implementations across the large MOOC platforms face some challenges. PA is the subject of active research, which attempts to find new ways of presenting, conducting, and structuring peer assessments to overcome its current limitations. Based on this research, the paper at hand presents a concept that incorporates the state of the art of peer assessment implementations of selected MOOC platforms and explores new ideas, which are added throughout the various steps of the workflow. This concept has been implemented on our own MOOC platforms. Three courses, which have piloted in employing this technology have been evaluated.

The rest of this paper is structured as follows: Section *Foundations* presents a summary on theoretical background, advantages, didactic importance, and common criticisms of peer assessment. Section *State of the Art and Best Practices* provides an overview on current practices of peer assessment on selected MOOC platforms. Section *Our Implementation* presents our concept and its implementation of a peer assessment system. Section *Evaluation* evaluates our system based on feedback from participants in several peer assessment pilots that we have conducted until the time of writing. Finally, the last two sections present the work that remains to be done and sum up our contribution and findings.

FOUNDATIONS
Benefits of peer assessment include improvement of higher order thinking skills, consolidation of topical knowledge, and individualized feedback for each participant [10, 14]. Learning effects can thus not only be seen as welcome byproducts of the process itself, the learning might even be put in the foreground. Educational assessment has the purpose of deepening a student's understanding, measuring student achievement, and evaluating the effectiveness of an educational program [22]. PA as a form of educational assessment is very flexible and can be used to serve either purpose–summative or formative assessment–or even both at the same time by combining several components [33]. Students reviewing each other's work and giving written feedback is a widely accepted application of formative PA [12, 32]. Summative PA of fellow students' work is a more complicated matter and requires careful guidance by a teacher, since grades should be fair, consistent, and comparable for all students [1, 32, 9].

Rubrics
A common way to enable students to peer-grade other students' work is to use teacher-designed grading rubrics. Depending on

the task at hand, an assignment can be objective or subjective. Objective assignments have clearly defined what is a right or a wrong answer, which in its simplest form could be a yes-or-no test. Subjective assignments have no clear way of expressing a correct answer, meaning that the student has multiple ways to solve the task at hand [31]. Creative writing is an example of a highly subjective task. Gauging the quality of such a piece of work through PA is difficult and highly subjective. On the other hand in a MOOC environment, such tasks are the ones that most likely will end up to be handled by peer assessment, as the massive nature of these courses forbids a manual grading by the teaching team, and an automatic grading of creative work is only hard to imagine. Rubrics counteract the subjectiveness during the grading by providing students with teacher-designed categories that communicate the quality expectations that a piece of work should fulfill [31]. They seek to guide students through the grading and often elaborate on the criteria, e.g. by giving examples how many points to award for which expertise and completeness displayed in the work of a peer [23].

Knight and Steinbach divide peer assessments into three guidance categories: (i) open-ended, where little guidance, e.g., in form of rubrics, is given, (ii) guided, where general hints and questions to consider are provided, and (iii) directed, which provides reviewers a detailed, checklist-like guidance to grade peers. They argue that directed peer assessment is superior to the other categories, since it also enables less knowledgeable students to assess their peers' work [14].

Self Assessment

A special type of assessment, often mentioned in conjunction with PA, is self-assessment. Having seen and assessed the work of their peers, students evaluate their own work on the same criteria that they used to evaluate the work of their peers [4]. Due to similar didactical and cognitive benefits and emerging synergies they are often used together [25, 3].

Studies examining student's performance improvements through PA participation report varying results. The consensus being that performance improvements largely depend on the specific application and learning environment where PA is employed [26, 27]. If applied responsibly, students have been found to improve in overall course performance if they previously participated in PAs for this particular course [26, 27]. Feedback in general is perceived useful by students. Some studies suggest that in some cases, students take comments from their peers more seriously than teacher comments [9, 25, 26]. Accurate grades have been reported for both peer and self-assessment, with more reviews increasing the accuracy relative to an accepted standard, such as teacher-assigned grades [26, 27].

Responsibly-applied PA should have explicit training or workshop sessions beforehand to increase student eligibility and confidence to assess peers [27]. The biggest concerns voiced regarding PA are grading bias and rogue reviewers, which both are related to the question whether or not students are eligible to assess peers.

Issues

Although large in-person classes also can amount to several hundreds of students, according to Suen [30], PA in this setting mostly has been employed in the context of smaller groups guided by a teacher or teaching assistant and often as a supplement to teacher assessment. In the context of MOOCs, increasingly heterogeneous groups of students participate in PA. Due to the different backgrounds and knowledge of students, student eligibility and grading accuracy is doubted and PA itself, as a valid assessment form, is sometimes being challenged by course participants [14, 30, 11]. Therefore, it depends on the teaching teams to narrow down quality expectations, for example by providing detailed rubrics to ensure the success of PAs and to keep assessments comparable, consistent, and fair [9, 27]. Students' subjectiveness based on their culture, education, and knowledge of the topic at hand will influence the way a student grades to a certain degree [16]. Bias can partially be counteracted with anonymity, multiple reviews per peer (averaging a grade), clear expectations, and trainings [14, 3].

Another factor linked to the problem of student eligibility are rogue reviews [26]. Rogue reviews are insufficient reviews caused by laziness, collusion, dishonesty, retaliation, competition, or malevolence [14, 26]. These were always a problem for PA, but have found to be a bigger problem online due to increased anonymity and a decreased feeling of community affiliation [12, 18].

STATE OF THE ART AND BEST PRACTICES

This section explores best practices and the state of the art of peer assessment implementations on Coursera, edX, and Iversity[1]. We have selected these MOOC platforms for the quality of the peer assessment tools that they feature.

Platform-specific Features

Across all platforms, PA is implemented as a work-flow consisting of several steps that have to be completed one after the other. The essential parts of the PA workflow on all platforms are a submission step, followed by a peer evaluation step, and finally a result step.

Coursera and edX additionally offer a calibration and a self-assessment step. On Coursera, these are optional [6, 5]. Iversity offers a Cloud Teaching Assistant System (CTAS) for customers that have voted to pay for this option [35]. In this model, freelance teaching assistants–hired by Iversity–are assigned to the course and grade the submissions of the participants. Thus providing sort of a missing link between crowd-sourced peer-grading and classic instructor-based grading. Vogelsang and Ruppertz [35] admit that it merely was assumed that these assistants (CTAs) possess the required qualities due to their professional status. In an experiment they conducted, CTAs and peers graded rather different from the course instructor but close to each other. In terms of the examined MOOC platforms, a step unique to edX is Artificial Intelligence (AI) grading, which allows to machine-grade essays based on advanced machine-learning algorithms [6, 7].

[1] Iversity is the largest German MOOC platform. https://iversity.org

Coursera offers a self-assessment step for the students to rethink their submission. As an incentive for doing self-assessment accurately, the maximum of both grades will be taken as the final grade if a participant grades herself within a 5% distance to the grade received from the peers [5].

Submission handling

Missing a deadline has different consequences across the platforms. On Iversity, no points are awarded if any deadline has been missed, whereas Coursera awards no points if participants missed the submission deadline, but only penalizes the final assessment grade by 20% if the evaluation deadline has been missed [5, 13].

edX offers the participants a plain text input field and the possibility to upload a file to submit their work. Iversity and Coursera offer the possibility of multiple subquestions per assignment, each one with an input and file upload. All platforms allow to save drafts as long as the submission deadline has not yet passed. The participants are required to explicitly submit their work at the end of the submission step to reduce the amount of empty submissions to be offered for grading. edX employs a quality filter, which determines, by using metrics, such as word diversity and text complexity, if a submission is accepted [6]. Based on the work of Kulkarni [16], Coursera was the first MOOC platform to use calibrated peer review (CPR) [5, 2], which transfers the idea of training sessions to online environments [2]. Participants learn to use grading rubrics correctly by comparing their grading to a grading sample of the teaching team. This allows them to adjust their grading, which leads to improved grading accuracy [2]. Coursera determines a competency index for participants, which is then used as a weight for the actual grading [2]. edX requires participants to reach an accuracy threshold before they can proceed. For the actual reviews Coursera and edX both advise teaching teams to opt for three to five reviews, whereas Iversity usually requires people to review seven peers [6, 5, 13]. Coursera and edX also offer motivated participants the possibility to grade additional reviews beyond the required amount.

Review distribution

A participant retrieves submissions to review one after another (edX, Iversity) or as a set to grade (Coursera) [7, 5, 13]. Exact details of how reviewers are mapped to reviewees are scarce. Several sources hint that Coursera and Iversity have a fixed mapping, which in turn means that if a reviewer fails to review all peers, reviewees might receive less than the required reviews [5]. edX on the other hand uses a submission pooling principle, where participants pull a submission from a pool and, thereby, lock the submission for everyone else. If it has been reviewed or 30 minutes have passed, the submission automatically returns to the pool [7]. The review process itself is double-blind without exception. Double-blind peer reviewing allows participants to give more critical feedback and freely express their opinions without having to consider interpersonal factors, which in turn results in more honest and, ideally, more useful reviews [18, 28]. To report code of honor violations, submissions can be flagged during the peer evaluation. Iversity has no obvious way to report submissions for misconduct other than plagiarism, whereas edX and Coursera allow further distinction, such as explicit content.

Grading

If participants have finished all reviews in time, they qualify for a grade, which is shown together with individual grades and comments received from their reviewers. For grade computation, Coursera and edX use the median to catch gradings too low or too high, whereas Iversity uses the average of reviewer grades [6, 5, 13]. As shown by Kulkarni [16], the median performs better than the average in this context. Raman [24] suggests to employ ordinal instead of cardinal grading. Each participant orders the submissions she has been assigned to for grading in the form of *a better than b better than c*. On the basis of these "local" orderings, a "global" ordering of all submissions is estimated and from this the cardinal grades are derived.

All platforms offer the possibility to request a re-grading. Coursera and edX suggest posting submissions and reviews in the discussion forums to get further feedback [7, 5]. Iversity offers a built-in re-grading tool [13].

EdX also employs an AI grading step that uses technology commonly referred to as Automated Essay Scoring (AES) [7, 2]. Statistical machine-learning models are employed to predict human-assigned scores. These models are trained based on teacher-assigned grades for a set of submissions and automatically extracted text features, such as number of words, orthographic or grammar errors, word frequency, or sentence complexity. AES dates back to the work of Page [21] in the 1960s and has been been an issue of continuous research since then [29]. Besides the high time investment that is required for training, the results are still problematic, as machines are not able to understand and interpret texts the way humans do [2].

The standalone tool Peerstudio[2], which can be added to any platform that supports the Learning Tools Interoperability (LTI) interface, takes a completely different approach on peer assessment. It focuses on enabling students to give immediate formative feedback on work-in-progress. Kulkarni et al. report that the grades of students that had received fast feedback were significantly higher than the grades of those students who did not receive feedback at all or after a too long time frame. [17]

OUR IMPLEMENTATION

Based on the state of the art PA implementations shown in the previous section, our core design is a workflow model that encapsulates a series of steps.

Basic Workflow

Submit work, *review peers* and *see results* are the core steps of the workflow. A training unit and a self-assessment step can additionally be activated by the teaching team. The additional steps can be mandatory or optional for the user. An unlock date and a deadline can be set for each of the steps. If the deadline of any mandatory step has been missed, the participant has failed the assignment. If the deadline of an optional step is missed, the participant is forwarded to the next

[2]https://www.peerstudio.org

step and can no longer complete the missed step. To start a peer assessment, participants have to acknowledge the code of honor. Furthermore, the system provides the option to create a best-of gallery. The participants, therefore, either have to acknowledge that their work can be used as an example in the gallery or opt-out from being featured in this gallery.

Peer Evaluation–The Core Feature

The system allows the teaching teams to define a summative and a formative part of the PA. The summative part is handled via grading rubrics. Defining the grading rubrics is one of the key tasks for the teaching team during the creation of a PA. A rubric consists of three components: An (ideally) self-explanatory title (e.g., "Writing Style" or "Creativity"), an explanatory text, and rubric options. The explanatory text can be used to give additional hints for the grading. This serves for a better guidance of participants, which helps to understand the rubrics and aims to reduce grading bias. Rubric options represent the different levels of attainment for their respective rubric. The scoring scale of the rubric options is not required to be linear and can weight levels differently, e.g., 1, 2, 4 points, or can be an interval, e.g., 0, 5, 10 points. Rubrics and rubric options are defined by the teaching team according to their needs for each PA.

Participants grade a submission based on the available rubrics. Additionally to this summative feedback, the participants are encouraged to give their peers formative feedback in the form of free text reviews. All reviews are double-blind to protect peers' identities from each other and to prevent call-outs or conflict escalations outside of the peer assessment. Participants who have completed the required reviews in time, advance to the next step. Participants who do not, receive zero points for the assessment. Voluntary additional reviews up to the number of required reviews can be handed in as long as the deadline has not passed.

A large amount of reviews has the advantage of increasing the probability that the average grade of a submission is close to the grade teachers would assign [26, 27]. However, time should be provided for those willing to write thoughtful reviews. With too many reviews to write, participants will rush through the process, which likely lowers the quality of the feedback overall. Therefore, we have designed the system to have a preset of three reviews as the default amount to be completed during the evaluation step. We recommend to increase this amount only if the peer assessment spans multiple weeks, only has a few rubrics to grade, or has a less demanding assignment.

In the following, we will focus on presenting some of those features that we added on top or that we have improved.

1. **A step in the workflow to train the participants in the summative part of the assessment.**
2. **A distribution mechanism that boosts the priority of the work of participants that already did a review.**
3. **Review rating, additional points for writing good reviews.**
4. **Transparent grade computation and re-grading option.**

Training Step

The teaching team has the possibility to add a simple training step to the PA workflow. This training step can be optional or mandatory for the participants, defined by the settings of the teaching team.

The teaching team grades at least 10 samples of the participants' submissions for the current PA to ensure a more diverse training pool. A diverse set of samples benefits the training as it provides the participants with examples for each level of quality. While a sample submission is being reviewed by a teaching team member, it is blocked for all other teaching team members to ensure that it is not accidentally graded twice.

As soon as the training step has been opened for the participants, the submissions that already have been graded by the teaching team are presented to the participant one after the other. Initially, the students only can access the submission, but not the grading of the teaching team. This view is more or less identical to the view of the actual evaluation step. As soon as the participant herself has graded the sample, she is presented an overview, which shows the teaching team's comment and adds indicator arrows to the rubric options that have been selected by the teaching team and those that have been selected by the participant. This way, the participant can easily detect scoring differences.

If the training step is mandatory, the teaching team can define the amount of training reviews that have to be done. If a participant still feels insecure in using the rubrics after grading the required amount of samples, she is allowed to grade as many additional samples as there are left in the pool.

Distributing Submissions to Peers

The distribution mechanism that maps submissions to peers is the core of the evaluation step. Our goal is that each participant receives sufficient feedback. Each participant is required to write a certain amount *(n)* of reviews, which means that each participant ideally receives that amount of reviews in return. The size of *n* is defined by the teaching team.

We are using a dynamic mapping approach that assigns submissions on demand from a pool of available submissions. This allows to rebalance review counts for submissions on the fly as the current submission distribution state can be considered. With additions such as review expiration, the problem of redistributing submissions is solved without requiring heuristics that determine when submissions are considered for redistribution.

Our implementation of the pooling approach introduces a *submission priority principle* to balance submission distribution and the possibility that a submission is reviewed by several reviewers in parallel (see Figure 1).

Particularly, the *submission priority principle* is a novelty that deserves some more detailed explanation. Submissions are assigned a *priority*, which influences their likelihood to receive reviews, and they have a *required reviews counter* to indicate how many reviews are still required for this submission. As soon as a submission is inserted into the pool, both the required

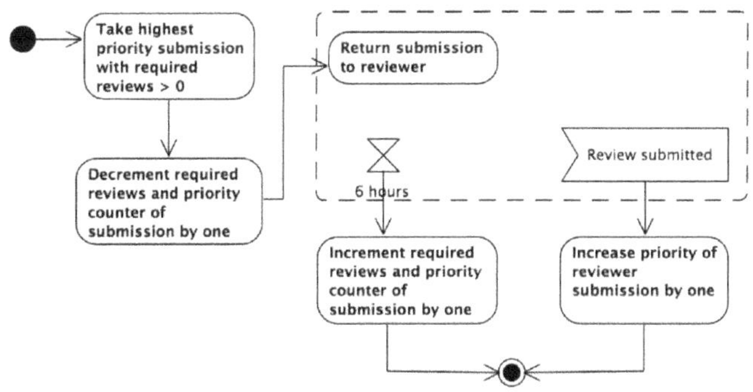

Figure 1. Activity diagram summarizing the distribution mechanism. The dotted line marks the time range from the start to the end of the actual review process. This time range starts when a participant requests a submission to review and ends either when the review is submitted or after 6 hours if the participant fails to return the review in time. A submission is the work that has been submitted to the system by a participant a needs to be reviewed.

reviews counter and the submission priority are initially set to the required amount of reviews of the PA *(n)*.

Submissions with the highest priority that still require reviews are retrieved first. If there are multiple submissions with the same priority, the retrieval of these is randomized to spread reviews more evenly. Retrieving a submission reduces both its counters by one, which means that other submissions are now more likely to be retrieved next, as they now have a higher priority relative to the retrieved one. Reducing both counters before a review is submitted, ensures that a submission cannot accidentally receive too many reviews, since it can be retrieved at most n times before other submissions are retrieved next. Otherwise, the balance of the mechanism can be disrupted due to one submission receiving too many reviews, which are then "missing" for other submissions in the worst case.

When a review is submitted, the reviewer's own submission receives a priority boost of one. The philosophy behind this boost is that those who write reviews deserve to get reviews in return, while those who do not should receive less. If a participant does not submit a review within six hours, it will expire. If a review expires, the priority and required reviews count of the corresponding submission are restored by increasing each by one again. Without review expiration, reviewers who forget about their reviews would leave their peers at a disadvantage, because they would no longer be able to receive the required number of reviews.

Review Rating

In the result step, participants can see the reviews they received and–as soon as the deadline for the evaluation step has passed–their final grade for the assessment. Our system introduces the option to report received reviews for misconduct, analog to reporting submissions in the evaluation step. A further improvement is the possibility to rate the received feedback.

Current platforms lack incentives to write thoughtful reviews, as well as a way for peers to give feedback on received reviews [36, 20, 34]. Participants are practically defenseless if the reviews they receive are not worthy of a report, since teaching teams have only limited capacities and cannot investigate minor incidents. Lu et al [19] have conducted an experiment to "grade the graders". They report particularly positive results when the graders receive grades for their grading and also grade the grading of others.

We, therefore, decided to go for a feedback rating approach, which has already been used in online and classroom peer assessments [10, 12]. The basic idea is to allow participants to actually make an impact and "defend" themselves by influencing the grade their reviewer receives, thus motivating reviewers to write more detailed and helpful reviews [14]. We have transferred the idea of feedback rating to MOOC peer assessment by allowing participants to earn up to one bonus point for each review they write. The receiving participants rate reviews on a scale from zero to three stars, based on how useful they perceive the review. Guidance on what a good review looks like is provided during the rating.

A four-point scale has been chosen and translates into no point for zero stars, 0.3 for one star, 0.7 for two stars, and 1.0 for three stars. This bonus can accumulate to a notable amount of points, even considering that participants already can earn a significant amount of base points for their submission in the PA compared to other assessment forms on our platform. This may seem to be a rather high bonus. However, reviews are an integral part of peer assessment and its learning experience. Hence, reviews are small but important work artefacts of a peer assessment process that require a considerable effort to be written in high quality, for which feedback rating can be seen as an appropriate reward. Until the participant has rated the feedback, we only show her the overall grade but not the individual grades that have been assigned by the peers. As soon as the written part of a review is rated, we also show the individual grade given by that peer. This is an attempt to make sure that participants only rate the usefulness and quality of the written review and not the grade that they received from their peer. Furthermore, this method uses the inherent curiosity of the participant as an incentive to rate the reviews.

Grade Computation

We originally opted for an experimental weighted average approach taking multiple factors into account. Some of these were intended to serve as long-term adjustments to reduce the impact of rogue reviewers and reviewers who constantly deliver poor review quality. In the end, however, we skipped that plan as this calculation would have become absolutely intransparent for all stakeholders, such as teaching team, helpdesk, and participants. Kulkarni et al [16] have already shown that simply using the median is good enough in most cases and will be only marginally improved by employing complex weighting mechanisms.

We use the average for those rare cases when a submission receives less than three reviews and the median when it receives three or more reviews.

The final grade consists of multiple components, which are transparently communicated to the participant in the result step:

- Median of review grades (base points)
- Self-assessment bonus points

Figure 2. Perceived learning effects for doing the assignment and reviewing peers (OSAP1: n=54, OSAP2: n=463).

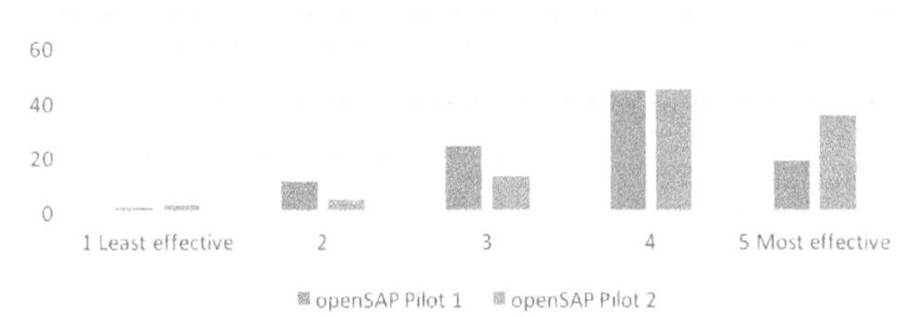

Figure 3. Perceived learning impact of peer grading assignment compared to other assessment types used on our platforms, such as quizzes (OSAP1: n=54, OSAP2: n=467).

- Review feedback rating bonus points
- Grading delta

The median of the review grades is calculated per rubric. We then sum up these values to the final amount of points for the participant[3].

The grading delta can be set by the teaching team members during conflict reconciliation. This delta can be relative or absolute. A relative delta adds a fixed amount of points to the base points, bonus points are left untouched and are added on top. The absolute delta sets the overall grade to a fixed amount of points, ignoring the originally received base and bonus points.

EVALUATION

We will now evaluate the implemented PA design based on surveys we conducted among the participants of our first PA pilots and on an analysis of some key factors of the data that we collected during these pilots. In total we have conducted five PAs in four courses, two on openSAP and two on openHPI, in a variety of settings up to now. The review distribution mechanism has been employed in all of the PAs, the other key features will be listed per PA in the following section.

Key Features of Examined PAs

Introduction to SAP Fiori UX (OSAP1)

- Enrolled participants: ~21,000
- Task: creative design challenge to create an SAP Fiori application
- Extra Steps: none
- Minimum reviews: 3

[3]See: https://open.hpi.de/pages/p_a_grading

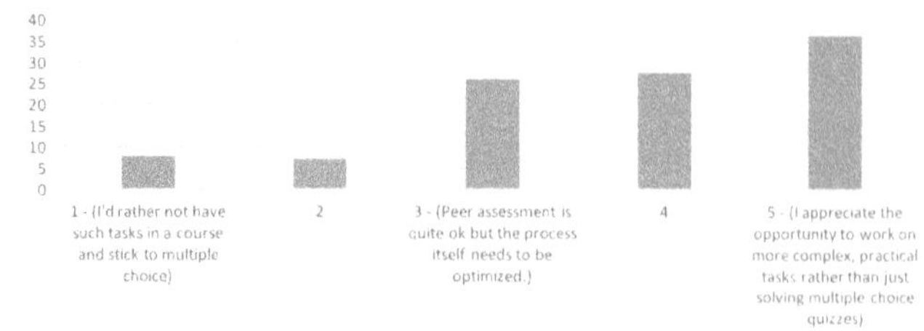

Figure 4. The participants of OHPI2 appreciated the opportunity to work on more complex practical tasks, enabled by the PA system (n=466).

- Rubrics: 8 (target group definition, creativity, simplicity, delightfulness, etc. (subjective))
- Timeframe: 5 weeks (submission), 1 week (peer assessment)
- 30 bonus points (course total: 360)
- Submissions: 149, qualified for grade: 116, survey: 54 (43%)

SAP experts reviewed the highest ranking submissions and chose three winners who were rewarded with a tablet computer.

Build Your Own SAP Fiori App in the Cloud (OSAP2)

- Enrolled participants: ~18,000
- Task: creative design challenge to create an SAP Fiori application
- Extra Steps: training, self-assessment, both mandatory
- Minimum reviews: 5
- Rubrics: 8 (Story, Persona, User Experience Journey, User-centricity, Look and Feel, etc. (subjective))
- Timeframe: 2 weeks (submission) + 1 week (training, peer- and self-assessment)
- 150 regular points (Course total: 450)
- Submissions: 1529, qualified for grade: 1332, survey: ~470 (~30%)

SAP experts reviewed the highest ranking submissions and chose three winners who were rewarded with a laptop.

Java for Beginners(OHPI1)

- Enrolled participants: ~11,000
- Task: modeling an object-oriented application, class diagram
- Extra Steps: self-assessment, optional
- Minimum reviews: 3
- Rubrics: 6 (mostly just checking if something useful had been delivered (yes or no) (objective))
- Timeframe: 3 weeks(submission), 1 week(peer- and self-assessment)
- 10 bonus points (Course total 103 + another 8 bonus points)
- Submissions: 337, qualified for grade: 297

Web Technologies(OHPI2 CSS/Pong)

- Enrolled participants: ~10,000
- Task1: create an HTML page including some CSS formatting according to a given design
- Task2: second task was to complete a given Javascript example
- Extra Steps: self-assessment, optional

Figure 5. Comparison of the openSAP pilot surveys (OSAP1: n=54, OSAP2: n=464) with Kulkarni's findings on perceived learning by assessing peers.

Figure 6. Comparison of the OSAP2 survey (n=469) with Kulkarni's findings on perceived learning by assessing one self.

- Minimum reviews: 3
- Rubrics: 3/6 (mostly simple yes or no questions to check if a certain feature exists or not (objective))
- Timeframe: 3/2 weeks (submission), 1/1 week (peer- and self-assessment)
- 7/9 bonus points, (Course total 180 + another 15 bonus points)
- Participants in assignment: 1371/1010
- Submissions: 761/567, qualified for grade: 476/592

General Feedback

Figure 2 shows how participants perceived the two key steps of the PA tasks in OSAP1 and OSAP2. Both–working on the assignments and reviewing the peers' submissions–were perceived by the participants as having a strong impact on their learning. These results validate PA usage in a creative design challenge context as given in those pilots. This impression is further reinforced by Figure 3, showing that the learning impact of PA is also perceived positively in comparison to other assessment types that are employed on our platforms.

The participants of OHPI1 stated in the course end survey that they appreciate the opportunity to work on more complex practical tasks, enabled by the PA system, instead of doing multiple choice tests (see Figure 4). This finding is also supported by participants' comments, throughout all of the examined courses, which generally expressed appreciation of the activity-driven assessment variation that has been introduced into the courses.

Comparing the survey results of OSAP1 and OSAP2 (in terms of perceived learning impact of assessing peers or one's own) with Kulkarni's results [16] (see Figure 5 and 6) shows at least very similar tendencies.

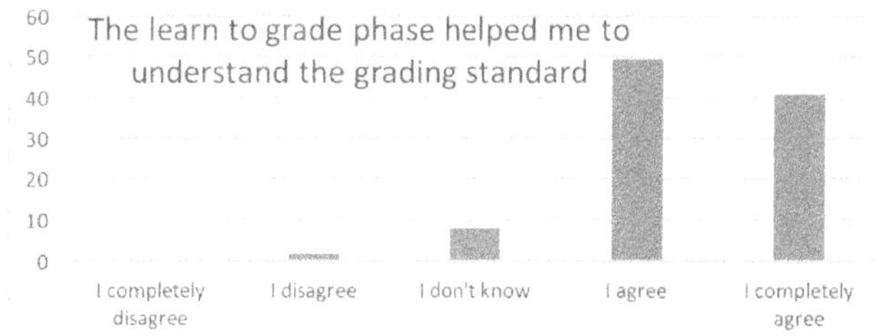

Figure 7. The training step helped me to understand the standards (n=468)

Evaluating the Novelties of our Implementation

Training Step

Almost 90% (n=54) of the participants of the OSAP1 survey stated that they would have preferred to have a training step before the actual peer grading step.

Figure 7 shows that the majority of participants of OSAP2's post-course survey perceived the offered training step as very helpful to understand the expected grading standard. In both pilots almost all participants perceived themselves to have given fair and detailed feedback (OSAP1: 94%, n=54, OSAP2: 96%, n=466). The perception of the received feedback, however, differs significantly between the pilots (OSAP1: 64%, n=54, OSAP2: 85%, n=466). While the difference between the perception of given and received feedback can be accounted to a well-known phenomenon in behavioral psychology (compare e.g. [15], [8]), the improvement in OSAP2 might be a sign for improved grading abilities due to the training step. However, there are too many factors involved to make a definitive statement here.

Distributing Submissions to Peers

Figure 8 shows that, except for OSAP1, the distribution mechanism worked quite well[4]. Starting with OSAP2 we can see a similar tendency throughout all the examined courses, showing that those participants who wrote the minimum amount of reviews, have also received a sufficient amount of reviews, while fewer reviews were "wasted" on those that did not write sufficient reviews. At least for the summative part of the PA the data shows that the distribution works sufficiently well. It has been suggested, however, that strong students are more likely to write reviews than weak students. Therefore, a concern might be that strong students get more reviews that way while weaker students get less. The formative part of the PA thus might increase the "learning gap" between good and bad performers.

Review Rating

Our review rating mechanism has been received very positively as a motivator for review quality. About 80% of the participants of the OSAP1 (n=54) and OSAP2 (n=472) surveys stated that our review rating implementation motivated to write useful feedback and was a good way to review the reviewers. More than 70% of the participants in the OSAP1 survey stated that the feedback they received motivates them to improve their reviews in the future.

[4]During OSAP1, the system was in a very early beta state and a lot of adjustments still needed to be performed

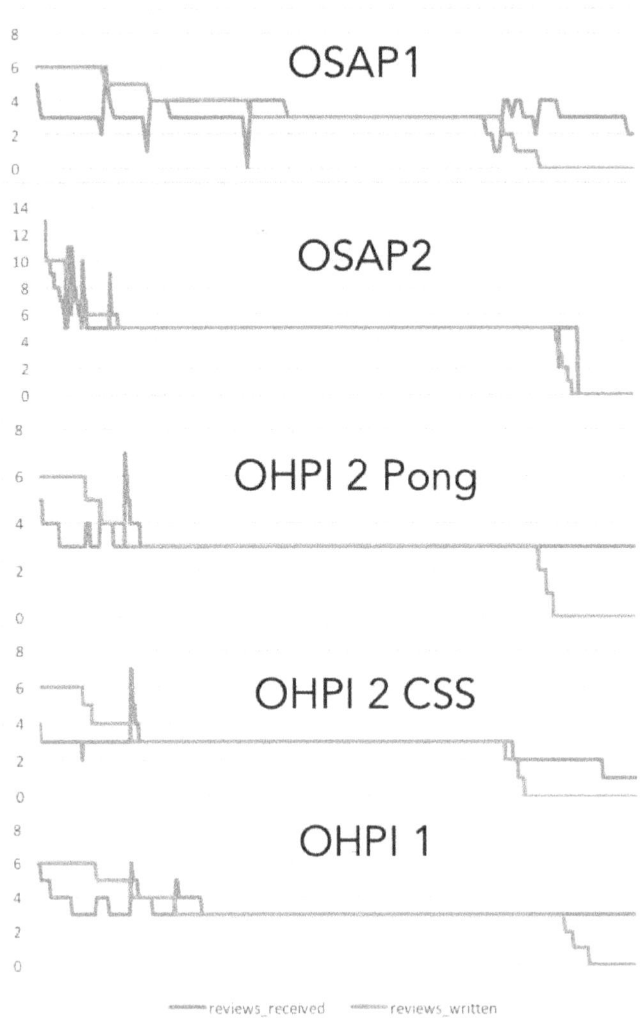

Figure 8. Ratio reviews written to reviews received in all of the examined courses. From top down (required reviews, submissions, sufficient amount of reviews: (3,149,116), (5,1529,1332), (3, 567, 476), (3, 761, 592), (3,337, 297))

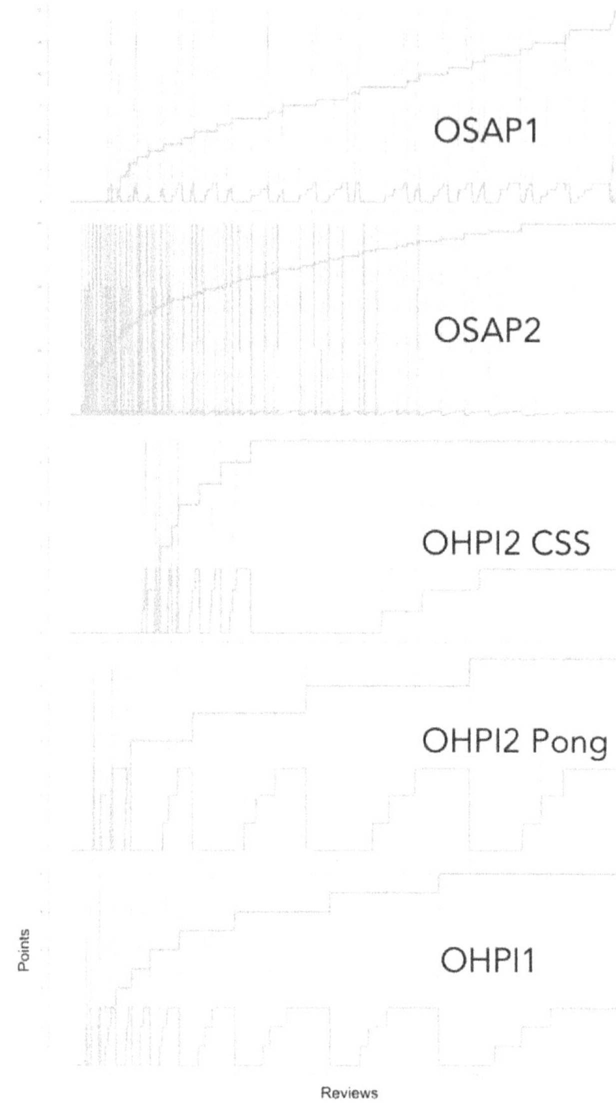

Figure 9. Orange: Points for submission, Blue: Review Rating, Grey: Review rating normalized (blue*maxOrange/maxBlue)

There is an objection that the introduced review rating might lead to a "Tit for Tat" situation where good grades instead of good reviews are rated good. We, therefore, analyzed the data in the the examined PAs to see if we can find evidence for this assumption. First, we compared the points a participant received for the submission to the rating she gave to the review. Figure 9 shows that we can observe a very similar trend in all of the examined courses. The feedback points that a review received, in general, is not related to the amount of points a reviewer gave. We then compared the reviews word count, as a very basic factor for review quality, to the received rating. Figure 10 at least implies that there is a certain relation between the length of a review and the rating it receives.

FUTURE WORK

It has been suggested that the review distribution mechanism might increase the "learning gap" between good and bad performers. A potential tweak in the process might be to explicitly inform the participants about the option to improve their chances for a review by writing reviews themselves. Furthermore, we need to further investigate how to provide a re-grading mechanism that is smart enough to decide who is eligible for a re-grading and who is not. Raman's approach of ordinal grading [24] might be a starting point worth investigating.

CONCLUSION

The paper at hand described the importance of peer assessment for scaling formative assessments and more challenging and engaging assignments in large online learning environments. A peer assessment workflow concept based on research findings, platform implementations of large MOOC platforms, and participant feedback has been presented, which incorporates the state of the art of MOOC peer assessment and adds several technical improvements to the process. Feedback rating has been introduced, which is a concept to let peers rate the reviews

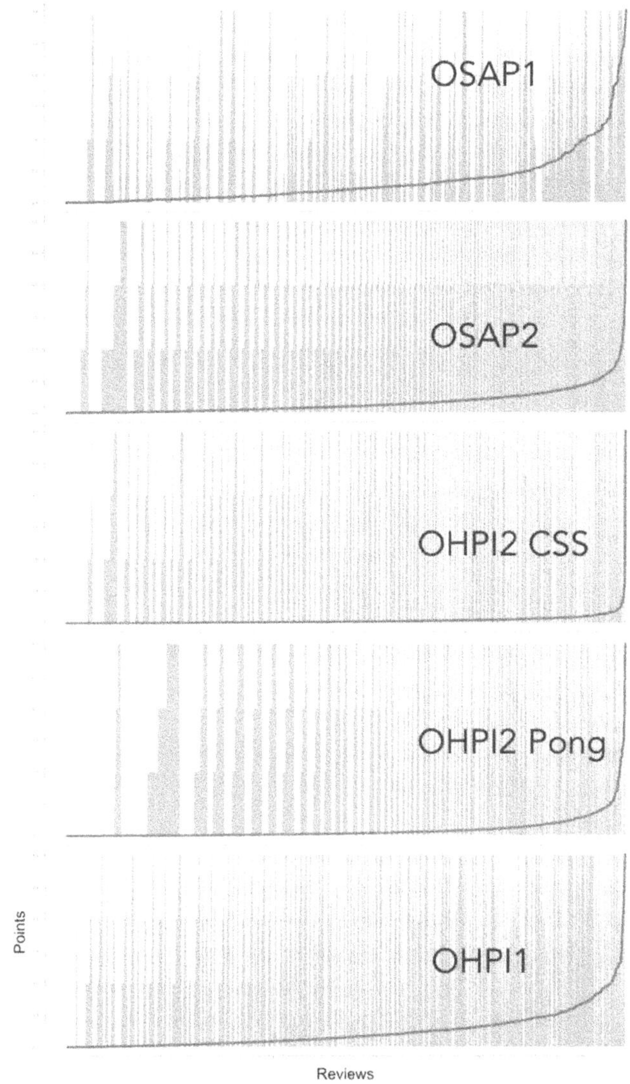

Figure 10. Orange: Review rating, Green: Review word count normalized (green*maxOrange/maxGreen)

they received, with the intention to provide incentives for reviewers to improve their review quality. Rated reviews award reviewers bonus points based on the rating, which is not only meant to motivate reviewers to write better reviews, but also to allow participants to defend themselves against poor review quality. Submission pooling has been developed as a dynamic algorithm that takes the current submission-distribution state into account and balances distribution of submissions on the fly, based on priority and reviews needed per submission. An evaluation based on peer assessments with different settings in four courses on two of our MOOC platforms marked a success of the implemented PA workflow with largely positive feedback from participants. Finally, our implementation is perceived as on-par with other implementations and many participants expressed their appreciation of a more activity-driven and creative challenge, wishing to have more of those in future courses.

ACKNOWLEDGMENTS
We thank openSAP, particularly Katrin Elk, for sharing their insights and the overall great collaboration.

REFERENCES
1. John R. Baird and Jeff R. Northfield. 1995. *Learning from the PEEL experience*. School of Graduate Studies, Faculty of Education, Monash University.
2. Stephen P. Balfour. 2013. Assessing writing in MOOCS: Automated essay scoring and Calibrated Peer Review. *Research & Practice in Assessment* (2013), 40–48.
3. Stephen Bostock. 2000. Student peer assessment. http://www.reading.ac.uk/web/FILES/engageinassessment/Student_peer_assessment_-_Stephen_Bostock.pdf. (2000). Online; accessed 14-September-2015.
4. David Boud. 1995. *Enhancing Learning Through Self-assessment*. Taylor & Francis.
5. Coursera. 2014. Coursera Peer Assessment Student FAQs. http://help.coursera.org/customer/portal/topics/521177-peer-assessments. (2014). Online; accessed 3-November-2014.
6. edX. 2014a. Open Response Assessment Problems. http://edx-partner-course-staff.readthedocs.org/en/latest/exercises_tools/open_response_assessment.html. (2014). Online; accessed 3-November-2014.
7. edX. 2014b. Open Response Assessments for Students. http://edx-partner-course-staff.readthedocs.org/en/latest/students/ora_students.html. (2014). Online; accessed 3-November-2014.
8. Joyce Ehrlinger, Kerri Johnson, Matthew Banner, David Dunning, and Justin Kruger. 2008. Why the Unskilled Are Unaware: Further Explorations of (Absent) Self-Insight Among the Incompetent. *Organizational behavior and human decision processes* 105, 1 (01 2008), 98–121.
9. Jan Fermelis, Richard Tucker, and Stuart Palmer. 2007. Online self and peer assessment in large, multi-campus, multi-cohort contexts. In *Providing choices for learners and learning Proceedings ASCILITE Singapore 2007*. 271–281.
10. Edward.F. Gehringer. 2000. Strategies and mechanisms for electronic peer review. In *Frontiers in Education Conference, 2000. FIE 2000. 30th Annual*, Vol. 1. F1B/2–F1B/7 vol.1.
11. David Glance, Martin Forsey, and Myles Riley. 2013. The pedagogical foundations of massive open online courses. *First Monday* 18, 5 (2013).
12. John Hamer, Kenneth T. Ma, and Hugh H. Kwong. 2005. A Method of Automatic Grade Calibration in Peer Assessment. In *of Conferences in Research and Practice in Information Technology, Australian Computer Society*. 67–72.
13. Iversity. 2014. P2P Grading: Assessing Globally. https://iversity.org/blog/p2p-grading/. (2014). Online; accessed 3-November-2014.

14. Linda Knight and Theresa Steinbach. 2011. The pedagogical foundations of massive open online courses. *Journal of Information Technology Education* 10 (2011), 81–100.
15. Justin Kruger and David Dunning. 1999. Unskilled and Unaware of It: How Difficulties in Recognizing One's Own Incompetence Lead to Inflated Self-Assessments. *Journal of Personality and Social Psychology* 77 (1999), 1121–1134.
16. Chinmay Kulkarni, Koh Pang Wei, Huy Le, Daniel Chia, Kathryn Papadopoulos, Justin Cheng, Daphne Koller, and Scott R. Klemmer. 2013. Peer and Self Assessment in Massive Online Classes. *ACM Trans. Comput.-Hum. Interact.* 20, 6, Article 33 (Dec. 2013), 31 pages.
17. Chinmay E. Kulkarni, Michael S. Bernstein, and Scott R. Klemmer. 2015. PeerStudio: Rapid Peer Feedback Emphasizes Revision and Improves Performance. In *Proceedings of the Second (2015) ACM Conference on Learning @ Scale (L@S '15)*. ACM, New York, NY, USA, 75–84.
18. Ruiling Lu and Linda Bol. 2007. A comparison of anonymous versus identifiable e-peer review on college student writing performance and the extent of critical feedback. *Journal of Interactive Online Learning* (2007), 100–115.
19. Yanxin Lu, Joe Warren, Christopher Jermaine, Swarat Chaudhuri, and Scott Rixner. 2015. Grading the Graders: Motivating Peer Graders in a MOOC. In *Proceedings of the 24th International Conference on World Wide Web (WWW '15)*. 680–690.
20. Debbie Morrison. 2013. Why and When Peer Grading is Effective for Open and Online Learning. http://onlinelearninginsights.wordpress.com/2013/03/09/why-and-when-peer-grading-is-effective-for-open-and-online-learning/. (2013). Online; accessed 2-November-2014.
21. Ellis B. Page. 1967. Statistical and Linguistic Strategies in the Computer Grading of Essays. In *Proceedings of the 1967 Conference on Computational Linguistics (COLING '67)*. Association for Computational Linguistics, Stroudsburg, PA, USA, 1–13.
22. James W. Pellegrino, Naomi Chudowsky, and Robert Glaser (Eds.). 2001. *Knowing What Students Know: The Science and Design of Educational Assessment*. The National Academies Press, Washington, DC.
23. Nancy Pickett and Bernie Dodge. 2007. Rubrics for Web Lessons. http://webquest.org/sdsu/rubrics/weblessons.htm. (2007). Online; accessed 14-September-2015.
24. Karthik Raman and Thorsten Joachims. 2014. Methods for Ordinal Peer Grading. In *Proceedings of the 20th ACM SIGKDD International Conference on Knowledge Discovery and Data Mining (KDD '14)*. ACM, New York, NY, USA, 1037–1046.
25. E.F. Redish, M. Vicentini, and Società italiana di fisica. 2004. *Research on Physics Education*. Number v. 156 in International School of Physics Enrico Fermi Series. IOS Press.
26. Ken Reily, Pam Ludford Finnerty, and Loren Terveen. 2009. Two Peers Are Better Than One: Aggregating Peer Reviews for Computing Assignments is Surprisingly Accurate. In *Proceedings of the ACM 2009 International Conference on Supporting Group Work (GROUP '09)*. ACM, New York, NY, USA, 115–124.
27. Philip M. Sadler and Eddie Good. 2006. The Impact of Self- and Peer-Grading on Student Learning. *Educational Assessment* 11, 1 (2006), 1–31.
28. Martyn Shuttleworth. 2008. Double Blind Experiment. https://explorable.com/double-blind-experiment. (2008). Online; accessed 8-November-2014.
29. IEEE Intelligent Systems staff. 2000. The Debate on Automated Essay Grading. *IEEE Intelligent Systems* 15, 5 (Sept. 2000), 22–37.
30. Hoi Suen. 2014. Peer assessment for massive open online courses (MOOCs). *The International Review of Research in Open and Distributed Learning* 15, 3 (2014).
31. Germaine L. Taggart, Sandra J. Jones, and Judy A. Nixon. 1999. *Rubrics: A Handbook for Construction and Use*. Rowman & Littlefield Education.
32. Keith Topping. 1998. Peer Assessment between Students in Colleges and Universities. *Review of Educational Research* 68, 3 (1998), pp. 249–276.
33. Stephan Trahasch. 2004. From peer assessment towards collaborative learning. In *Frontiers in Education, 2004. FIE 2004. 34th Annual*. F3F–16–20 Vol. 2.
34. Gregor Ulm. 2012. A Critical View on Coursera's Peer Review Process. http://gregorulm.com/a-critical-view-on-courseras-peer-review-process/. (2012). Online; accessed 3-November-2014.
35. Tim Vogelsang and Lara Ruppertz. 2015. On the Validity of Peer Grading and a Cloud Teaching Assistant System. In *Proceedings of the Fifth International Conference on Learning Analytics And Knowledge (LAK '15)*. ACM, New York, NY, USA, 41–50.
36. Audrey Watters. 2012. The Problems with Peer Grading in Coursera. https://www.insidehighered.com/blogs/hack-higher-education/problems-peer-grading-coursera. (2012). Online; accessed 8-November-2014.

Graders as Meta-Reviewers: Simultaneously Scaling and Improving Expert Evaluation for Large Online Classrooms

David A. Joyner[1,2], Wade Ashby[1], Liam Irish[1], Yeeling Lam[1], Jacob Langston[1], Isabel Lupiani[1], Mike Lustig[1], Paige Pettoruto[1], Dana Sheahen[1], Angela Smiley[1], Amy Bruckman[1], & Ashok Goel[1]

[1]Georgia Institute of Technology
School of Interactive Computing

[2]Udacity, Inc.

{david.joyner, mashby6, liam, yeeling.lam, jlangston9, isabel.lupiani, mikelustig, ppettoruto6, danasheahen, smiley}@gatech.edu; {asb, ashok.goel}@cc.gatech.edu

ABSTRACT

Large classes, both online and residential, typically demand many graders for evaluating students' written work. Some classes attempt to use autograding or peer grading, but these both present challenges to assigning grades at for-credit institutions, such as the difficulty of autograding to evaluate free-response answers and the lack of expert oversight in peer grading. In a large, online class at Georgia Tech in Summer 2015, we experimented with a new approach to grading: framing graders as meta-reviewers, charged with evaluating the original work in the context of peer reviews. To evaluate this approach, we conducted a pair of controlled experiments and a handful of qualitative analyses. We found that having access to peer reviews improves the perceived quality of feedback provided by graders without decreasing the graders' efficiency and with only a small influence on the grades assigned.

Author Keywords

Peer review; online education.

ACM Classification Keywords

K.3.2. Computer and Information Science Education.

INTRODUCTION

Recent trends in the development of higher education have introduced significant questions about scaling traditional university offerings. Massive open online courses (MOOCs) can draw tens of thousands of students each paying little to no money, making a traditional manual grading process using expert graders impossible. Many of these courses have opted to use peer grading to replace expert grading in assessment, and some studies suggest peer grading can be as reliable as expert grading under the right circumstances [6, 7, 21].

L@S 2016, April 25 - 26, 2016, Edinburgh, Scotland , United Kingdom.

ACM 978-1-4503-3726-7/16/04…$15.00 .
DOI: http://dx.doi.org/10.1145/2876034.2876044

However, increasing class sizes is not limited only to MOOCs; traditional educational offerings have begun experimenting with scaling up as well. The Georgia Tech Online Masters of Science in Computer Science (OMSCS) program is one such experiment. While neither Massive[1] nor Open[2], the program is still very large for a Master's program, with individual classes typically drawing between 200 and 500 enrollees. In the first two years of the program, there have been 11,000 individual course enrollments from 3,000 students. Although this large size is due in large part to the affordability (the entire Master's degree is around $6,600 [12], or $200 per month including fees assuming one class per semester), it also comes from an intentional decision by Georgia Tech to admit any qualified applicant rather than admit applicants based on the number of available seats.

These large class sizes, coupled with the drastically lower tuition cost, make scaling a key concern for educational programs such as Georgia Tech's OMSCS. However, given that these classes are often for credit for a Master's degree that is equivalent to the on-campus degree (rather than an implicitly weaker "online" degree), we argue that Georgia Tech cannot rely solely on peer grading to generate class grades. Part of the reputation of the Georgia Tech Master's degree is the trust that a graduate's work has been evaluated by experts. Heavy use of peer grading would compromise that reputation in the absence of systematic assurances of the equality of peer and expert grading.

Thus, the Georgia Tech OMSCS needs to scale up assignment assessment, yet it cannot use MOOCs' peer grading method for scaling! In this work, we investigate a novel compromise: could peer review be used to support, rather than supplant, expert grading? By equipping expert graders with peer reviews, we aim to make graders more like meta-reviewers in the traditional academic peer review process. Graders still assign the ultimate grade on every

[1] In its second year, the program has nearly 3000 students, making it the largest graduate program on campus [8], but much smaller than many MOOCs [13]. The program also hires TAs at a rate proportional to student enrollment.

[2] Participants in the OMSCS program must apply and be accepted to Georgia Tech.

assignment, but the feedback written by graders is informed by the feedback students received during peer review. We hypothesized that graders, now acting as meta-reviewers, may help students focus on the most important points from the peer reviews, resolve disagreements between peer reviews, and leverage peer reviews in writing their own feedback for the student. More importantly for scale, graders may ensure all students receive adequate feedback without spending additional time on grading: they may simply confirm strong peer reviews left by some students and devote more time to providing quality feedback to students who did not receive strong peer reviews.

To investigate the effects of reframing expert grading as meta-reviewing, we set up a pair of controlled experiments as well as gathered considerable additional data. We wanted to investigate several variables potentially affected by treating graders as meta-reviewers, including the quality of written feedback graders gave to students, the efficiency of the grading process, and the ultimate grades assigned by graders. We also wanted to investigate several interesting effects present in this data, such as the overall correlation between peer-assigned and expert-assigned grades, the potential biasing effect of seeing peer-assigned grades during expert grading, and the subjective impressions of graders on changing their role to meta-reviewers.

RELATED WORK

We want to contrast peer-to-peer feedback with peer assessment. In peer-to-peer feedback, students evaluate and give feedback on one another's work, but their evaluation does not affect the recipient's grade. In peer assessment, the peer's assigned grade is actually used in the calculation of the recipient's class grade. These terms are often used interchangeably in the community, but here, we will strictly use 'peer assessment' to refer to workflows wherein peer reviewers have influence over the recipient's grade.

Peer-to-peer feedback is well-documented to have a strong positive effect on learning [4, 19, 27] in a variety of contexts, including second language learning [23], college-level writing [31], and high school computing [28]. It is sometimes assumed that the main learning that occurs during peer-to-peer feedback is from the feedback one receives from one's peers; however, the literature and our experience both tell us that one of the most significant benefits of peer-to-peer feedback is in giving feedback [20].

Peer assessment has also been researched thoroughly. Existing studies suggest that it is possible to design assessments and associated grading instructions that will lead to peer-assigned grades being as reliable as expert-assigned grades [7]; however, these studies also point out that this reliability is not guaranteed, and that there are numerous instances where peer-assigned grades are not reliable replacements for expert-assigned grades. Notably, peer-assigned grades were found to be more valid replacements for expert-assigned grades in science and engineering and in more advanced courses [6]. Specifically applicable to the scale of this program, research has been generally positive on peer grading in MOOCs [21], and significant efforts have been devoted to increasing the reliability of peer grading specifically for this purpose [18, 25, 30], including through machine learning [24].

Whether or not the grades generated by peers are reliably similar to grades generated by experts is only one factor worth considering, however. Student perception is also an important factor. A recent study indicated that reliance on peer grading is one of the top drivers of high MOOC dropout rates [22]. This problem may be addressed by reintroducing some expert grading where possible.

BACKGROUND

This experiment took place in the Summer 2015 CS7637: Knowledge-Based Artificial Intelligence course [9, 10, 11] at Georgia Tech as part of the Georgia Tech's OMSCS program. 400 students enrolled in the 12-week summer offering of the course; 370 remained through the end of the initial drop/add week, and 280 completed the class.

The Course

CS7637 is a graduate-level course on the cognitive systems side of artificial intelligence. It is broken up into units on knowledge structures, learning, and reasoning, including analogical reasoning, metacognitive reasoning, and case-based reasoning. Originally offered in the OMSCS program in Fall 2014, it has become one of the program's highest-rated courses, earning its instructor and teaching assistant institute awards for the Fall 2014 offering.

In Summer 2015, CS7637 was offered as a 12-week course. As an online course, students do not attend synchronous lectures. Instead, lecture videos were produced and provided in partnership with Udacity. All videos were provided at the start of the course, along with a calendar of recommended viewing dates. Links to all course videos [9] and Summer 2015 course materials [14] are available in the references.

In addition to the pre-produced lecture videos, students participated in class discussions on a Piazza online forum [26]. Students were responsible for ~8500 contributions to the class Piazza forum, including proposing over ~750 discussions on their own, suggesting an active student community. For their work in the course, students completed three assignments, three projects, an unproctored final exam, and roughly 30 peer reviews.

The Assignments

Two types of written assignment were required in CS7637 in Summer 2015: written assignments [15] and project reflections [16]. Links to the descriptions of these assignments given to students are in the references section. Briefly, the written assignments all asked students to write ~1000 words applying certain course concepts to specific real-world problems. The project reflections asked all students to write ~1500 words reflecting on the successes and failures of their project and the relationship between their agent and human cognition. Both these assignments are open-ended, and although multi-point rubrics are given to evaluate the assignments, grader subjectivity does come into play (although we conjecture that grader subjectivity is the same across all assignments). All analyses below are based on the written assignments; no experiments were conducted on the project reflections.

We assigned six written assignments, and students chose three to complete in a paired fashion (e.g. each student chose to complete either assignment 1 or assignment 2, 3 or 4, and 5 or 6). All students completed three peer reviews on *each* of the six assignments, however, and so students received an average of six reviews per written assignment they completed while giving three reviews for each assignment. All students completed all three project reflections and completed three project reflection reviews, and thus students both gave and received an average of three peer reviews on project reflections. Projects were submitted between each pair of assignments.

	Online Summer '15	On-Campus Fall '14
% over years 25 old	88%	18%
% female	14%	24%
% previously obtaining a Master's degree	29%	6%
% previously obtaining a Doctoral degree	8%	0%
% international students*	13%	68%
% working full-time	90%	5%
Predicted hours per week spent on the course	11.2 (5.6)	7.9 (4.0)
Years of programming experience	10.6 (7.4)	5.3 (2.9)

Table 1. Demographic differences between online students in the Summer 2015 class and on-campus students in the Fall 2014 class.

Student Demographics

The nature of the online Master's program dictates that the student body of the class was significantly different from that of traditional on-campus programs [17]. Table 1 above compares the demographics of the Summer 2015 course with the Fall 2014 on-campus offering of the same course. Statistics marked with an asterisk were not collected per-course, and instead are derived from official Georgia Tech statistics [8] or other sources. Numbers in parentheses are standard deviations where appropriate.

As shown, students in the online program are significantly older, more educated, and more experienced. They are also, arguably, busier: most have full-time jobs, and anecdotally, most have families. Given that this experiment is built around peer reviews written by students, these different demographics may have a significant impact on the generalizability of the results observed here.

About the Graders

During the summer 2015 semester, the class employed ten teaching assistants, nine of whom participated in the assignment grading described here. All nine graders were current OMSCS students who had received an A in the class in either Fall 2014 or Spring 2015. All of these graders had previously received Bachelor's degrees, and two had previously received Masters degrees in other fields. Six were working full-time during the summer semester while working as a teaching assistant, while three were not. Four were taking other classes in the OMSCS program while working as a teaching assistant, while five were not. Altogether, four were both working full-time and taking other classes while working as teaching assistants, exemplifying the need for efficiency in grading duties. Additionally, three had formal teaching experience, one as an adjunct instructor at the undergraduate level, one as a teaching assistant and music teacher, and one as an undergraduate teaching assistant. Two also had prior experience with teaching online, one within a university and one through Coursera.

PEER FEEDBACK

To support this experiment in having graders act as meta-reviewers, we used a tool developed at Georgia Tech called Peer Feedback. Peer Feedback was originally developed to support peer-to-peer reviews in online and on-campus classes. Students enroll in a class section on Peer Feedback and can then either submit assignments directly through the tool or have their assignments ported over from a learning management system (in our case, Sakai [29]). After the assignment deadline passes, the teaching team runs the pairing process, where each student in the class is randomly assigned three classmates to review. These pairings are not bidirectional: students are not necessarily evaluated by the same classmates that they evaluate. Peer review is also not anonymous: feedback authors and recipients knew one another's identities to emphasize collaboration and discussion rather than numeric scores. In fact, one of the most common requests of students is the ability to more easily continue the conversation with their peer reviewers. Note that this structure differs from the "on-demand" pairing used by many online courses, where a student is assigned a classmate to review when they begin the peer review process (e.g. [21]).

In addition to the peer review function that gives Peer Feedback its name, the tool also comes equipped with a grading workflow. In the grading workflow, graders can be added to the class, and are assigned assignments to grade just as peers arc assigned peers to evaluate. Graders in the workflow grade on the same rubric as peers. When available and enabled, graders can also view the peer reviews that a student received while grading that student's assignment.

Peer Reviewing

Participation in peer review accounted for 15% of each student's grade. A 'peer review' comprises two pieces: scores on a scale of 0 to 5 in each of seven (for project reflections) or eight (for written assignments) rubric categories and written feedback. Peers and graders evaluate projects according to the same rubrics; for the remainder of this paper, we will discuss only the total scores assigned by peers and graders, not the individual rubric scores.

For the Summer 2015 section of CS7637, students were informed that they would be graded in part on the quality of the written feedback they provided in their peer reviews. Students were not given explicit instruction on how to write good peer reviews, but were provided with exemplars of high-quality peer reviews from past sections of the class. Anecdotally, noting that reviews would be judged for their quality in addition to their completion led to a significant uptick in review quality. A simple indicator of this is the increased average length of peer reviews, from a couple dozen words in past semesters to roughly 100 words in Summer 2015.

All assignments in the course were due on Sunday night; on Monday mornings, students received pairings for their peer reviews. Peer reviews were due by seven days following the original assignment due date. Peer reviews were made available to students the moment they were received from peer reviewers. After receiving a peer review, the recipient had the option of leaving 'meta-feedback' evaluating the feedback they received on a scale of 1 to 7, with 1 meaning the least helpful and 7 meaning the most helpful; individual labels were not attached to each number to avoid challenges with numerical analysis on otherwise ordinal data, although such challenges may still persist. Students could also leave written commentary. These ratings and commentary were only seen by the teaching team. Leaving meta-feedback was strictly voluntary, although students were encouraged to do so several times throughout the semester. Students were also informed of the way in which meta-feedback ratings would be used in order to encourage further participation. Although students providing meta-feedback may not be representative of the class as a whole, we do not anticipate a systematic bias toward one condition or the other unique to those students providing meta-feedback. In this paper, 'meta-feedback score' refers to the numeric component of meta-feedback.

Expert Grading

After the due date for peer reviews (that is, seven days after the original submission deadline), grading began. This delay was to allow the graders to have access to peer reviews when grading. At the beginning of the semester, graders underwent a training exercise where all graders independently evaluated assignments from previous sections and discussed their disagreements. During actual grading with peer reviews, graders were asked to read the peer review feedback students had received when considering their own review. Graders were given some basic suggestions on how peer reviews might help them compose their own feedback: they might emphasize strong feedback that was received in the peer reviews, help resolve conflicts or disagreements among peer reviews, and leverage peer review comments in the feedback that they themselves provided for the student. This last dynamic represents some strong potential for scaling assessment to larger classrooms: by opening the possibility for graders to 'crowd-source' written feedback and simply pick feedback from the available strong reviews, they can grade more quickly and focus more time on those students that did not receive quality peer reviews [2]. Importantly, graders were explicitly told they should not automatically agree with peer review feedback or scores.

Graders were given seven days to finish grading their allotted assignments. At the conclusion of the grading process, a simple normalizing function was applied to smooth inter-grader differences in assigned scores, and then grades were released, two weeks after the original assignment deadlines. As with peer review, students had the opportunity to leave meta-feedback for the TAs evaluating them. This meta-feedback was seen only by the course instructor. Students were encouraged to participate in meta-feedback, but were not required to do so.

EXPERIMENTAL DESIGN

The experimental design merged design-based research [1] and controlled experimentation. Each pair of assignments was treated as an individual controlled experiment investigating a particular treatment and its impact on notable dependent variables. The data from each experiment were then analyzed, and the results informed the structure and questions for the next experiment. The calendar of deliverables allowed a week for analysis of the previous week's experiments while project reflections were graded. No experiments were performed on project reflection grading.

The primary function of these experiments was to improve the class itself; we wanted to know whether treating grading as a process of meta-reviewing benefited students and/or improved grading efficiency. To ensure fairness during this semester, grades were normalized within each assignment and within, rather than across, treatments (although later analysis proved this was largely unnecessary). We also asked students to consent to user research as part of their participation in the class; only those students who consented to participate in this research are included in the data for this analysis. This was a large majority of the class.

Experiment 1

The first experiment asked the most fundamental question of the study: does equipping graders with peer reviews improve the grading process without compromising the integrity of the assigned grades?

Experiment 1 Design

To investigate this question, we conducted a controlled experiment. Each assignment was randomly assigned to either the control or experimental condition. In the control condition, graders evaluated assignments the way they have done in past semesters, without peer reviews. In the experimental condition, graders had access to peer reviews while evaluating assignments. Thus, the independent variable was access to peer reviews during grading. Three dependent variables were examined: time spent grading each assignment, grade assigned to each assignment, and meta-feedback score received based on each assignment.

Experiment 1 spanned two assignments, Assignment 1 and Assignment 2. In Assignment 1, all graders were assigned roughly 18 assignments to grade. Half the graders were randomly assigned to grade their 'control' assignments first, and half were assigned to grade their 'experimental' assignments first. In Assignment 2, all graders were assigned roughly 23 assignments to grade, and all were assigned to switch the order of evaluation (control first or experimental first) compared to Assignment 1. Thus, each grader graded 41 assignments between Assignment 1 and Assignment 2, with approximately an equal number in the control and experimental conditions while alternating which batch of assignments was graded first to correct for ordering effects. 343 total assignments were graded for Experiment 1, with one more experimental assignment than control assignment.

Experiment 1 Results

Experiment 1 revealed that having access to peer reviews during the grading process had no statistically significant effect on the grades that graders assigned and no consistent effect on the time graders spent grading each assignment. However, access to peer review did lead to a statistically significant increase in the meta-feedback score assigned by students to the graders.

Of the 343 assignments graded for Experiment 1, 90 received meta-feedback (26%); 42 control assignments and 48 experimental assignments received meta-feedback. The average meta-feedback score across all assignments was 5.84 (σ = 1.38). The average meta-feedback score for control assignments was 5.43 / 7.00 ($\sigma = 1.80$, $n = 42$), and the average meta-feedback score for experimental assignments was 6.21 / 7.00 ($\sigma = 0.74$). Testing for the difference of these means gives $t = 2.75$ ($p < 0.01$), demonstrating that assignments graded after seeing peer reviews received a statistically significantly higher average meta-feedback score than assignments graded without seeing peer reviews. The 95% confidence interval for the difference in meta-feedback score between the control and experimental conditions is 0.20 to 1.36. Described differently, students rated the feedback they received from graders as 11.1% better when the grader had access to peer reviews, with a 95% confidence interval of 3% to 19%.

The second dependent variable we investigated was grading efficiency. Of the nine graders, seven graded their assignments in such a way that we were able to glean reliable statistics from Peer Feedback about how long they spent grading their assignments. The graders varied significantly in the difference in the amount of time spent grading control and experimental assignments; three graders spent more time on average on control assignments, while four graders spent more time on average on experimental assignments. A *t*-test comparing the average time spent per assignment per grader found no statistically significant difference ($t = 0.88$, $p > 0.10$) in the amount of time a grader spent on assignments in one condition over the other.

The third dependent variable we investigated was grades assigned. We wanted to ensure that having access to peer reviews during grading did not systematically bias graders in favor of or against the students' work. Analysis found that assignments in the control group received an average grade (out of 40) of 28.81 ($\sigma = 6.63$), while assignments in the experimental group received an average grade of 28.38 ($\sigma = 5.74$). A *t*-test comparing these means showed $t = 0.6517$ ($p > 0.10$), providing no evidence to support the idea that assignments graded after seeing their peer reviews received systematically higher or lower grades.

In regards to these last two, it is important to note that absence of evidence is not evidence of absence; these analyses are not sufficient to prove that grading time or average grades assigned remain equal when equipped with peer review; proving equality would require different analysis. However, these tests do fail to find evidence to support the hypothesis that access to peer review during grading influences grading efficiency or average grades assigned.

An additional possible criticism of this analysis is that it tests only whether access to peer review makes graders more generous or strict on average, not whether access makes them converge onto the peer-assigned grades. This suggestion is examined further under Further Investigation.

Experiment 2

Due to the perceived positive effect of having graders act as meta-reviewers over peer reviews, we decided all assignments for the remainder of the semester would be conducted in this fashion to maximize student learning. Although we observed no statistically significant difference in the grades assigned to assignments in the control and experimental conditions, students expressed concern that seeing the rubric results from peer reviews would influence the grader's opinion of the paper. So, in Experiment 2, we decided to ask: does equipping graders with only the text of peer reviews preserve the benefits seen previously while removing a perceived source of grader bias?

Experiment 2 Design

To investigate this question, we conducted another controlled experiment. Each assignment was randomly assigned to either the control or experimental condition, without concern for the condition to which the corresponding student's assignment was assigned in Experiment 1. In the control condition, graders evaluated assignments the way they had in the experimental condition in the previous experiment, with access to both written peer reviews and peer-assigned rubric scores. In the experimental condition, the peer-assigned grades were hidden, and graders could only see the written feedback. Thus, the independent variable in Experiment 2 was access to the peer-assigned rubric scores. Two dependent variables were examined: grade assigned to each assignment and meta-feedback score received based on each assignment. Time spent grading each assignment was not examined in order to allow the graders to use more natural workflows (such as previewing all assignments before beginning to grade) rather than grade each assignment in one sitting.

Like Experiment 1, Experiment 2 spanned two assignments, Assignment 3 and Assignment 4. In Assignment 3, all graders were assigned roughly 12 assignments to grade. Half the graders were randomly assigned to grade their 'control' assignments first, and half were assigned to grade their 'experimental' assignments first. In Assignment 4, all graders were assigned roughly 21 assignments to grade, and all were assigned to switch the order of evaluation (control first or experimental first) compared to Assignment 3. Thus, each grader graded 33 assignments between Assignment 3 and Assignment 4, with approximately an equal number in the control and experimental conditions while alternating which batch of assignments was graded first to correct for ordering effects. Fewer submissions were observed in assignments 3 and 4 together due to class withdrawals. 296 total assignments were graded in assignments 3 and 4, with an equal number of assignments in each condition.

Experiment 2 Results

Experiment 2 found no evidence to support the hypothesis that access to peer-assigned grades affects the meta-feedback scores received or the grades assigned by graders compared to access to the textual peer reviews without the peer-assigned grades.

We first examined meta-feedback scores between the control and experimental groups. 87 students left meta-feedback on the grades and written feedback they received from graders. Feedback on assignments graded in the control group (with peer-assigned grades and written comments) received an average meta-feedback score of 5.60 / 7.00 ($\sigma = 1.47$; $n = 47$). Feedback on assignments graded in the experimental group (with peer review written comments, but without peer-assigned grades) received an average meta-feedback score of 5.95 / 7.00 ($\sigma = 1.45$; $n = 40$). A t-test comparing these gave $t = 1.128$ ($p > 0.10$), providing no evidence for the hypothesis that access to full peer reviews would affect meta-feedback scores compared to access to written comments only.

We then examined the grades assigned by graders to assignments in Experiment 2. Assignments graded in the control group received an average grade (out of 40) of 28.98 ($\sigma = 6.40$; $n = 148$). Assignments graded in the experimental group received an average grade of 29.32 ($\sigma = 6.88$; $n = 148$). A t-test comparing these gave $t = 0.4461$ ($p > 0.10$), providing no evidence for the hypothesis that access to full peer reviews systematically affected grades assigned to those assignments compared to grades assigned to papers graded without seeing the peer-assigned grades.

As with Experiment 1, the structure of this experiment is insufficient to categorically prove that access to rubrics has no effect on meta-feedback or assigned grades compared to grading without rubrics. However, this investigation gives no support for the hypothesis such a relationship exists.

Grading Workflow Evaluation

Experiments 1 and 2 found that having graders operate as meta-reviewers over peer-assigned reviews had a statistically significant positive effect on the quality of reviews students received as assessed by the assigned meta-feedback ratings, while not influencing the time spent grading assignments or the grades ultimately assigned by graders. Discussion of the results of these experiments revealed, however, that a possible notable factor of the grading process was the different workflows in which each grader graded. Thus, during grading of the final two assignments, we developed a typology of the grading workflows in which graders engaged. This followed a qualitative research design. Graders for this experiment were instructed to carefully document their grading process, including each time they opened an assignment, reviewed an assignment, read a peer review, issued a grade, and revised a grade. These nine accounts of the grading process were gathered and summarized.

Typology of Grading Workflows

Analysis of the self-reported grading processes revealed considerable overlap, but also notable differences. All graders reported beginning the grading process by first reviewing the recorded lectures for the topics covered by that assignment, as well as the directions for the assignment itself. From there, the workflow split: seven graders began grading, while two graders first took a cursory look over all their assignments to set their overall expectations before returning to the first assignment and beginning to grade. Each grader then reported participating in a roughly similar process for each individual assignment: they initially read over the peer reviews, then the paper itself. All graders reported writing comments and composing their rubric scores while reading the paper. At the conclusion, the workflow branched again: five graders reported a phase at the end of revisiting their earlier grades (or leaving open the option to do so) to modify them as necessary if their attitudes changed based on grading the subsequent essays.

Thus, two of the nine graders previewed all assignments initially; five of the nine graders left room to return and revise their grades at the conclusion of grading; and two graders graded each assignment in order with no previewing or revisiting. Interestingly, however, all graders participated in generally the same process of reviewing each assignment's peer reviews before reading and grading the assignment.

There are two main takeaways of this evaluation. First, that some element of internal normalization happened within the majority of graders: seven of nine graders built in the ability to revise their grades based on their experience grading other assignments. Second, the location of peer reviews in the evaluation workflow was consistent across all graders, even without explicit instructions. All graders reviewed peer reviews prior to the student's assignment, rather than reading and grading the assignment prior to reading the peer reviews.

FURTHER INVESTIGATION

The previous experiments addressed the core question of this research: these experiments suggest that equipping graders with peer reviews during the expert grading process improves the quality of feedback students receive without affecting the average grades assigned or the average time spent grading. However, none of these experiments addressed the possible connection between peer and expert grades. If, for example, peer grades were found to be highly correlated with expert grades, an argument could be made (as has been made in the past [6, 7, 21]) that peer grades could supplant expert grades as a reliable grading mechanism. There would also be arguments that our analysis above was not sufficient to rule out a biasing effect of exposure to peer review results, as well as that meta-feedback is not a useful metric as they are likely to be more positive in response to positive grades and negative in response to negative grades.

Expert Grades vs. Peer Grades

Initially, we wanted to determine if peer grades were good predictors of expert grades. During the semester, 1751 submissions received a combined total of 7287 peer reviews. A scatterplot showing the plot of expert grades (y) as a function of average peer review grades (x) is in Figure 1. Linear regression revealed an R^2 value of 0.3769, with a regression equation of $y = 0.8235x + 6.936$. This R^2 value suggests a moderately strong relationship, but one that leaves too many outliers on either side to support using peer grading in lieu of expert grading. A follow-up analysis calculating coefficients of determination solely within written assignments and project reflections found similar results; for written assignments alone ($n = 907$), $R^2 = 0.2836$ ($y = 0.8399x + 6.602$), and for project reflections alone ($n = 844$), $R^2 = 0.4608$ ($y = 0.7972x + 7.465$).

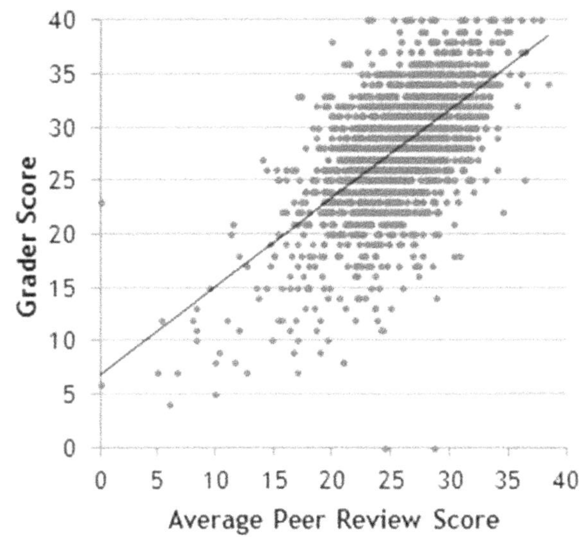

Figure 1: Average grader-assigned scores plotted against average peer review scores (n = 1751). The maximum grade was 40 points.

Bias Effects of Peer Reviews

The structures of Experiment 1 and Experiment 2 are not sufficient to completely rule out the hypothesis that access to peer review during grading biases graders to agree with the peer reviews. These analyses are only performed on the average grades assigned on all assignments. If biases existed in both directions within the experimental groups, they may cancel each other out, leading to no average difference in assigned scores despite the presence of differences in grades assigned to individual assignments.

To examine this, the above investigation comparing expert and peer grades was extended to compare the control and experimental groups within each experiment. If access to the peer-assigned rubric scores biases graders to agree with the peer reviews, we would expect to see a greater correlation between peer- and expert-assigned grades in the experimental group from Experiment 1 and the control group in Experiment 2 (that is, the two treatments where graders had access to peer-assigned rubric scores). We may also expect to see greater correlation in the control experimental group in Experiment 2, where although graders did not see rubric scores, they nonetheless saw written feedback that likely indicates the reviewer's attitude.

Table 2, below, provides the coefficients of determination (R^2) between average peer grades and expert grades within each experiment and condition.

These data suggest that a small biasing effect does exist when expert graders have access to the rubric scores assigned by peers during peer review. The highest coefficients of determination were seen for those groups of assignments that were graded with access to the rubric scores assigned during peer review. The effect of this bias was relatively small. The overall coefficient of determination between peer grades and expert grades when peer-assigned grades were visible during expert grading was 0.3203 (that is, putting together all treatments where peer-assigned grades were visible), indicating that access to peer-assigned grades during expert grading raised the coefficient of determination between peer-assigned grades and expert grades by 0.06 in these experiments compared to grading with no peer reviews available. This represents an average difference of roughly a point on these assignments. A higher coefficient of determination between peer-assigned grades and expert grades was observed for project reflections ($R^2 = 0.4608$); we speculate, however, this is due to project reflection grades being higher and less varied overall. Most notably, this effect disappeared when peer-assigned grades were hidden during expert grading, while in Experiment 2, meta-feedback scores did not decrease when peer-assigned grades were hidden. Therefore, the maximum possible benefit can be observed by equipping expert graders with written peer reviews, but hiding peer-assigned grades; this removed the bias of seeing peer-assigned grades while preserving the higher feedback quality associated with meta-reviewing as assessed by meta-feedback scores.

	Coefficients of Determination (R^2)	n
Experiment 1, Control Condition	0.2616	171
Experiment 1, Experimental Condition	0.3264	172
Experiment 2, Control Condition	0.3412	148
Experiment 2, Experimental Condition	0.2028	148

Table 2. Coefficients of determination between peer-assigned graders and expert grades within each experimental condition. A small increase in correlation is seen in those conditions where graders could see the rubric scores assigned during peer review.

Expert Grades vs. Meta-feedback

During our analysis, we speculated that there may also be an interaction between the grades assigned by graders and the meta-feedback scores returned by students. Specifically, we conjectured that students may be more likely to give higher meta-feedback scores when they received good grades, and lower meta-feedback scores when they received bad grades. To look for this effect, we performed a linear regression between expert-assigned grades and meta-feedback scores. Because written assignments and project reflections were graded on different scales, we performed these two analyses separately. For written assignments, we found $R^2 = 0.0923$ ($n = 241$); for project reflections we found $R^2 = 0.0187$ ($n = 190$). Thus, we determined there was no correlation between expert-assigned grades and meta-feedback.

Grader Impressions

Separate from the effect of access to peer review during grading on assigned grades, grading efficiency, and meta-feedback scores, we were also interested most subjectively in how the graders perceived access to peer reviews to affect their grading process. At the conclusion of Experiment 1, we conducted a short survey of the graders who had graded assignments 1 and 2 alternating between seeing and not seeing peer reviews during grading. Eight of the nine graders completed this survey. Based on this survey, graders reported that access to peer review was useful, but that it did not make their jobs easier; rather, they felt it was useful in improving the quality of their feedback. This corresponds to the opinion given by students through the meta-feedback ratings. The data and survey responses agree that access to peer review did not improve grader speed or efficiency, but it did improve the quality of feedback that students receive.

OPEN ISSUES

A few open issues remain that affect the generalizability of the conclusions observed in these analyses. First, as mentioned originally, the student body in this class is significantly different from the student body even in typical graduate-level classes, let alone undergraduate or K-12 classes [17]. These students are older, more professionally experienced, more educated, and more dedicated (based on how many hours they predicted they would spend on the course) than typical Masters students. We conjecture that this leads to improved peer review quality. Fortunately for this class, this would improve the amount of learning students receive from the peer review process, but it also means the usefulness of peer reviews may not extend to other classes and programs. Research applying these principles to other student bodies would be necessary to ensure this generalization.

Second, just as the student body in this study was rather unique, so also the graders were unique – all graders in this study were themselves students in the OMSCS program. All nine graders involved in this study demonstrated a significantly higher level of commitment to improving the class than graders the instructor had seen in past sections. Less-dedicated graders may react differently to access to peer reviews during grading. We have two hypotheses in this area. First, we hypothesize that less-committed graders would experience the benefits of access to peer review in their efficiency rather than their review quality. Second, we hypothesize that the commitment of the graders in this experiment led to a higher baseline for meta-feedback scores, and that less-committed teams of graders may actually experience greater relative benefit due to a lower baseline. In other words, the quality of graders in this experiment left relatively little room for improvement based on access to peer reviews; other teams may have more room for improvement. Additional research would be necessary as well to identify whether the effects seen here are universal to all graders or are a function in part of the unique qualifications and dedication of the graders participating here.

Third, as noted, access to peer reviews was shown to have a small biasing effect on the grades awarded by graders. This biasing effect should be resolved by hiding peer-assigned grades during expert grading. However, given that peer-assigned grades ought to be hidden during expert grading, should peers assign grades at all? Should peers instead focus only on providing written reviews instead of rubric scores? Research has already suggested that expert grades can undermine intrinsic motivation [5] and diminish the receipt of written feedback [3], and so focusing peer review on written reviews rather than peer-assigned grades could improve the learning that results from peer review while still allowing graders to act as meta-reviewers.

Last, this solution to scaling feedback while preserving expert evaluation assumes that a program like Georgia Tech's OMSCS cannot use peer assessment while maintaining its rigor and reputation. This assumption may not be accurate; after all, if peer-assigned grades *are* perfectly reliable duplicates of expert-assigned grades, then peer assessment is effectively as good as expert assessment. Research indicates this may be possible [6, 7], but considerable attention must be paid to designing assessments and accompanying grading workflows whose grades will retain their reliability when evaluated by peers. In this study, for instance, while peer and expert grades were somewhat correlated, the correlation was not sufficient to replace expert grades with peer grades. Machine learning may provide a mechanism to realize this, however, by seeding peer assessment activities with assignments with known expert evaluations, and using peers' assessments of those assignments to evaluate their individual reliability as graders overall. This method would also build a consistent account for why individual peer assessment grades are reliable, rather than relying simply on prior data indicating the reliability of peer assessment.

CONCLUSIONS

This study examines the benefits and drawbacks of structuring assignment grading as a process of meta-reviewing in an online graduate-level class. In traditional grading, graders see only the paper itself when evaluating and writing feedback. In a meta-review, a meta-reviewer sees the original submission as well as a collection of peer reviews. The meta-reviewer's feedback, then, is informed by the feedback written during peer review. The meta-reviewer can acknowledge important pieces of feedback the student has received, resolve disagreements amongst the peer reviews, and ensure that all students receive good feedback by focusing more time on those students who did not receive useful feedback during peer review.

Our experiments and analyses identified a notable benefit, a potential drawback, and an important recommendation for treating grading as meta-review. First, treating graders as meta-reviewers led to better feedback, as evaluated by the students. Students rated the feedback from graders acting as meta-reviewers as 11% better than feedback from graders grading more traditionally. There was no observed decrease in graders' efficiency nor any overall biasing effect on grades due to meta-reviewing. However, a small biasing effect was observed on individual assignments: there was a slightly greater correlation between peer-assigned grades and expert grades when expert graders could see the peer-assigned grades while grading. This small biasing effect disappeared while the higher meta-feedback ratings remained when peer-assigned grades were hidden but written peer reviews remained available to graders.

Therefore, this work concludes that treating grading as meta-reviewing has significant potential to help large programs scale by improving the quality of feedback students receive without compromising the efficiency of the grading process. Additional research would be necessary to ensure that the same effects observed here are observed at different levels of education and with different levels of commitment from graders. In future work, we will evaluate how to distribute the benefits of this approach across the target outcomes. While improving feedback quality without decreasing efficiency is a good outcome, it will be useful – especially as courses and programs scale up – to create improvements to efficiency as well. Specifically, we will examine whether or not different teams of graders, different guidelines in grading, or different evaluation workflows increase efficiency while preserving review quality.

ACKNOWLEDGMENTS

We are extraordinarily grateful to Joe Gonzales for developing the Peer Feedback tool and equipping it with the features necessary to perform this work. We are also grateful to Bryan Wiltgen, another teaching assistant during the class that did not participate in this grading, for his support. We are also grateful to the innumerable people at the Georgia Tech College of Computing, Udacity, Georgia Tech Professional Education, and AT&T for their support of this class and this program.

REFERENCES

1. Barab, S., & Squire, K. (2004). Design-based research: Putting a stake in the ground. *Journal of the Learning Sciences*, *13*(1), 1-14.
2. Basu, S., Jacobs, C., & Vanderwende, L. (2013). Powergrading: a clustering approach to amplify human effort for short answer grading. *Transactions of the Association for Computational Linguistics*, *1*, 391-402.
3. Black, P., Harrison, C., Lee, C., Marshall, B., & Wiliam, D. (2004). Working Inside the Black Box: Assessment for Learning in the Classroom. *Phi Delta Kappan*, *86*(1), 8-21.

4. Boud, D., Cohen, R., & Sampson, J. (2001). *Peer Learning in Higher Education: Learning from & with Each Other*. Psychology Press.
5. Butler, R. (1988). Enhancing and undermining intrinsic motivation: The effects of task-involving and ego-involving evaluation on interest and performance. *British Journal of Educational Psychology*, *58*(1), 1-14.
6. Falchikov, N., & Boud, D. (1989). Student self-assessment in higher education: A meta-analysis. *Review of Educational Research*, *59*(4), 395-430.
7. Falchikov, N., & Goldfinch, J. (2000). Student peer assessment in higher education: A meta-analysis comparing peer and teacher marks. *Review of Educational Research*, *70*(3), 287-322.
8. Georgia Tech Fact Book. (2014). Graduate Enrollment by College, Ethnicity, & Gender [Web Site]. Retrieved from http://factbook.gatech.edu/admissions-and-enrollment/graduate-enrollment-by-college-ethnicity-gender-table-4-15/
9. Goel, A. & Joyner, D. (2014). CS7637: Knowledge-Based AI: Cognitive Systems [Online Course]. Retrieved from https://www.udacity.com/course/ud409
10. Goel, A. & Joyner, D. (2014). Putting Online learning and Learning Sciences Together [Video]. Presented to the Georgia Tech GVU Brown Bag. Retrieved from https://www.youtube.com/watch?v=N56ghCGmWWQ
11. Goel, A., & Joyner, D. (2016). An Experiment in Teaching Artificial Intelligence Online. In D Haynes (Ed.) *International Journal for the Scholarship of Technology-Enhanced Learning(1)* 1.
12. Grimmelmann, J. (2014). The Merchants of MOOCs. *Seton Hall L. Rev.*, *44*, i.
13. Hu, H. (2013). MOOC migration. *Diverse Issues in Higher Education*, *30*(4), 10.
14. Joyner, D. (2015). CS7637: Knowledge-Based AI Summer 2015 Class Documents [Google Folder]. Retrieved from http://bit.ly/1PRZTCb
15. Joyner, D. (2015). CS7637: Assignment 6 (Summer 2015) [Google Document]. Retrieved from http://bit.ly/1XAkdtb
16. Joyner, D. (2015). CS7637: Project 1 (Summer 2015) [Google Document]. Retrieved from http://bit.ly/1jSOyF6
17. Joyner, D. (2015). The Impact of the Students in the Georgia Tech OMSCS [Video]. Presentation given to the GVU Center Brown Bag Seminar series. Retrieved from https://youtu.be/2u2dQOVyen4
18. Kotturi, Y., Kulkarni, C., Bernstein, M. S., & Klemmer, S. (2015). Structure and messaging techniques for online peer learning systems that increase stickiness. In *Proceedings of the Second ACM Conference on Learning @ Scale.* ACM. 31-38.
19. Kulkarni, C., Bernstein, M. S., & Klemmer, S. (2015). PeerStudio: Rapid Peer Feedback Emphasizes Revision and Improves Performance. In *Proceedings from The Second ACM Conference on Learning @ Scale.* ACM. 75-84.
20. Li, L., Liu, X., & Steckelberg, A. L. (2010). Assessor or assessee: How student learning improves by giving and receiving peer feedback. *British Journal of Educational Technology*, *41*(3), 525-536.
21. Lu, J., & Law, N. (2012). Online peer assessment: effects of cognitive and affective feedback. *Instructional Science*, *40*(2), 257-275.
22. Onah, D. F., Sinclair, J., & Boyatt, R. (2014). Dropout rates of massive open online courses: behavioural patterns. *EDULEARN14 Proceedings*, 5825-5834.
23. Paulus, T. M. (1999). The effect of peer and teacher feedback on student writing. *Journal of Second Language Writing*, *8*(3), 265-289.
24. Piech, C., Huang, J., Chen, Z., Do, C., Ng, A., & Koller, D. (2013, July). Tuned Models of Peer Assessment in MOOCs. In *Proceedings of the 6th International Conference on Educational Data Mining*. Memphis, Tennessee.
25. Raman, K., & Joachims, T. (2015). Bayesian Ordinal Peer Grading. In *Proceedings from The Second ACM Conference on Learning @ Scale.* ACM. 149-156.
26. Sankar, P. (2013). Piazza: Our Story [Web Site]. Retrieved from https://piazza.com/about/story
27. Topping, K. (1998). Peer assessment between students in colleges and universities. *Review of Educational Research*, *68*(3), 249-276.
28. Tseng, S. C., & Tsai, C. C. (2007). On-line peer assessment and the role of the peer feedback: A study of high school computer course. *Computers & Education*, *49*(4), 1161-1174.
29. The Sakai Project. (2014). Sakai 10. Retrieved from https://sakaiproject.org/sakai-10
30. Waters, A. E., Tinapple, D., & Baraniuk, R. G. (2015). BayesRank: A Bayesian Approach to Ranked Peer Grading. In *Proceedings of the Second ACM Conference on Learning @ Scale.* ACM. 177-183.
31. Xie, Y., Ke, F., & Sharma, P. (2008). The effect of peer feedback for blogging on college students' reflective learning processes. *The Internet and Higher Education*, *11*(1), 18-25.

Learning Transfer: does it take place in MOOCs?
An Investigation into the Uptake of Functional Programming in Practice

Guanliang Chen*, Dan Davis†, Claudia Hauff and Geert-Jan Houben
Delft University of Technology
Delft, the Netherlands
{guanliang.chen, d.j.davis, c.hauff, g.j.p.m.houben}@tudelft.nl

ABSTRACT
The rising number of Massive Open Online Courses (MOOCs) enable people to advance their knowledge and competencies in a wide range of fields. *Learning* though is only the first step, the *transfer* of the taught concepts into practice is equally important and often neglected in the investigation of MOOCs. In this paper, we consider the specific case of `FP101x` (a functional programming MOOC on edX) and the extent to which learners alter their programming behaviour after having taken the course. We are able to link about one third of all `FP101x` learners to `GitHub`, the most popular social coding platform to date and contribute a first exploratory analysis of learner behaviour beyond the MOOC platform. A detailed longitudinal analysis of `GitHub` log traces reveals that (i) more than 8% of engaged learners transfer, and that (ii) most existing transfer learning findings from the classroom setting are indeed applicable in the MOOC setting as well.

INTRODUCTION
The rising number of MOOCs enable people to learn & advance their knowledge and competencies in a wide range of fields. *Learning*, though, is only the first step; the *application* of the taught concepts is equally important, as knowledge that is learned but not frequently applied or activated is quickly unlearned [28, 6, 25].

Existing investigations into student learning *within* MOOC environments are commonly based on pre- & post-course surveys and log traces generated within those environments by the individual learners [15]. While student learning is indeed an important measure of success, we argue that another key measure is the amount of **learning transfer** [17] that is taking place: do learners actually utilize the newly gained knowledge in practice? Are learners expanding their knowledge in the area over time or do they eventually move back to their pre-course knowledge levels and behaviours? These are important questions to address in the learning sciences, and their answers will enable us to shape the MOOCs of the future based on empirical evidence.

The main challenge researchers face in answering these questions is the lack of *accessible*, *large-scale*, *relevant* and *longitudinal* data traces outside of MOOC environments. While learners can be uniquely identified within a MOOC platform, at this point in time we have no general manner of capturing their behavioural traces outside of these boundaries.

Not all is lost though. Social Web platforms (Twitter being the prime example) have become a mainstay of the Web. They are used by hundreds of millions of users around the world and often provide open access to some — if not all — of the data generated within them. While most of these platforms are geared towards people's private lives, in the past few years social Web platforms have also begun to enter our professional lives.

One such work-related social Web platform is `GitHub`[1]; it is one of the most popular *social coding* platforms worldwide with more than 10 million registered users. Hobbyists and professional programmers alike use `GitHub` to collaborate on programming projects, host their source code, and organize their programming activities. As `GitHub` was founded in 2007, we have potential access to log traces reaching several years into the past; moreover, its continuously increasing popularity will enable us to observe our learners over years to come. The potential of `GitHub` for behavioural mining has long been recognized by the software engineering research community where `GitHub` is one of the most popular data sources to investigate how (groups of) people code.

Thus, for MOOCs with a strong focus on programming concepts, we consider `GitHub` to be one of the most detailed and openly accessible sources of learners' relevant behavioral traces outside of the MOOC environment itself. Concretely, we analyze `FP101x`[2], an edX MOOC covering basic functional programming concepts. Of the 37,485 learners that registered for `FP101x` we matched

*The author's research is supported by the *Extension School* of the Delft University of Technology.
†The author's research is supported by the *Leiden-Delft-Erasmus Centre for Education and Learning*.

L@S 2016, April 25–26, 2016, Edinburgh, UK.

http://dx.doi.org/10.1145/2876034.2876035

[1] `https://github.com/`
[2] `https://www.edx.org/course/introduction-functional-programming-delftx-fp101x`

12,415 (33.1%) to their respective `GitHub` accounts, enabling a first large-scale analysis of the uptake of taught programming concepts in practice.

Here, we are foremost interested in exploring to what extent the course affects learners *after it has ended*. We are guided by the following three **R**esearch **Q**uestions:

RQ1 *To what extent* does the transfer of learned concepts take place?

RQ2 What *type of learners* are most likely to make the transfer?

RQ3 How does the transfer manifest itself *over time*?

Based on these guiding questions we have formulated seven research hypotheses which build on previous research efforts in work-place and classroom learning. In contrast to our work though, in these settings, the investigations are mostly based on questionnaires and interviews instead of behavioural traces. To the best of our knowledge, learning transfer has not yet been investigated in the context of MOOCs. Gaining deeper insights about the (lack of) learning transfer in MOOCs will lead to more informed discussions on the practical purposes and benefits of MOOCs. The main contributions of our work can be summarized as follows:

- We investigate to what extent learning transfer insights gained in work-place and classroom settings hold in the MOOC context. We find that the majority of findings are also applicable in the case of MOOCs.
- We introduce the use of *external* social Web-based data sources to complement learner traces within MOOC environments as a means to capture much more information about MOOC learners.
- We introduce `GitHub` as a specific large-scale data source to mine relevant longitudinal behavioural traces about learners before, during and after a programming-oriented MOOC.

BACKGROUND

Meaningful, robust educational experiences transcend rote memorization of facts and leave the learner empowered to take on new problems and practice novel ways of thinking. In tracking student activity from the learning context (edX) to a real-world, practical one (`GitHub`) over a period of three years, the present study observes the first two of the three criteria of *robust learning* as outlined in [17]: (i) application in new situations different from the learning context, (ii) retained over the long-term, and (iii) prepares for future learning. Gaining a better understanding of how students apply what they learn in online learning environments over an extended time frame enables instructors to design future courses that induce more robust learning.

Some researchers [27, 26] have begun to look beyond traces generated in online learning environments, by utilizing post-course surveys or conducting post-course interviews with MOOC students.

Although the early studies of transfer stemmed from educational issues, the majority of recent learning transfer research literature is concerned with work-place training in Human Resource Development (HRD) [7]. With the recent influx of student activity data generated from digital learning environments, we can now empirically measure not only the rate of transfer, but other contributing factors as well. That, in tandem with the established surveying strategies used by HRD, promises to fundamentally change the way we think about measurable learning outcomes.

Learning transfer is the application of knowledge or skills gained in a learning environment to another context [2]. While training situations in professional environments have a clear target context (the job), this is not the case with most academic learning situations. Students are generally taught a broad set of skills and knowledge which they may apply in countless ways. This deliberately broad definition encapsulates both *near transfer* (to similar contexts) and *far transfer* (to dissimilar contexts) [4] and avoids the subjective question of *how* similar or different the learning context is from the target context, as we are only concerned with whether the student transferred the learned skills or knowledge beyond the learning context.

Due to their rising popularity as a professional development tool and their roots as an educational resource, MOOCs serve as an ideal source of information to gain new insights on learning transfer. Studies have begun to discuss the learners' intention to apply what they've learned in MOOCs but do not continue to track student activity beyond the learning platform [12]. The present research aims to reoperationalize [10] the understanding of learning transfer given the emerging possibilities of user modeling and learning analytics from the current standard of *reported* learning transfer towards *observed* learning transfer.

Yelon & Ford [29] offer a key distinction in transfer that differentiates *open* and *closed* skills. Open skill training programs include "leadership and interpersonal skills training," and typical closed skill trainings include "various technical training and computer software training." This emerges as an important distinction. In a study in which Blume et al. [7] found post-training knowledge (PTK) and post-training self-efficacy (PTSE) to have similar correlations with learning transfer, PTK and PTSE for closed skills resulted in lower correlation coefficients than for open skills. Independent of performance, self-efficacy is a person's self-reported ability to successfully complete a future task [3]. Knowledge is measured as a result of a task—answering a quiz question correctly indicates possession of that knowledge [7].

Regarding the maintenance and persistence of learning transfer over time, Blume et al. analyzed how the *amount of time* (the "lag") between the end of training and the beginning of the transfer study affects learning transfer. They found that in studies with at least some lag time between training and testing, learners exhibited significantly lower post-training knowledge and post-training self-efficacy than those that tested students immediately following training [7].

In their survey of training professionals from 150 organizations, [24] report that 62% of employees in their organization *"effectively apply what they learned in training"* to their job immediately, 42% after six months, and 34% after one year. Other studies directly survey students in gathering self-reported data about learning transfer [19]. Another manner by which researchers have measured transfer is through assessment questions following instruction that, in order for students to answer correctly, would have to apply what they learned to a new context or problem [20, 1]. The present study examines transfer as a more naturally occurring, un-elicited phenomenon that the learners undertake and exhibit on their own accord.

FP101X

Introduction to Functional Programming (or short `FP101x`) is a MOOC offered on the edX platform. The course introduces learners to various functional programming concepts; all programming is performed in the functional language *Haskell*.

The first iteration of the course ran between October 15, 2014 and December 31, 2014. As is common in MOOCs today, learners were invited to participate in a pre-course and a post-course survey containing questions on the motivation of the learners, the perceived quality of the course, etc. In August 2015 we approached a subset of learners for an additional post-course survey.

The course was set up as an xMOOC [23]: lecture videos were distributed throughout the 8 teaching weeks. Apart from lectures each week, exercises ("homeworks" and "labs") were distributed in the form of multiple choice (MC) questions. While homework questions evaluated learners on their understanding of high-level concepts and code snippets (e.g. *"What is the result of executing [...]?"*), labs required learners to implement programs themselves. To enable fully automatic evaluations, all lab work was also assessed through MC questions. Each of the 288 MC questions was worth 1 point & could be attempted once. Answers were due 2 weeks after the release of the assignment. To pass the course, $\geq$ 60% of all MC questions had to be answered correctly.

Overall, 37,485 users registered for the course. Fewer than half (41%) engaged with the course, watching at least one lecture video. The completion rate was 5.25%, in line with similar MOOC offerings [18]. Over 75% of the learners were male and more than 60% had at least a Bachelors degree.

METHODOLOGY

We first outline and justify the seven research hypotheses upon which we ground our work. Next, we describe in detail how to verify them empirically based on course questionnaire data, edX logs and `GitHub` data traces.

Research Hypotheses

Based on prior work we can make the following hypothesis related to **RQ1**:

H1 *Only a small fraction of engaged learners is likely to exhibit learning transfer.*
While previous works, e.g. [24], note transfer rates of up to 60%, we hypothesize our rate to be much lower, due to the natural setting we investigate, the difficulty of the topic (closed skills) and the generally low retention rate of MOOCs.

A large part of existing literature has focused on the different dimensions of a learner that may be indicative of a high or low transfer rate. Thus, the following research hypotheses are all related to **RQ2**, which focuses on the *type* of learner exhibiting transfer.

H2 *Intrinsically motivated learners with mastery goals are more likely to exhibit learning transfer than extrinsically motivated learners.*
[22] found that, in academic settings, mastery goals are more consistently linked to transfer success than performance goals. This was measured by instructors guiding students through either mastery- or performance-oriented experimental conditions and comparing their assessment scores. In line with intrinsic motivation, mastery goals are characterized by a learner's intention to understand and develop new knowledge and abilities. Performance goals, extrinsically motivated, are those sought after in order to obtain positive judgements from others [9].

H3 *Learners expressing high self-efficacy are more likely to actively apply their trained tasks in new contexts.*
In other words, in both academic and professional settings, if you believe that you are able to do something, you are more likely to try it [13, 14, 16, 22].

H4 *Experienced learners (high ability levels) are more likely to transfer trained skills and knowledge in order to maintain and improve performance levels* [13].

H5 *Learners reporting a high personal capacity (time, energy and mental space) for transfer are more likely to actually exhibit learning transfer* [16].

H6 *Learners exhibiting a high-spacing learning routine are more likely to exhibit learning transfer than learners with a low-spacing learning routine.*
Here, high-spacing refers to a larger number of discrete learning sessions than low-spacing with few learning sessions each lasting a long time (i.e. "cramming") [21, 11, 5].

Finally, for **RQ3** we investigate the following hypothesis:

H7 *The amount of exhibited transfer decreases over time* [24].

From Hypotheses To Measurements

Table 1 shows an overview of the data sources used to investigate each research hypothesis.

	Pre CS	Post CS	edX Logs	GitHub Logs
H1			✓	✓
H2	✓	✓		✓
H3		✓		✓
H4	✓			✓
H5		✓		✓
H6			✓	✓
H7				✓

Table 1. Overview of the different data sources used to investigate each research hypothesis. *CS* refers to the conducted Course Surveys (before and after the course).

To explore **H1** we relate learners' performance during the course (as found in the edX logs) to their development activities on GitHub.

To determine the impact of learners' motivation on learning transfer (**H2**), we distinguish learners based on their answers to several pre/post-course survey questions we manually established as being motivation-related. To determine *intrinsic motivation* we identified six question-answer pairs including the following two[3]:

- What describes your interest for registering for this course?; Answer: My curiosity (in the topic) was the reason for me to sign up for this course [Pre CS, 5-point Likert]
- Express your level of agreement with the following statement.; Answer: Course activities piqued my curiosity. [Post CS, 5-point Likert]

Similarly, for *extrinsic motivation* we determined nine appropriate question-answer pairs, including:

- What describes your interest for registering for this course? Choose the one that applies to you the most; Answer: My current occupation motivated me to enroll in the course. [Pre CS, 5-point Likert]
- Considering your experience in this, how much do you agree with the following statement?; Answer: The course was compulsory for me [Post CS, Multiple choice]

Learners' belief in their ability to complete a task (**H3**), can be inferred based on a question asking the learners to express their level of agreement with a set of statements from the validated General Self-Efficacy Scale [8]:

- I can describe ways to test and apply the knowledge created in this course. [Post CS, 5-point Likert]
- I have developed solutions to course problems that can be applied in practice. [Post CS, 5-point Likert]
- I can apply the knowledge created in the course to my work or other non-class related activities. [Post CS, 5 point Likert]

The prior expertise of learners (**H4**) can both be inferred from survey questions as well as from the GitHub logs. The questions utilized are:

- Is your educational background related to (Functional) Programming? [Pre CS, 5-point Likert]
- Do you have professional experience in this field? [Pre CS, 5-point Likert]

The personal capacity (**H5**) of a learner is inferred based on two questions:

- Did any of the following negatively affect your participation in the course? [Post CS, 5-point Likert]
- Considering your experience in this course, how much did each of the technical issues affect your participation? [Post CS, 5-point Likert]

Responses to these questions allow learners to share which factors inhibited and distracted them from engaging with the course. Examples of responses to these questions range from personal problems, such as family obligations and medical issues, to technical trouble, such as slow Internet or hardware problems.

H6 considers the manner in which learners learn and can be inferred solely based on edX log traces which will be explained in more detail in the section below. Finally, **H7**, the extent to which functional programming is employed and applied by the learners over time can be inferred from GitHub logs alone.

edX Logs

For each learner, we collect all available traces (between October 1 and December 31, 2014), such as the learner's clicks & views, provided answers to MC questions as well as forum interactions. Using the MOOCdb toolkit[4] we translate these low-level log traces into a data schema that is easily queryable.

To investigate **H6**, for each learner the learning routine is determined based on their edX logs. We partition the learners into low-spacing and high-spacing types following [21]. Initially, all learners are sorted in ascending order according to their total time on-site. Subsequently they are binned into ten equally-sized groups. Within each group, the learners are sorted according to the number of distinct sessions on the site and based on this ordering divided into two equally-sized subgroups: learners with few sessions (low-spacing) and learners with many sessions (high-spacing). In this manner, learners spending similar amounts of time (in total) on the course site can be compared with each other.

GitHub Logs

We identify edX learners on GitHub through the email identifiers attached to each edX and GitHub account. A third of all learners that registered to FP101x are also active on GitHub: 12,415 learners in total. This is likely to be an underestimate of the true number of GitHub users (people generally have multiple email accounts), as we did not attempt to match accounts based on additional user profile information.

GitHub provides extensive access to data traces associated with *public* coding repositories, i.e. repositories

[3]Due to space constraints, only a subset of the identified question/answer pairs are shown.

[4]http://moocdb.csail.mit.edu/

visible to everyone[5]. `GitHub` is built around the `git` distributed revision control system, which enables efficient distributed and collaborative code development. `GitHub` not only provides relevant repository metadata (including information on how popular a repository is, how many developers collaborate, etc.), but also the actual code that was altered. As the *GitHub Archive*[6] makes all historic `GitHub` data traces easily accessible, we relied on it for data collection and extracted all `GitHub` data traces available between January 1, 2013 and July 21, 2015. We then filtered out all traces that were *not* created by our edX learners, leaving us with traces from 10,944 learners. Of the more than 20 `GitHub` *event types*[7], we only consider the `PushEvent` as vital for our analysis.

```
{
  "_id" : ObjectId("55b6005de4b07ff432432dfe1"),
  "created_at" : "2013-03-03T18:36:09-08:00",
  "url" : "https://github.com/john/
          RMS/compare/1c55c4cb04...420e112334",
  "actor" : "john",
  "actor_attributes" : {
       "name" : "John Doe",
       "email" : "john@doe.com"
  },
  "repository" : {
       "id" : 2.37202e+06,
       "name" : "RMS",
       "forks" : 0,
       "open_issues" : 0,
       "created_at" : "2011-09-12T08:28:27-07:00",
       "master_branch" : "master"
    }
}
```

Figure 1. Excerpt of a `GitHub` PushEvent log trace.

Every time code is being updated ("pushed" to a repository), a `PushEvent` is triggered. Figure 1 contains an excerpt of the data contained in each `PushEvent`. The most important attributes of the event are the `created_at` timestamp (which allows us to classify events as before/during/after the running of `FP101x`), the `actor` (the user doing the "push") and the `url`, which contains the URL to the actual *diff file*. While the `git` protocol also allows a user to "push" changes by another user to a repository (which is not evident from inspecting the *diff file* alone), this is a rare occurrence among our learners: manually inspecting a random sample of 200 `PushEvents` showed 10 such cases. A *diff file* shows the difference between the last version of the repository and the new one (after the push) in terms of added and deleted code. An example excerpt is shown in Figure 2. For each of the identified 1,185,549 `PushEvents` by our learners, we crawled the corresponding *diff file*, as they allow us to conduct a fine-grained code analysis. As a first step, we identified the additions and deletions a user conducts in each programming language based on the filename extensions found in the corresponding *diff file*. We consider code updates in the following nine functional languages as clear evidence for functional programming: *Common Lisp, Scheme, Clojure, Racket, Erlang, Ocaml, Haskell, F#* and *Scala*. We also log changes made in any of the other 20 most popular programming languages found on `GitHub` in the same manner. Any filename extension not recognized is first checked against a blacklist (which includes common filename extensions for images, compressed archives, audio files, etc.) and if not found, the change is classified as *Other*.

```
diff --git a/viewsA.rb b/viewsA.rb
index e37bca1..3ad75e4 100644
--- a/viewsA.rb
+++ b/viewsA.rb
@@ -26,6 +26,16 @@ def new
     @shift = Shift.new
   end
...
diff --git a/config/routes.rb b/config/routes.rb
index e576929..27ce68f 100644
--- a/config/routes.rb
+++ b/config/routes.rb
@@ -29,6 +29,7 @@
       put 'secondary'
...
```

Figure 2. Excerpt of a *diff file*. Two files were changed (*viewsA.rb* and *routes.rb*). The extension `*.rb` indicates code written in Ruby.

RESULTS

We first present some basic characteristics of `FP101x`, before delving into the analyses of our research questions and hypotheses.

FP101x Overview

We partition our set of all *registered* `FP101x` learners according to two dimensions: (i) learners with and without a `GitHub` account, and (ii) learners with and without prior expertise in functional programming. In the latter case, we consider only those learners that could be identified on `GitHub`. We define **Expert learners** as those who used any of our nine identified functional programming languages before the start of the course to a meaningful degree (i.e. more than 25 lines of functional code being added). The characteristics of these learner cohorts are listed in Tables 2 and 3.

When considering the `GitHub` vs. non-`GitHub` learners, we observe significant differences along the dimensions of engagement and knowledge:

- `GitHub` learners are on average **more engaged** with the course material (significantly more time spent on watching lecture videos and significantly more questions attempted).
- `GitHub` learners exhibit **higher levels of knowledge** (significantly more questions answered correctly).

Zooming in on the `GitHub` learners and their functional programming expertise, we find the differences to be enlarged: Expert learners have a higher completion rate (more than double that of non-Expert learners), attempt

[5]Data traces about private repositories are only available to the respective repository owner.
[6]`https://www.githubarchive.org/`
[7]`https://developer.github.com/v3/activity/events/types/`

to solve significantly more problems and are significantly more accurate in answering. Experts are also more engaged in terms of forum usage - 8% post at least once compared to 4% of the non-Expert learners.

	All Learners	GH Learners	Non-GH Learners
#Enrolled learners	37,485	12,415	25,070
Completion rate	5.25%	7.71%	4.03%
%Learners who watched at least one video	40.84%	50.58%	36.02%
Avg. time watching video material (in min.)	31.87	44.56 †	25.59 †
%Learners who tried at least one question	23.28%	31.94%	18.99%
Avg. #questions learners attempted to solve	22.07	31.29 †	17.51 †
Avg. #questions answered correctly	18.30	26.54 †	14.22 †
Avg. accuracy of learners' answers	16.36%	23.41% †	12.86% †
#Forum posts	8,157	3,726	4,431
%Learners who posted at least once	2.84%	4.27%	2.13%
Avg. #posts per learner	0.22	0.30 †	0.18 †

Table 2. Basic characteristics across all learners and their partitioning into GitHub (GH) and non-GitHub learners. Significant differences (according to Mann-Whitney) between GH and non-GH learners are marked with †($p < 0.001$).

	Expert Learners	Non-Expert Learners
#Enrolled learners	1,721	10,694
Completion rate	15.05%	6.53%
%Learners who watched at least one video	64.44%	48.35%
Avg. time watching video material (in min.)	69.61 †	40.53 †
%Learners who tried at least one question	48.69%	29.24%
Avg. #questions learners attempted to solve	57.86 †	27.02 †
Avg. #questions answered correctly	50.24 †	22.73 †
Avg. accuracy of learners' answers	37.96% †	21.06% †
#Forum posts	1,612	2,114
%Learners who posted at least once	7.55%	3.74%
Avg. #posts per learners	0.94 ‡	0.20 ‡

Table 3. Basic characteristics when partitioning the GitHub learners according to prior functional programming expertise. Significant differences (according to Mann-Whitney) between Expert and Non-Expert learners are marked with †($p < 0.001$) and ‡($p < 0.01$).

Finally, we note that we repeated this analysis on the subset of *engaged* learners only, where we consider all learners that attempted to solve at least one MC question or watched at least one video. While the absolute numbers vary, the trends we observe for the different partitions of learners in Tables 2 and 3 remain exactly the same.

Learning Transfer

Let us first consider the general uptake of functional programming languages. We can split each learner's `GitHub` traces into three distinct sequences according to their timestamp: traces generated *before*, *during* and *after* `FP101x`. We are interested in comparing the before & after and will mostly ignore the activities generated during `FP101x`.

Expert Learners

Overall, 1,721 of all `GitHub` learners have prior functional programming experience (our **Expert learners**). 1,165 of those are also *engaged* with `FP101x` (the remainder registered, but did not engage), leading to nearly a third (29.4%) of all engaged `GitHub` learners having pre-`FP101x` functional programming experience.

Most of our `GitHub` learners though are not continuously coding functionally: Figure 3 shows for each month of `GitHub` logs (January 2013 to July 2015) the *unique* number of `GitHub` learners programming functionally - while in 2013 less than 250 of our `GitHub` learners were active per month, by 2015 this number has increased to nearly unique 600 active users a month. Thus, the trend to functional programming is generally increasing. Most learners though are not actively using functional languages on a monthly basis.

How much functional code do our engaged Expert learners produce over time? An answer to this question delivers Figure 4: here, for each month, the functional coding activities (calculated as the additions made in functional languages as a fraction of all additions made in recognized programming languages) are averaged across all engaged Expert learners. Again we observe that over the years functional programming has become more popular. By September 2014 (right before the start of `FP101x`), on average more than 36% of coding activities are functional. What is surprising (and somewhat counter-intuitive) is the steady decline of functional activities after the end of `FP101x`. If we restrict our engaged Expert Learners to those 542 learners with functional traces before *and* after `FP101x` (Figure 5), the results are more in line with our expectations: functional programming is continuously gaining in popularity and a peak in activities is observed in the two months following `FP101x`[8]. Thus, 46.5% of engaged Expert learners did continue to program functionally after the end of `FP101x`.

Novice Learners

Most interesting to use are the **Novice Learners**: to what extent do learners that did not program (meaningfully) in functional languages before `FP101x` take it up afterwards? We find 522 such learners — 4.3% of all `GitHub` learners. If we restrict ourselves to engaged `GitHub` learners, we are left with 336 Novice learners (8.5% of all engaged `GitHub` learners). Figure 6 shows

[8]The drop in July 2015 is explained by the non-complete log coverage of July (the log ends on July 21, 2015).

the evolution of their functional programming usage over time: the uptake after the end of `FP101x` is substantial, on average more than 35% of all activities are conducted subsequently in functional languages! While there is no substantial increase after the initial uptake over time, there is also no significant drop. Since the average can only provide limited insights, we drill down to the individual user level in Figure 7: the usage of functional programming is highly varied; 50% of the Novice Learners use it for less than 10% of their programming activities, while some learners almost exclusively code in functional languages. Finally, we also consider which functional languages these Novice learners code in. Figure 8 shows that a month after `FP101x` ended (January 2015), Haskell contributions made up 48% of all contributions, but continued dropping to a low of 14.5% in June 2015. Scala on the other hand (the most popular functional language in industrial settings) slowly rises in popularity over time and by June 2015 makes up roughly half of the functional contributions. Other functional languages play less of a role. Conducting a similar analysis on our engaged Expert learners (not shown here), we find that on average across all months, 47% ($\sigma = 7.4$) of all functional activities are in Scala, whereas 24.0% ($\sigma = 5.5$) are in Haskell. The distribution of functional languages is stable over time. The only outliers can be found in the three months of `FP101x`, where Haskell contributions rise significantly.

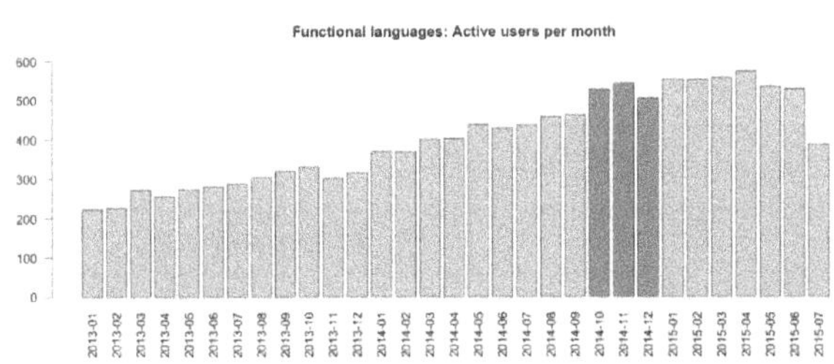

Figure 3. Number of unique users actively using a functional language. `FP101x` **ran during the highlighted region.**

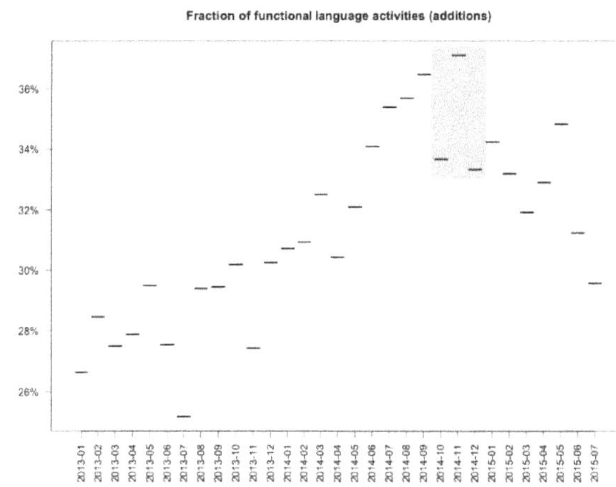

Figure 4. Fraction of functional programming activities among the 1,165 engaged Expert Learners. `FP101x` **ran during the highlighted region.**

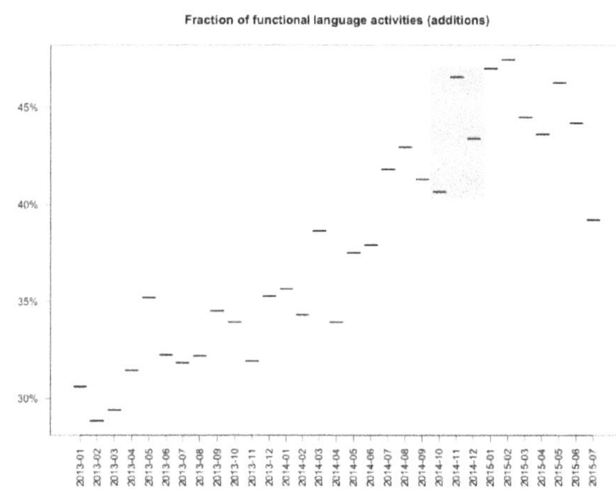

Figure 5. Fraction of functional programming activities among the 542 engaged Expert Learners with functional activities before & after `FP101x`**.** `FP101x` **ran during the highlighted region.**

Transfer Learning Hypotheses

On which learners should (or can) we investigate our seven research hypotheses? Ideally, we rely on all learners that engaged with the course and for whom `GitHub` traces are available. However, for Expert learners we are unable to determine the amount of transfer: since our analysis of functional coding is based on activities in functional languages (instead of a more fine-grained analysis of the type of functional concepts employed), we are not able to determine whether learners that programmed functionally before acquired knowledge in `FP101x` and applied it in practice (a direction of future work). Only for the engaged Novice learners can we be confident that `FP101x` actually impacted their programming practice and that the observed transfer is likely a result of `FP101x`.

Considering **H1**, we observe a **transfer rate of at least 8.5%** (i.e. among the 3,965 engaged `GitHub` learners we found 336 Novice learners that began programming functionally after `FP101x`). This percentage can be considered as a lower bound, as we (due to the reasons listed above) do not consider engaged Expert learners here. Only a minority (70) of the 336 engaged Novice learners did pass `FP101x`, indicating that transfer and pass rate are related but not synonymous. In fact, while the 70 Novice learners that successfully completed the course remained mostly active until the final course week (Figure 9), nearly 40% of all engaged Novice learners became inactive after week 1.

To investigate **H2, H3, H4, H5** and **H6**, for each hypothesis, we partition our 336 engaged Novice Learners who made the transfer according to the investigated dimensions (e.g. intrinsic vs. extrinsic motivation). Recall that the partitioning of the learners relies on their self-reported abilities in the pre- and post-course surveys. Similar to the retention rate, the return rate for

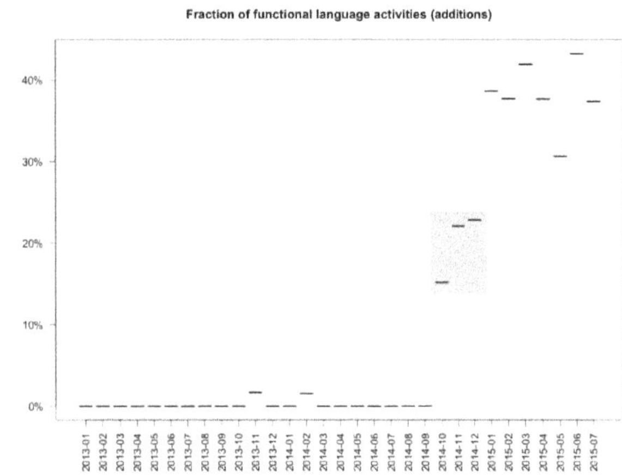

Figure 6. Fraction of functional programming activities among the 336 engaged Novice Learners with functional activities after FP101x. FP101x ran during the highlighted region.

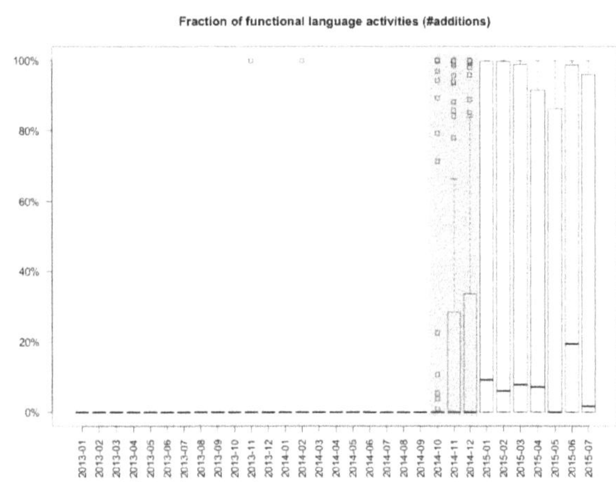

Figure 7. Distribution of functional programming activities among the 336 engaged Novice Learners with functional activities after FP101x. FP101x ran during the highlighted region.

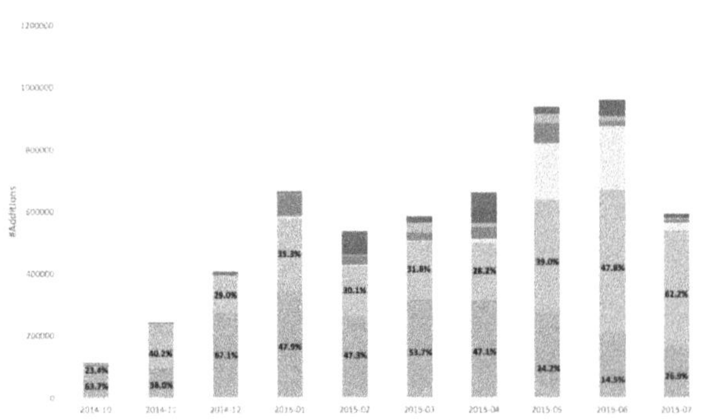

Figure 8. Functional languages used by the 336 engaged Novice Learners during and after FP101x. Best viewed in color.

such questionnaires is very low and many learners do not participate in these surveys for a variety of reasons. Table 4 shows the partitioning of our engaged Novice

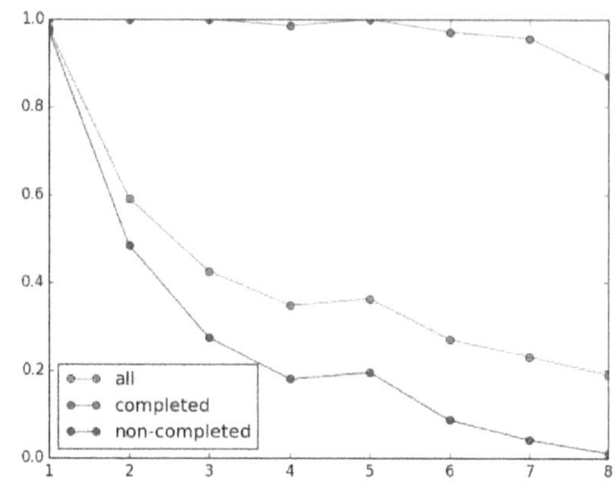

Figure 9. Fraction of the 336 engaged Novice learners remaining active in each course week. 70 Novice learners completed FP101x successfully, 266 did not complete it.

learners based on their survey data. The majority of learners cannot be assigned to a dimension due to a lack of data. Despite the low numbers, we do observe that the transfer learning hypotheses seem to hold in FP101x (for those learners for which it is possible to measure their effect): learners are more likely to make the transfer if (i) they are intrinsically motivated, (ii) have high self-efficacy, (iii) are more experienced programmers, and (iv) report a high personal capacity. Even though the number of learners we were able to investigate are small, we consider this as first evidence that transfer learning hypotheses also hold in the MOOC setting.

	Dimensions		N/A
H2 Motivation	Extr.: 12	Intr.: 28	296
H3 Self-efficacy	High: 23	Low: 5	308
H4 Experience	A lot: 42	Little: 25	269
H5 Personal capacity	High: 22	Low: 10	304

Table 4. Partitioning of the 336 Novice learners according to several dimensions. The last column shows the number of learners that could not be assigned (N/A) to a dimension.

Groups	Low spacing	High spacing
0	2	2
1	9	9
2	6	16
3	10	20
4	21	21
5	19	16
6	19	22
7	20	22
8	16	29
9	27	30

Table 5. The number of Novice Learners falling into spacing groups.

To answer **H6** (high-spaced learners are more likely to transfer), we binned all GitHub learners according to their total time and number of distinct sessions in the FP101x edX environment, as outlined earlier. This creates 10 groups, with learners in *Group 0* spending the least amount of time and learners in *Group 9* spending the most amount of time on the course site. Thus, each group contains those learners that roughly spent the same amount of time on the site. Further, within each group, learners are divided according to the number of distinct sessions. In Table 5 we report how many engaged Novice learners fell into each group and which part of the group — the high-spacing or the low-spacing one. While 187 engaged Novice learners are classified as high-spacing, 149 are classified as low-spacing. Thus, there is some indication that **H6** holds. However, the observed difference is rather small.

To conclude this section, we lastly consider **H7**. In contrast to the hypothesis (transfer decreases over time), we neither observe a significant decrease nor increase after the initial uptake as evident in Figures 6 and 7.

A Qualitative Analysis

We have found similarities and differences between transfer in classroom learning and our MOOC. Instead of speculating about the reasons for these differences, we designed a follow-up survey (containing 10 questions about learners' functional programming experiences before and after FP101x) and distributed it to subsets of GitHub learners in August 2015[9]. A second purpose of this questionnaire is to verify whether GitHub logs offer a good approximation of our learners' true behaviour. We partitioned the *engaged* GitHub learners into eight categories:

A **Novice** learners that **completed** the course but did **not transfer** (i.e. we did not observe functional GitHub traces after FP101x). #Survey responses: 131 (32% return rate).

B **Expert** learners that **completed** the course but did **not transfer**. #Survey responses: 15 (39%).

C **Novice** learners that **completed** the course and **transferred** (i.e. we observed functional GitHub traces after FP101x). #Survey responses: 11 (61%).

D **Novice** learners that **did not complete** the course, but **transferred**. #Survey responses: 1 (3%).

E **Expert** learners that **completed** the course and **continued programming functionally** (did they transfer?). #Survey responses: 20 (56%).

F **Expert** learners that did **not complete** the course but did **program functionally** after FP101x. #Survey responses: 8 (16%).

G **Novice** learners that were engaged in the course (but not completed) and did **not transfer**. #Survey responses: 93 (6%).

H **Expert** learners that were engaged in the course (but not completed) and did **not transfer**. #Survey responses: 4 (7% return rate).

How accurate are GitHub traces as approximation of learners' functional programming activities? Of those learners we had identified as Novices, 63% also self-reported as such. Of the learners we estimated to have some prior functional programming experience, 77% self-reported prior experience. In particular, the latter number is intriguing: based on our stringent methodology, we can be confident that all of our identified Expert learners did indeed functionally program before FP101x, though about a quarter self-reports otherwise. Of the learners we identified as having demonstrated learning transfer, 88% also self-reported as doing so. Of those we identified as not having demonstrated learning transfer, only 37% self-reported of not having applied anything they had learnt. An explanation for this discrepancy is based on the non-exclusive use of GitHub: while 73% indicated that they use GitHub for either work or personal coding projects, 65% use a Private/Employer's repository service, and 39% use BitBucket. While 73% is promising in that it accounts for nearly three quarters of all learners, we could only detect users who use the same email address for both their edX and GitHub account.

[9] All contacted learners had consented to additional contact.

What are the main reasons for learners not to transfer their acquired functional programming skills? 80% of learners reporting a reason for not transferring their acquired skills report a lack of opportunities. Many learners go on to explain that the programming language standards in their work-place do not allow them to practice what they have learned. Another common sentiment is that it is difficult for some experienced programmers to suddenly change their ways. For example, when asked why they did not apply what they learned in FP101x to either work or personal projects, one respondent shared, "It takes time and effort to change old programming habits." And another shared a similar sentiment: "[It's] hard to think functionally after 25 years of imperative [programming] experience."

CONCLUSIONS

We have investigated the extent of learning transfer in the MOOC setting and introduced the use of a social-Web based data source (i.e. GitHub) to complement the learner traces collected within MOOC environments. Focusing on one-third of FP101x learners we were able to link to GitHub, we made several important findings:

(1) Most transfer learning findings from the classroom setting translate into the MOOC setup; large discrepancies were only found for **H1**: the amount of observed transfer and **H7**: the development of transfer over time.

(2) The observed transfer rate in MOOCs is low. We found that 8.5% of engaged learners were indeed exhibiting transfer to varying degrees in our GitHub traces. We acknowledge that a substantial amount of programming occurs outside of GitHub (e.g. in private employer repositories). While the traces we gather offer many new insights by following learners beyond the MOOC platform for an extended period of time, considering one external data source alone is a limiting factor.

(3) The amount of transfer, operationalized as the fraction of functional coding is varying highly: about 50% of the learners transferring code less than 10% of the time functionally, while a small minority almost exclusively turns to functional languages.

(4) After the end of `FP101x`, learners making the transfer quickly identified the most industrially-relevant functional language at this moment (Scala). Over time their activities in Scala increased significantly, while their activities in Haskell (the language of `FP101x`) decreased. Overall though, after the initial uptake of functional programming, the fraction of functional activities (between 35%-40%) of all coding activities remained constant.

The limitations of the current study (only 33% of learners could be coupled to a `GitHub` account and our exploratory analysis has been conducted on the programming language type level) naturally lead to three directions for future work: (i) instead of focusing on the amount of code added per language, a more detailed analysis will determine the particular functional concepts employed and match them with the course material, (ii) programming languages are taught in a variety of MOOCs, it is an open question whether the same methodology is applicable across a variety of courses, and lastly, (iii) we will move beyond the `GitHub` platform and consider alternative external data sources.

REFERENCES

1. Adams, L. T., Kasserman, J. E., Yearwood, A., Perfetto, G. A., Bransford, J. D., and Franks, J. J. Memory access: The effects of fact-oriented versus problem-oriented acquisition. *Memory & Cognition 16*, 2 (1988), 167–175.
2. Baldwin, T. T., and Ford, K. J. Transfer of training: A review and directions for future research. *Personnel Psychology 41*, 1 (1988), 63–105.
3. Bandura, A. Self-efficacy: toward a unifying theory of behavioral change. *Psychological review 84*, 2 (1977), 191–215.
4. Barnett, S. M., and Ceci, S. J. When and where do we apply what we learn? a taxonomy for far transfer. *Psychological bulletin 128*, 4 (2002), 612–637.
5. Bjork, R. A. Memory and metamemory considerations in the training of human beings. *Metacognition: Knowing about knowing* (1994), 185–205.
6. Bjork, R. A., and Bjork, E. L. A new theory of disuse and an old theory of stimulus fluctuation. *From learning processes to cognitive processes: Essays in honor of William K. Estes 2* (1992), 35–67.
7. Blume, B. D., Ford, K. J., Baldwin, T. T., and Huang, J. L. Transfer of training: A meta-analytic review. *Journal of Management 36*, 4 (2010), 1065–1105.
8. Chen, G., Gully, S. M., and Eden, D. Validation of a new general self-efficacy scale. *Organizational research methods 4*, 1 (2001), 62–83.
9. Darnon, C., Butera, F., and Harackiewicz, J. M. Achievement goals in social interactions: Learning with mastery vs. performance goals. *Motivation and Emotion 31*, 1 (2007), 61–70.
10. DeBoer, J., Ho, A. D., Stump, G. S., and Breslow, L. Changing "course": Reconceptualizing educational variables for massive open online courses. *Educational Researcher 43*, 2 (2014), 74–84.
11. Donovan, J. J., and Radosevich, D. J. A meta-analytic review of the distribution of practice effect: Now you see it, now you don't. *Journal of Applied Psychology 84*, 5 (1999), 795–805.
12. Fidalgo-Blanco, Á., Sein-Echaluce, M. L., García-Peñalvo, F. J., and Escaño, J. E. Improving the mooc learning outcomes throughout informal learning activities. In *TEEM '14* (2014), 611–617.
13. Ford, K. J., Quinones, M. A., Sego, D. J., and Sorra, J. S. Factors affecting the opportunity to perform trained tasks on the job. *Personnel Psychology 45*, 3 (1992), 511–527.
14. Hill, T., Smith, N. D., and Mann, M. F. Role of efficacy expectations in predicting the decision to use advanced technologies: The case of computers. *Journal of Applied Psychology 72*, 2 (1987), 307–313.
15. Ho, A. D., Chuang, I., Reich, J., and Coleman *et al.*, C. A. Harvardx and mitx: Two years of open online courses fall 2012-summer 2014. *SSRN 2586847* (2015).
16. Holton III, E. F., Bates, R. A., and Ruona, W. E. Development of a generalized learning transfer system inventory. *Human resource development quarterly 11*, 4 (2000), 333–360.
17. Koedinger, K. R., Corbett, A. T., and Perfetti, C. The knowledge-learning-instruction framework: Bridging the science-practice chasm to enhance robust student learning. *Cognitive Science 36*, 5 (2012), 757–798.
18. Koller, D., Ng, A., Do, C., and Chen, Z. Retention and intention in massive open online courses. *Educause Review 48*, 3 (2013), 62–63.
19. Lim, D. H., and Johnson, S. D. Trainee perceptions of factors that influence learning transfer. *International journal of training and development 6* (2002), 36–48.
20. Lockhart, R. S., Lamon, M., and Gick, M. L. Conceptual transfer insimple insight problems. *Memory & Cognition 16*, 1 (1988), 36–44.
21. Miyamoto, Y. R., Coleman, C. A., Williams, J. J., Whitehill, J., Nesterko, S. O., and Reich, J. Beyond time-on-task: The relationship between spaced study and certification in moocs. *SSRN 2547799* (2015).
22. Pugh, K. J., and Bergin, D. A. Motivational influences on transfer. *Educational Psychologist 41*, 3 (2006), 147–160.
23. Rodriguez, O. The concept of openness behind c and x-moocs (massive open online courses). *Open Praxis 5*, 1 (2013), 67–73.
24. Saks, A. M., and Belcourt, M. An investigation of training activities and transfer of training in organizations. *Human resource management 45*, 4 (2006), 629–648.
25. Thorndike, E. L. *The psychology of learning*. Educational Psychology. Teachers College, Columbia University, 1913.
26. Veletsianos, G., Collier, A., and Schneider, E. Digging deeper into learners' experiences in moocs: Participation in social networks outside of moocs, notetaking and contexts surrounding content consumption. *British Journal of Educational Technology 46*, 3 (2015), 570–587.
27. Wang, Y., Paquette, L., and Baker, R. A longitudinal study on learner career advancement in moocs. *Journal of Learning Analytics 1*, 3 (2014), 203–206.
28. Willingham, D. T. What will improve a student's memory? *American Educator 32*, 4 (2008), 17–25.
29. Yelon, S. L., and Ford, K. J. Pursuing a multidimensional view of transfer. *Performance Improvement Quarterly 12*, 3 (1999), 58–78.

The Role of Social Media in MOOCs: How to Use Social Media to Enhance Student Retention

[1]Saijing Zheng, [2]Kyungsik Han, [1]Mary Beth Rosson, [1]John M. Carroll
[1]College of Information Sciences and Technology
The Pennsylvania State University
{suz128, mrosson, jcarroll}@ist.psu.edu
[2]Pacific Northwest National Laboratory
kyungsik.han@pnnl.gov

ABSTRACT
The Massive Open Online Courses (MOOC) have experienced rapid development. However, high dropout rate has become a salient issue. Many studies have attempted to understand this phenomenon; other have explored mechanisms for enhancing retention. For instance, social media has been used to improve student engagement and retention. However there is a lack of (1) empirical studies of social media use and engagement compared to embedded MOOC forums; and (2) rationales for social media use from both instructors' and students' perspectives. We addressed these open issues through the collection and analysis of real usage data from three MOOC forums and their associated social media (i.e., Facebook) groups as well as conducting interviews of instructors and students. We found that students show higher engagement and retention in social media than in MOOC forums, and identified both instructors' and students' perspectives that lead to the results. We discuss design implications for future MOOC platforms.

Author Keywords
Massive Open Online Course; MOOCs; Social Media; Facebook; Coursera; Mixed Method.

INTRODUCTION
Massive Open Online Courses (MOOCs) are a recent innovation in online learning and distance education that has developed rapidly and garnered extensive attention from a broad range of populations. The MOOCs paradigm is built on the principal belief that knowledge should be shared freely, and that learning aspirations should not be constrained by socioeconomic or geographic limitations [18]. In comparison to conventional online courses, MOOCs are in massive scale and distributed worldwide across a variety of educational platforms (e.g., Coursera, edX, Udacity, etc.) with no physical presence restrictions.

Recent work has shown that people who join MOOCs have diverse motivations, which lead to a variety of learning behaviors and innovative uses of MOOCs [13, 24]. For example, some students enroll in a MOOC is to meet social needs (e.g., make friends) rather than to learn *per se* [13, 24]. Others participate in MOOCs for both learning and entertainment [13]. As more MOOCs are emerging and as they are being used to meet more diverse goals, it seems that the online courses should no longer be viewed simply as a means of disseminating educational content, but rather as a *virtual organization* where people learn individually and collaboratively, make friends, exchange learning insights, and interact with people who come from different countries and disciplines [24, 25].

However, current MOOCs platforms are limited to playing videos, sending announcement, and hosting a discussion forum; there is little support for social activities [25]. A vast body of literature regarding classroom learning and distance learning has shown the importance of forming a sense of community [9], enhancing social interactions [9], and encouraging collaborations [24] to improve student retention and program success. Indeed, as retention issues become increasingly prominent in MOOCs [1, 4, 8], studies have identified the lack of one's sense of community, and ineffective social interactions and collaboration contribute to the high dropout rate in MOOCs [24, 25].

To cultivate an active learning environment, MOOC instructors have often recruited a variety of external tools, such as Facebook, Twitter and Google plus, etc. into their MOOCs [24, 26, 29]. However, these initiatives have not yet presented in-depth analyses of social media usage, the relationship of usage between a MOOC platform and social media and the rationales of the social media use from both instructors' and students' perspectives. Thus, there are not many insights that we could consider in order to provide design principles for the future MOOC platform and to help instructors and students better use social media to enhance engagement and retention.

In this paper, we investigate the role of social media in the context of MOOCs. We applied quantitative and qualitative methods through the analysis of usage log data of three MOOCs from Coursera and each MOOC's Facebook groups. We present comparative analysis results regarding the level of usage and engagement between two platforms. We also interviewed 4 instructors and 12 students of three

L@S 2016, April 25-26, 2016, Edinburgh, Scotland, UK.

DOI: http://dx.doi.org/10.1145/2876034.2876047

MOOCs to unpack their motivations and experiences in both platforms.

Our comparative analysis shows that although there were more people enrolled and more posts shared in Coursera relative to the smaller group of people who joined the Facebook groups, when it comes to user engagement, Facebook was a more attractive place for them to stay actively and longer. Our interviews with students highlight four main reasons of why they prefer to use Facebook — *a real community in Facebook, instructor imitated discussion forum, a better collaborative place, and more convenient to communicate with others.* Our interviews with instructors unveil four main motivations of using Facebook from their perspectives — *enhancing student retention and engagement, cultivating a sense of community, advertising their MOOCs*, and *being creative*.

BACKGROUND

Garrison et al.'s [31] Community of Inquiry research establishes a conceptual framework that informs the design of the online learning tool and also represents a process of creating a deep and meaningful learning experience through the development of three interdependent, mutually reinforcing elements: *social* [30], *cognitive* [31] and *teaching presence* [31]. Meanwhile, the research in social learning and online communities demonstrates important roles of online communities and helps us understand why these online communities have early gains in learners' engagement and retention.

Lucas and Moreira have noted that utilizing informal social media in a formal learning setting promotes informal interactions that students describe as having a significant impact on their formal learning outcomes [17]. A recent study has documented the broad research on the positive impacts of applying informal online learning strategies (i.e., using social media on learning) [7]. This study delivers a framework from a pedagogical perspective for using informal learning approaches to create Personal Learning Environments that combine formal and informal learning format by using social media.

Recent research on the effectiveness of learning communities found that learning communities play very important roles during learning process. For example, they could affect the flow of thoughts across group members and help to form highly creative groups and deliver collaborative work [2, 21, 23]. The term Community of Practice (CoP) coined by two cognitive anthropologists describes the fact that a group of "people who share a concern or a passion for something they do and learn how to do it better as they interact regularly" [15]. Thus, learning could be the main motive that the community forms together, or it could be an incidental product resulting from diverse interactions among members of the community. The emergent practices of a community could be one indicator of its effectiveness as a community.

In the research of Massive Open Online Courses (MOOCs), some literature found social media is important to enhance sense of community in MOOCs [11, 24] and instructors use social media as a second channel to communicate with MOOC students [3, 11, 26]. Also, an appropriate selection of social tools could be helpful to engage students and improve their retention during the course [3, 11]. However, these studies are lack of in-depth analysis of social media usage, the relationship of usage between a MOOC platform and social media and the rationales of the usages from both instructors' and students' perspectives. Thus, little insight that we could achieve exists to provide design principles for future MOOC platforms and help instructors and students to better utilize social media to enhance user engagement and retention.

In our study, we investigate the role of social media in the context of online education through the collection of usage logs from three MOOCs and the associated social media groups and through the comparative analyses on the level of usage and engagement between two platforms. We also conduct interviews with instructors and students to investigate their perspectives on using social media for MOOCs.

RESEARCH METHOD

We applied a mixed method to understand the role of social media. We first employ a quantitative method to look at student engagement both on Coursera and Facebook. Then we conducted interviews to find out the motivations for instructors to use social media and for students to join the official Facebook groups of the MOOCs and whether their experiences met their expectations.

The Study Settings

MOOC platforms normally include built-in social tools such as forums to centralize learners' contributions, and discussions; but also, instructors may suggest alternative tools to effectively build connections and collaboration among learners.

Coursera Forum (used as Coursera in this paper) is a tool for learners to participate in discussions on selected course topics. The forum needs to be maintained by both students and instructors who can define new threads and make comments. This forum is also for learners to raise questions about the enactment of the course, the contents of the modules or platform. The instructors and other participants may answer the questions or vote them as relevant to gain visibility.

Official Facebook Group (also used as Facebook) is Facebook group constructed by MOOC instructors or/and teaching assistants. Instructors may post announcements, foster course discussions, or share additional multimedia resources with learners who can contribute to the discussion and share new resources too. Note that using Facebook group is optional for MOOC instructors. Also, students can construct Facebook groups based on their interests but are not accounted in *official* Facebook groups. In our paper, we only focus on official ones.

Three MOOCs were offered by a large public university in the Northeastern United States. We chose three types of MOOCs to avoid any possible result biases on a particular type of MOOC. The first MOOC was an arts course (Arts, May – July, 2013). Students learned different skills to make art crafts and learned how to appreciate arts. The second MOOC was a qualitative course (CIC, July – September, 2014), which guided students to use different tools and mental models to become more creative. The third MOOC was a quantitative course (Geo, April – June, 2014), which taught students how to build a map using programing languages.

Data and Data Collection

Our data include three types. The first type is student usage data on Coursera of three different MOOCs. The usage data consists of click stream data, which documented students' all posting activities (e.g., posts, comments, and votes) on Coursera and the time of each activity occurs.

The second type is student usage data from three official Facebook groups of the three MOOCs we mentioned above. We collected Facebook usage data by two ways. We used Facebook API to crawl activities in the groups. We also collected summary data directly from the group page because the first author is the admin of all these three courses on Facebook. As we obtained the unique ID for each user (any user identifiable information was not used for preserving privacy), we processed different types of activities (e.g., the number of posts, comments, likes, etc.) for each user. As each post contains the timestamp, we measured a level of activities over time for both Coursera and Facebook.

The third type is the interview data from instructors and students of the three MOOCs. We recruited 4 instructors (one is from Arts MOOC, one is from Geo MOOC and the other two are from CIC MOOC) and 12 MOOC students. We send messages to students through Facebook to invite them join our study and we randomly chose 12 students from responders. Our data was collected by semi-structured interviews. At the beginning of each interview, we gathered social-demographic information about the participant (e.g., gender, age, general teaching duration, Facebook using frequency and routine). We then asked the participants about their general MOOC experiences (e.g., how many MOOC sessions they have taught/learned, how long they have been using MOOCs and social media, etc.). For instructors, our questions focus on the motivations of using Facebook, the teaching activities on Facebook, and their perceptions of using both Coursera and Facebook. For students, our questions focus on their motivations, expectations, and perceptions of joining and being engaged in Facebook.

We summarized the general profile of 12 participants (students): our interviewees included 5 undergraduate students, 4 graduate students, 1 housewife and 2 employees; 5 females and 7 males; 4 participants use Facebook daily, 5 participants login Facebook occasionally but check it frequently during the MOOC they took, 3 participants registered Facebook because the MOOC put the Facebook group link.

The interviews ranged from approximately 40 minutes to 2.5 hours. All interviews were audio-recorded, annotated, and transcribed for further data analysis.

Data Analysis

This paper proposes a deep analysis on how social tools are perceived and utilized by MOOC learners in order to shed some light on their selection process. Particularly, this analysis involves two different tools on three MOOCs. One tool is a built-in forum on Coursera, and the other one is an external social media group — Facebook. The analysis on these tools includes a level of usage and engagement from the actual usage logs and comparison between the two platforms.

For qualitative data (i.e., interviews), we use thematic analysis and grounded theory, which underlines the concurrent processes of data collection and analysis [10]. After conducting a small number of interviews with students, we took an initial data analysis session to identify core themes. Once these themes were identified, we employed axial coding to further generate categories and sub-categories. Themes and categories were refined by an iterative coding process that involved the first author and another coder. The preliminary results offered a coding guideline for the next round of coding for each new set of interviews. When following rounds of analysis were not able to discover new themes or categories any more, this demonstrated saturation of theory [10]. This happened after we conducted our 11th student interview. Our 12th interview further confirmed that the saturation of the theory had been reached. Thus, we stopped conducting more interviews with students.

RESULTS

We first present descriptive statistics of course enrollment, and use and engagement from posting activities in Coursera and Facebook. We then present how a level of engagement changes over time and compare the results between the two platforms. We next move to our qualitative analysis reports from a total of sixteen participants, presenting instructors' and students' perspectives of social media for MOOCs.

Engagement in posting activities

For each MOOC, we first measured the number of people who joined Coursera and those who joined Facebook. As summarized in Table 1, we can see that different numbers of people joined Coursera and/or Facebook and much fewer people joined Facebook than Coursera. Several reasons might lead to this result. First, Coursera is the official platform to carry the course and every student has to register for the course, watch lectures and submit homework on Coursera; Facebook is more like a second channel for student to connect with classmates and instructors. Also, students should find or become aware of the Facebook page after they joined Coursera. Second, not all of the students who registered for the course have Facebook account or are active users in Facebook, though Facebook has most large user population. Third, students have diverse motivations to join a MOOC [24]. For example, students who just want to audit a course may not participate social activities.

		Art (%)	CIC (%)	Geo (%)
Total users	C	69,867	155,237	25,837
	F	20,344	8,800	4,758
Engaged users	C	7,416 (10.6)	2,189 (1.4)	2,898 (11.2)
	F	3,524 (17.3)	2,841 (34.7)	1,547 (32.5)

Table 1. Summary of total users and engaged users (C: Coursera, F: Facebook).

		Art (%)	CIC (%)	Geo (%)
Total posts	C	29,876	7,945	16,710
	F	1,345	117	50
Comments added to posts	C	22,292 (0.74)	5,580 (0.70)	5,842 (0.34)
	F	2,538 (1.88)	123 (1.05)	64 (1.28)
Votes or Likes added to posts	C	40,304 (1.34)	6,306 (0.79)	5,121 (0.30)
	F	8,296 (6.16)	1,387 (7.83)	509 (10.1)

Table 2. Summary of post-related activities.

We considered a level of engagement and investigated how people exhibited different engagement levels in Coursera and Facebook. Here we defined *engaged users* who shared posts, comments, or votes in Coursera or Likes in Facebook at least once (if not more than once) during the course. With this rational, we measured how many users engaged in posting activities everyday. We were aware of a possibility of having more enrolled users after the class starts, which leads to having the different number of enrolled people on a daily basis. Again, from instructors, we were told that there was some increase in enrollment for the first two weeks, but the increase became negligible after then. In this sense, our analysis on engagement may not perfectly depict a trend but provides a general insight. Overall, as shown in Table 1, the result indicates that only around or less than 10% of users on Coursera posted content while there were more engaged users on Facebook. Especially, people in the CIC course were much more engaged in Facebook than Coursera compared to other two courses.

Along with total and engaged users, we also calculated the number of comments and votes/likes added to the posts and compared the results between Coursera and Facebook. Here we considered votes in Coursera equivalent to Likes in Facebook. Even if there are down-votes, we found only few cases in our samples where people added down votes to the postings. As shown in Table 2 and Figure 1, from all three courses, people tended to add more comments for each post in Facebook than Coursera as well as much more Likes for each post in Facebook than Votes in Coursera, showing higher engagement in social media. Students in Facebook seem to be more active and engaged than Coursera users.

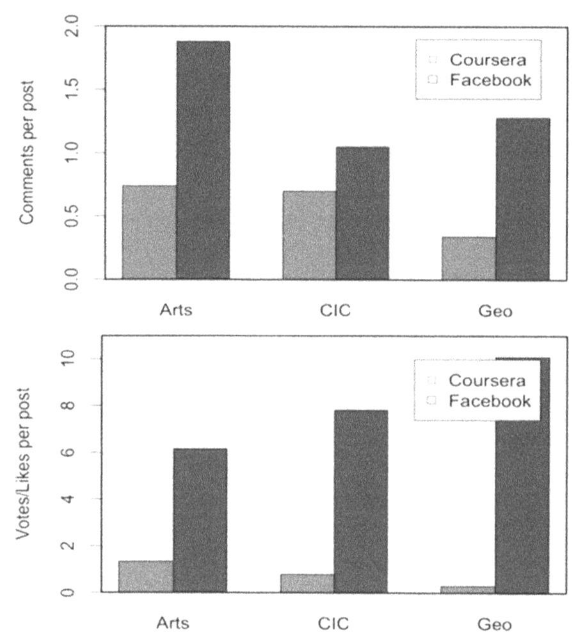

Figure 1. Summary of commenting (top) and Voting/Liking (bottom) activities.

Engagement over time

For the last measurement on engagement, we took the timestamps in the posts, calculated the number of posts for each day, and plotted a ratio of engagement by day. We also computed a linear trend model for the percentage of the total number of posts given day to compare the variance of engagement overtime more directly. As illustrated in Figure 2, we can see that the engagement in Coursera significantly dropped (especially well exhibited in Arts and CIC) after two or three weeks. According to linear trend model results, engagement decreased more rapidly in Coursera ($p < 0.001$) than in Facebook. It also appeared that there were active posting activities in Facebook before the class started for all MOOCs. The main reason is, in Coursera, students can register a MOOC several weeks before the course officially starts but they cannot access to the course until that day. Instead, during this period of waiting time, they could visit official Facebook group associated with the MOOC, which is built by instructors (we will have detailed rational in interview and discussion part). Additionally, we found that there were still activities in Facebook even after the MOOC finished, shown more obviously in CIC and Geo.

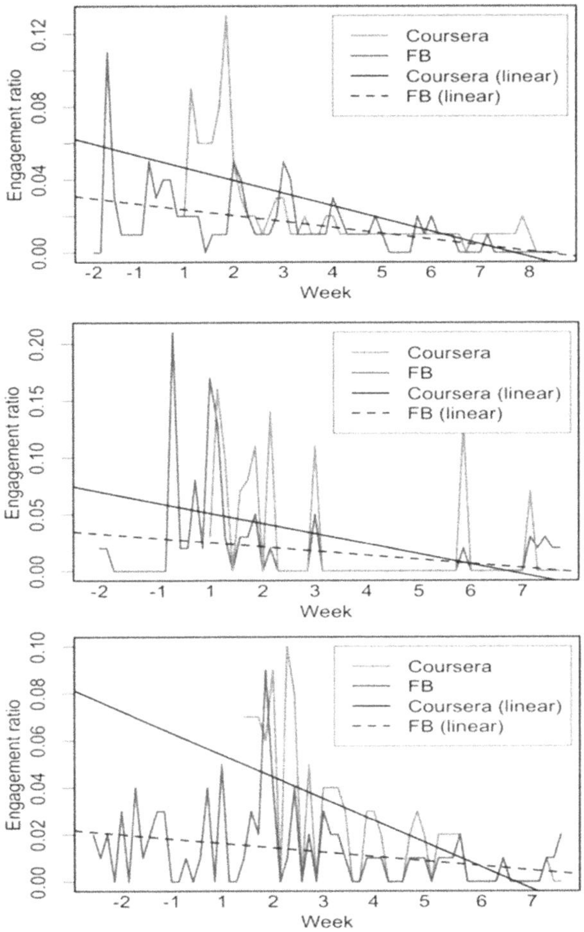

Figure 2. The level of engagement over time on Coursera and Facebook (FB) from three courses ((top): Arts, (mid): CIC, and (bottom): Geo).

Overall, our comparative analyses from the real usage data in the two different platforms clearly showed that, even if there were more people enrolled and more posts shared in Coursera and much fewer people joined in Facebook, when it comes to a level of engagement, Facebook seems a more attractive place to stay longer and engage more.

From these empirical results, we were motivated to study the following questions: *Does social media play different or unique roles in making people more engaged in an online course compared to official forums? Can we identify some of those elements from social media and think about a better approach to enhance students' retention, which will be both beneficial for instructors and students?* However, these are the questions that we could not answer just from a quantitative approach. To have better understandings of these questions we designed and conducted interview studies by recruiting four instructors and twelve students and asked their own perceptions and behaviors on Facebook and Coursera.

Students' Perspective: Learning Experiences between Facebook and Coursera

We interviewed 12 students of the three MOOCs with respect to their motivations and experiences in using Facebook and Coursera during learning. Our intention was to uncover how their reflections would match our quantitative findings and the discrepancy of using Facebook and Coursera between instructors and students.

From interviews, 11 students like Facebook more than Coursera. They admitted the role of Facebook and Coursera should be different, for example, Facebook should be more social orientated but Coursera should be more problem solving orientated. But in fact, the role is not clearly divided.They would rather stay in Facebook to follow the announcements and have discussions with students and the instructor. We have generated 4 themes that students made the comparisons between Facebook and Coursera forum based on their experiences.

A Real Community in Facebook

All 12 participants believe Facebook give them a sense of community. In Facebook, they know some "real" amazing people, have follow up conversations and discussions, gain more quick feedback and attentions, and also have fun moments, all of which are hard to find in Coursera forum.

"*I lost my interests in the Coursera forum after one week because it was very chaos. I didn't know people there because I guess most of them were not willing to make friends. They used fake name, which made me feel untrusted. So later, I used a fake name too. Also, I rarely received replies from them on Coursera and when I answered some questions, no thanks received. It's not like a human being interaction place. So I went to Facebook group, where I saw a totally different atmosphere...* "[P3]

"*Although I also introduced myself in Coursera but no people would carefully read it, which makes the introduction useless.*" [P7]

Indeed, in Coursera, students are allowed to use any names that are not real to represent themselves and it is optional to fill out their profile information. Trust would be hard to build in this case. Moreover, Coursera did not provide a course roster; thus, it is hard to maintain a conversation or a friendship there.

Also, our participants believe Coursera is just a short-term place to stay depending on the length of the course (usually 4 to 8 weeks). Thus, they do not treat Coursera as their "home" or "territory" and are not willing to put more efforts into the discussion forum. In contrast, even after the MOOC finished, they could still maintain friendship with students and track the materials or discussion in Facebook.

"*People will leave Coursera right after the course finish. Everything would be gone. So I didn't want to contribute much in the forum... At the beginning the course, I frequently asked questions on Coursera but no answers.*

After a while, I chose to ask questions on Facebook and it worked. Actually, I like answering question on Facebook, as least I received some thanks and we can have real interactions." [P11]

These factors make the Coursera not well suited for social connections and thus hard to build a sense of community. In addition, our participants felt hard to keep passion on the Coursera when their questions or actions constantly cannot receive feedbacks or attentions. This affects both social and learning aspects. Discussion forum is a crucial place for students to digest challenging knowledge and keep learning motivation. The current obstacles have made the expected functionality of the forum tarnished.

More Convenient to Communicate with Others in Facebook

All of participants consider convenient access is a big factor they visit Facebook group more than Coursera. Since our participants have much longer usage experiences on Facebook, and they are very comfortable to communicate with others and also potentially have more trust on other Facebook users. They have Facebook mobile app on their phone and keep Facebook website open on their PC, which make them receive any notifications or messages from the Facebook MOOC group anywhere and anytime. They could utilize a small chunk of time to join discussions. In doing so, they check the Facebook group much more often than Coursera. Although some participants said they also have and use a Coursera app on their phone, they mostly use the app to watch lectures and not necessarily to read posts, add comments, and so on.

"*I wish I could use my Facebook account to login Coursera. I think I will have more visits on Coursera when they save the extra step for me to login.*" [P5]

"*I frequently forget my password or account name. I know this is stupid, but it happens frequently not just on me but on many of my friends!*" [P4]

"*Sometimes, I actually want to reply or make some updates on Coursera, but when I think I need to login on my computer, I postponed doing it and then I forgot to do it later.*" [P12]

All of our participants believe Facebook plays an important role to remind them to visit Coursera. Since MOOCs are optional, most of students who registered MOOCs drop off in the middle [24] and lots of students cannot follow the course schedule. But when our participants received notifications from Facebook, they began to think of going to Coursera to catch up the course schedule. In other words, because of the reminders and course related posts on Facebook, our participants visited Coursera group more often than they would have.

"*I usually forgot to check the Coursera and follow the MOOC schedule, especially when I was busy. But Facebook group posts and notifications would encourage me to squeeze sometime to watch more course lecture on Coursera and catch up the course schedules.*" [P2]

Better Place for Collaboration in Facebook

All our participants believe Facebook is a better place to collaborate with group members comparing with Coursera because there is no build-in tool in Coursera to collaborate. Instructors usually encourage student to construct groups based on the project or their mutual interests. Students usually construct groups actively on Facebook because they feel this is the most "natural" tool they could think of. Usually, they recruited group members from the official Facebook groups first. After identifying the group members, they build their own private groups on Facebook. For example, in Art MOOC, they construct different Facebook groups based on their preferred materials to make crafts, different ages groups and with or without disabilities. Our interviews show that they had very satisfied and successful experiences to collaborate with team mate and finish their group projects in this way.

Although three of our participants tried to use Coursera to recruit group members and have group activity on Coursera by constructing a new thread, they ended up with using Facebook. The reason is, not like Facebook having privacy groups setting, people who do not belong to their group still could visit and comments on their thread on Coursera, which makes them hard to maintain their group activities.

"*What we need is a place to collaborate on our group project but Coursera is really not an ideal one. Since there is no collaboration feature on Coursera, we appropriated the forum and added a new thread on the forum to divide some place for our project discussion. But we cannot control the access to the thread. We experienced lots of interruptions. So we gave up and adopted Facebook.*" [P8]

Instructors/TAs Initialed Discussion in Facebook

Our participants believe it is beneficial to build professional relationship with the instructor. But it is very difficult to have conversations with the instructor on Coursera. One reason is that there is no specific communication channel to the instructor. There are also massive amount of messages on Coursera, making instructor hard to check/read them all. On the other hand, in Facebook, instructors or TAs usually initiate posts first and students could have comments under the post. This gives students the feeling that they have the direct interactions with the instructors. More importantly, our participants believe the posts proposed by instructors or TAs read important or interesting, which are more attractive and valuable for students to look at and discuss.

"*I like reviewing Facebook posts and joining discussions with classmates, instructors and TAs there. The posts are usually interesting, for example, the instructor would share some useful materials or learning topic related knowledge. It is beneficial. Even just reviewing the discussions, I could learn more. I also received more replies from instructors and TAs than that on Coursera.*"[P1]

Instructors' Perspective: Motivation and Perception of Using Facebook and Coursera

We interviewed 4 instructors of the three MOOCs with respect to their motivations of and perceptions in using social media and Coursera during teaching.

Motivations

Improving Retention and Engagement

All of our instructors said their primary goal of using social media was to enhance student retention and engagement. They believe the ideal online learning requires active engagement on the part of the student. Although each MOOC serves a large scale of students, they still hope their students to be active learners in the learning process not passive recipients of transmitted knowledge. Also, from the course data, they found only the small number of students could finish the course and receive a certificate. They hope more students could keep passion on the course. Together with students they hope to cultivate an active and friendly learning environment.

"*Ideally, I hope students can be engaged in MOOCs just like face-to-face class. Social media, such as Facebook may help to improve the engagement.*" [Instructor 2]

Cultivating a Sense of Community

In general, all our interviewed instructors believe cultivating a sense of community is imperative for a successful learning process. However, our instructors believe it is very challenging because MOOCs students are massive and from all over the world. Building groups and a community is the most effect way to make student have a sense of belongings. Facebook is suitable, because it not only allows in-depth and formal discussion over the learning topics bus also supports creating an environment for informal conversations more smoothly and naturally. In other words, the affordances of Facebook are appropriate for building a sense of community among students and instructors. In contrast, Coursera does not seem to be well designed to support these needs.

"*Cultivating a sense of community is definitely important for students, especially for MOOC student! I was forced to open a Facebook account to remind and encourage more students to participate our course activities. I don't know how effective it is but worth to try.*" [Instructor 1]

"*Facebook is a very useful tool to enhance student communication quality and quantitate. Although Coursera has provided a discussion forum for students and instructors to communicate, I still feel hard to take effective and efficient communications.*" [Instructor 2]

Advertising the Course

According to our instructors, another important role of Facebook is to advertise their MOOCs before MOOCs officially started. In Coursera, students cannot access the course until the start date. Thus, our instructors usually construct the official Facebook group several weeks before the course was launched. During this time, instructors virtually introduce themselves (i.e., text post and making a video) and also encourage students to do self-introduction. They would also make a more detailed introduction of the course and give students some suggestions to learn this course well. They will also post something interesting to remind student that the course will be available very soon.

"*Facebook is a great place for students and instructors to build some connections before the course. Since the MOOC usually only span 4 to 8 weeks, which is relatively short comparing with traditional course. Thus, it will be challenging to create a good learning environment. Building a Facebook group several weeks before the course start potentially gives students more time to cultivate a community*" [Instructor 4]

Being Creative

The enemy of creativity, according to Robinson, is standardization [20]. MOOCs today rely heavily on standardized tests because the massive scale makes personalized learning impossible. Our instructors believe this is not an ideal way to teach students. They hope students can understand divergent thinking and seek multiple answers to a problem. They believe utilizing social media could drive students to be self-starters and have the potential to encourage them to be creative.

"*In Facebook, they have the opportunity to connect to fellow students to work on collaborative projects just as they will in the career world. This could help student have critical thinking and broaden their scope of current understanding. I am not saying the Coursera forum cannot do this, but I think social media can do a better job.*" [Instructor 3]

Perceptions

More Positive Feelings in Facebook

The instructors perceived a more friendly environment in Facebook. They found there are full of the warm words in Facebook, such as "thank you" "this is helpful", but in Coursera, complains and rude words frequent appear. One instructor even kicked out some students on Coursera because of their bad behaviors.

"*I don't know whether this is because of the anonymous feature that allow students make a comment anonymously, I found students have very mean comments on both instructor and other students on Cousera. But in facebook, every one is very nice. I can always see very effective and meaningful discussions. I really hope the community is healthy and positive. I was actually disappointed when I go through the comments on Coursera.*" [Instructor 2]

More like a community in Facebook

All our instructors believe Facebook did a better job in terms of cultivating a sense of community. Instructors said there are still many activities going on in Facebook even after the courses were finished. For example, in the Art MOOC, students would continue share their art crafts on Facebook group and many prior students would comment under the picture. When instructors have some learning information or materials, they would still post in the Facebook group.

"*I think a good community could arouse students interests and make students feel happy and comfortable to share their learning experiences. Students should have a kind of attachment to the community and would like to contribute their efforts and benefit others. I think the Facebook group of my course is a very successful community in this case. I was always inspired by their words.*" [Instructor 1]

Chaos Discussion Forum in Coursera

Our instructors believe the structure of Coursera forum is chaos, though they have tried to divide various discussion areas for different topics; for example, each week's topic has a separate space to discuss. However, the structure is hard to maintain. Students do not follow the rules but post on the area they believe most people could see it. Besides, the design of forum is unaesthetic, even instructors consider the design is boring, which become more salient when there are a massive number of comments.

"*You cannot imagine how painful I was when I tried to look through the comments. The design of the forum is very boring, especially when I need to go through so many comments... Also, the structure of the forum is chaos. I need to answer the same question repeatedly in different threads. Why don't pull them together?*" [Instructor 4]

"*I doubt Facebook can do a better job if all the MOOC students joined in and had discussions in Facebook. But Facebook definitely looks better in terms of design, at least you won't feel bored.*" [Instructor 3]

DISCUSSION AND DESIGN IMPLICATIONS

Facebook cannot take over the role of Coursera, because the forum is still the main interaction hub for MOOC students. The number of participants and posts shows the importance of this functionality that is built into Coursera. However, students did not very engaged in their Coursera discussions, because of a lack of efficient communication, no features supporting collaboration, convenient access to the platform, aesthetic and structured design, and other issues. In contrast, although Facebook groups tended to be smaller in number, students using them felt more engaged. Thus, we should consider how to gain inspiration from Facebook for the better design of Coursera forums.

Social Presence in MOOCs

Both students and instructors believed their Facebook group was formed as a real community, since students used their real identities, communication was more efficient, and learners received more attention from peers and instructors, etc. From our quantitative analysis, we also found that activity patterns on Facebook were more stable and students were active even before the MOOC started and near to the time when it finished. In contrast, in the Coursera forums, students do not trust others, which inhibits effective communication; the activities also showed a steep decline after the first week and had almost no activity close to the MOOC's ending date. All these findings reflect the significant role of social presence in MOOCs. Social presence is defined as the ability of participants to identify with the community, communicate purposefully and meaningfully in a trusting environment, and develop interpersonal relationships by way of projecting their individual personalities [32]. Affordances of Facebook provide students a relatively trusting environment and foster more interactions between students, thus helping them to form a healthy community – all of which are lacking in Coursera.

We suggest MOOC carriers and designers should seriously consider the importance of social presence and use this concept to guide future design efforts. For example, it is beneficial to ask students to register using their real name to avoid issues of interpersonal trust. MOOC platforms could also consider a formal connection with Facebook as most people use their real identity in Facebook. This would also offer students a more convenient way to access MOOC platforms without constructing a new account and building a new profile. Besides, we also found instructors construct a Facebook group site and pages several weeks before the course begins since that period of time provides a good opportunity for students to "meet" each other earlier and begin to cultivate a sense of community. From our quantitative analysis (see figure 3, 4, & 5), we can also see students were very active even two weeks before the course started. Both quantitative and qualitative analyses show the importance of pre-course activity. We suggest Coursera allows instructors to open a forum and build a new social place before the course officially begins. Although Facebook works well, not all students have a Facebook account and are likely to join a Facebook group.

Teaching Presence in MOOCs

Our analysis also revealed an important distinction between Facebook groups and Coursera forums. In Facebook, all posts were initiated by the instructors and the students made comments to the posts. In contrast, the posts in Coursera were primarily student-initiated. This distinction results in different perceptions from students' perspectives. For example, the student participants felt that the content in Facebook groups was of higher quality and more attractive. On the other hand, this also demonstrates the involvement of instructors and TAs is important to make the forum popular and reliable. Although instructors are considered as a facilitator of their MOOC [18], we found students still have high expectations to be more connected with instructors. These findings further confirm the importance of the *teaching presence* in MOOCs [31]. This also implies that MOOC instructors' role is critical to enhance student retention and engagement. Prior studies have found similar results in the context of traditional online courses; teaching presence is critical for development of social presence [31] and also highly correlated with students' retention and learning outcomes [19]. Thus, we suggest rethinking the position of instructors and TAs [26]. From design perspective, it would be beneficial to open a sub-forum on Coursera to pull out all the instructors threads, which may makes the forum more effective and popular.

Pedagogy Matters
Both students and instructors we interviewed complained about the design of the discussion forum in Coursera including comments that it is boring, difficult to navigate with respect to content of interest, too many posts about the same content, unaesthetic forum design, no support for collaborations, and so on. These issues have been mentioned by prior literature [24, 25], and researchers also have begun to provide design suggestions for the forum. From our analysis, it seems the immature design of the forums has somewhat reduced students' motivations for using and being active in Coursera.

In contrast, discussions in Facebook were perceived as organized, meaningful and attractive. One of the big differences between the two communication spaces is that in Facebook, instructors design/select the outline of the discussion topics and lead the discussion but in Coursera, the forum is student initiated and develops on its own. The results demonstrated that discussions need to be pedagogically designed. While some literature does show that social media may foster and amplify social interactions over conventional discussion boards when equivalent pedagogical approaches are used (e.g., [28]), how to design and lead discussions matters more. As our results indicated, the students believed the content posed by instructors in Facebook groups had higher quality and were more interesting. Thus, we should also see the important role of pedagogy played during teaching and learning instead of merely relying on the technology and trying to find every answer from it.

LIMITATIONS AND FUTURE WORK

Although we have presented a comprehensive set of analyses based on three MOOC courses in different types and interviews, and have discussed several interesting and meaningful insights, we acknowledge our study has some limitations. First, our results may not apply to the entire genre of MOOCs, because there are many other courses with different goals and scopes that may attract many engaged students. Second, we only studied Facebook and did not include other communication options (e.g., Twitter or Google plus) because Facebook is the only one used by all the three MOOCs and is also most popular. But it is possible that other MOOCs are more successful on using Twitter and Google plus, etc. We plan to expand our work to other MOOCs to look for similar patterns, and to include other social media platforms in the analysis to study various roles of social media for the success of MOOCs.

Additionally, our findings may suffer from self-selection bias. Since we were not able to link the same users from Coursera and Facebook because of a lack of user information (e.g., same ID or username used in Coursera and Facebook), we cannot identify the different behaviors between Facebook user and non-Facebook user. We could only see the overall usage and engagement differences. Bias may exist; for example, people who join Facebook may be more active in communication than who do not. Future work could explore learning and social behaviors of different groups of students (Facebook user VS. non-Facebook user; heavy Facebook user VS. light Facebook user, etc).

Third, we found the motivation of some students joining Facebook is to have more interactions with instructors instead of purely being attracted by the affordances of Facebook (e.g., better communities, convenience of communication and better place for collaborations). Our usage data are limited to show the weights of these different reasons to result in different usage patterns. A large-scale survey could be used in the future to explore student motivations for joining a Facebook group when taking a MOOC.

CONCLUSION

In this paper, we employed mixed methods to understand social media use and engagement compared to official MOOC forums and also demonstrated the rationales of social media use from instructors' and students' perspectives. We first present the comparative analysis of usage log data of three MOOCs regarding usage and engagement between Coursera and the associated Facebook groups. We also interviewed four instructors and twelve students of three MOOCs to understand their motivations and experiences in both platforms. We found that students showed higher engagement and retention in social media than the forums, and identified *four reasons* that lead to the results including a real community in Facebook, instructor initiated discussion forum, a better place for collaboration and more convenient to communicate with others. Our interviews with instructors unveil *four motivations* of using Facebook including enhancing student retention and engagement, cultivating a sense of community, advertising their MOOCs and being creativity. Through the comparison between Facebook and Coursera, our research attempts to provide several design guidelines for the next generation of MOOCs.

REFERENCES

1. Adamopoulos, P. 2013. What Makes a Great MOOC? An Interdisciplinary Analysis of Student Retention in Online Courses, *In Proc. ICIS.*
2. Brown, J.S. and Duguid. P. 2000. Mysteries of the region: knowledge dynamics in Silicon Valley. *The silicon valley edge*. 16-45.
3. Carlos, A., Pérez, C. M. and Muñoz, M. 2013 Analysing the impact of built-in and external social tools in a MOOC on educational technologies. In *Scaling up learning for sustained impact*, 5-18.
4. Clow, C. 2013. Moocs and the Funnel of Participation, *In Proc. LAK.*pages 185-189.

5. Conrad, D. 2005. Building and maintaining community in cohort-based online learning. *Journal of Distance Education, 20(1), 1-20.*
6. Dahlstrom, E. D., Brooks, C., and Bichsel, J. 2014. *The Current Ecosystem of Learning Management Systems in Higher Education: Student, Faculty, and IT Perspectives*. Research report. Louisville, CO: ECAR, September 2014.
7. Nada, Dabbagh, and Anastasia Kitsantas. 2012. Personal Learning Environments, social media, and self-regulated learning: A natural formula for connecting formal and informal learning. *The Internet and higher education* 15, no. 1. 3-8.
8. Downes. S. S. 2010. Learning Networks and Connective Knowledge, Collective intelligence and e-learning (2), 1-26.
9. Du, H., Rosson, M.B., Carroll, J. M. and Ganoe, G. 2009. I felt like a contributing member of the class: Increasing class participation with Class Commons, *In Proc. GROUP,* 233-242.
10. Corbin, J. and Strauss, A. 2007. Basics of Qualitative Research: Techniques and Procedures for Developing Grounded Theory. *Sage Publications, Incorporated.*
11. Khalil, H. and Ebner. M. 2013. Interaction Possibilities in MOOCs–How Do They Actually Happen. In *International Conference on Higher Education Development*, pp. 1-24.
12. Kizilcec, R. F., Piech, C. and Schneider, E. 2013. Deconstructing disengagement: analyzing learner subpopulations in massive open online courses. In *Proc LAK.*170-179.
13. Kizilcec R. F. and Schneider, E. 2015. Motivation as a lens to understand online learners: Toward data-driven design with the OLEI scale. *ACM TOCHI, 22(2), 6.*
14. Kop, R. Fournier, P., Sui, J., and Mak, F. 2011. A pedagogy of Abundance or a Pedagogy to Support Human Beings? Participant Support on Massive Open Online Courses. *International Review of Research in Open and Distance Learning 12(7), 74–93.*
15. Lave, J and Wenger, E. 1991. *Situated learning: Legitimate peripheral participation*. Cambridge university press,
16. Johnson, R. D., Hornik, S., & Salas, E. 2008. An empirical examination of factors contributing to the creation of successful e-learning environments. *International Journal of Human-Computer Studies, 66(5), 356-369.*
17. Lucas, M. and Moreira, A. 2009. Bridging formal and informal learning–A case study on students' perceptions of the use of social networking tools. In*Learning in the synergy of multiple disciplines*. 325-337.
18. Means, B. Bakia, M., and Murphy, R. 2014. Learning Online : What Research Tells Us About Whether, When and How.
19. Richardson, J.C. and Swan, K. 2003. Examing social presence in online courses in relation to students' perceived learning and satisfaction.
20. Robinson, K. 2005. How Creativity, Education and the Arts Shape a Modern Economy.
21. Salomon, G. 1993. No distribution without individuals' cognition: A dynamic interactional view. Distributed cognitions. *Psychological and educational considerations. 111-138*
22. Scardamalia, M. and Bereiter, C. 1996. Engaging students in a knowledge society. *Educational leadership* 54(3). 6-10.
23. Smith, B. L., MacGregor, J., Matthews, R. and Gabelnick, F. 2009 Learning communities: *Reforming undergraduate education.*
24. Zheng, S. Rosson, M. B., Shih, P. C. and Carroll, J. M. 2015. Understanding Student Motivation, Behaviors and Perceptions in MOOCs, In *Proc CSCW.*
25. Saijing Zheng, Mary Beth Rosson, Patrick C. Shih and John M. Carroll. 2015. Designing Massive Open Online Courses as Interactive Places for Collaborative Learning. *In Proc LAS.*
26. Zheng, S., Wisniewski, P., Rosson, M.B. and Carroll, J. M 2016 Ask the Instructors: Motivation and Challenges of Teaching Massive Open Online Courses, *In Proc CSCW, In Press.*
27. Thoms, B., & Eryilmaz, E. 2014. How media choice affects learner interactions in distance learning classes. *Computers & Education, 75, 112-126*
28. Joksimovic, S., Dowell, N., Skrypnyk, O., Kovanovic, V., Gasevic, D., Dawson, S., & Graesser, A. C. 2015. How do you connect?: analysis of social capital accumulation in connectivist MOOCs. *In Proc LAK.* 64-68. ACM.
29. Rourke, L., Anderson, T. Garrison, D. R., & Archer, W. 2001. Assessing social presence in asynchronous, text-based computer conferencing. *Journal of Distance Education, 14(3), 51-70.*
30. Anderson, T., Rourke, L., Garrison, D. R., Archer, W. 2001. Assessing Teaching presence in a Computer Conference Environment. *Journal of asynchronous learning networks, 5(2), 1-17.*
31. Garrison, D. R., Anderson, T., & Archer, W. 1999. Critical inquiry in a text-based environment: Computer conferencing in higher education. *The internet and higher education, 2(2), 87-105*

Practical Learning Research at Scale

Ken Koedinger
Professor of Human Computer Interaction and Psychology
Director, Pittsburgh Science of Learning Centre
Carnegie Mellon University, USA
koedinger@cmu.edu

ABSTRACT

Massive scale education has emerged through online tools such as Wikipedia, Khan Academy, and MOOCs. The number of students being reached is high, but what about the quality of the educational experience? As we scale learning, we need to scale research to address this question. Such learning research should not just determine whether high quality has been achieved, but it should provide a process for how to reliably produce high quality learning. Scaling practical learning research is as much an opportunity as a problem. The opportunity comes from the fact that online courses are not only good for widespread delivery, but are natural vehicles for data collection and experimental instrumentation. I will provide examples of research done in the context of widely used educational technologies that both contribute interesting scientific findings and have practical implications for increasing the quality of learning at scale.

BIOGRAPHY

Dr. Ken Koedinger is Professor of Human-Computer Interaction and Psychology at Carnegie Mellon. His research has contributed new principles and techniques for the design of educational software and has produced basic cognitive science research results on the nature of student thinking and learning. Koedinger directs LearnLab (learnlab.org), started with 10 years of NSF Center funding and is now the scientific arm of the Simon Initiative (cmu.edu/simon). LearnLab has created a social-technical infrastructure to support data-driven investigations in education and, more generally, to leverage collaborations of scientists and practioners toward understanding the conditions that cause robust student learning. Koedinger's publications include the

- Knowledge-Learning-Instruction Framework http://pact.cs.cmu.edu/pubs/KLI-KoedingerCorbettPerfetti2012-pre.pdf
- Cognitive Science, 2012) and Instructional Complexity http://pact.cs.cmu.edu/pubs/Koedinger-Science-2013.pdf (Science, 2013)

See http://pact.cs.cmu.edu/koedinger.html for more.

L@S 2016, April 25–26, 2016, Edinburgh, UK.
ACM 978-1-4503-3726-7/16/04.
http://dx.doi.org/10.1145/2876034.2876054

Author Index

www.ingramcontent.com/pod-product-compliance
Ingram Content Group UK Ltd.
Pitfield, Milton Keynes, MK11 3LW, UK
UKHW051412290926
15471UKWH00009B/1567

9 781450 344777